Robert Ashton was Professor of English History at the University of East Anglia from 1963 to 1989 and is now Emeritus Professor. He is the author of *The Crown and the Money Market 1603–1640*, *James I by his Contemporaries*, *The City and the Court 1603–1643*, *Reformation and Revolution 1558–1660* and *Counter-Revolution: the Second Civil War and its Origins 1646–8*.

The English Civil War

Conservatism and Revolution 1603–1649

Robert Ashton

Emeritus Professor of English History
in the University of East Anglia

To Peggy, Rosalind and Celia

A PHOENIX GIANT PAPERBACK

First published in Great Britain by Weidenfeld and Nicolson in 1978
This revised edition first published in 1989
This paperback edition published in 1997 by Phoenix, a division of
Orion Books Ltd,
Orion House, 5 Upper St Martin's Lane, London WC2H 9EA

A CIP catalogue record for this book is available from the
British Library.

ISBN: 1 85799 184 2

Printed and bound in Great Britain by
The Bath Press
Bath

Contents

Preface

In early modern historiography the years around 1640-2 have become something of a watershed. For some time now it has become relatively unusual for those working in the period before 1640 to push their researches beyond that date, and for those working in the middle decades of the century to make investigations in depth of the period before the 1640s. In the latter case, in so far as historians of the Civil War have concerned themselves with earlier decades, they have done so primarily from the standpoint of the *terminus ad quem*, which, if the paradox may be permitted, formed the starting-point of their enquiries. The most obvious danger of such an approach, though one which has not always been avoided, is that the period before 1640 can too easily become, in Professor Elton's phrase, a 'highway to Civil War', that is that the decades before 1640 are interpreted in terms of their assumed outcome in the 1640s. Even in cases where the worst excesses of this neo-Whig approach are avoided, there is sometimes a failure to do justice to the complexity of the developments of earlier decades, and a tacit assumption that because a particular state of affairs obtained in 1642 it also characterized, with only minor variations, most if not all of the preceding two or three decades. This questionable assumption has characterized the often very cursory and over-simplified sections which deal with the decades before 1640 in many otherwise admirable studies of the Civil War.

The fact that this book differs from such histories – though doubtless having its own peculiar deficiencies – reflects in some measure the fact that its author's main historical interests have hitherto lain in the half-century or so before the outbreak of the war, but are currently in process of moving forward into the middle decades of the century.

Although Clarendon's great *History* has been my constant guide and companion, I am not one of those who, like Clarendon, believes that the origins of the war can be explained without reference to the period before the accession of Charles I. While rejecting the approach which sees the reigns of the first two Stuarts simply in term~ of their outcome in the Civil War, I nonetheless believe that one needs to go back beyond 1625 to understand the factors which gave rise to the great upheaval. Accordingly, far from offering one short chapter giving an over-simplified account of the complex developments of the period before 1640, I have devoted most of the first part of the book to this period. This has inevitably meant that, given the economies of modern publishing, I have had far less space to devote to the events of the 1640s than I would otherwise have liked, and that some important developments – for instance the growth of extra-parliamentary radicalism in the later 1640s – have received less attention than their importance merits. Since, however, there are many – too many, it might be argued – admirable (and many not so admirable) studies of the Levellers and Diggers, and since (to my mind) few, if any, modern histories of the Civil War give to the decades before 1640 the attention they deserve, I am convinced that the sacrifice has been worth making in the interests of the general balance of the work. Indeed, it could be argued that the enormous amount of ink which has been spilt on the subject of the Levellers and the Diggers in recent years reflects more nearly current interests in the origins of radical politics, and the political ideas appropriate to them, than the contemporary significance of such movements, important though they undoubtedly were.

With regard to the material used in this book, one area where I have knowingly and deliberately laid myself open to criticism is that of my failure to consult more than a few of the hundreds of doctoral and other theses on Civil War topics which are to be found in university libraries all over the country and in America, but more especially in the Bodleian Library. This is in no way to play down the significance of such work. Indeed one of the main reasons for my unwillingness to make extensive use of such material is that much of it is of such fundamental importance as to be difficult to use without laying oneself open to the charge of creaming off information which rests on solid, painstaking and often brilliant research, the fruits of which ought first to be made available to the reading public as the published work of those who originally undertook it. That said, however, I must confess that another factor which deterred me was the sheer bulk of unpublished thesis material. Quite early on I had to make a decision whether to cut down on my investigation of primary, and especially manuscript, source materials in order to cope with unpublished thesis material. Rightly or wrongly, I decided not to do so. Whether this was a correct decision is for the reader, not for me, to say.

The greatest of my many debts of gratitude to individual scholars is that owed to my colleague Professor J.R.Jones, who has read the original draft of most of the book and made a number of valuable suggestions for improvement. I have learnt an immense amount about local, regional and, above all, county history by contact over the years with my colleague Dr A.Hassell Smith, and not least from teaching a Special Subject with him. It is not only Chapters 3 and 10, however, which have benefited from his advice and criticism. Another eminent county and regional historian Dr J.S.Morrill, of Selwyn College, Cambridge, was kind enough to read and offer valuable criticism of the first draft of Chapter 10. I was able to draw on the expertise of Dr W.Lamont of the University of Sussex, whose own work on Puritanism and religious history I have long admired, and who kindly read and provided abundant and valuable comments and criticisms of an early draft of Chapter 5. The passages dealing with art historical themes in Chapter 2 were read by Professor Peter Lasko and Mr John Newman of the Courtauld Institute of Art, University of London, and by Dr John Onians of the University of East Anglia; those on music in the same chapter by my colleague Professor Peter Aston. Besides their invaluable general comments, they all helped to save me from committing elementary errors in areas in which both my approach and my knowledge are all too amateur.

Those whom I have benefited from conversations with about innumerable topics include the Master of Balliol, Dr Christopher Hill, who will, I fear, not approve the thesis of this book, but whose work has stimulated me profoundly, if on occasions to disagreement, and who has always been generous of time and advice; also at Oxford, Mr Keith Thomas of St John's College, Dr Blair Worden of St Edmund Hall and Dr Kevin Sharpe of Oriel. I have learnt much about local history and other topics from Dr Gordon Forster of the University of Leeds, and have benefited from interdisciplinary teaching at the University of East Anglia with Professor Lasko and Dr Onians in Art History, Professor Aston in Music and Professor Nicholas Brooke, Professor J.B.Broadbent and Dr R.I.V.Hodge in English Literature.

I would also like to express my gratitude to Professor Jack P. Greene of Johns Hopkins University for his encouragement. I must record my deep gratitude to the University of East Anglia for allowing me two periods of sabbatical leave, the first to engage in research and the second during the first two terms of the current academic year for the completion of research and writing. The Warden and Fellows of All Souls College did me the honour of electing me a Visiting Fellow of the College in 1973-4, which made it possible for me to spend an extended period working on the magnificent material in the Bodleian, and notably on the Tanner, Rawlinson, Clarendon and Walker collections, as well as putting at my disposal the resources of the Codrington Library. I have also had particular occasion to value my extended rights at All Souls on the occasions of subsequent returns to Oxford for further work in the Bodleian.

Three final debts remain: to Mrs V. Durell who has typed this entire book from my execrable manuscript with unfailing patience and astonishing accuracy; to Mrs Susan Loden, Mrs Gila Falkus and Mr Benjamin Buchan who saw it through the press and whose patience was no less monumental; and to my family who have suffered the normal fate of families when books are being written, and to whom my debt is very inadequately expressed in the dedication.

R.A.

BRUNDALL, NORWICH, 1977

Preface to Second Edition

SINCE THIS BOOK FIRST appeared in 1978 it has been reprinted several times. In the meantime the spate of publications on early Stuart history has not abated and there is a consequent danger that without serious revision in parts the study will become seriously out of date. I do not, however, believe that the very important additions to our knowledge which have come, for example, from the work of John Morrill and Nicholas Tyacke on religious history, Clive Holmes and Ann Hughes on county history, Ronald Hutton on the royalists and Mark Kishlansky and Austin Woolrych on the parliamentary army and radicalism, have necessitated any fundamental changes in the general interpretation which characterized the first edition of my book a decade ago. Such new work has involved me in making fundamental revisions in my treatment of individual episodes and developments but has not led me to alter my interpretation of the significance of the conflict as a whole. Quite apart from the stimulus of such important new contributions to knowledge I have some additional personal debts to acknowledge. The first one again is to the Warden and Fellows of All Souls College for electing me to a Visiting Fellowship a second time in 1987. Even though most (though not all) of the work I did in Oxford in 1987 was in connection with a forthcoming book on Counter-Revolution in the later 1640s, the result of such research was obviously relevant to this revised version of my earlier book. My second debt is to the University of East Anglia for granting me sabbatical leave on this and other occasions. My third is to Vera Durell who has painstakingly and uncomplainingly typed many revisions of passages which she had originally typed many years ago. My fourth is to Juliet Gardiner of Weidenfeld for encouragement and assistance. Finally there are my debts to my students and to my wife. When the first edition of this book appeared I had only recently changed over to teaching a Special Subject on the Great Rebellion. I am now indebted to scores of undergraduates at the University of East Anglia who have shared and stimulated my enthusiasm for the subject, the best of whom have since themselves engaged in research in one aspect or another of it at Oxford, Cambridge and other universities including U.E.A. My debt to my wife is as great as ever.

ROBERT ASHTON
BRUNDALL, NORWICH, 1988

I Court and Country 1603–42

ONE *Monarchy and Society*

The State of MONARCHIE is the supremest thing vpon earth: for Kings are not onely GODS Lieutenants vpon earth, and sit vpon GODS throne, but euen by GOD himselfe they are called Gods.

> James I, *A Speach to the Lords and Commons of the Parliament at White-Hall On Wednesday the XXI of March, Anno 1609* [10] in *The Political Works of James I*, ed. C. H. McIlwain (New York 1965 edn.), p. 307.

A King is a thing men have made for their own sakes, for quietness' sake.

> John Selden, *Table Talk* (1696 edn.)

As in natural things, the head being cut off, the rest cannot be called a body: no more can in politick things a multitude, or commonalty, without a head be incorporate.

> *Examples for Kings: or Rules for Princes to Govern By* (1642)

I

ON 30 JANUARY 1649 the English cut off the head of their king. This was not, of course, the first time that an English king had been done to death by his subjects. But what differentiated it from earlier acts of regicide, such as the murder of Edward II in 1327 and of Richard II in 1399, was that Charles I was not furtively murdered in a dark and secret place but executed on a public scaffold in Whitehall after a trial which, although he denied the legality of the court, was, it was claimed, conducted according to due process of law. In more modern times the executions of anointed monarchs – the public execution of Louis xvi in Paris in 1793 and the murder of the Tsar Nicholas ii and his family in an obscure Russian provincial town in 1918 – have been held to symbolize the passing of an old order and the inauguration of a new one. There can be no doubt that some, though by no means all, of that minority of revolutionaries who were responsible for the regicide of 1649 intended that it, too, should be symbolic of the birth of a new era, and many historians have been disposed to accept them at their word.

This chapter seeks to examine the significance of the monarchy whose dramatic abolition in 1649 marks both the beginning and the end of this book. In many ways it is a much easier task than it would have been several decades ago, not only on account of the mass of research which has been done on the period during the intervening years. For, partly perhaps as an indirect consequence of the increasing radical challenge to our contemporary political institutions, historians have become more interested in the institutions which were challenged by seventeenth-century radicals and the ideologies which were employed in their defence. Thanks above all to Mr Laslett, Sir Robert Filmer is no longer dismissed as the tenth-rate apologist of patriarchal absolutism worthy of mention only because his absurd ideas provided the occasion for Locke's Second Treatise on Civil Government.[1] There has been a revival of interest in the Divine Right of Kings and, following the lead given by historians of literature, the Great Chain of Being. Even the political ideas of James i are finding defenders, and indeed we may perhaps expect, at any time, a long-overdue reappraisal of his contribution as a statesman.[2]

II

In the speech quoted at the head of this chapter, James i offered for Parliament's contemplation three 'similitudes', as he called them, with the institution of monarchy. One of these was the correspondence between the role of the monarch and that of the head of the human body. This was a commonplace of contemporary social and political thought[3] in which elaborate analogies were drawn between the functions of the limbs or members of the human body and those of the body politic, each under the direction of the head: 'The head cares for the body, so doeth the King for his people. As the discourse and direction flowes from the head, and the execution thereunto belongs to the rest of the members, everyone according to their office: so it is betwixt a wise Prince and his people'.[4]

More interesting is the correspondence between kings and God, 'for that they exercise a manner or resemblance of Diuine power upon earth: for if you will consider the Attributes to God, you shall see how they agree in the person of a King.'[5] Within the microcosm of his realm the king's power is analogous with that of God in the macrocosm of the universe. As James pointed out in the work which he wrote for his eldest son, Prince Henry had the greater reason to love God since God had made him both a man and 'a little GOD to sit on his Throne, and rule over other men'.[6] In these circumstances it is hardly surprising that the scriptures were seen as offering unquestionable proof of the divine preference for the monarchical form of human government. The thirteenth chapter of St Paul's Epistle to the Romans was probably the most frequently cited of all biblical texts in support of the duty of subjects to render obedience to constituted authority, in this case to the Roman monarch. No doubt it could be argued that what the epistle required to be rendered unto Caesar would be as appropriately rendered to quite different sorts of authority under other political systems; but against this there was abundant evidence in the Old Testament to support the thesis that monarchy was the form of government most acceptable to the Almighty. It was God, argued Filmer, who had 'endued not only men, but all creatures, with a natural propensity to monarchy', and it was this that caused the Israelites to plead with Him to give them a king. But it was God, and not the people, who chose Saul to be king, and who laid down the hard conditions of their complete subjection to him.[7]

As a divinely ordered institution, kingship is endowed with formidable charismatic and supernatural powers. The anointing of kings with holy oil is a vital part of the coronation rite, and 'not a meere outward solemnity but ... significant of the spirit of God in a more especiall manner given unto them'.[8] One of the most spectacular manifestations of this was the power of magical healing and more particularly, that of touching for the king's evil.[9] Incongruously numbered among contemporary sceptics about the efficacy of such magical cures was that passionate believer in the godlike attribute of kingship, James I himself, who publicly expressed doubts about a practice which he nevertheless found it expedient to continue; and that most irreverent of republican radicals, Henry Marten, who scoffed at the scrofulous multitudes flocking to Holdenby House in the spring of 1647 in search of a cure from the captive king, suggesting that a parliamentary ordinance might be devised to transfer the requisite magical powers from the monarch to the great seal. Not everyone took it so lightly, and the continued recourse of sufferers from scrofula and similar complaints to the king, whose willingness to oblige them earned him the epithet of 'the Stroker' from some of his guards, was a matter of very deep concern to the parliamentary commissioners at Holdenby.[10] As well it might be, since it testified to the charisma and mystical aura which still attached themselves even to a defeated king. For, like modern miracle cures, the failures were easily forgotten so long as there were some successes, whether attributable, by modern science, to psychosomatic considerations, to physical remissions or to improvement in the illness itself. In these circumstances the royal power of mystical healing becomes a touchstone of legitimacy, something which, like the Divine Right from which it flowed, is transmitted in the strict line of hereditary succession and by no other means.

No king could divest himself of the supernatural qualities of his office and become a private person. When Shakespeare's Richard II is asked by the usurper Bolingbroke whether he is content to resign the Crown, he replies, 'Ay, no; no, ay; for I must nothing be.' He then embarks on a solemn and awe-inspiring coronation ritual in reverse, divesting himself of all the sacred marks of kingship:

> Now mark me how I will undo myself.
> I give this heavy weight from off my head,
> And this unwieldy sceptre from my hand,
> The pride of kingly sway from out my heart,
> With mine own tears I wash away my balm,
> With mine own hands I give away my crown,
> With mine own tongue deny my sacred state,
> With mine own breath release all duteous rites,
> All pomp and majesty I do forswear.[11]

The result is the loss not only of his kingly but also of his human identity.

> . . . I have no name, no title,
> No, not that name was given me at the font,
> But 'tis usurp'd.[12]

Richard II, who makes his first appearance in the play in the full panoply of kingly glory, ends the deposition scene as something less than a man. With the destruction of both regality and humanity goes the destruction of that divinity which hedges kingship. The Bishop of Carlisle likens the resulting state of England to 'the field of Golgotha and dead man's skulls',[13] and the deposed king sees himself as a Christ-figure, betrayed by Judases and delivered to his 'sour cross' by Pilates.[14] Shakespeare's analogy would doubtless acquire additional poignancy to contemporaries after the regicide of 1649 and the appearance of the *Eikon Basilike* with its reference to Charles's 'kingdom of brambles' and its clear and unmistakable comparison between the ordeal of Calvary and that of the scaffold in Whitehall.[15] James I had remarked on the correspondence between sedition and blasphemy.[16] To more than one person who lived through the events of 1649, regicide was in itself a blasphemy.[17]

III

'Even the power which God himself exerciseth over mankind is by right of fatherhood,' wrote Filmer in 1652.[18] Just as God is the father of mankind, argued James I, so 'the stile of *Pater patriae* was ever, and is commonly used to Kings'. Thus 'as the Father . . . is bound to care for the nourishing, education, and vertuous gouernment of his children; euen so is the king, bound to care for all his subjects.'[19] In its fully developed Filmerian form the patriarchal theory of royal authority was to prove a powerful argument both against the idea that government originated in a political contract between ruler and ruled and against the far more influential notion that representative government and the limitations which it placed on the royal exercise of power were immemorial features of the constitution.[20] There was yet another and more venerable political tradition to which patriarchalism also ran counter. The idea that human subordination to government was a direct consequence of the sin in the Garden of Eden was one of the liveliest and most persistent intellectual inheritances of the early modern world from the medieval past. While it might offer a firm justification for government and subordination in an imperfect world, there was always a danger that men might strive to re-attain a state of pre-lapsarian perfection. If Adam had sinned, Christ had redeemed men from the consequences of sin. To such dangerous notions patriarchal doctrine offered as firm a challenge as it did to theories of the contractual origins of government or the immemoriality of representa-

tive institutions. For, argued Filmer in 1648, subjection to government
was a pre-lapsarian characteristic, since 'Eve was subject to Adam
before he sinned'.[21] If any sort of government could be said to have
resulted from the Fall, John Maxwell had argued four years earlier,
it was not monarchical government proper, but those perversions
of true government: aristocracy, democracy and mixed monarchy.[22]

The distinction between fully developed Filmerian patriarchalism
and James I's rather commonplace argument from the correspondence
between kingly and paternal power, while of great moment to historians of political theory,[23] need not bother us unduly here. Indeed,
although Filmer's basic ideas were developed before 1640, they were
not to be published for another decade. But in practical terms the
humdrum nature of James's arguments was a strength rather than a
weakness in their role as – to adapt Mr Laslett's suggestive description
of Filmer – a codification of 'conscious and unconscious prejudice,'[24]
and a ranging of it behind the *status quo*. For it gave to heads of
households, as it were, a personal stake in the monarchy. Just as kings
were little Gods,[25] so were fathers little monarchs. He who does not
honour the king, maintained Thomas Jordan, cannot truly honour his
own parents, as the fifth commandment bids him. So, in his speech on
the scaffold in February 1649, the royalist Lord Capel affirmed 'very
confidently that I do die here . . . for obeying that fifth commandment
given by God himself.'[26] Monarchical and traditionalist authoritarian
regimes have always been careful to foster parental authority, seeing its
fortunes as inextricably bound up with their own. For 'this subordination of children is the foundation of all regal authority, by the ordination of God himself.'[27]

But the above argument related to a great deal more than the authority of kings and fathers. *All* authority was, in fact, paternal in
character. When Archbishop James Ussher referred to a household as
a little commonwealth and a commonwealth as a great household, he
meant by 'household' not only the nuclear family but something a
great deal wider than what we understand by that term today.[28] To
contemporaries the relationship between the domestic servant, or the
farm employee living on his master's premises, and his employer was
not basically different in kind from that between child and father.
Moreover, the fact that most industrial production was domestic rather
than factory-based also made for the prevalence of familial relationships between industrial masters and their dependants even in cases
where the latter were not their children.[29] The *raison d'être* of the craft

guild and apprenticeship, more honoured in the breach than in the observance in rural industry, but still an important force to be reckoned with in the towns, stretched beyond considerations of technical training to considerations of public order. Here is one of the numerous authoritarian relationships of Tudor and Stuart England in which the phrase *in loco parentis* requires to be taken quite literally. Like the schoolmaster, the university don, the householder, the civil magistrate and the king himself, the master wields an authority which is in essence paternalistic and contributes to the maintenance of order in society as a whole. For order is indivisible.

IV

As well as being the keystone of the arch of order, the monarch was also the source of all privilege, inequality and social distinction. Deference and privilege pervaded the social arrangements of the seventeenth century to an extent which requires a real effort of the historical imagination for us to appreciate. Anyone who thought himself a cut above his fellows or who enjoyed more or less exclusive privileges of any sort felt to a greater or lesser degree a community of interest with the monarchy which, as well as being the fount of honour – 'regardingly vnto the merits of the vertuous'[30] – was also the supreme symbol of order and human differentiation and as such stood for something of which all but the bottom layers of society, from village constable and master-craftsman upwards, felt themselves to be the beneficiaries.

Nor is it necessarily true that the higher one moved up the social scale, the more powerful were the ties of interest and sentiment which bound one to the monarchy. Certainly some, but by no means all, of that minority of peers who sided with Parliament in the Civil War were persons who, in one way or another, had felt themselves cheated of their 'honorable deseruings'. Thomas Hobbes remarked upon what he saw as the singular failure of the House of Lords to give thoroughgoing support to the king in the Civil War.[31] If so, it was not for want of trying on the part of the king, whose message to the House on 22 April 1642, requesting that it take action against a seditious pamphleteer, reminded the peers 'how much their own particular Interest (as well as the publike government of the Kingdome) is, and must be, shaken, if such Licence shall bee permitted to bold factious spirits.'[32] And when in September of the same year the king requested a loan from the Earl of Kingston, he was at pains to stress that 'all persons of your fortune and quality . . . are not altogether unconserned in my necessety'.[33] The royalist Sir John Berkeley quoted no less a person than Oliver Cromwell as saying that 'no men could enjoy their Lives and Estates quietly without the King had his Rights.'[34]

V

Absolute power, whether of fathers or of kings, was not at all the same thing as capriciously exercised power, and James I was at particular pains to make the distinction between an absolute king, 'who acknowledgeth himselfe ordained for his people', and a tyrant, who 'thinketh his people ordained for him, a prey to his passions and inordinate appetites . . .'.[35] To the distinction between kings and tyrants, James I added a further and connected distinction between what kings might do in the far-off times when they first exercised regal power and what they might do in what he called 'the state of setled Kings and Monarches, that doe at this time gouerne in ciuill Kingdomes.' In the former times law was synonymous with the king's will, but once there had grown up a body of such king-made law, his successors became bound by their coronation oaths to observe it, and any king who neglects to do so 'leaues to be a King, and degenerates into a Tyrant'. But he was answerable for his misdeeds to God alone, though tyrants ought to be aware that the punishment meted out to them by the Almighty would be in proportion to their exalted position.[36] Thus Woodstock's widow fails to persuade John of Gaunt to avenge her husband who had been murdered by the king's command, for

> God's is the quarrel; for God's substitute,
> His deputy anointed in his sight,
> Hath caused his death; the which if wrongfully,
> Let heaven revenge, for I may never lift
> An angry arm against his minister.[37]

Revolt even against a tyrant was unthinkable, for revolt simply compounded the disorder created by the tyrannical actions which produced it. King James, who had had his bellyful of plots and conspiracies as King of Scotland, encountered no less than three during his first three years as King of England,[38] and who to the end of his days lived in terror of more, was at great pains to emphasize this point. Revolt was not justifiable even against an Ahab, a Nebuchadnezzar or a Nero. Daniel submitted to the punishment of the lions' den; Shadrach,

Meshach and Abednego to the burning fiery furnace. David refused to harm the tyrant Saul, who was also the Lord's anointed, when he had him at his mercy, and himself slew the Amalekite who had killed Saul even though he had acted on that king's request. In any case another reason why it was wrong to rebel against tyrants was that tyranny might well be a just punishment visited by God upon a sinful people. Moreover, to concede the right of rebellion raised the difficult question of in whom lay the right to decide whether a ruler were a tyrant or not. To make this a matter of individual judgement was to open the floodgates, and one of the reasons that James I loathed and feared the Jesuits was their alleged justification of tyrannicide. And to restrict the right of decision to inferior magistrates, as advocated by the celebrated Huguenot theorist of the right of revolt, the so-called Junius Brutus, was hardly better, whether this right be vested in the nobility or in parliaments. Better by far to insist that kings, even if they were also tyrants, were responsible only to God.[39] As the royalist commander Sir Marmaduke Langdale, endeavouring to bring Colonel John Hutchinson and two of his Roundhead colleagues to a realization of the wickedness of 'that rebellious course of life you seeme to glory in', was to put it in a letter of 18 December 1643:

> ... if you please to reade all the histories of this nation from the conquest to this time ... you shall find all rebells pretences of taking vp armes against the sacred person of the King varnished ouer with the title of loue to the lawes of the land, liberty of the subject and loyaltie to his Majestie ... yet the authors had cause to repent commonly before their deathes, and certeinly their [sic] neuer was yett law of this land nor religion publiquely proffessed here did euer allow subjects to take vp armes against their naturall Soveraigne.[40]

Scripture might abound with inconvenient examples of rebels executing God's will upon unrighteous princes, but this was in no way to justify the act of revolt *per se*. Among the more mysterious ways in which God moved was his willingness to 'use and turn men's unrighteous acts to the performance of His righteous decrees'.[41] The most that might be permitted in cases when the demand of a tyrannical ruler offended against conscience and appeared to be transgressing against divine law was refusal to obey followed by passive submission to the punishment inflicted for such conscientious disobedience. This was the so-called doctrine of passive obedience. But the Civil War would never have been fought if all men had found adequate this quietistic mode of satisfying conscientious scruples about royal policies. The problem which was to be faced by the English Parliament in 1642 had first been faced by the Scots in the later 1630s. 'I was latelie in the minde,' wrote one of them on 12 February 1640, 'that, in no imaginable case, any prince might have been opposed; I inclyne now to think otherwayes.'[42] Faced by what to a godly Scots Presbyterian seemed to be a royal attempt to subvert the whole basis of the Scottish Reformation, Robert Baillie's change of heart about passive obedience is not altogether surprising. Indeed although he specifically disclaimed being influenced by the arguments of George Buchanan and Junius Brutus, the latter's advocacy of the right of revolt which had been the condition of the survival of French Protestantism might appear to be no less applicable to the plight of Scottish Presbyterians in the later 1630s. They were shortly to fall on receptive ground in England also.

VI

But to view these matters as a clear-cut choice between the two polarities of acceptance of absolute monarchy and revolt against it is to run the risk of reading the inevitability of conflict so far back into the seventeenth century as to obviate the need for complex historical explanation of a situation in which, in actual fact, a far greater number of options seemed to be open until at least quite late in the period. Unlike France, Tudor England had not experienced the trauma of decades of sanguinary civil war, from which the French had emerged with a strong and entirely understandable inclination to welcome an absolute monarch as the new messiah. Englishmen had far less reason and inclination to resign themselves to the protective custody of the new Leviathan and more reason to appreciate the value of what their less fortunate neighbours might be inclined to regard as an outmoded concept of the nature of the body politic as a *dominium politicum et regale*, that is as a constitutional rather than an absolute (*dominium regale*) monarchy. The English constitution, boasted Thomas May, 'is by wise men esteemed one of the best in Europe, as well for the strength and honour of the Prince as the securitie and freedome of the people.'[43] Both people and king benefited, for parliament safeguarded the essential freedoms of the former while the power of the latter was at its greatest in parliament.

Limited or mixed monarchy, it was argued,[44] utilized the best and

cast aside the worst features of unmixed political systems. The characteristic advantage of monarchy was that it provided an unrivalled focus
for national unity; of aristocracy that it associated the ablest persons
with the highest councils of state; and of democracy that it fostered
'liberty and the courage and industry which liberty begets'. By contrast, the prevalence of any one of these systems in an unmixed form,
unchecked and unbalanced by the others, allowed free play to its
characteristic vices; in the case of monarchy, a tendency to tyrannize,
for, as the great Tudor writer on government Sir Thomas Smith had
put it, 'the frailtie of mans nature . . . cannot abide or beare long that
absolute and uncontrowled authoritie, without swelling into too much
pride and insolencie';[45] in that of aristocracy, faction, and, in that
of democracy, 'Tumults, Violence and Licentiousnesse'. When monarchy is mixed, however, each element in the constitution does what
best befits it. The executive power, for example, is vested in the king,
while the House of Commons, 'an excellent conserver of liberty but
never intended for any share in government or the chusing of them that
should govern', controls the granting of taxes and exercises a measure
of control over ministers of the Crown via the process of impeachment.
The constitution is a finely wrought system of checks and balances
which certainly did not afford a completely free rein to the wills and
desires of *Rex Solus*.

In constitutional terms, however, the English Civil War is not a
struggle between the adherents of mixed and absolute monarchy. Before the war had broken out, the king's party had seized upon the idea
of mixed monarchy and, as the masterly royal reply to the Nineteen
Propositions of June 1642 shows, was exploiting it as an attractive
ideology of constitutional propriety against parliamentary usurpa-
tions.[46] But this was a constitutional stance which had developed out of
the stresses of the events of the first two years of the Long Parliament
and was very different from the views of the nature of monarchical
power which high prerogative men had expounded in better days. A
brilliant parliamentary lawyer such as James Whitelock might argue in
the great debate on impositions in the House of Commons in 1610 that
'the power of the King in Parliament is greater than his power out of
Parliament, and doth rule and control it', but four years earlier Chief
Baron Fleming had handed down a judgement in Bate's Case on the
same matter of impositions; although like Whitelock's it distinguished
between two forms of royal power, it came to radically different conclusions on their relative priority. In this view, the king's 'ordinary power

is for the profit of particular subjects, for the execution of civil justice, the determining of *meum*,' and is exercisable through the courts and can be altered only by Parliament. The absolute power, by contrast, 'is only that which is applied to the general benefit of the people and is *salus populi*'. It is in no way dependent on the common law and may be varied 'according to the wisdom of the King for the common good'.[47] There were not wanting those who were prepared to go even further and declare the king's power as absolute, irrespective of the use to which it was put.[48]

More surprising, however, is the fact that the greatest parliamentary opponent of royal policies in the 1620s, Sir John Eliot, held similar views about the powers vested in *Rex Solus*. 'Practically every word Eliot wrote in his work,' claims a modern biographer, 'would have received the enthusiastic approbation of the first Stuart King of England'.[49] The work in question is *De Jure Maiestatis*, written when the author was imprisoned in the Tower after the dissolution of Charles I's third parliament in 1629, and it is not impossible that it may have been composed with an eye to making his peace with the king and obtaining his release. But at least one historian has seen the work as symbolic of a state of affairs in which, as a consequence partly of the Stuart exaltation of royal power and partly of the tendency to cry up the importance of case-made at the expense of statute law, the idea of mixed monarchy was at a low ebb.[50] Conceivably the king might be blamed – or rather the fault might be seen to lie in those who exercised influence over him – for heeding the advice of his favourites rather than that of his parliaments. That much must needs be conceded, given the history of Eliot's own parliamentary career. But what is crucial is the absence of any notion of the king's power as such being controllable by Parliament. In his important revaluation of early Stuart parliamentary history, warning us of the dangers of seeing the variety of claims made by parliamentarians in the course of the 1620s as indicative of an articulated policy of general constitutional aggression, Professor Conrad Russell provides some salutary observations on the significance of some of these events.[51] His argument serves to remind us that although the royal need for war finances over these years did result in parliamentary claims to control the appropriation of its grants (a suggestion which, however, emanated from the Court not from the Commons); to impeach ministers (though successfully only when in alliance with powerful Court faction); and to limit royal freedom of action via the Petition of Right of 1628, the constitutional significance both of its claims and its achievements has been exaggerated. Too many historians' views of the 1620s have been distorted by the hindsight which is a product of their knowledge of what was to follow in the 1640s.

At the beginning of 1629 Charles I embarked on what turned out to be eleven years of non-parliamentary rule. Was he trying to regain ground lost during the 1620s, or did he aspire to create a new monarchy on the French model? Whichever view comes nearer to the truth, both protagonists in the constitutional conflicts of the early seventeenth century chose to present themselves as the upholders of tradition rather than as innovators. The chapter which follows is concerned with this matter of tradition and innovation not simply in the field of constitutional, but in the more general areas of social and cultural history and in that of Court and Country as well as Crown and Parliament.

TWO *Tradition and Innovation*

... Now concerning customs, this must be considered that for every custom there was a time when it was no custom, and the first precedent we now have had no precedent when it began. When every custom began, there was something else than custom that made it lawful, or else the beginning of all customs were unlawful. Customs at first became lawful only by some superior power which did either command or consent unto their beginning. And the first power which we find ... is Kingly power ...

Sir Robert Filmer, *Patriarcha*, ch. XXVII.

I

ALTHOUGH THE WHIG INTERPRETATION of history is nowadays out of fashion, there are still many historians whose approach to the history of the seventeenth century owes more to the teleological Whig historical framework than they would care to admit, or, perhaps, are even aware of. For it is the essence of the Whig view that it is those historical figures whose actions led to the checking of royal power and fostering the growth of representative institutions to whom the historian should look as the true innovators and harbingers of progress. Conversely, their opponents are the traditionalist resisters of change. It is true that the greatest of Whig historians was concerned to emphasize that both elements were vital in the evolution of that English constitutional equilibrium which was the end-product of their interaction. Innovation and liberty without tradition and order would lead to anarchy;

tradition and order without innovation and liberty would lead to tyranny. Nevertheless no one can be in doubt with which element Whig sympathies lie and to whom especially they attribute that progress which is the central theme of Whig historiography.[1]

The Whig view of the seventeenth century as a crucial stage in constitutional progress has some important features in common with the most influential of non-Whig interpretations, that held by Marxist historians. For they too see the seventeenth century as the great heroic age in the growth of representative institutions and the emergence of modern liberalism. And even if they claim to look beyond liberal institutions and ideologies to the capitalist organization of production which they see as their material foundation, this is simply to add an extra dimension to the analysis, so that the innovators become bourgeois as well as constitutionalist, and their opponents feudalists as well as traditionalist royalists. This prompts the observation that the Marxist interpretation of history is open to the same criticism which Sir Herbert Butterfield levelled at the Whig – that it makes the principal participants in the historical events which it describes the agents of a process of which they themselves were totally unaware.[2]

How then did they see themselves? Certainly the innovators and progressives of the Whig and Marxist pictures regarded themselves in a very different light. Conservatism and tradition rather than innovation is the keynote of the attitude of most of the principal opponents of royal policies in the 1630s and 1640s. The fact that the same is not true of all of them is, of course, important, but not the least significant of the effects of this was to confirm and heighten the conservatism of the majority. From their point of view it was the Crown – influenced by its evil advisers – which was the innovator, and it is only the fact that Whig interpretations are embedded so deeply in the historical consciousness of all of us that blinds us to what seemed an obvious and alarming fact to most contemporary parliamentarians: that it was absolute monarchs who were the innovators *par excellence*; and that everywhere, or nearly everywhere, in Europe representative institutions appeared to be on the retreat.

According to the Kentish antiquary Sir Roger Twysden, limited monarchy was the traditional form of English government, for 'wise antiquity did conceive of lawes . . . for the moderating the exorbytancies greatnesse aptly falls into.' Conversely absolute monarchy was a relatively recent innovation, and 'this latter age hath produced some of

the opinion [that] no kings can be limited.'[3] Innovations in government was one of the headings proposed by Sir John Strangeways
at a committee of the House of Commons on 6 June 1628 discussing
the contents of a proposed parliamentary remonstrance to the king.
Among these innovations he placed the grievances of billeting and
martial law which were to figure so prominently in that very conservative document the Petition of Right of the same year.[4] The succeeding
twelve years were to see a plethora of such innovations. In a speech
to the House of Commons in the early days of the Long Parliament,
Sir John Holland, MP for the Norfolk constituency of Castle Rising,
denounced

> the late & great Invndation of the Prarogatiue [sic] Royall which
> haue broke out & almost overturned all our libertyes even those
> [which] were best and stronglyest fortefyed : The Grand Charter
> itself, that which haue been soe often, soe solemnly confirmed
> . . . founded by the wisdom of former ages . . . the best & choysest
> part of our Inheritance haue been infringed, Broken . . . & sett
> at nought.[5]

Holland's mention of Magna Carta would strike a familiar chord in the
minds of those who heard his speech. In his brilliant study of the
historical ground where seventeenth-century politics and historiography meet, Professor Pocock has demonstrated that, while 'a vitally
important characteristic of the constitution was its antiquity,' it was
not enough to trace its existence back to a remote date. It had to
be demonstrated to have existed from time immemorial.[6] Thus when
those who took this view made use of precedent, this was not done to
prove the coming into existence of particular rights or privileges, but to
demonstrate their existence prior to that time. For to be able to trace
their precise historical origins was to ascribe them to the action of some
human agency, and, more particularly, to concessions made by a king.
And what one king could grant another could revoke.[7]

In this view of constitutional history Magna Carta played a key
role as the most celebrated link in the chain whereby the liberties
of immemorial antiquity were confirmed and passed on to future
generations.[8] For Magna Carta did nothing new. It simply did what
William I had allegedly done when he confirmed the laws of the Confessor;[9] what Henry I had done in his coronation charter; what
Edward I was to do when he confirmed the charters in 1297; and
what parliament was to ask Charles I to do in 1628 when it presented

him with the Petition of Right. As John Pym himself observed in
a justly celebrated speech,

> ... those commonwealths have been most durable and perpetual
> which have often reformed and recomposed themselves
> according to their first institution and ordinance, for by this
> means they repair the breaches and counterwork the ordinary
> and natural effects of time. ... There are plain footsteps of those
> laws in the government of the Saxons. They were of that vigour
> and force as to overlive the Conquest; nay, to give bounds and
> limits to the Conqueror. ... It is true they have been often
> broken, but they have been often confirmed by charters of Kings
> and by Acts of Parliaments. But the petitions of the subjects
> upon which those charters and Acts were founded, were ever
> Petitions of Right, demanding their ancient and due liberties,
> not suing for any new.[10]

Not all contemporary champions of parliamentary rights and privileges insisted on their immemorial character, however. For instance
the author of a parliamentary tract written shortly before the outbreak
of the Civil War was content to claim an antiquity of a mere five
centuries for parliamentary rights and privileges.[11] The great antiquary Sir Robert Cotton went further, and, like Sir Henry Spelman
before him, was at pains to emphasize that Anglo-Norman society and
institutions were too far removed in time and character from those of
his own day for the consideration of them to be of any relevance to
contemporary constitutional controversies. Far from having their immemorial freedoms confirmed in 1066, 'the People [were] brought
vnder the sword ... to a subiected vassilage.'[12] William Prynne, in his
treatise on Ship Money, is more confused, at one point arguing that
Danegeld could hardly be a precedent for Ship Money, since it was
imposed in a period of unsettled government before the power of kings
to impose taxes had been circumscribed; and, at another, inclining
towards Selden's view that Danegeld had been imposed with the consent of an Anglo-Saxon parliament.[13] It could be that some of these
contemporary commentators failed fully to grasp the significance of the
distinction between the ancient and the immemorial. But it would be
wrong to lay too much stress on the contradictions and logical imper-
fections which characterize the arguments of many of them. What
is really important is their appeal to history as a means of harmonizing
the constitutional case for controls on royal power with instincts which
were deeply conservative. The idea of an ancient and an immemorial

constitution – as exemplified in William Hakewill's account of the existence of modern parliamentary institutions and parliamentary consent to taxation under Edward the Confessor[14] – was designed to lend the respectability of antiquity to constitutional practices and attitudes which had far more of innovation in them than their proponents cared to admit.

The last point is, of course, important, but it is too easy to dismiss the parliamentary emphasis on tradition and the antiquity of the constitution as the conservative disguise of an innovating opposition, pointing to the celebrated English propensity for clothing revolutionary change in traditional garb. Now while there may be an element of truth in this, it is at best no more than a half-truth. As we shall see later,[15] those who went to war against Charles I in 1642 – or, as they significantly put it, those who fought for King and Parliament – were for the most part deeply conservative men who sincerely believed they were defending ancient and traditional rights. It is true that there were others who scorned the appeal to history and tradition, but they were emphatically the exception rather than the rule. If the majority was 'revolutionary' it was 'revolutionary' in the seventeenth-century rather than the Whig or Marxist sense of the term,[16] desiring not violent social and political upheaval but a return to those fundamental constitutional principles which had been violated by arbitrary royal rule.

Needless to say the Crown did not willingly accept the innovatory role attributed to it by its critics. To the claim that the proposed changes of 1641-2 in the constitutional balance between Crown and Parliament in favour of the latter were no more than a restoration of the ancient constitutional equilibrium, the king opposed the view that these changes usurped royal rights which were themselves of immemorial antiquity.[17] An innovation, the king's advisers remonstrated, was not rendered less of an innovation 'by the meer averring it to be according to the fundamentall Laws of this Kingdom.' Far from being immemorial, such things were 'a totall Subversion of the Fundamentall Laws, and that excellent Constitution . . . which hath made this Nation . . . both famous and happy.'[18] It was natural that the king should resort to such arguments in the circumstances of 1642 when, in the course of his advisers' battle with John Pym for the soul of the political centre, they devised arguments which were designed to appeal to a basically conservative political nation and win back support which had been lost during the period of the royal offensive during the eleven years of non-parliamentary rule before 1640. In truth, Pym's claim that the constitutional innovations of 1640-2 were simply restoring the ancient constitutional balance was as difficult to sustain as the elaborate historical justifications which had been dragged up by Attorney General Noy and others for the royal innovations of the 1630s. By contrast, royal Me-Tooism was likely to be more effective in circumstances where it was the Parliament and not the Crown which was on the offensive, but this should not blind us to the fact that in the decades before 1640 royal claims had been far less dependent on arguments from immemorial antiquity than had those of Parliament. The Divine Right of Kings itself, quite apart from its novelty as a doctrine,[19] was in no way crucially dependent on historical arguments. When James I had recourse to an argument from history in his celebrated speech to the Parliament of 1610, the essential feature of the argument was that historical circumstances alter cases,[20] a doctrine which is inimical to the defence of constitutional rights in terms of their historicity.

II

The compartmentalization of different aspects of life and knowledge which is one of the features of the modern world and a notable product of the Renaissance had already made some spectacular advances by the early seventeenth century. For example, many thinkers, statesmen and men of affairs had already accustomed themselves to considering economic and political matters in autonomously economic or political terms, and to this extent the unifying force presented by the great overarching considerations of moral theology was weakened. On the other hand it is too easy to make insufficient allowance for the resilience of the traditional world view. For example, the ideas about the antiquity of the constitution which have been considered above found extremely significant analogies in the field of religious and ecclesiastical controversy which are treated in a later chapter.[21] Ulysses' famous utterance about degree in Shakespeare's *Troilus and Cressida*[22] testifies to the power of the notion that nothing was fully compartmentalized and that events on one plane of activity produce parallels upon others. The intimate connection between the world of religion and politics and that of thought and culture, which the historian neglects at his peril, is perhaps even more rewarding of study in the age of Shakespeare, Milton and Inigo Jones than at any other time in English history, partly because great artists, far from detaching themselves from the central political and religious issues of their day, were passionately concerned with them. The case for Crown and Court as innovators is reinforced when we turn from considerations of politics to those of culture.

Certainly under the first two Stuart kings, and especially during the reign of Charles I, it is reasonable to speak of the emergence of a distinctive Court culture. This was a peculiarly self-contained, even introspective, phenomenon, which, unlike its Elizabethan equivalent, was unconnected with the need to publicize the monarch and his role to the political nation in general. In addition those who indulged in it were minority groups of cultivated men and women rather than the Court as a whole. On many of the courtiers who thronged to Court masques, for example, the neo-Platonic subtleties of the art form must have been completely lost, and the experience analogous to the unlikely occasion of a visit by a modern rugby club outing to the Covent Garden ballet. Nevertheless if the connoisseurs and virtuosi were in a minority at Court, they were a creative minority who influenced profoundly the whole character of the Court. Sir Oliver Millar has described Charles I as 'the most enthusiastic and discerning patron of the arts to grace the English throne', and his collection as 'unequalled in the history of English taste'.[23] And around the king was a small but select circle of collectors and patrons, the so-called Whitehall group, of whom the Earl of Arundel was the most discerning and erudite collector and the Duke of Buckingham the most lavish. The extent to which their collections were the product of genuine aesthetic interests or of the mania for collecting *per se* and, in the king's case, a desire to vie with other royal collectors, which may have been one product of his visit to Madrid in 1623, cannot easily be determined, and on the whole art historians have opted for the more generous interpretation.

But if those courtiers who shared the king's love of art or of collecting were a small minority whose tastes were not appreciated by most of their fellow-courtiers, they were the object of profound suspicion to some of the inhabitants of the world outside the Court. This is not altogether surprising, for the Catholic element at Court centering around Henrietta Maria lost no opportunity of exploiting the royal taste for the art of Counter-Reformation Italy and the Southern Netherlands. They were aided at Rome by the Pope's nephew, Cardinal Barberini, who, among other things, was instrumental in getting the great baroque sculptor Bernini to do the bust of the king. Whatever exactly went on at the negotiations conducted by papal agents in

London, ostensibly about artistic matters, there can be no doubt that many Englishmen feared the worst; among them that indefatigable Protestant and conservative, William Prynne, who was deeply suspicious of what he saw as a plot 'to seduce the King himself with Pictures, Antiquities, Images & other vanities brought from *Rome*.'[24] The art historian may be correct in asserting that 'Charles I's achievement was to set England for a tragically short period within the orbit of most of the contemporary artistic movements on the Continent.'[25] But to the majority of Englishmen this made him an object of suspicion rather than of admiration.

'At this time in England . . .,' wrote the late Sir Ellis Waterhouse, 'collecting and the patronage of the living painter went hand in hand.'[26] The beginnings of the process whereby England was brought into the mainstream of European art are normally associated with the arrival of the Netherlandish painters Paul van Somer and Daniel Mytens in England around 1617–18.[27] From here grew the association of the English Court and monarchy with high baroque painting which was to culminate gloriously in the royal and courtly patronage of Rubens and, especially, of Van Dyck. But their significance extends beyond this, for both in Rubens' ceiling canvases in the Banqueting House in Whitehall and in Van Dyck's equestrian portraits of Charles I, the connection between artistic innovation and politics becomes apparent, for both give unforgettable expression to the aspirations of the Stuart monarchy. Indeed Van Dyck's equestrian portrait, now in the National Gallery, links Charles I with one of the most ancient traditional representations of the imperial theme, revived in the Renaissance with Michelangelo's dramatic *mise en scène* on the Capitol of the equestrian statue of Marcus Aurelius to greet the arrival of the Emperor Charles V at Rome, and with Titian's celebrated equestrian portrait of the same emperor, with which Charles I must have already been familiar from his visit to Madrid as Prince of Wales in 1623.[28] Van Dyck's mastery of the techniques of baroque portraiture produced a dazzling picture of majesty, however far removed the representation might be from the reality. The gulf between the two is well brought out by the well-known story of the disenchantment of Charles I's niece, Sophia, who was ultimately to become, appropriately enough, the mother of the first of that Hanoverian dynasty which was finally to put paid to Stuart hopes in the next century. Hitherto acquainted only with Van Dyck's enchanting portrait (we do not know which) of Henrietta Maria, the princess was astonished when she encountered at the

Hague in 1642 'a small woman . . . with long skinny arms and teeth like defence works projecting from her mouth'.[29]

III

Nothing like Charles I's patronage of great foreign artists had been seen since the days of the employment of Torregiano and Holbein at the Court of Henry VIII. The same is true of architectural innovation, though here some credit must also go to James I who renewed the role of the monarch as builder in the grand style which had virtually lapsed under Henry's daughters. Here the prime object of royal patronage was not a foreigner but an Englishman, or rather Welshman, but for all that an artist of comparable stature, 'an architectural Rubens' as he has been described by Sir John Summerson, emphasizing the need to see his work in a European rather than a native English context.[30] Contemporary Italians familiar with the high baroque creations of Bernini and Borromini would probably have boggled at the idea of Inigo Jones as a significant architectural innovator. They would certainly have regarded his Palladian inspiration – and indeed his insistence in searching back beyond Palladio and rejecting what he regarded as mannerist excrescences marring the work of the Vicenzan master – as distinctly old-fashioned, already at least a century out of date, revolutionary and unfamiliar as Jones's creations might appear to contemporary Englishmen. Looked at from another perspective, however, the verdict is different, and if Jones's work was old-fashioned to contemporary Italians it was to be a source of wonder and inspiration to the neo-classical pundits of the next century. How much Jones owed to his native genius and how much to Italian models – not simply to Palladio, but also to others, and perhaps especially to Scamozzi, in his rejection of the mannerist elements in Palladianism – is a matter for the art historian.[31] His reputation as an innovator in an English context is hardly at stake, and anyway what he produced were never slavish copies of Italian models but a genre which was at one and the same time both strikingly new and unequivocally English.

Few contemporary Englishmen would have agreed with this last statement, and it may be that our consciousness of Jones's Englishness derives less from considerations like the horizontal accentuation of his work emphasized by some architectural historians[32] than from retrospective, and therefore unhistorical, insights which are derived from an English tradition, to which he was an inspiration, but which can

hardly be said to have begun until the eighteenth century. Most contemporary Englishmen who were aware of Jones's work were probably
far more conscious of its un-English novelty and its total incongruity
within an English setting than of the classical chasteness and unfussi-
ness which strike the modern, as they struck the eighteenth-century,
observer. Moreover, like Prynne in the matter of the royal collection
of paintings, they concentrated less on matters of style than on matters
of use. And consider the uses to which some of Jones's most famous
buildings were put: a wildly eccentric garden house at Greenwich built
for a papist queen, the centre of Catholic intrigue at Court; chapels
at Somerset House and in St James's, where not only the queen, but
many courtiers worshipped in accordance with the hated Roman rites;
the Banqueting House, the setting for masques, those expensive and
immoral inportations from Catholic France and Italy; and a new west
front for St Paul's Cathedral, with a giant portico, the highest north of
the Alps. This latter provided a suitable façade for that temple of the
Arminian liturgical and ceremonial innovations introduced by William
Laud, who was Bishop of London from 1628 to 1633, and whose
pressure, both before and after his elevation to Canterbury, on both
Londoners and provincials to contribute towards the cost, as well as his
ruthlessness in sweeping aside adjacent dwellings and shops and even
one parish church to make room for these changes, made it certain
that they would be attended with the maximum amount of hostility.[33]
For, regrettably no doubt, it is considerations such as these, rather
than matters of form and style, on which the historian needs to concentrate his attention if he seeks to probe the general historical significance
of the phenomena which are the subject matter of cultural history.

The number of contemporary buildings which tradition ascribes to
Inigo Jones is in all around 120,[34] but this reflects the posthumous fame
of the architect rather than his popularity even in courtly circles in his
own time. The private houses in which he had a hand, such as the Earl
of Pembroke's Wilton and perhaps, as has been argued by Professor
Stone, the south front of the Earl of Salisbury's Hatfield,[35] were relatively few. For most of the others the only evidence for attributing
design to the master is the existence of some classical features even
if these are incongruously mixed with distinctly un-Jonesian elements.
In general the most distinctive feature of courtly houses was to be found
less in their architectural style than in their sheer size, marking them
off from the more modest houses of country gentlemen. However a
word of caution is necessary here. It would certainly be dangerous to

accept the phenomenon described by Sir John Summerson as the 'prodigy house' as a simple expression of courtly conspicuous consumption. The variety of buildings included under this heading and the variety of their owners in terms of the undoubted connection of some and the highly tenuous connection of others with the Court makes it difficult to find a factor common to them all, unless it be the need of their owners to give expression to relatively newly acquired status. For on the whole the older aristocracy eschewed such things, and if it be argued that a Talbot was responsible for Hardwick and a Howard for Audley End, this objection can fairly easily be countered by the argument that Hardwick was the creation not of the Earl of Shrewsbury but of his parvenue wife, and that the fortunes of the Howards were enjoying a spectacular revival in the early years of the reign of James I after decades in the political wilderness.

The novelty which contemporary opinion attached to such houses related more to their social than to their aesthetic significance. Or, to put it another way, the innovatory features remarked upon by contemporaries were considered significant because they were thought to reflect more fundamental things. Such features were the altered disposition of the great hall and the stress on ornamental elaboration, whose details were often derived from Serlio, De Vries and Dietterlin, whether via pattern-books or through the influence of alien craftsmen,[36] and appeared to betoken an obsessive concern with ornament at the expense of function. Such things were especially worthy of remark because they had a significance which transcended aesthetics and reflected a scale of social values which was felt to be diametrically opposed to the traditional virtues of the paternalistic estate owner.[37] But it would be unwise to stress too strongly this notion of the indivisibility of the idea of tradition and innovation across all forms of activity. For example, to his Puritan and other critics in matters of ritual, Church government and doctrine Laud was an innovator and they the preservers of ecclesiastical tradition.[38] But if we expect this to be reflected in Laud's own aesthetic tastes, as witnessed by Canterbury Quadrangle at St John's College, Oxford, or the rebuilt church of St Katherine Cree in London; whose high-Laudian reconsecration provided Prynne with the opportunity for a more than usually effective lampoon,[39] we shall be disappointed. In the one project where the names of Laud and Inigo Jones are coupled, the rebuilt west front of St Paul's, the choice of the architect can surely be ascribed to the king rather than to the bishop.

IV

An interesting parallel with the achievement of Inigo Jones in the sphere of Court architecture is provided by the case of William Lawes in that of Court music. Although Lawes' music was far more strongly influenced by fashionable baroque tendencies than was Jones's architecture, the part of his output which excites the greatest interest and admiration of modern musicologists is the instrumental Consort Suites which, as in the case of Jones's neo-Palladianism, the contemporary enthusiast for the high baroque probably found old-fashioned but which have riveted the attention of modern scholars on him as one of the most important influences of the period on the future development of English music and a precocious anticipator of the music of the post-baroque era.

The historical context in which both architect and musician flourished was the royal Court, the centre *par excellence* of cultural innovation. Security of position, more substantial and regular payment, the greater availability of high-class instruments and singers, even immunity from the vagrancy laws, were all factors of crucial importance in attracting the best available musicians to the Court and the royal service.[40] Referring to one of the outstanding musical innovations of the period, the free declamatory style of writing for solo voice which was employed, though certainly not introduced, by Lawes, his biographer stresses the fact that this was 'an exclusive art form designed for a small coterie of intellectuals, nobility, poets, wits, musicians and artists who adorned the sophisticated chambers of the Court.'[41] During the later years of Elizabeth's reign more than half of the musicians at the English Court were foreigners[42] and the foreign influx continued under the Stuarts. Nor was religion always a bar to royal patronage as the Elizabethan patents conferred upon William Byrd and Thomas Morley demonstrate.[43]

What the King's Musick did for secular the Chapel Royal did for sacred music. It was especially here, and to a lesser extent, in some of the cathedrals and in those Oxford and Cambridge colleges which had not succumbed to Puritan influence, that music figured prominently in liturgical practice. Outside the Chapels Royal, the Caroline period was not a time of notable innovation with regard to the composition of sacred music, but it is significant for what amounted to an attempted extension of the norms of courtly practice into wider spheres as part of that process of Laudian ritualistic and ceremonial innovation which aroused such widespread resentment in the country. A *cause célèbre* in which musical and other forms of innovation were significantly linked was the dispute between the Laudian John Cosin and the Puritan prebendary Peter Smart over the innovations favoured by the former in the services in Durham Cathedral. Among the things to which Smart took objection was that Cosin and his supporters claimed 'for your noveltyes the imytation of the Court, as if every preist or prelate may be so sawcy as to imitate the King'. Mixed in with the objections to the replacement of communion table by altar, 'ducking', (viz. bowing) and the use of crucifixes, candles and communion wafers was 'the horrible profanation of both the sacraments with all manner of musick, both instrumentall and vocall, so lowde that the Ministers could not be heard'. But it would be wrong to see this sort of objection simply as an apt illustration of Puritan philistinism. Of crucial importance in Smart's objections are the drowning of the voice of the minister and the obscuring of the meaning of the service. Not every sort of music was objected to, but it was alleged against Cosin that

> ... you have not only banished the singing of psalmes, in the vulgar tunes, by authority allowed ... before and after sermons; but you have so changed the whole liturgie, that though it be not in Latin, yet by reason of the confusednes of voices of so many singers, with a multitude of melodius instruments (directly contrary to the Injunctions and Homilyes) the greatest part of the service is no better understood, then if it weare in Hebrue or Irish.[44]

To the Puritan conscience, organs, choirs and polyphony were no less offensive than the altars, wafer-cakes and crucifixes with which they were as inextricably associated as were the neo-Palladian creations of Inigo Jones with the world of the Counter-Reformation.[45] All were clear signs that powerful elements at Court were pushing England hard in the direction of Rome.

V

In the realm of drama no great claim can be advanced for the Court as a centre of vital cultural innovation. The greatest early Stuart dramatists found their audiences at the public theatres on Bankside and – to a lesser extent – in the northern suburbs, as well as at the far more expensive and exclusive private coterie theatres such as Blackfriars and

Salisbury Court. Nevertheless, as Professor Harbage has shown, during the reign of Charles I the Court came to exert a more marked influence on the theatre than ever before, and a distinct genre, Cavalier drama, made its appearance;[46] originally the product of amateur courtly dramatists but coming to exercise an important influence on professional playwrights also. After the early Jacobean achievements of late Shakespeare and early Jonson, it would obviously be absurd to attach the same sort of claim for the Court as an innovatory force which can be so convincingly made in the fields of portraiture, art collecting, architecture and music, not to mention politics and religion. But, as in these other cases, such cultural innovation as was fostered by the environment of the Court has an interest for the historian which transcends its importance for the student of drama. For it came to reflect both the best and the worst characteristics of the Caroline Court. The Court of James I, presided over by the homosexual monarch, as well as being the scene of so many heterosexual scandals of which the Essex divorce and the Roos scandal are only the most unsavoury, was a very different place from that of his son. During the reign of Charles I, and perhaps especially after the removal of the Duke of Buckingham in 1628, no effort was spared to clean up the life of the Court. If Puritan moralists were horrified by courtly – as indeed by all – drama, this was not because it anticipated the comedy of manners of the post-Restoration period with its emphasis on ribaldry, the cuckolding of country yokels and the seducing of country wives by licentious and sophisticated Court gallants.[47] Apart from their objection to the appearance of women in plays[48] – Prynne's notorious *Histriomastix* was sparked off by Henrietta Maria's appearance in Wat Montagu's *Shepherd's Paradise* in 1633 – there was little for them to cavil at in terms of sexual immorality. As Professor Harbage has pointed out, the very presence of Court ladies at such entertainments as well as their occasional participation as performers was a safeguard against that.[49] It was platonic, not corporeal love which occupied the centre of Cavalier dramatic attention. 'Cavalier plays are clean because the court was beginning to boast a veneer of refinement, and court ladies must needs be protected against embarrassment.'[50] But if the Caroline Court was a more refined and wholesome place than its Jacobean predecessor, its social tone was, if anything, more exclusive, aristocratic and authoritarian.[51] Of those qualities the first two are abundantly reflected in Cavalier drama, the *dramatum personae* of which are frequently 'the exemplars and expositors of a body of faddish notions about etiquette, ethics and the emotions.'[52]

But nothing better epitomizes the ethos and aspirations of the Stuart Court than the art form which attained its glorious climax in this period and environment: the Court masque. Here was a closed world, a world of illusions and splendour, which, unlike that of Cavalier drama, at its best was the product of the collaboration of two men of genius, Ben Jonson and Inigo Jones - at least until their celebrated quarrel in the 1630s - and a world as ephemeral as it was prodigiously expensive. 'Onely the enuie was, that it lasted not still, or (now it is past) cannot by imagination, much less description, be recouered to a part of that spirit it had in the gliding by.'[53] Like most forms of Court art, the masque has a profound significance for the student of contemporary politics and institutions. Not political propaganda in the normal sense of that term, since its limited courtly audiences did not need to be persuaded of the validity of its political message, it was, nevertheless, a morale-boosting exercise, even if a distinctly narcissistic and inward-looking one. Its potency operated via the intimate tripartite connection between the subject of the masque, the masquers themselves (often including members of the royal family) and the audience. What was portrayed behind the proscenium arch was not a separate world from that which was inhabitated by the onlookers, but an ideal neo-Platonic representation of it. And ideal and illusion merge with reality when the noble masquers descend from the stage and invite leading members of the audience to join them in the dance - the dance itself the symbol of order, authority, decorum and concord.[54] As Professor Orgel brilliantly puts it in his perceptive and seminal study of the Jacobean masque, 'what the spectator watched, he ultimately became.'[55]

The climax of the masque is the ritual glorification of the monarch. If the king himself was one of the masquers, as was Charles I on a number of occasions, this was relatively easy to contrive, but Charles did not take part in every masque and his father took part in none of them. However, far from the latter situation being a major obstacle to the achievement of the climax, it afforded an opportunity of exploiting that conjunction of illusion and reality which is the essence of the masque as an art form. For example, in the masque *Pleasure Reconciled to Virtue*, which Jonson and Jones put on in 1618, there comes a point at which one jeof the masquers in the role of Mercury contrives that the audience's attention be diverted from the masquers - of whom the Prince of Wales was one - to the king sitting off-stage and suddenly assuming the role of 'Hesperus, the glory of the West'.[56] From this point the attention of the audience would be divided between the prince and the eleven other noble masquers on stage and the king off-stage, until, of course, the descent of the masquers from the stage and the interpenetration of masquers and audience presages the culmination of the entertainment in the rendering of homage to the person of the monarch.[57]

It is not altogether without significance that, in the Twelfth Night performance of this masque, just as the climactic moment was approaching, and the principal masquers, including Prince Charles and Buckingham, had descended from the stage and were about to initiate that merging of illusion and reality which is the culmination of the masque as an art form, 'the King who is naturally choleric, got impatient and shouted aloud "Why don't they dance? What did they make me come here for? Devil take you all, dance!"'[58] The king's precipitate and indecorous behaviour shattered both the illusion and its intended conjunction with reality and therefore the *raison d'être* of the whole performance.

Nor was it simply such incidents which prevented masques from always carrying full conviction. In the achievement of the overall purpose of the masque, the episodes known as anti-masques had a crucial function to perform. For in the anti-masque is portrayed the antithesis of everything that courtly society and courtly virtue should stand for, and on more than one occasion the anti-masque was used as a medium for pillorying the enemies of the regime, including one who had already been pilloried in the literal sense of the term. The masque *The Temple of Love*, created by Jones and D'Avenant in 1635, contains reference to Puritan critics of the regime, among whom one can surely be identified as William Prynne, 'a modern devil, a sworn enemy of poesy, music and all ingenious arts, but a great friend to murmuring, libelling and all seeds of discords, attended by his factious followers, all which was expressed by their habits and dance'.[59]

But if the anti-masques were designed to portray the antithesis of courtly virtues, there was more than one occasion on which they bit dangerously near the courtly bone. The anti-masque which opens *Pleasure Reconciled to Vertue* personifies gluttony and disorder in the person of Comus:

> . . . the bouncing belly
> First father of sauce and deviser of jelly.[60]

Here is a world of excess and lack of restraint in which men can become 'living measures of drink and can transform themselves into Bottles or Tuns when they please'.[61] Such is the allegorical significance of another anti-masque, part of the same masque, described by Sir Edward Harwood in a letter to Sir Dudley Carleton as consisting of 'litle boyes dressed like bottells & a man in a great tonne which the bottells drew out & tost too and froe . . .'[62] The disappearance of this world and its replacement by the world of virtue, restraint and order is heralded by the appearance of Hercules, who scatters the anti-masquers whom he roundly denounces as 'burdens and shames of nature' wallowing in 'the sty of vice'. However some observers might be forgiven for finding the realities of Court life echoed at least as much in the anti-masque as in the masque proper. For the gluttony which was a product of the pursuit of pleasure totally unreconciled to virtue and portrayed in the anti-masques described above found notorious exemplification at Court, most spectacularly of all in the so-called ante-supper at which one supper was thrown away and replaced by another even more magnificent meal – the invention of that byword in Jacobean courtly prodigality, James Hay, later Viscount Doncaster and Earl of Carlisle. Nor did any anti-masque portray anything more vulgar and grotesque than the drunken orgy which served for an entertainment given at Theobalds in 1606 to mark the visit of Christian IV of Denmark, the king's brother-in-law, and, amongst his other accomplishments, probably the most intoxicated crowned head in Europe.[63]

There were other matters in which the world of the anti-masque came dangerously near to portraying all too familiar aspects of courtly vice. Despite Professor Leach's assertion that the anti-masque of projectors which was a prominent feature of Jones's and D'Avenant's masque *The Triumph of Peace*, which was mounted in 1634, was 'harmless in its satire because these would-be monopolists are crazed inventors of impossibilities,'[64] one has only to recall Ben Jonson's highly effective satirization of Court projects in *The Devil is an Ass* by his juxtaposition of the real and the fantastic[65] to become aware that, in an age when such rackets were popularly, and quite correctly, connected with the Court, there was abundant scope for the vices portrayed in this anti-masque to be identified with the seamier side of the economic operations of many courtiers.

Nothing perhaps better illustrates the enormous gulf that was fixed between the world of reality and the illusory world of the masque than the contrast between the ignominious English defeats at the hands of the Scots and the image of victorious monarchy which was presented in the last and perhaps the most spectacular masque of all. This was Jones's and Davenant's *Salmacida Spolia* which was put on in 1640, on the eve of the disappearance for ever of that rarefied world of which the masque was perhaps the most eloquent cultural expression.

> ... the King's Majesty and the rest of the masquers were discovered sitting in the Throne of Honour, his Majesty highest in a seat of gold and the rest of the Lords about him. This throne was adorned with palm trees, between which stood statues of the ancient heroes. In the under parts on each side lay captives bound, in several postures, lying on trophies of armour, shields, and antique weapons.[66]

The masque is our last example of that courtly cultural innovation which helped to mark out the life of the Court from that of the Country. Like Jones's architecture it derived its inspiration from abroad and especially from France and Italy. As such it was an obvious target for that xenophobia which never lay far below the surface of Country opposition to the Court. Worse than this, the area of inspiration was, as in so much else in the culture of the Court, the baroque world of the Counter-Reformation, which connected it in the popular mind with Popery and unspeakable forms of Italianate vice. As if all this was not enough, the masque was also prodigiously expensive. 'The more money that is spent on things of this sort,' wrote Serlio, that highly influential Italian authority on courtly art and culture, 'the more deserving they are of praise, for in truth they are to be associated with magnanimous princes and noble lords to whom ugly Parsimony is an evil Stranger.'[67] Those who had to foot the bill by contributing towards the subsidies voted by Parliament to defray a royal debt which had risen alarmingly because of James I's hardly surprising inability to live of his own, no doubt had very different views about such matters. The taxpayer did not need to know the precise details, such as that 2142 ounces of silk were supplied by the queen's silkmen for the costumes of fourteen masquing ladies and that £249 was spent on three masquing suits alone for *Pleasure Reconciled to Vertue*.[68] The masque was quite simply and obviously one of the prime examples of that royal prodigality which became increasingly a cause of complaint from such country gentlemen who were excluded from its benefits as Thomas Wentworth, MP for Oxford, who protested in the House of Commons in 1610 that 'he would never give his consent to take money from a poor frieze jerkin to trap a courtier's horse withal. And therefore he wished that we might join in humble petition to his Majesty that he would diminish his charge and live of his own without exacting of his poor subjects ...'[69]

This is, of course, a protest against courtly extravagance in general, rather than the masque in particular. Ironically enough the most telling and penetrating criticism of the masque from the point of view of the country gentlemen who, in one form or another, had to foot the ultimate bill, comes from the greatest of masque librettists, Ben Jonson. For what would have made the masque especially shocking to country gentlemen saving to make ends meet was the combination of the enormous expense of these Court spectaculars and the ephemeral nature of the occasions. Many masques were put on only once and few more than two or three times. The anti-masque never sailed more dangerously near the wind than it did in *Love Restored*, where Jonson puts the following sentiments into the mouth of Plutus:

> I tell thee, I will have no more masquing; I will not buy a false, and fleeting delight so deare: The merry madnesse of one hower shall not cost me the repentance of an age. . . . I will no more of these superfluous excesses.[70]

Even though such sentiments must be viewed in the context of the anti-masque as the vehicle for the enunciation of graceless, perverse and uncourtly opinions, they were probably a by no means inaccurate articulation of what was in the minds of many, not necessarily Puritanical, country gentlemen.

VI

If the masque is the most eloquent expression of the ethos of monarchy and Court, it is useful to set it against a literary genre which expresses in a similarly idealized way the contrasting ideals of the Country. This is best found in the great series of 'Country-house poems' which begins with Jonson's 'To Penshurst and 'To Sir Robert Wroth', continues in Herrick's 'Panegyricke to Sir Lewis Pemberton' and Carew's 'To Saxham' and culminates in Marvell's 'Upon Appleton House, to my Lord Fairfax', where, after the first dozen or so stanzas, the classic theme is transcended, and the poet turns to profounder and more personal issues.[71]

In 'To Penshurst' the contrast between the ethos of Court and Country is explicitly made from the beginning by the emphatic assertion of what Penshurst is not:

> Thou art not, Penshurst, built to envious show
> Of touch or marble, nor can boast a row

> Of polish'd pillars, or a roofe of gold.
> Thou hast no lantherne, whereof tales are told;
> Or stayre, or courts. . . .[72]

The contrast is clearly with the prodigy house, built to impress, in which use is sacrificed to ornament and where nature is violated for the sake of spectacular effect. The house grows, as it were, organically out of the countryside in the midst of which it is situated. Like the architecture of the house the animal and vegetable life of the estate find their *raison d'être* in use. Fish leap gladly into nets and pheasant and partridge find fulfilment in being served at dinner. The life of the countryside centres around the estate, for its lord is resident and not an absentee,[73] and his house is neither built nor maintained on the profits of oppressive estate management.

> And though thy walls be of the countrey stone
> They are rear'd with no mans ruine, no mans grone,
> There's none that dwells about them, wish them downe.[74]

The resident landlord who lives at home and practises the ancient patriarchal virtues lives off his estate and does not oppress his tenants. How different the absentee who evicts and racks the rents of tenants of whose existence as persons he is hardly aware, in order to finance a rake's progress of luxury at Court. The juxtaposition of images of courtly luxury and economic oppression is perhaps the most striking feature of Herrick's poem to Pemberton, who, like the owner of Penshurst, is presented as the antithesis of all these things:

> Safe stand thy Walls, and Thee, and so both will
> Since neithers height was rais'd by th'ill
> Of others; since no Stud, no Store, no Piece,
> Was rear'd up by the Poore-mans fleece:
> No Widowes Tenement was rackt to guild
> Or fret thy Sealing, or to build
> A *Sweating-Closset*, to annointe the silke-
> soft skin, or bath in *Asses milke*:
> No *Orphans* pittance, left him, serv'd to set
> The Pillars up of *lasting* Jet,
> For which their cryes might beate against their eares,
> Or in the dampe Jet read their Teares.[75]

It is often not until traditional virtues are under serious threat that they achieve widespread recognition as virtues, and it may be that the domestic and charitable activities of a Sidney, a Wroth or a

Pemberton had never been so generally practised as social commentators suggest, and that by now they had become distinctly exceptional. There can also be little doubt that the picture of open-handed generosity freely and ungrudgingly dispensed, equally from highest to lowest, is overdone. But it would be foolish to rush to the opposite extreme and to deny any element of truth in such accounts, which undoubtedly acquired additional poignancy as descriptions of a way of life which, however far its practice fell short of the ideal, was now passing away. And for all the open-handed generosity of the ideal old-fashioned landowner, decorum and moderation ruled in the well-ordered household. 'The rout of rurall folke' might throng into Sir Robert Wroth's house, and Pemberton might dispense wine

> As the *Canary* Isles were thine:
> But with that wisdome, and that method as
> No One that's there his guilty glasse
> Drinks of distemper, or ha's cause to cry
> Repentance to his liberty.
> No, thou know'st Order, Ethics, and ha's read
> All Oeconomicks....[76]

Of course, drunken orgies were not unknown in the country, but the picture conveyed in these poems is deliberately intended to be set beside courtly riots of conspicuous consumption, of which the orgy at Theobalds in 1606 is only one of many examples. '*O rus quando te aspiciam*', the words with which Sir John Harington, the shocked survivor of what was coming to be regarded as the period of Elizabethan courtly decorum, ended his description of the goings-on at Theobalds in 1606, may serve to point the contrast.[77]

VII

Another area of behaviour in which it became normal to contrast the life of the Country with that of the Court, and in which the latter was charged with deviating from traditional standards of behaviour, was that of sexual morality. Unquestionably the chief culprit here was the Jacobean Court. We have already had occasion to remark on the fact that the high moral tone of Caroline courtly drama reflects the very real improvement of standards at the Caroline Court. In this at least the lives of Charles and Henrietta left nothing to be desired as examples of chastity and family devotion to be held up to the nation. But, in so far as the popular image of the Court was concerned, by this time the damage had been done as a result of the notorious scandals of the Jacobean Court, all of which lost nothing in the telling, and no doubt tended to be regarded as the mere tip of a vice-ridden iceberg.

While the contrast between Court and Country in sexual as in other fields was accentuated by Puritanism, it existed irrespective of the Puritans. No one was less of a Puritan than Ben Jonson. Yet he commends that staunch, old-fashioned parliamentarian Sir Robert Wroth, who:

> ... Though so neere the citie and the court
> art tane with neithers vice, nor sport.

While of Lady Sidney at Penshurst, that epitome of the old-fashioned country house, he says:

> Thy lady's noble, fruitfull, chaste, withall
> His children thy great lord can call his owne;
> A fortune, in this age, but rarely knowne.[78]

Lady Sidney, Jonson's exemplar of the noble country wife, was not only chaste. She was also fruitful, like the estate on which she dwelt. But the object of courtly love was very different, as he makes clear in another poem:

> Fine Madame Would-bee, wherefore should you feare
> That love to make so well, a child to beare?
> The world reputes you barren: but I know
> Your 'pothecarie and his drug sayes no.
>
>   . . . .
>
> What should the cause be? Oh you live at court:
> And there's both losse of time, and losse of sport
> In a great belly. Write then on thy wombe,
> Of the not borne, yet buried, here's the tombe.[79]

In the Jacobean play *A Chaste Maid in Cheapside* by Thomas Middleton we catch a glimpse of a different and probably more common view of the sex-life of the court. During a particularly nasty scene in which Sir Oliver and Lady Kix are engaging in mutual recrimination about responsibility for their childless marriage, Lady Kix indignantly repudiates her husband's allegation that the fault lies in her, since she is barren.

> ... I barren!
> 'Twas otherways with me when I was at court,
> I was n'er called so till I was married.[80]

Middleton is here making an interesting comment on licit Country and illicit Court fruitfulness. But Jonson's contrast between fruitfulness and voluntary barrenness goes deeper, for it is an oblique and penetrating judgement on the artificiality of Court as distinct from Country life.[81]

In sexual mores as in so much else the accent of the Court was on sophistication and vice and of the Country on innocence and virtue; or so it seemed to those who celebrated the influence of the latter and deprecated that of the former. Perhaps the most striking literary expression of this contrast is by Robert Herrick, praising his brother, who:

> Could'st leave the City, for exchange, to see
> The Countries sweet simplicity:
> And it to know, and practice; with intent
> To grow the sooner innocent.

The modern mind might boggle at the idea of growing innocent, but it lies at the heart of that pastoral tradition which was, both in this complex and sophisticated form, as well as in less refined forms, to be an important ingredient of the ethos and ideology of the Country. It is the peculiar nature of this pastoral existence that it cleanses and purifies all who experience it. And so Herrick's sister-in-law surrenders her virginity not once but on every occasion on which she has sexual intercourse with her husband.

> Nor has the darknesse power to usher in
> Feare to those sheets, that know no sin.
> But still thy wife, by chast intentions led,
> Gives thee each night a Maidenhead.[82]

VIII

So far cultural innovation has tended to be associated with the Court and cultural conservatism with the Country, so that, under the guise of discussing the perennial dichotomy which gives the title to this chapter and which is so central to cultural history, we have also been throwing some light on another which has in recent years come to the forefront of the attention of historians of the politics of the period: that between

Court and Country. But the distinction between what was traditional and what was innovatory, and its identification with the distinction between Country and Court, was in reality much more complex than the treatment of the theme so far in this chapter might suggest. This can be illustrated by a few examples. Among those who sat for the great Court painter Van Dyck were three peers who sided with Parliament in the Civil War, the Earls of Northumberland, Pembroke and Warwick, and Arthur Goodwin, friend of John Hampden and, like him, a noted Buckinghamshire parliamentarian. The only Englishman known to have sat for Bernini was the Suffolk gentleman Thomas Baker, who also fought on the parliamentary side.[83] Inigo Jones has been treated in the context of his Court masques, his magnificent Banqueting House where they were mounted, the Palladian mansion built for a Catholic queen, and the private chapel where she and some of her courtly co-religionists worshipped. But he was also the architect of the first Protestant church to be built in London, St Paul's, Covent Garden, built, using the appropriately primitive Tuscan order, for the Earl of Bedford, a nobleman out of favour at Court and the political associate of Pym and Hampden during the 1630s. Jones was also the key figure in the Earl's development of the piazza at Covent Garden in which the church was situated, though how far Bedford was acting from free choice and how far from the need to associate the royal surveyor with this highly innovatory piece of town planning is a question.[84] The importance of the masque in the creation of courtly myths has been stressed, but the greatest masque of all was written by John Milton. Ben Jonson, the foremost exponent of the Court masque before he fell out with Inigo Jones, was also the author of two of the finest country-house poems which extol the virtues of the Country as opposed to the Court life. But again when considering the pastoral tradition of which this genre is a prime example, it is important to be aware not only of the importance of the pastoral existence in contradistinction to that of the Court, the life of contemplation as opposed to action, but also of its role as a cleansing and refreshing agency which renders those who experience it the more fit for the responsibilities of the courtly and governmental life.[85] And Ben Jonson himself was the author both of a poem to his muse which expresses self-disgust at the servility involved in obtaining a courtly patron and of numerous begging letters in verse to, among others, the Earls of Pembroke, Aubigny and Portland, and both of the first two Stuart kings.

Similarly, rural oppression was not simply the product of absentee landlordism and the need to finance a life of luxury at Court. Not all rack-renters, depopulators and other grinders of the faces of the rural poor were absentee courtier landlords. Not all non-courtly resident landowners were men of the stamp of Jonson's picture of the Sidneys of Penshurst or Herrick's of Sir Lewis Pemberton – model hospitality-dispensing, socially responsible, paternalistic landlords. Not all owners of prodigy houses were unmindful of their duties to the local rural community. Generous allowance must be made for the hyperbole employed by the country-house poets in developing, in their elaborate, versified thank-you letters, an important aspect of what could be described as the myth of the Country. For in so far as the prodigy houses which are eloquently depicted in these poems were testimony to the social importance of relatively newly arrived families, such arrivistes were the more likely to be susceptible to the social pressures which demanded the exercise of the traditional housekeeping virtues. No doubt Barnaby Rich's picture of the hospitality dispensed at the greatest of all Elizabethan prodigy houses, Sir Christopher Hatton's Holdenby, which 'giveth daily relief to such as be in want for the space of six or seven miles compass',[86] is overdone, but it serves as a useful corrective to the unforgettable passage in Herrick's *Pemberton* which has already been cited as linking economic oppression with courtly luxury and absentee landlordism.

Equally in need of modification is the distinction between the Court as the centre of sexual promiscuity and sexual deviation and the Country as the home of sexual purity. Many contemporaries who would not have quarrelled with the former identification would have been astonished by the latter. Shakespeare's picture of the life of the forest in *As You Like It*, where it is deliberately set in contradistinction to the Court, sees it not simply as the world of contemplation and pastoral refreshment, but of unbridled – if unsophisticated – sexual licence – the world of Touchstone and Audrey. In his great ode on Charles I's proclamation of 1630 Sir Richard Fanshaw makes no bones about the fact that the world to which the gentry and aristocracy were commanded to return from London was by no means a world of sexual innocence and purity, even if it is also not a world of sophistication. For

> There shall you see the nightingale
> The harmless siren of the wood,
> How prettily she tells a tale
> Of rape and blood.

In a word, the worlds of Court and Country were inextricably intertwined. The Country was interpenetrated by the Court, by courtly houses such as Burghley, Holdenby, Hatfield and Audley End, and interpenetrated politically by the fact that failure to obtain office rather than ideological objections was a main cause of political alienation in early Stuart England; and, as is demonstrated by the cases of Sir Edward Coke, William Hakewill, Sir Dudley Digges, William Noy and a host of others of whom the most spectacular example is Thomas Wentworth, some of the most fervent opponents of government were quick to change their tune when sweetened by the rewards of office. The Country was interpenetrated by the Court also through the way in which courtly factions used the Country opposition as a means of asserting their preponderance and bringing down their rivals at Court, as did Coke and Cranfield against Bacon in 1621, Buckingham and the Prince of Wales against Cranfield in 1624 and (though in this case unsuccessfully) Pembroke and other outraged courtiers against the upstart Buckingham in 1626.[87] Finally, as the next chapter will show, the Country was interpenetrated by agencies of royal centralization, many of which were to be found within the ranks of the local magistrates themselves.

There was in fact a great deal more to-ing and fro-ing between the worlds of Court and Country than is allowed for by the notion of a strict dichotomy between the two.[88] Nevertheless, when all this has been said, the fact remains that the distinction is something not drawn by a modern historian but part of the normal currency of contemporaries, who in turn tended to identify the Country with the maintenance of traditional standards and the Court with cultural, political, religious and numerous other varieties of innovation. The distinction may have something of the character of a myth, but the most important thing about myths is not that they are not founded upon complete historical truth, but that they are widely believed, in which circumstances they become historical facts in their own right which historians neglect at their peril. Those who went to war against Charles I in 1642 may have been revolutionaries in the sense that they were taking arms against their sovereign lord; but unless this truth is tempered by the knowledge that in their own view they were fighting not to innovate but to restore an old and better order which royal innovation had been well on the way to destroying, a very distorted view of their aims and aspirations will result.

THREE *Centralism and Localism*

Thus you see how by the only default of jurors and inquests the native liberty and ancient pre-eminence of the English policy is . . . very like . . . in short time to be utterly lost and taken from us if you lay not better hands and hold upon it. Which thing if it should happen in our days (as God forbid that it ever happen at all) we shall be condemned by all posterity to have been the most ungracious and base-minded age of men that have lived here since the general conquest of our nation and country.

Stand fast, therefore, stand fast, I say, in this liberty whereunto you are born and be inheritable . . . which your forefathers, not without sweat and blood, have recovered and left to descend to you.

> William Lambarde, 'Charge to the
> Michaelmas Sessions of the Peace,
> at Maidstone, 28 February 1591, et
> 33 Elizabethae Reginae', printed in
> C. Read (ed.), *William Lambarde and
> Local Government* (Ithaca 1962), p. 108.

I

IN JULY 1610 the House of Commons was treated by the Government to an account of the current inadequacies of local government consequent upon what it regarded as the failure of local magistrates to attend properly to their duties.[1] The subject of this chapter is the interplay between the Government's attempts to remedy this situation and the passionately held beliefs that these were putting hardly won and deeply cherished freedoms to hazard; the freedoms of a high degree of local self-government exercised by what it has become normal to call the community of the county. This concept has been subjected to sharp criticism by Dr Clive Holmes on grounds both of the alleged failure to stress the importance of the extra-county connections and aspirations of the county gentry and of the opposite error of neglecting more local foci of interest and activity – for example, the parish – than that of the shire. But, as Professor Fletcher has observed, far from being mutually exclusive, such foci and loyalties were overlapping and complementary.[2] Certainly it is no longer appropriate to regard the Commission of the Peace and the Quarter Sessional system of local government associated with it as the more or less willing workhorse of an exigent central government which was resolved to make its will effectively felt in the provinces. To achieve this end Stuart governments were prepared to adopt old and to devise new institutional means which were seen as offering a threat to what were regarded as the time-honoured powers of local magistracy. Such expedients testify not so much to local domination by central government as to a degree of localist independence of central government: a preparedness to go along with it where its policies were acceptable, but a propensity to drag feet where they were not.[3] Some of the most important constitutional and political controversies which were to culminate in civil war were themselves the product of stubborn local resistance to encroaching central power, and Parliament itself, packed as it was with country gentlemen, was the medium through which a wide variety of such local grievances were, as it were, nationalized. It is in many cases misleading to place 'national' in sharp contradistinction to 'local' issues, since, at least as often as not, the former grew out of, and were an amalgam of the latter.

II

Far from being innovations, some of the administrative procedures employed by the government to remedy the deficiencies of the local magistracies lay ready to hand. Elizabethan government had made regular administrative use of the assizes held in every county by judges on circuit to exercise a general oversight over the way in which JPs were performing their duties, and these arrangements continued under the Stuarts.[4] In 1635, for example, letters were sent by the Privy Council urging all assize judges on circuit to take special care to observe that JPs efficiently administered the Council's Orders and Directions relating to the provision of adequate supplies of corn and other foodstuffs and the administration of the Poor Law. The assize judges were to see to it that the JPs returned certificates testifying to the action taken by them, and were, if necessary, to punish defaulters or certify their names to the Council.[5] Indeed, quite apart from the assize judges, a formidable apparatus of centralized control was built up around the Caroline Orders and Directions of the 1630s, and unusual steps were taken to prevent 'the frustratinge of the sayd orders . . . from the negligence of the Justices of the Peace'. In 1630 a special committee of the Privy Council had been designed as commissioners for the poor, and these commissioners were in turn divided into sub-committees, each with a watching brief over a particular assize circuit. In addition, they delegated powers to local commissioners who were distinct from, though overlapping with, the Commission of the Peace. In the early 1630s the responsiveness of the local magistracy and the pressure to which it was subjected from central government was probably greater than it had been for at least a century. While some historians have expressed justified scepticism about the extent to which the 'improvement' was sustained throughout the decade,[6] there can be little doubt about the widespread resentment bred by the attempt. For example, when confronted by a Council order of 1631 that all corn in Norfolk should be brought to specified market towns for sale, which, they claimed, would interfere with a long-established and smoothly working system, the Norfolk magistrates must have experienced great difficulty in restraining themselves. The Council was read a polite but firm lecture about the geography and agrarian economy of the county and informed that 'this particular part of the Kingdome neuer changed their auntient vse in his behalfe'. In other words, old and well-tried ways were best.[7]

III

One agency of centralized control which acquired great notoriety under Elizabeth and James I, but which seems to have been seriously curtailed as a result of the Statute of Monopolies of 1624, was the administrative patent. The government's pursuit of mutually inconsistent objectives by resorting to methods of economic and social control which were also designed to act as a form of courtly out-relief helped to make of patents an important anti-Court issue, for they were one of the most powerful challenges to the traditional system of local controls exercised through the Commission of the Peace and the Quarter Sessions.[8]

Needless to say, the incongruity of an administrative procedure which was designed to produce a more efficient and centralized form of control by specifically linking public control with the pursuit of the patentee's private profit was fair game for critics. In 1610 the House of Commons informed the king that the execution of penal statutes was vested in him alone and could not be alienated to anyone.[9] However, there were ways around this difficulty. Patentees could be given the role of Commissioners acting in the royal name instead of their own, which in every sense except the necessary legal one amounted to virtually the same thing.[10] One of the reasons why parliament disliked the system was that it put effective enforcement of some of the legislation which it had passed into the hands of private individuals who, more often than not, profited by dispensing with the operation of statutes rather than by enforcing them. Another was undoubtedly the parliamentary influence of the local magistracy, who would have hated patentees as much for enforcing statutes as for dispensing with them, since they were thereby trespassing on the functions of the JPs.

In his interesting account of the working of the penal statutes, Professor Beresford has shown how by the statute of 1624 the number of cases actionable in the central courts at Westminster was spectacularly reduced, and that this removed 'the tariff of distance and expense' which had been a primary reason why so many hapless individuals had consented to compound with patentees for their offences.[11] He does not, however, mention that the other chief gainers from the legislation of 1624 were the JPs, who rejoiced in what they saw as a triumph of localism over centralism. In a speech in the House of Commons on 22 February 1621 against the patent for licensing alehouses, Sir Edward Coke significantly linked the authority of JPs to license alehouses and issue recognizances to licensees with parliamentary, that is, statutory, authority.

> ... This recognizance [is] to be certified to the Sessions and there to be kept that the justices may know when it is forfeited, which they cannot do if these patentees ... keep them in London, which was never the intent of the lawmakers; this therefore is a wrong to the justices. ... The justice *in proprio comitatu* was all for the common good, but these [projectors] travel into 52 countries for their private benefit. ... Besides the justices upon the matter are but these projectors servants. For ... they have put in their patent a command upon the justices of peace to be assistant unto them. What a base thing is that.[12]

What a base thing indeed! Apart from their usurpation of the statutory functions of the local magistrate, the patentees added insult to injury by requiring him to be at the beck and call not only of them, but also of their deputies, men 'of very mean condition and report,' as was remarked of the deputies of the alehouse patent.[13] 'No government in the Country', argued Sir Edward Giles with pardonable exaggeration on 19 February 1621, 'if the Ministers of Justice should be thus contemned.' Sir Robert Phelips complained of the same patent that he 'never knew government receive so great a wound,' for 'whereas the King hath referred a great part of the government of this kingdom to the justices of peace, this dishearteneth them, for it maketh a justice of peace to be buffeted by a base alehouse-keeper.'[14]

But perhaps most resented of all was the ability of some patentees to find places for 'base and unworthy men', who would do them service, on the Commission of the Peace itself, or even to suborn existing justices and use them for their own ends. As will appear more than once in the course of this chapter, the Commission of the Peace was by no means monolithic in its attitude to royal centralizing processes. An excellent example of its infiltration by the enemy in the case of patents is provided by Mompesson's notorious creature, Sir Francis Mitchell, who was degraded by the House of Commons from the dignity of knighthood and declared unfit to be a member of the Commission. One of the things which was held very much against him was the allegation that he 'hath no land nor annuitie, and lives of his Justice-ship.' Similar considerations no doubt prompted the proposal of Sir Dudley Digges on 22 February that the king should be petitioned for stricter control of the numbers of the JPs 'for some justices were so mean as there is a contempt of them and some so poor that they project such things as these.'[15]

Another objection which was frequently brought against patentees was their total lack of the necessary technical know-how to perform the duties stipulated in their patents, and therefore also adequately to supervise any deputies whom they might appoint to do so. 'And is Sir Henry Goldsmith a fit person to judge who shall be a rat-catcher, tinker, etc. that was never brought up in the trade?' Such was the acid comment in the Commons in 1621 against one of the holders of a patent of 1619 concerning offences against the apprenticeship clauses of the Statute of Artificers of 1563.[16] But the argument cuts both ways, and was hardly less applicable to the qualification of an ordinary JP than to those of a courtly patentee. In September 1616 the Merchant Adventurers' Company, itself in a sense a semi-official government agency for the export of cloth, wearied by the lack of effective response to its complaints about the quality of Gloucestershire cloth, produced an alarmingly radical proposal that its members should be allowed to nominate a merchant to visit the western clothing counties to supervise the JPs' performance of their statutory functions in connection with the manufacture of cloth and, in particular, to see that they appointed suitably knowledgeable overseers. For the JPs to have their actions supervised by low-born central snoopers was bad enough. But the Merchant Adventurers' proposals went much further than this, for the efficient prosecution of the merchant's duties was to be facilitated by – outrageous suggestion! – his recruitment on to the Commission of the Peace for Gloucestershire, and three neighbouring clothing counties.[17] It was again at the request of the Merchant Adventurers that in 1630 the Privy Council appointed two commissioners charged with examining and reforming abuses in cloth production. One of these men met with stiff resistance from the locally appointed searchers in Gloucestershire, who were backed up by Nathaniel Stephens, a local JP whose example appears to have spread to other local magistrates, who objected strongly to the oath which the Commission administered to searchers, without which the Commission would have been hamstrung. The recalcitrant magistrates had to be summoned before the Privy Council before they submitted.[18]

The discussion in the last paragraph, centering around the problem of the technical competence of the executants of government policies, moved from the consideration of administrative patents to other forms of control foisted upon an allegedly inefficient local magistracy. Magisterial opposition to all these methods was inevitable, given the clear implication – and indeed, frequently the explicit assertion – by the Government that they had their origin in the manifold deficiencies of magisterial regulation. It was, moreover, as we have seen, exacerbated by the requirement that the JPs cooperate with – and on occasions subordinate themselves to – patentees and their deputies,[19] who added to the injury of being strangers to the counties where they operated the insult of lowly social origins. In a famous declaration to the Long Parliament in 1642, John Pym referred with approval to an incident which had taken place in the third year of the reign, when a respected MP had referred to the requirement that JPs should render assistance to patentees as 'a great dishonour to those Gentlemen which are in Commission to be so meanely imployed.'[20] Social snobbery and wounded *amour propre* are among the more neglected factors in the evolution of both local and parliamentary opposition to Stuart government.

IV

To the operation of the administrative patent with its basic assumption that the pursuit of the private profit of the patentee was entirely compatible with the public ends of centralized economic and social control, a notable contrast was presented by another agency of control, the lieutenancy. Of course, the two functions were by no means mutually exclusive and it was not unknown for lord lieutenants and their deputies also to be patentees. Sir Arthur Heveningham, a deputy lieutenant in Elizabethan Norfolk, had no compunctions about employing his lieutenancy powers to implement his patents, while Sir Francis Mitchell, Mompesson's creature in the enforcement of his numerous patents, as well as being a JP, was reported in 1621 to have threatened recalcitrant alehouse-keepers in the metropolitan area who were protesting against the abuses of the alehouse patent that 'he was a deputy Lieutenant and would scatter them with Musquets.'[21]

With the Tudor origins and early history of the lieutenancy we need not here be concerned,[22] and it is enough to note that by the end of James i's reign it was distinctly unusual for counties not to have lieutenants, though some lieutenants served several counties.[23] First and foremost the lord lieutenant was responsible for the military preparedness and defence of the county, but his functions flowed fairly naturally over from this into a number of other spheres. If, as Miss Scott Thomson suggests, one of these was 'that the counties might be kept in quiet and order,'[24] it was not altogether unreasonable to interpret this as involving more than a mere supervision of militia training and military affairs narrowly conceived. The need to maintain order among the pressed levies within the county under the lieutenant's jurisdiction was an obvious case for the legitimate exercise of his authority, and it was chiefly to this end that lord lieutenants had appointed those Provost Marshals whose activities were the occasion of so much disquiet to so many JPs in the 1590s and after.[25] For what more natural than that the Provost Marshal's functions should be extended from an oversight of those under arms to disbanded men on their way home or seeking employment; and, in turn, from them to the mass of vagrants from whom they were not always easily distinguishable?

It is somewhere along this line of gradually and hardly perceptibly extended jurisdiction that the authority of the Provost Marshal began to tread heavily on the toes of the Commission of the Peace. These incursions were less frequent in the conditions of peace in the reign of James I than they had been in the later years of Elizabeth, but they became more marked after 1624 during the years of war.

The case of the office of Provost Marshal provides an excellent example of the extension of the powers of the lieutenancy into areas which the local magistracy regarded as its peculiar administrative territory. But at least in this case these powers had followed naturally enough from a widening of the bridgehead represented by the lord lieutenant's military authority. But there were numerous other functions exercised by the lieutenancy for which it would not be easy to find such a justification, including *inter alia*, the enforcement of the recusancy laws, the supervision of the machinery for collecting Forced Loans, and even of the extent to which the royal wishes about the planting of mulberry bushes had been observed. Additional ground for magisterial fear and resentment was the fact that the lord lieutenant was an obvious source of information for the Government as to the composition of the Commission of the Peace itself.[26] In such circumstances with the lord lieutenant or his deputies interfering in a wide variety of matters hitherto considered as falling within his exclusive jurisdiction, and casting a very long shadow over virtually the whole of the remainder of his functions, the local magistrate may be excused a certain apprehensiveness that, as in the case of patents, he was being reduced to the status of a mere administrative assistant at the beck and call of a higher, centrally oriented authority. Thus, even when, in 1636, the Kentish lieutenancy was performing what was beyond doubt a lieutenancy function in urging JPs to see that the beacons were properly manned, there were among the Kentish JPs those who entertained very serious doubts about the propriety of accepting orders from the deputy lieutenants, who had in former times 'prayed' the JPs to take action, but now 'required' them to do so. The change of words might not signify much in terms of the deputy lieutenants' objectives, but it was open to any number of unfavourable interpretations by touchy and status-conscious local magistrates. The previous year had seen a similar incident in Somerset – the attack at the midsummer sessions of the peace on the orders transmitted from the deputy lieutenants to the JPs to assist them in the matter of Ship Money.[27]

There can be no doubt both that the lieutenancy was conceived by the Government to be a prime instrument for the breaking down of local particularism in the interests of efficient centralized control, and that most of the local magistrates were heavily tarred with the particu- larist brush. The lieutenant, by contrast, was normally a man of stand- ing at the Court, often himself a Privy Councillor and as such a member of that government which was seeking to impose its will on the provinces.[28] From the localist point of view, the dangers of this aim being effectively accomplished were increased as a result of the early Stuart tendency to appoint a greater number of lord lieutenants than had been normal under Elizabeth with the intention of increasing the effectiveness of their control. For example, until his death in 1601, the Earl of Pembroke had been Lord Lieutenant not only of Wiltshire and Somerset but also of the Welsh counties and (at least for part of the time) of four of the counties on the Welsh border. But the authority of his successor, the Earl of Hertford, as Lieutenant of Wiltshire and Somerset was confined to these two adjacent counties, which ought to have made for a far greater concentration of administration and control.[29]

A crucial consideration was the extent to which lord lieutenants were served by efficient and devoted deputy lieutenants. The deputy lieutenants were drawn from the ranks of the élite country gentry, and were normally, if not quite invariably, themselves members of the Commission of the Peace; so that, in so far as they were devoted to their superior and to their office, their views on the need for centralized con- trol were markedly different from those of most of their colleagues on the Commission of the Peace. Self-evident as it may seem, however, and true as it probably is in the majority of cases, this proposition needs to be advanced with caution, since not all deputy lieutenants were so devoted to the cause of centralized control as might appear at first sight. The battle between localism and centralism in Elizabethan Norfolk has become familiar through the work of Professor Hassell Smith – with Sir Nathaniel Bacon of Stiffkey, though himself the son of an Elizabe- than lord keeper, the champion of local particularism; and Sir Arthur Heveningham, deputy lieutenant, and also for most of the period also a member of the Commission of the Peace, his main centralist oppo- nent. But some of the force of this classic dichotomy is diminished by the fact that Bacon himself became a deputy lieutenant in the next reign, and the strength of his localist convictions appears not to have diminished one iota.[30] An even more striking example is the case of Sir Richard Knightley, deputy lieutenant for Northamptonshire, who had been fined both under Elizabeth I for involvement in the publication of the seditious Marprelate tracts, and in 1605 for signing a petition protesting against the suspension of nonconformist ministers, for which offence he was also deprived of his deputy lieutenancy and struck off the Northamptonshire Commission of the Peace. This record of Puritan opposition did not, however, prevent his reinstatement as a deputy lieutenant in 1612; not, if his subsequent behaviour is any guide, an indication that he had been effectively brought to heel.[31]

Prominent among the reasons which impelled country gentlemen to accept deputy lieutenancies were the advantages flowing from establishing intimate connections with the influential magnate who served as lord lieutenant; among which were the opportunities for an increase in personal power, social prestige and (not least) the wreaking of one's will in faction-ridden county society. For some no doubt an additional inducement was the opportunities which the office provided for corrupt personal gain. Sir George Sadler, a deputy lieutenant of Wiltshire, made money out of overpressing for military service in the 1620s and, if the accusations made in 1627 by Sir John Hobart, himself a deputy lieutenant for Norfolk, are to be believed, three of his less scrupulous colleagues had engaged in similar practices.[32]

But it would be very misleading to give the impression that the motives which impelled members of the county élite to become deputy lieutenants ranged between, at best, the desire to enhance their personal standing and, at worst, the opportunities for corrupt gain which the office afforded. Some responded – often reluctantly – to what they saw as the call of duty rather than to considerations of 'reputation or . . . profit . . . or both'. Nor did all deputy lieutenants cling tenaciously to office once they had acquired it, though it was not always easy to back out. It was not until 1609 that the Lord Lieutenant of Wiltshire allowed one of his deputies, Mr Thomas Horner, to resign, though the latter had been pleading old age and infirmity as an excuse for the past four years at least. A plea on similar grounds made by Sir Nicholas Hawlswell, a deputy lieutenant for Somerset, in 1608 may have stood more chance of prompt recognition, since it was corroborated by the unimpeachable evidence of that lynch-pin of the lieutenancy in the matter of military training, the county muster-master, Captain Norton: '. . . truly my lord, if you had seen in what paine he was in at these musters, you would much have pittied him.'[33]

The dependence of the deputies on the lord lieutenant turned to some extent on whether the office of deputy lieutenant was in his gift or not, and here there was, at least down to 1623, room for different practices in different counties.[34] In 1623 there was a reversal of what seems to have been the tendency of earlier years for nominations of deputy lieutenants to be increasingly left to the lord lieutenant. In that year new lieutenancy commissions were issued for all the counties, and except for the case of Yorkshire, the names of the deputies were specified in the deputation clauses rather than left to the lord lieutenant. But the change, whatever its cause, was short-lived, and there was a reversion to the practice of allowing formal nomination by the lord lieutenant of his deputies in the first commissions issued in the new reign. But it is perhaps easy to make too much out of this distinction between different modes of formal appointment of deputy lieutenants. Even in those cases where formal nomination of deputies was not left to the lord lieutenant, there was obviously scope for him to influence the choice of names which went into the deputation clause, and it is surely unlikely that such choice would be made without prior consultation with him.

The deliberate emphasis which has so far been placed upon the lieutenancy as a centralizing institution has tended to obscure an element of genuine ambivalence in the position of the lord lieutenant, which is well brought out in Mr Murphy's observation that 'the essence of his function was to represent the Crown to his district and his district to the Crown'.[35] One aspect of the former function was to act as the propagandist for royal policies to countrymen who were all too likely to misconstrue them. Grieving at the differences which had arisen between Charles I and his subjects in the first year of that king's personal rule, a veteran of service of the days of Elizabeth I urged that lord lieutenants (and bishops) be instructed to perform their traditional role as explicators of royal policies in the areas under their charge.[36] With regard to the second function of representing his county to the central government, there were numerous occasions on which the lord lieutenant is to be found attempting to relax the rigour of the application of central government policies in what he conceived to be the interests of his charges, even if such actions were likely to be misinterpreted by those whom they were designed to benefit and occasioned sharp rebukes from the central government whom it was their object to convince. The account of the operations of the lieutenancy which follows will afford some illustrations of its Janus-like role. But when all is taken into account, there can be little doubt that, of the two ways which it faced, it was as an agent of royal centralization and an antidote to local particularism that it attracted most attention.

V

The lieutenancy's role in the creation of a state of national military preparedness provides a classic example of the incipient conflict between national needs and local inclinations. It was not so much that, if pressed, those local JPs who were profoundly suspicious of the growth of central power would not concede the need for military training and preparedness against the dangers of foreign invasion, but rather that they refused to recognize either the need for close central supervision and control of the training of the local militia or the fact that local gentlemen, some of whom would have been members of the Commissions for Musters which had been superseded by the lieutenancy in control of military training,[37] were not necessarily the best agencies for bringing English practice into line with the needs of modern warfare. The control of the militia, which was to be a crucial issue over which the final break between the king and his opponents came in 1642, had, though in a different form, already been an issue for decades. In these circumstances the apparently outrageous claims of Pym and his colleagues in 1642 may have evoked a more sympathetic response than might normally be expected from traditionalist country gentlemen.

Down to 1604 the obligation to provide arms and undergo military training was statutorily defined. It was true that the Marian legislation[38] on which these obligations rested was by the beginning of the seventeenth century hopelessly out of date in terms of current continental military practice, and there can be no doubt that, during and after the Armada crisis, many of the demands made by the lieutenancy in a great number of counties were far in excess of what was required by statute. It was no doubt the inadequacy of this legislation which caused the repeal of the Marian statute in 1604.[39] It is in fact true that if an efficient militia were to be maintained, both before and after 1604, it could be done only on the basis of extra-statutory authority. But Englishmen were likely to be even less tolerant of such burdens in times of peace than they had been during the long Elizabethan war against Spain. Moreover, the constitutional position *ex post* 1604 was much starker and relatively more straightforward compared with the Elizabethan situation. It is true that the legislation which was repealed in 1604 had carefully laid down the obligations of every sort and condition of man so that any demands in excess of these were hardly likely to go unnoticed. But after 1604 the basis for any type of levy for military purpose or military training rested clearly on the prerogative and not on parliamentary statute. The government had perhaps made a conscious decision that, in the absence of new legislation which would lay arealistic military and financial burdens on the subject, the repeal of the existing legislation would at least prevent the making of appeal to statute as the natural recourse of the countrymen when the statutory limits were exceeded, as they would have had to be if the nature of the provision was to be realistic in terms of military need. But the result of the decision, if conscious decision it was, was of momentous significance, for it emphasized starkly the prerogative-based power of the lieutenancy in this the most central of its functions. Thus the local resistance to military exactions came to acquire a general significance as part of the struggle over the prerogative and the constitution, and a variety of motives, ranging from the blatantly self-interested to the idealistic defence of local custom and parliamentary statute, went into the melting-pot with the other ingredients which were to make up the cause of the 'Country'.

To the devotee of the ideal of military efficiency, national uniformity and central control, the key figure in the process whereby country yokels were to be transformed into formidable trained fighting men was the muster-master. He was the military expert, the seasoned warrior, the epitome of military professionalism when set against the pathetic playing at soldiers by local amateur captains and their dependent rustics. And there can be no doubt that many muster-masters were worthy of these expectations. Others unfortunately were not. As Gervase Markham observed, many a muster-master 'neither was souldier, is Souldier, Nor will Indeavor to be a souldier,' but sought only profit and prestige. Markham was tactful enough to ascribe such cases to the 'abroad imployments & necessarye absence' of the lord lieutenants, who in consequence might be ill-informed about the cases in question.[40] But in reality their personal responsibility for such shockingly inappropriate appointments sometimes went further, for the post of muster-master was a useful piece of lieutenancy patronage. Josias Kyrton, muster-master of Wiltshire in the early years of James I's reign, appears to have had no qualifications for the office beyond the fact that he was a client of the lord lieutenant, the Earl of Hertford. Both Thomas Hodson, muster-master of Durham in the next decade, and the muster-master appointed by the Earl of Northampton for Pembrokeshire seem to have been equally unsuited for the post. On the other hand Hertford's appointee as muster-master for the neighbouring county of Somerset, Captain Samuel Norton, was the very best sort of incumbent; a local gentleman and an experienced and efficient soldier to boot, and the same was true of Charles Wogan, who replaced Northampton's original and unsuitable appointment in Pembrokeshire.[41]

But it took more than such qualities, admirable though they might be, to make the muster-master and all he stood for acceptable in local society, and it must not be thought that the Nortons and Wogans escaped the sort of opposition which was no doubt richly deserved by the Kyrtons and Hodsons. What was the precise nature of the opposition of local gentlemen to them? It has already been suggested that the repeal of the Marian statute in 1604 offered golden opportunities to link local opposition to central interference to larger constitutional issues. The Deputy Lieutenants of Norfolk excused the inadequate state of the county militia and the lax observance of the musters by reference to the fact 'that noe Lawes for seruice eyther with Horse or foote are at this time in force'. There was an abortive attempt to alter this state of affairs in the Parliament of 1624, which failed because a majority 'thought it not good to strengthen the power of the Lievtenantes by any such Lawe'. For the government the only valid alternative to accepting statutory controls on lieutenants and muster-masters was to rely on the prerogative.[42] And what was true of military obligations in general applied *a fortiori* to the raising of a local rate for the muster-master's pay. The objections to the rate for the Durham muster-master voiced by Sir Henry Anderton in 1619 centered on the absence of statutory authority for his office, as did those of the defaulting Dorset gentry according to the complaints of the unfortunate muster-master of that county, whose pay was two and a half years in arrears around 1630. In addition Anderton had even claimed that 'giving Warrant for paying the [muster-master's] office is a direct Praemunire'.[43]

Perhaps most significant of all was the tendency to link the absence of parliamentary (viz. statutory) authority with the absence of Quarter Sessional approval for the levying of a rate and the issue of instructions to high constables. In both Wiltshire and Somerset in 1605 and Northamptonshire in 1613 the Commission of the Peace and Quarter Sessions were deliberately by-passed by the lord lieutenants in question,[44] who were no doubt exasperated by magisterial foot-dragging. The practice seems to have become widespread in later decades, to judge by the numbers of complaints about it. Such flagrant disregard of Quarter Sessional authority had explosive potentialities, and produced some

notable constitutional arguments which, since they are cast within
a local institutional framework, have tended to be ignored by constitutional historians. For instance, an interesting variation on the celebrated argument which was to be employed more than three decades
later by Oliver St John in the Ship Money case – that the king's
command can operate only through the appropriate legal channels
– was used by some of the inhabitants of Warminster hundred as
early as August 1605, when they refused to pay their quotas for the
muster-master on the grounds that 'it is not his Majesties comaunde-
ment yt should be soe, for the justices did not alsoe comand it, nor
did procure the people thereunto'.[45]

There is abundant evidence to suggest that the attempt of the lieutenancy to by-pass Quarter Sessions was widely regarded as a form of
arbitrary taxation analogous with extra-parliamentary levies on the
national front. In October 1633 when the Earl of Bridgwater, President
of the Council of Wales and Lord Lieutenant of Herefordshire, urged
upon his deputies in that county the need to make adequate financial
provision for the muster-master, they went to great pains to emphasize
that 'the vsuall and accustomed Course in this Countie' was to make
such provision 'by the joynt Act of the Deputy Lieutenants and Iustices
of Peace at the Quarter Sessions'. This decision was arrived at after
employing arguments from custom and precedent not dissimilar from
those used on the national front in defence of parliamentary rights.[46] If
the history of the Wiltshire and Somerset lieutenancy in the first decade
of the century and that of Gloucestershire in the later 1620s is anything
to go by, however, the opponents of the muster-master were equally
ready, when it served their turn, to argue that precedent pointed to
levies for this purpose being raised voluntarily and not through a
compulsory rate levied in Quarter Sessions.[47]

The linking of local custom with national constitutionalism finds
striking expression in the parliamentary campaigns against prerogative levies under James I. But in addition, less lofty and disinterested
motives are not far to seek. Asked whether the office of muster-master
was necessary, the Norfolk deputy lieutenants replied emphatically
that it was not, and that the job could be done as well and much less
expensively by those local gentlemen who were captains of the county
trained bands. Similar assertions were made in 1603 by the inhabitants
of Thornbury in Gloucestershire, by the Lord Mayor and Aldermen of
London in the 1630s and by the Bishop of Durham in 1630, and are
clearly implied in the statement by the Shropshire Grand Jury at the

Easter session in 1635 that the muster-master's stipend was a grievance and his office superfluous.[48] While it might be difficult to sustain the argument that military training could be carried out as efficaciously by local gentlemen as by a professional muster-master, it was incontestable that it could be carried out a great deal more cheaply. High-sounding appeals to custom, tradition and constitutionalism were often to no small extent devices to shroud simple reluctance to meet the bill arising out of the creation of a state of military preparedness, as this was conceived by the government; more particularly, during the years 1624–30, when the counties were subjected to a succession of prerogative levies for items such as Coat and Conduct Money, billeting, Forced Loans and (in the maritime counties) Ship Money. But at least the government could plead the necessities of war over these years. By contrast, no such sense of national urgency could be evoked during the two decades of peace which succeeded the Treaty of London of 1604, or during Charles i's personal rule in the 1630s, during which time he persisted in his attempts to create the 'exact' or 'perfect' militia and aroused widespread local opposition in the process.[49] The clearest exposure of the less respectable motives of the local opponents of military improvements comes from the earlier period, in a statement by the hard-pressed Lord Lieutenant of Wiltshire and Somerset in the autumn of 1604. Petitioning the king about the dangers arising out of magisterial opposition to the muster-master and the prerogative powers of the lieutenancy, the Earl of Hertford produced a very shrewd and suggestive analysis which identified what he regarded as fractious opposition in the locality with the same phenomenon in parliament. For the dissident JPs were 'endevouring . . . to tye and confine your commands to the rules of the common lawes or to statutes to be in parliament *whereunto all theyr assents must be gained*'. Far from being based on lofty constitutional principles or relief of the county as a whole, their opposition to the muster-master was rather 'for each man's own particular [advantage]'. For the close scrutiny of the certificates of the muster-master was a means of bringing to light shocking cases of underassessment of themselves by the magistrates and 'overcharging . . . the poorer sorte (for theyr own case) in higher measure than theyr small habilities can performe'.[50]

The offence of the muster-master whose activities so disturbed local custom and tradition and upset local susceptibilities was often compounded by the fact that, as a stranger to the county where he exercised control, he was insensitive to the peculiarities and rhythms of local life which were so important to residents of long standing. In March 1627 the Privy Council, acting on local complaints, urged the Lord Lieutenant of Norfolk to make sure that the next musters were called around Whitsuntide and not, as had been the case in recent years, at peak periods of agricultural activity such as seed-time and harvest.[51] But what rankled most with the county magistracy was the total lack of respect and deference shown to them by some muster-masters, of which 'the insolent, unmannerly and unrespective usage' offered to the Wiltshire magistrates at the Marlborough Quarter Sessions in 1604 and on other occasions is a good example. It is difficult to exaggerate the impact which such behaviour would have had on the outraged local magistrates confronted by the insolence of this individual who, moreover, kept his hat on in their presence.[52] Although Kyrton's case may be an extreme one, there can be little doubt that his behaviour was activated by that sense of independence *vis-à-vis* the magistracy which his position as the client of the lord lieutenant and the agent of royal centralization imparted to him.

VI

Another issue of the late 1620s which occasioned localist opposition to the lieutenancy was the billeting of troops, which, especially before and after the expeditions to Cadiz in 1625 and the Isle of Rhé in 1627, plagued the lives of many of the inhabitants of the southern counties. Whether it was Irishmen in Essex and Norfolk, Scots in the Isle of Wight, or Gloucestershire men in Devon, the fact that many of the troops billeted were not local men but strangers certainly did not help matters in an age in which most men's horizons were bounded by their counties. Ultimately, of course, billeting, along with martial law, forced loans and imprisonment without trial, was one of the great national issues which found expression in the Petition of Right in 1628. In this, as in so much else, Parliament was performing its classic role as the blender and nationalizer of local issues. But to appreciate this process it is important not to underestimate the extent to which initially opposition was essentially local and, far from being viewed as a national grievance, billeting was seen as a case in which a burden was shared very unequally between counties. The Devon gentleman who demanded how much longer his shire would continue to 'bear the charge for all England' probably had many no less aggrieved counterparts in other English counties which felt that they were carrying a disproportionate share of the national burden.[53]

The lieutenancy, somewhat undeservedly, became the focus of local discontent. Caught between the two fires of central pressure and local dissatisfaction, it was the recipient both of government complaints about local dilatoriness, such as were meted out to the deputy lieutenants of Cornwall in June 1629, and of local complaints that it was nothing more than an instrument of the central government and totally unresponsive to local hardships and difficulties. Yet there is abundant evidence of the concern of both lieutenants and their deputies for the burdens which were being heaped upon their counties, in for example Norfolk, Gloucestershire, Somerset, Devon and the Isle of Wight. But the lieutenancy's fulfilment of its classic mediatory function between the Court and Country simply exposed it to cross-fire from the two opposing camps. However persistent its attempts to make the central government aware of the hardships being borne in the counties, they are no guarantee that it would not be exposed to local criticism which was the more pungent and effective when, as was the case with the Somerset lieutenancy, it was delivered by a former deputy lieutenant, Sir Robert Phelips, who, in the great debate in the House of Commons on 2 April 1628, charged the Somerset deputy lieutenants with illegally raising the county rate for billeting. A similar charge was made against the Norfolk deputy lieutenants at a public sessions at King's Lynn in the summer of 1628 by a man 'graue in yeares, learned in the Lawes and by his callinge a Serieant'.[54] Billeting was only one of a number of charges which were piled upon the counties between 1624 and 1629 and which contributed, as Professor Barnes has demonstrated in his study of Somerset, to the growing unpopularity of the deputy lieutenants. Others included alleged electoral malpractices by deputy lieutenants who, in Cornwall, put pressure on candidates not favoured by the central government to withdraw, and, in Somerset, made unscrupulous use of their control of billeting as a means of winning votes.[55] It has been pointed out that all the various local discontents against billeting, martial law, coat and conduct money and forced loans, some of which find celebrated constitutional expression in the Petition of Right of 1628, have as their common feature the unpopularity of the lieutenancy as the agency of central government in such matters,[56] an unpopularity which was as great with municipal as it was with county magistrates. Thus the Mayor of Southampton complained in December 1624 that the Hampshire deputy lieutenants were infringing that borough's charter in the matter of conscription of its inhabitants, while the Privy Council in 1635 brought to book the two Norwich aldermen who had argued that the writ of the lord lieutenant of Norfolk did not run in that city. They were left in no doubt that any such action in the future would render the Norwich municipality liable to quo warranto proceedings.[57]

VII

There was therefore nowhere within a county that the lord lieutenant's writ did not run, but in some remote counties, in the north of England and in Wales and the four border counties of Shropshire, Worcestershire, Herefordshire and Gloucestershire, the power of the lieutenancy ran in tandem with that of regional councils. The Lord President of the Council of the North seated at York was in fact more often than not the Lord Lieutenant of Yorkshire, while the same office in the Council in the Marches of Wales seated at Ludlow was normally held by the lord lieutenant of the four English border counties.[58] In the opening years of the seventeenth century there was a notable increase in the activities of the latter council, consequent upon the appointment of a quorum of four lawyers as its permanent judges. Paid by the fines imposed by the Council, these judges had an obvious personal interest in its increased judicial activity, and the fact that the greater part of the fines came from the inhabitants of the English border counties rather than from the Welsh gives additional point to the agitation of those four counties to be freed from the Council's jurisdiction. In the parliament of 1610 there were representations that inhabitants of the four counties were effectively being denied their fundamental right of recourse to common law, on account of technical difficulties in obtaining writs of prohibition transferring cases from the Council to a court at Westminster.[59] Criticisms were again heard during the parliaments of the 1620s, but, oddly enough, it was the period of Charles I's personal rule after 1629 which was to see a marked reduction in the Council's power and influence, not least because it had powerful enemies at Court as well as in the Country. In these years opposition to the Council seems to have intensified, for despite its diminished effective power and the increasing difficulty it had in enforcing its will, 'The gentlemen and greate men are eclipsed in their firmament, their swaye, by the neighbourhood of such a Courte of Justice; they like not such a superintendent'.[60] Such is the account of one observer in 1641, the year in which the Council was abolished, although he also made it clear that in his view the need for such a Council was directly proportionate to the amount of opposition it provoked from local notables.

Many of the gentry of the north entertained similar views about the Council of the North. Edward Hyde, chairman of the parliamentary committee on the matter, won (if his own account is to be believed) golden opinions from the local MPs when he emphasized, at a conference with the Lords in the Painted Chamber on 26 April 1641, the legal disabilities suffered by the inhabitants of the northern counties, 'left to the arbitrary power of a President and Council, which every day procured new authority and power to oppress them'. In contrast with the case of the Council of the Marches in the 1630s, the impression of a progressive tightening of conciliar control conveyed by this and other evidence is almost certainly the correct one. Under Wentworth as Lord Lieutenant of Yorkshire and Lord President of the Council of the North, the Council was, despite his absence in Ireland for much of the time, an important means of increasing royal control over the activities of the JPs and curbing the 'humoure and libertye I find raign in these parts, of observing a superiour commande noe farther than they like themselves'. When the Council of the North reprimanded Sir Ferdinando Fairfax and two other Yorkshire JPs for taking action against a constable for misappropriation and failing to inform the Council, Fairfax, while agreeing on the desirability of informing the Council, went on to assert that 'to make it a thing of absolute necessity, and solely to depend on their directions' was an unwarranted innovation. But that, as Wentworth might well have replied, was what 'Thorough' was all about.[61]

VIII

Even though the years of Charles I's personal government were a time of peace, when the financial burdens heaped upon counties were less varied and probably less heavy than during the preceding decade, there were any number of issues which helped to keep the flame of opposition burning fiercely over these years. The prerogative courts, and notably Star Chamber, were very active, and the well-meant but not always well-executed efforts of the Privy Council and Depopulation Commissioners to prevent or alleviate a variety of economic hardships seem to have got the worst of both worlds by alienating the articulate country gentlemen whose activities they restricted, without, it would seem, eliciting the gratitude of those who ought to have been the beneficiaries of such policies. But much the best known and, in terms of its political significance, much the most important issue of these years is Ship Money, which also raised questions of considerable interest in connection with the theme of this chapter. For Ship Money provides an excellent illustration of how local resistance to central government measures achieves respectability by being identified with the defence of traditional ways of doing things. Back in March 1627 twenty-three Somerset JPs had contrasted their reluctance to undertake the business of Ship Money with the fact that their county 'hath not byne backwarde in publique services when custome and aunciente usage hath byne the grounds of those comaunds'. Similarly, in reply to the Ship Money writ in November 1634, the Common Council of London informed the Government that what it was demanding was contrary to 'their auntient liberties, Charters and actes of Parliament', thus neatly dovetailing local and national constitutional objections.[62]

The county lieutenancy, preoccupied with the highly contentious business of creating the 'exact militia', probably had no regrets that the central figure in the arrangements for Ship Money was the sheriff, that traditional representative of royal power in the shires whose importance had recently been eclipsed by the rise of newer central agencies. And it was against the sheriff that local animus was mostly directed. For, in attempting to find the money required by the Government in the most efficient and equitable way sheriffs were sometimes impelled to adopt rating systems which differed from those which were hallowed by long usage. Thus the sheriffs of Northamptonshire in 1635 and of Nottinghamshire in 1638 were sharply criticized by local notables – in the latter case by JPs – for assessments which allegedly discriminated against some of the divisions in their counties. However, as Dr Lake has brilliantly demonstrated in his study of the Ship Money dispute between the city and the county of Chester, such issues might redound to the advantage of the central government, whose performance of the role of arbiter between such local disputants, put a premium on the need for them to demonstrate unequivocally their own zeal in its service.[63]

Besides inequalities of burden as between different districts, there was also the matter of equity of assessment in terms of the real burden borne by rich and poor.[64] Given the Council's concern, emphasized in the careful analysis made by Miss Gordon many years ago,[65] that rates should be both realistic and equitable, it may be that objections against the social inequity of the tax need to be taken with more than a grain of salt. Professor Barnes's admirable account of the collection in Somerset makes it perfectly clear that the determined advocacy of localism and traditionalism in the matter of assessment was first and foremost designed to frustrate shrieval attempts to tap the real source of wealth in Somerset in a way in which the customary rates emphatically did not.[66] On the other hand, the Privy Council in this case, departing in some measure from its stated principles about equitable assessment, demanded that realistic assessment should be extended both in the direction of the wealthy and in that of poor cottagers and the like. The former would clearly excite the disapproval of the comfortably off who escaped lightly under the traditional rating system. But the latter also was unlikely to be popular with landowners who may have been adversely affected by the squeeze exerted on the liquidity of their tenants and their consequently diminished ability to pay their rents.

Opposition was not confined to private gentlemen. As in so many other of the issues dealt with in this chapter, it extended to the local magistracy, sometimes, as in Essex in 1627 and Northamptonshire in January 1640, extending to formal protests made by the Grand Jury at Quarter Sessions, egged on or at least not positively discouraged by the JPs.[67] Nor was that citadel of centralism, the lieutenancy, by any means solidly behind the Government in this matter. In November 1636 the Privy Council ordered that lord lieutenants and deputy lieutenants (as well as JPs) who refused to pay Ship Money should be discharged from their offices.[68] There are, of course, cases which run true to the classic pattern of the complaint of the Montgomeryshire deputy lieutenants against the lukewarmness of one of the JPs in the matter of Ship Money;[69] against which we must set Professor Barnes's findings for Somerset that three of the JPs who complained about Ship Money in March 1627 were deputy lieutenants, and that at least two Somerset deputy lieutenants were connected intimately with the agitation of the succeeding decade.[70]

It may be the fact that their role in connection with Ship Money was less central than in many aspects of royal policy which afforded to deputy lieutenants the opportunity of indulging in the luxury of opposition. By contrast the role of the sheriff, dragged back into the limelight, was an unhappy one. Subject to repeated prodding from the Council, liable to be held personally responsible for any arrears during his shrievalty, plagued by the defection and lukewarmness of his subordinates from constables to under-sheriffs, sometimes unable to rely on the cooperation of his predecessor in office, as was the case with the

High Sheriff of Lincolnshire, Sir Anthony Irby, in 1637,[71] his lot was unenviable and his office something to be avoided if at all possible. An extreme case was the treatment meted out by the Privy Council to two successive sheriffs of Northamptonshire, each of whom was made to go about the royal business in the county in the custody of a sergeant-at-arms, who was 'soe to attend him from place to place ... as he may perfecte the said seruice'.[72] Nor did the Government receive whole-hearted cooperation from all of the sheriffs of London, which was the first local authority to raise objection to Ship Money as a levy which violated local custom, an argument which was of far greater import-ance than the historian of London's role in the origins of the Great Rebellion gives it credit for.[73] They were sharply rebuked in February 1638 for their dilatoriness in the service, and their participation in the house-to-house search in the service of the levy in June 1640 seems to have been undertaken with extreme reluctance. Along with their counterparts in Middlesex and – rather unfairly – the enthusiastic mayoral supporter of the Government Sir Henry Garway, they were marked down by the Attorney General as candidates for prosecution in the Star Chamber.[74]

IX

To what extent are the palpable cracks in the edifice of centralized royal control revealed by an examination of the evidence in the case of Ship Money apparent in connection with other matters? Is there any evi-dence, for example, that the lieutenancy was as (or more) divided in relation to those matters in which, unlike Ship Money, it was the main agency of centralized royal control in the localities? Before proceeding to an examination of the evidence it is perhaps as well to sound a warning note. For not all splits which the evidence reveals within the ranks of the lieutenancy are ascribable to issues of principle; many of them are explicable in terms of factional rather than political consider-ations, though sometimes, as in the classic case of the Somerset lieuten-ancy, faction-fighting is inextricably enmeshed with, and not just masked by, issues of high constitutional principle.[75]

The evidence of deputy lieutenants offering resistance to, or at the very least lukewarmly administering, the policies which it was their duty to implement is too abundant to be cited in detail. There are, for example, a great many cases of differences of opinion between lord lieutenants and their deputies as well as of sharp rebukes being administered by lieutenants to some of their deputies for their dilatoriness over military training and the musters: in Wiltshire in 1605, where the lieutenant complained to his deputies of 'a great contraryetie betweene you and me'; in Northamptonshire in 1613 and 1629; in Suffolk and Dorset in 1625; in Gloucestershire in 1629; in Norfolk in 1631, when the Earl of Arundel informed his deputies that the shocking example of disobedience set by them was likely to spread down the whole chain of command to the lowest constable; in Herefordshire in 1633 and in Bedfordshire in 1635, to quote but a few examples. If the Deputy Lieutenants of Durham were, by contrast, not in disagreement in 1630 with the bishop who performed the duties of a lord lieutenant in the county palatine, over the issue of the muster-master, this was not because they both supported the Government attitude on the matter – quite the reverse, in fact. If reports made by the military commanders Sir Jacob Astley and Captain Henry Waite in the early months of 1639 are to be believed, the Deputy Lieutenants of Yorkshire, Cumberland and Westmorland had left a great deal to be desired in the matter of the creation of the king's much-cherished 'perfect militia' in these counties, being more concerned with pleading difficulties and putting obstacles in the way of the desired improvements than with bringing the militia of these crucially important northern counties up to scratch.[76] The connection between the military débâcle of 1639–40 and the disintegration of the machinery whereby the royal will was enforced in the provinces is close and intimate. The MPs who came up to Westminster in 1640 determined to put paid once and for all to royal innovations, including, as they saw it, central interference with time-honoured local rights were in fact about to deliver a *coup de grâce* to a system which was already on its last legs.

X

The emphasis which many historians, following the pioneering work of Professor Everitt, are now placing on the community of the county as a vital focal point of political aspirations raises questions about the nature of and relations between both national and local movements, which have tended to be ignored both by more old-fashioned political historians whose approach is virtually uninfluenced by the new school of county and regional historians and by some of the members of that school themselves, whose horizons, like those of the objects of their study, tend to be limited by regional or county boundaries. One conclusion which is perhaps suggested by the material which has been treated in this chapter is that there may be something to be said for the old-fashioned view that royal policies played a crucial role in the process of state-building and the breaking down of provincial infra-national barriers. A main theme of the chapter has been the resistance to this development at the level of the locality and the county, and this in turn raises further questions about the nature of and relationship between the county community and that great community of communities, Parliament itself. Was the idea of the county community, the near autonomy of the county, something existing prior to and independently of the royal centralizing tendencies which form the subject of this chapter? Or was it a product of, a response to (or at the very least, enormously heightened by) such pressures? What was the role of Parliament? The forum for the expression of diverse, if connected, localist aspirations? Or the means of blending them into a whole which was greater than the sum of its parts?

Parliament was, of course, only one, albeit the most important, of a number of agencies which historians have designated as creators of something which can be described as a national political consciousness. Prominent among the others were those social institutions which were the product of the charitable benefactions studied by Professor W. K. Jordan,[77] which increasingly followed patterns set more particularly by the merchants of contemporary London, and which, in his view, with their emphasis on careful, well-ordered capital endowments and secular philanthropic objectives, laid 'the foundations of a new England and of a new kind of society, a society animated by values which were all but unknown to medieval men'.[78] Among such benefactions were the educational endowments to which in recent years historians have come to attach great importance as agencies in the growth of national consciousness. And connected with this is the well-known phenomenon of the large-scale invasion of the universities by the gentry and aristocracy and the importance of the Inns of Court in London as providing, if not an adequate legal training for men who would meet legal problems as landowners and magistrates rather than professional lawyers, at least a sort of postgraduate finishing-school where a young gentleman from one county might meet and discuss the problems of the day with his counterparts from others. While there is more than a grain of truth in these by now very familiar arguments, it cannot be said that all of the propounders have been altogether guiltless of over-simplifying what are, in fact, extremely complex phenomena. Were, for instance, the establishments which form the subject of Professor Jordan's enquiry designed to break down or to foster local and regional pride and consciousness? How far were they the products of the philanthropic endeavours of men, who, given the prevailing discontinuity of mercantile fortunes, hoped to end their days in their region of origin, living a life which was distinguished from that of the established local élite only in that greater emphasis laid upon the maintenance of the traditional *mode de vie* which is to be expected of parvenus? The rôle which is normally ascribed to the universities in the process of creating a national consciousness has also been sharply questioned by Dr Victor Morgan, who sees many colleges at Cambridge (and no doubt the same was true of Oxford) as fostering rather than breaking down county particularism via, *inter alia*, the links provided by the lands with which they were endowed and the statutory limitations relating to the areas from which both undergraduates and fellows could be recruited.[79] Professor Prest refuses to accept the applicability of such an argument to the Inns of Court,[80] pointing out that the 'regional attachment of the societies never became so pronounced as to direct all entrants from one locality to a particular inn at the expense of the rest'. But neither was this true of colleges at either of the universities, and it needs to be remarked that history does not work within such closed categories, and that another historian of the legal profession takes a rather different view of the significance of the experience of life at the Inns of Court in terms of local and national influences.[81] At the very least it can be confidently asserted that the regional connections of some of the inns may have been a factor which attenuated or counteracted to some degree any influence which they might have had as a 'nationalizing' influence.

But one must beware of dichotomizing too rigidly between the two sets of influence. And nowhere is this more important than when we turn to the greatest of these allegedly nationalizing agencies, the House of Commons itself. 'We all that sit here for our country must have a fellow feeling of the grievances of the same,' declared Sir George Moore, MP for Guildford, in the House of Commons debate of 14 February 1621. Moore was complaining of the decline of the clothing towns in his county and was particularly concerned to pin at least some of the blame on a recent royal imposition, the so-called pretermitted customs. In the debate which followed, Moore's experience was borne out by the observations of members sitting for other clothing districts in other parts of the country – by Wentworth for Yorkshire and Neale for

Dartmouth in South Devon; while Sir Robert Crane, speaking for Suffolk, drew attention to the restrictive practices of the Merchant Adventurers as a prime cause of the trouble.[82] Similarly in other matters, for example, patents such as Sir Robert Mansell's glass patent, by acting as members of select committees or simply listening to the reports made by such committees in the House, MPs would become acquainted with the contents of a wide variety of petitions emanating from different parts of England or with the gist of evidence given before committees about the effect of different patents in different areas.[83] Sometimes MPs themselves, even when they had come up to Westminster armed with the grievances of their constituents, were asked to investigate the effects of a particular measure, such as the alehouse patent, in their constituencies and to report back;[84] a process which afforded opportunities to become aware both of the factors peculiar to different regions and of the factors which they had in common in relation to such matters. Of course the circumstances and complaints of some constituencies were sometimes peculiar to them or very nearly so, in which case it was far more difficult, though not necessarily impossible, to formulate general parliamentary attitudes based on widely shared experiences. A good example is provided by the peculiar grievances of the four border counties against the Council of the Marches which was brought up by local MPs in the House of Commons in 1610. The problem here was how to make a general issue out of an institution whose operations affected only a remote part of the realm. It might be relatively easy to enlist the sympathies of some northern gentlemen who regarded themselves as the victims of a similar institution. But for the remainder it was necessary to demonstrate that the thin end of the wedge of despotism had been inserted into the border counties whose failure to obtain their desired exemption from the Council of the Marches 'may in future times give countenance to the erecting of like jurisdiction in other places'.[85]

The House of Commons in the early seventeenth century was the agency of a subtle alchemy whereby the MPs who came up to Westminster armed with the grievances of their constituents came via a process of shared experiences to contribute to the emergence of a national or 'Country' attitude. The process whereby these often widely divergent local attitudes and grievances were blended into what has become customary to describe as the view of the 'Country' as opposed to that of the Court is one of the least understood aspects of seventeenth-century history. Historians have paid, and are paying, too much attention to the imagined dichotomy between the local and the national, as opposed to studying the process whereby the latter emerged out of the former. Of all aspects of the political history of the period, it is perhaps that which presents the most fertile ground for research.[86]

FOUR *Gentlemen and Bourgeois*

If thou endeavour to make a *Republique* in a Nation where the *Gentry* abounds, thou shalt hardly prosper in that designe; and if thou wouldst erect a *Principality* in a Land where there is much equality of people, thou shalt not easily effect it: the way to bring the first to passe is to weaken the Gentry; the means to effect the last, is to advance and strengthen *turbulent* and ambitious Spirits. . . .

The lower sort of people are desirous of *Novelties*, and apt for Change, weighing Government with the scales of their owne Fortunes: they are too sensible of evills in present to feare worse in future.

> Francis Quarles, *Observations Concerning Princes* (1642), pp. 14, 24.

I have heard My Lord say,

(i)

That those which command the wealth of a kingdom, command the hearts and hands of the people.

(ii)

That he is . . . a wise monarch, that imploys his subjects for their own profit (for their profit is his), encourages tradesmen, and assists and defends merchants.

. . . .

(v)

That great princes should not suffer their chief cities to be stronger than themselves.

> Margaret, Duchess of Newcastle, *The Life of the Duke of Newcastle* (1667, Everyman edn. 1915), pp. 149, 150.

MATERIALIST EXPLANATIONS AND LANDED SOCIETY

I

THE EMPHASIS upon the fundamental and determinant importance of material factors in history, which is one characteristic feature of the historiography of our time, is a product both of the rise of the study of economic history as an academic discipline or sub-discipline and of the growing historiographical influence of Marxism, even though by no means all historians who stress the significance of those factors are Marxists. In the Marxist interpretation of history the English Civil War plays a crucial part in the transition from 'feudal' to 'bourgeois' society. Capitalistic forms of production and exchange had, of course, existed for centuries within the framework of a 'feudal', non-capitalist or even anti-capitalist society; that is, a society whose institutions, ideologies and theories on the role of private enterprise and private property, far from being designed to facilitate economic growth and capital accumulation, were at best indifferent and at worst actively hostile to that process. According to Marxist historians the Civil War was the crucial event in the transfer of authority from one social class to another, and was in a very real sense a revolt of property-owners against the restraints on their freedom of employing their property which were imposed by a 'feudal' government.

Now there were many people on both sides in the Civil War who argued that the defence of private property was one of the main principles of the cause which they had espoused. The king claimed that the individual's right to property was under serious threat as a result of the example set by the parliamentary seizure of his own property and its illegal ordinances, passed without his consent, raising levies from the subject. But, needless to say, there were not wanting parliamentary opponents of the king who made the most of what they regarded as the absurd new-found royal tenderness for property, the strange product of 'the same shop from whence issued forced loans, Knighting money, benevolences and Ship Money.... For is it in earnest to be thought that the destroyers of property are now suddenly become the patrons of property?'[1] Indeed perhaps the most striking impact of the royal exactions of the 1630s on the consciousness of the political nation had been the menace which they offered to the property of the subject. One of three heads of grievances to be considered at a conference between the Commons and Lords in the abortive Short Parliament of April 1640 was 'the propriety in our goods', and included in the matters for discussion under this head were monopolies and other restraints on trade, Ship Money, the exactions of royal forestry commissioners, and miscellaneous military charges.[2] Striking testimony to the importance of this issue is provided in a speech made in the Commons debate on the Triennial Bill on 19 January 1641 by Lord Digby of all people, a nobleman who was to become one of the most intransigent and extreme of royalists in the Civil War. When Digby spoke of 'the liberty, the property of the subject fundamentally subverted, [and] ravished away by the violence of a pretended necessity', he was referring not to unconstitutional parliamentary exactions but to those of Charles I's personal government during the previous decade.[3] After this it comes as no surprise to find the great leader of the parliamentary cause in its early years, John Pym, in a celebrated 'Declaration of the Grievances of the Kingdom' delivered in the House of Commons in the following year, laying stress on a number of other threats to individual property rights such as the activities of the Building Commission in London and the Depopulation Commission in the countryside.[4] There is in fact abundant evidence to support the Marxist contention that the threat offered by arbitrary royal government to private property owners was a very important factor in the isolation of the King and Court in 1640.

In the Marxist canon, then, the events of the 1640s and 1650s in England constitute the first revolution whose achievement was to break down the 'feudal' and to substitute for it a 'bourgeois' order, which far from being at worst inimical to, or at best not actively encouraging to, capitalist activity is, in fact, sensitively geared to it. This is a transformation which, it is argued, could come about only by revolutionary means as a result of the effective transfer of political power from one social class to another. Capitalism had now outgrown the stage in which it could expand with reasonable comfort within the framework of a non-capitalist 'feudal' society, and its progress would have been fatally arrested if Charles I had won the Civil War.[5] This particular emphasis is uniquely Marxist, but Marxist historians were by no means the first to emphasize the importance of material and social factors in the genesis of the Civil War. Indeed, there is a real sense in which the familiar neo-Whig interpretation of what was significantly called the Puritan Revolution by great Victorian and post-Victorian historians such as S.R.Gardiner and his pupil, Sir Charles Firth, with their stress on the importance of constitutional and religious at the expense of economic and social issues, was something of an historiographical aberration which had lost sight of the fact that many of their seventeenth-century predecessors had laid considerable stress on material factors. For instance, during the 1650s James Harrington in a variety of ways significantly anticipated some of the central features of Marxist historical analysis. Harrington saw the distribution of property – and especially landed property, since the society of his day was a preponderantly agrarian one – as the foundation on which political institutions and the distribution of political power are based. To him as to Marx, the fundamental engine of political change was change in the distribution of property, and just as Marx postulated the necessity of revolution when the existing 'feudal' relations of property became positively inimical to further capitalist growth, so does Harrington postulate a similar necessity when the distribution of political power ceases to correspond with the distribution of landed property.[6]

If the emphasis of contemporaries on the importance of material factors in the political conflicts of the seventeenth century had been confined to an oddball figure such as Harrington – a man with, as it has been argued,[7] a very personal axe to grind – we might perhaps dismiss such observations without further ado. But it is emphatically not confined to Harrington, and its significance can perhaps best be stressed by reference to a contemporary statesman and historian whose views were at the very opposite political pole to his – Edward Hyde, Earl of Clarendon. While it is true that Clarendon offers no clear-cut, synthetic account of the relationship between material factors and political change such as characterizes the theses of Harrington or of Marxist historians, there are a great many ways in which this greatest of all historians of the Civil War, in his analysis of the motivation of individuals, penetrates to the importance of the material factors which often underlay more lofty considerations. Prominent among such considerations were the threat to private property which has already been emphasized, manifested in such things as Forced Loans, the Ship Money judgement of 1637, the Court of Wards and the restriction on freedom of land use by commissions of depopulation and forests; the dislike of the older – often not very much older – nobility for such upstart jacks-in-office as the royal favourite, Buckingham, in the 1620s, and for the attempts of the low-born Archbishop of Canterbury after

1633 to emphasize the unique position and dignity of Churchmen and to devise ways of making the voice of the Church on social and other matters heeded by the highest laymen in the land. Far from being obsessed with individual characters to the neglect of general factors, as Firth alleged, Clarendon was anxious to explore every conceivable facet and association of factors which too many of his Victorian successors were content to treat as unconnected. It would not be altogether unjust to apply Firth's criticisms of Clarendon to his own interpretation on the grounds that the general factors whose importance Firth stressed were in fact insufficiently inclusive: in a word they were not general enough.[8]

II

One predictable response of historians to the challenge offered by the Marxist version of events is virtually to ignore it without subjecting it to any sort of critical examination. The eminently readable and justly popular account of the Civil War of Dame Veronica Wedgwood[9] is written in the clearly admitted belief that in order to explain *why* events took place, it is sufficient to describe *how* they took place, a corollary of which view is that it is perfectly legitimate to begin an account of the causes of the Civil War with the years immediately preceding its outbreak. But not all of the modern non-Marxist interpretations of these events neglect material factors and social causation. For instance if the very different theses associated with the names of Lawrence Stone and H.R.Trevor-Roper have anything in common with each other and with the Marxist explanation to which they are alternatives, this is to be found in the crucial importance which each of them, in quite different ways, lays upon material factors, even though they do not necessarily accord complete primacy to such factors:[10] Stone stresses the variety of ways in which individuals can be classified: 'as gentry, bourgeois, country, capitalist and puritan, each valid for certain analytical purposes, none adequate as a single, all-embracing characterization'. In so far as he lays emphasis on material factors, it is not as preponderant causes or determinants of events but as a part of a complex whole, so that if there is an appropriate social science from which tools of analysis may be drawn to elucidate it, the methods and concepts of the economist are likely to be less illuminating than those of the sociologist.[11]

Emphasis on the significance of material factors is perhaps more striking in the interpretation of H.R.Trevor-Roper, but he too develops his thesis with reference to notions about group social behaviour, and frustrated rising and stable status expectations, though his work owes less to borrowings from the social sciences than to acute and penetrating historical insight. He sees the economic crisis of the 'mere' gentry, who were wedded to socially compulsive patterns of expenditure and the need to keep face by maintaining their 'port', but lacked supplementary sources of income, as a major factor in the onset of political crisis. To some extent the 'mere' gentry owe their economic difficulties to the fact that they were 'out'. The more comfortable economic position and the more ample *mode de vie* of the office-holding landowners and their connection with a government which, during the reign of Charles I, was imposing increasing burdens often of doubtful constitutional legality on the country, offered a very obvious target for social envy. The Civil War provided the opportunity for the 'outs' to enjoy the innings which had been denied them for so long.

The contrast of such notions with the Marxist interpretation hardly needs emphasis. Far from being made by an economically rising and 'progressive' class whose operations were frustrated by the obstacles placed in its way by a royal government which found its natural supporters among the lazy, feckless, inefficient and ultra-conservative elements in society, the most dynamic opponents of the Crown in the Civil War are to be found among the economic backwoodsmen, who were experiencing economic decline as a result of their inability to buttress inadequate landed income by income from other sources. Trevor-Roper shares with Marxist historians the belief in the importance of material factors in producing the line-up of forces in 1642, even though the interpretation which he gives to these developments is very different from – indeed diametrically opposed to – that of the Marxist.

III

There are some notable general difficulties in the way of acceptance of the Marxist notion of the war as the means whereby a bourgeois replaced a feudal order. In the seminal article from which Marxist historians drew their ideas of the economically progressive rising gentry as a sort of agrarian wing of the bourgeoisie, R. H. Tawney gave a very short shrift to this distinction between 'feudal' and 'bourgeois' landowners, insisting that 'patrician and parvenu owed their ascent to causes of the same order. Judged by the source of their incomes, both were equally bourgeois.'[12] To this charge the Marxist historian would doubtless reply that, in referring to a landlord as 'feudal', he does not intend to indicate one who drew a preponderant part of his income from feudal labour rent exacted from a personally unfree tenantry (as in thirteenth-century England or seventeenth-century Pomerania) or personal seigneurial exactions (as in pre-revolutionary France). Such arrangements may be classically feudal, but it is not necessary for a society to be characterized by them in order for it to be 'feudal'. Any economy which is based upon agriculture and in which political power is monopolized by a landowning class living off the rent (money rent if necessary) paid by a dependent peasantry is in fact 'feudal'.[13] Now this definition is clearly applicable to landlord-tenant relations in early Stuart England. But the difficulty is that it is no less applicable to the England which succeeded, as well as that which preceded, the Civil War; or indeed to the England which succeeded as well as that which preceded the Reform Bill of 1832. In these circumstances it is not easy to see how the Civil War could be the agency whereby a feudal was replaced by a bourgeois order, since the society which outlived it by a couple of centuries was, on this definition, a 'feudal' one.[14]

Mutatis mutandis, there are also general difficulties of a similar sort in the way of giving full credence to Trevor-Roper's suggestion that the most dynamic elements within the ranks of the king's opponents in the war were the 'mere' gentry. At the heart of this thesis is the notion that landed incomes alone were insufficient to sustain a rise in gentry economic fortunes. Each of the twin arguments on which this proposition is based, the first relating to the income and the second to the expenditure of landowners, raises fundamental questions. With regard to income, if the thesis is to be sustained, it must necessarily assume that such landowners were in fact rentiers, for it is based upon the stickiness of rents, that is, their unresponsiveness to changes in the price level. But what if a country gentleman drew the greater part of his income not from rent but from the direct exploitation of his demesne, and, like a good yeoman farmer, geared the production of his estate to a market in which the prices of food and raw materials emphatically led other prices? There is no reason to believe that such cases were either exceptional or even unusual.[15]

A crucial element in Trevor-Roper's arguments is that the socially compulsive need to maintain an extravagant life-style made it necessary for successful gentlemen to supplement their landed income by income not derived from the land; and that it is the fact that the most spectacular example of the latter sort of income was that derived from

office under the Crown which produced the intolerable tension between those who were fortunate enough to possess such offices and
those who were not. There are a number of simple but fundamental
objections which can be raised to this brilliantly argued thesis. In the
first place, the central controlling idea behind it is of a uniform pattern
of gentry 'port' or expenditure, applicable both to 'mere' and to office-
holding gentlemen. For it is, in this view, the attempts of the former to
live at the same rate as the latter, without their advantages of extra-
agricultural forms of income, which brought about their economic
downfall or, at best, ruled any improvement in their economic position
out of the question. Now while it is unquestionably true that there were
'mere' country gentlemen who aspired to a *mode de vie* way above their
economic capabilities and who ruined themselves in consequence,
there is no reason to assume that these were the rule rather than the
exception, for in general the style of life deemed appropriate to the
great office-holder was different from that of the 'mere' gentleman.
Moreover, in the vast majority of cases the information which is available to the historian is totally insufficient to allow of a thorough-going
breakdown of the income of landowners into its constituent parts. Now
this is a matter of crucial importance for without such hard information
about the proportions of their income drawn from different sources it is
begging the question to assume that in the cases of gentlemen whose
economic fortunes are improving and who are also office-holders, the
second of these facts stands to the first as cause to effect. There were
undoubtedly office-holders among the gentry who owed their rise
almost entirely to office.[16] But though the calculation of the economic
value of office is a hazardous business, full of pitfalls for the unwary,
G. E. Aylmer's very guarded, cautious and invaluable treatment of this
problem clearly suggests that the relationship between the amount of
income available from office to the number of gentry office-holders was
such that, in the vast majority of cases, it could have made only a
marginal difference to their economic position. This leads him to
the inevitable conclusion that 'it is impossible to identify the rising
with the office-holding gentry'.[17]

Finally, it may be asked whether the struggle in which Englishmen
spilt one another's blood and ultimately that of their king is explicable
simply in terms of frustrated ambitions for place and income. Such
things may perhaps serve for explanations of relatively minor revolts
such as the Essex Revolt of 1601 or the Bye and Main Plots of 1603. In
relation to an event of the magnitude and importance of the Civil War,

while being factors which the historian neglects at his peril and which were certainly more important for some men than for others, they can never be more than very partial explanations.

IV

Although Marxist historians quite properly lay stress on the fact that the part of the country from which the parliamentary cause drew its chief strength was the economically advanced south and east, while the royalist strength lay more especially in the more economically backward north and west, the available evidence does not suggest any uniform identification of any of the competing political groups with any identifiable economic or social interest. Indeed even the familiar geographical dichotomy is a good deal less rigid and straightforward than is often assumed, and there were important and powerful pockets of royalism and neutralism in Kent and in the heart of what was to become that parliamentary stronghold, the Eastern Association; and of parliamentary support in Somerset, to cite but a few of many examples.[18] The fact is that rising, declining, 'mere', office-holding, entrepreneurial, rentier, backward and innovating gentry are found in abundance on both sides. In their study of the members of the Long Parliament, Messrs Brunton and Pennington found little difference between the landed economies of those who fought on either side in the Civil War.[19] In another collaborative study, Mr Pennington and Professor Roots discovered that in Staffordshire 'neither the demonstrably rising nor the demonstrably declining gentry were wholeheartedly for one side or the other'. However, not all accounts, either by contemporaries or by modern county historians, are quite so negative in their conclusions. In Cornwall, according to Clarendon, 'the major and most considerable part of the gentry and men of estate were heartily for the king', though he admits that there were 'others of name, fortune and reputation with the people' who supported the parliament. A contemporary account of events in Gloucestershire gives a similar picture, while attaching great importance to the fact that most of that county lay in royalist hands, a factor which was probably of at least equal significance in Cornwall. Of course, there is no easy way of identifying the size and character of the parliamentarian minority in such counties, and estimates are likely to err heavily in the direction of understatement. The same is true of a parliamentarian county such as Suffolk, where the majority party, led by the formidable

Sir Nathaniel Barnardiston of Kedington, included some of the most substantial members of the élite class of gentry who ruled the county in the absence of any resident aristocratic landowner. Many of them were entrepreneurial gentry engaged in large-scale dairying operations. By contrast, the line-up in Leicestershire was dominated by the long-standing aristocratic feud between the two magnate families of the Greys and the Hastings. Although more than twice as many of those gentlemen whose allegiance in the struggle can be identified took the side of the king (and the Hastings) as those who fought for the Greysnand the Parliament, most of the former were relatively small landowners whose families had, moreover, settled longer in the county than those of their opponents, while, according to Alan Everitt, a much higher proportion of Leicestershire parliamentarians was drawn from the 'brisker, newer and more dynamic' landowners. Such people may have been less prevalent or at least less spectacularly successful in neighbouring Nottinghamshire, where the members of the large and powerful resident nobility, including the royalist commander the Earl of Newcastle, took the king's side, as did the bulk of the greater gentry. The ranks of their parliamentarian opponents, while containing a few substantial gentlemen, including two sons of the royalist Earl of Kingston, were characterized far more by men of modest wealth and social position. If the large acreage of woodland in Northamptonshire made that county particularly desirable as an aristocratic and courtly playground, it was also the county of pasture enclosure *par excellence*, offering abundant scope for the emergence of a class of rich entrepreneurial gentry whose sympathies were to be preponderantly parliamentarian in the Civil War. On the other hand, while the historian of the Yorkshire gentry has demonstrated that a substantially higher proportion of parliamentary than of royalist gentry had increased their holdings of land since 1603, and that, conversely, a far higher proportion of the landowners who were to be royalists in the war had been in financial difficulties over the two previous decades (a circumstance which finds close parallels in recent studies of Cheshire), there were nevertheless notably rising as well as notably declining gentry to be found among the Yorkshire royalists. And by no means all of these were perquisite-laden courtiers. Both sides in both Yorkshire and Cheshire included entrepreneurial gentry of the first order, a situation which affords scant encouragement to the view that such persons were overwhelmingly parliamentarian in their sympathies. While go-ahead entrepreneurial landowners such as Sir Marmaduke Langdale and Sir Henry Slingsby may have been outraged by the misdeeds of royal personal government in the 1630s, their alienation was not permanent, and they were among the most fervent and devoted adherents of the king in the war.[20]

V

While some parts of the evidence cited above point in the direction indicated by the Marxist interpretation of events, others suggest quite opposite conclusions. Nor is the evidence any more conclusive when used to test the alternative hypothesis that those gentlemen whose income from land was supplemented by income from office were an obvious source of support for the king, while the 'mere' gentry, whose fortunes were allegedly declining or, at best, static, as a result of their failure to supplement landed by non-landed income saw in the war the opportunity of ousting their more fortunate neighbours. In Yorkshire, for example, 'mere' gentlemen were found in abundance on both sides of the struggle, while if they preponderated in any group in Kent it was among those 'moderate' gentlemen who, if circumstances forced them to take sides, did so without enthusiasm and often with extreme reluctance. In that county extra-landed sources of income seem, on the other hand, to be a common characteristic of those who actively supported both sides in the war. A substantial majority (twenty-five) of those Yorkshire gentlemen who drew some part (how great a part?) of their income from office lined up with the king in 1642, though six supported Parliament. Of course, it needs to be remembered that both were a small minority on both sides.[21] Among MPs in the Long Parliament, the proportion of office-holders who bit the hand which had fed them was notably higher. Out of twenty-seven MPs in the Long Parliament in 1640 who were also office-holders of one sort or another, only about half were royalists, while as many as ten supported the Parliament.[22] And in this for once the behaviour of MPs appears to mirror that of the political nation, for in general a significant minority of Caroline officials opposed the king in the Civil War, while many others were neutrals or trimmers. This at first sight astonishing fact is at least partly explicable in terms of what must already be becoming a familiar phenomenon which will receive still further exemplification before this chapter is finished; the astonishing propensity of the Caroline government to alienate many of those who should have been its natural allies. Among the factors at work here was the threat posed to the security of tenure of many of those officials who held their offices for life. This may have been designed to bring to heel office-holders who had survived from the very different days of the hegemony of Buckingham, and who, especially after 1635, found themselves increasingly out of sympathy with the policies which it was their duty to administer. Another factor was the economic threat to the office-holding class posed by the activities of the Royal Commission on Fees. The 'doublethink' which characterized this aspect of royal administrative reform and its use as a fiscal device to screw composition money out of officeholders makes it perhaps surprising that even greater numbers of them were not alienated. A final factor which may have swayed some officials in 1642 was the parliamentary control of the capital and the machinery of government from which they drew their livelihood.[23]

Finally, does the evidence offer any support to the arguments of Lawrence Stone about the importance of the status uncertainties of upwardly and downwardly mobile social groups as a factor which the historian of the Civil War needs to take into serious account? There are, of course, very real problems relating to the employment of modern sociological concepts which have been designed to illuminate the social processes of an historical situation which is radically different from that which prevailed in the period here under discussion, problems to which the enthusiastic advocates of the use of the social sciences in historical research too often pay insufficient attention.[24] Nevertheless, if used with caution and a due regard for these differences, such concepts can afford insights into the motives of some of the participants in seventeenth-century conflicts. For example, the parliamentarianism of some of the rising entrepreneurial gentry of Northamptonshire which was noted earlier might conceivably owe something to their resentment at their inability to penetrate into the ranks of the élite of this county *par excellence* of enclosure, prodigy houses and Puritanism. But the classic case is Clarendon's description of Somerset. In that county,

> ... though the gentlemen of ancient families and estates ... were for the most part well affected to the King, there were a people of an inferior degree, who, by good husbandry, clothing, and other thriving arts had gotten very great fortunes, and, by degrees getting themselves into the gentlemen's estates, were angry that they found not themselves in the same esteem and reputation.[25]

Such social resentments might operate equally strongly in the case of families of recent settlement in the shires who found it no less difficult to penetrate the county oligarchy than did indigenous families which had been newly gentilized. For many counties such factors can probably be written off completely. Such a case is Cheshire, where there was no notable difference either in antiquity of gentility or of residence as between royalist and parliamentarian gentry. In Kent both Cavaliers and Roundheads tended to come from newcomers and only four of the latter came from old county families. The situation in Hertfordshire, where there was a relatively large number of parvenus and newcomers, mostly from neighbouring London, and where only one-tenth of the gentry came from families which had held land in the county in the Middle Ages, may however have afforded some scope for the status frustrations whose importance is stressed by Professor Stone. In Yorkshire 28 per cent of the royalist gentry had entered the county since 1558 as opposed to 32 per cent of the parliamentarian gentry, while 18.8 per cent of the latter had acquired gentility since 1558 as opposed to only 13.2 per cent of the former. These differences are insufficiently great to be in any way conclusive, and indeed one question which they leave unanswered is why, if status frustrations were an important ingredient in the parliamentarianism of some of the gentry, the admittedly lower proportion of royalist newcomers or newly gentilized royalist landowners did not experience the same frustrations, or, if they did, why they did not take the same political expression.[26]

VI

Below the ranks of the gentry we move quickly out of the sphere of the political nation, although the voice of some of these members of the lower orders was to make itself heard at election times, especially in county elections, and to become increasingly a factor to be reckoned within the policies of the mid-1640s. Dr Hill has seen in 'the industrious sort of the people' some of the most solid supporters of the parliamentarian cause, though this view of them, as the dynamic, forward-looking element in the economy as compared with the concessionary mercantile interest which had grown up within, and which was totally dependent on the continuance of the 'feudal' framework of society, perhaps owes too much to a view of the nature of the economy of the period which sees industrial rather than commercial growth as the leading sector of economic change, and which few economic historians of the period would now accept.[27]

More useful conclusions about the political attitudes of the manufacturing classes can probably be drawn by examining areas where the fortunes of war were uncertain and fluctuating rather than areas such as Norfolk and Suffolk which remained under firm parliamentary control, and where it may be that the apparently parliamentarian sympathies of clothiers and weavers were as much due to their desire to be left unmolested as to positive political sympathies, however much these might be induced by economic self-interest. Large parts of the most important and developed regional sector of the woollen cloth industry, in Wiltshire, Gloucestershire and Somerset, fall into the former category, as do the less important but rapidly growing textile centres of the West Riding of Yorkshire. Although the royalist gentry were thicker on the ground in the West Riding than in any other part of Yorkshire, there was a solid parliamentarian preponderance among the cloth producers of the area. Similarly, Professor Underdown has indicated the impressive support for the parliament which was evinced by the cloth manufacturers of northern and eastern Somerset. But there were some prominent west-country clothiers, such as Henry Hawkins of Chippenham, with royalist sympathies to set against the likes of the pertinacious John Ashe of Freshford, one of the most notable Somerset parliamentarians. A recent historian of the west-country cloth industry suggests that most of the clothiers of the region were inclined to support Parliament, though anxious as far as possible to avoid embroilment; while the historian of the Wiltshire woollen industry has argued that it is extremely difficult to discern a notable preference for either side among the bulk of the manufacturers in this most highly capitalized and developed of all textile counties.[28]

Some of this scepticism is perhaps open to the criticism that it makes too much of exceptional cases. But whatever may be said for or against the identification of clothing regions with the parliamentary and puritan cause – and on the whole the evidence in favour of the identification is impressive – Professor Underdown's more recent extension of the thesis in his detailed study of Wiltshire, Somerset and Dorset, to areas of wood pasture in general, whether or not these contained pockets of textile production, raises additional questions. Underdown sees such districts as characterized by an individualistic popular culture which chimed in well with the puritan ethos; in contrast to the traditionalist, deferential and closely-knit character of areas in the same counties where open-field husbandry, nucleated villages, smaller parishes, and the more pervasive influence of squire and parson prevailed. This argued connection between distinct farming regions and distinct popular cultures finds further striking expression in an admittedly rough and approximate fit 'between pre-war [popular] culture and civil war allegiance'. While it must be admitted as Dr Morrill has conceded, that this is a more sophisticated and less procrustean account of the social and economic bases of the political antagonisms of the Great Rebellion than the all too familiar Marxist dichotomy between the 'feudal' and backward north and west of England and the economically advanced south and east, Underdown's thesis must for the moment be accorded the status of a highly stimulating hypothesis which still requires much more detailed research. For even if one accepts the argument that the traditional festive and paternalist culture flourished best in areas such as the nucleated downland villages of the west country, where deference was a more potent feature than in clothing or forest communities, it still does not necessarily follow that this was a factor making for predominantly royalist sympathies in the former areas, even if we take full account of Puritan antipathy to popular festive culture. And, needless to say, whatever one makes of Underdown's identification of distinct farming regions with distinct popular cultures and political sympathies in these south-western counties, the identification has no necessary application to other parts of England, as he himself readily admits. To cite a fairly obvious example, it is obviously inapplicable to the political allegiance of, on the one hand, the sheep–corn husbandry and nucleated villages, and, on the other, the wood pasture with its pockets of dairying, leather and textile production, in Roundhead East Anglia during the Great Rebellion.[29]

The common identification of the middling sort or people with parliamentary puritanism which has received renewed emphasis in recent studies[30] finds some support in a contemporary account of allegiance in Gloucestershire. The author contrasts the royalist sympathies of the bulk of the substantial gentry with the parliamentarianism of 'Yeomen, Farmers, petty Free-holders, and such as use Manufactures that enrich the Country, and passe through the hands of a multitude, a generation of men truely laborious . . . whose principall ayme is Liberty and Plenty . . .' Rather than follow the gentry, the most prominent and numerous of whom, fearing for the integrity of their estates in a county where the balance of advantage lay with the royalists, had espoused the royalist cause, these men, 'the true Commons of the Realme . . . the most vehement assertors of Publicke Liberty', tended to follow the lead of the clothiers, 'those men by whom those manufactures were maintained that kept them alive'. This picture of the attitude of the middling and the manufacturing sort of people is one to delight the heart of Dr Christopher Hill, even though it may be true that their political sympathies are attributable at least as much to the economic inconveniences consequent upon the disruption of the vitally important outlet for their products through parliamentarian London. Be this as it may, it would be wrong to write off completely this contemporary contrast between the independent attitude of such people and the alleged pusillanimity, of on the one hand, the invertebrate Gloucestershire gentry, and on the other, 'the dreggs of the people ... the first rise of Tyrannicall Government, and the foot-stoole upon which Princes tread when they ascend the height of Monarchy'.[31]

CITIZENS AND CONCESSIONAIRES

I

Just as the Court penetrated the County, via, as was shown earlier, the official sources of income of some landowners, so did it also penetrate the City of London.[32] This was a period in which the leading sector of the non-agrarian economy was to be found not in industry but in commerce, and one of the most spectacular economic developments of the Tudor century had been the centralization of a great deal of commercial business on the metropolis where there emerged a business concessionary interest linked with the Court by close and intimate ties of economic interest, which arose out of the Government's employment of private enterprise to provide machinery for the enforcement of some of its economic policies, and the use of the same medium by courtly concessionaires who unloaded their valuable economic privileges on the business world.

Some of the members of this business concessionary interest confined their interests to one or to a small number of economic concessions; others, the greatest among them, had their economic eggs distributed over a wide variety of concessionary baskets. Broadly speaking, the concessions fall into two main categories, those connected with foreign commerce and those relating to domestic matters. The former find their origin in the area monopolies of overseas trade exercised by trading companies which owed their exclusive privileges to the Crown. Among the main domestic concessions were licences *non obstante* penal statutes, domestic patents of monopoly and customs farming concessions. In all of them the relationship between the courtier who obtained the concessions and the man (often a London busi-nessman) who exploited them was close and intimate. Sometimes the courtier held a rentier interest, receiving the concession in the first instance and sub-letting it at a profit to the business interest which actually exploited it directly, though there were on occasion rings of business speculators who separated the original grantees from the final recipients of the concessions. On other occasions, the courtier's role was akin to that of the broker who negotiated concessions on behalf of business interests which then farmed them direct from the Crown. In either case it was clearly in the interests of both parties to perpetuate the arrangements and for so long as a reasonable *modus vivendi* could be maintained between them, it is proper to speak in terms of a com-munity of interest between the Court and at least an important sector of the City.

Thus, far from being opposed to government restraints on the free-dom of economic enterprise, many of the most prominent businessmen of the day stood to gain spectacularly from associating themselves with these restrictions. This important fact has now found general recogni-tion from historians. However, the associated view that business con-cessionary interest lined up firmly with the Court in 1640[33] raises some fundamental questions. In the first place, if it is correct, then the attitude of concessionaires stands in marked contrast to that of almost every other sector of the political nation, including many of those who, as has already been suggested, would in normal circumstances be the natural allies of the government, but were now alienated from it. Secondly, it raises the question of the extent to which the interests of different sorts of concessionaire were in fact mutually harmonious or whether they might not be, in certain circumstances, mutually con-tradictory. There is in fact a danger that the previously exploded ortho-doxy which assumes that businessmen were *ipso facto* opposed to a government which imposed restrictions on the freedom of economic enterprise should be replaced by another orthodoxy that the ties which linked the concessionary business élite of the day to the Court were indissoluble and that their relationship with the Crown remained in basic essentials the same throughout the first four decades of the century.

The truth is more complex, more interesting and more in line with what we know of the general attitude of the political nation in 1640. Despite the existence of what might be described as interlocking con-cessionary holdings by magnates who were also multi-concessionaires with fingers in a wide variety of concessionary pies, there was plenty of scope for conflict of interest amongst concessionaires.[34] There were conflicts between members of the same chartered companies and between different companies such as the Levant and Merchant Adventurers' Companies. In addition there were disputes between courtly concessionaires and their business sub-lessees such as that between the Duke of Richmond and Lenox and the Merchant Adventurers in the 1630s about the price demanded by the duke for his cloth export licences.[35] And there are any number of examples of conflict between the customs farmers and other domestic concessionaires such as monopolists and the great chartered companies with area privileges of foreign trade.[36] Nevertheless, despite such conflicts, so long as the attacks on the concessionary interest in parliament were indiscriminate rather than selective and they were all grouped together as the agents of a sort of metropolitan plot to drain away the economic life blood of the outports, there was bound to be some closing of the ranks of concessionaires who, in other circumstances, might have been at daggers drawn. For as long as every sort of concessionaire owed his privileged position to and continued to receive the unstinted support of the government, and also continued to be the object of indiscriminate hostility from the opposition to government policies in the House of Commons when parliament was meeting, they would, in the nature of things, tend to lean towards the Court rather than the Country. But this classic situation was not permanent and the consequent split in the ranks of the concessionaires is a development of first-rate importance which has received scant attention from historians.

The 1620s were the great climacteric decade in this matter also. It was during this decade that the loyalties of the most numerous sector of the concessionary interest were subject to the severest test that they had yet experienced. As a result a new and highly significant realignment of forces emerged, whereby the sympathies of the great chartered companies moved away from the Court and towards the Country, effecting a reconciliation with the parliamentary opposition which, from Sir Edwin Sandys's Free Trade Bill of 1604 down to the strictures of Neale, Digges and Alport in the parliament of 1621 on the companies' restrictive practices, had hitherto been implacably opposed to them. There was, however, little or no sign of this in the parliament of 1621, when the hostility of the Commons to privileged economic concessionaires was greatly exacerbated by severe economic depression, and no concessionary interest was safe from attack. In general the concessionary interest was in a state of disarray, its various elements lumped together for indiscriminate condemnation.[37] There were also attacks on a number of companies in the parliament of 1624. Nevertheless the temper of the Commons was notably less fierce, and for instance in the inclusion of some of the complaints of the Merchant Adventurers and the Levant Company in the parliamentary petition of grievances presented to the king, it is perhaps not unreasonable to see some measure of reconciliation in contrast to the unrelenting parliamentary hostility to the companies in 1621.[38]

But what makes the contrast between the parliaments of 1621 and 1624 especially striking is that the latter parliament witnessed the significant beginnings of a fissure within the ranks of the concessionary interest between, on the one hand domestic concessionaires and on the other the chartered overseas trading companies. In this respect, much the most significant event of the parliament was the famous Statute of Monopolies.[39] Ever since 1604, when the great chartered companies had come near to being swept away on the backwash of the anti-monopoly agitation in parliament, there had been a tendency to group the two sorts of restrictive practice together as fit subjects for parliamentary denunciation, a development which culminated in the parliament of 1621. The Statute of Monopolies, by contrast, via its specific exemption of corporate bodies from its provisions, sharply distinguished between the two sorts of concessions, and marks the beginning of a new and more realistic differentiation by opposition MPs between different sectors of the concessionary interest. This was not an ephemeral phenomenon. For not only were the attacks on chartered companies, which had been a notable feature of the economic attitudes of the opposition in James I's parliaments, notably absent from those of his son, but some companies discovered an unwonted and, no doubt, astonishing sympathy with their problems among persons who had previously been among their most implacable opponents. Examples were the encouragement given by Sir Dudley Digges to the East India Company's petition to parliament in 1628, and the favourable response of the Commons to the Company's case, a significant contrast with the rebukes which had been administered to the directors by the Privy Council; also the favourable reception given to the complaints of the Somers Islands Company in the same year against the tobacco monopolists which issued first in a parliamentary petition to the king on the company's behalf, on the failure of which a bill was introduced in its favour the following February.[40]

Parallel with the cessation of parliamentary attacks on the companies and the favourable response of the House of Commons to the difficulties of some of them was their alienation from their traditional ally, the Crown. The irresponsible policies associated with the hegemony of the Duke of Buckingham, who during the years between the declaration of war in 1624 and his assassination in 1628 exercised a stronger and more disastrous influence on royal policy than ever before, had adverse repercussions on some of the companies, as was the case with Buckingham's extraction of £10,000 from the East India Company as the price of its seizure of Ormuz in 1624, and his confiscation of the goods of a French ship allegedly carrying contraband of war which precipitated the French seizure of the English wine fleet at Bordeaux in 1626. The latter incident achieved the near miracle of uniting the London merchants of the French Company and the merchants of the south-western outports in protest against the ham-handed actions which had precipitated this disaster.[41] Of all companies, the East India Company was probably the most sorely tried over these years and it has already been seen that its difficulties evoked a great deal more sympathy in the House of Commons than on the Privy Council. Among them were the Government's failure to take a consistently firm line with the Dutch over restitution for the massacre at Amboina; the royal encouragement of the agitator Thomas Smethwicke in the attacks he was mounting on the company's directorate in 1628 and during the following decade; the outrageous proposal advanced by Smethwicke and others that the king be credited with a free adventure of £10,000 in the company; and, during the 1630s, courtly and royal support both for the privateering expedition of Kynaston and Bonnell, and for the East India association formed by the adventurer Sir William Courteen, both of which did untold harm to the company's fortune and reputation.[42] The view which sees the directorate of the East India Company and Charles I as natural allies does not accord very well with these uncomfortable facts.[43]

It has been shown that the splitting of the different elements in the concessionary interest and their realignment in respect of the struggle between Court and Country was begun by the Statute of Monopolies of 1624. It was completed five years later by the tonnage and poundage dispute in Charles I's third parliament, the events of which brought to boiling-point the long-simmering antagonism between the chartered companies and the farmers of the royal customs. In concentrating their attack on a small but wealthy and influential sector of the concessionary interest, domestic monopolists in 1624 and customs farmers in 1629, the Commons carried with them those far more numerous sectors of the concessionary interest to which they had before 1624 shown at least an equal hostility. And in the strike in the payment of unparliamentary customs duties which followed the dissolution of parliament, members of the Merchant Adventurers' and Levant companies were among the most prominent adherents of the famous resolution which condemned not only collectors but also payers of such duties. It was not, however, as collectors in government employment that the customers were attacked, but as persons to whom the king had alienated his interest in the customs, the collection of which was therefore regarded as being in their own, private, and not in the royal, interest. The tonnage and poundage dispute widened irreparably that breach in the business concessionary interest which survived more or less unchanged through the 1630s, so that the Long Parliament began at exactly the point where the parliament of 1629 had left off.[44]

The evidence does not suggest that those companies which had been alienated from the Court and had found new allies in Parliament had reason to alter their attitude during the succeeding decade of non-parliamentary rule.[45] This is not to imply that there was a complete identity of interest between them on all matters. Nevertheless, the broad dichotomy between the attitudes of concessionaires in foreign trade and those of domestic concessionaires which was the most significant product of the events of the 1620s is not less true of the following decade, even though there continued to be a number of individuals whose interests were spread across these groups. There was, for example, continued hostility to the customs farmers for their role in exacting burdensome and 'unconstitutional' duties, as well as to the proliferation of domestic corporate monopolies, which militated hardly less against the interests of some of the chartered companies for overseas trade than against those of consumers and of the producers who were displaced by these monopolies or who had to pay through their plebeian noses for the privilege of doing what they had every reason to regard as their right to do.[46] This book already abounds with examples of Charles I's alienation of large numbers of what ought in normal circumstances to have been his natural allies during the 1630s: deputy lieutenants, local magistrates, sheriffs and government servants, to mention but a few. But in no field is the king's prodigal dissipation of the natural sources of support for his regime more apparent than in that of the business concessionary interest. The events of the 1620s had marked off the domestic concessionaires from the more numerous concessionary groups with area privileges of foreign trade whose rapprochement with parliament had been one of the most important, as it is one of the most neglected, features of the decade.

II

One of the main reasons the Civil War was lost by Charles I was that his opponents had at their disposal the wealth and resources of London. This fact naturally prompts the question of how far the alienation of important sectors of the London concessionary business interest, and especially those of them who were City fathers, that is aldermen and common councilmen, and especially the former, can be held responsible for this development. If we take the aldermen of 1640–1,[47] it immediately becomes apparent that the great majority of them, twenty-seven out of thirty, had concessionary interests of one sort or another, and some had multiple concessionary interests. This might be regarded as strong supporting evidence for what has become the orthodox thesis that the municipal governors of London in 1640 were tied by powerful links of economic self-interest with the Crown and Court. But the evidence becomes less impressive in direct proportion as credence is attached to the argument of the preceding pages that the bulk of the concessionary interest, those engaged in foreign trade as distinct from those holding domestic concessions (the two categories were not, of course, mutually exclusive), had been alienated from their traditional alliance with the Crown in the course of the decade and a half after 1624. Indeed, of the twenty-seven concessionaires among the aldermen of 1640–1, only nine of them held *domestic* concessions of any sort, so that, if the argument of the preceding pages carries any weight, the percentage of aldermen who were clearly linked by any sort of ties of economic interest with the Crown shrinks from 90 per cent to 30 per cent.

It is not intended to argue that the economic interests of the aldermen were the only force determining their political stance, and that the disillusionment created by their experience as entrepreneurs and concessionaires might not perhaps be offset by their views on religious and constitutional matters, and more particularly, in their capacity as City fathers, on the problem of authority and obedience. It is therefore important to examine their position as City fathers as well as their position as concessionaires, and to look carefully at the relation between the City government and the Crown during the years of Charles 1's personal government.

The view that these relations were amicable and that disputes between Crown and City were of relatively minor importance simply will not stand up to the overwhelming evidence of acrimonious disputes between Crown and City during the 1630s. In other words, it is arguable that any doubts which the bulk of the aldermen may have experienced in their capacity as business concessionaires would be reinforced by their experiences as City fathers. The numerous disputes between the Crown and the City may broadly be divided into two categories, the first of which is of disputes peculiar to the relations between Crown and City, and the second the wider issues which also affected the remainder of the political nation.[48]

The first of these two categories may be further subdivided into issues which were settled – or, more appropriately, patched up – during the summer of 1637, by the City's consenting to compound for its admitted offences.[49] The best-known of these issues is probably the bitter dispute over the Londonderry plantation, which culminated in the celebrated Star Chamber case of 1635 resulting in the forfeiture of the City's Irish lands, the imposition of a fine of £70,000, which, like most Star Chamber fines, was later reduced, and, not least important, the public humiliation of the City in the process.[50] Hardly less humiliating had been another case brought against the City three years earlier by the Attorney General, this time in the Court of Exchequer, relating to the alleged breach of trust by the City and its Land Sales Committee in connection with the sale of royal lands conveyed to it as a means of satisfying the subscribers to City loans to James I and Charles I.[51] Other issues patched up in 1637 were the royal contestation of the City's right to certain casual revenues, the estreats under the greenwax, which it had taken as a matter of course ever since the reign of Henry VI, and the renewal of royal claims to the fines imposed for encroachment on the wasteland and streets of the City, which the Crown had dropped in the second decade of the century but revived in 1636.[52] The aldermanry may, as Dr Pearl suggests,[53] have been anxious to come to terms with the Crown in respect of the issues which were patched up by 1637, but this anxiety is hardly evidence of enthusiasm for royal policies, and the settlement was achieved only as a result of the prolonged and relentless pressure to which they had been subjected.

This general impression is reinforced when one turns to issues which had not been settled by 1637. The royal policy with regard to the City guilds was certainly one of these and the occasion of serious misgivings on the part of the lord mayor and aldermen on account of the breach when they threatened to force in the oligarchic citadel. The most contentious issues here were the favour which the Crown showed to splinter incorporations of master-craftsmen attempting to break away from their parent guilds, and the royal encouragement of the attempts of many of the minor crafts, in violation of the so-called custom of London, to obtain the literal enforcement of a rule whereby all guildsmen should belong to the guild appropriate to the craft which they pursued. In both of these matters the lord mayor and his colleagues engaged in a determined exercise of foot-dragging and obstructionism which occasioned numerous clashes with the Crown.[54]

A further threat to the power and prestige of the City government came from the royal creation of a Corporation of the Suburbs in 1636, ostensibly to deal with the growing and neglected problems posed by these totally unregulated pockets of disorder. An additional blow was the Government's insistence, despite earlier assurances to the contrary, that the inhabitants of the so-called 'liberties' which lay between Temple Bar and Aldgate and therefore geographically within the City – and even of those 'liberties' over which the City had acquired control by virtue of its charter of 1608 – must become members of the new corporation or relinquish the right to do business in these places.[55] Another serious and more long-standing grievance was the operations of the Royal Commission on Buildings. In both cases the royal motives were at least as much concerned with financial gain as with the need to regulate the abuses in question. Established in 1615, the Building Commission was an object of the suspicions of municipal authorities from the beginning, even though they were represented on it. Indeed the City fathers were acutely embarrassed by the fact that it quickly became common knowledge that they found its operations irksome. But although they made some attempt to dispel this impression, its truth seems to be attested by the fact that they were responsible for bringing royal building controls as a grievance before the parliaments of 1621 and 1624. Their disquiet increased in the next decade which saw a notable stiffening of the reinforcement of the royal building regulations.[56]

Nor was it only in the matter of local disputes peculiar to the relations between Court and City that the latter had cause to resent the policies of the former. In the discussion of Ship Money in the last chapter, it was observed that the City of London was in the very forefront of the process of articulating constitutional opposition to the innovatory royal demands, as indeed it had been in a previous ship levy of 1626.[57] Similarly it was not just ordinary citizens but also the lord mayor and aldermen who received sharp conciliar rebukes for their lack of cooperation in connection with the Forced Loan of 1626–7.[58] And there are other issues in which the City fathers found themselves ranged alongside other parts of the political nation which, in other circumstances, might have been expected to be firm pillars of support for royal policies, but had now been alienated by them. For example, they shared the widespread general dislike for the royal demand that they contribute to the creation of the 'perfect militia' and for the expense of meeting the salary of the muster-master, and their obstinacy in this matter occasioned royal and conciliar reprimands on more than one occasion.[59] And in a variety of ways they fell foul of William Laud in his capacity both as Bishop of London before 1633 and as Archbishop of Canterbury afterwards. The issues here ranged from Laud's determination to screw up the revenue from tithes in the city, perhaps intended as a national test-case, and both the Privy Council's and Archbishop's castigation of the civic authorities for their lukewarmness about Laud's great scheme for the re-edification of St Paul's, to more narrowly local concerns such as mayoral attempts to exercise civic jurisdiction in St Paul's church-yard and the dean and chapter's opposition to the bearing of the lord mayor's ceremonial sword at the head of the civic procession entering the cathedral. In these and other matters the lord mayor and aldermen shared the antipathy of most of the political nation to Laudian clerical pretensions, and the fact that they had to tone down some of their sabbatarian and anti-clerical instincts in face of pressure from the hierarchy can hardly be regarded as betokening approval of Laudian policies.[60]

Nothing better indicates the alienation of the civic authorities from the government by the end of the period of Charles I's personal government than their attitude over the proposed financial levies to meet the charges of the war against the Scots. The City's response to royal demands for aid in March 1639 was totally inadequate and there was a plan to present the derisory sum of £5,000 along with a petition against monopolies and high prices, to which was to be added the localist demand that the Londoners pressed for military service should be employed solely in the defence of the capital. Instead of his hoped-for loan of £100,000 in June the king had to content himself with a free gift of £10,000, as well as to put up with the recalcitrant and positively

uncooperative attitude of many of the aldermen which prompted Strafford's notorious remark about the desirability of hanging some of them
– in full aldermanic robes – to expedite matters. When the City did
finally consent to lend £200,000 in 1640, it was effectively on condition
that parliament be called, and the provision for installed payments at
well spaced out intervals was a guarantee that this was not to be another
Short Parliament.[61]

The civic authorities who complained dragged their feet and in so
doing played a significant part in bringing about the calling of the Long
Parliament were in no sense radicals, any more than they were out-
and-out sympathizers with the aims of Charles's personal government,
as they are usually represented. Like the majority of the political nation
and of the MPs who came up to Westminster at the end of 1640, seeing
in the summoning of parliament the essential remedy for eleven years
of tyrannical government, they were moderate men, many of whom
were to side with the king in the Civil War. But some time was to elapse
and a great many things were to happen before they were driven to take
up this position. It is true that the ranks of the aldermen in 1640
contained a very small minority of men such as the notorious wine
monopolist William Abell, and the lord mayor of 1639–40 Sir Henry
Garway, a man with extensive domestic concessionary interests, who
had every reason to fear that they would be among the first objects of
parliamentary vengeance. But to the great majority of the City fathers
the calling of the Long Parliament brought renewed hopes of better
times following the battering which they had received during the previous two and a half decades in their twin capacities as businessmen
and municipal governors.

The moderate parliamentary sympathies of the bulk of the London
aldermen were to fade over the ensuing months as events began to
take an increasingly radical turn, so that London's parliamentarian
allegiance in the Civil War was ultimately achieved only as a result of a
revolutionary change in the personnel of the Common Council and
Court of Aldermen.[62] Until studies of the personnel of the governing
class of many more provincial towns have been made, it is impossible
to say how far the situation in London was paralleled in the provinces.
In Newcastle-upon-Tyne and Chester, where municipal government
was in the hands of the royalists in 1642, the persons in question seem to
have been in each case a small but cohesive minority group – in the case
of Chester a minority of racketeers whose royalism was based on their
determination to keep their hands on the lucrative economic con-

cessions which they derived from the Crown, even though the support of the Privy Council for their privileged position seems at various times during the 1630s to have been less than enthusiastic. The ruling clique which controlled Newcastle consisted almost entirely of mercers and coal traders and not of economic concessionaires, in the sense that William Gamull and his associates in Chester were concessionaires. Nevertheless they seem to have regarded support for the royal cause as the surest way of safeguarding their position against the attacks of their enemies in the town. The royal distrust of the temper of municipalities, even in a town which declared for the king in 1642, is clearly manifested in the refusal to entrust effective government of Chester to native Cestrians at any time during the war. The Crown was all too aware that municipal governors with compelling reasons to take the King's side against Parliament were usually minority groups, even though their numbers may have increased, in provincial towns as in London, in the period between the calling of the Long Parliament and the outbreak of the Civil War.[63]

FIVE *Religion and Politics*

It hath been ever held a rule or Maxime amongst all Nations to make the defence of Religion the chiefe ground or cause of their Warre; sometimes for meere politick ends and by respects, sometimes to regulate it where it is.

A parallel betweene the late troubles in Scotland (1642) p. 1.

I have heard My Lord say

(xx)

That there should be more praying, and less preaching; for much preaching breeds faction; but much praying causes devotion.

. . . .

(xxiv)

That all books of controversies should be writ in Latin, that none but the learned may read them, and that there should be no disputations but in schools, lest it breed factions amongst the vulgar; . . . also that prayer-books should be writ in the native language; that excommunications should not be too frequent for every little and pretty [*sic*] trespass; that every clergyman should be kind and loving to his parishioners, not proud and quarrelsome.

Margaret, Duchess of Newcastle, *The Life of the Duke of Newcastle* (1667, Everyman edn. 1915), pp. 153, 154.

Let the King have his due,
Lest the dangers of Strangers ensue,
Though ye had a Laud and Wren,

Bishops may be honest men,
And preach almost as well as you.

Thomas Jordan, *Rules to know a royall
king* (1642), p. 6.

I

FEW OF THE CONTEMPORARIES of that vastly experienced parliamentarian, Sir Benjamin Rudyerd, MP for Wilton in the Long Parliament, would have disagreed with his description of religion in his
speech of 7 November 1640 as 'our *premium quaerite*, ffor all things are
but &c. to it,'[1] or with Edward Bowles's statement some six years later
that it was 'the foundation and perfection of the Kingdomes happi-
nesse'. Yet Bowles went on to argue that 'if I were asked the ground
of the Parliaments taking up armes *de facto* I should not answer the
reformation of Religion'. There were many, among them Oliver
Cromwell himself who would have agreed with him.[2] There were, in
addition, many contemporaries who were prepared to argue from a
quite different point of view that the war was not about religion. Such
were royalist sympathizers for whom the spiritual zeal of the godly
Puritan was a bogus disguise for the pursuit of personal gain under
the cloak of religion: 'Al lands & revenues of the Churche, in their
opinion, are the fleshe of the whore of Babylon, & they will eate the
fleshe of the old whore, & devour the bones.'[3] To accept such views
at their face value would be to reduce the religious genius of Puritanism
to the lowest common denominator of land, place and money grabbing.
Nevertheless, when it is recalled that some notably godly predecessors
of the Puritans of the revolutionary years, from the radical separatist
John Penry in the 1590s to the ultra-respectable Dr John Preston in
the 1620s, had not been above dangling the prospect of tasty pickings
of ecclesiastical revenues and lands before the aristocratic notabilities
whom they attempted to interest in the cause of religious reform, it
would clearly be rash to rule out the possibility that the clouds of smoke
emitted by anti-Puritan writings may have betokened the existence
of at least some fire.[4] Nevertheless, as will be argued later in this
chapter, the intimate connection between religious and secular issues
can also be viewed as testifying to the fundamental importance of the
former rather than to their subordination to the latter. Moreover, the
temper in which religious matters *per se* were discussed and the passions
which they aroused have led Dr John Morrill to argue forcefully and

convincingly for their primacy as divisive issues leading to civil war. 'The English Civil War', he confidently concludes, 'was not the first European revolution: it was the last of the Wars of Religion'.[5]

II

One of the most potent sources of misunderstanding of the nature of the Puritan challenge in the decades before 1640 is the failure of many historians to recognize that the Puritan mainstream was not Presbyterian or anti-episcopalian, especially following the crushing of Cartwrightian Presbyterianism by Archbishop Whitgift in the closing decades of Elizabeth's reign. To the mainstream Puritan, King and Bishop were the allied central figures through whose joint agency godly reformation was to be brought about. Episcopacy was not a divinely ordained institution, but it was more than simply a convenient and appropriate way of organizing the Church in a monarchical society. It was an institution which had proved its Protestant worth in the fires in Balliol ditch in the reign of Mary.[6] Even if some of the first generation of Elizabethan bishops, hot from Zurich, Frankfurt, Basle and Strasbourg (if not from Geneva) had been succeeded by men cast in a very different mould – the good shepherds Grindal and Parkhurst by the persecuting Whitgift and Freake – the genus and the tradition were very far from extinct. As late as March 1641 Robert Abbot, vicar of Cranbrook in Kent, in a letter to Sir Edward Dering, contrasted the formidable intellectual contributions of godly bishops such as Ussher, Morton, Davenant, Downham and Archbishop Abbot in the battle against Popery with the paltry contribution of the Presbyterian church of Scotland.[7] Indeed moderate episcopacy was still to find some staunch defenders among the less extreme Puritans in the debates on religion in the early days of the Long Parliament.[8] If their numbers were now smaller and their voice less powerful than would have been the case at the beginning of the reign, this is attributable to what amounts to yet another example of that now familiar prodigality of the Caroline regime in alienating potential sources of support: in this case the Puritan mainstream, one of the most notable of whom was William Prynne.[9] Awkward and cross-grained though Prynne's personality may have been, his brand of Puritanism was very different from that of his fellow sufferer, the radical anti-episcopalian Henry Burton. One might indeed be tempted to ascribe the punishment of these two on the same scaffold in 1637 either to the Government's insensitivity to fundamental differences between its critics, or to the clumsy attempt to tar them all with the extremist brush, were it not for the fact that Burton was at great pains to conceal his anti-episcopal views at this time. As to Prynne, nothing could be further from the truth than Cottington's statement in the earlier Star Chamber case of 1634 that 'Mr Pryn would have a newe churche, newe government, a newe kinge, for hee would make the people altogether offended with all thinges att the present.'[10] It is true that Prynne's way of drawing attention to what he deemed to be gross abuses and ungodly practices condoned by authority was infuriatingly tactless. But in his view the programme of reform for which he stood did not involve innovation; it was innovation against which he was protesting. Far from advocating disobedience to the king, it was the king on whom he rested his hopes as the prime agent of godly reformation. Far from opposing episcopacy as an institution, he looked, mostly in vain, to the Caroline successors of the Marian martyr-bishops to join with their sovereign in bringing about the glorious work. A government which made implacable enemies of such persons was likely to run extremely short of friends.

III

This view of the conservative nature of the Puritan mainstream differs from that held by some historians. Professor Michael Walzer, for instance, argues that it was 'the Calvinists who first switched the emphasis of political thought from the prince to the saint (or band of saints)'.[11] He points, for example, to the challenge offered by Puritan teaching to the traditional world-order by the dissociation of the role of the king from that of the paterfamilias and the refusal to admit that the king was God's analogue.[12] The formidable Puritan propagandist Henry Parker argued in 1642 that kings were most unlike gods, and that although they were 'sanctified with some of God's royaltie', this was solely directed to the 'extrinsecall' end of the prosperity of God's people. Parker gives even shorter shrift to the parallel Jacobean correspondences between the king as the head of the body politic and the head of the human body, and between the authority of kings and paternal authority.[13] Another line was to deny not so much the analogy between kings and fathers as the absolute power possessed by the latter over their children, arguing that children and servants had the right to resist violent or tyrannical parents and masters. On this reckoning, if the king's power corresponded with that of a father, both were analogous with that of the master of a ship who may be restrained by his crew

if his actions are imperilling the safety of the vessel, the traditional
metaphor of the ship of state being here put to a distinctly radical use.[14]
And before the end of the 1640s one writer (Henry Parker?) was performing a radical intellectual conjuring trick by deftly reversing roles
in the correspondence between kings and fathers:

> ... in the relative Offices of Prince and Subject, the Prince lookes
> lesse tenderly upon the people as being his root or parent, whilst
> yet the people lookes more tenderly upon the Prince as its owne
> stemme and issue.[15]

The above examples have all been drawn from the revolutionary
decade of the 1640s, and it needs to be pointed out that there is a very
real danger, of which not all students of Calvinism have shown themselves sufficiently aware, of reading back such ideas into historical
situations to which they are not applicable, and to distort the significance of earlier decades by seeing them simply as, in Sir Geoffrey
Elton's phrase, a 'highway to Civil War'. But even if examples of such
ideas can be found in the decades before 1640 there still remains the
question of whether they can be regarded as typical of the Puritan
mainstream. It may be true, for example, that the Puritan 'saint' was
a significant anticipation of the dedicated revolutionary fanatic of
modern times, but concern with this blueprint of revolutionary psychology can easily obscure the fact that certainly before, and probably
after 1642, this is the psychology of Puritans who lay well to the left of
centre, not only of the religico-political spectrum as a whole but even of
the Puritan part of it.[16]

To say that is not to deny the importance of a number of factors
which are common to all Puritans and which have potentially radical
implications. Among these is the Puritan insistence on the importance
of spiritual and intellectual understanding for all believers, which
prompted, *inter alia*, the insistence on the crucial significance of preaching, and which would militate strongly against viewing the subjects of
the Prince as simple children whose main duty was obedience.[17] As
such, it contrasts with the emphasis laid by the ruler and by most of the
hierarchy, including Archbishop Abbot, a primate who was by no
means out of sympathy with many of the views of moderate Puritans,
but who, in a pastoral letter of 1622, argued that preachers should avoid
'a soaring up in points of divinity too deep for the capacity of the
people'.[18] Not altogether unconnected with this was the Government's
dislike of what it regarded as the sedition-mongering sermons of

many Puritan preachers and lecturers, 'furious promoters of the most dangerous innovations which were ever induced into any State'.[19] But such complaints ought not to be taken as proof of the revolutionary temper of such people; they could at least equally well testify to the alienation of moderate Puritans as a result of royal and episcopal innovation in State and Church.

IV

The salutary emphasis of Patrick Collinson and William Lamont on the conservative rather than the revolutionary characteristics of mainstream Elizabethan and early Stuart Puritanism, and on its support for, rather than subversion of, the existing order is not necessarily in any way incompatible with the familiar commonplace about its significance as an ideology of opposition. But opposition to what? To Christopher Hill it was the ideology of the bourgeoisie and, more especially, of 'the industrious sort of the people' against a regime which posed serious obstacles to the exercise of the bourgeois virtues and the growth of capitalism. To Lord Dacre (Hugh Trevor-Roper) it was a perfect ready-made ideology of exclusion for those who did not enjoy the economic and other benefits of the Court – an ideology of 'outs' desperately concerned to get themselves an innings. To Alan Everitt, perhaps, and certainly to some county historians it could easily be turned into an ideology of localism against centralism. Granted that there was greater scope than is sometimes realized for these characteristics to overlap, the overlap was a great deal less than complete. Nor even if one were to settle for one of these alternatives to the exclusion of the others, is the range of possibilities exhausted. For example, among those historians who stress Puritanism's significance as a bourgeois ideology, Dr Hill sees it playing this role from, at the latest, the closing years of Elizabeth I, while Professor George postulates a sudden, dramatic (and largely unexplained) leap from a movement whose social content was conservative before 1640 to one which formed a powerful ideology for an insurgent bourgeoisie thereafter.[20]

Certainly, the specific teachings of mainstream Puritan divines on social and economic matters before the Civil War were as orthodox and unexceptionable as their views about political or episcopal authority. A useful touchstone is the teaching of William Perkins, who died in the year before the accession of the first Stuart king, but who Dr Hill sees as 'the dominant influence in Puritan thought for the forty years after his death'.[21] Hill perceives the whole content and tone of Perkins's teaching as offering encouragement to the growth of economic individualism and providing an illustration of his view that the 'fundamental concepts of Puritan thought *are* bourgeois'.[22] But it is possible to see these teachings and those of other Puritan writers which are cited in support of the thesis in a rather different light. A case in point is the doctrine of the Calling of which Max Weber made so much,[23] and to which Perkins devoted a whole treatise. It is, of course, undeniable that the doctrine of the Calling had distinctly revolutionary potentialities not least in giving to its adherents an almost Hegelian sense of having History (or God) on their side – that in making 'a conscionable Enquiry which way God calleth us',[24] they were exercising that true revolutionary freedom which is the recognition of the necessity of aligning themselves with God's will. But it is by no means clear how the allegedly Puritan emphasis on the equal worth of all callings in the eyes of God differs from the non-Puritan Anglican view of the matter: the difference between Perkins's 'Neither is there so much as a bondslave, but he must . . . by his faithful service to his master serve the Lord,'[25] and George Herbert's

> A servant with this clause
> Makes drudgery divine,
> Who sweeps a room, as for thy laws,
> Makes that and the action fine.[26]

Moreover, far from Perkins's hostility to beggars and vagrants, 'rotten legges and armes that droppe from the body', denoting a harsh attitude to poverty as such, it was precisely because the exercise of charity, which he enjoined on all, would be fruitless 'if the bold instant beggar gets all and the rest have nothing', that penal treatment of vagrants was necessary. If he also attacked indiscriminate charity because it fostered idleness, this was a vice which was no more strongly deplored by Puritans than by contemporary legislators, whether Puritan or not, if the preambles to statutes of the realm are anything to go by.[27] Finally, in his attitude to the conscienceless, oppressive landowner Perkins's ideas are basically similar to those found in any contemporary traditionalist treatise on the subject or in 'country-house poems' such as *Penshurst* or *Pemberton*, in terms both of his stern disapproval of oppression and of his quietistic exhortation to the oppressed tenant to pray that God would soften the heart of the oppressor.[28]

A study of Puritan teaching on the socially inflammable issue of usury yields similar conclusions. Great significance has been accorded to the limited condonation of interest by Calvin and its being repeated by scores of Puritan divines.[29] But Calvin, as one of them put it, dealt with usury 'as the apothecarie doth with poyson',[30] and if the result of his teaching was that businessmen took note of the slight concession and forgot the major qualifications, this is surely more reasonably interpreted as the result of miscalculation by Calvin and his Puritan followers of the effect his teaching was likely to have rather than a firm evidence to be used in support of the argument that they were the advocates of a notable relaxation of traditional economic ethics in favour of free enterprise.

But the case which Max Weber and other writers have advanced that Calvinism in general and English Puritanism in particular fostered the growth of economic individualism does not rest solely, or for that matter even primarily, on the teaching of Calvinist divines on specific aspects of economic and social behaviour. More fundamental, and arguably more important, in this context, are the implications of theology *per se* and the distinctive world-view of the Puritan. Of course, one must beware of too close an identification between Calvinism and Puritanism. Puritans were Calvinists, but not all Calvinists were Puritans. It is difficult to speak of a distinctively Puritan theology, for the difference between Puritans and non-Puritan Anglicans did not extend to matters of theological dogma. Even after Laud and his followers had made a clean break with Calvinist orthodoxy, theirs was emphatically a minority view, and the majority of English churchmen, including many who could not by any stretch of the imagination be described as Puritan, were in no sense Laudian. It is fatally easy to see the Caroline ecclesiastical spectrum in simple terms of a polarity between Laudians and Puritans and to neglect the middle ground, most of whose occupants were Calvinist to their very marrow.[31] What happened during the reign of Charles I was that there was a dangerous narrowing of the ecclesiastical ground occupied by the Court, and a corresponding widening of that occupied by the Country, as more and more basically moderate men – in both the secular and the ecclesiastical sense – were alienated from the regime. This is the situation which afforded scope for Calvinism – led by the Puritans as the Calvinist ginger-group – to act as an ideology of opposition in contrast to the days when Calvinist theology had been the common property of the majority of both 'ins' and 'outs'.

But to admit this is not to identify Calvinism with the bourgeois virtues. It is, of course, true that the Calvinist insistence on diligent application in one's worldly calling and abstinence in the expenditure of its fruits could act as a powerful ready-made ideology of capitalist accumulation. Lord Dacre (H.R.Trevor-Roper), as might be expected, takes a different view, arguing that it was a more appropriate ideology for poor gentlemen saving to make ends meet than for rich capitalists saving to invest.[32] But might it not serve both purposes: both to act as a medium which assisted in the conversion of the traditional vice of parsimony into the capitalist virtue of thrift, and to encourage declining mere gentlemen to make a virtue of what had been forced upon them by economic necessity?

One factor which brought together many different sorts of discontent, among them those of religious dissidents, businessmen, landowners, and, not least, common lawyers, was the operation of the prerogative courts. While the antipathy of Puritans and common lawyers to prerogative justice might derive from quite distinct causes, the former would clearly share the latters' approval of practices such as the calling of cases from ecclesiastical to secular courts by the use of writs of Prohibition. Indeed many a common lawyer may have been drawn towards the Puritan persuasion on account of its compatibility with his professional interests. Of course, such careerist considerations might work in the opposite direction for those making a career in the government service. Of the seventy-five barristers who sat in the Long Parliament in 1640, thirty-three were ultimately to be royalist and forty-two parliamentarian in the war. However, in his analysis of the probable ultimate allegiance of a random sample of 115 barristers, Professor Wilfred Prest discerns notably stronger anti-royalist leanings – thirty-four Roundheads as against fifteen Cavaliers – than was the case with those barristers who were also MPs. Not surprisingly, among the élite of the profession, those of Prest's sample who were benchers, the parliamentarian predominance is far less marked. Of all these groups, as of most others, there would certainly be a far higher proportion of anti-Court men in 1640 than there was to be in 1642.[33]

Conversely, professional and careerist considerations would tend to produce a dislike of Puritanism among the vast majority of civil lawyers who found their most spectacular career opportunities in the ecclesiastical courts, which were so detested by common lawyers and religious dissidents alike. In his admirable study of the profession Dr Levack finds only three civil lawyers classable as active parliamentarians as against eighteen active royalists. However, some civilians continued to work, *faute de mieux*, for the parliamentary government after 1642, their course of action doubtless directed by their continued need to earn a living.

The most familiar stereotype of the Puritan is that which links his radical Protestant piety to a distinct culture, in its crudest terms the anti-festive culture of the killjoy: a culture which despised and fiercely attacked that traditional festive communal culture which owed a great deal, like so much of the ceremonial and ritual emphases which one associates with anti-Puritan churchmanship from Matthew Parker to William Laud, to pre-Reformation survivals. As such it was open to the Puritan criticism that it was part of the inheritance of Antichrist. There have been some suggestive, though tentative and certainly by no means conclusive, attempts to link each of these contrasting cultures with economic differences. For instance, it has been argued that in the south-west, Puritan anti-festive culture, Puritan religious practice and Puritan magistracy, with their emphasis on strict social control of the lower orders and the reformation of the manners of the unregenerate, found their strongest expression in the clothing districts of Wiltshire and Somerset and were far slower to penetrate the arable regions of north-western Wiltshire or even the pasture areas of north-east Wiltshire, south Somerset and north Dorset; and slowest and weakest of all in the heartland of the traditional communal and festive culture, the downland areas where traditional open-field farming, seigneurial dominance and social control went together, neither welcoming nor needing the ministrations of Puritan churchmanship or the efforts of Puritan magistracy. Indeed the traditional festive culture, symbolized by Maypoles and church-ales, was anathema to the Puritan conscience.[34]

It remains to inquire how far Puritanism acted also as an ideology of that localist resistance to royal centralization which formed the subject of the third chapter of this book. In his study of Elizabethan Norfolk, Professor Hassell Smith has remarked on the significant connection between religious radicalism and local opposition to centralizing patents, licences, lieutency rates and Ship Money, a connection which suggests that Dr Walzer's argument that Puritanism was a solvent of the reliance of individuals on factors such as kinship and local association is open to very serious question.[35] It is true that magisterial power was often used for personal advantage, and considerations of personal rivalry and personal ambition were often masked by pious professions of concern for the public good. It was precisely this concern for private advantage which was castigated by Thomas Scot, a celebrated moderate Puritan divine, in this sermon before the magistrates at Thetford in Norfolk in 1620 :

> He is vnworthy of his place, who attaines it onely for his owne grace, to hurt his enemies, profit his followers, to vphold his faction and partie; and therefore attends his profit or pleasure rather than his calling ... ; the Church, the Commonwealth expects more of you.[36]

This reads like a comment on the factional jostling on the bench of Norfolk justices as described by Hassell Smith. But local magistrates were not the only persons in authority who jeopardized the common good by their pursuit of private advantage. The same was true, as Scot emphasized in a more famous sermon delivered at Norwich assizes in the same year, of those agencies of centralism which were interfering with the proper fulfilment of the godly magistrate's functions. Scot roundly denounced the '*Proiectors* [who] have eased him [viz. the JP] in his Office, and set vp Alehouses (those schooles of misrule) vnder the authoritie of the broad Seale and so left him little to do'.[37]

If Puritanism could provide an ideology of localist resistance to central administrative innovation, it fulfilled a similar function with regard to opposition to unparliamentary taxation. The best-known treatise against Caroline Ship Money was, of course, written by that most famous of the Government's Puritan victims, William Prynne.[38] As Professor Lamont has pointed out, such high-church Laudian divines as Sibthorpe and Mainwaring, in preaching the duty of 'Apostolike Obedience' in the matter of Ship Money, gave clear scope for their Puritan opponents to identify their opposition to high Laudian episcopacy with their opposition to unparliamentary taxation.[39] It is not always clear whether the clergymen who preached against Ship Money, such as Giles Randall, the Huntingdonshire parson who in November 1636 described it as one of the causes of God's wrath against the nation,[40] can justly be described as Puritans. At first sight Richard Powell, vicar of Puttishall in Northamptonshire, who was hauled before the Privy Council in July 1638, seems a likely candidate, since his offending sermon had attacked bishops as well as Ship Money, but the fact that he was also accused of drunkenness perhaps suggests the need for caution about making such an identification, as does the testimony given in his favour by the impeccably anti-Puritan Robert Sibthorpe, who on other occasions showed himself only too eager to identify

opponents of Ship Money with Puritans.[41] Northamptonshire's reputation as a hotbed of Puritanism finds clearer expression in the infor-
mations relating to the village of Kilsby near Daventry which are
headed 'Disloyal and seditious words of certain Nonconformists
against his Majesty's proceedings about the ship money and the Scots
rebellion'.[42]

As to laymen other than Prynne, and especially lay magistrates,
there were certainly some Puritanically inclined sheriffs, such as
Thomas Wrothe in Somerset and Thomas Windham in Norfolk, who
got into hot water for their alleged dilatoriness in raising Ship Money.
But, of course, many magistrates who could not by any stretch of the
imagination be described as Puritans also opposed the levy, and there
is at least one case of an active Puritan, Robert Bewick in Northumberland, who appears to have been diligent and active in its collection.[43]
While Bewick's case is a salutary warning against assuming an inevitable and unvarying connection between Puritanism and opposition to
the Court, there can be no doubt that a strong case can be made out for
the extra-religious significance of the movement as an ideology of
opposition on a variety of fronts.

To leave matters like this, however, would be a crude over-simplification of an extremely complex reality, as if the significance of Puritanism was simply to act as a professional, bourgeois or localist ideology
or an ideology of exclusion from the sweets of office and Court connection, according to the nature of the soil in which it took root. Far from
detracting from the central importance of religion in the seventeenth
century, the intimate connection between it and the everyday affairs of
men and women enormously enhanced that importance. It is perhaps a
natural response of our own age in which religion has lost this central
significance as a force in men's lives, to emphasize the secular, at the
expense of the spiritual, elements in the mixture. However, in the
matter of the argued connections of Puritanism with secular considerations, the process whereby private advantage and ambition became
adequately reconciled with higher spiritual considerations, cannot be
summarily disposed of by cynical observations about the need to cloak
these motives in respectable guise. The precise admixture of godly zeal
and personal advantage would vary enormously from person to person, but it is all too easy to play down the former. For instance,
passionately concerned with personal status and local rivalry though
they might be, magistrates such as Sir Nathaniel Bacon, who aspired
to create the new Jerusalem in the flinty, wind-blown villages of north

Norfolk, and Sir Richard Knightley and Sir Richard Grosvenor who laboured diligently for the cause in Northamptonshire and Cheshire, were men who saw themselves as epitomes of 'the Magistrate who bears not the sword in vaine, but must either smite where he findes *sinne*, or be smitten with it to his owne *shame* and dishonour'. As Scot emphasized, the godly magistrate was 'Hee who makes a conscience of the calling'.[44]

As well as spiritualizing secular impulses, religious considerations could act autonomously to impel men to take up attitudes which were contrary to, not consonant with, their economic and professional interests. For instance, among the civil lawyers were to be found some notable Puritan opponents of the Court. Such a man was Calibute Downing, the Puritan vicar of Hackney, who preached the notorious sermon to the Honourable Artillery Company in 1640 justifying resistance to government. Another was Isaac Dorislaus, whose dangerously republican views brought about his dismissal from Fulke Greville's lectureship in history at Cambridge in 1627, and his assassination by royalist exiles at the Hague in 1649 for the part he had played in preparing the legal case against Charles I earlier that year.[45] Similarly, while there were many who were Puritans because they were 'out', there were others who were 'out' because they were Puritans. Such a man was the opposition peer Lord Saye and Sele, and the testimony that his 'ambition would not be satisfied with offices and preferment without some condescensions and alterations in ecclesiastical matters' is the more credible since it comes from a political opponent who detested him as 'the oracle of those who were called Puritans in the worst sense'.[46]

V

In Elizabethan times the Puritanism of a peer like Saye and Sele would not *per se* have been the bar to preferment that it clearly became under Charles I. During the earlier reign courtly Puritans abounded, among them holders of high office such as Leicester, Walsingham and Huntingdon. Perhaps the last glimmering of this older Elizabethan tradition before it was snuffed out for ever was the strange alliance in the closing years of James I's reign between the royal favourite, Buckingham, and one of the most celebrated Puritan divines of the day, Dr John Preston, in association with parliamentary Puritans such as Lord Saye and Sele and Sir Richard Knightley. Indeed Preston was for a time chaplain to the Prince of Wales himself.[47] The alliance with Preston and his Puritan associates was, however, not long to survive the accession of Charles I, during whose reign the ground was cut from beneath the feet of those who upheld the mainstream Puritan tradition which looked to King and Bishop as the initiators of godly reformation.

This vitally important turn of events clearly requires careful explanation, for its chief product was the complete alienation of the moderate Puritans, so that, the way of advance via the Court being blocked, Puritanism became increasingly an ideology of the 'Country', which, as earlier chapters have suggested, was itself being alienated from the Court. Historians should be wary of ascribing great and complex developments to single causes. Nevertheless if there is one person to whose actions and policies the fall of the Stuart monarchy can be attributed, that person is William Laud, Bishop of London from 1628 to 1633 and from the latter year Primate of All England. Laud is in many ways a genuinely tragic figure. A good and honest man, an idealist whose aims were not without some true notes of nobility, and whose spiritual temper was, as Professor Lamont has perceptively suggested, in some respects similar to that of the Puritans whom he drove into the wilderness,[48] Laud was more than any other person responsible for irrevocably closing the door on reconciliation with the moderate Puritans, and therefore for the fact that, when the Long Parliament met in November 1640, the formerly moderate Puritan aims were already in process of being transformed into something more akin to those of the Presbyterian extremists of the 1570s and 1580s who had been quelled by Whitgift. In the words of a member of that parliament, Sir Harbottle Grimstone, in a speech of 18 December 1640, Laud was 'the stye of all the pestilentiall ffilth that hath infected the state & goverment [sic] of this church & common wealth . . . he is the man the only man that hath rased & advanced all those that together with himselfe haue bin the authors & causes of all our . . . miseries'.[49]

The words of this essentially moderate MP underline vividly the fear and horror which Laud and his aspirations generated, and help to explain why this powerless, forlorn and feeble old man, no longer capable of hurting or influencing anyone, was sent to the block amid universal execration in 1645.

'The Catholic Church of Christ is neither Rome nor a conventicle.'[50] Far from seeing himself as an extremist, Laud's vision of the English Church was of a mean between extremes, the mean described in George Herbert's sublime poem:

A fine aspect in fit array,
Neither too mean, nor yet too gay,
    Shows who is best :
Outlandish looks may not compare ;
For all they either painted are
    Or else undrest.[51]

But the Laudian attempt to bisect the difference between the Catholic
and what he regarded as the Puritan extremes, or, as the Laudian
divine, Richard Montague was to put it, 'to stand in the gapp against
Puritanisme and Popery, the Scilla and Charybdis of antient piety',[52]
was to deal what ultimately proved to be a fatal blow not to Puritan
extremists but to the moderate Puritan mainstream. Laud warned
Charles I of the danger that the Church was 'between these two factions
[viz. Puritanism and Catholicism] and unless your Majesty look to it,
she will be ground to powder', but it was he who, more than anyone
else, had placed her in this vulnerable position. For there can be little
doubt that whatever arguments could be advanced in favour of the
Laudian aim of restoring 'Church government as it hath been in use in
all ages and all places where the Church of Christ hath taken any
rooting',[53] to most of his critics he was a dangerous innovator responsible for the introduction of new doctrines and liturgical practices
which 'serve to terrifie and scandalize tender consciences'.[54] More than
this, these innovations were seen as part of an international papist
conspiracy to weaken Protestant unity by the introduction of Romish
practices into the English church. The resolutions of the sub-committee of the House of Commons on Religion of 24 February 1629 came
very near to identifying Arminianism with Popery,[55] and the identification was soon to become a matter of common Puritan knowledge ; so
that a Hampshire petition to the Long Parliament could complain
about 'the Malignant opposition of the Popish & prelaticall party',
as if the two things were one and the same.[56] The Laudians were
seen as a sort of popish fifth column designed to soften up Protestant
resistance in preparation for the ultimate Catholic triumph.

Nothing, of course, could be further from the truth. Laud's concern
with ceremony and ritual might lay him wide open to such charges, but
there is no need for the historian to take anything but literally his own
moving confession to the king of his belief that the Church of England
had been drawn into contempt by its neglect of 'uniform and decent
order' and of the need for 'the inward worship of the heart' to find
external expression in ceremonies which emphasized the beauty of

holiness.[57] But, when this has been said, it needs to be added that the Laudians hardly put themselves out to attempt to dispel the popular identification of Laudian with popish practice or indeed that they showed moderation, tact and proper caution in introducing such practices. It is true that Laudian clergymen, including Laud himself, might enter the lists of controversy against the papists. But many of the arguments which they employed were as unacceptable to the Puritans as those which they were designed to controvert. What was needed as proof of Protestant mettle was an unequivocal identification of Rome and Antichrist. Laud's insistence that the Roman church was 'a true church' as opposed to being 'the right Church ... and in some times right and in some times wrong'[58] was at best too tame and unemphatic, and at worst might be interpreted as an apology for the Catholic Church. To the Puritan mind the most striking thing about Richard Montague's notorious treatise of 1624[59] was not what it condemned but what it condoned in Romish practice. The Roman Church was corrupt, but it was not Antichrist; pictures and images should not be the objects of worship, but their moderate use was acceptable and even useful; auricular confession ought not be compulsory, but was nevertheless beneficial in certain cases. Similarly, John Cosin sincerely intended his Book of Devotions of 1627 as a distinctively Anglican substitute for Catholic private devotional practices, but it was the similarities, not the differences, which struck most Protestant observers. Again, however much Laud might himself deplore the fashionable Catholicism of certain elements at Court centering around the person of the queen, once Buckingham was dead and Charles's devotion to his wife grew daily, the last thing the Primate could do was to wage war on the pernicious influence of the royal consort, that other primary architect of royal misfortunes.[60]

It requires a real effort of the historical imagination to appreciate the startling novelty presented by the Laudian ritualistic revival to a generation of churchgoers which had been starved of such things. Starved or not, for every worshipper who welcomed such innovations there were probably scores who identified them with popish practices, or, at the very least, saw the Laudians as 'true-cousin-germans' to the papists,[61] and the disciplinary action taken against those who opposed them as indistinguishable from the persecution of good Protestants by the Inquisition. There must have been many witnesses of the punishment of Laud's most distinguished victims, Prynne, Burton and Bastwick, in 1637 who took literally the remark of one observer that 'if soe they would turne Catholiques they neede feare none of this punishment'.[62] One imagines what use the Puritans would have made of Montague's jocular observation in a letter to John Cosin that 'it will never be well till we have our Inquisition'.[63] The complaints which were made by a clerical convert from Catholicism, Richard Carpenter, in the mid-1630s are also drawn from private correspondence, but there is good reason to believe that the person to whom they were addressed (probably the Kentish squire Sir Edward Dering) was by no means the only recipient of Carpenter's information. He alleged that he had been told by the bishop's chaplain that in his recantation sermon he '*must not speake revengefully and ungratefully against the Church of Rome*', and that he must include in the sermon a passage emphasizing that a prime reason for his conversion had been '*the sight and loue of the orders and ceremonies newly begun in the Church* of England; a thing which (the Lord knowes) had not entered into my thoughts before this admonishment'. More, he claimed that he was later to incur a sharp rebuke from the Primate himself on account of the strongly Protestant tone of the references in his sermons to his conversion from Rome.[64]

Such were the stories and incidents which fed the Puritan belief that Laud was guiding the English Church along the road to Rome. According to some Puritan critics Laudianism and Popery were also virtually identical in the exalted views which the adherents of both held about the status and role of the priesthood, and the need to keep the control of the Church out of secular, and especially parliamentary, hands.[65] There had, in fact, been a complete reversal of roles since the days when Archbishop Whitgift had defended an Episcopal but Erastian Church settlement against the theocratic onslaughts of Cartwrightian Presbyterian Puritans. Now it was not the Archbishop but the Puritans who were arguing for the need for ecclesiastical government to be brought into conformity with civil government.[66]

But Laud's vision was not that of two strictly separate kingdoms. 'Jerusalem,' he affirmed, 'stands not . . . for the City and the State only . . . nor for the Temple and the Church only; but jointly for both . . . both are but one Jerusalem.'[67] It was Laud who, in his response from prison to Lord Saye and Sele's outraged observations in 1641 about the meddling of bishops in secular affairs, maintained that bishops might preach the gospel as effectively via their actions in court and councils as in their sermons from the pulpit.[68] Far from renouncing secular functions, the godly divine should embrace such duties with enthusiasm, be they those of JP or Privy Councillor. The creeping back of clerics into

secular office, of which the most spectacular example was the appointment of Laud's successor in the see of London, William Juxon, as Lord
Treasurer in 1637, was a cause of alarm to many who saw in it a
dangerous revival of the hold exercised by churchmen on affairs of
state in pre-Reformation days, before the large-scale expansion of the
numbers of the educated laity had allowed of a spectacular measure of
secularization of offices of state. Clerics were everywhere, complained
one Puritan, with pardonable exaggeration:

> In the High Commission, at the Councell Table, in the Star-
> Chamber, and the Chequer, Churchmen are now more active
> than their own Consistories, and yet their ambition further aimes
> (as 'tis said) to the Chancery, Court of Requests &c. which could
> not chuse but redound to the scandall of Religion, the obstruction
> of Iustice, and Vexation of the subject.[69]

That such posts would normally have been filled by clerics before the
Reformation served further to point the direction which Laudian policies appeared to be taking, and to arouse the anxiety not simply of
radical Puritans like John Ley and Lord Saye and Sele, but of persons
almost right across the spectrum of political and religious opinion.

VI

Another way in which the Laudian church obtruded increasingly on
the lives of laymen related to the jurisdiction of the spiritual courts.
'The time is now come in this kingdom,' preached Laud to a largely
unsympathetic audience at the opening sermon to the second parliament of the reign on 6 February 1626, 'that the civil courts are as [*sic*]
much too strong for the ecclesiastical, and may overlay them as hard.'[70]
It was another of Laud's missions in life to remedy this situation. A
wide variety of cases, some of which are now heard in secular courts
and others, concerning such matters as 'swearing, ribaldry and usury'
which are no longer offences at all, fell within the province of the
spiritual courts in the early seventeenth century.[71] The line between
the spiritual and the proprietorial was often so thin as to be impercep-
tible to the unschooled observer, and there can be no doubt that the
royal pressure on temporal judges not to issue writs of Prohibition
calling cases out of ecclesiastical courts and Laud's own strongly expressed views on this matter[72] were further contributory factors to the

unpopularity of both the government and the Primate. Among the principal victims of ecclesiastical jurisdiction were property-owners and, not least, businessmen, for, as Nathaniel Fiennes observed in 1641, 'Titles concerning *Wills* and *Legacies, Tythes, Marriages, Adulteries* ... are no more of spiritual Consideration than Rapes, Thefts, Felonies or Treasons may be.'[73] Other victims of the same jurisdiction, besides the adulterers, blasphemers and those who engaged in slovenly practices, such as urinating against a pillar in St Paul's Cathedral or christening a cat,[74] were Puritan objectors to Laudian ceremonial innovation. Along with the professional objections of common lawyers, these considerations contributed powerfully to the moulding of a number of diverse interest groups into a unified opposition. Finally, Laud's archiepiscopate also saw energetic attempts to tighten up the operation of the ultimate spiritual sanction of excommunication[75] and the extended membership and use of the High Commission, including the resuscitation of its lapsed powers of visitation,[76] developments which, as Clarendon emphasized, aroused a great deal of resentment.[77]

VII

The increased power of the spiritual courts was only one of a number of ways in which Laud sought to enhance the prestige of the Church and to restore at least some of its lost medieval glory. No one was more aware than he of the extent to which wealth was an index of that prestige, and none of his policies occasioned more resentment and swelled the ranks of his opponents more effectively than those which were designed to improve the economic position of the Church. Prominent among them was the determined attempt to realize the full potential of ecclesiastical revenues from lands which were leased out by bishops and capitular bodies. What Laud, with the full cooperation of the king, sought to discourage was the tendency of some ecclesiastical landlords, who, of course, had no hereditary interest in their lands, to make hay while the sun shone and lease their lands on low reserved rents for long periods – and notably for a number of lives – in return for substantial fines. This was, of course, to sacrifice future income for immediate capital, and the interests of one's successors to one's own personal gain. Richard Montague, as Bishop of Chichester and later of Norwich, and William Peirs, Bishop of Bath and Wells, were among the ecclesiastics who had occasion to rue the self-regarding behaviour of some of their predecessors along these lines.[78]

Laud's attempt to put an end to these practices involved the enforcement of severe restrictions on the terms which ecclesiastical landlords were allowed to offer to their tenants in future. Short leases were to be the rule and leases for life were forbidden.[79] While one aim of this policy was to realize the income potential of these Church lands, Laud's contemporary biographer, Peter Heylin, regarded this simply as 'the outside of the business', pointing to another, and what most contemporary gentlemen would regard as more sinister, motive: 'that the gentry and yeomanry (and some of the nobility also) holding lands of these churches, might have a greater respect to the church and churchmen, when they must depend upon them from time to time for renewing of their said estates at the end of every ten or twelve years at the most'.[80]

Another aspect of Laud's determination to redress the unfavourable economic balance between Church and State, which was one of the most spectacular products of the Reformation, was his attitude to impropriated tithes. The supreme though unattainable objective of which he never completely lost sight was the resumption by the Church of all the economic assets which it had lost to the laity, both lands and impropriations. But in the event of this aim's falling short of complete success – and in practice it enjoyed very indifferent success – there was the not contemptible *pis aller* of inducing lay impropriators to devote a more substantial and appropriate part of their ill-acquired gains to the spiritual uses for which they had originally been intended. This policy was pursued more successfully than the larger objective of the wholesale resumption of former ecclesiastical property, but property-owners could hardly be unaware of the Primate's hopes and aspirations which they may well have viewed as a more ominous portent of the Romeward drift of the Church than the ritualistic innovations which were all of a piece with them.[81]

It must however, have been the occasion of much bitterness and frustration to Laud that his attempts to restore lay impropriations to the Church were attended with such indifferent success when compared with the efforts of a private body, the so-called Feoffees for Impropriations, which was created in 1628 and dissolved in 1633 as a result of a case brought in the Court of Exchequer at the instance of the Primate.[82] While the aims of both Laud and the Feoffees were similar in so far as both desired the restoration of impropriated revenues to spiritual uses, there was a world of difference between them in every other respect, and this in itself provides yet another instance of Laud's high-flying notions of the role of the Church and churchmen *vis-à-vis* the laity. For what the Primate found especially objectionable in the practice of the Feoffees was that they did not apply the impropriated revenues which they acquired by purchase to the original parishes to which they had appertained, except in the rare cases when the views of the local parson in question coincided with, or approximated to, their own. Far more frequently, the revenues were applied to the financing of 'dative lecturers' who were often appointed over the heads of the incumbents, a practice which provided a potent cause of 'difference and jarring'. And these lecturers were at least as much anathema to Laud as were the Puritanical parsons whose stipends the Feoffees did choose to augment out of the impropriations which they acquired. This was because, in addition to the fact that the lecturers were normally of a strongly Puritan disposition, they were also in the pay and therefore at the mercy of the lay Feoffees who controlled their stipends, which of course, also applied to lectureships endowed by any lay persons and not simply by the Feoffees. On occasions, when the views of the local parson were acceptable to those who controlled the purse-strings, the lectureship was conferred on him, providing a useful augmentation to his stipend. But what made the practice abhorrent to Laud was that the control of finance was a means whereby laymen exercised control of the views of the lecturers. For example in the case of the lectures endowed in the parish of St Bartholomew-by-the-Exchange by the will of the London citizen Richard Fishbourne, dated 30 March 1625, it was stipulated that if the parishioners did not wish the parson to be lecturer, 'they [are] to make Choice of *some other*, as they in *their discretion* shall think fit'.[83]

A similar set of objections might, *mutatis mutandis*, be levelled against the institution of lay patronage of the clergy, even though, once the parson had been appointed at the choice of the owner of the advowson, the latter did not, in theory at least, exercise any control over the exercise of his functions. At first sight lay patronage might appear to be as objectionable to the views of Puritan critics of the hierarchy as to the theocratic notions of the Primate. One such critic, a certain Augustine Skinner, wrote from the depths of rural Kent to Sir Edward Dering, his MP at Westminster in January 1642, both commending him for his 'assault on the Goliah [*sic*] of Hyerarchicall Episcopacy' and complaining of the palpable scandals such as the simoniacal practices

whereby lay patrons unashamedly sold benefices to the highest bid-
der.[84] But confronted by a choice between the two extremes of lay patronage and the choice of incumbents by diocesan bishops, who as like
as not would be Laudians, there was no doubt which alternative a radical Puritan would prefer.[85] The choice, of course, never came to that,
though there were non-Laudian bishops, such as John Williams of Lincoln, who certainly felt that Laud was playing a very dangerous game
in poking his nose into a problem which was none of his concern. But
to Laud, lay patronage accorded ill with the idea of the Church as
an independent witness and provided an example of that subordination
of Church to laity which he loathed with every fibre of his being. His
intransigence afforded to his Puritan critics another opportunity of
assuming the role of defenders of private property – for what is an
advowson if not a piece of private property? – against clerical attacks
and the status quo of the parish against Laudian innovation.[86]

VIII

It is a fact which affords some scope for reflection on the social significance of seventeenth-century conflicts that a prime reason for the violent dislike which Laud had aroused was the contrast between his high
notions of clerical status and the humble origins both of himself and of a
number of other Laudian bishops, '*ex faece plebis, humi serpenti*, of the
lowest of the people', in the words of that aristocratic radical (in ecclesiastical, though apparently not in social matters), Robert Greville,
Lord Brooke.[87] Men of similarly humble origins had, of course, at
all times risen to eminence in the Church. Latimer, for instance, had
been proud to describe himself as a yeoman's son and Whitgift was
the son of a Grimsby merchant. But the social origins of some Laudian
bishops – Laud was the son of a Reading draper, Neile of a tallow-
chandler, Peirs of a hatter and Wren of a London merchant[88] – were
a matter for comment precisely because of the Laudian attempt to exalt
clerical status. 'A fellow of mean extraction and arrogant pride', was
how the Primate was described by the wife of a regicide, who was,
however, also the daughter of a Caroline office-holder and courtier.[89]
The juxtaposition of the two qualities is of profound significance.

Himself a socially graceless man who did not move easily in courtly
society, Laud was no doubt especially vulnerable to such taunts,
which pursued him down to and even beyond the grave. Only three
weeks after his execution on 10 January 1645 some satirical verses

appeared which laboured the same distasteful point which had been made so often in his lifetime by patrician snobs in both Court and Country.

> You that so proudly th'other day
> Did rule and the King's country sway,
> Must trudge to know the other place;
> Remember now from whence you came,
> And that the grandsires of your name
> Were dressers of old cloth:
> Go bid the old men bring their shears
> To dress your cloth and save your ears,
> Or pawn your head for bot.[90]

The jumped-up prelate had at last got his deserts, not only for his attempts to exalt the status of churchmen, but also for his outrageous interference with the rights of gentlemen as impropriators, patrons of benefices, or property-owners menaced both by interference with the free use of their land and by the encroaching power of ecclesiastical courts:

> Persons of honour and great quality ... were every day cited into the High Commission court, upon the fame of their incontinence, or other scandal in their lives ...; and ... the shame (which they called an insolent triumph upon their degree and quality, and levelling them with the common people), was never forgotten....[91]

Nor did the parallel with another proud prelate of humble origins escape contemporaries. Laud and Wolsey, as one hostile critic observed, were both 'the sons of mean and mechanick men, Wolsey of a butcher, Laud of a cloth worker'.[92] The parallel could be pushed still further, for just as the low-born cardinal's concern – however sporadic – for social justice, as evidenced by his role in connection with the Commission for Depopulation of 1517, had enraged patrician landowners and contributed powerfully to the unpopularity which helped to bring about his downfall,[93] so, in Clarendon's view at least, did Laud also 'a little too much countenance the Commission for Depopulation',[94] which aroused resentment, primarily no doubt because it interfered with landowners' freedom of action in the matter of their landed property, but also because it was yet another example of clerical interference in secular affairs.

IX

None of the pretensions of the Laudian episcopate provoked more resentment than what its enemies conceived of as an arrogant insistence on its title by divine right. However, recent treatment of this theme has made it clear both that belief in episcopacy *iure divino* was not the exclusive property of Laudian churchmen and that it was rather the manner in which it was asserted by them than the claim itself, which they shared with other protestant divines, which excited hostility.[95] Elizabeth I's cousin, the erastian Sir Francis Knollys, no doubt believed, as he emphasized in a letter to Lord Burghley in August 1598, that episcopal claims to hold by divine right short-circuited the royal supremacy, and that the bishops were, as the ecclesiastical lawyer Dr John Hammond had assured him, 'wholie her [Majesty's] creatures and not the immediate creatures of God at all'.[96] But this alleged incompatibility of divine right episcopacy with the royal supremacy ignored the fundamental distinction between spiritual power *per se* – the *potestas ordinis* – which the monarch did not have and the bishops did, and supreme power *over* spirituals which rested in him and not in them. Like many moderate Puritan churchmen Laud's case rested on this dualism, in which circumstances there is no incongruity about the Laudians being at one and the same time upholders of both divine right episcopacy and divine right monarchy and the royal supremacy. Indeed some of Laud's enemies erroneously asserted that he denied, as the sixth article of his impeachment put it in 1641, that 'the power of prelacy [came] from the King',[97] while others saw his alleged encouragement of the king to act as if his will was law as part of a deliberate plot to divide him from his subjects, from which the main gainers would be those who held 'that the king's septre [*sic*] ought to submit to Aaron's rod'.[98] The point was, of course, more than a trifle strained, and the reality was nearer to Laud's newly formulated assertion of the familiar Jacobean principle of the interdependence of monarchy and episcopacy, in a sermon before the second parliament of the new reign on 6 January 1626. Here he emphasized that they 'that would overthrow ... "the seats of ecclesiastical government" will not spare, if they ever get power, to have a pluck at the "throne of David"'. Parity in the Church would inevitably lead to parity in the State.[99]

Moreover, if no bishop meant no king, the converse was perhaps even more true. Thanks to Laud's firm alliance with his royal master, English Arminianism had none of the treasonable associations of its

Dutch equivalent, which had brought about the fall and execution of Oldenbarneveldt and the despatch by James I of an anti-Arminian delegation to the Synod of Dort in 1619. So long as bishops and king were interdependent, the former stood to benefit from the support of all those who looked to monarchy as the keystone of order and authority,[100] and who, like Lord Falkland in the parliamentary debate on episcopacy in February 1641, had a profound distrust of any 'mutations' which threatened that order, of which they themselves were – however modestly – the beneficiaries.[101] Richard Hooker, who had lived through an earlier assault on the institution of episcopacy, had also been concerned to stress the far-reaching social implications of such attacks.[102] To abolish episcopacy would be simply to begin with the tenderest branch of the social tree, and the next branch to attract attention might well be the nobility. Much later Thomas Hobbes was to express surprise at the House of Lords' countenancing attacks on episcopacy, while to Clarendon, the depriving of bishops of their votes in parliament was the removal of a notable social landmark, for 'the ecclesiastical and civil state was so wrought and interwoven together ... that, like Hippocrates' twins, they cannot but laugh and cry together'.[103] The connection had been denied by the Elizabethan Presbyterian Thomas Cartwright, and was again to be denied by the exponents of the root-and-branch extirpation of episcopacy in parliament in 1641, and outside parliament, in, *inter alia*, John Milton's polemical tracts where he argues that, far from episcopacy and monarchy being complementary, monarchy could only benefit from the abolition of episcopacy.[104] The fixing of popular attention upon an institutional scapegoat to which all the evils of the day may conveniently be attributed is a characteristic of the revolutionary temperament in most ages. To the radical of the modern far left it is capitalism which stands between society and the achievement of the millennium; to his mid-seventeenth-century equivalent – at least in the context of 1640–2 – it was episcopacy, blamed by the London apprentices in 1641 and the mariners in 1642 for the economic depression; and by the Root and Branch Petition of 11 December 1640 for a wide variety of evils ranging from the licensing of lewd publications to monopolies and inflation. Such arguments – if they can be dignified by that name – provided a sitting target for Lord Digby's formidable powers of ridicule in the debate on the petition in February 1641,[105] but it was the fact that they were nearer to half-truths than to downright absurdities, that probably won them so many adherents. For instance, in so far as

Laudian prelates had enjoined that resistance to the king was in all circumstances a damnable sin and that the king could raise what taxes he wished without parliamentary consent, the notion that such bishops bore at least some responsibility for monopolies, Ship Money and the rise in prices was by no means entirely absurd. What was more unfair was the attribution of such evils not simply to Laudian but to all bishops. This spelt the doom not only of episcopacy as an institution but of mainstream Foxeian, episcopalian Puritanism. These were the twin casualties of the Laudian episode and its aftermath. 'Reduced' or 'primitive' episcopacy continued to have influential adherents such as Williams among the bishops and Falkland among the laity, but in revolutionary situations the centre tends to be squeezed by both extremes. For the logic of Laudianism was the logic of polarization, and, as one royalist writer was later to admit, the work of the root-and-branchers had been greatly facilitated by 'the rash and furious carriage of some of the Episcopal clergy'.[106] Laud's failure to distinguish between moderate and extremist Puritans was matched by the failure of Milton and the proponents of root and branch reform to distinguish between prelacy and primitive episcopacy.

X

Although a good deal has been said in the foregoing pages about the Puritan tendency to identify Laudianism with Catholicism, or, at the very least, to see Laudian innovations as facilitating the ultimate triumph of Popery by creating divisions among Protestants and fatally weakening the Protestant cause, little has been said about the Catholics themselves. Generations of historians have readily assumed that the king was able to draw upon the unquestioning support of his Catholic subjects when it came to civil war. However, Dr Keith Lindley has argued that such historians have been too uncritical in their acceptance of the plausible allegations of parliamentarian supporters and propagandists.[107] Of the sample of 1511 Catholics whose allegiance in the war he examines, he finds that an astonishingly high proportion of almost 82 per cent took a neutralist stance. Of particular interest is his contention that in Lancashire and Yorkshire, both predominantly royalist counties early in the war, the vast majority of Catholics stood aloof from the royalists, despite the hotly canvassed contentions of the king's Roundhead and Scottish opponents that the Earl of Newcastle's army was crammed with papists. But Lindley's thesis has not gone unchal-

lenged, and there is real force in the objections of Dr P.R.Newman
that his dependence on sources such as the records of the parliamentary
Committee for Compounding has the inevitable effect of understating
Catholic support for the royalist cause, since Catholics were, in the
nature of things, much less strongly represented in such sources. This
is because their religion was itself often deemed an argument for not
according to them the opportunity to take the relatively favourable
alternative of compounding for their delinquency – that is, to pay a
fine, rather than to have their lands sequestered. Additionally perhaps,
the very fervour of Catholics for the royalist cause may have been,
religious considerations aside, an additional factor pointing to the
same conclusion. In the northern counties, where Catholicism was
especially rife, Newman's findings are far more in line with the traditional picture than those of Lindley. For instance, of 102 northern
colonels whose religion can be identified, as many as 39 were Catholics; of 59 northern lieutenant-colonels 26 were Catholics; and of 48
northern majors 22 were Catholics. He concludes that 'the Catholic
commitment to armed support of the King was out of all proportion to
the size of the [Catholic] community as such, and was, furthermore,
most marked in the upper echelons of the army in terms of rank, and in
the élite arm, the cavalry.'[108]

Newman's statistics appear to bear out the familiar conclusion
which shines out of the abundance of more literary evidence about the
strength of Catholic support for Charles in the war. In some cases this
may have been a case of Hobson's choice for there is no reason to
assume that during the years of personal government in the 1630s
country Catholics in general, as distinct from fashionable courtly
Catholics, had any great cause to feel satisfied with their lot. One small
straw in the wind relates to complaints about the differential treatment
not of courtly and country Catholics but of men with Catholic wives.
John Hilton, who in 1634 found himself debarred from becoming
Mayor of Appleby on account, so he claimed, of his wife's Catholicism,
pointed a telling contrast between the treatment meted out to him and
that obtaining at Court where some Privy Councillors and even the
king himself had Catholic wives.[109] This contrast can be extended to
the treatment of Catholics themselves. In his admirable study of the
Caroline Catholics Professor Havran draws a similar distinction to that
made by the outraged Hilton.[110] It was almost as if Laud, frustrated by
his total inability to do anything about fashionable Court Catholicism
as well as infuriated by the fact that some of the Court's reputation for

encouraging popery was rubbing off on him, turned with particular vehemence upon those Catholics who did not enjoy this protective aura. At any rate, country Catholics in the 1630s, disillusioned by the failure of the king's Catholic marriage to yield its expected fruit, had reason to contrast the relaxation of the application of the recusancy laws in the later years of the reign of James I, with the harassment and fiscal penalization to which they were subjected under his son. But they knew that things would be immeasurably worse if Charles's and Laud's Puritan opponents should ever gain control.

XI

If the identification of Laudianism with Catholicism was a crude – and, in some cases, disingenuous – over-simplification, it might be pleaded that it was no more so than the Laudian failure to distinguish between moderate Foxeian and radical anti-episcopal Puritans, which drove the former into closer association with the latter. The common ground which the two elements came to occupy may well have included reference to the practice of remote antiquity as the key to the appropriateness of contemporary ecclesiastical practice and organization. Just as the constitutionalist opponents of the government from Sir Edward Coke to Pym and Hampden saw their task as the restoration of the immemorial constitution in the face of the depredations of a royal innovator, or at least of his evil advisers,[111] so did radical Puritan reformers seek to justify their programme, if not in terms of immemorial antiquity, since after all, the Christian Church did not exist before Christ, at least in the ordering of the Church in apostolic times, with additional help from the Old Testament where appropriate. The analogy between these two lines of thought, constitutional and ecclesiastical, is significant, and there may have been some cross-fertilization between them. In a speech made on 4 January 1642, on the day of Charles I's abortive attempt to arrest him and his five other parliamentary colleagues, John Hampden significantly coupled the defence of the ancient constitution with that of the true religion which was known and tested 'by searching the sacred Writings of the old and new Testament',[112] while in the following year Lord Saye and Sele countered arguments about the antiquity of the secular employment of bishops with the firm assertion that '*this is not so antient but that it may truly be said* Non fuit sic ab initio'.[113]

Just as there is a significant parallel between the biblical literalism of the Puritans and the Cokeian notion of the immemorial constitution, so is there an equally striking parallel between the political and the religious views of the upholders of the high monarchical and anti-Puritan viewpoints. Attention has already been drawn to James I's argument that the powers which it was appropriate for kings to wield in one set of historical circumstances might not be appropriate in others.[114] This is paralleled by Hooker's gentle *reductio ad absurdum* of Puritanical biblical liberalism – 'that in tying the Church to the orders of the Apostles' times, they tie it to a marvellous uncertain rule' – and his distinction between things of eternal and immutable significance and those where change was not simply appropriate but lack of change would invite justified ridicule.[115] The Hookerian argument remained the basis of the anti-Puritan position and was held tenaciously by Charles I to the very end. Even in the final desperate negotiations at Newport in the autumn of 1648 Charles insisted that it was necessary to distinguish between the form of organization appropriate to a Church under a Christian Prince and that used 'when Christians lived among Pagans and under persecution'.[116]

It was emphasized earlier that not every proponent of the virtues of the ancient constitution insisted on its immemorial character.[117] Similarly, there were Puritan sympathizers, among them John Ley, who advanced strikingly Hookerian arguments both about the unreliability of evidence relating to the apostolic organization of the Church and about its relevance to contemporary needs.[118] It is clearly important not to be too dogmatic in characterizing the ideas and ideology of either side in the religious no less than the political aspects of the conflict. Conceivably the argument based on historicity was losing its attractiveness for some people, at least by the 1640s. But this is in no way to deny its crucial importance in the process whereby Puritanism became the ideology of opposition to the Court and based its appeal to no small extent on its assault on innovation and its fervent defence of tradition.

II King and Parliament 1640–9

SIX *From Consensus to Confrontation 1640–2*

They sat-down in November, and now it was May; and in this Space of Time . . . they won from the King the Adherence which was due to him from his People; they drove his faithfullest Servants from him; beheaded the Earl of Strafford; imprisoned the Archbishop of Canterbury; obtained a triennial Parliament, after their own Dissolution, and a Continuance of their own Sitting, as long as they listed; which last amounted to a total Extinction of the King's Right, in case that such a Grant was valid; which, I think, it is not, unless the Sovereignty itself be in plain Terms renounced. . . .

> Thomas Hobbes, *Behemoth*, in
> Maseres, *Select Tracts*, II, 526–7

. . . whether the way to preserve this [royal] power be not to give it away. For the people of England have ever bin like wantons which will pull and tugg as long [as] the Prince have pulled with [viz. against] them; . . . But when they [viz. the kings] have let it goe, they come and put it into theire hands againe that they may play on. . . .

> *Letter from Sir John Suckling to*
> *Henry Jermyn,* 1640–1; Bodleian Library,
> Tanner MSS. 65, fo. 33.

I

THE BROAD CONSENSUS which existed among about 400 out of the 493 MPs elected to the Long Parliament in the autumn of 1640[1] is a very different phenomenon from the kind of 'consensus' with which Sir

Geoffrey Elton's work has familiarized us.[2] Far from being the product of contented subjects working harmoniously with the monarchy in the interests of the common weal, it was the product of that conflict between ruler and ruled whose existence, as Elton insists, is a clear indication not of the health but of the degeneration of the body politic. Its origins lay in the shared belief of the great majority of MPs that the previous eleven years had witnessed a disastrous shift away from the traditional balance in the direction of royal absolutism on the continental model. These men assembled at Westminster in November 1640 determined to restore what they described as the traditional constitution, to weaken the force of central government and to restore the health of the time-honoured institutions of county and locality; to arrest the Romeward slide of the Church; and to reform the Court: in a word to restore the ancient harmony between King and Parliament which, though differing substantially from Elton's picture of consensus, was by no means entirely a figment of the romantic parliamentary imagination.

Nothing could be further from the King's initial intentions in calling the Parliament. Conrad Russell has convincingly argued that it was Charles's belief that recourse to parliament was, following the victory of the Scots at Newburn in August 1640, a way of carrying on the same Scottish policy by other means, and that he had deluded himself into thinking that, if the Scots were not compliant with his unchanging demands, parliament would be willing to make the money available for further campaigns against them. Not only was this view in sharp contrast to that of the reform consensus in parliament; it was almost certainly not shared by many of the remainder of the MPs nor by the Council of Peers which had recommended the calling of Parliament, nor even by all of his own councillors. To cite but three examples, the elder Sir Henry Vane, and the earls of Bristol and Northumberland seem clearly to have recognized that the Bishops' Wars had given the final quietus to Charles's Scottish policies, and that the calling of parliament, far from offering him the opportunity of pressing such policies further, afforded a convenient means of disengagement from them. Thus the opening weeks of the Long Parliament saw both an apparently solid parliamentary consensus for reform and a divided Court and government.[3]

The aspirations and temper of MPs in November 1640 are explicable not simply in terms of their experience of the so-called eleven years' tyranny but also in terms of the failure of the Long Parliament's predecessor in the spring of the same year. This had occasioned profound gloom and despondency among many moderate men. On the other hand (if Edward Hyde's account is to be believed) a moderate and judicious assembly such as the Short Parliament, by no means suited the book of those who were to become his parliamentary opponents. Airing his misgivings about the dissolution of the Stuart Parliament to one of them, Oliver St John, Hyde received the sharp answer 'that it must be worse before it could be better; and that this Parliament would never have done what was necessary to be done.'[4]

In retrospect, it was both easy and convenient for future royalists like Hyde to play down the large measure of general agreement which united them with those who were later to become their bitter opponents. At the time of the calling of the Long Parliament what united the great majority of MPs loomed far larger than the considerations which were later to divide them, many of which had in any case not yet made an appearance. But the idea of such a consensus did not marry at all happily with that of the rebellion as a deeply laid and long-maturing conspiracy – a notion which royalists shared, *mutatis mutandis*, with their opponents. For it involved acceptance of one of two almost equally distasteful alternative corollaries; either that those who were later to be royalists had, by sharing in the consensus, shared in the conspiracy; or that they had been duped by the conspirators. If the historical piece was to have real villains, it was important to dissociate oneself from them at every stage. The truth is, however, more complex and more interesting.

II

In this chapter an attempt is made to distinguish between certain broad political groupings and to observe the changing patterns of political affiliation between the opening of parliament in November 1640 and the early weeks of 1642.[5] It is perhaps easiest to make a beginning with those sixty-four MPs whose courtly sympathies clearly put them outside the range of the broad anti-Court consensus, and there is a strong likelihood that this may also have been true of a further sixteen, though the evidence is not so clear and unequivocal in their case.[6] Out of the seventeen MPs who were disabled from sitting in the House, sixteen were clearly Court men, as was the unpopular secretary of state Sir Francis Windebank, who anticipated disablement or worse by fleeing abroad.[7] Eight were expelled for their activities as government con-

cessionaires,[8] all of them being monopolists, while two of them, Sir
John Jacob and Sir Nicholas Crispe, had also been heavily involved in
royal customs farming and other economic concessions;[9] three for
election irregularities;[10] four for complicity in the Army Plot in the
summer of 1641,[11] and one for incautious and intemperate criticism
of the parliamentary proceedings against the Earl of Strafford in May
1641.[12]

Among those 'courtly' supporters who retained their seats well into
1642, and in some cases almost until the outbreak of war, were professional courtiers such as Endymion Porter (Droitwich); John Ashburnham (Hastings); Philip Warwick (New Radnor); the two Thomas
Jermyns, father and son, both of whom sat for Bury St Edmunds; Sir
George Goring, whose propensity for rapine and pillage was later to
help bring disgrace to the name of Cavalier and who was the son of one of
the most voracious of Caroline courtly concessionaires; and John
Griffith, MP for Caernarvonshire, who was, however, to move over
to the opposition early in 1642, following the queen's thwarting of his
ambition to obtain a place in the household of the Prince of Wales.[13]
Other MPs whose views mark them down clearly as supporters of the
Court in 1640 included a group of four Yorkshire gentlemen, three of
them relatives of Strafford, and all of them beneficiaries of his ascendancy;[14] and two notorious sympathizers with Laudian church innovation, Robert Hyde, Recorder of and MP for Salisbury, and a
relative of Edward Hyde, though, unlike him, a Court man from the
beginning, and Orlando Bridgman (Wigan), the son of the Bishop of
Chester.[15]

Office-holding MPs are another group who, other things being
equal, might be expected to lean towards the Court either because they
feared that radical changes might threaten their position, or because,
like Secretary Windebank, they were deeply implicated in the formula-
tion or implementation of unpopular royal policies. But while it is
reasonable to entertain a cautious presumption in favour of the likelihood of office predisposing the holder to the Court rather than to the
Country, there are a surprising number of exceptions to this rule, as
the work of Gerald Aylmer has demonstrated: among them Sir Robert
Pye, the father-in-law of John Hampden, and Auditor of the Receipt,
who continued to sit for New Woodstock until 1648; Sir Benjamin
Rudyerd (Wilton), the celebrated 'silver trumpet' of the House of
Commons, who, as Surveyor of the Liveries, is included in a list of
fourteen officials of the Court of Wards who refused to join the king at

Oxford after the beginning of the war; and no less a person than John Pym himself (Tavistock), who had held minor but quite lucrative offices under both the king and the queen.[16]

If Dr Aylmer's revelations about the pressures to which office-holders were subjected in the 1630s has seriously modified notions about the political sympathies of this group, similar considerations are applicable to the arguments about the royal economic concessionaires which were advanced in the fourth chapter of this book, where it was argued that the rapprochement between the parliamentary opposition and the chartered companies, coupled with the royal neglect of, and pursuit of policies inimical to the interests of, the companies, made for a split within the concessionary interest which was prolonged into the Long Parliament.[17] Continuing where its predecessor of 1629 had left off, the parliamentary opposition, now a substantial majority of the House, violently attacked monopolist and customs farming interests, while, again like its precedessor, affording some encouragement to the great chartered companies in overseas trade. The fact that a relatively small proportion of aldermanic economic interests was tied up in mon-opolies and customs farms, and that, quite apart from their changing relations with the Crown as business concessionaires, the aldermen had come into bitter conflict with Charles I during the 1630s in their capacity as City fathers casts serious doubts on the argument that they were predominantly Court men in 1640.[18] But to argue thus is emphati-cally not to turn them into radicals. The contrast between their views and those of the three radical City MPs elected in 1640 is not a contrast between polarities. There were many varying degrees of opposition to the Court among the governing classes of the City in 1640, and the moderate reformism of aldermen such as Sir John Gayre, Sir Nicholas Rainton and Sir James Campbell had more in common with the views of the fourth City MP, Alderman Thomas Soame, than with either the courtly sympathies of the wine monopolist Alderman William Abell and the multiple-concessionaire Alderman Sir Henry Garway or, on the other hand, with the views of the three radical City MPs and those City merchants with interests in colonial and especially transatlantic trade, on whose activities the researches of Dr Robert Brenner have thrown such important light.[19] The fact that a municipal revolution was necessary in 1641–2 in order to win the City for Parliament does not mean that the City was governed by supporters of royal absolutism in 1640. What happened was that the political sympathies of most of the aldermen, like those of many other people, had moved back towards the king under the stress of events which took place not before but after the calling of the Long Parliament.[20]

III

The numerical disproportion between the at least 399 'Country' and at least sixty-four and perhaps as many as eighty 'Court' MPs was to be somewhat lessened by the end of 1641. The first and most obvious group of 'Country' opposition men in 1640 comprises those who were to fight for Parliament in the Civil War. This covers an enormously wide group ranging from radicals, such as the later republicans and regicides like Henry Marten (Berkshire) and Miles Corbet (Great Yarmouth) to about thirty-five men who were to go over to the king during the course of the war, such as the Hothams, father and son (Beverley and Scarborough), and Sir Hugh Cholmeley (Scarborough). The second category consists of MPs who were Country opposition men in 1640, but who went over to the king before or at the outbreak of the war, and this in turn lends itself to subdivision between those who the evidence suggests were moving away from their oppositionist position during the first session of the Parliament, that is before the recess in September 1641; and those whose alienation appears to have occurred at some time during the second session and before the outbreak of war. The combined numbers of these two groups were between fifty-five and fifty-seven, but it is impossible to be more than very loosely approximate about the division of this number into the sub-categories of those alienated before and after the recess. Before making a very tentative attempt to do this, it is necessary to examine the main reasons why the oppositionist consensus came to melt at the edges.

One central problem in dealing with this question is pinpointed by the two quotations which stand at the head of this chapter, both of which were the views of men whose inclinations were royalist rather than parliamentarian in 1642. Were the defections from the ranks of the anti-Court MPs the result of the dislike of what were regarded as outrageous inroads made on the king's prerogative rights, even during what is normally regarded as the period of consensus reform during the first session of parliament – à la Hobbes? Or were they due to royal concessions which won over those moderates who had been alienated by the arbitrary rule of the 1630s but who now rallied to a reforming monarch working hand-in-glove with a reforming parliament – à la Suckling? It would be surprising if either of these views were com-

pletely correct to the total exclusion of the other, but in so far as historians have seen the first session of the Long Parliament as an important
stage in the building up of support for the king, they have tended to
emphasize the pull of royal constitutional concessions rather than the
push of parliamentarian radicalism and the other extremist actions
which dominate their account of the second session.

This dichotomy is true only in the very broadest sense. Many of the
seeds of later divisions were sown in the earlier session, and the process
of attraction of former anti-Court MPs to the certainties presented by
the monarchy in an increasingly uncertain political world was not
simply a matter of grateful response to the reforms which were willingly accepted by the king, important though this factor is. In general
the achievements of this session may be divided into three parts. First,
the destruction or neutralization of the personnel (Strafford, Laud,
Windebank, Finch, the customs farmers and the monopolists, etc.)
and machinery (Privy Council, Star Chamber, lieutenancy, High
Commission, Councils of the North and of Wales) of personal government, though not all these had their origins during the years of
personal rule. Then there was the condemnation of the measures and
policies associated with arbitrary government (Ship Money, forest
fines, fines in distraint of knighthood, patents, monopolies and
Laudian ecclesiastical innovations, etc.). Finally there were the
positive reforms such as the Triennial Act, the Act that the parliament
should not be dissolved without its own consent and the attempt to
associate prominent members of the Country group with the government service.

It is certainly true that the reforming measures of the first session
commanded a more general assent than those of the second. Hyde was
later to argue that if there were a pretty general consensus in the earlier
session, it was built upon dissimulation and deceit, and that Pym and
his associates 'pretended . . . only the reformation of disapproved and
odious enormities, and dissembled all purposes of removing foundations'.[21] The reforms were represented as being designed not to create
a *tabula rasa* as the necessary prelude to radical institutional innovation
but as the restoration of the ancient constitutional equilibrium, following the innovatory assaults of royal personal government. But for all
that, it is possible to overestimate the element of consensus. Certainly
some of those who had been numbered among the opponents of the
Court developed serious misgivings about the methods which were
employed and the extremities pursued even against those individuals

whose names were intimately bound up with the eleven years' tyranny. The destruction of Strafford is a case in point. No one, with the possible exception of his friend Laud, could be more unpopular than this alleged apostate from the parliamentary cause. Nor can it be said that Strafford's apostasy had made him as popular in Court as it had made him unpopular in Country circles. Hamilton, Holland, Arundel, Newcastle, Leicester, and perhaps most fatal of all, Secretary of State Sir Henry Vane the elder, all hated him, and the queen herself favoured supple and unprincipled courtiers such as Holland rather than Strafford and Laud, the men of unbending principle and proponents of 'Thorough'. Similarly, among Strafford's opponents in the Commons were such men as Falkland and Hyde and Hopton, who while numbered among the anti-Court men in 1640–1 were ultimately to take the king's side in the war.[22] Yet for all this, his resolute and brilliant conduct of his defence at his trial in April 1641, the obviously unfair methods employed by his adversaries, and the ultimate injustice of the resort to a bill of attainder when the trial appeared to be going in his favour – St John's outrageous 'it was never accounted either cruelty or foul play to knock foxes and wolves on the head ... because they be beasts of prey.'[23] – won Strafford supporters such as George Digby and even John Selden from those who might be expected to be among his greatest enemies. Had it not been for the intimidation by the London mob and the belief that the bill would either fail in the Lords or be vetoed by the king, the list of fifty-six 'Straffordians *Betrayers of their Country*' posted on the wall of a house in Old Palace Yard at Westminster would probably have been much longer.[24] But these fifty-six members of both Houses are in themselves testimony to the serious disquiet which the judicial murder of Strafford aroused, not only among the courtly party but also among those who hated everything that he had stood for.

The case against Strafford also touched on a number of the institutions of royal centralization which were among the main objects of the Country party's attack. Most notably, he had been not only Lord Deputy of Ireland,[25] but also Lord President of the Council of the North and Lord Lieutenant of Yorkshire. Both the regional councils and the lieutenancy were marked down for special parliamentary attention.[26] For all the bitter hostility of so many country gentlemen to the lieutenancy as the agency of what was widely regarded as central interference with country affairs, it had not played a notable role in connection with the most outstanding of the grievances of the 1630s,

Ship Money, and it will be recalled that some deputy lieutenants had got into trouble over their lukewarm or even positively hostile attitude to government policy not only on this but on a variety of other matters.[27] However, such considerations were insufficiently weighty to deter the Commons from appointing a committee on 14 December 1640 to examine the conduct of the lieutenancy and to prepare a bill for regulating and controlling it in the future. If Clarendon is to be believed, however, one effect of this attack on 'the prime gentlemen of quality in all the counties of England' who had been lieutenants or deputy lieutenants and – especially in connection with their role in respect of Ship Money – sheriffs, was the way in which many of those gentlemen who felt themselves to be most deeply implicated in such matters sought safety by allying themselves with the Country opposition. Clarendon picks out the Yorkshire gentleman, Sir John Hotham the elder, who was to take over Hull for parliament early in 1642, as a case in point, though it is a case whose force is somewhat weakened by the fact that by 1639 Hotham, who had earlier incurred great unpopularity as a sheriff for his determined collection of Ship Money, was numbered among the Yorkshire opponents of the levy.[28]

The alleged oppressions of the High Commission and the Star Chamber and, on 21 January 1641, the 'undue proceedings' of the Privy Council were also brought within the purview of the same parliamentary committee. There is no doubt that the resultant abolition of the first two of these bodies met with general approval, and the same is true of the attack on the measures which were the product of Caroline personal rule. The condemnation of Ship Money, forest fines, fines in distraint of knighthood, monopolies and the expulsion of monopolist MPs, the sequestration of the customs farming leases and the imposition of a fine of £150,000 on the farmers for their delinquency were clearly popular measures. But none of the measures passed in the first session of parliament was attended with more general approval than those specially designed to prevent a recurrence of non-parliamentary rule. In the debate on the Triennial Bill on 19 January 1641 Digby answered Solicitor General Herbert's argument that the provision for the automatic recall of parliament three years after its predecessor's dissolution 'tooke from the king one of the supreame prerogatives of his crowne' by stating simply that it was open to the king to employ his veto if he thought so. Whatever Charles may have thought, he vetoed neither this bill nor the bill that the present parliament could not be dissolved without its own consent which received the royal assent in

May 1641 at about the same time as the Bill of Attainder against Strafford was going through the Lords. Both bills received the support of future Cavaliers such as Falkland and Hyde as well as of future Roundheads such as Hampden and Pym. For all the arguments that such measures were rooted in tradition, both were radical innovations of crucial significance; the latter especially since it ensured that this parliament would not suffer the fate of so many others – abrupt dissolution once its proceedings became displeasing to the king.[29]

Complementing these measures were the attempts to remove those advisers of whom Parliament disapproved and to associate prominent anti-Court politicians with the business of government. In the debate on the Triennial Bill on 19 January 1641 Digby, who was soon to become the prime candidate for the role of evil counsellor, argued that the passage of the bill would effectively curtail the operations of evil counsellors, 'the proximate cause of our miseries', by holding over their heads the imminent threat of parliamentary impeachment. As William Strode insisted in the House of Commons in May 1641, it was because the king was encompassed by evil councillors that he 'understandeth not what treason is'; a convenient fiction no doubt, but one which, though absolving the king from blame was hardly conducive to the maintenance of royal dignity, since its necessary corollary was a view of the monarch as a cipher, or an individual of very feeble understanding, capable of being led by the nose by unscrupulous advisers whose defects were obvious to almost everyone but himself; by, to quote, Sir Benjamin Rudyerd's typically flowery metaphor, 'grosse condense bodies' which 'obscure and hinder the Sunne from shyning out'.[30]

It was not only via the threat of impeachment that parliamentary control over ministers of the Crown was sought. From John Pym's Ten Propositions of June 1641 to the Nineteen Propositions a year later the attempt of parliament to influence the appointment of ministers was a central feature of the constitutional struggle. The proposals relating to choice of ministers in the earlier propositions were mild enough, their essence being that the king was to be trusted to appoint 'such officers and counsellors as his people and Parliament may have just cause to confide in'. It was the royal failure to live up to these modest hopes which led to the far more drastic (and totally unacceptable) propositions of a year later, whereby parliament demanded the right to approve the royal choice of ministers.[31]

Moreover, far from being a product of the destruction of evil ministers, the proposal in the early summer of 1641 to associate prominent anti-Court politicians with the government of the realm was in fact the price which the king was prepared to pay for the saving of the life of Strafford and the preservation of episcopacy. Rumours that some of the most prominent oppositionists were to obtain preferment had been circulating since the previous December, and were given further credibility by the appointment of Oliver St John, who had achieved national celebrity by his defence of Hampden in the Ship Money case of 1637, as Solicitor-General 29 January 1641; and, three weeks later, by the appointment to the Privy Council of a number of opposition peers including the Earls of Bedford, Essex and Warwick and Viscount Saye and Sele. By early May when the Strafford business was entering its final phase, a wholesale ministerial reorganization was widely expected. Bishop Juxon, it was rumoured, was to be replaced by Bedford as Lord Treasurer; Cottington as Chancellor of the Exchequer, by Bedford's client and associate, Pym, and, as Master of the Court of Wards, by Saye and Sele; Lord Kimbolton was to succeed his father, the Earl of Manchester, as Lord Privy Seal, as soon as could be decently arranged; and the secretaryship of state vacated by Windebank's flight was to go to Denzil Holles. Three of these aspirants to office were to be among the parliamentarians whom Charles I was to attempt to arrest in January 1642, while the fourth, Saye and Sele, was the most implacable of Puritan peers. The fifth, and much the most moderate, Bedford, was the key to the whole operation on account of his influence – real or imagined – over his client Pym, and his death on 9 May was a crucial blow to the plan.[32]

There is no need to attach much credence to Clarendon's suggestion that one reason for the failure of the strategy of bridge-appointments was that it came too late, in that by the early summer Pym, Hampden and Holles had already gone too far with their 'desperate designs' to pull out, and that the royal strategy would have succeeded only if they had been preferred along with St John in January.[33] Clarendon's argument turns too much on his obsessional *ex post facto* notion of a long-standing conspiracy. In reality, the failure of the royal initiative of the early summer is explicable in terms partly of Bedford's death; partly of the impossible *quid pro quo* demanded by Charles, who hoped to use it to save Strafford's life; and, partly of the king's disingenuous pursuit of an alternative and violent means of achieving this end by a coup at the Tower connected as this had originally been with a plot to bring the disgruntled and long unpaid army south. This in turn was popularly – and mistakenly – construed as a conspiracy to secure the

sinister popish ends of Henrietta Maria, to whom the saving of Strafford's life was at most a very minor consideration. To the queen and
her courtly following, men such as Holland, Cottington and Vane, the
death of the great proponent of 'Thorough' was a matter indifferent.
That the split within the Court extended as far as the policies of the king
and his consort is probably another factor of no small significance in
the disastrous failure of the royal attempts to establish a *modus vivendi*
between the Court and the Country in the summer of 1641.[34]

IV

Most accounts of the history of the two years before the outbreak of the
Civil War emphasize the second parliamentary session which opened
on 20 October 1641 as the decisive period for the disintegration of the
anti-Court consensus. From very early on the business of the session
was conducted against the background of the revolt in Ireland, and it is
difficult to exaggerate the impact of this terrifying revelation of what
was seen by English Protestants as the true face of Catholic frightful-
ness. It totally transformed the political situation, and threw into sharp
relief crucial issues of power and sovereignty, the contesting of which
was to lead relentlessly on to civil war: the control of the militia, the
lieutenancy, the navy, the magazines and strong places and their
commanders. Pym might argue with some force that in these new
circumstances he had no choice but to break the letter of the constitution in order to preserve its spirit and to avoid putting the constitutional achievements of 1640–1 in jeopardy. But it was not only the
small minority of Court men whom he failed to convince. He also
alienated a number of those moderate reformers who had warmly
welcomed the achievements of the first session, but who were now
concerned that the advocates of further constitutional change were
passing over from the role of restorers of the ancient constitution to that
of constitutional aggressors.

Clearly the idea that the second session of parliament was a time of
stark confrontation and party conflict, leading more or less relentlessly
to the Civil War, in contrast with the high degree of consensus among
reformers during the first session, has some basis in fact. But this
distinction can be pushed too far. One reason why the importance of
the earlier session in connection with the break-up of the reforming
consensus has tended to be played down lies in the nature of the
evidence relating to the political attitudes of individual MPs. It is only

in the cases of such outstanding figures as Pym, Hyde and Holles, to take examples from what were to become widely differing sectors of parliamentary opinion, that it is possible to trace the evolution of their views with any degree of certainty. By contrast, as we have seen, for many it is impossible to be certain about their attitudes at the outset, let alone to trace the evolution of their views over the succeeding months. Had we extensive division lists for the period, the task would be much easier, but, as it is, apart from such exceptional evidence as the lists of Straffordians and of those taking the Protestation in May 1641, we have to rely on such information as membership of parliamentary com-mittees – which can be very misleading – and on speeches made in the House. Most MPs spoke rarely, and, when they did, not always unam-biguously. By contrast, the one matter about which we can be certain in the majority of cases is the side taken by individual MPs during the war. In the case of the fifty-five or more MPs who can reasonably be described as anti-Court men in 1640 but whom we know to have been royalist by August 1642, it has normally been assumed that the reforms of the first session represented the consummation of their aims and that it was the developments of the second session which pushed them into the royalist camp. The truth is not always quite so simple as this, and there were probably many cases where the process of alienation began during the earlier session and was apparent in varying degrees before the high summer of 1641.

Some indication of this process may be derived from an examination of the attitude of MPs to the attainder of the Earl of Strafford. But the evidence needs to be treated with caution, for, quite apart from Denzil Holles, who does not appear on the list of 'Straffordians'[35] but was related to the Earl by marriage and did his utmost to save his life, the names of the 'Straffordians' include six MPs who were to remain at Westminster after the outbreak of war and may therefore be presumed to be parliamentarian rather than royalist in sympathy.[36] Indeed, three of them were to retain their seats after Pride's Purge and the execution of the king. These were John Selden (Oxford University), the man who had been the colleague of Pym and Eliot in the parliamentary struggles of the later 1620s; Robert Scawen (Berwick) and Sir Richard Wynn (Liverpool).[37] The vast majority of the 'Straffordians' were, of course, more straightforward and consistent cases in that they had been Court rather than Country men from the outset. There were, however, some MPs whose attitudes to the attainder had something of the genuinely climacteric about it. Selden, Scawen and Wynn were clearly shocked by the management of the case against Strafford and the recourse to attainder on the apparent failure of impeachment into taking a line which was totally out of accord with their normal political stance, into which, however, they lapsed again after the event. But for other MPs Strafford's case was simply the most important of a number of developments during the first parliamentary session which pointed the way clearly to the abandonment of their anti-Court sympathies. There are four quite spectacular examples of such transformation of political attitudes, though the first of these cases, the celebrated Dr Samuel Turner (Shaftesbury), who had leapt spectacularly into the limelight with his accusation of the Duke of Buckingham in the parliament of 1626, is the weakest, since Turner's reputation as a fashionable physician in great demand at Court may have severely tempered his oppositionist enthusiasm long before 1640. The others, however, had impeccable anti-Court credentials. Sir John Strangeways (Weymouth) had been a stalwart of the parliamentary opposition in the 1620s, in the forefront of parliamentary debate on almost every great issue. George Digby (Dorset) was, of course, later to be the most extreme of Cavaliers, but at this stage was popularly connected like his father, the Earl of Bristol, who had been a notable victim of Buckingham's megalomania during the 1620s, with the Country rather than the Court. He had opposed Ship Money and other royal exactions in the 1630s and had spoken enthusiastically in favour of the Triennial Bill. The anti-Court reputation of our fourth example of defecting MPs, Robert Holborne (Mitchell), rested chiefly on his role, with Oliver St John, as counsel for Hampden in the Ship Money case of 1637, and while too much weight ought not to be attached to what was, after all, a professional brief in what turned out to be a case of outstanding political significance, Holborne's connection with the Earl of Bedford suggests that his anti-Court reputation may not have been unfounded. The factors involved in the defection of these men were complex and numerous. Dislike of the course taken by the proceedings against Strafford was certainly common to all of them, though they all regarded themselves as enemies of the despotism associated with Strafford's name. Digby indeed had described Strafford as 'the *most dangerous* Minister, the most unsupportable to free subjects that can be charactered'. Digby, Strangeways and Holborne were also profoundly alarmed by the Root and Branch petition with its attack not simply on Laudian prelacy but on episcopacy in general, while the two former more than once expressed horror at the licence given to the London mob and the use made of tumultuary petitioning by Pym and his colleagues as an exercise in political intimidation, of which Strangeways was later to have unpleasant personal experience when attacked by the mob for his part during the debate on the secular employment of the bishops in January 1642. And, as far as the king was concerned, the end of Strafford was as decisive a climacteric as the army plot had been to Strafford's opponents. As Professor Fletcher observes, 'he would not employ men whom he regarded as Strafford's murderers'.[38]

V

It has been seen that at least fifty-five of the anti-Court reforming MPs of 1640 were to fight for the king in the Civil War. Of how many of them can it be said that, like Digby, Strangeways and Holborne, their alienation was effectively complete before the end of the first parliamentary session? Excluding Samuel Turner, who may have left his 'Country' sympathies behind before 1640, there were as many as fifteen MPs of whom there is a very strong likelihood that this is true,[39] eleven about whom no confident statement can be made as between the two sessions on the decisive period of their alienation;[40] and a further twenty-eight or twenty-nine MPs about whom there is no evidence of alienation before the second session – which is not to deny that the process may have begun earlier. These latter include some of the most spectacular defectors, most notably Hyde and Falkland, who helped to fashion the attractive image of constitutional monarchy which was a potent factor in winning support for the king both in and out of parliament in 1641-2.

These cases of defection to the Court find mention in every textbook on the period, though it was not until the appearance of Mr Wormald's subtle and penetrating study of Hyde that it was realized how complicated and long-drawn-out a process this was, in the case of this most important of all the defectors to the Court.[41] But there were other cases which contemporaries may have found more spectacular. Sir Francis Seymour (Marlborough), who was removed from the limelight by his elevation to the Lords at the beginning of 1641, had like Strangeways played a central part in the parliamentary opposition in the late 1620s, and began in 1640 where he had left off in 1629, with blistering attacks on Catholics, Laudians, monopolists and other delinquents. Unlike Strangeways, however, there is no evidence in Seymour's case to suggest defection from the ranks of the opposition before 1642.[42]

The Grand Remonstrance, that controversial document with its synthetic history of the reign, account of royal misgovernment and radical recommendations for reform,[43] is usually and correctly designated as the great climacteric of the Long Parliament, and indeed, since the Remonstrance passed the House of Commons on 22 November by only eleven votes, it is clear that it raised doubts among many more MPs than those who ultimately defected to the Court. One member for whom the Remonstrance was certainly a moment of truth was Sir Edward Dering, the former proponent of Root and Branch.[44] Another was Geoffrey Palmer, the MP for Stamford. Hitherto a sensible, moderate reformer, anti-Laudian and anti-Straffordian, who, as one of the managers of the case against Strafford, had earned the disapprobation of some of his colleagues for showing courtesy and consideration towards the Earl, Palmer was to earn a spell in the Tower in November 1641 for insisting on his right to protest against the decision to print and circulate the Remonstrance.[45] The royal cause could only benefit from the acquisition of such supporters. This was no less true of another anti-Straffordian reformer who also spent some weeks in the Tower. Sir Ralph Hopton, who was later to be the most efficient and successful royalist commander in the south-west, had, though a deputy lieutenant in the 1630s, distinguished himself by taking the Puritan side in the notorious Somerset church-ales controversy in 1633, as well as by his advocacy of the customary rating system, which would militate against the obtaining of the maximum returns from Ship Money, in Somerset. Hopton's most recent biographer has suggested that the debates on the Grand Remonstrance in November 1641 were as crucial in his defection from the anti-Court ranks as they were in Palmer's and Dering's cases. But the evidence suggests that Hopton's defection may have come later. On 23 November, the day after the Remonstrance passed through the Commons, he made a sharp attack on the misdeeds of Lord Keeper Finch, and he was, moreover, to be chairman of the parliamentary committee which presented the Remonstrance and an accompanying petition to the king on 1 December. A stronger case can be made for January 1642 as the crucial month in Hopton's defection, which, once begun, was very quickly accomplished. By March his new-found sympathies, expressed in his vote against the expulsion of the renegade Dering from the House, and, even more significantly, his resolute defence of the king's attempted arrest of the five members, had landed him in the Tower, and characterized him definitely as an intransigent royalist.[46]

VI

The Grand Remonstrance was probably Pym's answer to the threatened disintegration of the anti-Court consensus as well as his justification for the racial programme on which he was about to embark. A somewhat ambivalent attempt to foster alarmed awareness of crisis and to consolidate conservative opinion and maintain the consensus for reform, it presented the king's advisers with an opportunity which they were quick to take. The royal declaration in answer to the Remonstrance, produced in December 1641, was the first of a remarkable series of able, moderate and conciliatory appeals to the political centre, designed to accelerate the process of defection from the anti-Court ranks which, as we have seen, had begun, however modestly, during the previous session. It emphasized the king's cooperation in the reforms of that session, and, more particularly, that he had never refused 'to pass any Bill ... for Redress of those grievances mentioned in the Remonstrance'. As to religion, the declaration hit out shrewdly at extremists at both ends of the spectrum, denouncing both the Catholics and those sectaries whose excesses were causing many moderate men to entertain the most serious doubts about the advisability of departing further from the established forms of Church government. It concluded with a forthright denunciation of the Irish rebels and an indignant repudiation of their claim to be acting in the king's name.[47]

The declaration was a masterpiece of conciliation and reasonableness and seemed clearly to indicate the king's willingness to listen to moderate counsel.[48] Crucial to its significance as a foundation document of constitutional royalism is its assertion that it had been published with the advice of the Privy Council. This attempt to dispel the well-founded rumour that Charles was still subject to the backstairs influence of favourites was to be coupled at the beginning of 1642 with a further instalment of the policy of bridge-appointments, when Falkland and Culpepper were admitted to the Privy Council as Secretary of State and Chancellor of the Exchequer respectively. It is true that the appointment of men who were cut off from Pym and his supporters by the great divide of the Grand Remonstrance cannot be regarded in quite same light as that of St John in the previous year. However, the latter office was said to have been offered to Culpepper only after Pym had refused it, which if true, suggests that a serious resumption of the policy of bridge-appointments was envisaged.[49]

If the image of constitutional monarchy which the king's moderate advisers were striving to create was to have the maximum impact, it had to be exemplified consistently by royal behaviour. But consistency of purpose was the quality which Charles most conspicuously lacked, and the work of Hyde and his colleagues was bedevilled by the king's propensity to waver between moderation and extremism – between the policies of Hyde and Falkland and those of the queen and the now ultra-royalist Digby. This inconsistency was the main reason why the full potential of the situation arising out of the widespread dislike of the Grand Remonstrance was never realized, and the break-up of the anti-Court consensus was not so extensive as might otherwise have been the case. The astonishing tactlessness of Charles's appointment of the swashbuckling Cavalier Lunsford as Lieutenant of the Tower, on 23 December 1641, and the dismissal on the following day of his superior, Newport, a man in the complete confidence of the anti-Court party, as Constable of the Tower, were actions which totally belied the impression of royal moderation and conciliatoriness which Hyde and Falkland had been at such pains to build up, and which could not be restored at a stroke by Lunsford's dismissal on 26 December, since this was all too obviously a royal response to popular protest and demonstration.[50] No less harmful to the desired image of moderation was the royal countenancing of the protestation made by the twelve bishops on 29 December concerning their exclusion from the House of Lords. For the bishops to protest against their exclusion from the House by the London mob, encouraged no doubt by Pym and his supporters, was one thing, and unquestionably their exclusion was an outrageous popular infringement of parliamentary privilege. To demand on that account that the votes of the Upper House during their enforced absence should be null and void was quite another, and Charles's apparent countenancing of the bishops' outrageous protest had two important and unlooked-for consequences. In the first place it reconciled the Lords with the Commons, with whom they had been at odds since the Lower House had insisted on going it alone on the Grand Remonstrance. The second consequence went deeper and related to the serious implications of the bishops' protest for the reforming achievements of parliament to date. The use which Pym made of popular demonstrations as a means of bringing pressure to bear on parliament was to become one of the most powerful arguments of his opponents, designed to appeal to erstwhile reformers who were becoming increasingly alarmed at the course taken by events. But the bishops' claim that their enforced absence invalidated the business done during that period had disturbing implications in respect of the achievements of the first parliamentary session. For it might be the thin end of a wedge which when rammed home would invalidate these achievements. The trial of Strafford had been only the most notable occasion when intimidation of MPs had been openly practised. How many other measures had been passed as the result of such intimidation? How much of the reforming legislation of the first session might be invalidated if the decision about the bishops' case went in their favour? Might not the king himself claim that his own consent had been extorted, and, in the light of this, how convincing was the brand-new image of the king as the moderate monarch who desired nothing more than to preserve these reforms?[51]

To those who entertained such doubts, the events of 4 January 1642 must have come as a horrible confirmation of their worst fears. Charles's attempt to arrest Lord Kimbolton and the five members – Pym, Hampden, Haselrige, Holles and Strode – appeared to be the living confirmation of the thesis of the Grand Remonstrance and refutation of the moderate royal reply to the Remonstrance. For here in all too solid flesh were the courtly villains, the threatening, trigger-happy, Cavalier ruffians – many of them allegedly papists – of popular rumour. Here, assuredly, was the true face of the Court. In these circumstances those moderate men who had lately been admitted to the Privy Council, and who in actual fact had been in complete ignorance of the king's extremist intentions, must have appeared either as accomplices of, or as fools who had been duped by, the king. The attempted royal coup of 4 January was thus a heaven-sent opportunity which Pym was not slow to exploit. Here was a marvellous justification of the need for parliament to keep the control of the militia in its own hands, a point which the opening section of the Militia Ordinance of 31 January was careful to emphasize.[52] The attempted arrest of Pym and his five colleagues was treated as a clear indication that the king was clay in the hands of those who wished to return to the arbitrary royal rule of the 1630s, and that the reforms of 1640-1 were therefore in jeopardy.[53] The incident, argued a parliamentary declaration of 9 March, not only 'exceeded all former breaches of Priviledges of Parliament'. It was in addition a part of a design of 'diverse bloudy and desperate Persons . . . to have massacred and destroyed the Members of that House'.[54] Such allegations called to mind the equally unsuccessful coup of 5 November 1605, as they were no doubt intended to do, for there were not wanting attempts to link the events of 4 January with the Irish revolt itself as 'an effect of the bloudie Courses of Papists'.[55]

Here was the great ground-bass on which Pym was to elaborate a series of wonderfully resourceful and ingenious variations over the next few months, perhaps most notably in his brilliant speech to a conference between the two Houses on 25 January. Here he made use of petitions from London and the Home Counties which brimmed over with apprehension of the dangers of Catholic conspiracy, and which possibly had been drafted at least partly by his agency.[56] The theme was to be a constant element of anti-Court propaganda in the months both before and after the outbreak of the war, when a great deal was made of the alleged courtly complicity in the Irish revolt and (later) about the employment of papists in the army commanded by the Earl of Newcastle, despite royal statements to the contrary in each case.[57] The effect of the events of 4 January was to lend plausibility to the most fantastic and lurid rumours of malignant Cavalier conspiracy against Protestantism and the ancient constitution, and to make it necessary for the moderate royalists to resume *ab initio* their Sisyphean labours which had begun to promise so well in the previous December. The net result of the king's paying heed to the voice of Cavalier extremism was that the moderate royalists had to begin again from scratch, while to Pym and his supporters the king's action might well appear to have saved the anti-Court consensus from the disintegration which had seemed imminent at the time of the Grand Remonstrance.

VII

That the task facing the moderate royalists, though formidable, was not impossible was due in no small measure to events which took place outside rather than within parliament. Pym's constitutional pro-gramme might excite some alarm among moderate men who had welcomed the measures of the first parliamentary session, but the events of 4 January had provided Pym with a powerful counter-argu-ment in favour of the need for further constitutional advances in order to protect what had already been achieved. But however powerfully the king's recourse to extremist courses might impress itself on the minds of moderate men, they had no less, and perhaps more, cause for alarm in the apparent effect of radical policies on the populace and the appar-ent willingness of Pym and his associates to make use of tumultuary assemblies and so-called tumultuary petitioning to further their own political ends.

During the intervening months between the dissolution of the Short and the meeting of the Long Parliament, the London mob had burst into frightening prominence. The first outbursts in the early summer of 1640 had been unorganized and uncoordinated. This, however, did not make them any the less alarming, for although the London apprentices played a prominent part, the disturbances took on a far more threatening aspect than the letting off of adolescent steam normally associated with Mayday and other apprentice demonstrations. For the apprentices were joined by large numbers drawn from the metropolitan proletariat, and notably by the leather workers of Southwark and Bermondsey, in an attempted assault on the Primate at Lambeth on 11 May, and the breaking open of gaols three days later, while on 28 October the proceedings of the High Commission were interrupted by the mob as the Court was about to sentence a Separatist. On the following day the rabble invaded St Pauls.[58]

Over the next few months the London mob was to become a formidable instrument in the hands of the radical group in the House of Commons. In a well-known passage, Clarendon described how Pym and his associates organized mass petitions, the intimidation which was practised on people to make them sign, and the fraudulent means employed to obtain signatures to petitions which were often quite different from those which were finally presented.[59] Quite distinct from this were the alarming social implications of mass petitioning.[60] On 15 March 1641 Sir John Danvers drew Sir Edward Dering's attention to the fact that 'the Monstrous Easye receit of Petitions at the standing Committees makes Authority declyne and the threatning of lewd persons to petition the parliament seeme of too great power & Encouragement for an invndation of Beggars.'[61] The implication clearly was that such petitions had their origins elsewhere than in the minds of the petitioners.

Tumults with or without petitions became an increasingly familiar feature of political life whereby the outer world impinged itself alarmingly upon the political nation. While it is true that the recurrence of the phenomenon became more frequent during the second session of the parliament, it was sufficiently prominent in the first session to give rise to considerable alarm. The prime example occurred during the crisis days of May 1641, when the Bill of Attainder against Strafford was being debated, and the organizers of anti-Strafford demonstrations skilfully rang the changes between respectable bourgeois and proletarian demonstrators. One report tells of a gathering of the 'ordinary

Canallie [*sic*] mecanicke people' who replied to the soothing assurance of the Lord Chamberlain that justice would be done on Strafford with the threat 'that if they had it not . . . they would come thrice as many with swords and clubs', which was apparently carried out.[62] The manipulation of such assemblies became part of the stock-in-trade of Pym and his associates. It is impossible to say how far they were aware of the risks they were taking or if they ever paused to consider whether they had called into being a Frankenstein monster which might ultimately refuse to play their game and turn upon them also. What can be said with confidence, however, is that, while their use of tumults helped them to secure their immediate political ends, it also swelled the ranks of their opponents more particularly during the second session of the Parliament when such demonstrations became more frequent. At times no one who was not of Pym's party seemed safe. Sir John Strangeways was surrounded by a threatening mob in Palace Yard; the bishops were prevented by the mob from taking their seats in the House of Lords in December 1641; and Lord Mayor Gurney 'was most violently assaulted by a multitude of Rude Citizens and . . . vncivill women', who broke his chain of office and tore his gown from his back, when he was returning from escorting the king to Whitehall after Charles' visit to Guildhall on 5 January 1642. Perhaps most sinister of all was the hardly veiled threat of the London porters on 2 February 1642, who demanded strong measures against 'that adverse, malignant, bloodsucking, rebellious party' in default of which they should be forced to 'extremities not fit to be named, and to make good that saying that *Necessity hath no law*'.[63]

The increasing number of such incidents in the course of 1642 was to provoke many moderate men to demand that 'some exemplary Punishment may be inflicted upon the principall fomenters of them' as well as the demonstrators themselves.[64] But who exactly were these 'principall fomenters'? Few knowledgeable men had any doubt that tumults had become a standard weapon in the armoury of Pym and his associates, who, as a petition from Herefordshire bluntly put it, afforded 'Private if not publique encouragement' to 'the mutinous rabble'.[65] The evidence provided by members of Grays Inn about the way in which Captain Venn, one of the radical MPs for London, whipped up a demonstration to bring pressure to bear on parliament when it was debating whether to send Geoffrey Palmer to the Tower in November 1641 was, whether true or false, entirely credible:

... there came into one Lavenderes shopp a seruant from Mr.
Venn and told him that in the House of Commons ... the worse
partie were like to gett the better of the good partie, therefore
he was desired from Captaine Venn to come to Westminster with
his armes to helpe the good partie, accordingly he presently tooke
his sword and went away.[66]

A certain verisimilitude was given to these allegations by a phenomenon which, *mutatis mutandis*, is by no means peculiar to seventeenth-
century disorders; the mealy-mouthed response of men in whose political interest it might be to encourage, but whose duty was to discourage these excesses of the multitude.[67] Pym's celebrated speech at a
conference between the two Houses on 25 January 1642 is typical
enough, with its token denunciation of tumults but extenuation of
them in terms of the economic hardship which the current economic
depression was visiting upon humble people, and attribution of these
in no small measure to the political uncertainty of the time.[68] Pym's
message was that the surest way of stopping such disorders was to press
for radical reforms which would remove such uncertainties and make
for confidence and economic recovery. While there can be little doubt
that his dangerous strategy involving the use of popular demonstrations as a political weapon was a factor in drawing some moderate
reformers into the royalist camp, there is no need to dispute Dr Manning's argument that there were others who accepted Pym's view that
a strong dose of further radical reform was a necessary condition of
the restoration of both economic confidence and political peace.[69]

The connection between economic distress and popular discontent
at this time is not in doubt. There is plenty of evidence of serious
unemployment in England in the late autumn, winter and spring of
1641-2. A Hampshire petition at the end of 1641 complained of the
disastrous decline of the cloth trade.[70] The Lord Mayor of London, in a
speech before the king at Guildhall on 5 January 1642, referred to the
high level of unemployment due to the decay of trade,[71] as did a pro-
royalist petition from Kent in the spring of 1642.[72] As may be imagined
from the nature of these sources, not all of them stress the connection
between economic distress and political uncertainty which was a staple
ingredient of Pym's rhetoric. Some, however, did. As we have already
seen,[73] the London apprentices at the end of 1641 and the mariners and
miscellaneous London poor in January 1642 all laid at least some of the
blame for the economic depression at the door of failure to deal decis-
ively with 'the Papists and Prelates and the Malignant Party which

adhears unto them'.[74] More neutrally, the clothiers of Leeds in their petition of 14 April, bewailed the fact that they had jumped out of the frying-pan of exactions by courtly promoters into the fire of economic stagnation and unemployment arising out of political uncertainty which made merchants reluctant to take up their cloth.[75]

Many profoundly worried contemporaries must have pondered both Pym's diagnosis of the causes of popular tumults and that which was put out by his opponents; that the phenomenon was a natural consequence of the loosening of the reins of authority from which everyone who was anyone had a great deal to lose. The dangers of mob rule and the driving of the king and many of those who opposed Pym's policies from London was to be one of the most frequently reiterated themes of royalist propaganda in the months both before and after the outbreak of the war.[76] There was an ever-present danger that the encouragement of popular action might lead to a situation in which the attentions of the multitude might turn from communion rails, altars and vestments to private property. As Clive Holmes has shown, the rioters in the Stour Valley in August and the early autumn of 1642, at first attacking 'delinquents' such as the future Cavalier Sir John Lucas of Colchester and Catholic landowners such as Lady Rivers and Sir Thomas Audley, soon became less discriminating in their choice of victim, though in the circumstances of that time this was a factor which helped to drive the alarmed gentry of the region more firmly into the parliamentary orbit.[77] Indeed, once the king had left London in March 1642, the fear of popular disorder was as likely to work in favour of his opponents who in some areas appeared as the only effective guardians of public order. This is, however, in no way to deny the importance of this factor in the earlier movement of sympathies back towards the king among men whose minds had already been made up by March.

VIII

Fears about the social and political implications of religious radicalism were another factor which helped to frighten many moderate men away from the implications of further reform. Something has already been said in the last chapter about the widespread belief among many of those who had no sympathy with Archbishop Laud's ritualistic innovations and attempts to exalt the social status of the clergy that the Church in a monarchical society must be organized on an episcopal basis and that to do away with bishops would threaten the very existence of monarchy and with it the whole structure of social degree, priority and place. This was the thesis that was savagely attacked in John Milton's intemperate treatise *Of Reformation in England* which was published in 1641, and in a number of his other contemporary tracts. For in them Milton challenged not only Laudian prelacy, which had few defenders by this time, but the whole Foxeian notion of godly Prince and godly (*iure humano*) Bishop as the joint agents of godly reformation more sharply and effectively than it had been challenged since the Presbyterian heyday of Cartwright and Travers in the 1570s and 1580s. Episcopacy, he argued, was a free-standing institution whose destruction would have no harmful implications for monarchy and the social order; the reverse in fact. Eight years later when both bishops and king had been removed from the scene, the same author was to take a rather different view. In his *Eikonoklastes*, written to counter the influence of the *Eikon Basilike* with its moving account of the last days of the martyr-king, Milton was to find no difficulty in making the connection which he had formerly repudiated between 'the civil kind of idolatry, in idolizing kings' and 'the prelates and their fellow-teachers . . . whose pulpit-stuff . . . hath been the . . . perpetual infusion of servility and wretchedness to all their hearers'. But in all conscience his position in 1641 was radical enough. Prelacy and primitive episcopacy were lumped together for indiscriminate abuse. The Marian martyr-bishops – 'It was not episcopacy that wrought in them the heavenly fortitude of martyrdom' – were not the only sacred cows of the Foxeian tradition on whom Milton heaped ridicule. Despite his specific dissociation – in the context of 1641 though not, as has been seen, of 1649 – of the fate of the king from that of his bishops, the legend of the monarch as the English Constantine received as short shrift as that of the Marian martyr-bishops.[78]

However, the doubts which Milton's treatises of 1641 were designed to allay persisted. For what was to replace an episcopal organization of the Church? Digby referred to the Root and Branch Petition for the abolition of episcopacy as a comet with 'a terrible tail . . . pointed to the North'. There can be no doubt that for many moderate men the abandonment of episcopacy and its replacement by fully fledged Presbyterianism *à l'écossaise* represented a leap in the dark which they were extremely reluctant to take. For example, a petition to the House of Lords from the gentry of Cheshire on 27 February 1641 expressed serious alarm at what its authors deemed to be the social implications of Presbyterian discipline administered by 'a numerous Presbytery, who together with their ruling elders, will arise to near forty thousand Church governors', a form of ecclesiastical policy which was, the petitioners claimed, inconsistent with monarchy, 'dangerously conducible to an anarchy', and to 'the utter loss of learning and laws, which must necessarily produce an extermination of nobility, gentry and order if not of religion'. In the Root and Branch debate Sir John Strangeways, moderate Church reformer though he was, argued that 'if wee made a paritie in the church wee must at last come to a paritie in the Commonwealth', thus echoing the sentiments of a Laudian sermon of 1626 and evoking spirited denials from, amongst others, Oliver Cromwell, Denzil Holles and John Pym.[79]

Sir Edward Dering had proposed in a speech of 21 June 1641 an ingenious way out of the difficulty in the form of a compromise between primitive episcopacy and Presbyterianism in which dioceses were to be reduced to be conterminous with shires, in each of which a presbytery of 'Grave Divines' would be presided over by an Overseer, Moderator or Bishop. Here, he argued, was a Church polity which, while going some way in the direction of Presbyterianism, would avoid the dangerous social consequences of the adoption of a full-blown Presbyterian system.[80] Like many other gentlemen of moderate reforming inclinations, Dering was even more alarmed at the activities of extremist sectaries, a phenomenon about which he was the regular recipient of information via the anguished letters of Robert Abbot, the moderate reforming vicar of Cranbrook in his native county of Kent. On 15 March 1641 Abbot had written about the increasing prevalence of sectaries in Kent. Such persons were not simply anti-episcopalian, but 'They would haue euery particular congregation to be independent, and . . . the votes about euery matter of Iurisdiction . . . to be drawne vp from the whole body of the church . . . both men and women . . . They would haue none in the commission [of the Peace?] but by solemne Couenant.' Compared with such a terrifying prospect, the contents of a later letter of 5 July from the same correspondent, complaining that he was also under pressure from 'the middle sort of the parish' to abandon the use of the Common Prayer Book, the tolling of the bell at funerals and the churching of women, all to the detriment of the incumbent's income, might seem trivial, but to Dering, a man of deeply conservative instincts for all his radical flourish as the former propounder of root and branch, they were yet another sign that society was sliding away from time-honoured practices, abandoning the social certainties symbolized by immemorial rites of passage and creating a vacuum which would be filled by heaven knows what.[81] Similarly, it was not long before men who had voted joyfully for the abolition of the spiritual courts, became aware of the dangerous vacuum which they had created, in that not only heresy and schism, but offences such as adultery, incest and non-payment of tithes would go unpunished.[82]

On 20 November 1641, Dering made a speech in the House of Commons which is a classic example of the attitude of the erstwhile reformer who has consented to the opening of a religious and social Pandora's box and is horrified at the awful consequences of his action. All certainties were gone, social no less than religious certainties. His horror at 'all mens venting their severall sences (senceless senses) in matters of Religion' as instanced by his encounter with a 'bold Mecanike', who reproached him for his mistaken religious beliefs, was probably shared by an increasing number: among them the members of the Inns of Court who petitioned parliament on 11 January 1642, that it should not allow 'learning to be defaced nor discountenanced by the ignorant'. It was certainly no accident that this clause in the petition was followed by another complaining of 'the exorbitancies of the Separatists and disorderly persons'.[83]

The spiritual outpourings of mechanics and labourers were not confined to chance encounters such as that related by Dering. They issued from the very pulpits themselves. The desecration of the pulpit by being occupied by base-born lay preachers who saw themselves as the mouthpieces of the Almighty was to many gentlemen an abomination whose implications were at least as much social as religious. If spiritual functions could appropriately be exercised by untutored illiterates, what other dignities could be denied to them? 'How fit would these men be for State imployment too?' enquired one satirical pamphleteer. 'Would not *How* the Cobler make a speciall Keeper of the great Seal in regard of his experience in Wax? ... Who fitter to be Master of the Horse than my Lord *Whatchicallums* Groom?' Lay preachers, moreover, included not only mechanics, but also women, who indulged, it was said, in sexual excesses with their male colleagues 'in a joynt labour for the procreating of young Saints to fill up the numbers of the new faith'.[84] No doubt many of the horrified readers of the account took such details literally, as indeed they were intended to.

No less alarming than the personnel of the lay preachers was the content of their sermons. To the frightened minds of respectable men and women there was nothing extravagant in the statement that 'all Sectaries and Schismatickes ... would have no King at all over them on Earth, nor Church.'[85] Indeed it was no doubt true of some of them. It was only to be expected that people with such strange and heterodox religious beliefs should be politically subversive also. Writing from London to his wife at home in Norfolk on 18 May 1642, Thomas Knyvett reflected sadly on the connection between religious heterodoxy and the decline of monarchical authority:

> Poore King, he growes still in more contempte & slyghte heer every day . . . ; And no wonder when the reverence & worshipp of the King of Kings comes to be constr'd superstitious & Idollatrus, yet no worshipp to much for the sonns of men.[86]

To many men who had been enthusiastic supporters of moderate reform in 1640, their whole ordered world, and more especially the deference and obedience due to them from their inferiors, appeared to be crumbling. They had supported reform to restore what had been lost, not to destroy the landmarks of order and civilization. In such circumstances some of them turned naturally for comfort to the monarchy as the symbol of that threatened order and authority. In turn, most of the others who remained, however uneasily, in opposition sought not for principles which would enable them to dispense with royal authority, but for assurances that they were not in fact defying the king's authority but upholding it. These assurances they received in abundance from their leaders, who moved from cold to hot war in 1642, asserting their determination not to turn the world upside down but to defend what they had rightfully restored.

SEVEN *Conflict 1642–6*

> ... who can stretch forth his hand against the Lord's anointed, and be guiltless?
>
> 1 Samuel 26 : 9.

> ... The matter, with us, is quite and generally mistaken, and the question altogether wrong stated, viz. Whether we should obey the king or parliament? For the king and parliament are not like two parallel lines, which can never meet, nor like two incompatible qualities, which cannot be both in one subject; nor like the Ark and Dagon, whom one house will not hold; nor like God and Mammon, which one man cannot serve: For by siding with ... the parliament, in those things which are according to law, we side with, and serve the king.
>
> *The vindication of the Parliament and their*
proceedings (1642), *Harleian Miscellany,* V
(1810), 292.

I

THE CONVENTIONAL DATE for the opening of the Civil War is 22 August 1642, when Charles I raised his standard at Nottingham. But the idea that this symbolic act was succeeded by a period of armed conflict and preceded by something less than this, albeit of undoubtedly worsening relations between Charles and his Parliament, does not altogether fit the facts. On the one hand the events of the preceding weeks had been punctuated by a number of armed clashes and a petition from Hertfordshire on 7 June, with its reference to 'the great Effusion of Blood made betwixt your Majesty's own Subjects' gives the impression of the war being already very much in progress.[1] On the other hand, far from being a period of unremitting armed conflict, the next few years were punctuated by a succession of admittedly abortive peace negotiations. This helps to explain why so many of the more moderate opponents of the king insisted on the strict observance of constitutional proprieties which seem to the modern reader to be inappropriate to a state of war.

Since the king's departure from London for York on 3 March, Englishmen had been increasingly dividing into two armed camps. According to Clarendon, who argues strongly for the advantages of the royal move to York, Charles had not only moved from hostile to friendly territory, but, once in York, acted as a magnet, drawing to his person not only the notables of the northern counties but also 'many persons of condition from London and those parts who had not the courage to attend upon him at Whitehall'. But on balance it seems likely that the move did more harm than good to the royalist cause. For in so far as moderate MPs were drawn in increasing numbers from Westminster to York, the opportunities for a royalist offensive in Parliament were lessened and Pym's task was made easier. Those who did remain were the more easily subjected to the varied forms of intimidation and persuasion of which Pym and his city allies were past masters.[2] Moreover, the king's removal to the north unquestionably diminished the attractiveness of his image in the more populous parts of the country as the symbol of order and authority, and many of those who were seriously alarmed at the popular excesses of 1641-2 felt abandoned in consequence. For every gentleman who forsook his 'country' in the south and east to join his royal master, there were thousands who stayed at home, for whom - for better or worse - Parliament and not the king was henceforth to be the one effective source of authority and protection. As was shown earlier, the popular excesses in Suffolk and Essex in the late summer and autumn of 1642 were an important factor in drawing the local gentry into the parliamentarian orbit.[3] For since March the king had been a very long way away.

But in the last resort 3 March is no more convincing as the climacteric date than is 22 August. For the events which followed it were not in essence new developments so much as the acceleration of a process which had begun at least as far back as the debates over the Grand Remonstrance in November 1641 and the mounting crisis of confrontation which had been broken by the king's attempted seizure of Lord

Kimbolton and the five members on 4 January 1642. The immediate response of Pym and his supporters to the tactical advantage conferred upon them by the royal adoption of extremist courses had been measures such as the Militia Ordinance and the parliamentary appointment of lord lieutenants and military commanders which spectacularly widened the gap between them and their opponents, and which were in a real sense a significant step along the road to civil war.[4] On 11 January, parliament ordered Sir John Hotham to occupy Hull, and on 23 April the civil war scenario was anticipated when the king stood outside that town and was refused entry by parliamentary commanders. Such parliamentary actions were clear breaches of the prerogative as it had hitherto been understood. There were no doubt some persons who had been profoundly shocked by royal extremism and wished to be reassured that Parliament was not embarking on a revolutionary course who were prepared to swallow whole Pym's arguments that these palpable invasions of the royal prerogative were justified by tradition and custom.[5] But not everyone was deceived. In making their unprecedented claims for the power of the two Houses at the expense of the monarchy, Pym and his colleagues had laid bare a vulnerable flank. The question was how far those who had striven to avert a breach between Charles and his Parliament but had been dispirited and disillusioned by the events of late December and early January were capable of seizing the opportunity which was thus presented to them.

II

In the opening days of 1642 the policy of moderation associated with Falkland and Hyde lay in ruins. Hyde's own *History* is eloquent about the dejection of its principal proponents, who had striven so hard to project the attractive image of a reforming monarchy which had been mocked by the king's recourse to extreme measures entirely without their privity, among them the attempted arrest of Kimbolton and the five members, the appointment of the Earl of Newcastle as Governor of Hull, and the royal attempt to take over the magazines there and at Kingston-upon-Thames. In the face of such discouraging portents it would hardly be a matter for surprise if the hurt and disillusioned moderates had retired from the political scene in despair. Instead they set to work to piece together the fragments of a policy which had been shattered by the events of late December and early January.[6]

The two central features of the political history of the subsequent months were the battle of the moderates and the extremists for control of royal policy, and, given the ascendancy of the former, their battle with Pym for the soul of the political centre. As to the first of these struggles, while, following the disastrous failure of the extremist courses of early January, the fortunes of the moderates were mostly in the ascendancy at court, the king's lack of fixed purpose and his tendency to vacillate between the policies associated with the queen and Digby on the one hand and those of Hyde and Falkland on the other was at times the latters' despair, and ensured that the trickle of returning sympathizers with the royal cause never became a flood.[7]

Pym was naturally determined to press home the advantage which had been presented to him on 4 January by the re-emergence of Cavalierism red in tooth and claw, and to use this and other incidents as arguments for further parliamentary encroachment on the prerogative. So long as the counsels of the queen and Digby could plausibly be represented as continuing to prevail at Whitehall – so long, as a later parliamentary declaration put it, as the arrest of the five members could be represented as 'but the prologue to a bloody tragedy'[8] which might yet be played out, it was not difficult to make out a rational justification for Pym's policies. If, however, the king could be won back to moderate causes, it was just possible that skilful parliamentary tactics which took the maximum advantage of even the slightest tendency of Pym and his associates to overplay what was undoubtedly a very strong hand might succeed in retrieving the situation.

For both sets of contestants the stakes were frighteningly high. After 4 January, Pym, Hampden and their associates could have no illusions about the price of failure. But again, as a consequence of these same events, any adviser on royal policy, however moderate his advice, was inevitably tarred with the Cavalier brush. It was not for nothing that Hyde urged the king early in March to burn a paper of his advising on policies, even though its contents were the pure milk of moderation. The paper emphasized that the king's greatest strength lay in the support of 'those persons who have been the severest assertors of the publick liberties . . . and value their own interests upon the preservation of your rights'. Hyde's paper hit a crucial nail squarely on the head in his assertion that Cavalier extremism suited Pym's book far better than the royal pursuit of moderate policies.[9] Pym could, of course, point out that the king's profession of the best of constitutional intentions was pure moonshine. He had given the impression of a moderate constitutional monarch in the previous year only to revert to type in late December and January. What had happened then would happen again. To cite the king's consent to bills as evidence of his intentions was absurd, argued a parliamentary declaration of 26 March, for at the very time that the bills were becoming law, royal designs were afoot to render them nugatory and to restore the *status quo ante* 1640.[10]

The first essential element in the attempt of the constitutional royalists to win back moderate men was an unequivocal repudiation of the extremist policies which had driven so many into Pym's camp. Above all, the *locus classicus* of royal extremism, the attempt on the five members, had to be disavowed. It was not enough for Charles to aver that 'he had no other Design upon that House ... then to require ... the Persons of those five Gentlemen'. Nothing less than a royal assurance that the charges had been totally abandoned was requisite to the purpose. A very reluctant king had to be made to eat humble pie. Although the opposition continued to insist on citing the events of 4 January as unequivocal evidence that royal policies could not be trusted and that further parliamentary encroachment on the prerogative was therefore necessary, it is not unlikely that the continual harping on the incident lost Pym some support. Some moderate men were reassured by royal acts of contrition, and by the king's plea early in March that even 'if the breach of Priviledge had been greater than hath beene ever before offered, our acknowledgment and retraction hath beene greater than ever King hath given'. There were still plenty of men who were desperately anxious to trust their king, even if Charles had given them ample grounds to distrust him.[11]

It was at such persons that the king's moderate advisers pitched their appeal. In doing so they did not scruple to employ some of the tactics of their opponents. Pym's skilful use of petitions, which often had their origins at least as much at Westminster as in the localities from which they purported to come has already been remarked, and there is no better example of the use to which he put them than his great speech of 25 January, a brilliant but not completely successful attempt to prevent a royalist parliamentary recovery from the self-inflicted wounds of the first week of that month. However, the exhaustive examination of the petitions to parliament which has been made by Professor Fletcher has led him to the conclusion that historians have been far too ready to attribute their origin to central direction. By contrast, he has stressed the need to see them as 'an authentic expression of deeply felt local opinion'. In the nature of things the evidence is not always conclusive, and it may be that Fletcher's revisionist view, while a useful corrective, swings too far in the opposite direction. While it is undoubtedly one of the great contributions of county and regional historians to make us more aware of the importance of local and regional initiatives in national affairs, many such initiatives in the matter of the petitions of 1641–2 probably owed something to factors ranging between gentle encouragement and positive pressure from Westminster.[12]

Such petitions continued to come in throughout 1642, but the succeeding months were also to see a number of petitions of a quite different sort, expressing serious disquiet at Pym's policies and supporting the moderate royalist programme. Falkland and Hyde seem in fact to be taking a leaf out of Pym's book, and – *pace* Fletcher – it is more than likely that some of these petitions originated at Whitehall, Hampton Court and – from March onwards – York. Pym's supporters certainly seem to have thought so, though the pamphlet which describes such petitions as 'pretended (though falsely) to have beene delivered to his Majestie and other to his Privy Council' was decidedly a case of the pot calling the kettle black.[13]

With the possible exception of the Kentish petition, the most remarkable document of this sort emanating from the provinces was technically not a petition at all, but a declaration in the summer of 1642 from Herefordshire which so clearly reflects the ideas associated with Hyde and Falkland that it is difficult not to discern the influence of at least one of them in its composition. With what seemed impressive impartiality it condemned both the arbitrary royal policies of the 1630s and those which were currently being pursued by Pym and his colleagues. It called for the maintenance of the Protestant religion, the king's just power, the laws of the land and the liberty of the subject – unexceptionable aims it would seem – but went on to itemize the ways in which Pym's policies were doing violence to all of these things: by encouraging sectarian excesses and tumultuous assemblies; by disregarding Magna Carta and the Petition of Right in the matter of arbitrary imprisonment; and by encouraging petitions from 'the mutinous rabble', while disregarding the complaints expressed in petitions such as those from moderate royalists in London in February. No less alarming to Pym than the petitions themselves was the fact that the royalists were seeking to emulate his tactics by encouraging not only petitions but the demonstrations which accompanied them. The assembling of thousands of Kentish gentlemen at Blackheath on 29 April and their selection of 280 of their number to carry their petition to Parliament bore a suspicious resemblance to the intimidatory tactics which Pym and his colleagues had employed on numerous occasions. Their reaction was swift and brutal. The Kentish ringleaders were arrested, as was Sir George Benion, the main spirit behind one of the London petitions. Benion was fined and imprisoned, and the authorities discreetly looked the other way when his splendid London house was looted and defaced. According to Professor Everitt, the imprisonment of Kentish moderate leaders had the effect of putting protest in that county into the hands of royalist ultras, a development which may not have been altogether displeasing to Pym.[14]

The royal replies to petitions are models of moderation and conciliatoriness, whether dealing with strongly royalist petitions such as that from the gentlemen of Cornwall; or loyal petitions which yet express serious disquiet at the rift between king and Parliament, like those from Lancashire and Hertfordshire on 6 and 7 June, when the king joined his own regrets to those of the petitioners, carefully pointing out that blame for this state of affairs rested with the men at Westminster rather than with him; or more sharply critical petitions, like that from the town of Lancaster on 11 May, where the royal reply gently pointed out that the arguments were based upon misinformation, and attempted to put the record straight.[15]

In general, then, the strategy of royal moderation which took over in mid-January 1642 was twofold. In the first place, it offered reassurance to the political nation on those matters where extremist royal actions had given rise to serious alarm and the defection of moderate men, however unwillingly, to the opposition camp. Secondly, it sought to make maximum political capital out of those opposition policies which, whatever justification was offered for them, could most plausibly be labelled as arbitrary and innovatory. The royalists in short sought to steal their opponents' clothes and present themselves as the guardians of tradition and liberty against innovation and arbitrary rule. The royal instructions to the assize judges in the spring emphasized the need to punish both sectaries and recusants in the spirit of the royal promise to defend the Protestant settlement 'without declining either to the right hand or to the Left', and to uphold the privileges of Parliament without yielding to 'any suche vnwarrantable power in either or both howses of Parliament which in some thinges hath bene lately vsurped'.[16] Such professions would not have cut much ice if made in the opening weeks of the year. Made when the king seemed to be striving to live up to the image of a constitutional monarch in which he had been cast by his moderate advisers, they were likely to command more attention.

While it was important to challenge Pym and his associates on every issue on which it could be claimed that they were guilty of constitutional innovation, it was no less important to give the impression not of mere stonewalling resistance but of genuine willingness to entertain the possibility of compromise. A good, if at first sight rather surprising, example is the king's attitude to the control of the militia. Charles had indicated his willingness to compromise within limits early in February, and on 11 March his own Militia Bill was introduced in Parliament. It was only after it had been altered out of all recognition in parliamentary committee that he exercised his veto. As he later claimed in a declaration of 17 May, 'We never denied the thing, onely denied the way'.[17] The militia issue touched the royal prerogative at one of its tenderest points, but the wisdom of the royal policy of showing some willingness to compromise must be apparent to readers who recall how militia control and training had been one of the primary issues of localist resistance to the centralizing tendencies of the decades before 1640.[18]

By the time that Parliament introduced the Nineteen Propositions on 3 June, the parliamentary and royal positions had clearly become irreconcilable and conflict was virtually inevitable.[19] Historians of political thought now recognize the masterly royal reply to the Nineteen Propositions as a document of crucial importance,[20] and it is certainly a crystal-clear statement of the moderate royalist position. The reply was not an outright rejection of every one of the parliamentary propositions, on some of which the royal tone is conciliatory and even enthusiastic; for example, the proposals for the education of the children of Catholics in the Protestant faith[21] and the recommendation of an alliance with the United Provinces.[22] But Charles was adamant in those matters where the propositions sought to make further substantial inroads on his prerogative; the control of the militia and navy, of commanders of ports and strong places, the demand for the dismissal of the royal guard, the curtailment of the prerogative of pardon in so far as it extended to popish priests and recusants, and, the last straw, parliamentary control of the education and marriage of the royal children.

Of these parliamentary demands none was more crucial than the propositions dealing with the choice and responsibility of ministers. No one had laboured more diligently than Hyde to persuade Charles to make bridge-appointments acceptable to Parliament, but it was a central feature of Hyde's policy that the king must be trusted to make such appointments himself. This was worlds removed from the demand of the first of the propositions that ministers should be removed if not approved by Parliament and that all future nominees must be so approved. While it could be argued that this was a somewhat less extreme position than had been canvassed earlier in the year – that Parliament should actually nominate ministers as distinct from having a negative voice over their appointment – it was only marginally so. On the whole question of ministerial responsibility, the royal reply to the propositions is seen at its most subtle and persuasive. The masterstroke of the argument was to cite the right of impeachment as the reason why the desired parliamentary control of ministerial appointments was unnecessary as well as constitutionally objectionable. Given the Triennial Act, and, perhaps even more, the act that the present Parliament could not be dissolved without its own consent, the reality of impeachment, coupled with the royal assurance that ministers would not be allowed to plead the royal command in defence of their actions, were, it was argued, as ample an assurance against ministerial delinquency as any reasonable Parliament could desire. However, the force of this argument was somewhat weakened by the royal refusal to consent to that part of the second proposition which stipulated that no public act of the Privy Council might be deemed to carry royal authority unless done with the consent of a majority of Privy Councillors and *attested under their hands*. It was true that this was a startling innovation. It was no less true that to refuse to consent to it would make it highly unlikely that sufficient evidence could be accumulated for a successful ministerial impeachment.[23]

The royal answer to the Nineteen Propositions is an eloquent manifesto of constitutional royalism which emphasizes the abandonment of that Cavalierism which had prevailed so disastrously in early January. From the time of the royal reply to the Grand Remonstrance in the previous year both sides had been increasingly engaged in that process of appealing 'downwards to the people' which had so profoundly disturbed Sir Edward Dering and other moderate, conservative gentlemen. These declarations and counter-declarations were designed to be read not only by MPs but by private gentlemen; read not only in the privacy of the study, but aloud from the pulpit. Hyde complains, perhaps a trifle disingenuously, that while the king desired that both points of view should be freely heard and openly discussed, 'the agents for the Parliament took as much care to suppress the King's [declaration] as to publish their own.'[24] The reply to the Nineteen Propositions is probably the most significant of all those royal declarations demonstrating the gulf between the king and his opponents and the grounds on which he based his appeal to the political nation; not as the innovating despot of Pym's picture, but as the exponent of the ancient English concept of *dominium politicum et regale*, or mixed monarchy.[25] The royal argument depicts Pym and his colleagues as having gone beyond the point at which the proper constitutional equilibrium between King, Lords and Commons had been re-established following the personal rule of the 1630s, to encroach materially upon a moderate royal prerogative as defined in the theory of mixed monarchy. To cite but one example drawn from the argument of the *Answer to the Nineteen Propositions*: while the Commons unquestionably had the right to impeach ministers, and the Lords to judge them, their *appointment* was a royal prerogative and Parliament had no negative voice in the matter. But while the king took his stand on the powers traditionally assigned to him according to the theory of mixed monarchy, he was emphatically not prepared to countenance their reduction to dimensions more appropriate to a Duke of Venice than a King of England: to remain the ceremonial centrepiece of the pomp and majesty of the monarchy, but 'as to true and reall Power . . . but the outside, but the Picture, but the signe of a King'. In taking this firm, if conciliatory, line, and resting his case on the statement *Nolumus Leges Angliae mutari* Charles was trenchantly asserting that his adversaries' claim to be the defenders of the ancient constitution against innovating monarchy was the reverse of the truth. Indeed it is more than likely that his *Answer* may have had an impact on the more moderate MPs and have influenced the parliamentary modification of the Propositions during the closing week of June; not least in crucial matters such as the withdrawal of the limits on the size of the Privy Council and the parliamentary veto on some ministerial appointments, including that of privy councillors.[26] Conceivably the nucleus of what was shortly to become the peace group at Westminster was making a final and unavailing attempt to avoid war.

III

One product of some of the developments described above was the promulgation of mutually contradictory claims on the obedience of the subject: as evidenced by the refusal in March of some of the king's nominees to bring in their lieutenancy commissions to Parliament for cancellation;[27] by the rival claims of the Earl of Newcastle and the elder Sir John Hotham as royal and parliamentary Governors of Kingston-upon-Hull, and of Sir John Pennington and the Earl of Warwick to command the royal fleet. When ordered by the king to give way, Warwick gave what was to become a classic reply that 'he cannot doe it without the consent of that power which had reposed that trust in him'.[28] Hotham offered similar excuses and on 23 May treated some Yorkshire gentlemen who had accepted his invitation to Hull for the occasion to a disquisition on 'why the Subject being Commanded by the Parliament ought not to disobey, though by the King commanded the Contrary'. The Hull business was to feature prominently in the controversy between king and parliament, the king arguing that the withholding of his property from him boded ill for the property rights of the subject, and Parliament, in the person of its most able propagandist, Henry Parker, not only denying the validity of the royal argument from property rights, but claiming that, far from being withheld from the king, Hull and its contents were being 'reserved for him, in better hands than he would have put them'.[29]

As tension mounted in the high summer of 1642, more and more people were confronted by this problem of competing authority, and nowhere was the issue more spectacularly and agonizingly pinpointed than in the mutually contradictory claims of the parliamentary Militia Ordinance and the royal Commission of Array. The use of Commissions of Array arose out of uncertainty about the status and loyalty of the lieutenancy following Parliament's tampering earlier in the year. But recourse to this 'old ordinary way for the Preservation of the King and Kingdom' would probably never have been adopted if the king's advisers had been aware, as they ought to have been, of the hornets' nest they were stirring up by their researches into the early Tudor and Medieval past before the Marian establishment of the lieutenancy. The analogy with the historical justifications advanced for expedients such as Ship Money and forest fines in the 1630s ought to have been sufficient to deter them. The royalists argued that the Militia Ordinance was illegal since it lacked the royal consent; Parliament claimed that the Commissions of Array were illegal, since they had been abolished by the Marian statute. As to the abolition of that statute in the first Parliament of James I, it was surely unlikely that Parliament would do away with the statute which carefully limited the military obligations of the subject in order to re-establish a pre-existing state of affairs which 'did establish a Power in the King without Limitation . . . for such is the Power of the Commission of Array'. As was shown earlier, this in fact had been the effect of the Jacobean statute which substituted prerogative for statutory control.[30] In an argument reminiscent of St John's defence of Hampden in the Ship Money case of 1637, one parliamentary pamphleteer argued that, while power over the armed forces of the realm rested with the king, this must be exercised 'by lawfull meanes and not by Commission of Array', recourse to which was a clear indication that the king had again fallen under the sway of evil advisers. Herein lay the justification for vesting control of the militia in parliamentary hands 'until such time as the King be better informed, and the Common-wealth . . . setled againe in peace and safety'. Such arguments told more heavily than the studied impartiality of the great legist John Selden, who no doubt as much delighted his old parliamentary colleague Pym by his declaration that the Commissions of Array were illegal in one speech, as he infuriated him by reaching the same verdict about the Militia Ordinance in another. Such objective judgements were regarded as out of place in an emergency situation.[31]

The great Victorian historian of the period, whose verdicts one never challenges lightly, was surely wrong to describe the controversy over the Commission of Array as 'of no practical importance whatever'.[32] To many people both the unfamiliarity and the antiquity of the device told heavily against it. Reporting his impressions to Secretary Nicholas, following his completion of the west country circuit in the summer of 1642, the justice of assize Sir Robert Foster remarked on how he had been pressed on several occasions – without success – to give an opinion against the Commission of Array. The general impression which Foster had obtained while on circuit was that both the Commission and the Militia Ordinance were very unpopular. On the other hand, he reported that the moderate tone and contents of royal pronouncements and policies over recent months had met with general approval, a royal advantage which might easily be dissipated by the fears aroused by the Commission of Array that the king was about to revert to extremist policies. Parliamentarian propaganda made the most of such fears, a declaration of 1 July denouncing the Commission of Array as 'a heavier yoke of Bondage . . . than . . . Ship Money'. Certainly in Devon there were future royalists as well as Roundheads who saw the Commission as offering a dangerous threat to property, while in Somerset such views found expression in a petition from the Grand Jury at Bath assizes on

25 July. It was rumoured in Somerset that the Commission of Array would be made the pretext for arbitrary taxation and the exaction from poor people of labour services on military works one day in every week.[33] In Kent, however, the Commission of Array was supported by some who were later to be Roundheads. Conversely in Suffolk not all of those who gave their support to the parliamentary Militia Ordinance were enthusiastic parliamentarians. In each case considerations of public order may have been paramount for the Commission of Array was implemented before the Militia Ordinance in Kent, while there was little possibility of the royalists exercising effective sway in Suffolk. The latter county was, of course, soon to become part of the entrenched parliamentarian stronghold of the Eastern Association, though on 1 September Sir Nathaniel Barnardiston, the most important parliamentarian in the county, warned against the danger that troops raised under the authority of the Militia Ordinance might be put to a very different use if and when the Commissioners of Array got to work in Suffolk. The danger never materialized and attempts to implement the Commission in East Anglia were totally damp squibs.[34]

Things were less quiet elsewhere. According to an admittedly biased account emanating from the Cheshire Commissioners of Array, Sir William Brereton, who was to become the leading parliamentarian in Cheshire, attempted to put the parliamentary Militia Ordinance into execution in Chester and 'had bene puld in peices by the Cittyzens had not the Maior and Recorder . . . Conveyed him away with a gaurd [sic]'. The parliamentary commissioners were no less frustrated in their attempt to raise men at a clandestine meeting near Nantwich.[35] There were violent scenes in Leicester in late June when the long-standing feud between the Greys and the Hastings took a new turn with the Earl of Stamford, as the Parliament's lord lieutenant, attempting to muster men under the Militia Ordinance, and Henry Hastings, son of the Earl of Huntingdon, reading the Commission of Array supported by armed miners from his coal-pits.[36] Attempts to read the Commission of Array in various places in Devon between July and September were frustrated by mass demonstrations,[37] while Lord Chandos's efforts to do the same for Gloucestershire at Cirencester were 'stifled in the birth and crusht by the rude hand of the multitude', an account which is the more credible since it proceeded from the hand of a parliamentarian supporter.[38] At least twenty-five people died in a clash between the contending parties at Marshall's Elm in Somerset on 2 August, but ultimately the temporarily victorious royalists were dis-

persed, some with the Marquis of Hertford across the Bristol Channel
to South Wales, and others under Sir Ralph Hopton to Cornwall in
an attempt to recoup royalist fortunes from a new base in the far south
west.[39] In Cornwall parliament's deputy lieutenants and a group of
local royalist MPs who were expelled from Parliament in consequence
of their action both had meetings to implement the Militia Ordinance
and the Commission of Array respectively, and the deadlock was not
resolved in favour of the royalists until after the arrival of Hopton and
his small but determined band of royalist fugitives from Somerset at
the end of September.[40]

IV

The clashes between Commissioners of Array and parliamentary Militia Commissioners were mostly confrontations between determined
men who knew their own minds. But there were many people in
responsible positions for whom the issues were by no means straightforward, and who experienced agonies of indecision when subjected to
intense pressure from both sides. Although the Commission of Array
had bypassed the lieutenancy, the role of lord and deputy lieutenants
was especially vulnerable in view of their importance in connection
with the Militia Ordinance. The Earl of Leicester, Lord Lieutenant
of Kent, who was certainly not an out-and-out Cavalier, ultimately
resigned rather than execute the Militia Ordinance.[41] Lord Paget,
Lord Lieutenant of Buckinghamshire, despite having executed the parliamentary Militia Ordinance in his county, finally resigned his post
and joined the king in June 1642 on the grounds that the Parliament
was clearly undertaking 'a preparation of arms against the King' under
the shadow of loyalty.[42] On the other hand, the Lord Lieutenant of
Lincolnshire, Lord Willoughby of Parham, a young and inexperienced
man in his early twenties, refused to yield to intense royal pressure
to desist from implementing the Militia Ordinance. Willoughby wrig-
gled, pleading his tender years and the fact that the Ordinance had
passed both Houses with the support of persons much better qualified
to judge its legality than himself. There was, he groaned, 'nothing of
greater Heaviness to me than to receive a Command from your Majesty whereunto my Endeavours cannot give so ready an Obedience as
my Affections'. Torn between conflicting loyalties, he begged the king
not to command him to do what 'must needs render me false to those
that rely on me, and so make me more unhappier than any other

Misery [that] can befal me'. His mind was made up, but the decision had clearly not been altogether easy and a residual ambivalence shines out of every line of his letter.[43]

Willoughby refused the royal clemency which had been offered to him on condition of the return to his proper allegiance. Such offers were an important part of the royal strategy and were undoubtedly intended not only to bring about defection from, but also have an unsettling effect upon, the ranks of the king's opponents, ranging from the most exalted – as in the case of the royal declaration of 9 August which offered a pardon to the Earl of Essex (and to his subordinate officers) on condition that he laid down his arms within six days[44] – to the relatively obscure (at least in national terms) Cheshire gentleman Sir George Booth, who was subjected to similar pressure. The royal letter of 16 August to Booth is a good if unsuccessful example of the exercise of the subtle art of winning men. It expressed shocked surprise at Booth's apparent defection, while charitably assuming that he had been deluded into implementing the parliamentary Militia Ordinance by 'those plausible Artifices of our Adversaries ... practiced to deceaue our people'. The exercise of moderation and patience was similarly urged by the king on his Cheshire commissioners, but, if any credence is to be attached to the complaints against them, they did not always observe these admirable precepts.[45]

V

'Oh sweete hart, I am now in a great strayght what to doe.' Thomas Knyvett's *cri de coeur*, in a letter of 18 May from Westminster to his wife as Ashwellthorpe in Norfolk, tells of his own personal agony of indecision, after having been presented with a commission from the Earl of Warwick, the parliamentary Lord Lieutenant of Norfolk, to take up his company under the Militia Ordinance, and a few hours later reading the king's declaration 'point Blanck against it'.[46] Knyvett's anxious consultations 'with some vnderstanding men' about the appropriate course of action to take were, his letter suggests, paralleled by countless other protracted conversations between friends and neighbours talking perhaps into the early hours. On 19 August Sir John Holland sought the counsel of his fellow MP and Norfolk militia-commissioner, Sir John Potts, about how to 'frame & fashion my carriage heere to the advantage of what becomes every Honest Man to Endeavour, the Peace of his Country'. It was no doubt as a result of such discussions that the abortive plan for a neutrality pact in Norfolk emerged.[47] Similar canvassing of opinion took place in Kent. In letters of 18 June and 20 July Henry Oxinden of Deane wrote to his cousin of the same name, who dwelt at Barham in the east of the county, asking for his views on the same matter and more particularly soliciting information on the state of opinion in his part of the county about whether the Militia Ordinance would be obeyed.[48]

Among those imprisoned for causing the king's proclamation against the Militia Ordinance to be read was the Lord Mayor of London, Sir Richard Gurney. This occurred on 11 July, when Gurney was dispatched to the Tower, and a month later he was dismissed from office and replaced by Pym's ally, Alderman Pennington, one of the radical London MPs.[49] It was argued earlier that the prelude to these events, the capture of the Court of Common Council by the radicals in the election of December 1641, was not a revolt against a municipal government which had been an ally of the Court from the beginning, but arose rather out of the need of Pym and his city friends to counter a flow of sympathy back towards the Court among those who had lent support to the early reforms of the Long Parliament; a movement which is apparent not only in the City of London but in the country in general and Parliament in particular.[50] The radical change in the sympathies of the majority of the Common Council was followed by a stream of measures in which the power of the Lord Mayor was curtailed and that of the lower City court increased; a period in which the lord mayor and aldermen on the one hand, and the Common Council on the other, were at daggers drawn. The removal of Gurney and his replacement by Pennington ends the first stage of this development. Previous to this, the position of the lord mayor and his aldermanic colleagues was threatened, not simply by the replacement of a moderate reforming by a radical Common Council, but also by developments in Parliament itself, whereby Pym and his associates delivered a number of attacks, as fierce as they were unwarranted and unjust, upon the City fathers' alleged support for royal tyranny during the 1630s. The whittling away of the royal prerogative was paralleled by the whittling away of the municipal prerogatives of lord mayor and aldermen. The controversy over the control of the militia presents a particularly significant parallel between events in Parliament and in the City. Parliament's usurpation of the royal control of the militia is paralleled by the Common Council's creation of the City Committee of Safety, which took control of the London trained-bands out of the hands of the lord mayor. In these circumstances it is hardly surprising that Gurney actively opposed the Militia Ordinance, and his removal from office was essential if the City were to be made safe for Pym.[51]

VI

The argument of the earlier part of this chapter has emphasized the importance of both the new-found royalist moderation and the increasingly radical policies of the opposition in winning support for the king in the weeks and months before the war. In the last resort, however, there were probably many people who were more moved by instinctive loyalties of a sort which had bound man and lord from time immemorial. Sir Edmund Verney, who was to die for his king bearing the royal standard at Edgehill, confessed that he would have been content for the king to yield to the demands of his opponents. But in the last resort he had no choice but 'in honour and gratitude to follow my master', whom he had served and whose bread he had eaten for nearly thirty years.[52] The motives of Lord St Leger are less clear, but may well have been similar. His support for the policies of the king's opponents had lost him 'allready my mothers blessing and purchased all my friends curses', as he wrote to Secretary Falkland on 11 August, informing him that, following an interview with the king at York, he was prepared to bring over to the royal camp not only himself but also his troop of horse.[53]

Despite the importance of family ties in the political connections of the seventeenth century, one of the most disturbing aspects of the Civil War was the way in which it so frequently split families. Sir Edmund Verney might not approve of the policies for which he and the royalists fought, but he was grief-stricken at the fact that his son, Ralph, chose to serve against the king and therefore against both his father and his younger brother.[54] Clarendon remarks on how, among the noblemen who fought under Essex's command at Edgehill on 23 October, were Lords Rochford and Fielding 'whose fathers, the earls of Dover and Denbigh, charged as volunteers in the King's guards of horse'.[55] No less inimical to considerations of social order and obedience, when viewed in the light of the observations in an earlier chapter about the *in loco parentis* relationship of masters and their apprentices, was the parliamentary ordinance of 1 November 1642, securing apprentices who joined up from legal action by their masters for the violation of their indentures, and providing that their time spent in the forces should be counted as part of their apprenticeship. The ordinance, in Clarendon's view, was in practice derogatory not only to the authority of masters over their apprentices, but also of fathers who had procured apprenticeship indentures for their children, and 'by this means many children were engaged in that service not only against the consent, but against the persons, of their fathers'.[56]

For many and probably most of the combatants in the war the side on which they fought was not a matter of personal choice – a luxury confined chiefly to the propertied classes – but something for their betters to decide. In many parts of Lancashire, for instance, the Stanleys were supreme and 'looked upon as of absolute power over that people'. As lord lieutenant of the county, James Stanley, Lord Strange, who succeeded to the earldom of Derby in 1642, was a fanatical royalist, who took care that like-minded people were appointed as his deputy lieutenants. Together they wielded power over the lives of a great many people, both their tenants and other persons, many of whom later claimed that they had been forced to fight for the king against their will. Adam Martindale tells how his brother, Henry,

> knew not where to hide his head for my Lord of Derby's officers
> had taken up a custom of summoning such as he and many other
> persons, upon paine of death, to appeare at generall musters and
> thence to force them away with such weapons as they had, if they
> were but pitchforks, to Bolton; the reare being brought up with
> troopers that had commission to shoot such as lagged behind. . . .

Yet it would seem that the Stanley power, which, as Clarendon admitted, 'depended more upon the fear than love of the people', was by no means an unmixed blessing to the royal cause. The Cheshire Commissioners of Array related how, on their way from York to their native county, they stopped at Manchester, where they found '500 men in Armes to keep out ye Lord Strange'. But access was not denied to the Commissioners who were dined in the town and were very impressed by the fact that the hostility of the inhabitants was reserved for the person of Strange and extended neither to the king nor to themselves.[57]

An admittedly hostile and therefore biased account of a meeting of Somerset royalist notables at Ham in August, in order to consider the implementation of the Commission of Array, reports Lord Poulett as claiming to exercise a similar if less extensive sort of power over humble people in east Somerset, while in the west of that county, Sir John Stawell is credited by the same account with a brutally frank assertion of the realities of hierarchy and tenurial dependence as a prime factor in securing a following for the royalist cause. Stawell observed that 'he hath great Lordships and Mannors about the West part of the shire, and . . . his Tenants most of them holdeth their Lands by Rack-rent; so that if they would not obey his command, he might out with them'.[58]

Professor Underdown's contention that there was a connexion between local economies and topography on the one hand and popular culture and political allegiance on the other in this part of England, has already been remarked on in another context. Its significance in this is that he also employs it to emphasize the importance of 'plebeian culture', as distinct from 'patrician leadership', as a determinant of the political attitudes of ordinary people, which operated independently of the more commonly emphasized considerations of deference and hierarchical authority. Historians have always differed in their estimates of the extent to which those who bore arms did so out of enthusiasm for one or other cause or simply because their betters told them to do so, and it may be that, in the inevitable absence of conclusive proof, they have been too ready to attach weight to the latter consideration. But all in all, it seems not improbable that sheer indifference was the most common of all attitudes among those who bore arms on both sides. The view that a necessary ingredient of any efficient army is a high degree of popular identification with one or other of the causes being contested and understanding of the issues at stake is one that overstates the idealism and commitment of common soldiers while underrating the efficacy of strict military discipline in welding such men into a fighting force, as any person who has served in any war knows well. That there were ordinary men who took sides in the war with zeal and enthusiasm and that this might infect their less politically conscious comrades is not for a moment in doubt. But that such persons were more than a small minority of those fighting on both sides is surely unlikely. As Professor Underdown himself admits, many even of that minority of the male population who bore arms 'had very low levels of commitment'.[59] Roundhead and Cavalier soldiers, like most of their successors in wars down to our own time, fought prompted not by enthusiasm or understanding but by that combination of deference to and fear of authority which is the prime cohesive force of all armies in all ages.

The territorial influence of royalist magnates like the Earls of Derby and Newcastle in the north was paralleled on the parliamentarian side by that of the Earl of Warwick. Warwick's power in Essex, like that of Derby in Lancashire, flowed more from the long ascendancy of his family in the county than from his official position as parliamentary lord lieutenant. Warwick never dominated Norfolk, of which he was also parliament's lieutenant in opposition to the royal nominee, the Earl of Mowbray, to anything like the same degree. But in Essex he was supreme. A newsletter of 7 June reported that his deputies, doubting their own ability to weld the county into an armed camp for Parliament, had persuaded the authorities in Westminster to recall him temporarily from his command of the fleet in the Downs 'to cum to animate his Countrymen'. There can be no doubt that Warwick's personal authority and local and national prestige was at least as important a factor as political, religious and ideological commitment to the parliamentarian cause in making Essex perhaps the most solidly Roundhead county in England.[60]

VII

To people brought up on horror stories about the Thirty Years War in Germany and the civil strife from which England had been rescued by the Tudors, Civil War was a dreadful prospect. Moreover, in addition to the terrors of rapine and pillage, war disrupted everyday life; reduced landowners' income; rendered them liable to crippling taxes; separated areas of commodity production from markets and export outlets; and set members of the same family at each other's throats. This sort of consequence was understood only too well by unpolitical persons such as Lady Anne Maynard, who, in a letter of 18 October 1643 to Sir Thomas Barrington, the foremost of the Essex deputy lieutenants, asking for a reduction in her assessment, pleaded her own inability 'to discover the depth of this great and unhappy Contestation ... that requiringe the helpe of a Braine farre surpassing that of a womans weaknesse'.[61] Such lack of understanding was not, however, confined to her sex. And some who comprehended cared nothing for the issues. If many of the active participants on both sides knew little and cared less about these issues, there were others whose neutralism was a positive force to be reckoned with, as distinct from the passive grumblings which characterize the utterances of hapless conscripts in any war in any period.

It is far too easy to forget that the primary concern of most Englishmen during the war remained what it had always been, whether or not the war impinged on their daily lives. In the early months of the war many Oxfordshire gentlemen seem to have been far more concerned with their own farming than with the king's military needs, or such is the impression given by the complaints about the requisitioning of horses for the royal service heard by the Oxfordshire Grand Jury.[62] Similarly on the other side both of the country and of the conflict, Sir Thomas Barrington complained that if the requisitioning of horses by the Lord General's officers were not curtailed in Essex, 'our Harvest must perish and truely ye Countries will not be continewed in their affection'.[63] Of course, failure to get in the harvest could be disastrous to the war efforts of both sides. Nevertheless there were times when response to the peak periods of demand for agriculture labour overrode everything else, including military discipline and military security. For example, the plans to send troops from Essex in August 1643 to counter the royalist threat to Cambridge; to raise troops in Cheshire to attack Nantwich in the spring of 1644, or in Yorkshire to guard against a threatened royalist attack in August of the same year, were all put in jeopardy by the natural preference of local soldiers for following the plough over military campaigning.[64]

VIII

The transition from cold to hot war brought, if anything, an intensification of the propaganda struggle which had been waged since the royal reply to the Grand Remonstrance in the late autumn of 1641. Of the two contending parties the Roundheads probably had the more difficult task in that Hyde and Falkland, while having to contend with the revival of militant Cavalierism as an expected consequence of war, did their best to see that royalism presented a moderate and attractive face to the world. Both the content and the tone of most royalist pamphlets suggest that they were aimed especially at the sort of conservatively minded country gentlemen who had disliked the policies and exactions of Charles's personal government in the 1630s, and were therefore the more susceptible to arguments that Parliament was now guilty of similar and more serious illegalities. Many of them were convinced by the portrayal of the Crown as a bulwark against the threats to order, hierarchy, property and social and religious decency posed by tumultuous mobs and frenzied sectaries – the direct consequences, it was claimed, of revolt against royal authority.[65]

Royalist propaganda was the more effective in that it frankly admitted the royal mistakes of the past; more than that, it even endeavoured to make political capital out of them. In the 1630s, it was now freely admitted, the danger to Englishmen's liberty and property had come from the monarchy, guided by evil advisers and encouraged by Laudian churchmen. In continually drawing attention to these past tendencies, which had unfortunately surfaced again for a brief moment in January 1642 Pym and his friends were, it was argued, attempting to divert attention from their own irregularities. In a brilliant passage Clarendon describes their employment of 'the same principles . . . to the wresting all sovereign power from the Crown, which the Crown had a little before made use of for the extending of its authority and power beyond its bounds to the prejudice of the just rights of the subject'.[66] Moreover, as any number of royal declarations and royalist pamphlets emphasized, the Roundheads had gone much further in this direction than the king had ever done, and in matters such as arbitrary imprisonment and illegal taxation had flagrantly violated that Petition of Right which had been intended to curb the arbitrary behaviour not of parliaments but of kings. The declaration of 8 December 1642 made a great show of hoisting the king's opponents with their own petards by citing against them what it described, with heavy irony, as 'that excellent Speech of Mr Pym's' on the subject of the dire consequences of disregarding the law.[67] Needless to say, the parliamentarians pleaded dire necessity as justifying these and other legal and constitutional irregularities, as well as pointing out that the king himself was by no means guiltless of similar practices. 'If the nature of War be duly considered', argued a parliamentary declaration of 27 March 1643 in the course of negotiations with the king at Oxford, 'it must needs be acknowledged that it is incompatible with the ordinary Rules of a peacable Government.' As Clarendon gleefully pointed out, similar arguments from 'supposed necessity' had been advanced in favour of royal encroachments on the liberty of the subject during the 1630s.[68]

The safety of the kingdom might be the supreme law, but what rendered the measures of the Parliament especially open to criticism was the patent incompleteness of the body which promulgated them – 'no more [a] Parliament than a Pye-powder Court at *Bartholomew-Fair*', as one royalist pamphlet was to put it in 1647. It was incomplete in the double sense of having neither 'fulnesse of Members nor . . . any head at all'.[69] The restoration of a full parliament by the re-admission of the now absent MPs was one of the conditions insisted upon by the king in the spring of 1643 before he would agree to the disbanding of the armies as the prelude to peace.[70] For some time following December 1643, when Charles summoned the excluded and other MPs to meet in a so-called 'Parliament' at the royalist headquarters in Oxford, he had a further weapon at his disposal. For it could be argued that although the ranks of the Commons at Oxford were a good deal thinner than those at Westminster, there were far more peers at Oxford, and, of course, there was the king himself without whom no Parliament had any constitutional standing.[71]

A pamphlet of 1642 which dismissed the king's legitimate, and hitherto, unquestioned, claims to be an essential part of Parliament as a recent innovation was not likely to carry much conviction.[72] Others treated the absence of the king, the great majority of the peers, and many of the Commons, from Westminster as part of a deliberate design to render Parliament incomplete and unrepresentative, and therefore nugatory.[73] Yet another line, at least as far as the king's absence was concerned, was the broad, down-to-earth view taken by a parliamentary declaration of 3 November 1642 that it was absurd to let the country go to the dogs because the king 'seduced by wicked Counsell, will not hearken to us'. Parliament as the representative body of the kingdom was obviously a much better judge than the king of what was required for the safety of the kingdom, though how far it was absurd to regard this truncated body as representative of the realm was a question left unanswered.[74] Another ingenious argument which equated the king's physical absence with 'the want of his voluntary concurrence' with, for instance, the reforms of 1641, was open to the obvious criticism that there was a world of difference between his consent to measures such as the Triennial Bill and the attainder of Strafford, however much he may have disliked them, and his complete refusal to concur, however unwillingly, with later measures such as the amended Militia Bill.[75]

The events of 1642 and the controversies around them raised in an acute form the problem of the locus of sovereignty in England. Royal declarations and royalist pamphlets had been quick to point out that the effect of the Nineteen Propositions was to rob the king of all real power and to place sovereignty in Parliament. Their opponents were not unduly worried by the charge, for they had accepted the idea of parliamentary sovereignty as early as 26 May 1642 in the parliamentary remonstrance defending Hotham's actions at Hull.[76] The idea was sometimes rather incongruously and dangerously coupled with the notion of Parliament's deriving its power from the people, though in such cases parliamentarian writers, of whom the ablest and most prominent was Henry Parker,[77] went to great trouble to stress that this must not be interpreted to mean that they favoured democracy, a form of government 'when meane persons and of base condition are set over the rest'.[78] But even this carefully made qualification, intended to underline the social and political conservatism of the parliamentarians, was made skilful use of by royalist propaganda. A royal declaration of May 1642 made great play with Parliament's equation of itself with the kingdom as a whole, 'so by the word *Kingdom* they intend to exclude all Our people who are out of their walls'.[79] The fact that no one could possibly suspect the royalists of arguing in favour of democracy or popular sovereignty gave them an advantage over their opponents, whose insistence that sovereignty rested in Parliament laid them wide open to the charge that it was not only the king but the electorate whom they excluded from effective power and influence.[80]

The emphatic disavowal of any democratic implications for their doctrine of parliamentary sovereignty was intended to reassure men of substance that their conservative instincts were shared by the parliamentarians who could be relied upon to prevent things getting out of hand. It was for this reason that they attached such enormous importance to the support of noblemen such as Essex, Salisbury, Pembroke, Northumberland, Warwick and Saye and Sele for the cause, and that Pym was determined to back Essex as Commander-in-Chief of the parliamentary army through thick and thin, despite the latter's near-defeatism and mediocre military talents.[81] It was for similar reasons that the New Model Army, with its military careers immeasurably more open to low-born talent, was to produce such misgivings and alarm among the Parliament's more conservative supporters.[82] But the New Model was not created until 1645, and not until it had become abundantly clear that the war could not be won without a radical military re-organization. The war was begun, however, with strong emphasis on the King as the innovator and Parliament as the preserver and restorer, which, considering Pym's radical incursions into the royal prerogative in 1642 and Hyde and Falkland's determination to stress the king's role as the defender of traditional constitutional freedoms, was becoming a good deal more difficult to sustain.[83] Nevertheless, under the guise of the defence of tradition and backed by copious reference to alleged precedents, there were few powers which could not be claimed for Parliament. Kings, it was argued, were bound by their coronation oaths to sign all bills sent up to them.[84] Parliament could always be summoned without the royal consent and was omnicompetent.[85] The monarch's power was in essence fiduciary, argued others, and trusts, as Henry Parker put it, were 'commonly limited more for the use of the party trusting than the partie trusted';[86] and, as another writer ominously declared, kings who were guilty of breaches of trust might forfeit their kingdoms.[87] A more convincing, if daring, argument was provided in the parliamentary declaration of 26 May 1642, which frankly admitted that parliament had had no choice but to depart from precedent – to break the letter of the constitution in order to preserve its spirit – in face of unprecedented royal attacks on parliamentary privilege and the liberty of the subject. 'If we have done more than our Ancestors have done', it argued, 'we have suffered more than ever they have suffered.'[88] A pamphlet of 1643 makes the same point, while taking a strikingly Hookerian view of the limitations of precedent:

> ... if they have made any presidents this Parliament, they have made them for posterity; and upon the same or better reasons or law then those were upon which their predecessors first made any for them; and as some presidents ought not to be rules for them to follow; so none can be limits to bound their proceedings, which may and must vary according to the different condition of times.[89]

But this last was a most untypical departure from the Cokeian view that parliament was not creating new precedents but following old ones, and that these in turn had not been creations of new law but evidence of immemorial practice.

IX

But the greatest political problem facing the king's opponents in the autumn of 1642 was not so much that of bringing their constitutional innovations within the canon of custom or justifying them in terms of unprecedented royal aggression, but to find ways of stilling the doubts of its potential supporters about the dire consequences of taking up arms against the Lord's anointed. It was, of course, by no means difficult to find examples in the recent past of English monarchs encouraging the subjects of foreign princes to do just that.[90] Moreover, what could be justified out of recent history could also be justified out of Scripture. Far from obeying the precepts of passive obedience when 'Ahab sent a Cavaliere ... to take away the Prophet *Elishas* head', the prophet justifiably offered resistance and called on others to support him.[91] Even the *locus classicus* of Scriptural non-resistance, David's refusal to harm Saul when he had him at his mercy, was turned to good use. For while no one wished to harm the person of the king, it was absurd to argue that David was not in revolt against Saul. If he was not, 'what did he with 600 men about him? He might have fled from Saul ... without such a train and guard of men attending him.'[92] This argument induced a snort of contempt from loyal royalist nostrils. Was the dominion of Charles I, the constitutional monarch, really comparable with the crazed tyranny of Saul? For had David encroached upon Saul's prerogative? Had he encouraged tumultuous assemblies, slanderous pamphlets and declarations, and denied the king access to the citadel at Jerusalem?[93]

Neither David nor Elisha was an ordinary and private man, and it was not easy to adduce a general right of revolt from their cases. But neither was it desirable. The more circumscribed the right of revolt, the more it was likely to find acceptance among those who harboured serious misgivings about the consequences of disobedience as opening the floodgates of democracy. In justifying their own revolt in the Bishops' Wars the Scots had taken one argument straight out of the book of their French co-religionists in the sixteenth century. This was to make a distinction between revolt by private persons and by what were described as the 'inferiour Magistrates', an idea which derived some of its force from the Calvinist notion of the godly magistrate.[94] When the orders of the Prince conflicted with the law of God, the godly magistrate in England and Scotland must not hesitate and, unlike the private person, must not confine his action to disobedience and passive acceptance of its consequences. His right – more, his duty – was to offer resistance which in itself legitimized, indeed required, the resistance of his inferiors acting on his command.

Clearly if Parliament were sovereign, it could hardly also be a collectivity of inferior magistrates, unless it was argued that the whole was more than the sum of its parts, or a distinction was drawn between the rights of individual magistrates and the rights of Parliament to initiate revolt. But these were academic points ignored by the royalists, who concentrated on other and more practical criticisms of this theory. It was, they maintained, patently absurd for inferior magistrates to claim the right to resist the supreme magistrate from whom they derived their authority and without whose sanction that authority could not be said to exist at all. They were, it was argued, public magisterial figures only in relation to their inferiors, and private men *vis-à-vis* the monarch.

Perhaps most telling of all was the assertion that 'those that in degree are nearest to their soveraigne ought to be so much the more loyall, faithfull and constant to him'.[95]

The last argument probably touched many a well-born Roundhead on the raw. It would be wrong to interpret the occasional waverings and defections of parliamentarian aristocrats such as Northumberland, Bedford and Holland entirely in terms of calculated self-interest. Such people, and perhaps especially Essex, the parliamentarian commander-in-chief, must have experienced some profoundly uneasy moments when reflecting on their rejection of the principle of the indivisibility of obedience on which they had been reared. Accordingly it is not altogether surprising that a doctrine which figured more prominently than that dealing with the rights and duties of inferior magistrates – though not basically incompatible with it – was that which insisted that Parliament was not in fact fighting the King at all. Pym was not being altogether disingenuous when he affirmed in March 1643 that he 'neither directly nor indirectly ever had a thought tending to the least disobedience or disloyaltie to his Majestie'.[96] Thus, in such a view, Hotham had been acting not against the king but in the royal interests when he shut him out of Hull;[97] the deputy lieutenants of Devon implementing the parliamentary Militia Ordinance in August 1642 described that contentious measure as being 'for his Majesty's service and the good of your Countrye'.[98] Parliament, in short, was fighting not against but for the king. 'All that beare Armes *against the King*,' observed one pamphleteer, 'are Rebells all, but we beare Arms for the King and the Parliament, therefore we are good subjects all.'[99] In 1643 parliament's Scottish allies joined in the exercises in self-deception, and the allies pledged themselves in the Solemn League and Covenant to 'preserve and defend the Kings Majesty's person and authority'.[100]

Needless to say, the convenient fiction that Parliament was protecting the king by taking up arms against him presented glorious opportunities to the royalists which they were not slow to exploit.[101] 'Whoever knows what danger Our person was in, on Sunday the 23 of October', stated a royal declaration referring to the battle of Edgehill, 'can never beleive [*sic*] that the Army which gave Us Battle was raised for Our defence & preservation.'[102] The parliamentary reply drew the somewhat unconvincing analogy with a hypothetical occasion in which the king had fallen into the hands of thieves, from whom he had to be rescued by giving them battle. Here was a variation on the familiar theme, reiterated over and over again by parliamentarian propaganda, of the king's enslavement by evil advisers who were the real architects of royal policy.[103] Clarendon tells how, on the eve of the battle of Edgehill in October 1642, the parliamentarian commander, the Earl of Essex, loudly contradicted the royal herald's affirmative reply to his question whether the king was present in the opposing army, 'for care had been taken that the soldiers should think that they fought against those malignants who kept the King from the Parliament'. Similarly, Clarendon ascribed Essex's concentration on besieging Reading in the spring of 1643 rather than directly advancing on Oxford, which, he claims, would have been a far more efficacious strategy, to the Earl's disinclination to 'besiege the very place where the King himself was', and his fear that the parliamentary soldiers might not easily be restrained.[104]

If Parliament were fighting for and not against the King, it followed that his followers were fighting against him. Parliamentarian apologists attempted to turn the deep-seated horror of rebellion to advantage by arguing that it was not they but their opponents who were the rebels.[105] But given Charles's inevitable denial that he was a cipher or a mere puppet dancing to the tunes played by his evil advisers, parliamentarians had to devise some way of dealing with the royal insistence that those whom they described as evil advisers were in fact nothing of the sort, but were faithful servants obeying the royal commands. The answer to this was that the king had been deceived both into trusting such persons and into making such commands. Around this simple idea was erected the elaborate and sophisticated doctrine of the king's two bodies.

This doctrine was put as succinctly and clearly as anywhere in the parliamentary declaration of 3 November 1642 which argued that: 'the levying of Forces against the personall commands of the King ... and not against his Lawes and Authority, but in the maintenance thereof ... is not levying war against the King. ... Treason is not committed against the King's Person, as he is a man, but as he is a King, and as his Person hath relation to his Office. ...'[106]

As early as 18 June 1642 a royal proclamation attacked this almost Hegelian distinction between the king's personal and his regal will,[107] making it clear that the subjects owed allegiance 'unto the naturall Person of their Prince and not to his Crown or Kingdom distinct from his naturall Capacitie'.[108] But the most effective royalist weapon against the notion was not learned exegesis of the law of treason but well-directed shafts of ridicule. One of the most effective of these *reductiones ad absurdum* is to be found in the royalist pamphlet of 1643 called *The Rebels' Catechism*:

> For by this strange division of the King from himself, or of his person from his power, a traitor may kill Charles, and not hurt the King: destroy the man, and save the magistrate; the power of the King in one of his armies may fight against his person in the other army, his own authority may be used to his own destruction, and one may lawfully set upon him, beat, assault and wound him, in order to his preservation.[109]

X

One of the papers captured by the victorious New Model Army at Naseby in June 1645 was a copy of a letter from Charles I to his uncle, Christian IV of Denmark, declaring that parliament was pursuing a 'great designe of exterpating the Royall Blood and Monarchie of England'.[110] Allegations about the regicidal and republican intentions of their enemies were bandied freely about by the royalists in an attempt to horrify both foreign and English opinion. They could also be used to generate misgivings among the Scottish allies of the English Parliament, more particularly towards the end of the war. On 23 March 1646 Charles wrote to the Scottish commissioners in England alleging the growth among their English allies of 'a potent faction which desires the exterpation of Monarchy and particularly of our Family'.[111] But far from being a potent faction, those holding republican views were a tiny and uninfluential minority. Nevertheless, the neo-republican sentiments of a few pamphleteers, however untypical, and the outrageous utterances of men such as Henry Marten and Sir Henry Ludlow,[112] were very embarrassing to the parliamentarian leadership, and Pym underlined his own position by sharply rebuking Marten in the House of Commons on 1 May 1643 and helping to bring about his expulsion and dispatch to the Tower for a notorious speech on 16 August 1643 in defence of a radical clergyman who had argued that 'it were better that one family were destroyed than the whole kingdom should perish'.[113] No one appreciated better than Pym the need to repudiate radical republican solutions if the invaluable support of noblemen like Essex were to be retained; indeed there were other magnates far to the left of Essex to whom any suggestion of republicanism was anathema. Of Lord Saye and Sele, Clarendon remarked that 'he had not the least thought of dissolving the monarchy, and less of levelling the ranks and distinctions of men: for no man valued himself more upon his title, or had more ambition to make it greater. . . .'[114]

It is one of the main tenets of this book that radical, republican solutions were always, even in 1648–9, the views of a minority, pressed forward against the opposition of the vast majority of the political nation. This said, however, it is almost certain that there was a growth of such sentiments as the war progressed. Denzil Holles was later to claim that the parliamentary victory at Marston Moor in July 1644 was a crucial turning-point after which the fiery spirits began 'to spit out their venom against Monarchy . . . Nobility and Gentry'. The next landmark noted by Holles on what he saw as the slippery slope towards republicanism was the foundation of the New Model Army early in 1645. Here was the first public indication, he tells us, of the republican intentions of his parliamentary opponents, the so-called 'fiery-spirits', for, in the commission to Sir Thomas Fairfax as commander-in-chief of the new army the usual words about the preservation of the king were omitted, as was the reference to King and Parliament, 'as . . . before under my Lord of *Essex*, who otherwise would not have meddled with it'.[115]

Long before these events Holles, the one-time firebrand, had become a proponent of peace at almost any price and one who saw republicans under every camp-bed. The historian of Cromwell's army is right to emphasize that the army as such was not an independent force in politics before 1647,[116] and Holles was wrong to see the leaders of the new army and their parliamentary allies as espousers of republican policies. Even in the autumn of 1647 Cromwell and Ireton were fiercely defending monarchical institutions in the famous debates at Putney,[117] and no trace of republicanism attached to Fairfax at any time. But what is true of the commanders of the army does not necessarily apply to all middle-ranking and junior officers or to the rank and file. When the Presbyterian divine Richard Baxter visited the army two days after its crushing defeat of the royal forces at Naseby in June 1645, he was horrified not only by the toleration of heterodox religious views among a minority of officers and men, but also by the widespread expression of republican sentiments.[118] The army as a whole might continue to obey the commands of its parliamentary master, but Holles is surely right to see its foundation as a climacteric. For here was indeed a New Model Army, in which career was enormously more open to low-born talent than is true of any of its predecessors, and in which the sectarian excesses so deplored by a pious Presbyterian like Baxter have a significance which goes far beyond religion and which has profound political implications. To appreciate the full significance of these things, it is necessary to turn aside from the ideological considerations which have dominated the latter part of this chapter to examine the nature of the political struggles not simply between King and Parliament, but also between competing elements in the Parliament itself, and this is the subject of the chapters which follow.

EIGHT *The Political Spectrum at Westminster and Oxford 1642–4*

It is a damnable and cursed policy, by dispencing with anything which God hath commanded to be done for his house, to seek after peace and deliverance. It was the policy of *Jeroboam*, & it turned to his ruine. . . . Thou thinkest to turn away wrath by the neglect of Religion & of the house of God, but God hath said, that wrath shall be upon the Kingdome, unless what he hath commanded be done for his house. Art thou wiser than he? . . .

> *A Sermon preached to the Honourable House of*
> *Commons at their late solemne Faste, Wednesday,*
> *December 27, 1643 by Alexander Henderson Minister*
> *at Edenbrugh* (1644), in *Fast Sermons*, IX, 184.

. . . a Civil War never ends by Treaty without the Sacrifice of those who were on both Sides the sharpest . . .

> Thomas Hobbes, *Behemoth*, in Maseres,
> *Select Tracts*, II, 566.

I

ALTHOUGH THE PARLIAMENTARY RIGHT WING had been weakened by defections to the king in the summer of 1642,[1] there remained at Westminster at the outbreak of war a substantial and very vocal group of MPs who followed Pym's path only with extreme reluctance, and who required constant reassurance that it did not stray beyond the limits of the fundamental law and the ancient constitution. Nor were all of them convinced in the long run, for forty-four more MPs were to go over to the king during the course of the war.[2] The fact that at least twenty and perhaps as many as thirty-two of these defections took place in 1643 is not surprising, since this was the year in which parliamentarian fortunes were at their lowest ebb, more especially during the summer months, from May to July, which saw the crushing victories of Newcastle in the north and Rupert and Hopton in the south-west, culminating in the fall of Bristol on 26 July. It was not until September, the month which saw the relief of Gloucester by the Earl of Essex, the brushing aside of the royal army which barred the parliamentarian general's return to London at Newbury, and the final conclusion of the alliance of the parliament with the Scots, that the downward slide was arrested, and even then the real fruits of the last and most significant of these events were not reaped until the following year.

Among the defectors were men who had distinguished themselves by their anti-Court activities, whether during the parliaments of the 1620s, like Sir Guy Palmes (Rutland), who defected before the end of 1642; or like John Fettiplace (Berkshire), who went over in 1643, by opposition to the arbitrary exactions of the 1630s, including Ship Money; or, the most spectacular case of all, by taking up arms for Parliament and defying the King before the outbreak of the war, like the Hothams, father and son (Beverley and Scarborough). For others such as Richard Shuckburgh (Warwickshire), who was shamed into joining the king when on a hunting expedition on the eve of the Battle of Edgehill, and Thomas Coke (Leicester), the son of the former Secretary of State, Sir John Coke, it is difficult to find any reasons other than sheer inertia for their not joining the king earlier than they did.[3]

There were at least four defectors in 1643 from whose actions the king benefited not at all. Ralph Verney refused to take the Covenant, but went into exile rather than join the king. The active parliamentarian Sir Alexander Carew,[4] who was entrusted with Drake's Island, which commanded the seaward approach to the vital parliamentarian port of Plymouth, and the two Hothams, whose detention of Hull from the king had been one of the spectacular set-pieces of 1642, all ended on the scaffold as a result of the failure of their plans to betray their charges to the king. If Clarendon is to be believed, the elder Hotham had taken on a great deal more than he had realized when he became parliamentary governor of Hull, banking on a peaceful solution of the problems of 1642 and an appropriate reward for his services. The defection of his friend Sir Hugh Cholmeley, another Yorkshireman and, like the younger Hotham, MP for Scarborough, and an active opponent of the Court in the 1630s and the early days of the Long Parliament, was more successfully accomplished, and brought with it the valuable prize of Scarborough Castle, of which he had been the parliamentary governor.[5]

II

Armed revolt simply emphasized more starkly the issue of disobedience and its possible social consequences which had driven many to defect to the king before the war. Ranking high among these consequences were the disorders which the royal reply to the Nineteen Propositions had pinpointed as the inevitable consequence of disobedience and parliamentary innovation, as a result of which Hodge ewould come to rule the field, and the common people would 'Destroy all Rights and Proprieties, and Distinctions of Families and Merit.'[6] Not everyone was convinced by the careful distinction made by the parliamentary declaration of 3 September 1642 between legitimate measures such as those taken against Sir John Lucas and other Essex Cavaliers and the other 'violent actions . . . unwarrantably committed' to which they had all too easily given rise, and which merited exemplary punishment, not least because they brought the parliamentary cause into disrepute with respectable people.[7] Another declaration, probably of the next month, was particularly concerned to deny the charge that parliament was endeavouring 'to raise an implacable malice and hatred between the Gentry and Commonalty'.[8] But the charge stuck, and there were probably many gentlemen who saw the supreme act of disobedience to the king as having repercussions right through society; or at the very least, like Anne Lady Maynard in a letter of 18 October 1643, blamed the war for the uppityness of their tenants and their unwillingness to pay rent.[9]

In the circumstances it is hardly surprising that emphatic disavowal of 'any popular or plebeian sway'[10] became an important feature of parliamentarian propaganda. Nevertheless the fear that the rebellion encouraged the excesses of the multitude was probably one of the most important factors encouraging both defections to the royalists and, among those who did not defect, the strengthening of the resolve and swelling of the numbers of those who were prepared to opt for peace at almost any price. Sir Simonds D'Ewes is an excellent example. His long speech of 22 December 1642 in the debate in the Commons over peace propositions to be offered to the king is eloquent of the fears aroused by popular disturbances such as those in the Stour valley in the late summer and autumn – D'Ewes was himself a Suffolk man. He dwelt at length on the expense of the war and the economic dislocation which it produced. In addition, even at this early stage in the war, he deplored the growth of the power of the military, and prophesied that they would before long be in a position to dictate to parliament what peace terms it should accept. More to the particular point here at issue, he dilated upon the horrific social consequences of the power of the army in the Roman Empire, its deposition and murder of emperors, and raising to the purple 'not onely blackesmithes and other tradesmen but euen slaves and fforainers'. Moreover, the economic dislocation engendered by war would bring the poor to such an extremity 'as they will bee enforced to take some violent course for the releife of them selues and to spoile the richer and abler sort'. Connected with the fears of a Jacquerie was the dreaded spectre of Anabaptism and Jan of Leyden, who would 'have made a parity of all men', a likely enough consequence, to the conservative D'Ewes, of parliament's failure to put an end to sectarian and lower-class excesses.[11] In a similar plea to the Upper House three days later for accommodation with the king, the Earl of Pembroke emphasized that he had a great deal 'more to lose than many of those who so hotly oppose an Accomodation'.[12] Denzil Holles was another prominent conservative politician who – in his case later in the war – was to identify the supporters of peace with 'gentlemen who had estates which required their looking-after', and their opponents with persons of lower social and economic status 'having a greatness far above the sphere they had formerly moved in'.[13] It was certainly substantial men of property who had most to lose from the continuance of the war, especially in so far as this was accompanied by an increasing radicalization of politics and the unleashing of dangerous forces of social disruption as a means of achieving the political objectives of Pym and his successors. Mrs Mulligan has advanced the interesting suggestion that those parliamentarians with estates lying in royalist or contended territory were more likely to be among what has come to be called the war party than those whose lands lay mainly in parliamentary territory, some of whom may have been deterred from joining the king at Oxford mainly by the knowledge that a consequence of taking this step would be the sequestration of their estates. The latter were therefore likely to be found among those who favoured peace on very easy terms. Her tentative attempt at analysis of the economic interests of MPs, which she claims confirms her findings for the 'war' and 'peace' parties and finds the MPs who occupied the middle ground in a position midway between them in respect of the location of their estates, is open to criticism for the rather crude methods used to compute landed wealth (notably a variation on the discredited method of counting manors). However, her findings concerning the location of estates – irrespective of their size – are in themselves quite suggestive, and they are worth serious attention when considering the reasons men took the line they did.[14]

As the war proceeded, there was an increasing number of measures which were distasteful to many substantial property-owners. Something is said in the next two chapters about the significance of the creation of the New Model Army and the changes in county government in this respect. One measure in the period which is here under discussion was the ordinance relating to the sequestration of royalist lands. D'Ewes describes how, during the debate on the Sequestration Ordinance on 28 March 1643, 'a gentleman who sate by mee saied wee haue most of the men of great estates with vs heere . . . I answered that the meane . . . fellowes on the other side [*viz.* of the House] weer those who vnited vs, for . . . hauing been mechanicks & . . . men of meane fortune, [they] weere not soe sensible of the destruction of the Kingdome as wee who had estates to loose.'[15] In actual fact considerations of class solidarity and of neighbourliness and local pride in the face of the encroaching power of central governments often tempered the severity of the application of such policies.[16] But this hardly lessened the doubts of men of substance about the intentions of the central government which initiated such policies or about their effects in terms of the decline of respect for rank and hierarchy. 'I thought it a crime to be a nobleman,' wrote Lord Willoughby of Parham despondently to the Earl of Denbigh on 30 June 1644. 'Nobility and gentry are going downe apace.'[17] The misgivings of the likes of Willoughby and Denbigh were soon to be increased immeasurably when the foot-dragging aristocratic leadership of the parliamentarian forces, and the gentlemanly conduct of the war associated with it, were to be swept aside by the foundation of the New Model Army.

III

It is, of course, impossible to dissociate the fear of social from that of religious disorders, not least because many of those engaging in the latter were themselves low-born persons, whose acts of sacrilege and iconoclasm were regarded as a threat to order and decency in general.

Royalist propagandists naturally sought to tar all opponents of episcopacy with the extreme sectarian and Anabaptist brush. Their stock response to their opponents' reiterated allegations about the multitude of papists in the royal armies was to emphasize such things as 'the profane and odious licence which the rabble of Brownists, Anabaptists and other Sectaries took to themselves . . . of suffering Mechanick ignorant fellows . . . to preach and expound the Scripture'.[18] Parliamentarians might reply to such smear tactics by insisting that most of the opponents of prelacy, far from being wild-eyed sectaries, were in fact earnest conservative gentlemen who were implacably opposed to innovation in ecclesiastical as in other matters.[19] But the presence of smoke did presuppose the existence of at least some fire. The mechanic preachers complained of were not always casual, part-time operators. According to some of the inhabitants of Harwich, who petitioned the House of Commons in October 1643, a certain Mr Wood, who had been authorized by the House to receive the income of the vicarage of Dovercourt and the chapel of Harwich, far from being 'a right godly, Learned and able devine', as his supporters claimed in a counter-petition, was in fact 'never brought up in any Schools of Learneing but is meer Mecanick'. He inveighed against the authority of the Church of England, refused to conduct services of baptism, marriage and burial, and had confessed to the deputy lieutenants that he was in fact a Separatist. He gave encouragement to two local Anabaptists, a tailor and a seaman, who had preached in several houses and whom he urged the authorities not to molest on the grounds that they were children of God. All of a piece with this, and perhaps most objectionable of all, he 'rayleth against the Maiestrates and gouerment of the Towne'.[20]

The orgy of destruction and iconoclasm in the name of godliness prompted similar misgivings and extended to some of the great cathedral churches themselves. There were scenes of wholesale desecration and vandalism at Canterbury and Worcester in 1642 and at Norwich and Wells in the following year. Among many other horrific acts of desecration at Canterbury, Colonel Sandes's troopers took pot shots at a statue of Christ in the south gate, 'triumphing much when they did hit it in the head or face'.[21] At Somerset House in March 1643 the vandals hurled into the nearby Thames not only the popish images in the Queen's Chapel but a no doubt equally popish Rubens painting from over the altar.[22] Further encouragement seems to have been given to such excesses both by the appointment on 24 April of a House of Commons committee charged with the destruction of idolatrous monuments, which was followed by an iconoclastic orgy in the capital; and by the parliamentary ordinance of 28 August 'for the utter demolishing removing and taking away of all monuments of superstition and idolatry'.[23] But long before then incidents like those described in the correspondence of Nehemiah Wallington, a junior officer in Essex's army, of the vandalism accompanying the progress of the parliamentary army in the early autumn of 1642 – stained glass and communion rails broken, churches despoiled, surplices cut up to make handkerchiefs – were more or less everyday occurrences,[24] encouraged by the fact that the parliamentarian soldiers were in the happy position of being able to indulge in wanton vandalism in the name of godliness. Needless to say, rapine and plunder were not confined to the parliamentarian army, but this particular form of vandalism aroused special attention[25] and undoubtedly contributed both to the drain of men to the king and to the clamourings for peace at Westminster.

IV

There can be no question of the parliamentary right wing, or peace party, being depleted *pro rata* with its losses via defections to the royalists at Oxford. For, as the war dragged on, many of those who had been numbered among the radicals in 1640–2 became increasingly uneasy both about the ends for which it was being fought and about the radical measures which were necessary if it were to be won, and came to swell the ranks of those who were prepared to accept what many would regard as abject peace terms. The outstanding example of this tendency is Denzil Holles. Holles had been a notable figure in the parliamentary opposition of the 1620s; one of the principal actors in the dramatic scene in 1629 when the Speaker had been forcibly held down while the Commons' Protestation was put to the question. Unlike men such as Strangeways and Seymour, he had maintained his radical stance in the early days of the Long Parliament. He was one of the five members singled out by the king for arrest on 4 January 1642, but was, in the early days of the war, to part company with the other four and assume the leadership of the peace party.

The use of this term is likely to beget some confusion unless it is realized that the word 'party' is not here employed to describe a firm and cohesive political organization with disciplined membership and consistent political behaviour. No such organization existed in the Long Parliament, and indeed the majority of MPs probably had no affiliation, however vague and indefinite, with any of the rather amorphous political groupings which it is convenient, if not altogether appropriate, to describe by this name. Until the appearance in 1941 of Professor J.H.Hexter's seminal study of parliamentary politics between the outbreak of the war and the death of Pym in December 1643,[26] it was customary to divide MPs into two main groups, leaving aside those independent members who certainly cannot be put into any such group. The first group was the peace party, led by Denzil Holles and John Maynard, and the second the war party, led by John Pym. Hexter replaced this dualism by a tripartite division, in which Pym is seen not as the leader of the war party, but of a middle group, even more indefinite in composition and less consistent in political behaviour, but yet sufficiently cohesive and consistent to merit consideration as a distinct political entity. The simpler, older and over-simplified dualism he regards as a product of the uncritical use by historians of D'Ewes's parliamentary diary with its built-in conservative distortions and notably the 'political foreshortening' which groups Pym almost invariably along with radicals such as Henry Marten and the younger Henry Vane.[27]

The first and most important issue over which these political groupings crystallized was that from which the two main groups take their names, the issue of peace and war, that is the attitude of MPs to the question of reaching agreement with the king, and the intimately connected matter of how the war itself was to be waged. An examination of debates on this issue clearly reveals the existence of a war group or party containing such men as Henry Marten, the younger Henry Vane, Alexander Rigby and William Strode, who pressed for vigorous and determined prosecution of the war with virtually no holds barred, leading to a dictated rather than a negotiated peace. While it would be an exaggeration to say that the aim of the almost equally cohesive group of MPs at the opposite political extreme was to obtain peace at almost any price, it certainly would not be going too far to say that they were prepared to accept or propose terms which were far less stringent than those rejected by the king in the Nineteen Propositions in the summer of 1642. The more nebulous and less consistent middle group was on most occasions ready to go along with the war party in voting for measures designed to increase the effectiveness of the parliamentary war effort, but differed from it in that it aimed, like the peace party, not at a dictated but at a negotiated peace. Accordingly a majority of middle groupers often supported the peace party, while recognizing that the weakness of the latter's position arose from its refusal to recognize that any peace not negotiated from a position of strength would be a surrender peace. Wishing for peace, it was necessary to be fully prepared for war in ways which horrified many of the peace-party men. As Pym himself put it in a famous speech at Guildhall on 10 November 1642, 'the King, having seen the Courage of his Subjects, having seen the Danger of his own Person, and so much Blood shed about him, he will be more tractable to good conditions of Peace than he would have been before. . . .'[28]

There is an element of hyperbole in Pym's statement, in that the king's situation was much stronger, not weaker, in November than it had been at the outset of the war,[29] when Parliament's peace terms had been even more stringent than those of the Nineteen Propositions.[30] Peace feelers in November, with royal forces only a few miles from London, proved abortive, sabotaged by Rupert's precipitate assault on Brentford on 12 November,[31] and the most significant attempt at peace of the first year of the war was the so-called Treaty (*viz.* treating) of Oxford in the winter and early spring of 1643. This was perhaps because negotiations took place at a time when royal and parliamentarian fortunes were more nearly balanced than at any other time before the late autumn of 1643. Although Charles had recovered spectacularly from what had seemed to be a near hopeless position at the outset of the war, the royal threat to London had been successfully beaten off in November 1642. The crushing royalist victories in the north and south west, which marked the nadir of parliamentarian fortune in the summer of 1643, still lay in the future. There can be no doubt that the terms offered by the parliament in February 1643 at Oxford were notably less severe than those of the Nineteen Propositions, more especially in the matter of control over the executive.[32] As such they were bitterly opposed by the war party at Westminster. However, they were still too stiff for the king, especially a king whose fortunes had undergone a dramatic improvement since the beginning of the war. In such circumstances Charles was unlikely to agree to the abolition of episcopacy, the removal of some of his councillors from his presence, and the exemption from pardon of two of his most devoted servants, Digby and Newcastle. On the other hand, some of the matters on which the king insisted would have been suicidal for the Parliament to accept. To abandon the negative voice in the appointment of councillors, on which it had insisted in the Nineteen Propositions, was one thing; to do the same in respect of the appointment of a Lord Warden of the Cinque

Ports and the governors of castles and fortress towns was quite another. The stock royal response (as in the answer to the Nineteen Proposi- tions) that the parliamentary remedy lay not in the right to veto such appointments but in taking legal action against those giving just grounds for offence, while having some force when applied to royal councillors, was unreal when applied to the control of vital military positions. As the parliamentary commissioners at Oxford mildly ob- served on 14 April, it was necessary that these should 'remain in the hands of such Persons with such powers, as both parties might believe themselves secure'.[33] If the peace party were prepared to trust the king on this, no one else was.

In the debate on the progress of the peace negotiations the delicately adjusted behaviour of the political weathercocks of the middle group bewildered some contemporaries.[34] D'Ewes, for instance, seems to have been genuinely mystified over the precise significance of Pym's proposal to the House of Commons on 10 April 1643 that the apparent deadlock at Oxford might be resolved by proceeding from hotly dis- puted matters on which no headway appeared possible to some of the less contentious resolutions :

> which motion of Mr. Pyms some conceived to bee made out of a
> desire to further the peace . . . but others conceiued that he did it
> to hinder any further time to bee giuen to our Committee at
> Oxford, soe as almost all men being iealous of his motion did
> oppose it and it came to nothing.[35]

While there is no reason to doubt that Pym was entirely capable of such Machiavellian behaviour as is suggested by the second of these alterna- tive possibilities, an essential presupposition of this explanation of his behaviour is that his aim was to find cogent arguments for abandoning negotiations and getting on with the war. This is all very well if one holds with D'Ewes that the only difference between Pym and fiery spirits such as Henry Marten lay in the greater subtlety of the former. If, however, Pym is seen as a politician who, as much as D'Ewes or Holles, wanted a negotiated peace, but, unlike them, was not prepared to accept an abject peace, the first of the alternative explanations is entirely plausible. Herein lies the main difference between the aims of the peace and the middle-groupers in respect of the pursuit of peace. Clarendon was not far wide of the mark when he described the former as men 'who really desired the same peace as the King did'.[36] The royal declaration of 3 June 1643, which ascribed the failure of negotiations to 'that violent Party which lookes upon Peace like a Monster', was calculated to strike a familiar chord in the consciousness of such men as D'Ewes and Holles, who no doubt felt increasingly that they had more in common with moderate royalists at Oxford than with extremists on their own side.[37]

V

Closely connected with the question of peace terms and overtures were matters relating to the war effort, ranging from the taxes to pay for the war to the conduct of the parliamentary armies in the field. It is obviously virtually impossible both to wage determined war and punctiliously to observe the letter of constitutional propriety. The necessary condition of the preservation of constitutional freedoms intact is the abrogation of some of them in situations of dire emergency, a thesis which is none the less true for having been used historically to justify any number of totalitarian excesses. But the peace party men consistently refused to accept the argument that 'the nature of War . . . is incompetible with the ordinary Rules of a peaceable Government',[38] and continued to voice pettifogging objections to a wide variety of measures without which the war could certainly not have been won and might very well have been lost. This included opposition to strengthening the fortification of a town in parliamentarian hands because this would involve an infringement of the royal prerogative,[39] and, perhaps most notable of all, opposition to the various measures of taxation without which the parliamentary war effort would have totally collapsed. On 10 February 1643 D'Ewes emphasized in debate in the House of Commons that one of the most desirable products of the return of peace would be 'the returne to the old way of collecting money by Act of Parliament'.[40] But this emphatically did not mean that he and his peace party colleagues were prepared on account of the emergency to acquiesce in financial measures such as the Sequestration Ordinance, the weekly assessment and the Excise, all of which they opposed.[41] D'Ewes tells how, at a Grand Committee of the House on 5 December 1642, a proposal was made for a tax at the rate of at least one-twentieth of annual income from land, with a higher rate for personal estate. What horrified him was not simply the penal rate of tax proposed but the voting of a tax 'by a meer Ordinance of both howses' as distinct from a proper Act of Parliament.[42] This sort of objection was typical of the lack of realism of men who consistently opposed virtually every measure which was necessary if the war were to be won by Parliament; to which criticism they would doubtless have replied that it ought to be Parliament's aim not to win the war but to establish a just peace.

At the opposite extreme, the war party held very different views. In a debate on taxation on 9 February 1643 Henry Marten advanced views which were to find their ultimate expression in Pride's Purge. Pointing out that there were MPs who had not yet contributed a penny to the war effort, he argued that 'they might haue no voice in the making of peace who had not had a hand in supporting the warre'. Marten was backed up by William Strode, another war-party stalwart, who voiced the similar view 'that as in a building men would looke to their materials and not take that which is vnfitt, soe we should doe with our owne members'. As so often, the war-party men had gone too far. It is true that D'Ewes' suggestion that inability rather than unwillingness might be the reason for some members' failure to contribute, 'or else they reserue themselves to contribute to better purpose, for peace is better then victorie' was hardly likely to rejoice the hearts of any but his own kind, but the intervention of John Maynard, another peace-party man, was much better judged and seems to have produced the isolation of Strode from all but his fellow extremists. This was not the sort of issue on which the war party could expect much support from the middle group.[43]

VI

While Pym and the middle-groupers tended to support the war party on matters relating to the resolute prosecution of the war, there was one matter in particular on which the two groups were, for most of the time, at complete variance. Of all English military commanders in any age few, if any, have been subjected to the constant sniping from his own side which was the unhappy lot of the Earl of Essex. Essex's dilatory generalship made him the war party's *bête noire* almost continually during 1643. The exception is the period of the negotiations at Oxford, when Essex's anxiety that the peace party would not pay due regard to essential conditions of military security in their eagerness to secure peace brought him the warm, if very temporary, support of the hard men of the war party, formerly, and subsequently, his fiercest critics. But this support evaporated with the renewal of fighting, the disasters of the summer, and the war party's discovery of a new saviour, Sir William Waller, if not for the role of commander-in-chief as originally designed, at least for the command of a separate army independent of Essex. But if the war party waxed hot and cold, and mostly very cold, in its attitude to Essex, Pym never faltered in his support for the Lord General, recognizing that his advantages as a respectable, aristocratic commander in helping to still the doubts of conservatively minded gentlemen outweighed the disadvantages of his somewhat mediocre military ability. It was due above all to Pym that it was Essex and not Waller – a less glamorous figure than previously, following his defeat at Roundway Down on 13 July – who led the parliamentary army to the relief of Gloucester in September.[44]

Pym's support for Essex ranged him temporarily alongside Denzil Holles, the peace-party leader. In the summer of 1643, the peace party was showing signs of a split between those who, like D'Ewes, opposed almost any design to increase the military effectiveness of the parliamentary forces, and whose pusillanimity at the time of the Oxford treaty had brought about the temporary rapprochement of Essex with the war party; and a group led by Holles, which was implacably opposed to Waller and any ordinance designed to strengthen the forces under his command, but not to Essex. As the allies of Essex, the commander whom they felt to be most sympathetic to their own very conservative interests, they cooperated with Pym, whose support did not, however, extend to aiding them in their attempts to hamstring Waller. Given the deep scars left by the political in-fighting at Westminster during the summer of 1643 and the continued animosity between the two generals, Pym's statesmanship is seen at its best in his attempts to reconcile the two, to secure the passage of the ordinances for provision of adequate resources for both, while insisting on the supremacy of the Lord General. His policy compares very favourably with those pursued by the parliamentary factions to the right and left. Even if, as subsequent events, culminating in Essex's disaster in Cornwall in September 1644 and Waller's alleged failure to afford him assistance, were to show, Pym was doing little more than papering over cracks, it is difficult to see what more he could have done.[45]

VII

The final and most important element in Pym's strategy for saving the parliament from the dangers which threatened from all sides in 1643 was the Scottish alliance which raised a variety of issues, contended over by different political groups both at Westminster and Edinburgh. From the beginning the Scots had assumed that the institution of a Presbyterian system *à l'écossaise* would be the inevitable product of the abolition of episcopacy in England,[46] and in the course of 1641-2 there were a number of official statements by King and Parliament which appeared to point clearly in this direction.[47]

From the outset of the Civil War the radical kirk party in Scotland had taken an interventionist line, arguing strongly for an alliance with the English Parliament.[48] In the view of such men as the Earl of Argyll and Johnston of Wariston, the religious and political concessions which the king had made on his visit to Scotland in 1641 were safe only so long as he was preoccupied by, or if he were defeated in, the war in England. A royal victory would be followed by a reversion to the familiar policies which had produced the National Covenant and the Bishops' Wars. As the price of their support for the English Parliament, the Scots should insist on the establishment of a full-blown Presbyterian ecclesiastical policy to be riveted immovably upon England as an ironclad safeguard against a repetition of the events of the 1630s.

It was, however, possible even for good Covenanters to make a completely different diagnosis of the situation and argue for a non-intervention policy. This alternative view rested on the assumptions that the king was a man of his word and that it was anyway in his interest to abide by the ecclesiastical and political reforms to which he had agreed in 1641. According to this view the greatest danger to that settlement came not from staying put but from entering the war against him, which might invite his just retribution later. The most important and influential advocate of this policy was Charles's own adviser on Scottish affairs, the Marquis (later Duke) of Hamilton. Hamilton was later to spend years in captivity in England on the charge of having tricked the king, but in so far as he was to blame his fault lay in his political misjudgment rather than political duplicity. He was the better able to reconcile his royalism with a non-interventionist policy, because, in the context of 1643, it seemed increasingly likely that the English royalists would win the war, provided that their opponents did not obtain help from outside.

That Argyll succeeded and Hamilton failed was due less to the impracticability of the latter's policies *per se* than to the inept behaviour of the king, which robbed them of any credibility they may have possessed. If Charles had played Hamilton's game properly, he would not have rejected with such contempt and contumely the offer of the

Scottish commissioners in England in the spring of 1643 to mediate between him and his parliament;[49] he would not have refused to discountenance the papists in Newcastle's northern army which caused such misgivings in Scotland; perhaps above all he would not have encouraged the so-called Antrim Plot, details of which were revealed to the English Parliament in June 1643 and quickly made available to the Scots. This was a plan to follow a cease-fire in Ulster by a descent of Irishmen on the west coast of Scotland, and its disclosure was wholly ruinous to Hamilton's plan. As a result most Covenanters came to accept Argyll's thesis that their ends could be achieved only by intervening against the king in the English Civil War.

The Scottish war aims were preponderantly religious in character. The Scots might deplore the delays of their godly English friends in bringing about the necessary transformation of their Church, but they were not unaware that the latter had to contend with the sons of Meroz and the locusts of the bottomless pit.[50] That incurable optimist Robert Baillie, who was very gradually to learn the complicated truth the hard way, gives no inkling in a letter to his cousin William Spang, on 18 February 1643, that he entertained any doubt that the English Parliament's affirmation of 'their earnest desyre to have their Church reformed according to the word of God' meant anything other than what any good Scottish Presbyterian would take it to mean.[51] The Scots were moved to intervene in the war both by the proselytizing zeal of true believers rejoicing in the opportunity of spreading the word of righteousness abroad, and by the notion that attack was the best form of defence. As the Scottish Committee of Estates declared in August 1643, 'if we upon so fair a Calling sit still and hold our Peace, the Kirk and Kingdom shall perish by the hand of the Same Enemy'.[52]

Most of the peace party at Westminster naturally disliked the Scottish alliance. As early as December 1642, D'Ewes had described it as the most dangerous of all the options open to Parliament, not least because it was likely to precipitate the calling in of foreign powers by the royalists.[53] Peace-party men were reluctant to take any step which would further antagonize the king by making the parliamentary war effort more effective, let alone being a party to the introduction of a foreign army to fight against him – an offence which was compounded by the fact that the foreigners in question were also his own subjects. In the memoirs which he wrote many years later, Denzil Holles, the peace-party leader, accused the leader of the parliamentary delegation to Scotland to negotiate the alliance, the war-party man, Sir Henry

Vane the younger, of blackening peace-party men in the eyes of the Scots and of lauding their parliamentary opponents. He also criticized the proponents of the alliance, and especially Pym, whose middle group was allied with the war party on the issue, for their readiness to 'promise any thing, offer any thing, do any thing . . . that the Scots would have them do'.[54]

But did the desperate plight of the English cause them to capitulate so completely to the Scottish demands as is often claimed?[55] Here the crucial text is the first clause of the Solemn League and Covenant which was agreed in Scotland in August and accepted, though in a significantly modified form, by the English Parliament on 25 September.[56] This bound the parties to the alliance to agree to the preservation of the Scottish Church. The fact that the English Commissioners in Scotland originally agreed to the description of that church as being 'according to the word of God', and the use of precisely the same words to describe the needed reformation of religion in England and Ireland, carried the clear implication that the former was the model on which the latter was to be based. This was only slightly toned down by Vane's persuading the Scots to agree to the addition of the words 'and the example of the best reformed Churches' in the latter case, though this did perhaps suggest that the word of God might be different in respect of different national traditions and environments, an implication which would be totally lost on the Scots. But this mild modification of the originally proposed clause was not enough for the English Parliament, which saw the danger of the exact repetition of the phrase about the word of God in respect both of the existing state of the Scottish Church and of the coming reformation of the English and Irish Churches. Accordingly it expunged the phrase in the former, and retained it in the latter case – hardly, it would seem, the action of a nation negotiating from a position of weakness with another negotiating from a position of strength. According to one contemporary memorandum on the subject, 'the endeauour of vniformity . . . is promisory in both Kingdomes *to meet each other* in such reformation as shalbe . . . agreeable to god's word'.[57]

The remaining clauses of the Solemn League and Covenant were less open to a variety of interpretations, and the argument of the above memorandum that the second clause, calling for the extirpation of (*inter alia*) episcopacy should not be interpreted as being against bishops *per se*, as distinct from their coercive powers, was far fetched. Although the peace-party man Maynard and the middle-grouper Glyn tried to push a similar view in one of the debates on the Covenant on 2 September, they were outvoted.[58] To the peace-party men in particular, the abolition of episcopacy was the erection of yet another barrier to the successful conclusion of peace with the king. So also was the final clause, binding the parties to the alliance not to make a separate peace with the king, which had the alarming consequence of multiplying enormously the matters on which agreement had to be reached before the peace, for which peace-party men longed above all else, could be attained.

The alliance with the Scots was John Pym's crowning achievement. That it was not bought at so high a price as is sometimes assumed made it the more acceptable, not only to most of the middle group but also to the war party, for many of whom Presbyterianism à l'écossaise was as unpleasant a prospect as it was to most of their opponents of the opposite parliamentary extreme.

VIII

The Scottish alliance was one of the main issues around which party differences at Westminster crystallized, but although the central war aims of the Scots related to religion, religion as such was not a party issue in 1642–3. This is not to say that there was no disagreement about religious matters in Parliament, but simply that such religious disagreements as appeared in the course of debate mostly cut across, rather than followed, party divisions. For example, in the debate over the bill to abolish the jurisdiction of bishops, deans and chapters and the like on 20 January 1643, the peace-party men, Maynard and Bagshaw, supporters of primitive episcopacy, who no doubt were playing for time, spoke firmly against immediate abolition, arguing that it was necessary to be clear about what exactly was to be put in place of episcopacy before inviting chaos as the inevitable product of the ensuing vacuum. On the other hand, D'Ewes, normally the most conservative of peace-party men, declared himself to be 'of the same minde I was from the beginning for the abolishing of Archbishopps [and] Bishopps with their whole dependencies in a parliamentary way'.[59] Similar cross-party divisions on religious grounds can be observed in the debate on the Covenant in the summer and autumn of the same year.[60]

If there is a central feature of the religious parliamentary history of the period between the beginning of the war and the publication of the Independent *Apologeticall Narration* at the beginning of 1644, it is the determined attempt to minimize the differences between the Presbyterians and Independents with their respective emphases on highly structured ecclesiastical centralism and loosely organized decentralization. In a real sense Pym may be said to have defused the issue in seeking as far as possible to relegate discussion of such matters to the Assembly of Divines whose proceedings opened at Westminster in July 1643. The main theme of the early sessions of that assembly over the remainder of the year was the attempt of the Presbyterian majority to win over the Independents by the force of argument. The Scottish representatives at the Assembly might be irritated beyond measure at the filibustering tactics of the non-Presbyterian minority. Nevertheless their strategy remained, in the words of one of them, 'to eschew a publick rupture with the Independents . . . [and] to go on hand in hand . . . against the common enemie'. Ultimately reason would prevail and 'the Independents will either come to us, or have very few to follow them'.[61]

But reason was very slow to prevail, and the idea that Scottish-type Presbyteriansim, with its 'Kirk-Officers and Kirk-Government by Assemblies higher and lower in their strong and beautiful Subordination', was '*Jure divino* and perpetual', as a declaration of the Scottish Assembly on 3 August 1642 had put it, was totally unacceptable to a minority of the Westminster Assembly. Such a system, they felt, smacked strongly of theocratic tyranny.[62] The English Parliament, whose creature the Assembly of Divines was, had only recently dealt the death blow to *iure divino* episcopacy, and was in no mood to tolerate the no less – and perhaps even more – theocratic pretensions of *iure divino* Presbyterianism. The subordination of the Assembly to the parliament in ecclesiastical matters amazed and horrified the Scots, and was yet another reason for striving to maintain the semblance of unity within the former body. The royalist observer Captain Thomas Ogle, who, in a report to the Earl of Bristol compiled on 17 October 1643, associated the Independents in the Assembly with 'some few and inconsiderable anabaptists and sectuarys', hit upon a truth which both Presbyterians and Independents found increasingly embarrassing, as sectarian excesses multiplied in London and the provinces.[63] The Presbyterians sought the more earnestly to play down the matters which divided them from their Independent colleagues, and the latter responded by dissociating themselves from their disreputable sectarian allies on their left. Dr Kaplan has suggested that the moderate Presbyterian minister Stephen Marshall played a Pym-like role in the Assembly, gathering around him 'a middle party of like-minded clergymen'. By these and similar means the lid was kept on, and a precarious peace preserved.[64]

But the strain was formidable, and no doubt more than one Presbyterian felt that the pact with the Independents rendered him guilty by association of condoning sectarian excesses and alarmingly heterodox opinions on all sorts of matters. Who could doubt, for example, that the outrageous views of John Milton about marriage and divorce, which appeared in print in 1643 and still strike the modern reader as advanced, were a consequence of the loosing of the reins of authority; that the threat to parental and husbandly authority was connected with the decline in ecclesiastical and royal authority? If anyone did doubt it, a glance at the text would make the connection abundantly clear. Divorce was the more necessary, argued Milton, on account of the 'savage inhumanity' of the institution of the arranged marriage. Marriage itself should be seen as a covenant, as dissoluble as an oath of allegiance in the event of the contract being broken.[65] To Pym, the painstaking builder of a parliamentary alliance based on respectability and conservatism, Milton's linking of the struggle against the royalists with a revolt against the authority of the family and the institution of marriage must have seemed an infuriating threat to all that he had so laboriously created. To moderate reformers the risk of being associated with such persons and their ideas was a perpetual nightmare, and the same considerations applied to the moderate divines in the Westminster Assembly. Even though the Assembly, in its report to the House of Commons on 4 December 1644 of its deliberations on the subject of marriage, condemned not only marriage without parental consent, but also 'Parents unjustly forcing their Children into Marriages against their own Consents', this was simply removing some of the grounds for Milton's advocacy of divorce, not condoning his conclusions.[66] In the same year the attempt to muzzle the propounders of such views was to produce in the *Areopagitica* a defence of the right to utter heterodox views which was no less shocking to most contemporaries.

IX

Before examining how far Pym's political system survived his death in December 1643, it will be convenient to turn from the political divisions at Westminster to those within the royalist camp at Oxford. While the onset of war seems initially to have given something of a boost to the fortunes of the peace party at Westminster, it had the opposite effect at

Oxford. Given the failure of the moderate policies pursued by the Crown under the advice of Falkland and Hyde, a resurgence of that Cavalier extremism, which had never been far below the surface since its last notable appearance on the scene in January 1642, was only to be expected. Paradoxically enough, the parlous military position of the royalists in the opening days of the war weakened the arguments of the advocates of conciliation, such as Southampton and Dorset. At this stage not all the royalists who, like Hyde, favoured peace on honourable terms threw their influence against the hardliners such as Bristol, Digby and Rupert. For the only peace terms available in the early autumn of 1642 were anything but honourable, in which circumstances the most sensible policy for a hard-headed royalist moderate was to support the building up of royalist military power so that negotiations could ultimately be undertaken from a position of greater strength.

In this respect the analogy with political attitudes and conflicting strategies at Westminster is striking, but it ought not to be pushed too far. One significant difference is that while the army of the parliament did not become a political force in its own right until after the end of the first Civil War, the same is emphatically not true of the royalist forces, or at least of their commanders. On a number of occasions in his great *History*, Clarendon, who as a civilian minister of the king was not, of course, a disinterested witness, emphasizes the undue influence of the military in the royalist councils, and how the king was normally strongly drawn towards their point of view, which, like that of the war party at Westminster, favoured the waging of war *à l'outrance*. The balance was tilted further in the direction of extremism by the death, at the first battle of Newbury on 20 September 1643, of Hyde's great ally, the statesmanlike and pacific Secretary Falkland. If Hyde's celebrated 'character' of Falkland is to be believed, his reckless bravery on the field of battle was attributable to his determination to discountenance the tendency of royalist *ultras* to associate political moderation with personal cowardice. If so, he was doing a disservice to the cause of moderation. For the king chose the *ultra* Digby as his successor as Secretary of State, though he also made Hyde Chancellor of the Exchequer. From that time on, the only civilians admitted to royal councils of war seem to have been Digby and Culpepper, both of whom favoured hardline policies. This tendency was to culminate in the short-lived alliance between Digby and Prince Rupert in 1644-5, but these two principal figures in what Ronald Hutton describes as 'the long-awaited ultra-royalist axis' had been too long at daggers drawn for their rapprochement to survive even the immediate military crisis which had originated it.[67]

The prevalence of extremists at Oxford was naturally made much of by parliamentary propagandists such as Henry Parker, who argued that moderates could not get a word in edgeways in the royal councils.[68] A special bogey was Prince Rupert, who with his brother Maurice brought to the conduct of civil warfare some of the ruthlessness and savagery associated with the Thirty Years War in Germany. One pamphlet of 1642 alleged that Rupert's ambitions did not stop short of the crown itself, to which end he was cultivating the support of the soldiers of fortune who flocked to him in great numbers.[69] On 26 June 1643 a horrified House of Commons was treated to a lurid account both of the hundred whores kept by the Prince, 'two of them . . . in boyes apparrell who constantly attended him', and of the 'horrible oaths and execrations' with which he terrorized the advocates of peace at Oxford into silence.[70] There is no doubt that Rupert had been the arch-enemy of peace from the moment he arrived in England. In the opening weeks of the war, as has been seen, he got some support from more moderate royalists such as Hyde who did not oppose negotiations but were against peace at any price and favoured negotiating from strength. Rupert, on the other hand, seems to have opposed negotiations in almost any circumstances, because he thought them likely both to hinder recruitment of troops and to sacrifice those who had already been recruited – the perennial suspicion of the soldier that he will be betrayed by civilian politicians. Rupert was later to claim that his reputation as the implacable enemy of peace was ruthlessly exploited by his enemies at Oxford, and notably by Digby.[71]

In the early days of the war, Hyde's consciousness of the need to build up royalist strength before negotiating had put him nearer to the hardliners at Oxford than to men such as Southampton and Dorset, and perhaps even Falkland, who some thought to be 'so much enamoured on peace that he would have been glad that the King should have bought it at any price'.[72] But as royalist power grew spectacularly, towards the end of 1642, the gap between Hyde's position and that of the hardliners widened and the different ends to which each envisaged royalist strength being put became starkly apparent.[73] The attitude of the hardliners, and, *mutatis mutandis*, its similarity with that of the war party at Westminster, is clearly exemplified by a statement made by the Earl of Bristol in February 1643, at the time of the peace negotiations at Oxford. The purpose of royalist strength, he argued, was to crush the king's opponents, not to serve as a position from which to negotiate. 'We have an Army . . . that by force can compel that which fair words cannot effect'. Long before the Oxford Treaty, Hyde and Falkland had deplored the opportunities for peace which had been lost; first, after Edgehill, when the royal army made for London instead of offering honourable peace terms to the Parliament; and secondly, by Rupert's precipitate action at Brentford in November. Bristol's statement at Oxford offers an eloquent contrast to their views of the use to which military strength ought to be put.

The opposite view, that of the Oxford counterparts to the members of the peace party at Westminster, was eloquently put by the Earl of Dorset in answer to Bristol. Dorset rejected the idea that the king should go all out for a crushing military victory as inappropriate to a commonwealth which, 'languishing with a tedious Sickness, must be recovered by gentle and easie Medicines . . . rather than by violent Vomits'. The comparison made by Bristol, a former ambassador to Spain, between the obedience of Spaniards and the rebelliousness of Englishmen was odious since the former were 'scarcely removed a degree from Slaves, nor the Soveraign from a Tyrant'. The similarity, *mutatis mutandis*, between Dorset's utterance and those of the peace-party men at Westminster hardly needs emphasis. Where the latter went out of their way to praise the pacific intentions of the king and opposed any measures which they thought might provoke him, Dorset took an exactly similar line towards the Parliament, which he believed to be, at heart, a loyal defender of the royal prerogative.[74]

Moderate royalist opinion inevitably attached some of the blame for the failure of the Oxford Treaty to the influence of intransigents such as Bristol, his son Digby, Jermyn, Rupert and, not least, the queen. Intransigents on both sides in fact did their best to wreck the negotiations. Some said that the Parliament's nomination of Lord Saye and Sele as one of the commissioners to negotiate at Oxford was a deliberate attempt of the war party to abort the negotiations, knowing that the king would never accept the nomination of Saye, whom he loathed and had specifically exempted from pardon. They may well have been right, though not in their calculation that the treaty would fail in consequence, since Saye was replaced by another commissioner more acceptable to the king. But an interesting light is cast upon the temper of what may be called the peace groups at both Westminster and Oxford by the fact that just as the original nomination of Saye disquieted the former as likely to put the treaty's success in jeopardy, so did the royal rejection of him disquiet the latter, and for much the same reasons.[75]

Frustrated all along the line by Cavalier and Roundhead extremists, it would not be altogether surprising if the peace-groupers at both Westminster and Oxford came near to thinking of one another as something like associates in a common enterprise, the pursuit of peace. Following the failure of the Oxford Treaty, the summer of 1643 was to see a spectacular attempt to exploit this community of interest which was foiled by the opportunism of Pym who turned it brilliantly to his own advantage. The incident in question was Waller's so-called plot, which was uncovered in May. In reality this was no plot at all, but the deliberate conflation by Pym of what were almost certainly two entirely separate and disastrously contradictory strands of royal policy. On the one hand there was the clandestine correspondence of the poet and peace-party MP Edmund Waller, with Secretary Falkland at Oxford, an exchange of views between persons in each camp aimed almost certainly at a concerting of efforts to bring about a successful peace. On the other hand there was the royalist plan, engineered by Sir Nicholas Crispe, the erstwhile customs farmer and monopolist, to execute a royal Commission of Array and provoke an armed rising in London. While the latter project was totally incompatible with the aims of Falkland, Hyde and royalist moderates at Oxford, the exchange of information between peace-groupers in both places was in no way incompatible with them, which makes the description of the 'plot' by Falkland's modern biographer as an attempt to combine the two things more than a trifle odd.[76] Clarendon assures us that Crispe's project for the Commission of Array was taken up by the king 'without the privity or advice of any one councillor or minister of state'. To both Hyde and Falkland it must have seemed that the disastrous pattern of royalist extremist mistakes which had brought the king to his knees at the beginning of 1642 was ominously repeating itself. Pym's version of Waller's Plot which deceived not only the middle and war groups at Westminster but also many of the peace group, not to speak of generations of subsequent historians, put paid to any possibility of coordinating a drive for peace from both Oxford and Westminster, and gave a notable fillip to the opponents of the peace groups in both places.[77]

Reconciliation and peace therefore became more unlikely from the summer of 1643. There is a sense in which the situation which had obtained at the beginning of the war was now reversed. In the summer of 1643, the time of one royalist military success after another, it was now Parliament which might expect impossibly hard peace terms, which circumstance doubtless explains Pym's determination to nail the peace party to the coffin of Waller's Plot. As to Oxford, those favouring total victory and a dictated peace were again in the ascendancy, and the death of Secretary Falkland in September and his replacement by Digby was a further blow to the cause of royalist moderation. The atmosphere at Oxford hardened as a result of military success. Even tough politicians like Hyde must on occasions have been near to despair, and more delicate creatures found the atmosphere unbearable. A good case in point is Sir Edward Dering, the sort of man who, an ornament to society in normal times, fits nowhere in a revolutionary situation. The erstwhile proponent of the Root and Branch Bill, Dering had lapsed into advocacy of primitive episcopacy and from being a parliamentary ally of Pym, he had been driven to the king in 1642 by what he regarded as the extremism of the prevailing party at Westminster. His main motive for defecting from the king at the beginning of 1644 may well have been the desire of a very sick man to end his days in his beloved Kent. But there can be little doubt that he was as much out of place among the roistering Cavaliers at Oxford or Arundel Castle as he had been at Westminster in the reign of King Pym. While there is obviously an element of self-justificatory rationalization in his petition of February 1644 asking for the protection of Parliament, there is no reason to doubt the impression which he conveys of a fear that the voice of reason and moderation – never very powerful at Oxford – was now in danger of being completely hushed.[78]

Yet at the end of the previous year Hyde had sought to counter such impressions by persuading the king to summon a 'Parliament' to Oxford. Dering's own unease seems in actual fact to have been compounded by the prospect of taking his seat in this 'Anti-Parliament', as he called it, an ominous sign perhaps that this bold royal initiative, which was pitched not only at those ex-Country MPs like Dering, who had already defected to the king, but also at peace-party men at Westminster, was likely to be attended only with limited success. Pym's exploitation of Waller's Plot had made it clear, however, that little could be expected in the way of peace initiatives from Westminster. Peace-party men had either been shocked into acceptance of Pym's version of the incident, or recognized their impotence in face of the prevailing opinion that royal peace moves were no more than a cover for attempted royalist *coups*.

Given the increasing prevalence of extremist councils at Oxford, it was a considerable achievement on Hyde's part to persuade the king to issue a proclamation on 22 December 1643, summoning a parliamentary assembly to Oxford.[79] During the summer it was only with difficulty that he had prevailed upon Charles not to dissolve Parliament at Westminster, an act which would have set the seal on royalist extremism by violating the statute of 1641 that the parliament could not be dissolved without its own consent, and therefore, by implication, placing the rest of the reforming legislation of the first session of the Long Parliament in jeopardy. Instead Hyde persuaded the king to content himself with a Proclamation in June, which, while declaring that Parliament was no longer free, specifically disclaimed 'the least intention to violate or avoyd any . . . Act passed by Us for the good and benefit of Our People this Parliament'.[80] Hyde had thus succeeded in turning a disadvantageous situation to the benefit of the hard-pressed moderates at Oxford. If the policy of summoning a parliamentary assembly to Oxford succeeded, their numbers ought to be substantially increased, even if an inevitable corollary of this would be a proportionate weakening of the peace party at Westminster. But it was the fact that the latter had been at a hopeless disadvantage since the discovery of Waller's Plot, which, along with the need for an augmentation of the strength of the moderates at Oxford, had brought about this imaginative royalist initiative in the first place. How far was it successful?

Clarendon's estimate that there were almost three hundred members of the House of Commons and more than sixty from the Upper House at Oxford, as opposed to less than a hundred of the former and a dozen of the latter at Westminster, has been shown by Gardiner to have overstated the number of commoners and understated that of the peers. A letter from the Oxford 'Parliament' to the Earl of Essex on 27 January 1644 is signed by 118 MPs and 44 peers, though an additional 57 commoners and 38 peers were absent mostly on one form or other of military service.[81] Some of the MPs at Oxford, such as Sampson Eure (Leominster) who acted as Speaker, the civil lawyer Dr George Parry (St Mawes) and the ex-monopolist William Watkins (Monmouth), had been closely linked with the Court from the beginning of the Long Parliament. It is highly unlikely that any of these were voices in favour of moderation. More was perhaps to be expected from former anti-Court men who had gone over to the king before the outbreak of war, of whom the three members for Weymouth and Melcombe Regis, one of them the celebrated Sir John Strangeways, may serve as examples; and still more perhaps from those who had defected after the outbreak of hostilities. The evidence is insufficiently definite to allow of defections being dated with precision, but it certainly does not suggest that, if the calling of the Oxford 'Parliament' was designed to attract peace-party MPs from Westminster, this aim was attended with any notable success. Roger Matthew, MP for Dartmouth, who had been active for Parliament in the early months of the war, and later claimed that he had gone to the Oxford 'Parliament' in the interests of peace, is the only really convincing example.[82]

One circumstance which may well have discouraged the large-scale defection of peace-party men to join the Oxford 'Parliament' was the icy reception which had been accorded at Oxford to three of the six peers who had gone over to the king immediately after the peace initiative favoured by the House of Lords had been frustrated in the Commons by the combined forces of Pym's middle group and the war party in August 1643. In Clarendon's view the cold shoulder which was offered to the queen's former favourite, the Earl of Holland, and the two other peers, Bedford and Clare, was a disastrous mistake in that it made 'the King and all those about him looked upon as implacable'. The three lords, and especially Holland, returned to Westminster burning with resentment and full of excuses which confirmed this damaging impression and no doubt helped to discourage the Earl of Northumberland from the defection which he was almost certainly contemplating at that time.[83]

Such things were not quickly forgotten, and presented the most unfavourable circumstances imaginable for the success of the Oxford 'Parliament', some of whose acts would undoubtedly have met the approval of the peace-party men at Westminster. This is certainly true of a declaration in February 1644 denouncing the calling of the Scots into the war, 'to drink our Blood, to divide our Possessions, to give us new Laws, and to rule over us'.[84] Although the same could not be said of the voting of supplies to the king, the use of a representative assembly, however incomplete, to grant taxes did at least help to soften the impression of a complete royal reversion to the arbitrary methods of the 1630s. The MPs at Oxford also emphasized their role as constitutional caretakers by requesting and obtaining from the king a specific disavowal of any intention of dispensing with parliament after he had won the war, as well as a promise that the emergency financial measures which were currently necessary to the royalist war effort would not be regarded as precedents to be used in peace time.[85]

It is noteworthy that Clarendon in his *History* went through complicated exercises in circumlocution to avoid describing the assembly at Oxford as a parliament. The view he seems to have taken is that two distinct sets of MPs were meeting at Westminster and Oxford in assemblies each of which fell short of full parliamentary status, but that it was hoped that the peace-loving members of both would reach out towards one another in gestures of peace and reconciliation, as they had done in the days before Waller's Plot. Not surprisingly, this view did not find acceptance at Westminster, even among peace-party men, since it clearly implied that the Parliament there was incomplete. The call of the Oxford 'Parliament' on 16 April for 'a free and full Convention of Parliament as the most hopeful Way to unite these unhappy Divisions' was therefore rejected with scorn since it 'puts them at Oxford into an equall Condition with vs.'[86]

Charles was able to turn such rebuffs to good effect as an argument why his Oxford assembly should grant him adequate supply, arguing on 7 February that 'this strange arrogance of refusing to treat with you can proceed from nothing but their contempt of our Forces . . .'[87] At the ending of the first session on 16 April 1644 and its adjournment to 8 October,[88] moderate royalists had some grounds for modest self-congratulation despite the failure to break through to a peace settlement via a 'free and full Convention of Parliament'. But not everyone at Oxford felt well disposed towards the assembly. Essentially the creation of royalist moderates who had persuaded a reluctant king to abandon his hardline attitude for the time being, it had made powerful enemies at Court, among them military commanders like Rupert and extremists such as Digby, who, while bitterly opposed to one another on everything else, were at least at one in their dislike of peace negotiations. This feeling may have been intensified by the fear of royalist extremists that a peace-seeking 'parliament' at Oxford might not be above giving an earnest of its pacific intentions by delivering to justice some of those – Digby, Bristol and Jermyn, for example – whom the parliamentarians of Westminster had designated as delinquents who could not be excepted from trial by any peace terms negotiated. If to such considerations is added the dislike on the part of courtiers and royal officials, who had too long been accustomed to the delights of irresponsible government, of parliamentary scrutiny of their expenditures and criticism of their procedures, it is not difficult to see why the 'parliament' quickly outlived its usefulness in the eyes of many royalists.[89] It is an unfortunate accident of history that all too little is known about its proceedings, since its records were burnt prior to the surrender of Oxford to the parliamentary army in 1646. But enough is known to permit the observation that it was not simply the disappointments about peace which caused the hopes of moderate royalists to turn sour. When Charles I adjourned – for the last time as it turned out – the assembly on 10 March 1645, he did so, as he informed his wife, with considerable relief at being 'freed from the place of base and mutinous motions – that is to say, our mongrel Parliament here'.[90] Was there even the slightest prospect that a king who found such an assembly irksome could live with any Parliament?

In the meantime, it has been argued, the hopes of royalist moderates were also being frustrated by developments in the conduct of the war and the nature of the royalist command. Dr Ronald Hutton has pressed the case that, as the war progressed, and especially from about the middle of 1643, command in the royalist army fell increasingly into the hands of seasoned professional soldiers, ruthless men often of relatively obscure social status and with few close ties with their regional and local communities. Aristocratic commanders of great social prestige and regional influence were increasingly being superseded by experienced soldiers of fortune, 'here today and God knows where tomorrow', as one of the former, the Earl of Worcester, put it to one of the latter, the king's commander-in-chief Patrick Ruthven, later Earl of Brentford,[91] who himself had in 1642 succeeded the Earl of Lindsey who was later killed at Edgehill in October. In the following year Lord Capel in The Welsh marches and the West Midlands was succeeded by Sir John Byron, and while the rise of the royal princes Rupert and Maurice at the expense of aristocratic commanders such as Hertford, Worcester and Newcastle, was obviously not a case of the triumph of military qualities over conditions of birth, the Princes' royal blood in no way detracts from their significance as ruthless soldiers with none of the close ties with regional communities which characterize native English grandees such as Hertford, Worcester and Newcastle.

It has been argued that Dr Hutton's dichotomy is too bold. Lindsey, for instance, may have been an aristocrat, but he was also a professional soldier of great experience, who was simply replaced by an even more experienced professional, Ruthven. Capel was a rich nobleman as well as an incompetent commander, but Byron, who replaced him, came from a Nottinghamshire family of high social standing. Moreover, from the beginning aristocratic commanders had worked closely with and relied heavily on more experienced subordinates, sometimes themselves men of local reputation and influence. The

Marquis of Hertford had used Sir Ralph Hopton,[92] the Earl of Cumberland had relied heavily on Sir Thomas Glemham, and the Earl of Newcastle on the Scotsman James King (later ennobled in the Scottish peerage as Lord Eythin). Professional competence and 'feral' behaviour were not so inextricably linked as Dr Hutton claims. His thesis that while a royalist victory in 1642 would probably have produced a settlement incorporating most of the royal constitutional concessions of 1641, such a victory two or three years later would have ushered in a thorough-going royal absolutism resting on the power of the sword, remains a matter for conjecture rather than a self-evident truth. It is, of course, one of the might-have-beens of history, significant largely in counter-factual terms, as shedding light on the temper of the royalist command in the later stages of the war, and even here a matter of some doubt and legitimate controversy. It is perhaps a feature of most wars, and in no way incompatible with the inevitable onset of war-weariness, that they tend to become more rather than less savage with the passage of time; a feature which is by no means necessarily connected with an increasing importance of professional military commanders of relatively obscure social status or without close regional ties. Such considerations are certainly not exclusive to the royalist army, though in the days following its disastrous defeat at Naseby and Langport in the high summer of 1645, royalist ferocity was undoubtedly accentuated by military desperation and precipitate and disorderly retreat.[93]

X

The above examination of affairs at Oxford has taken us beyond the point at which we left the political situation at Westminster: the death of Pym on 8 December 1643. It used to be claimed – and still is claimed by some historians[94] – that the middle group did not survive Pym, and that the other groups gained from its disintegration. But as Valerie Pearl has demonstrated, Pym did find a worthy successor, and the middle group a new leader, in Oliver St John, who like Pym was a former client of the Earl of Bedford, which gave him a host of influential connections in many parts of the country.[95] To the best of his ability St John followed in the steps of the master politician. For example there is nothing about his attitude to peace negotiations or the war effort which does not fit with the notion of him as Pym's political heir. In particular, his determination to negotiate only from positions of strength brought him – as it had brought Pym – into frequent alliance with the war party, and collision with the peace party. The same is true of St John's support for the ordinance establishing the Committee of Both Kingdoms in February 1644 as the central directing agency of the Anglo-Scottish war strategy. Here again he ranged himself alongside the war party against a peace party which could see nothing but bad in the proposed committee, both on account of what it regarded as its excessive powers and as the product of the Scottish alliance which its members had so bitterly opposed. On the former issue, and in particular the proposed right of the Committee to negotiate peace or war, St John, in marked contrast to the war-party radicals, displayed an instinct for compromise worthy of Pym himself, as a result of which the Ordinance went through and the committee was launched.[96] Another long-standing notion exploded by Dr Pearl is the view that the Committee was dominated by anti-peace and anti-Essex men, which again rests on the assumption that the middle group did not survive, and that any active politician not connected with the peace group was almost certain to be anti-peace and anti-Essex.[97]

But even if the Committee of Both Kingdoms was not dominated by anti-Essex men, it is arguable that some of the Lord General's intense irritation at the limitation of his strategic freedom by a mostly civilian committee – even though he himself was a member of it – would have rubbed off on the politicians of the middle group who had pushed for its establishment, and that this in turn would make continuity with Pym's policy of supporting Essex through thick and thin the more difficult to accomplish.[98] More than once the Lord General's smouldering resentment broke through to the surface, as in his irascible letter of 14 June 1644 which he signed as the Committee's 'innocent though suspected Servant', complaining of the orders which it had sent him, based, as he claimed, on misinformation, and attempting to divert him from his advance to the west, in order to relieve Lyme Regis, then under siege by Prince Maurice. In the same letter he gave vent to his long-standing grudges against his old rival, Waller, whom he petulantly accused the Committee of favouring at his expense.[99]

The mutual dislike of Essex and Waller was, of course, a problem which St John had inherited from Pym, and he tackled it in much the same way, though, it must be confessed, with less success. Like Pym, he strove to strengthen the forces not of one but of both generals, as well as of the army of the Eastern Association under the Earl of Manchester which had been created in the meantime. But, again, like Pym, he continued to support the Lord General against the almost perpetual sniping of the war party.[100] It is a very over simplified view which takes the middle-groupers' support for the armies of Waller and the Eastern Association as evidence of their hostility to Essex, even though the Lord General himself might regard it as such.[101] If this is true, then Pym himself cannot be acquitted of the same charge and on the same grounds. Indeed, as Dr Holmes has clearly shown, the problem of the attitudes of the political groups at Westminster to the different armies in the field is a highly complex one, in which localist issues are intimately involved. For instance, conservative gentlemen from East Anglia might, for good localist reasons, support the ordinance for the army of the Eastern Association more enthusiastically than that for the Lord General's army. In doing so, they would range themselves alongside the war party whose members had switched some of their support from their former hero Waller and his army to Manchester and the Eastern Association force, not least on account of its reputation for godliness and as a receptacle for radicals, Independents, sectaries and saints.[102]

XI

The excesses of the sectaries were a product of the vacuum created by the abolition of the machinery of ecclesiastical discipline and coercion and the failure, so deplored by strict Presbyterians, to put anything in its place. It is against this background that the end of the pact between religious Presbyterians and Independents which had been one of the achievements of Pym's reign should be viewed. The significance of the publication of the famous Independent tract *An Apologeticall Narration* in February 1644 is not so much that it initiated the end to the long truce as that it was in itself a response to the increasingly vocal Presbyterian disquiet, which was given eloquent expression in the Fast Sermon preached before the Parliament by Alexander Henderson on 27 December 1643.[103] But it was not only the Presbyterians who deplored the failure of the Westminster Assembly to achieve thorough-going reformation. As Dr W. Lamont has demonstrated, this failure was contributing to the growth of sympathy with Erastianism, that great English Protestant tradition which looked to the secular power to initiate and to complete godly reformation, and, at least after 1603, had looked in vain. Laudian episcopacy had, rightly or wrongly, been viewed as a departure from this great tradition, and Scottish Presbyterianism was no less, and perhaps even more, foreign to it. The failure of the English Constantine was succeeded by the failure of an assembly of divines as the motor of godly reformation. Was it not time to turn away from clericalist solutions back to the agencies which had initiated the Protestant settlements of 1549 and 1559? Where the godly Prince had failed, the godly Parliament would surely succeed.[104]

Faced with the sects on the one hand and the Erastians on the other, it was no wonder that the Presbyterians were desperately anxious to get on with the business of reformation in which they had been so consistently frustrated. However conscious they were of the responsibility of Independent members of the assembly for the delays, the publication of the *Apologeticall Narration* must nevertheless have seemed to them like a stab in the back. Although the pamphlet is for the most part a moderate and reasoned statement of the Independent position, there were some passages which could not but give deep offence to strict Presbyterians. To assert, for instance, that the primitive Church consisted of independent congregations was tantamount to claiming that Independency, rather than Presbyterianism, was, in fact, *iure divino*.[105]

Yet for all the obstructionism and delays, the righteous might yet prevail. On 7 June 1644 Baillie wrote home with much greater optimism than he had displayed for some time. Some progress, however slow, had at last been made in the Assembly. The Directory of Worship had gone through, admittedly after an unduly prolonged debate. No less encouraging, the Independents were being weakened by the defection of some of their number to the sects. If reason was at last prevailing in the Assembly, it would surely also not be long before the Presbyterian God of Battles provided unequivocal proof of the favour which he accorded to his saints. From the first the Scots had banked on military success such as they had experienced in the Bishops' Wars, as providing the most telling of all arguments for the righteousness of their cause. What they needed above all else was the spectacular military victory which had so far eluded them. This opportunity came and was taken at Marston Moor on 3 July. But, unfortunately for the Scots, it was taken at least as much by the godless sectaries and Independents of Manchester's Eastern Association army as by their own Covenanting army. Instead of being the finally convincing proof of the righteousness of the Scottish cause, Marston Moor was widely regarded as the triumph of Oliver Cromwell. Baillie's optimism of less than a month earlier evaporated. 'Our Independents,' he spluttered in a letter of 23 July, 'continews and increases in their obstinacie. Much is added to their pride and hopes by their service at the battell of Yorke [*viz.* Marston Moor]; albeit much of their valor is grounded on very false lies, prejudiciall to God, the author and to us, the true instruments, of that dayes honor.'[106]

One of the main issues on which opinion had been divided in the Westminster Assembly was toleration, which was supported, for obvious reasons, by the Independent minority and detested by the Presbyterian majority. If there was one treatise which made Presbyterian blood boil at an even higher temperature than Milton's divorce tracts it was Roger Williams's *The Bloudy Tenent of Persecution.*[107] It was, among other things, for a generous measure of toleration for non-Presbyterians that the *Apologeticall Narration* had been pleading. There is an important sense, in which, as Haller has suggested, the Independent advocacy of toleration reflects the different historical background against which English Puritanism and Scottish Presbyterianism had developed.[108] Those advocating toleration were in one sense propounding a dangerously innovatory notion, but in another were traditionalists who harked back to relatively easy-going, tolerant broad-Church attitudes of the days of Archbishop Abbot before the Laudian episode. It was the relative freedom to preach the word – relative, that is, to what had been experienced under Laud and what was to be expected under a tight Presbyterian system – rather than forms of Church government, which was for them the vital consideration. To a nation which had cast off *iure divino* episcopacy, *iure divino* Presbyterianism was hardly less inimical, for new presbyter was but old prelate writ large. This is not simply a metaphor, nor was this feeling confined to the Independents and the sectaries on their left. On 13 September 1644 in the debate in the House of Commons on the form of ordination proposed by the Westminster Assembly, that good anti-episcopalian conservative, Sir Simonds D'Ewes, gave expression to his worries about Presbyterian theocracy and his hope that the divines had no intention 'to introduce such a tyrannical power as the bishops had'. The outcome of that debate was the so-called Accommodation Order in which the Assembly was asked to bear in mind differences of opinion about Church government and, if agreement proved impossible, to make proper provision for tender consciences. Appropriately, it was St John who introduced the Order in the House, in response to a suggestion from the war-party man, Oliver Cromwell, but in typical middle-group style framing the Order in such a way as to gather support from a wide variety of MPs.[109] While 1644 did indeed see the end of the inter-denominational truce between Presbyterians and Independents and the re-opening of intra-Puritan polemical strife, this did not on the whole spill over into politics. The terms 'Presbyterian' and 'Independent' continued to relate to confessional differences only. To examine the political transformation whereby they also became the labels of political parties will be one of the main tasks of the chapter which follows.

NINE *The Transformation of Politics 1644–6*

For I assure thee, I put little or no difference between setting up the Presbyterian government or submitting to the Church of Rome.

> Letter from Charles I to Henrietta Maria,
> 19 February 1646, in *Charles I in 1646*, p. 19.

. . . since those men who were most averse to the coming in of the *Scots* . . . are so handsomely come about to an intimate conjunction with the *Scots, quid non speremus?*

> Edward Bowles, *Manifest Truths* (1646), p. 45.

I

THE PERIOD between the autumn of 1644 and the summer of 1646 saw the victory of Parliament in the first Civil War. This victory was in itself a product of a radical reorganization of the parliamentary high command accompanied by striking changes in the composition and alignment of the political groupings at Westminster. The tripartite division between peace, war and middle groups gave way to a two-party dichotomy with the middle group losing that completely separate identity which it had preserved, however precariously, during the months following the death of Pym. In the course of 1645 these two groups became increasingly known as Presbyterians and Independents. The significance and appropriateness of these terms will be discussed later in this chapter, along with the most important single factor around which these developments turned – the changed political orientation of the Scots. There was in fact a startling reversal of alliances, whereby the peace party, which had bitterly opposed the entry of the Scots into the war, now became their ally, while their former supporters in the war party became their opponents. This bald summary of the subject matter of the present chapter, however, obscures the complex nuances of developments which must now be traced in more detail.

II

During the late autumn of 1644, when Roundhead delight at the triumph of Marston Moor in July had turned sour as a result of the disaster to Essex's army at Lostwithiel in September and the disillusionment attendant upon the failure of parliamentary commanders to follow up the advantage gained at the second battle of Newbury at the end of October, the time seemed ripe for the replacement of diffident and allegedly defeatist aristocratic commanders by energetic and determined men with no inhibitions about carrying the war to the enemy. Three of the most important of these discredited commanders were, in ascending order of importance, the Earls of Denbigh, Manchester and Essex, and none of these cases is quite so straightforward as is sometimes assumed. Denbigh was Commander-in-Chief of the forces in the associated counties of the West Midlands between June 1643 and his dismissal in November 1644. His disputes with Colonel John Barker and the radical war-party MP William Purefoy in Warwickshire, and with the formidable Cheshire war-party leader Sir William Brereton in Staffordshire are sometimes treated as a simple case of aristocratic foot-dragging and incompetence versus the energetic radical pursuit of victory at all costs.[1] There is some truth in this verdict, but it is by no means the whole truth, at least in so far as the quarrels with Purefoy and Barker are concerned. These two seem to have ruthlessly exploited localist sentiments on the Warwickshire county committee in order to frustrate the Earl's attempts both to exercise control over the defences of Coventry and to get local troops to march on Shropshire to counter a royalist threat from Wales. In a sense these incidents stand on its head the orthodox notion of the war-party men as the opponents and the peace-party men the supporters, of that endemic localism which threatened to paralyse the parliamentary war effort. At any rate Denbigh's enemies succeeded in getting him removed from his command partly as the result of a snap vote taken in the House of Commons in November

1644, when some of those who might normally have been expected to support him were at dinner.[2]

Denbigh's enemies had also frustrated his ambition to obtain a parliamentary ordinance for his command similar to that of the Earl of Manchester for the Eastern Association. In contrast to their use of localist sentiments against Denbigh, Manchester's insistence on his obligations to the Eastern Association as an excuse for not advancing too far or too speedily approximate more closely to the orthodox picture, with localist sentiments used as a weapon against, rather than for, the war party. Manchester's strength at Westminster had, however, originally rested on the fact that he had replaced Waller as the favourite commander of the war party, while also drawing substantial support from the middle group. Yet in the closing months of 1644 he also fell victim to charges of 'continued backwardness to all action, averseness to engagement . . . neglecting opportunities, and declining to . . . pursue advantages upon the enemy', culminating in his alleged refusal to follow up the initial advantage gained by parliament at the second battle of Newbury. Of the eighteen principal witnesses who testified against him before the Commons committee chaired by the war-party man Zouch Tate, thirteen can be identified as war-party or middle-group supporters, with the former especially prominent.[3] Most prominent of all was Oliver Cromwell, not least because, as a recent reinterpretation of these events has suggested, as commander of the horse at Newbury, he was at least as vulnerable as Manchester to such charges.[4] Yet earlier in 1644 Manchester and Cromwell had worked together in broad agreement on, inter alia, the policy of officering the Eastern Association army on the basis of efficiency and zeal for the cause rather than of confessional distinctions. It was in fact his enthusiasm for an interdenominational Puritan army which had made Manchester the favourite commander of the war party. The original threat to that ideal had come from intolerant Presbyterian commanders such as the Scot Lawrence Crawford and the Lincolnshire gentleman Colonel Edward King. It was their measures against Independents and sectaries in their commands which sparked off Cromwell's abandonment of Puritan ecumenicism and his recourse to purging his command of religious Presbyterians and staffing it with Independents and sectaries which was one of the principal charges brought against him by his enemies.[5]

In so far as one can point to any single decisive event in the parting of the ways between Cromwell and Manchester, it was the battle of Marston Moor in July 1644. To Oliver, Marston Moor was one of those divine dispensations for which throughout his career he urged men to wait, while always doubting the ability of lesser mortals to recognize authentic revelation when vouchsafed to them. If Oliver needed any assurance that he and 'the Godly Party' were God's chosen instruments, Marston Moor provided it.[6] As to Manchester, Dr Kaplan's discrediting of the myth about the younger Vane's mission to the allied commanders before York to test their reactions to the idea of deposing the king[7] precludes the adoption of this convenient and dramatic explanation of the earl's change of heart and revulsion from the energetic prosecution of the war. But it does not rule out the view of Marston Moor as a climacteric event for Manchester also. Down to that time it had been the royalists who had won the crushing victories. Marston Moor, which put the vast bulk of the north under parliamentary control and sent into despairing exile the Earl of Newcastle, the royalist commander, whose advance through Lincolnshire had not long before threatened the heart of Manchester's Eastern Association itself, wonderfully concentrated Manchester's mind on the likely consequences of a complete Roundhead victory. It was not only Oliver to whom divine dispensations were vouchsafed. Manchester had looked into the abyss, where, though clouded with the dust of battle, he had discerned dim shapes to which the events of the succeeding weeks were to give increasing and horrifying substance. 'It was easy to begin a war,' one of his opponents reported him as saying, 'but no man knew where it would end'.[8]

Where indeed would it end? In social anarchy, the removal of hierarchical distinctions between men, perhaps in republicanism? To some conservative parliamentarians Cromwell's alleged disregard of considerations of social rank in his choice of army officers seemed to point clearly in the horrifying direction indicated by royalist prophecies of social disruption such as the royal answer to the Nineteen Propositions back in 1642. 'The wisest of men,' as one of Cromwell's most determined parliamentary opponents was later to put it, 'saw it to be a great evil that Servants should ride on Horses.'[9] It is important, however, to get this matter into proper perspective. Earlier in the war Cromwell had written to his relative, John Hampden, stressing the disadvantages under which parliament was fighting the war with armies full of 'old decayed serving men and tapsters and such kind of fellows'. These 'base and mean fellows' could never be a match for the spirited gentlemen who flocked to the support of the king. However, in so far as such ideal officer material was in short supply, 'better plain men than none', he argued in August 1643 in reply to complaints about his promoting such a man.[10] While even this might be sufficient to stamp him as a dangerous radical, Manchester and his supporters accused him of going much further, and of cashiering honest gentlemen under his command and replacing them with 'common men, pore and of meane parentage, onely he would give them the title of godly, pretious men'. Under his military governorship, they alleged, the Isle of Ely had 'become a meer Amsterdam', with soldiers preaching from church pulpits which orthodox parsons did not dare to enter, and men raised to be captains 'onely as I conceive because they proffess themselves Independents, and such as have filld dung carts before they were captaines and sinc [sic]'.[11]

The now familiar juxtaposition of social and religious radicalism will not have gone unobserved. Such statements, moreover, were all of a piece with Cromwell's alleged attitude to lords, urging on one occasion, it was reported, that 'God would have noe lording over his peopell'.[12] In the course of 1644 it became increasingly clear to men of Manchester's way of thinking where emphasis on winning the war at any cost was leading. The cost was in fact too high. When zeal for outright victory became the only test of eligibility to hold command, anything was possible. It was such considerations which turned Manchester, the hero of the war and middle groups at the beginning of the year, into the fearful and apprehensive conservative of the late summer. But to deal with Manchester simply as a case study in indecision, procrastination and failure of nerve is to fail to do justice to a gentle, idealistic man who was horrified by the carnage of the battlefield and no less horrified by the prospect of his own army's tearing itself to pieces as a consequence of the dissension and backbiting which had shattered his ideal of a united Puritan inter-denominational force. Like a number of other characters in this book, he presents the sad spectacle of an erstwhile radical overtaken by events. As to Cromwell, while his celebrated fire-eating statements about lords and the irrelevance of considerations of social degree may be hardly less apocryphal than his alleged concurrence in Vane's imaginary project to depose the king, one is nevertheless left with the impression of a man whose determination to win the war was blinding him to the possible social consequences of the policies necessary to win it – consequences which he himself was bitterly to regret later. Yet of the two men's diagnosis of the situation in the autumn of 1644, there can be no doubt that Cromwell's was the more realistic. The alternative to a radical change in the conduct of the war was still a royalist victory whose consequences would be as unwelcome to Manchester as they were to Cromwell.

What Newbury was to Manchester's reputation, Lostwithiel had been to that of the Lord General whose defeat in Cornwall in September had finally lost him the support which Pym's middle-group successors had continued to accord him against the snipings of the war party.[13] However, as Dr Holmes has clearly shown, Essex remained a force seriously to be reckoned with long after this.[14] In the first place, he did his utmost to ascribe the disaster to the failure of other commanders, Manchester, Middleton, and, needless to say, his old rival Waller, to come promptly to his assistance.[15] Secondly, the failure to follow up the parliamentary advantage at the second battle of Newbury and to prevent the king from relieving Donnington Castle on 9 November turned the spotlight away from the Lord General's failures. The parliamentary high command was now positively strewn with failures and reputations were lying all over the place. If the reputations of Waller and Cromwell could be destroyed along with that of Manchester, Essex would have been provided with a splendid platform from which to restore his own fortunes. Certainly some of his supporters, among them Sir Samuel Luke, the parliamentary governor of Newport Pagnell, were confident that a revival of his fortunes was imminent.[16]

It was therefore crucially important to both Cromwell and Waller that none of the blame for the depressing aftermath of the second battle of Newbury should be attached to them. According to Bulstrode Whitelock, it was Cromwell's attempt to ascribe some of the blame to the Lord General himself – even though he had been ill at the time of, and had played no part in, the Newbury campaign – which more than any other factor explains Essex's decision to call a meeting at his house in the Strand some time during the first week of December to consider whether to impeach Cromwell as an incendiary. Among those present were the Scottish commissioners in London and Denzil Holles and Sir Philip Stapleton, the latter a former middle-grouper but now associated with Holles in the peace party. Whitelock and John Maynard, who had been asked to the meeting as peace-party lawyers, to advise on the plan which they heard expounded by the Scottish Lord Chancellor, the Earl of Loudoun, pronounced it impracticable, doubtful in law and likely to boomerang. It was reluctantly abandoned, and the main interest of the incident for us is as an early instance of the peace party's and the Scots' consorting against the former's parliamentary opponents. It is therefore an interesting early indication of the changing political situation which was ultimately to bring about the great reversal of alliances.[17]

III

The royalists, who themselves were no strangers to bitter internecine disputes, must have rejoiced greatly at the spectacle of their most prominent opponents at each other's throats towards the end of 1644. This gravely serious situation for the parliamentary cause was saved only as a result of the imaginative expedient of the Self Denying Ordinance, which, by relieving serving officers who were also members of either House of Parliament of their commands, disposed of the contesting parties at one blow and made a fresh start possible. As Dr Cotton has convincingly demonstrated,[18] it also suited Cromwell's book by preventing the charges which he had made against Manchester in the House of Commons from going forward, and making it possible to treat them as privileged material, thus preventing the earl from carrying the war to Cromwell by counter-charges which he was only too anxious to make and some of which would probably stick. In these circumstances it is hardly surprising that the Ordinance, which in its original form was proposed by the war-party man Zouch Tate on 9 December, did not go unopposed. To some, as Robert Baillie reported, it was 'a most wise, necessar [sic] and heroick action'; to others, 'the most rash, hazardous and unjust action as ever Parliament did'.[19] War-party men such as Vane and Cromwell might stress that it was a compromise whose advantages enormously outweighed its disadvantages, but to their cautious and suspicious parliamentary opponents such as Holles and Whitelock, war-party compromises were *ipso facto* suspect and the ordinance a leap into the unknown, involving the sacrifice of tried and trusted commanders. But, their opponents urged, the whole point of the ordinance was that such men had not only been tried but had also been found woefully wanting, and the sacrifice of those who had served Parliament well was eminently worth making, not least since the ordinance allowed everyone to make his own judgement as to which commanders fell into which category. Mutual sacrifice was the condition of the restoration of internal peace in the parliamentarian camp, and, as Cromwell insisted, of the new modelling of the army, without which 'the People can bear the War no longer and will enforce you to a dishonourable Peace'. Ludlow was later to argue that the ordinance made Parliament the better able to resist such popular clamour, since it was no longer open to charges that it was obstructing peace initiatives because it was in the interests of a number of influential members to prolong the war.[20]

The subsequent exemption of Cromwell, and the refusal of Parliament to exempt Essex, from the provisions of the ordinance naturally gave rise to *ex post facto* allegations not only by the peace-party leader Denzil Holles, but also by the non-aligned MP Clement Walker, that this had been planned from the beginning, and no real mutual sacrifice was ever contemplated by the clauses of the ordinance.[21] Similarly, elaborate conjectures about the role of the ordinance in the revolutionary process came to be built on its rejection by the Lords, which necessitated the creation of a second ordinance which passed through the Upper House on 3 April 1645. The new ordinance preserved the substance of the old, while saving noble faces by allowing those peers who also held commissions to resign them rather than depriving them of them outright.[22] The peers had objected to the ordinance on the grounds that it deprived them 'of that honor which in all ages haue been giuen unto them'. No one, they argued, had to be a member of the Lower House, but peers had no choice about membership of the House of Lords and consequent exclusion from military employment under the terms of the Self Denying Ordinance. Added to such deeply felt objections was a certain shocked incredulity at the notion that it might be appropriate for anyone but a peer to command an English army, and that to deprive peers of the right to do so was to rob them of their essential *raison d'être*.[23]

Bulstrode Whitelock believed that the peers had good grounds for their apprehensions, notwithstanding a Commons declaration of 21 March that the members of the Lower House held themselves obliged to preserve the privileges of the Upper House.[24] Whitelock argued that the ordinance was, amongst other things, a weapon specially designed by the war party for use against aristocratic generals such as Essex, against whom they continued to pursue their long-standing vendetta, not simply because he was 'too much a favourer of peace (a good fault in a General of an Army)', but also, and more significantly, because he was 'too strong a supporter of Monarchy and of Nobility and other old Constitutions, which they had a mind to alter'. This view of the ordinance is obviously flawed by Whitelock's failure to shake off his own knowledge of the ultimate revolutionary outcome of the events of the 1640s which impelled him to yield to the temptation to search for republican origins in events which took place much earlier. This is not to argue that this and the parallel development of the new modelling of the army were not steps on the road which ultimately led to regicide and republicanism. But it is to question the imputation of such motives to those who sought to get such measures through Parliament in 1644–5, the vast majority of whom were neither revolutionaries nor republicans.

Similar arguments can be applied to the foundation of the New Model Army which the Self Denying Ordinance was to facilitate. Armed with the knowledge of its crushing victories at Naseby, Langport and elsewhere later in 1645, it is dangerously easy to see the ultimate military triumph of the New Model as inevitable. But before Naseby in June 1645 no one could be sure that commitment to wholesale military reorganization was not leaving the parliamentary flank dangerously exposed to a royalist offensive designed to take advantage of the existing state of uncertainty. It was considerations such as these which probably loomed at least as large among the early objections to the New Model as the more familiar fears about the social composition of its officer class and the heterodox religious practices with which it become increasingly associated.

Nor were either of these two latter characteristics peculiar to, or originated by, the New Model. It is broadly true to say that the structure of command in the case of the earlier parliamentary armies had mirrored pretty faithfully the gradations of rank in the local societies from which they were drawn. The local rustics were normally officered by social superiors previously known to them. Military discipline reinforced social subordination, and social subordination helped to cement military discipline. In Essex's army, for example, most of the regiments of foot were commanded by colonels who had recruited their men from their own local dependents. The crucial break away from this came not with the New Model, but with Manchester's Eastern Association army, which was in its turn to provide the nucleus of the élite corps of the New Model. Far more than Essex and Waller, Manchester seems to have drawn many of his officers from different localities from those of his other ranks and some of them from outside the eastern counties altogether. Some of his colonels were drawn not from the élite county gentry but from the lesser parochial gentry, while one of his lieutenant colonels, Hewson, had been a shoemaker in Westminster. Manchester's and Cromwell's emphasis first and foremost on godliness, which they both interpreted – at least down to July 1644 – in a generalized Puritan, rather than exclusively Presbyterian or Independent way, was a further consideration which often conflicted with that of social degree.[25]

This is important because considerations of social rank were significant on both sides in the Civil War. Too much attention ought not to be paid to Clarendon's notorious observation, after reviewing the names of the royalist notabilities killed at the second battle of Newbury in October 1644, that 'the officers on the enemy's side were ... for the most part of no better families than their common soldiers'[26] In most parliamentary armies before 1645 considerations of social rank counted for more than those of military merit and aptitude, which makes Manchester's and Cromwell's policy of opening up military careers to Puritan talent all the more worthy of notice. In a real sense the New Model took over this feature from the Eastern Association army rather than introducing it as a complete novelty. This, needless to say, did not commend it any the more to conservative parliamentarians. For instance, Denzil Holles, whose observations were, however, made in the context of 1647, when the army was bitterly at odds with his ruling Presbyterian faction in parliament, deeply deplored the social composition of the officers in the new army – 'most of the Colonels and officers mean tradesmen ...; a notable dunghill if one would rake into it, to find out their several pedigrees'. However, while some royalist observers viewed the element of social dilution in the officer corps of the New Model with no less distaste than Holles, they were also not unaware of certain advantages which it brought to their adversaries. A royalist account of the siege of Colchester in the Second Civil War in the summer of 1648 is at pains to contrast the habit and temper of 'many of our generall officers in the former warrs [viz. the First Civil War] [who] had such indulgence for their debaucheries that they adopted none to preferments but the companions of their pleasures'; with those of the Roundhead officers who, 'being mechanicks, of the meanest trades, understood no pleasures, soe that to them labour was naturall.' Since, the author concludes, 'in military affairs industry still triumphs over wit', this was by no means an unmixed curse to the Roundhead cause.[27]

However, in the earliest days of the New Model Army only seven of its thirty-seven colonels were not gentlemen by birth – though this proportion is remarkable enough in itself – while nine came from noble families. By the end of the war and in the later 1640s the number of officers and even of regimental commanders drawn from below the

ranks of the landed gentry had increased, a fact which again emphasizes the danger of reading back these conditions into 1645.[28] Similar
considerations apply to the phenomenal zeal, dedication and *esprit de
corps* of the new army. It is true that the typical parliamentarian soldier
before 1645 was a conscript, often the product of a process of impressment which was not basically different from that practised in the days
of Justice Shallow. There is a revealing letter from two Essex gentlemen
to Sir Thomas Barrington 21 August 1643, pleading for the release of
a man 'who through ye malice and ill will of ye Constable is impressed
for a souldier', and yet was known 'to be very honest or well affected
to ye Parliament beyond any of his Neighbours.'[29] Honesty and civic
virtue seem here to have been regarded as positive disqualifications
for military service rather than the reverse. The contrast between this
picture and that of the New Model soldier of the popular imagination
with a Bible as well as a field marshal's baton in his knapsack needs no
stressing.[30] But in actual fact the rank and file of the New Model, and
more especially of its infantry, were recruited from the existing armies
and the numbers made up by the same process of conscription which
had applied in the case of these armies. When the new army first took
the field in May 1645, more than half of the infantry were impressed
men.[31] The cavalry were admittedly different, but the nucleus of this
corps d'élite was the cavalry of the old Eastern Association army, whose
zeal for the godly cause and the leaning of so many of its officers and
men towards radical religious beliefs did not originate in 1645. Firth's
statement that Independency was not a prominent force in the army
before the New Model seriously underrates its significance in the army
of the Eastern Association.[32] It would probably be true to say that the
creation of the New Model ensured the continued encouragement of
that pre-existing radical religious zeal which had been such an important feature of Manchester's army but had been threatened by the
intolerance of Presbyterian officers such as Crawford and King.[33]
There can be no doubt, however, that the new army provided a fertile
ground for the planting out of these seeds of religious radicalism.
Richard Baxter stressed the absence of godly (i.e. Presbyterian) chaplains with the army as a crucial factor.[34] And when ordained ministers,
whether of an Independent or a Presbyterian variety, were absent –
or often enough when they were present too – there were not lacking
soldiers filled with the Holy Ghost who were only too anxious to preach
the word; and a very heterodox word it often was, whether preached by
Cromwell's soldiers from pulpits in the Isle of Ely in 1644 or, as in

December 1645, by a lieutenant at Bristol who 'delivers very strange things', including heretical mortalist notions, preaching in a scarlet coat with silver lace and the sword at his side.[35]

The creation of the New Model was one of a number of factors making for that transformation of politics whereby the peace-party men were increasingly aligning themselves with the Scots against the latter's former allies on the other side of the House. When the complaint of the Scottish commissioners in London against the dismissal of Scottish officers in the English service and their replacement in the new army by men hostile to the Scottish interest, religious Independents and worse, was debated in the House of Commons on 3 March 1645, Holles, Glyn and Stapleton spoke up in favour of the Scottish point of view and against that of the war party that the complaint was a breach of parliamentary privilege.[36] The officering of the new army was also a party issue quite irrespective of the Scots. On 7 February the Commons debated a proposal from the Upper House to insert a proviso into the New Model Ordinance which would give to Parliament the right to nominate all officers above the rank of Lieutenant. Cromwell, backed by the war party, tried unsuccessfully to insist on the right of the newly appointed commander-in-chief to appoint his own officers, as Lord General Essex had always done, though in his case in the teeth of the opposition of the same war party which was now screaming to Parliament to keep its hands off. The House finally settled for a compromise solution whereby the army commander nominated the officers but Parliament was given a negative voice. This seems to have been supported by the peace party for whom Stapleton and Reynolds acted as tellers in the division which was won by 82 votes to 63. The pattern of voting had been very different on 21 January in the case of the motion to appoint Sir Thomas Fairfax as commander-in-chief, when the number of votes cast was much larger, the motion passing by 101 votes to 69 with Holles and Stapleton acting as tellers against, and the war-party men, Cromwell and the younger Vane, for, the motion. Perhaps a greater number of non-aligned MPs voted in this division, but it could also be that a majority of the surviving middle-groupers were acting in a classic Hexterian manner, switching support from side to side according to the nature of the issue.[37]

If so, this was probably a late manifestation of the political distinctiveness of the middle group which by this time was in process of losing its separate identity. The association of the former middle-grouper, Stapleton, with the peace party is a significant straw in the wind. Along with the original peace-party leader, Denzil Holles, Stapleton was to act as teller for the peace (later Presbyterian) party in divisions in the Lower House more frequently than anyone else, while his former middle-group colleague Sir John Evelyn of Wiltshire was to perform the same function for the war (later Independent) party along with the original war-party militant Sir Arthur Haselrige. In the process whereby the parliamentary centre was being squeezed out of existence by pressure from both sides, those men who moved towards the peace party, like Stapleton, Sir John Clotworthy and Recorder Glyn, seem to have been more completely assimilated than those moving in the other direction. Among the latter were Evelyn, William Pierrepoint, John Crewe and, most notable of all, Oliver St John, Pym's successor for a time as middle-group leader. If, as Professor Underdown puts it, the middle group 'existed more as a state of mind than a party' by 1645[38] this mental distinctiveness was more apparent in those of its members who moved to the left. In so far as their middle-group attitudes survived their entry into what was to become the ramshackle Independent coalition – the word is more suitable than 'party' – they came to form the nucleus of what Valerie Pearl has taught us to call the 'royal Independents'[39] acting to some extent as, to use a common contemporary nautical metaphor, a *remora*, that is an agency which served to attenuate the radicalism of the alliance and to slow down its revolutionary impetus. They exerted their influence in the direction of favouring a vigorous and determined prosecution of the war as the best means of achieving a moderate and lasting peace.

IV

That moderation was hardly the keynote of the parliamentary peace terms debated at Uxbridge at the beginning of 1645 is explicable in terms of the peculiar political circumstances of this particular peace initiative.[40] The major difference between these circumstances and those of the treaty at Oxford two years earlier was that now the war aims of the Scottish, as well as the English opponents of the king had to be accommodated. The Treaty of Uxbridge was in a real sense a Scottish initiative, which fitted in well with the aims of the militants in the English war party, who, while they might suspect that the Scots would be prepared to abandon the civil provisions of the allied propositions if they could get the king to agree to a religious settlement along high Presbyterian lines,[41] did not share the optimism of the Scots about the likelihood of the king's agreeing to the establishment of a Presbyterian Church. In fact, the Scottish lack of realism on this matter was the best possible assurance to the war party that the negotiations would fail and that war à l'outrance would be resumed. Moreover, the failure of the treaty would increase the force of the arguments in favour of the Self Denying and New Model Ordinances, and enable the war party and the Scots to mend their damaged fences by demonstrating conclusively that the Scots could not hope to attain their ends except through military victory.

By the time of the Uxbridge treaty the military situation had altered dramatically in Parliament's favour as compared with the situation at the time of the Treaty of Oxford two years earlier. However, just as the Oxford negotiations had taken place before the king's fortunes had mounted to their zenith with the spectacular royalist victories of the summer of 1643, so did those at Uxbridge precede the great and decisive victories of the new parliamentary army in the summer and autumn of 1645. And just as the aftermath of the Oxford Treaty had been Waller's so-called Plot, which Pym had skilfully used to foil any attempt to create consensus between peace party men at Westminster and royalist moderates at Oxford, so was the Uxbridge treaty followed – at an interval – by the revelations of Lord Saville which were designed to have a similar impact on the fortunes of the peace party.

Preliminary peace ploys in the autumn of 1644, from the king's approaches to Parliament in September following his victory at Lostwithiel[42] to the preparation of grand full-scale negotiations by the sending of a parliamentary delegation to Oxford in November with proposals which were to form the basis of the Uxbridge Propositions, did not offer much hope of success except to the incurably optimistic. According to Lord Denbigh's account of the November mission,[43] the king told the parliamentary commissioners that there were three things with which he would never part; his Church, his Crown and his friends. It was the first and last of these things which boded ill for the success of the peace initiative for the Crown was hardly in jeopardy at this point. Republicanism was still the creed of cranks and way-out persons; nor was there any evidence of determined advocacy of the replacement of Charles by one of his family at this time, even assuming that a suitable candidate might be found. Charles's remark about his Crown might, however, be interpreted as a refusal to agree to terms which might be regarded as inconsistent with royal dignity and majesty, into which category parliamentary control of the militia and the renunciation of past royal actions and policies might be deemed to fall. As to Charles's second sticking-point, the renunciation of his friends, while the Oxford Propositions of 1643 had specified the names of only two royalists to be exempted from any subsequent pardon, there were fifty-seven such names in the Uxbridge Propositions, including not only notorious royalist extremists but moderate reformers, such as Hyde. Finally Charles's other views about the Church seemed to preclude any hope of satisfying the Scottish demands. Indeed, between the parliamentary propositions and the royal reply which was read in the House of Lords on 17 December 1644[44] followed by the king's own propositions of 21 January 1645, there was such an enormous gulf fixed that only a Scottish optimist or a war-party machiavel could look forward to the negotiations at Uxbridge with any confidence. On the Church, the militia, the navy, Ireland, the fate of royalist delinquents and virtually everything else the royal and parliamentary positions were poles apart.[45]

But the preliminaries to the Uxbridge Treaty, and the treaty itself, provide evidence of the at least partial revival of that consensus between members of the peace party at Westminster and royalist moderates at Oxford, which Pym had used Waller's Plot to scotch in the summer of 1643. During the visit of the parliamentary delegation to Oxford in November the king, according to Whitelock's account, did his utmost to capitalize on Denzil Holles' obvious dissatisfaction with the parliamentary terms, which, as Holles emphasized to him, were a majority view from which he and many others dissented.[46] Hyde tells how at the Uxbridge Treaty itself in February 1645 the Earl of Pembroke tried to persuade him to bring pressure to bear on the king to agree to the parliamentary terms, offering an assurance, which, if true, does that nobleman no credit, that the peace party would see to it that the king ultimately got back what he now conceded. The alternative was the triumph of extremism at Westminster and the creation of an army which would enforce an extreme solution on the country. Holles, Northumberland and the middle-grouper and future Independent William Pierrepoint, himself the son of an earl, did their best to impress on their royalist acquaintances the need to persuade the king to make some concessions over the militia.[47]

But all was to no avail and, despite a well-judged royal appeal on 5 February for the exploration of areas of possible agreement, and against letting disagreement on one or more articles prejudice reaching agreement on others,[48] the treaty ended in deadlock on 22 February, less than a month after it had begun. If a subsequent royalist pamphlet criticizing·the parliamentary attitude in general had been applied to the war party in particular, it would stand as a just epitaph on the incident, more especially in its condemnation of the limited scope given to the parliamentary 'Eunuch-Commissioners' to treat on propositions 'which they knew no man with *Honesty* or *Conscience* could *Grant'*.[49] The war party and those of the middle group who went along with them, in fact, got the best of all possible worlds by making sure that the negotiations would break down without appearing to oppose them. But, in fairness it ought to be added that a memorandum which fell into the hands of Parliament at Naseby reveals that the scope given to the royalist negotiators to depart from the letter of the royal propositions was hardly greater than that accorded to their parliamentary counterparts.[50]

This is hardly surprising for, at least on the matters of the Church and the militia, Charles continued for a long time to regard his Uxbridge terms as the maximum he was prepared to concede. This is the position taken not only in a memorandum by Secretary Nicholas on 29 March 1645, but, more significantly, after the royalist disasters of the summer when the war had entered into its final and decisive stage. In a moving letter to Prince Rupert in August, Charles admitted that his nephew's gloomy view of royal prospects was justified by events, 'yet as a Christian, I must tell you that God will not suffer Rebels and Traytors to prosper nor His Cause to be overthrown'. Notwithstanding the disastrous turn taken by events, it was the king's firm resolve 'that low as I am, I will do no more than was offered in my Name at Uxbridge'.[51]

V

Writing to Lord Fairfax on 14 January 1645, James Chaloner, MP for Aldborough, suggested that if the Uxbridge Treaty failed it would go ill with some peace-party men, 'when it should be held seasonable to call them in question'.[52] Chaloner's shrewd observation was prophetic of what was to be one of the most complicated and revealing episodes of the months following the Treaty of Uxbridge, the so-called Saville incident.

The details of this affair have been recounted many times,[53] and it must here suffice to dwell briefly on the light which it sheds on political affiliations and attitudes at Westminster. Lord Saville, an anti-Court man of 1640–1 who had joined the royalists in the early part of the war, was a very recent and highly suspect convert to the parliamentary cause. Just as Pym had used Waller's Plot in 1643 as a means of branding any exchange of views between Westminster and Oxford as treasonous complicity with the enemy, so did the war party make similar use of Saville's revelations in July 1645 about the alleged conversations of Holles and Whitelock with moderate royalists on their visit to Oxford as parliamentary commissioners the previous November, and their more discreet contacts during the negotiations at Uxbridge.[54] Saville's charges against Holles and Whitelock, and especially the former as the leader of the peace party, provoked a clear split in Parliament, with the peace party backing the accused, the war party backing the accuser, and the middle group splitting in a way which reflects the ultimate destination of each erstwhile middle-grouper in one or other of the two principal groups. Whitelock emphasized that he and Holles received solid backing from 'the Gentlemen of best interest and quality in the House', even down to those somewhat apathetic peace-party supporters whose greater appetite for dinner than for politics had brought about the downfall of Denbigh on a snap vote the previous November. The Earl of Denbigh was in fact one of the peace-party men who distinguished themselves in defence of the pair, by giving evidence of their exemplary behaviour in the discussions both at Oxford and Uxbridge. Former middle-groupers who were now well on the way to being peace-party men or, as men were increasingly calling them, Presbyterians, who also spoke in favour of the accused, included Sir Philip Stapleton, Sir William Lewis and John Glyn, the Recorder of London. Prominent among the war-party men who distinguished themselves on the other side were John Gurdon, who by introducing Saville's letter in the House on 2 July set the whole nasty business in motion; and Sir Peter Wentworth, who attempted to stop either of the accused from giving evidence in the presence of the other and who was an especially pertinacious questioner of Whitelock on another occasion. Also prominent on the same side were the former middle-groupers and future 'royal Independents', Oliver St John and Samuel Browne, the latter, if Whitelock is to be believed, a hostile and very partial chairman of the House examining committee on the matter. Their sympathies in this matter, like those of other former middle-groupers on the other side, are a clear pointer to their future political affiliations.[55]

Attempts to pin on their opponents the charge of treasonable complicity with the enemy were a recurrent feature of war-party/Independent tactics and the Saville affair was by no means the last instance.[56] But it is significant not simply as an episode in the recurrent attempts of the war party to blacken their opponents. It was also a smoke-screen put up by some of the more committed enemies of the peace party, and notably by Lord Saye and Sele, to obscure their own tentative gropings towards accommodation with the royalists. The issue is clouded somewhat by the additional and connected likelihood that they were also considering the possibility of action based on the improbable notion that some leading royalists, disillusioned by the king's refusal to yield an inch at Uxbridge, were preparing to defect, and even to betray royalist strongholds – including Oxford itself – to Parliament. In these very tentative and obscure moves can perhaps be discerned the origins of those Independent initiatives, which were to come to full fruition in 1647 when Cromwell and the army, who were ultimately to destroy Charles and the monarchy, made a determined effort to reach agreement with the king.

There is one more piece to fit to the jigsaw before the full picture of the Saville incident is complete. The charges levelled against the two peace-party men were to be an important factor in the restoration of that rapprochement between the peace party and the Scots which had received a setback as a result of the turn taken by events at Uxbridge early in the year. It was the Scots who finally cooked Saville's goose on 14 July by providing unequivocal evidence, in letters from him to Oxford which they had intercepted, of his own intrigues, both with the royalists and political associates of the accusers of Holles and Whitelock. Saville replied to the inevitable question of what he was doing communicating with the enemy by asserting that 'he was authorised to do this by the Sub-committee for private and secret intelligence for the Committee of both Kingdoms', mentioning Lord Saye in particular by name. The guilty secret was out.[57]

Each of the two possibilities which may have been contemplated by Saye and his colleagues – of coming to terms with the king or arranging for the surrender of Oxford to Parliament – was equally distasteful to the Scots. The collapse of Oxford would mean the effective end of the war and, if successful military endeavour were to be the measure of the degree of influence to be exerted in subsequent peace negotiations, then the bargaining strength of the Scots would be about as great as that of the Italians after the fall of France in 1940. Neither the terms on which Oxford might be betrayed nor such terms as might be agreed between Saye and his kind and Charles I were likely to have much in them for the Scots; certainly not the *sine qua non* of Scottish endeavour, the establishment of a high Presbyterian Church. Far more likely was a settlement which would secure a comfortable place in the sun for two elements which were equally disliked by the Scots and their high Presbyterian allies in the City of London; the bishops and the sects.[58]

One important consequence of the Saville affair, therefore, was to contribute powerfully to the revival of that sense of a community of interest between the Scots and the peace party which had begun to develop late in 1644 but had been seriously threatened by the events at Uxbridge at the beginning of 1645. But this revival and the consequent transmutation of the peace into the Presbyterian party in the course of 1645 was a development which raised new and formidable obstacles to the achievement of that goal from which the party had drawn its original name, since it became linked in the king's mind with the pursuit of the primary war aim of its Scottish allies, a settlement of the English Church along high Presbyterian lines. This was the situation which offered the opportunity for the peace initiative which the war party was contemplating in the summer of 1645. While a peace settlement achieved as a result of a war-party – or, as we must now call it, Independent – initiative might be tough to the king on civil matters, it was not unreasonable to assume that it might be more flexible on religion than any settlement to which the Scots were a principal party was likely to be; perhaps even to the point of allowing some form of episcopacy in return for religious toleration. While in the course of 1645 there may have been some episcopalians in England who were prepared, *faute de mieux*, to accept some form of Presbyterian settlement as a strong centralized safeguard against sectarian anarchy, Charles was emphatically not one of them. His wife, who was not one to draw fine distinctions between different varieties of Protestant heresy, was to fight a losing battle during 1645 and 1646 to persuade him to come to terms with the Scots on the matter as the one way of extricating himself from an otherwise impossible position. But the king was adamant and, in letter after letter to the queen, members of the royal family and others, he asserted the twin beliefs which it is arguable were more than anything else to bring him to the scaffold: that the maintenance of episcopacy was essential to, and the Presbyterian system of Church government incompatible with, monarchy.[59] His prejudices against the Presbyterians blinded him to the fact that, whatever their views about religion, they were of all his enemies the most deeply concerned for the maintenance of monarchical power and the traditional social order, though, as Hyde was to point out at the beginning of 1647, the notion that political Independency and republicanism went together was highly questionable, given the fact that the Independent leaders were substantial property-holders with every reason for opposing any threat to the existing order.[60] It is not extravagant to suggest that the king, like so many historians after him, was led astray by the titles by which the two principal political groups at Westminster were coming increasingly to be known. How significant were the terms Presbyterian and Independent as indications of the religious beliefs of the members of the two parties? And perhaps most important of all, how far did the alliance of the political Presbyterians with the Scots wed them to ideas of Church government and the relation between Church and State which the king found abhorrent?

VI

While there were, of course, some religious Presbyterians in the 'Presbyterian' party, this was no more a necessary characteristic of members of the group than it had been of the old peace party out of which it emerged. The leader of the party himself, Denzil Holles, whom Clarendon describes as being 'no otherwise affected to the Presbyterians than as they constituted a party upon which he depended to oppose the other'[61] was, if anything, an Erastian, as were many others of whom Bulstrode Whitelock and John Selden are notable examples. It was certainly not religious considerations which made a political Presbyterian out of Recorder John Glyn; nor of Sir William Waller and Edward Massey, both of whom were drawn to the party by their dislike of the new army, the creation of the Independents. Similarly within the Independent coalition were a number of persons who were not religious Independents, ranging from irreverent unbelievers such as Henry Marten and Thomas Chaloner to zealous thorough-going religious Presbyterians such as John Gurdon, Edmund Prideaux, William Purefoy and the London radicals Isaac Pennington and John Venn.

It was the appearance in 1938 of an article by Professor J. H. Hexter which first challenged the notion of an equivalence between religious denominations and political parties, which historians had until then taken for granted.[62] Hexter's startling discovery, from his study of the surviving lists of Presbyterian classes in seven counties, that a significant number of Independents were in fact Presbyterian elders shattered the symmetry and simplicity of the old view of an equivalence of religion and politics which was a staple ingredient of Firth's view of the Civil War as a fundamentally religious revolution. Ever since 1938 historians have been grappling with the problems to which Hexter's revelations gave rise. Professor George Yule, reverting to a near-Firthian emphasis on the primacy of religious considerations as determinants of political affiliation, sees Hexter's Presbyterian Independents as the conservative wing of the Independents, those who could not stomach the alternative of congregational separatism which more radical Independents such as John Blakiston, Miles Corbet and Sir John Bourchier embraced with such enthusiasm.[63] The difficulty about Yule's thesis is that it takes no account of undeniably radical Independents such as Gurdon, Prideaux, Purefoy and Pennington, who were also zealous religious Presbyterians. It is the existence of a large number of such awkward cases which argues strongly in favour of Professor Underdown's view that there is no necessary connection between the Independent and Presbyterian parties in Parliament and the religious denominations which bore those names,[64] and this is broadly the position adopted in this book. Professor Stephen Foster's contention is that the problem of the Presbyterian Independents is a great deal of ado about nothing, since from October 1645 all MPs were *ex officio* elders of Presbyterian classes and, since this removes the element of voluntary choice on their part, it also robs the eldership of any significance as an indicator of religious affiliation; this contention has been strongly challenged by a number of other historians who see it as based on a misreading of the evidence.[65]

Be this as it may, the discrediting of the notion that party divisions faithfully reflected confessional differences suggests that there must have been a good deal of cross-party voting on religious issues in parliament. The most important of these issues was, of course, the nature of the religious settlement. Was it to be the strict uncompromising high Presbyterianism seen by the Scots and some of their English co-religionists both as ordained by God and enjoined by the Solemn League and Covenant? Or was it to be a looser system with some measure of toleration for tender consciences in the spirit of the Accommodation Order of 13 September 1644?[66] In December 1644 some members of the (religious) Independent minority in the Westminster Assembly registered their protest against that body's recommendation to Parliament that a full Presbyterian system should be set up.[67] It was a Presbyterian form of government to which the king was asked to agree in the Scottish-inspired Uxbridge Treaty at the beginning of 1645, and it is interesting to find the sort of argument which was ultimately to prevail in Parliament being used at Uxbridge by the moderate royalist commissioner, Lord Hertford, against both the arguments of the Scots for Presbyterianism and those of Charles's religious advisers for episcopacy. With impressive impartiality Hertford pronounced both arguments inadmissible since both rested on unacceptable *iure divino* premises.[68] After the failure of Uxbridge, when the Scots finally brought themselves to think of peace initiatives again, the strategy they favoured was that there was to be scope for negotiation only on civil and not on religious matters. But the English parliament took a totally different view, and indeed was an inordinately long time deciding exactly what sort of a religious settlement it did want. On 29 August 1645 the Scottish Commissioners in London were complaining that the powers to be given to presbyteries and synods and, above all, 'whether they shall have dependance vpon the civill Magistrate' was still undecided. On 15 October they were bewailing the unsatisfactory nature of the ordinance on Presbyterian Church government which had just gone through the House of Commons, since it denied the right of Presbyterian elders to exclude notorious offenders from the sacrament save in the twenty-four cases of sin specified by Parliament.[69]

This was to become the main issue around which different opinions as to the nature of the new Church were to crystallize. When on 13 March 1646 an ordinance for the establishment of a Presbyterian form of Church government finally passed through Parliament, it gave little joy to the Scots and their high Presbyterian allies. What gave particular offence to them was the fourteenth clause of the ordinance of the previous October. Bodies of parliamentary commissioners in each province were now substituted for the standing parliamentary committee as the final authority on whether sins not enumerated by Parliament merited suspension from the Lord's Supper. But the similarities are far more important than these minor administrative differences, the point of prime importance being the responsibility of each of these bodies to Parliament.[70]

It is difficult to imagine a provision more designed to give offence to the high clericalist temper of theocratic Presbyterianism as expressed in the Westminster Assembly's belief in the '*jus divinum* of a power in Church officers to keep scandalous persons from the sacrament of the

Lord's supper'.[71] The prime object of the operation, as stated brutally clearly in the preamble to the ordinance was to prevent 'an indefinite and unlimited Power in the Eldership'. Nor was this the only sharp Erastian slap in the face for the supporters of *iure divino* Presbyterianism. When the Westminster Assembly, while being careful to congratulate Parliament for its zeal for true religion, petitioned against these provisions in April 1646, it was promptly put in its place, reminded that, as the creature of the Parliament, it was there to do as it was told, and reprimanded for acting in breach of parliamentary privilege.[72]

If the Church settlement was a triumph for anyone, it was a triumph for the Erastians. Ignominiously defeated in the Westminster Assembly,[73] the Erastian point of view nonetheless prevailed in Parliament. The new religious settlement marked in a very real sense a reversion from radical solutions – and in ecclesiastical terms Scottish Presbyterianism was a radical solution – and a return to the traditional Puritan mainstream view of the organization of the Church and the springs of religious reformation. In its religious settlement, Parliament had in fact selected the most conservative of all the available options, given the fact that an episcopalian solution was no longer a serious possibility. Equally out of the question was an ecclesiastical supremacy vested in *Rex Solus*, which dissident parliamentary Puritans, from Peter Wentworth under Elizabeth I down to the critics of Arminianism in the early parliaments of Charles I, had always been disinclined to accept, regarding the royal supremacy as having been established by Parliament. The vesting of ultimate ecclesiastical authority in Parliament, with which, following the conclusion of peace, the king might again be associated, must have seemed to many contemporaries an inspired solution along traditional lines, which, moreover, given the adoption of a Presbyterian Church structure, was not inconsistent with the Solemn League and Covenant. With this latter point, however, the Scots could hardly be expected to agree. On 26 March the Scottish commissioners in London gave vent to their contempt for what they regarded as the absurd notion 'that some few Civil Men, having no Calling from God, can be more able to judge of Matters of this Nature than the Assemblies of the Church'. 'The Pope and the King,' moaned the disgruntled Baillie, 'were never more earnest for 'the leadership of the Church than the pluralitie of this Parliament.' His view was echoed by the king himself, who, if he detested Scottish Presbyterianism, had no more time for its watered-down English equivalent with its transfer of the ecclesiastical supremacy from Crown to parliament.[74]

In his brilliant treatment of Erastianism, Professor Lamont is at pains to distinguish between true Erastians like Thomas Coleman and William Prynne, and the deliberately dirty connotation which the Scots tried to pin on the word by associating it with those whose sole aim was to subject the Church to the State with a minimum concern for spiritual ends. The distinction is important, as is Lamont's emphasis that recourse to Erastian solutions – Prynne is a good case in point – was a product of disillusionment at the wrangling in the Westminster Assembly and the failure of a clerical body to further the cause of godly reformation.[75] But some of those who were Erastians in the Scottish rather than the Lamontian sense were capable of quoting scripture for their purpose. For example on 3 September 1645, during one of the numerous debates on the suspension of sinners from the sacrament, two of them demonstrated an ability to deploy non-secular arguments which would not have shamed Coleman or Erastus himself. Drawing on his vast store of Hebraistic and patristic, as well as scriptural, learning, John Selden argued against the existence of suspension or excommunication in the primitive Church and argued that it was positively wrong to suspend anyone from the sacrament. Similarly, Bulstrode Whitelock, not normally thought of as the most spiritual of men, did an etymological exercise on the words 'pastors and elders', and declared it shocking that those urged to feed the flock should deny them spiritual food. Was this really the best way to encourage sinners to repent and mend their ways?[76]

It has already been suggested that of all the issues debated in parliament, religion was the one on which opinion was the most likely to cross what were anyway none too firm party lines. Divisions in the House of Commons are a very imperfect guide on this matter, since few division lists have survived and the historian has for the most part to be content with the names of the tellers. Moreover, for issues to come to a division was the exception rather than the rule, not necessarily because men did not feel strongly about the issues, but because they recognized the futility of dividing the House when the result was a foregone conclusion. But such divisions as did occur on matters relating to religion do admit of certain broad, even if tentative, conclusions.

In the debate on 3 February 1646 on the drafting of a declaration 'for the undeceiving of the People' on the matter of peace negotiations with the king, the Presbyterians moved what seems at first sight to be a minor amendment to a clause emphasizing the need to make allowance for tender consciences. The amendment took the form of adding the words 'and of the church' to the clause that toleration might be allowed in so far as it was compatible with the word of God and the peace of the kingdom. A small thing, perhaps, but in so far as it had any significance, this was to weaken the force of the declaration for toleration. The amendment was carried by 105 votes to 98, with Holles and Stapleton acting as tellers for, and the Independents, Haselrige and Sir Henry Mildmay, against it. Holles and Stapleton again acted as tellers in the more important division on 11 April when the Independents, with Haselrige and Evelyn as tellers, succeeded in getting the protest of the Westminster Assembly against the Church settlement declared a breach of parliamentary privilege, though by the narrow margin of eighty-eight votes to seventy-six.[77] The first of these two votes points to the Presbyterian dislike of religious toleration, but the second ought not to be interpreted as a declaration of the party's disapproval of the religious settlement. Undoubtedly there were some political Presbyterians who would vote against the motion because they were in agreement with the Assembly's objections to the settlement. So, no doubt, would some political Independents, 'Presbyterian Independents' like John Gurdon and Edmund Prideaux. But the settlement had been perfectly in accordance with the views of, for example, Denzil Holles, who indeed had carried the ordinance establishing it from the Commons up to the Lords. Why then did Holles vote against a motion condemning the Westminster Assembly's criticism of the settlement? One thing which the votes against toleration and against the condemnation of the Assembly's protest have in common is that both actions would commend themselves to the Scots. The latter vote can perhaps be interpreted as an attempt to wrest some advantage from a situation in which neither party had hitherto acquitted itself honourably in the eyes of the Scots on the religious issue.

VII

Relations with the Scots were the pivot on which the political transformation which is the main theme of this chapter turned. A number of factors contributed to the deterioration of Anglo-Scottish relations over this period and, consequently, to the growing unattractiveness of the Scottish connection to the war party as well as to making things difficult for those peace-party men who favoured a rapprochement with the Scots. Among the latter it is important to keep in mind the distinction between men like Holles and Stapleton, who were attracted to the Scots on account of their mainly conservative political aims, and those who, while sharing these views, were, like some political Independents who were also religious Presbyterians, positively attracted by the religious aspirations of the Scots.

Robert Baillie had always argued that the cause of Scottish Presbyterianism would best be served by striking contributions from the Covenanting army to the triumphs of the allied cause. Hence his chagrin when Cromwell appropriated the lion's share of the credit for the victory of Marston Moor in July 1644. Whatever the relative contributions of the English and Scottish armies on this occasion the contrast between the decisive victories of the English forces in the summer and autumn of 1645 and the inactivity of the Scots became painfully obvious. The Scots raised the siege of Hereford in September, and subsequently gave offence by their reluctance to move from Yorkshire to take an active part in the siege of the royalist stronghold of Newark. Most damaging of all, perhaps, was their withdrawal of a substantial number of men to meet the menace posed by the spectacular successes of the royalist Montrose at home. Far from affording the hoped-for assistance to their English allies, the Scots, it was rather unfairly argued, were incapable of defending their own land against a few highland and Irish barbarians, a criticism which provoked the obvious retort that it was only because they had come to the aid of the English Parliament that Scotland had been vulnerable to attack at all.[78] If the obligations of the two nations under the Anglo-Scottish alliance were mutual, argued the Scottish Chancellor, the Earl of Loudoun, before the English Parliament on 12 September, then the English ought now to be as ready to come to the aid of the Scots as the Scots had been to send their army to England in 1643.[79]

The decisive defeat of Montrose at Philiphaugh on 13 September removed one element of discord, but the others both remained and increased in intensity. Complaints from the far north against the depredations of the Scots which had become prominent in the latter part of 1644 rose in a crescendo in the summer and autumn of 1645. Finally relieved by the departure of the Scots southwards in October, the sorely tried countrymen of north Yorkshire had only just got their harvest in, when the locusts returned and proceeded to exact further cash contributions and free quarter in defiance of a parliamentary ordinance for the supply of the Scots by more regular means. And to add insult to injury, their army was quartered 'where it can give this County no Assistance against the enemy'.[80] In response to increasingly insistent complaints, especially from Yorkshire, the House of Commons on 13 October passed the first of a number of resolutions sharply critical of the behaviour and exactions of the Scots, which are the first official, as opposed to unofficial, indications of the almost total deterioration of relations between the two kingdoms.[81] The parliamentary resolution together with the official complaint from the County Committee of Yorkshire, which had given rise to it, was read from pulpits and other public places in north Yorkshire which gave the inhabitants of these parts every excuse for treating the Scots as hostile invaders rather than allies. The result, complained the Scottish commissioners on 1 November by which date their army should have been before Newark, was that 'most of the [Scottish] souldiers . . . are naked . . . [and] others walking without stockings or shoes'.[82] Nor did the final and very late arrival of the Scots before Newark produce any notable diminution of complaints against them. The geographical focus of complaint simply changed from the North Riding and further north to the West Riding and Nottinghamshire, though complaints from the north were to be heard again in 1646 and especially after the royal surrender of Newark in May. The matters complained of ranged from murder, rape, torture and pillage to illegal exactions and free quarter.[83]

But the grievances were not all on one side, and the Scots too had good cause to complain that the free quarter and other exactions – though not, of course, the worst outrages – complained of were the inevitable consequence of Parliament's failure to give adequate financial support in accordance with its treaty obligations.[84] Parliamentary pleas of lack of money cut little ice with the Scots, who complained that this did not prevent payments being made to the English armies. The parliamentary retort that, if such discrimination indeed existed, it could be attributed to the greater readiness of the taxpayer to contribute towards an active and successful army was hardly likely to placate the outraged Scots.[85] Despite parliamentary promises things were not better after the Scots finally arrived before Newark at the end of 1645. Scottish complaints continued to pour in during 1646 and the House of Commons finally cut the Gordian knot with a declaration on 19 May that England had no further use for the Scottish army which should be paid off and packed off home.[86]

Some of the other major causes of Anglo-Scottish disagreement have already been touched on elsewhere. First and foremost, of course, was the Scottish sense of betrayal at the religious settlement, against which they protested in vain in March 1646.[87] Then there was the Scottish dislike of what they regarded as the inflexible attitude of their allies to peace initiatives, and more particularly, the ruling out of negotiations with the king in favour of presenting bills for his simple acceptance or rejection. If Parliament was in the last resort prepared to negotiate at all, it was only on those very religious matters which the Scots regarded as non-negotiable. The indignation of the Scots overflowed in December 1645 when parliament sent a letter to the king which represented them as agreeing to certain propositions 'which had not been so much as offered to our Consideration', and it was increased rather than allayed by the smooth and plausible parliamentary reply to this protest.[88]

VIII

In these circumstances it is not altogether surprising that in the latter part of 1645 the rupture of Scottish relations with their former war-party allies figured more prominently than the rapprochement of the Scots with their old peace-party opponents. There appears at this time to have been something approaching a lull in the political atmosphere at Westminster, though Professor MacCormack's picture of a virtual truce between the parties[89] perhaps overstates the case and the truce at best was intermittent.[90] Nevertheless, the Independents appear at the time to have gone to some trouble to try to bring their opponents along with them in the matter of the peace terms to be sent to the king, and to have made a gesture of reconciliation towards them by offering them a share in the spoils of peace. The propositions which were put to the king by an Independent-controlled Parliament in December 1645 included the conferring of dukedoms on Essex, Pembroke and Northumberland, a marquisate for Manchester, an earldom for Willoughby of Parham and a viscountcy for Holles as well as similar, if on the whole, less spectacular, honours for Independents such as Saye and Sele, Wharton and Oliver Cromwell.[91]

It seemed likely that the Independent ascendancy would be further strengthened as a result of by-elections to fill seats which had been vacated as a result of the death or disablement of MPs. The Presbyterians opposed the issue of writs for such elections in the firm belief that they had everything to lose from them. The Independents supported them for the same reason, though Ludlow mentions the fears of some Independents that a large number of 'such as were more likely to be for peace upon any terms' would be returned.[92] At any rate the order for writs to be issued for elections at Bury St Edmunds, Hythe and South-wark passed by only three votes on 21 August 1645, inaugurating the first of a series of so-called Recruiter elections which were to continue over the next three years.[93] Professor Underdown's valuable study of these elections affords good grounds for believing that the Independents, largely through the skilful management of Edmund Prideaux, were the first to reap electoral advantage from this development, and that in so far as the 150 new MPs elected by the following spring had any political affiliations at all – and many of course, would not have – more would incline to the Independents than to the Presbyterians.[94] Against his last entry for May 1646, Whitelock observes that one of the most important factors preventing proper attention being paid to royal messages about peace was the fact that 'the new elected Members took in with those who were averse to a complyance with that which his Majesty proposed'.[95] By that time the war was to all intents and purposes over, and the Presbyterians were about to launch an electoral counter-offensive, which was to be reflected in Parliament in a series of votes between 1 September and 8 October whereby the control of the Great Seal, a vital consideration in determining the timing of elections, was wrested from the Independents;[96] and in an unsuccessful Independent attempt on 3 September to prevent a by-election from taking place in the borough of Kellington in Cornwall, a county where, as in the Welsh border counties, Presbyterian influence was especially strong.[97] This electoral counter-attack was to lay the basis of that Presbyterian parliamentary ascendancy, which was to last from the end of 1646 to Pride's Purge in December 1648, and which is a central feature of the last two chapters of this book.

IX

One very important element in the alliance between the Presbyterians and the Scots has yet to be considered. This was the City of London, which for much of 1645–6 outshone Westminster as the centre of the alliance, a development which owed much to the determined and untiring efforts of Robert Baillie.[98] To the City fathers Presbyterianism, with its emphasis on centralized and tightly controlled ecclesiastical organization, had obvious attractions. Not averse to making use of tumults for their own ends, as they had done in 1642 and were to do again in 1647, they were none the less acutely conscious of the need for a

discipline which would keep in place the turbulent passions and democratic notions encouraged by the wide ranging toleration of sectarian
activities favoured by the religious, and probably a large majority
of the political, Independents. There had, of course, once been a time
when the monarchy had been the keystone of the arch of order, subordination and social discipline, and it has already been emphasized that,
in rejecting Presbyterianism as incompatible with monarchy, Charles I
was significantly failing to align himself with a force which ought to
have been his natural ally. The City fathers made no such mistake.

To what extent did militant City Presbyterianism in alliance with
the Scots receive the backing of the political Presbyterians in Parliament? A petition from the Common Council of London asking for a
speedy settlement of the Church with greater power for ministers
andelders than had so far been accorded to them by Parliament was
rejected by the House of Commons on 19 November 1645, and the
petitioners rebuked for misrepresenting the proceedings of Parliament. On the same day a similar petition from the Presbyterian ministers of London was referred to the Committee of Examinations, more,
it would seem, with the idea of investigating the instigators of the
petition than of taking action on their recommendations. The ministers who had attended the House were curtly ordered home to look
to the charges of their congregations. In neither case was there any
attempt on the part of Holles and his colleagues to divide the House,
though they may have been responsible for the face-saving acknowledgement that the City petition had proceeded 'from the good intentions of the Common Council'.[99] If a division had taken place, there
would almost certainly have been some cross-party voting. By no
means all of those normally voting with the political Presbyterians
would have been happy about the theocratic implications of the petition, while, as Valerie Pearl has shown,[100] among Robert Baillie's
parliamentary allies at this time were the religious Presbyterians Zouch
Tate, Francis Rous and Edmund Prideaux, none of whom could be
described as political conservatives, and the last two of whom would
certainly vote with the Independents on most issues other than the
religious one.

In the summer of the following year, however, the Presbyterians in
Parliament were willing to take stronger action in favour of their City
allies by supporting a City petition and remonstrance in the House of
Commons on 26 May 1646. The document in question is an interesting
amalgam; pro-Scottish in its emphasis on the need to maintain friendly

relations with the Scots, and no less pro-Scottish in its high Presbyterian demands for sterner action against sectaries and the exclusion from office of all who were 'disaffected to the Presbyterian Government'. It also contained a number of autonomously City matters such as the businessman's perennial grievances about the 'protections' accorded to MPs and their servants against creditors, and the burden of taxation on enterprise, as well as stressing the need to apply the proceeds of delinquents' composition fines to defray the debts owed to citizens. The City ought to control its own militia and the hated Committee for the Advance of Money at Haberdasher's Hall, staffed by radicals and social upstarts should be dissolved. The Independents endeavoured unsuccessfully to frustrate the Presbyterian attempt to thank the petitioners and to take their petition formally into consideration, the motion being won by 151 votes to 108 with Stapleton and Holles acting as tellers in favour and Haselrige and Evelyn against. The size of the vote suggests that Holles and his colleagues may have received some support from non-party MPs, as well as from some 'Presbyterian Independents'. But on 2 June the authors of a counter-petition, signed, so the diarist Lawrence Whitacre suggests, by between five and six thousand persons, narrowly got the thanks of the House by 112 votes to 108, with the same individuals acting as tellers, though on different sides. In supporting the petition as a counter-stroke to their defeat on 26 May, the Independents were playing a dangerous game, lending countenance to extra-parliamentary radical forces which were later to threaten their own position. The petition of 2 June in fact marks the emergence of the Leveller movement in London.[101]

X

The progressive deterioration of Anglo-Scottish relations in 1645–6 seemed to Charles I and to the French diplomat Montreuil, who acted as go-between for the king in Oxford, the queen in France, and the Scots, to offer the one real hope that Charles might be able to extricate himself from a situation which had become hopeless in military terms long before the end of 1645. In the early months of 1646 when Parliament remained for the most part under Independent control, its relations with the Scots went from bad to worse. A complaint from the Scottish commissioners in London on 10 February unfolded the familiar catalogue of grievances, and events took a dramatic turn on 15 April when the House of Commons ordered that the recently published edition of the Scottish commissioners' papers should be burnt by the common hangman. This calculated insult was not altogether rectified by the Commons' later reluctant acceptance of the Lords' amendment that this ignominious fate should be reserved for the preface rather than the papers themselves.[102]

It is difficult to imagine a more favourable background against which to explore the possibility of a rapprochement between the king and the Scots which in turn would strengthen the latters' relations with Holles and his colleagues at Westminster. Indeed such a rapprochement might have been achieved earlier if it had not been for Charles's hopes of success for Montrose. But the efforts of the queen and Montreuil to bring about agreement with the Scots were frustrated by the king's refusal to countenance a Presbyterian Church settlement and the abolition of episcopacy. There was substance in Charles's assertion in a letter of 8 January that, even if he had wished to, he would never be able to force Presbyterianism à l'écossaise down the throats of the Erastians and Independents at Westminster, or even of the Presbyterians who 'will never admit of the Scotts' way'. The same cannot be said of his argument in a similar letter of 8 February that an agreement with the Scots about religion would remove all possibility of a royal rapprochement with the Independents.[103] As Montreuil himself pointed out, this was in reality no option at all, any more than the hopes which the king still entertained of foreign interference on his behalf, which would have the effect only of uniting the Independents and Presbyterians against the invader, even assuming that such hopes were anything more than pure moonshine. Charles's only sensible course was to trust Montreuil to persuade the Scots to agree to a less rigorously Presbyterian settlement on the grounds that, as the settlement of March was to demonstrate, even their English parliamentary allies would find it difficult to accept thorough-going theocratic Presbyterianism.[104] According to Clarendon, the king still hoped that a possible way out of the difficulty might be to give an assurance to the Scots that an English episcopalian system should not in any way prejudice the Scottish Kirk.[105] But this solution was impracticable for three reasons. In the first place, an episcopalian settlement in England would command insufficient support and provoke much violent opposition. Secondly, it assumed that the Scottish concern with the English Church settlement related only to considerations of their own self-defence, and completely discounted the Scottish missionary zeal to spread the word abroad. And finally, there can be little doubt that even an attenuated form of Presbyterianism in England was a greater safeguard for the integrity of the Scottish Kirk than a restoration of English episcopacy, even when accompanied by apparently ironclad guarantees. The Scots had not forgotten the lessons of the 1630s.

By the beginning of April, when Charles was perfecting his plans to slip out of Oxford and meet the Scots at Market Harborough, he was brimming over with new-found confidence that his intrigues would succeed in setting his English and Scottish enemies at each other's throats and that the Scots would be persuaded to 'employ their Armies . . . to assist us . . . in the Recovery of our just Rights'.[106] But his plans miscarried, due, as he claimed, to the bad faith of the Scots, 'abominable relapsed rogues', and when he finally surrendered his person to them at Southwell on 5 May, he was not given much grounds for hope that his plans to set them off against the English rebels would succeed.[107] The Scottish Commissioners may have been more than a trifle disingenuous in their letter informing the English Parliament that the king's arrival in their midst had filled them with amazement, and made them 'like men that dreame'. But there was no question of their going back on their alliance.[108] On the contrary, they were all too conscious of the fact that the king's surrender to them had strengthened their bargaining power as a means of securing what they regarded as the true aims of the alliance. The end of the first Civil War saw the Scots in a stronger position than they had enjoyed since the time of the Solemn League and Covenant. It remains to be seen how far they were able to take advantage of that situation.

TEN *Centralism and Localism 1642–8*

... every county had the civil war, more or less, within itself.

Lucy Hutchinson, *Hutchinson Memoirs*, p. 91.

The God of your Salvation ... hath now expelled your Adversaries: and brought us safe through the Red Sea of our Fears and Troubles, to the Borders of that sweet Canaan of our desired Peace; and what now remains ... but that ... in grateful Acknowledgement of the loving Affection of his People ..., the heavy Yoke should be loosed to which they so readily did submit their Necks; nay, desired you to put upon them for your Security and the Kingdom's Weal.

Petition of the Freemen and Citizens of London at large to the Parliament, December 1646, *Parliamentary History*, XV, 230–1.

I

MOST OF THE MPs who came up to Westminster in 1640 – indeed most of those who took sides with the Parliament at the outset of the war – aspired, if anything, to put the clock back rather than to innovate; to restore what they thought of – however mistakenly – as traditional local ways of doing things against royal centralizing innovation. As the mayor and jurats of the Cinque Port of Sandwich sharply reminded Sir Edward Dering on 14 January 1641, they had elected representatives not to further innovation but to see to the restoration of their ancient privileges and 'liberties', which had been violated by the Duke of

Buckingham as Lord Admiral in the 1620s and by the king in the following decade.[1] But over the next few years it was to be the Parliament rather than the king which was to acquire particular notoriety as a violator of such local privileges. The royalists were naturally not slow to take advantage of this. For instance, the royal letter sent to Leicestershire with the Commission of Array on 12 June 1642 made use of arguments which had, in earlier decades, been employed against the Crown's own nominees as lieutenants. It drew attention to the fact that many of Parliament's nominees – Lords Saye and Sele in Cheshire and Warwick in Norfolk are good examples – 'have no interest, nor live near to some of the counties to which they are nominated for the Lieutenancy'.[2] Local sentiment was already on the way to becoming a nuisance rather than an ally to the parliamentary leaders, who were at pains to stress that the central versus local issue was based on a palpably false dichotomy. This was the line taken, for example, by John Hampden in a letter to the Essex deputy lieutenant Sir Thomas Barrington on 9 June 1643, urging that the support of that county for the Lord General's army in terms both of men and money was 'for the good of the kingdome in generall, and so of Essex in particular'.[3]

II

More than one commander in the Civil War encountered serious difficulties arising out of the reluctance of local gentlemen – and of the troops themselves – to have local levies serving under any but local officers.[4] Their inability to see beyond their own county boundaries had, as will be shown at length, other grave disadvantages. On 4 August 1643 the Speaker of the House of Commons informed Colonel Oliver Cromwell 'that nothing is more repugnant to ye opinion and sence of this house and dangerous to ye kingdome then ye vnwillingness of their forces to March out of their severall Countys'.[5] The idea that local forces should be used exclusively for local defence died very hard indeed. It seems for example to have inspired a number of Norfolk gentlemen, including one of the MPs for the shire, Sir John Potts, to stipulate that their contributions of men and money should be employed 'for defence of this county not to be sent out'. As late as August 1648 a similar provision was made in respect of a revised Eastern Association committee with 'power to order the Souldiery as to the defence, and not to go out of the Association but by their consent, to meet an enemy or prevent his comming to [sic] near them'.[6] Fear of leaving the county at the mercy of the enemy was naturally the main consideration behind such localism. But the Cavaliers were not always the only danger. On 23 October 1643 the Mayor of Colchester and his colleagues begged for the return of their trained bands whose absence had rendered the town vulnerable not only to enemy attack, but - no less terrible - to 'our vnruly multitude whoe are ready vpon all occasions to worke mischeife by plundering or otherwise', a difficulty exacerbated by the fact that many of those serving in the trained bands were employers on whom the poor of the town depended for a living.[7]

Royalist commanders faced similar problems. Yorkshiremen were reluctant to leave the siege of Hull and march south with Newcastle in 1643 because of the fear of leaving their homeland vulnerable to attack from the Roundhead garrison; or to move south in 1645 from Leicester under Langdale in the campaign which culminated in Naseby. Montrose's highlanders melted away as he pushed his campaigns into the Scottish lowlands in 1645. Perhaps most familiar of all is the disinclination of Cornishmen to exercise their proverbial valour beyond the banks of the Tamar, and even when they did so, to go beyond Bristol - which must have seemed a very long way indeed - in 1643, or Taunton in 1645. They were the more insistent on returning home because of fears of the vulnerability of Cornwall to attack from the parliamentarian garrison of Plymouth, similar to those which lay behind the unwillingness of Newcastle's Yorkshire levies to accompany him deep into Lincolnshire.[8] The serious obstacles imposed by such considerations to strategic freedom of action find shrewd expression in some observations made by the royalist courtier William Davenant for the benefit of Prince Rupert in June 1644. The prince could be confident, observed Davenant, that if the king had to march northwards to join him, 'he will hardly be followed by those armies which consist of Londoners; for it was never heard that any force or inclination could lead them so far from home'. Similarly, however, if Rupert moved south towards the king's army, the northerners in his own force would quickly melt away.[9]

This phenomenon of large-scale desertion from both the royal and the parliamentarian armies is in one sense a further manifestation of localism in terms of the motives both of the deserters themselves, often enough bewildered and disoriented rustics operating in districts which seemed very different from their native heaths; and of the authorities in the places which harboured them. To be stationed within a few hours' walking distance from home did not make their surroundings any the more congenial to men whose horizons were often bounded by their native villages. It simply strengthened the incentive to desert. On 8 August 1643, Thomas Honeywood wrote despairingly to his fellow Essex deputy lieutenant, Sir Thomas Barrington, that almost the whole of the company of local men which he had not long before despatched to Cambridge, then believed to be under the threat of royalist attack, had returned home to their native country, 'and will not by no means be persuaded to returne'.[10] Despite the imposition of heavy fines not only on individuals harbouring deserters, but also on towns in which they were discovered, some local authorities – for example the Mayor and Corporation of Colchester and the committees of a number of eastern and southern counties – seem to have been less than completely cooperative with the military in apprehending the deserters in their midst.[11]

III

It could be argued that the most powerful expressions of localist senti-ment during the Civil War were neutralist movements of one sort or another. Dr Morrill has found evidence of attempted neutrality pacts in as many as twenty-two counties as well as in a number of boroughs.[12] Some of these were admittedly demilitarization pacts made between active participants, such as the royalist Commissioners of Array and the parliamentarian Militia Commissioners, and as such testify not to the basic lack of concern with the issues being fought or consciousness of their irrelevance to the county communities, but to consensuses of active royalists and active parliamentarians that there was nothing to gain and everything to lose by allowing the war to be fought out locally. Examples are the pact between the two sides in Cheshire negotiated at Bunbury on 23 December 1642 and the similar, if less formal, arrangement in Norfolk earlier in the year which royalist Norfolk squires such as Sir William Paston and Sir John Spelman were later to denounce as a Roundhead ruse to secure their quiescence rather than a genuine attempt to keep the war away from Norfolk.[13] Conversely in October 1642 Parliament administered a sharp rebuke to Lord Fairfax and other Yorkshire parliamentarians who had entered into a similar pact with their royalist neighbours since, in Parliament's view, a neutrality agreement in Yorkshire was likely to favour the royalists.[14] The Devon county committee received a similar reprimand from the parliamentarian commander Sir William Waller, on 29

March 1643, for their attempt to arrange a pact with the royalist gentry of Cornwall in an abortive effort to confine the parliamentarian interest to Devon and the royalist to Cornwall.[15]

More interesting than such local arrangements for cessation of hostilities made between committed supporters of both sides were deliberate attempts on the part of those wishing a plague on both contending houses to keep the war out of their counties. For instance, the Bunbury agreement between the contestants in Cheshire in December 1642 had been preceded the previous August by an attempt to keep the war out of Cheshire on the part of what can only be described as neutralist gentry, whose declaration denounced 'that dangerous and disloyal distinction (which rings twoe lowd in oure eares) vizt For the Kinge [or] For the Parliament'. Similar instances may be found in the declarations by the High Sheriff, Justices of the Peace and Grand Jury of Staffordshire on 15 November 1642 and by the actively neutralist sentiments of some Lincolnshire gentlemen who, pronouncing they were for neither side, proposed to raise a troop of horse, 'only for the preservation of peace within themselves'.[16]

Such moves were genuine predecessors of the neutralist activities of the so-called 'clubmen'.[17] Until recent years the activities of clubmen received little more than token attention from historians and it is significant that an important Oxford doctoral thesis by Dr Brian Manning was almost ignored and was never published. This neglect is the more remarkable when compared with the reams which have been written about the Levellers. Unlike the Levellers, whose journalistic and propagandist flair gave rise to a vast quantity of easily accessible printed material, the clubmen have little to offer the historian of radical political ideas. Yet, as a number of studies have clearly demonstrated, it is arguable that there is at least as much to be learned about the springs of political action in the seventeenth century from a study of their activities as from those of the Levellers. For the clubmen were a great deal more than the rustic Poujadists in which guise they were too frequently represented by historians. It may be true that their activities more often than not arose out of angry confrontations between sorely tried and justly exasperated villagers and disorderly soldiers; and that even when the former were joined by local gentry, their aims were often limited and severely practical, such as the primary aim of some Dorset clubmen on 28 May 1645, 'to preserue ourselves from plunder and all other vnlawfull violence.'[18] But even to do this presupposed an impressive amount of admittedly purely localist cooperation and organization. Moreover, as will appear, the aims of the clubmen often went far beyond this, and shed light on the temper and aspirations of local societies and the connection between localism and neutralism.

With one notable exception in Shropshire at the end of 1644, it was 1645 which saw the emergence of the clubmen in several parts of the country, and notably in the south and south-west, South Wales and the marcher counties. The clubmen's 'neutralism' was less than absolute. They sometimes leant towards and cooperated with one or other of the contending armies, normally on a very local rather than a county basis. As Dr Hutton has observed, there was a natural enough 'tendency of local people to withdraw support completely from defeated troops'[19] and, given that the main aim of the clubmen was to protect their much-enduring localities from further subjection to the horrors of war, co-operation with the obviously winning side was a logical enough extension of this tendency. In parts of the south-west, for example, during the campaigns of the summer and autumn of 1645, as Professor Underdown reminds us, 'the better discipline of Fairfax's troops . . . made their presence preferable to that of Goring's brutal rabble';[20] the latter rendered all the more brutal by the desperation induced by the decisive defeat at Langport in July and the fall of Bristol in September. For Fairfax Langport had been as decisive a victory as Naseby not only because it cleared the way to the conquest of the south-west, but also because it prevented thousands of Dorset and Wiltshire clubmen from joining forces with the royalists. On the other hand, the defeated Goring's fears that local clubmen would now happily cooperate with Fairfax were borne out, at least as far as the clubmen of east Somerset, Devon and Gloucestershire were concerned.

However, it would be wrong to assume that it was only in the face of such tactical considerations, which made support for the winning side the most effective way of bringing the war to a speedy conclusion, that the clubmen were less than completely neutral in their sympathies. The royalist inclinations of the Dorset and Wiltshire clubmen earlier in 1645 have among their main causes bitter disappointment at the failure of the Uxbridge Treaty and an eagerness for negotiation to be resumed, but only it would seem on such terms 'as may probablie find acceptance with his Majestye.'[21] The programme of one of the shortest-lived of the clubmen groups, from west Sussex, which lasted only four days after its first meeting[22] has a distinctly royalist flavour, adding to the limited and practical aims of clubmen everywhere with regard to matters such as free quarter and acts of plunder, a strong Anglican emphasis in such matters as the extrusion of local parsons and damage to the fabric of churches and a highly sophisticated and eloquently articulated constitutional localism. Particularly striking is the strong emphasis laid on customary rights in both a local and a national context. Rates are not to be levied contrary to Magna Carta or parliamentary ordinances, and those imprisoned for refusing to pay were to be allowed the right of appeal to a local body specially created for that purpose. Strongly stressed was the countryman's right to petition parliament against the oppression of centralist agencies, whether low-born excisemen or the county or rape committees. It is difficult to overestimate the significance of this attack on

> The insufferable, insolent, arbitrary power that hath bin vsed amongst us, contrary to all our auncient knowne lawes or ordinances of Parliament ... by some particular persons stept into authority whoe haue delegated theire power to men of sordid condicion whose wills haue bin lawes ... by which they haue overthrowne all our English libertyes ...[23]

As Underdown emphasizes, the Sussex clubmen, like those of Hampshire, 'were not trying to end the war by supporting the winning side; they were doing the opposite.' Nor should the resistance of clubmen to the depredations of royalist forces in Wiltshire, Dorset, Worcestershire and Herefordshire necessarily be taken as an indication of their anti-royalist proclivities. Two of the quite separate groups of Worcestershire clubmen were in fact endeavouring to secure the efficient enforcement of regulations for military discipline and order promulgated by royal proclamations and by the royalist 'parliament' at Oxford. Moreover, while the more genuinely neutralist clubmen of Herefordshire had strongly and successfully resisted Sir Barnabas Scudamore's foraging parties from the royalist garrison at Hereford – for which they were later to be savaged by Prince Maurice – they were also adamant in refusing to cooperate with the forces of Colonel Massey, the parliamentarian governor of Gloucester.[24]

Professor Underdown has offered an ingenious explanation of the alignment of clubmen towards one or other of the contending armies in cases where this is not explicable in terms of simple historical considerations. This is couched in terms of a distinction which he has since extended to provide a clue to the whole question of allegiance in the Civil War: that between the topography, culture and patterns of social obligation in downland/fielden and woodland/pasture regions; the former with their strongly traditional, hierarchical and deferential character, and the latter where the puritan ethos prevailed with its antipathy to the festive customs which flourished in the former. The argument is suggestive rather than conclusive. Underdown himself disarmingly suggests some notable exceptions to this rule and one might add that the phenomenon of deference might cut very much the other way, when the local magnate was a man of puritan sympathies.

As Dr Hutton points out, the factor of experience might be sufficient to explain such sympathies without reference to the differing regional cultures and topographies of the areas from which the various clubmen hailed. Just as the attitude of the east Somerset clubmen who cooperated with Fairfax in the New Model's western campaign of the late summer and autumn of 1645 can be explained in terms of the outrages they experienced at the hands of Goring's wild and despairing followers, the royalist sympathies of some of the Wiltshire and Dorset clubmen probably owed at least as much to their sufferings at the hands of retreating parliamentary troops the previous Spring as they do to their fielden environment, though it is true they had also been the victims of royalist depredations.

Whatever the reasons for their varying political sympathies, the localism of the clubmen looks both back to the resistance of the Country to the royal centralism and fiscal oppression of the 1630s and forward to the anti-centralist and anti-county committee agitation of the post-war years, as well as anticipating, especially in its mildly royalist manifestations, the movement which was to culminate in 1648 in the revolt of the provinces in the Second Civil War. It is to the institutional framework within which and against which such movements operated that we must now turn.

IV

Given the fact that the Civil War had originated partly in a revolt against royal centralizing pressures, it is ironical that, of the two contending forces in the war, the royalists seem to have shown more respect for local rights and local institutions than their opponents, though it is important to draw a distinction between the king and his council on the one hand and some of the wilder and less scrupulous royalist commanders – men like George Goring and Sir Richard Grenville – on the other. But while it may be true that the Cavaliers were responsible for the worst, though certainly not for all, excesses in the war, this is no more than an impression which it may be very difficult to quantify, and it ought not to be allowed to obscure the contrast between the king's attempt to work with local customs and institutions such as Quarter Sessions, Grand Juries and general meetings of freeholders, and Parliament's disregard for them.[25] The contrast was certainly not lost on many country gentlemen who, during the 1620s and 1630s, had been alienated by the royal disregard of the local institutions and susceptibilities for which the king was now showing such notable concern. It was probably sufficient to turn some old-fashioned country opponents of the Court into royalists, to turn others into royalist-sympathizing clubmen, and still others, fearful or disinclined to move so far, into out-and-out supporters of the peace party. But the type of Parliament man who most nearly represented the attitude and aspirations of the disillusioned man of the Country was probably not so much the peace-party, or later Presbyterian, MP such as Sir Simonds D'Ewes, as the non-party, non-aligned independent member. It is the minds of such persons which we must attempt to penetrate if we are to understand the disillusioned parliamentarian, who, in giving support to Parliament as the repository of constitutional freedoms which he too easily identified with his own cherished local customs and traditions, was soon to find that he had jumped from the frying-pan into the fire.

V

Although in the months before the war Parliament had taken over the control of the lieutenancy which had been one of the key agencies of royal centralism, its attitude to the institution, even when it was under its control, was shot through with ambivalence. It will be recalled that it had been the parliamentary pre-empting of control over the lieutenancy which had given rise to the disastrous royal expedient of the Commissions of Array. Nevertheless, it is significant that a parliamentary declaration of 18 January 1643 roundly condemning the Commissions of Array was a good deal less than enthusiastic about the lieutenancy.[26] Moreover there are a number of local echoes of the old fears about the lieutenancy's encroaching on local autonomy, such as the complaint of the Hertfordshire Militia Committee on 12 July 1644 that an ordinance of 5 July had taken control of the militia out of its hands and given it to the lieutenancy.[27] However, although in many counties there was a significant overlap between the personnel of the deputy lieutenants and of the new parliamentary county committees which had often developed out of regular meetings of the deputy lieutenants, it would be true to say that, apart from a county such as Cheshire, where the deputy lieutenants plus a few co-opted gentlemen performed the functions elsewhere exercised by the county committees,[28] the parliamentary reorganization of county government on balance detracted from rather than added to the powers of the lieutenancy. An important case in point is the sharply diminished military power of lord lieutenants in face of the powers of commanders of the armies of associated counties. The Earl of Manchester, who was later to exercise more power in this respect than the commander of any other association army, is reported to have observed in the House of Lords that since the powers conferred upon Lord Grey of Groby as commander-in-chief of the associated forces of Nottinghamshire, Derbyshire and other Midland counties at the end of 1642 'did interfeer with the power of the Lord Leiftenantes for those Counties', the latter would be desirous of relinquishing their offices in consequence. As Sir Simonds D'Ewes drily observed, this seemed clearly to indicate that 'the Lord Leiftenantes for those Counties are not much in loue with their Offices'.[29]

In a country divided by war, it was probably inevitable that, in royalist as well as parliamentarian areas, the county governors would have to be recruited to some extent from below the ranks of the élite county gentry from whom they had traditionally been drawn. This may have been truer of areas under parliamentarian than royalist control, though there is no need to take *au pied de la lettre* Clarendon's characteristically exaggerated account of the social composition of the Somerset deputy lieutenancy during the brief parliamentarian ascendancy in the county in the early months of the war – 'for the most part clothiers and men who, though they were rich, had not been before of power or reputation there'.[30] In neighbouring Gloucestershire, a contemporary describes the parliamentarian recruitment of deputy lieutenants from lower social echelons than the county gentry who 'drew back and shunned the employment', not altogether surprisingly in a county where the royalists were in a strong ascendancy.[31] Less than half of those twelve deputy lieutenants of Cheshire who constituted what Dr Morrill describes as 'the stable membership' of the Cheshire Lieutenancy Commission were county gentry of the sort who would have occupied the office before the war, while an even stronger impression of social dilution is apparent both from the names of the nineteen persons given in a document of 1645 as fit to be added to the Norfolk deputation, and of the fifteen other names held in reserve.[32]

Turning from the lieutenancy to the institution which, despite over-lapping membership, had been its great rival in the pre-war decades, the Commission of the Peace, it had always been regarded as axiomatic that, in John Pym's words, the JPs 'must be of the most sufficient, knights, esquires and gentlemen . . . of the county', – that is from the élite country gentlemen whose displacement from the local Commission of the Peace was among the complaints made by the Grand Jury at the Hampshire assizes on 18 July 1642.[33] In many counties a higher proportion of these 'natural rulers' would be of Cavalier rather than Roundhead sympathies. Even in Norfolk, a county lying in the parliamentary heartland, as many as seventeen of the pre-war bench were in one way or another involved in royalist activities during the war, nine of them in the local incidents at Lowestoft, Norwich and King's Lynn in 1643. Among the post-war Norfolk JPs it is interesting to find some war-time royalist sympathizers, not all of whom had, like Sir William Paston and Sir Thomas Pettus, pre-war magisterial experience.[34] But given the facts that these were exceptional cases which seem to have slipped through the net of the ordinances forbidding royalist delinquents from holding office, and that at least eleven former JPs had died between the outset and the end of the first Civil War, it was inevitable not only that the post-war Commission in Norfolk should contain many new names – at least thirty-eight of them between the end of the war and 1649 – but also that many of them should be drawn from below the social level traditionally associated with the magisterial class; from the middling and even the parochial gentry.[35]

Of those active JPs in Yorkshire in 1642 whose political views can clearly be distinguished, royalists predominated over parliamentarians by fifty-three to thirty-seven, and though the most dramatic changes were to come in 1649, the reconstitution of the benches of all three Ridings after the war inevitably meant the recruitment of some magistrates from below the ranks of the county gentry, the more so on account of the increased size of the post-war Commissions.[36] The Commission of the Peace in royalist Somerset in the two years following July 1643 contained the names of most, though not all, of the great county families, but, while there was inevitably some social dilution in the post-war commissions, they were not flooded by the sort of minor parochial gentry and townsmen who had helped the Somerset Independent political boss, John Pyne, to dominate the county committee.

As in Yorkshire a more drastic change came later, in this case in 1648 as part of Pyne's all-out offensive against his political opponents, many of whom had occupied seats on the bench.[37] In Sussex too the most notable changes came at the end of the decade rather than earlier. While all but one of the Sussex Commission of 1642 (thirty-six, or 97.2 per cent) were drawn from the county gentry, twenty-nine (85 per cent) of the slightly larger Commission of 1644 were drawn from the group, involving a noteworthy, but relatively modest, increase in the representation of those below the traditional governing class. In the 1649 commission, however, the proportion of those drawn from below the rank of county gentry had risen from 12 per cent in 1644 to 33 per cent – a notable increase though still – rather surprisingly – a minority.[38] When the Cheshire Commission of the Peace was reconstituted at the end of 1645, it still contained many representatives of the old closely knit magisterial élite which had dominated the county for generations, though after 1647 there seem to have been only two representatives of top Cheshire families among the active JPs.[39]

VI

It will have been noticed that a great deal of the above information about the social composition of Commissions of the Peace is drawn from the post-war years. During the war itself the Commission of the Peace in most parliamentarian counties took a back seat to the county committees. And almost everywhere many of the administrative and judicial functions of the JPs were being exercised by committee-men who, even if they were also JPs, were exercising power *qua* committeemen.

How far were these crucially important new organs of local government manned by members of the traditional county élites, and how far by new men? The situation differed from county to county. The élite county gentry were very strongly represented on the county committees of Norfolk and, especially, Suffolk.[40] The same seems to have been true of Sussex, where, however, the general committee of the county, consisting of about forty members, exercised only a very loose control over its subordinate committees in the rapes, or administrative sub-divisions of the county, which, especially in the west, contained a large number of lesser gentry and townsmen who thereby came to exercise important influence in county affairs.[41] By contrast, in neighbouring Kent the county committee, dominated by the formidable Sir

Anthony Weldon, kept a very tight rein on the subordinate lathal committees. Unlike Sussex, however, the process of social dilution in Kent can be seen at work within the main county committee itself. This was the product not only of the increasing size of the committee – from twenty-four in February 1643 to between fifty-six and sixty-eight in 1648 – but also of the adoption of more radical policies as Weldon's hold strengthened, with a consequent withdrawal of many of the representatives of the county gentry and their replacement by radicals and – by Kentish standards – new and lesser gentlemen such as the Independent stalwart and later regicide Sir Michael Livesey.[42]

The situation in Somerset offers striking parallels to that in Kent. Here too the county committee was dominated during the period of the brief parliamentarian ascendancy in the county in 1642-3 by men of substance, including some representatives of undoubted county gentry families such as Sir John Horner, even though the great majority of the top Somerset families were staunch royalists. But just as Weldon was to preside over the social dilution and political radicalization of the Kent committee, so is the same process observable in Somerset under the chairmanship of John Pyne, after the county fell once more into parliamentarian hands in 1645.[43] In Lincolnshire, as in Somerset, the social dilution of the county committee was at least partly a product of the fact that many of the county gentry were royalist in their sympathies. But more important was the succession of political squabbles which racked the county and resulted in the exclusion of many parliamentarian gentlemen also: first, the supporters of Lord Willoughby against the absorption of the county into the Eastern Association in 1643-4; and, later in 1645-6, supporters of Willoughby's great bugbear, Colonel Edward King, against King's radical opponents on the committee.[44]

The one factor common to all but one of the sixteen active members of the Nottinghamshire committee was that they all hailed from the south-west of the county within a radius of eight or so miles from Nottingham. After the summer of 1643 the committee contained only four members who could be described as county gentry. A further six came from middling and lower gentry families. Two more were lawyers and the remainder, including the Mayor of Nottingham, who sat on the committee *ex officio*, appear not to have been gentlemen at all. In normal times none but the top four, who included Colonel John Hutchinson, the Governor of Nottingham and later regicide, and Francis Pierrepoint, the third son of the royalist Earl of Kingston, would have been remotely in the running for the county magistracy, but Nottinghamshire, like Somerset, was a county in which the great majority of élite gentry fought for the king in the war.[45] The same may well be true of Staffordshire where the county committee had a similar preponderance of minor gentry and lesser figures over the county grandees and substantial gentlemen on the fringe of the county élite. This was even more marked in neighbouring Warwickshire where the composition of the county committee presents one of the most spectacular of all examples of the social dilution of the county governors as compared with those of the pre-war years. Moreover, unlike the cases of Kent, Somerset and Lincolnshire, this was not a progressive development over the 1640s but apparent almost from the onset of the war. Of the Warwickshire committeemen only William Purefoy, the radical Presbyterian Independent MP and later regicide, came from anything approaching the ranks of the élite county gentry, and even he from the fringes rather than the heart of this class. As Ann Hughes has demonstrated, while most of the élite gentry resided in the south of the county, the wartime and post-war committee was preponderantly recruited from relatively minor gentry from north and east Warwickshire, from Coventry men and even from outside the county altogether.[46]

In most parts of Wales, especially in Snowdonia and West Wales, the county gentry were not only in extremely short supply, but the sympathies of the overwhelming majority of them were steadfastly royalist. In any case the fact that the greater part of the Principality was in royalist hands during most of the war made it inevitable that – outside Pembrokeshire – county committees were non-starters in the early part of the war. The post-war committees inevitably had to rely to a very considerable extent on members of smaller gentry families and even on importations from England. On some Welsh county committees, for instance those of Denbighshire, Caernarvonshire, Anglesey, Carmarthen and Brecknock, former royalists were prominent, despite legislation disqualifying them. Presumably the advantages of the authority which went with social eminence often outweighed the disadvantages of having fought on the wrong side in the war. On the other hand there were counties, of which Suffolk, Derbyshire and Lancashire are examples, in which the creation of county committees consisting of supporters of Parliament seems to have been in no way incompatible with continued retention of control by traditional county élites.[47]

VII

The social composition of the county committees, and indeed of local organs such as the committees for sequestration and the auditing of accounts, was a matter of some importance in respect of their fitness to serve the purposes of the central government. While it might be essential for a committee to contain a minimum proportion of what were normally regarded as the natural rulers of the county - viz. the élite county gentry - it could sometimes be inconvenient, as Alan Everitt has demonstrated in the case of Kent, for this element to become dominant on county committees which would then be the more likely to offer stubborn localist resistance to some of the demands coming from Westminster. It is strikingly apparent that increasing social dilution of the membership of the Kent committee was both slackening its grip on the county community as a whole and making it less capable of resisting the dictates of the central government. This seems also to have been true of the Lincolnshire committee which was both increasingly dominated by lesser social figures and increasingly dependent on the central government. That this was not invariably the case, however, is clearly demonstrated by the fierce localism of the Warwickshire committee, which, as was shown earlier, was drawn overwhelmingly from below the ranks of the county gentry.[48] Indeed, as Dr Hughes has suggested, the élite gentry, long ousted from political control, probably viewed alliance with Denbigh against the localism of the committee as a golden opportunity to regain what they regarded as their rightful place in county government from the upstart committeemen.[49]

One factor in the growing unpopularity of the committees was their role in connection with taxation. If contemporaries sought to fix responsibility for a burden of taxation which made the so-called fiscal oppression of the 1630s seem mild by comparison,[50] the most visible culprit was not in Westminster but much closer at hand. Was this, men asked, what we went to war for: the establishment of a tyranny more grinding than that whose yoke we sought to throw off? Was there not a suspicious resemblance between the nature and administration of the parliamentary monthly assessment and that of the Ship Money, the most notorious of the fiscal devices of the eleven years' tyranny before 1640? Were arbitrary imprisonment, and the use of informers and interrogatories, condemned by all right-thinking men as abominations of the old regime, any the more excusable when exercised by county committees?[51] Propagandists for the government might argue that they were, since they were simply emergency measures designed to preserve and not to subvert freedom. In such a view allegations that Englishmen were '*in a worse case in respect of Liberty than formerly, by paralleiling Committees with the Star-Chamber, and Taxes with Ship-Money*' were palpably absurd.[52] But absurd or not, as time went by an increasing number of people would be found to agree with them.

Mr Pennington and Professor Roots have described the *raison d'être* of the county committees in terms which recall our remarks in an earlier chapter about the twofold function of the lieutenancy. They were designed to act as 'the representative of the County to the Parliament as much as of the Parliament to the County'.[53] But this Janus-like role was more difficult to perform and these two functions were less mutually compatible than this description perhaps suggests. To most locals the committees probably appeared more as the agents of centralism than of localism, but many of the parliamentarian leaders at Westminster took an opposite view. The Kent committee, for example, might incur enormous unpopularity locally as the result of its engrossing of power, but it would be a mistake to regard this power as being exercised consistently in the interests of central government control. Its emphasis was almost invariably on the decentralization of power – on itself, that is. Of its chairman, Sir Anthony Weldon, Professor Everitt writes that 'though faithful to parliament he was more faithful to Kent, and most of all to himself'.[54] By contrast, John Pyne, Weldon's counterpart in Somerset, seems to have consistently subordinated county to central interests.[55] But however strong the local complaints against the alleged subservience of the county committees to Westminster, from the point of view of the central government most county committees were much too heavily tarred with the localist brush. One of the most serious manifestations of this was the deep-rooted belief of many committeemen that the primary function of local levies of troops was strictly that of local defence, and their consequent reluctance to employ them outside the confines of the county. There might be some excuse for this attitude in war-torn centres such as Staffordshire or Wiltshire. But there was little or no excuse for the reluctance of the Essex committee to send troops in June 1643 to succour Cambridge, which occasioned a spirited rebuke to the deputy lieutenant, Sir Thomas Barrington, from his own wife, or for the objections of the Hertfordshire committee a year later to sanctioning the release of their troops to campaign under Major General Browne outside the county. The reluctance of the Warwickshire committee to cooperate with the Earl of Denbigh, commander of the West Midland Association forces, in his plans to use local troops to relieve Shropshire from the royalist threat from Wales has already been noted in another context.[56]

The localism of many county committees finds an equally eloquent expression in the matter of taxation, the more so since the committees' duties in respect of central government levies were one of the main causes of their growing unpopularity. As had been the case with the prerogative levies of the 1620s and 1630s, some counties complained bitterly that they had been very inequitably treated as compared with others. Such complaints came not only from Kent, Norfolk and Suffolk, the three most heavily taxed counties, but also from Bedfordshire, Buckinghamshire, Monmouthshire, Nottinghamshire, Devon and Yorkshire, the last the most frequent of all complainers.[57] It is difficult to read such complaints without becoming conscious of the fact that the idea of a national struggle for national objectives was very far indeed from the minds of many of the county governors. This is further exemplified by the frequently reiterated demands for local appropriation of locally raised taxes. There was, of course, something to be said for a measure of financial decentralization in view both of the dangers of transporting large sums over great distances and of the fact that taxes often needed to be disbursed in the localities where they were collected. But when pushed to extremes, such localism offered a serious threat to the pursuit of a national, or even a regional, strategy. Certainly treasurers sometimes experienced the greatest difficulty in laying their hands on locally assessed levies. The Staffordshire committee, for instance, seems to have ignored the government's instructions to send all the so-called Weekly Pay up to London, and instead disbursed it locally. Similarly the payment of locally based Warwickshire forces out of local appropriations of taxes helps to account both for their unwillingness to move further afield at Denbigh's behest and for their warm support for the county committee which authorised this appropriation, the collection of the taxes being put in the hands of the soldiers themselves. The rather loosely formulated terms of some parliamentary ordinances were sometimes cited in justification of such financial localism.[58]

The revenues from sequestration and composition present an interesting example of the struggle between financial centralism and localism. Following the order of 12 August 1645 which made provision for royalists to regain possession of their estates on compounding for their delinquency, there was a steady flood of complaints to Westminster over the next three years from the county committees. Such complaints were occasioned by the fact that while the rents for sequestered lands were administered locally, fines for compounding were imposed by and paid to the Committee for Compounding in London. The radical line taken by some of these complaints, that royalists ought to be made to suffer the full penalty of sequestration and not be allowed to regain their estates on payment of composition fines which in no way reflected the extent of their delinquency was no doubt genuinely advanced in many cases, but this should not be allowed to obscure the importance of localist motives in favouring such action. On the other hand, localism undiluted by other considerations lay behind the request of some county committees that the process of composition (as well as that of sequestration) should be decentralized on them, sometimes accompanied by the suggestion that this should also apply to taxes such as the Excise, the assessment money and the fifteenth and twentieth parts. To Sir William Brereton's moderate opponents in Cheshire, for example, the decentralization of compounding was the obvious solution to the problems arising out of their dislike of sequestration as too severe and of composition as benefiting the central government as opposed to the county.[59] General constitutional arguments were made to serve the ends of fiscal localism in the complaint by the Yorkshire committee on 25 April 1645 against the practice of army commanders in offering favourable capitulation terms to royalists, among which was the right to compound on relatively easy terms. That the practice would 'begett an opinion that the sword hath a power above the Lawe which will vtterly destroy the authoritie of parliament' was probably a matter of secondary importance to the objectors whose main concern was with the fact that the practice, by swelling the number of compositions, involved a further diversion of money from the counties to the metropolis.[60] In response to a number of such complaints Parliament took steps to prevent its commanders from granting such terms as of right, but permitted them to make recommendations for leniency which, to the disgust of many county committeemen, were often acted upon.[61]

If fiscal localism sometimes impelled committees to take a severe line with local delinquents, considerations of kinship and good neighbourliness frequently operated – at least among individuals – as a force working in the opposite direction. For instance, there were a number of complaints in 1643 and 1644 against the Earl of Manchester's lax operation of the Sequestration Ordinance against royalist gentlemen in the eastern counties.[62] Sir John Holland, MP for Castle Rising, wrote to Speaker Lenthall in September 1643, begging to be excused from implementing the ordinance against the royalists implicated in the comic-opera episodes at Lowestoft and Norwich and the more serious rising at King's Lynn – 'amongst whom there are, Sir, those to whome I have the nearest relations of Blood and obligation of friendship'.[63] It was the reluctance of gentlemen like Holland to engage wholeheartedly, if indeed at all, in the nasty business of sequestration which led to their being replaced on local sequestration committees by 'persons of inferior ranke', a development which was deplored by conservative parliamentarian gentlemen as one of the most unfortunate consequences of the war.[64] Nor was sequestration the only issue in which considerations of upper-class solidarity often reinforced those of good neighbourliness. They underlay, for example, the appeals made to Sir Thomas Barrington in the spring and summer of 1643 to afford his protection to three royalist Essex ladies, Lady Rivers, a notorious papist, Lady Conway and Lady Capel, in the last case against some eighty local rowdies who were 'resolved to come and make a very great spoile in my parke'.[65] While it is true that the Civil War was not a class struggle in that members of all classes were to be found on both sides, both Cavalier and Roundhead gentry were acutely aware of a common interest arising out of the danger that the lower orders might use the war as the occasion of an attack on the property of enemies, which might all too easily spill over into an attack on property in general.

VIII

Prominent among the correctives devised by Parliament to remedy the deficiencies of county committees as agencies of central control was the creation of regional associations of counties. Unlike the counties, these made some sort of military sense as strategic units, and it might have been thought to be a distinct advantage that they commanded none of the fierce localist loyalties which were seen as an obstacle to the evolution of a national war effort. But what their creators – like the creators of the new units of local government in our own time – failed to take into account was that the absence of any sense of regional, as distinct from county, identity was a fundamental obstacle to the regional associations achieving the ends which they were designed to serve.

Of the parliamentarian county associations set up in 1642-3, only one, the Eastern Association of the counties of Essex, Norfolk, Suffolk,

Cambridgeshire and Hertfordshire (joined later by Lincolnshire) can be described as an undoubted success, and then only for a limited time. Although in some cases the associations had been formed in the teeth of opposition from some of the counties which made them up, and in the case of the South-Eastern Association of Kent, Sussex and Hampshire only as a last resort in response to the imminent danger from Hopton's thrust into Sussex in 1643, the constructive role of the Suffolk committee in the building of the Eastern Association clearly demonstrated that some county committeemen were capable of seeing beyond their own noses.[66] But that others were not is clear from repeated reminders to county authorities of the need for inter-county cooperation.[67] More especially, but not exclusively, in 1643, the regional associations had to contend with a great deal of foot-dragging by county authorities. The Gloucestershire committee complained on more than one occasion in 1646 of the regular allocation of £194 of its weekly contribution for the maintenance of the Bristol garrison.[68] The Essex committee was repeatedly rebuked in 1643 for its dilatoriness in providing both men and money for service outside the county, and on one occasion in August for sending troops 'in so naked a posture that to imploye them were to murther them'.[69] It was perhaps some comfort to the Roundheads to know that the enemy experienced similar problems. In a letter of 30 August 1645 the royalist commander Lord Astley bemoaned the failure of his attempt to create an effective working association of the counties of Glamorgan, Brecknock and Monmouth, and by these means to collect a formidable force to march to the relief of Hereford. Instead 'each county draw [sic] their strengths apart for the defence of their several counties, and the fifth part of the men they have not armed'. The Glamorgan commissioners had failed to attend the appointed rendezvous at Abergavenny, and the remainder had made this their excuse for not signing the articles of association.[70]

The determined opposition of the Kent committee in 1644 to the commissioning of Kentish officers not by the committee itself but by Sir William Waller, the commander-in-chief of the forces of the South-Eastern Association, provides another apt example of the fear of county authorities of losing their identity by being merged in a wider and more amorphous regional association. Parliament's refusal to yield to this demand, on the grounds that no such conditions had been made by Sussex and Hampshire, brought the characteristic reply that 'there is not the same Reason for the other assotiated Countyes as for ours'.[71] Waller at least won this particular battle unlike his counterpart in the West Midlands Association, the Earl of Denbigh, who complained bitterly, and not without cause, of the Warwickshire committee's attempt to regain control of its troops serving under his command in other counties within the association.[72]

It will be recalled that one of the bitterest opponents of Denbigh's attempts to employ local troops outside the counties was Colonel Barker, the military governor of Coventry, who worked hand in glove with the county committee on this matter. This instance of a military governor's pursuing localist ends in alliance with the county committee against the commander of the forces of the regional association runs counter to the more normal situation where such governors were an agency working to break down county localism in the interests of wider regional or national strategy. 'The Committees in all places oppose themselves to the Governors', remarked one of the latter, Sir Samuel Luke, parliamentary governor of the strategically vital town of Newport Pagnell in a letter of 18 October 1644. Luke himself was having to contend with almost continual evasive action by the committees of the counties of the Eastern Association on the matter of their contributions to the maintenance of his garrison, as well as from the Buckinghamshire committee which calmly informed him on 24 September 1644 that it existed 'to contradict the exorbitant powers of Governors', which, in his case, were more appropriate to a commander in the Thirty Years War in Germany than to the English situation.[73] Colonel Edward Massey, military governor of Gloucester, waged an almost continual battle in 1644-5 against the obstructionism of the Gloucestershire committee;[74] as did Colonel John Hutchinson, the governor of Nottingham, against the Nottinghamshire committee. Despite the warm support for Hutchinson of Lord Fairfax and other influential persons, the compromise solution which was devised in November 1644 by the sub-committee of the Committee of Both Kingdoms created for this purpose, still left the governor's hands tied in certain crucial respects, though it at least defined the committee's obligations more specifically.[75] Further examples of clashes between authorities and military governors are those between the Earl of Manchester's two successive governors of Great Yarmouth in 1643 and 1644 and the municipal authorities of the town who found the appointments 'prejudiciall to our liberties and ancient government' and were backed by the county committee of Norfolk, on whose territory in the hundred of Flegg the governors' power encroached; between the Committee of the Isle of Ely and the military governor and deputy governor of the Isle,

Oliver Cromwell and Henry Ireton; and between Colonel Edward King, the governor of Boston and Holland and later of Lincoln, and the Lincolnshire committee.[76]

One of the most powerful factors favouring county localism against the subordination of county to wide regional and national interests was the – at least for the whole of 1643 – total financial dependence of the association committees on money raised through the county committees. Parliament's reluctance to grant the appropriation of funds to the former meant that the latter exercised effective control of the disposition of forces with, if they so desired, minimal reference to wider than local strategic considerations. But the Eastern Association did better than most other regional associations, at least after the passing of the parliamentary ordinance of 20 January 1644 which materially strengthened its financial position *vis-à-vis* the associated counties. Another triumph for regional control over county localism was Manchester's success in establishing that it was he and not the county committees who selected the representatives to sit on the association committee at Cambridge. Most of these representatives came from well below the ranks of the élite county gentry and were, to that extent, less likely to be devoted to the idea of county autonomy.[77]

The acceptance, however slow, of the need to subordinate county localism to wider regional considerations, though undoubtedly a significant step forward did not go nearly far enough for the radicals in the regions and at Westminster. To such persons the new regional maxi-localism, such as lay behind the objections of the Sussex and Essex committees to the employment of their troops beyond the boundaries of their respective county associations without the sanction of the county authorities concerned, was no less galling than the county mini-localism which it had replaced.[78] To the Westminster war party, the Eastern Association army in particular was regional only in the matter of the place of origin of its soldiers, not in terms of the geographical limits within which it operated. Excessive concern with such limits, they argued, could only have the effect of putting the whole national cause, to which all other considerations must be subordinated, in jeopardy. A splendid example is Cromwell's outburst on 6 August 1643 to the deputy lieutenants of Essex, whose localism was threatening the success of his operations in Lincolnshire, which at that time was still outside the Eastern Association:

Gentlemen ... is this the way to save a kingdom, where is the doctrine of some of your Countye concerninge the trayned bands and other forces not goeing out of the Association? ... Lord Newcastle will aduance into your bowells, better ioyne [battle] when others ... can ioyne with you, then stay till all bee lost.[79]

After the summer of 1644 the gentlemen of the eastern counties, who no doubt sincerely felt that they had made an enormous concession in subordinating county to regional localism, found a new ally in the Earl of Manchester, who in the campaigns following Marston Moor cited again and again the objections of the Eastern Association to the employment of its army far from its boundaries, whether in the north, in the west or in the south.[80] Under such a commander-in-chief, the Eastern Association army could not long remain the favourite force of the war party at Westminster, whose hopes turned to a new and truly national force. By contrast, when representatives of the Eastern Association counties met at Bury St Edmunds on 30 January 1645, they almost unanimously endorsed the idea of the purely defensive and regional role of the association's army, and expressed disquiet at the provisions of the New Model Ordinance which had not yet got through Parliament. The argument of the one dissentient representative from Hertfordshire that the ordinance ought not to be condemned outright 'in regard it might be for the safety of the kingdome' was met with what has since become the classic statement of near-sighted regionalism, that 'notwithstanding it might be for the safety of the Kingdome, yet that was not our worke, being then mett as committees for the Assocition'.[81] The Eastern Association, the object of county localist suspicions and the pride and joy of the radical win-the-war elements at Westminster in 1643, had become the prime instrument of localism, conservatism, and, in the eyes of its former radical supporters who now looked elsewhere for salvation, defeatism. The future lay with a truly national organism, the New Model Army.

IX

In the course of the war Parliament developed its own central agencies, the equivalent of the Caroline Privy Council and the Council of War at Oxford, whereby the will of the central government was transmitted to the provinces. The most important of these agencies were the Committee of Safety and following the entry of the Scots into the war, its successor, the Committee of Both Kingdoms. The former was much the less powerful of these two bodies, and its failure to bring effective pressure to bear on county and other local authorities may be accounted one of the reasons for the disasters attending the parliamentarian war effort in 1643.[82] Its successor, while having to face its share of localist evasion, exercised a strong and more consistent control on local authorities, employing a judicious combination of firmness, tact and persuasion, not least on occasions when its members must have been under strong temptation to resort to a more heavy-handed approach. A splendid example is its letters urging the county committees of Suffolk and Essex, whose members were still sore about the demise of the Eastern Association army and at best ambivalent about the New Model, to take elaborate measures to forestall a possible Cavalier thrust to the east during the edgy period between the sack of Leicester and the battle of Naseby in early June 1645. The records abound with examples of pressure exerted by the Committee of Both Kingdoms on county committees on a wide variety of other matters, including the punishment of deserters and anti-Scottish rioters, the protection of royalist houses from demolition, the settlement of local differences among committeemen, and above all the need to overcome localist objections to the movement of troops outside the boundaries of counties, or, failing that, of county associations. In such cases it was always careful to stress the short-sightedness of narrow localism, for 'your safety is best served when the war is furthest from you'.[83]

One very important agency of centralized control which operated in the all-important sphere of finance, was the so-called Committee for Taking the Accounts of the Kingdom, which was established in February 1644 with sub-committees in each of the counties under parliamentarian control. The sub-committees were empowered to demand accounts at ten days notice from anyone – from army commanders to local constables – or any institutions through whose hands public money had passed.[84] Early in 1647 the central Committee for Accounts produced an impressive catalogue of the forms of obstructionism experienced by its local sub-committees at the hands of county committees. These included refusal to make the necessary accounts and papers available; flagrant persecution of members of the sub-committees by assessing them for taxes for which they were not liable; refusing normal facilities for meeting-places; and intimidating witnesses and releasing persons whom the Accounts sub-committees had sent to prison.[85] This sort of thing went on despite the fact that some care seems to have been taken by the central Committee for Accounts to appoint, as far as possible, men to the sub-committee who would be acceptable to county committeemen. For example, in Suffolk, where the county committee and the Accounts sub-committee seem to have worked in harmony, the former had sent up lists of nominees or persons whom they regarded as suitable members of the latter and this had been accepted by the central Committee for Accounts.[86]

But the Suffolk county committee was a relatively homogeneous and unified body. In counties where, by contrast, the county committee was rent by faction, it was virtually impossible to appoint a sub-committee for accounts whose membership would be acceptable to all the county committeemen. In such circumstances it was all but inevitable that the sub-committee would become deeply embroiled in county faction politics, whether, as in Montgomeryshire, in alliance with local radical elements,[87] or, more often, as part of local campaigns against county committees or at least their control by radical caucuses. This seems to have been the case in Warwickshire and at least to some extent in Cheshire; also in Lincolnshire and Somerset under the guiding inspiration of Colonel Edward King and William Prynne, the latter also being one of the most active members of the central Committee for Accounts.[88] Nor was it necessary for the Accounts sub-committee to become deeply involved in factional politics for its operations to arouse the fury of local committeemen and to serve as a rallying ground for the growing local distaste for their operations. There was some mutual recrimination and victimization between the committee for Chichester rape in Sussex and the county sub-committee for Accounts.[89] In Kent, as in Sussex, the sub-committee's investigations yielded nothing notable in the way of malversation or fraudulence on the part of Sir Anthony Weldon and the county committee which he dominated. But the very existence of the sub-committee; its right to call county committeemen before it, often on very trivial matters; and, above all, in this home of county localism *par excellence*, its responsibility, not to the county committee, but to an organ of central government, wounded the localist susceptibilities and diminished the prestige and standing of members of the county committee, and more especially of its ruling caucus led by Weldon. For all its complaints of insufficient powers and inadequate funding, Professor Everitt sees in it a profoundly important influence in the disintegration of the power of the Kent county committee and in the train of events which led to the defection of so many Kentish men in the second Civil War.[90]

X

To the conservative-minded country gentlemen who had opted for the
Parliament rather than the King in 1642 – while steadfastly refusing to
recognize the reality of the antagonism between them – the main task
in hand following the end of the first Civil War in 1646 was the restoration of the traditional ways of conducting affairs which had been
usurped both by King and, under the stress of war, by Parliament.
One can sense the feeling of expectancy as early as 14 October 1645
in a petition from the Grand Jury of Staffordshire, a county where
the Commission of the Peace had been in virtual abeyance, 'That the
Commission of the peace may bee directed to some gentlemen of
quallity in the County'. From such persons, the natural governors of
the county, greater justice might be expected than from county committeemen, by no means all of whom were gentlemen of quality, and
many of whom had vested interests in the abuses they were asked to
redress.[91] But the return to normal was neither so rapid nor so complete as such petitioners and their like desired, and the county committees were a very long time dying. The committeemen were well
aware of the threat to their power posed by the prospect of the issue of
new Commissions of the Peace, unless they could find a way of influencing their composition. As Professor Underdown has pointed out,
this was not the least significant aspect of the parliamentary struggle for
the control of the Great Seal in the autumn of 1646.[92] But although the
JPs were appointed by the Commissioners of the Great Seal, there was
another factor to be taken into account. The practice employed was for
the MPs for constituencies within the county in question to submit the
names of suitable gentlemen for the Commission of the Peace to the
Commissioners of the Great Seal, who then issued the Commission.
For example, on 24 December 1647 the Speakers of both Houses asked
the MPs for the Kentish constituencies to pronounce on the suitability
of local gentlemen to serve on the Commission, both those who were
already JPs and those they deemed suitable to be JPs.[93] There was thus
ample scope for the ambitious plans of radical committeemen such as
John Pyne in Somerset to fill the Commission of the Peace with their
own supporters to miscarry. Indeed the first post-war Commission in
Somerset contained a number of Pyne's sworn enemies, including the
inevitable Prynne, though Pyne's efforts were more successful in 1648
when many more of his supporters got on to the Bench.[94] From what
was said of the composition of the post-war Commissions of the Peace

earlier in this chapter, it must be clear that, in many counties at least, the post-war conservative hopes that the issue of new Commissions heralded the return to normal were seriously eroded before the end of the decade, more especially when, as was often the case, Recruiter elections had strengthened the influence of the county bosses at Westminster.

XI

One important area of possible disagreement between a Commission of the Peace, whose membership reflected conservative yearnings for a return to normal, and the radical caucuses which controlled many county committees is pinpointed by a complaint made by three members of the Wiltshire committee to the Speaker of the House of Commons on 28 June 1647. The complainants alleged that the local JPs were giving far too much encouragement to 'scandalous ministers' who had been excluded from their livings and that they were totally unsympathetic to the complaints of officially intruded ministers about such matters as the withholding of tithes by their parishioners.[95] If these charges were indeed well founded, the JPs were probably on to a good thing, for in many cases, and perhaps especially in not notably Puritan shires such as Wiltshire, Cornwall and Kent,[96] the authority of county committees to eject so-called scandalous ministers from their livings and sequester their estates, sometimes leaving the cure of souls unattended and sometimes intruding an unwelcome newcomer, was an important contributory cause of their unpopularity. The ruthless displacement of parsons, by no means all of whom were Laudian high churchmen, occasioned a great deal of local resentment. Nor is there any reason to believe that the eviction even of Laudian parsons and their replacement by Puritans necessarily commanded general approval locally. What had been ritualistic innovations in the 1620s might in some cases have been drawn into local custom by the late 1640s, especially when the parson in question had earned the respect and affection of the parishioners. In such circumstances the introduction of the stark simplicity of Puritan worship might somehow be considered an intolerable interference with local custom, comparable with the Puritan questioning of a Sussex parson for observing the local wedding custom of breaking a cake over the bride's head.[97] Indeed, in the minds of locals, the two sorts of custom could all too easily be confused.

The extrusion of local parsons who were held in high esteem by their parishioners often gave rise to comparisons between extruded and intruded ministers in which fact was difficult to disentangle from fiction. In 1648 Joseph Maye, the much loved vicar of St Austell and St Neots in Cornwall from 1621 until his ejection in 1646, returned to his parish, from which his successor had fled in face of a visitation of the plague, and resumed the cure of souls, including the burial of the victims of the plague according to the forbidden Anglican rites. That he himself survived only to be ejected again on the return of the intruded minister once the danger of infection was past, gave rise to a local belief that he had been divinely protected. In cases where the eviction of the incumbent was brutally carried out, and, despite the provision for settling a fixed portion of the parish revenue on his dependents, he and his family were left destitute, local indignation frequently vented itself the more strongly on the intruded parson. A further exacerbating circumstance might be the fact that the latter was a stranger coming from outside the county. This was especially important in a county like Cornwall where there were a great number of 'malignant' parsons extruded after the county fell into parliamentarian hands at the end of the war, and a consequent difficulty in replacing them without importing foreigners. This epithet might be as appropriately applied to ministers imported from the neighbouring county of Devon as to the Scotsman, 'a meere stranger to the place gott into the Liveing by vertue of a forged peticion', who replaced Dr William Peterson as rector of St Breock. With the aid of a testimonial from 115 of his parishioners in 1646, testifying to his innocence and godliness, Peterson had managed to stave off sequestration until 1648, though he and his sick wife had on one occasion in 1647 been illegally evicted from his parsonage by soldiers. When final deprivation came in 1648, it occasioned a protest from twenty Cornish gentlemen, including the High Sheriff, three MPs and several members of the county committee itself.[98] Such expressions of protest by parishioners against the removal of beloved and respected ministers were certainly not confined to former royalist-dominated counties such as Cornwall. The eviction of John Large, whom we have already had occasion to notice as the cake-breaking vicar of Rotherfield in Sussex, occasioned a testimonial on his behalf from more than two hundred of his parishioners. Large was the victim, to some extent at least, of sordid log-rolling by influential persons who wanted his living for a relative.[99] Such considerations apart, there can be no doubt that a small minority of determined and active extremists could often bring about the displacement of parsons with whom the vast majority of their parishioners had no cause for quarrel. Thus Peter du Moulin complained to Lord Fairfax on 30 March 1645 that he had been evicted from his Yorkshire living at the behest of a family of Anabaptists 'against the many petitions, cries and fears of above two hundred communicants, good Protestants'.[100] Martin Blake, vicar of Barnstaple in North Devon, accused, *inter alia*, of betraying the town to the royalists as well as of attempting to persuade the mayor of his native Plymouth to surrender, protested that 'excepting two or three that are latelye become Anabaptistes & Brownistes, there are no such men in the whole town that have stirred against me in this business'. 'Anabaptist' and 'Brownist' were, of course, very emotive and dirty words, but whatever the truth of his charges against his enemies, it is clear that Blake was the victim of a small and determined band of extremists. Of the nine persons testifying against him, only two were his parishioners, '(none of the best neither), [and] the rest were fforeigners', one of whose names had anyway been given without his consent. Against this must be set the well attested petition of the inhabitants of Barnstaple for the return of Blake, 'our beloved Pastor, of whose abilities, industrie and integritie we have had so long experience'; another from the mayor and aldermen of the town; and, astonishingly, another from the Independent stalwart, Sir Hardress Waller, who testified to his 'great zeale to Gods people'. But all this availed Blake nothing, and he was suspended by the Devon county committee, whose unscrupulous clerk made matters worse for him by falsely entering the committee's decision as being one of sequestration. It is pleasant to record that he was restored in 1648, though he was deprived again in 1655.[101]

The protests of parishioners sometimes took stronger forms. In 1644 Thomas Ford, the intruded incumbent of the Northamptonshire parish of Aldwinkle St Peter, found his parishioners so hostile that he had to flee and take refuge in Newport Pagnell where he acted as chaplain to the garrison.[102] In Kent there are numerous examples of action, sometimes even amounting to physical violence, against intruded parsons, in which circumstances it is not altogether surprising that here, as in some former royalist counties such as Herefordshire and Northumberland, many Anglican parsons continued to operate unmolested.[103] Even in strongly parliamentarian Norfolk Nathaniel Gill, the eccentric and exceedingly high-Church parson of Burgh-next-Aylsham, continued to preach and administer the sacraments according to the old rites – '*sicut meus est mos*' – in the parish church from which he had been officially extruded. He could hardly have done this without the approval of the parishioners and the connivance of the churchwardens.[104] Most striking of all is the case of the arch-Laudian divine Henry Hammond, who, while living under virtual house-arrest in the Bedfordshire village of Clapham in 1648–9, officiated at services in the local parish church, using the Book of Common Prayer and the old rites.[105]

It would be rash, however, to take every case of defiance of sequestration orders and support for extruded ministers as a simple product of devotion to Anglicanism and loyalty to local parsons. No less powerful an influence might be exerted by the sort of fear that was played on by the extruded minister of Walton-with-Felixstowe in Suffolk, when he stressed, as a witness reported, that 'notwithstandinge the sequestration hee was still Viccar thereof, for that he hoped the times would soone turne, and therefore bid the Parishioners take heede what they did'.[106] The ordinance of 22 January 1644 laying down the procedure for dealing with scandalous ministers in the Eastern Association counties suggests that parishioners who failed to denounce such ministers were often prompted by base and self-interested motives, either being against godly reformation because 'loath to come under a powerfull ministry', or susceptible to bribes from delinquent ministers who excused them payment of their tithes.[107] The case of John Allen, the extruded minister of Capel in Surrey, provides an example of a different sort of cause of possible resistance to Puritanism. Given the steadfast hostility of the true Puritan believer to the semi-magical remedies which the local parson was often popularly expected to administer and which have recently received emphasis in the brilliant work of Sir Keith Thomas, the fact that Allen 'hath written a charme for the Tooth Ach, giving out that if ye Party greeved would believe, it would help him', doubtless told heavily against him in the eyes of those investigating his case if not in those of all of his parishioners. In addition, it was claimed, he was a drunkard, whose 'loose and debauched conversation' had made him a laughing-stock locally. Drunkenness was indeed one of the commonest of clerical vices mentioned in the charges against 'scandalous' ministers, and, as in the cases of John Aylmer, vicar of Melshbourne in Bedfordshire, and Thomas Walker, vicar of Winston in Suffolk, it was not unusual to couple this misdemeanour with Laudian ritualistic practices, seeking to discredit the latter by association with the former.[108]

Another of the religious tasks given to the county committees which was likely to meet with stiff local opposition, especially in counties where enthusiasm for strict Puritanism was not especially prominent, was the duty of making a division of the county into units suitable for use as Presbyterian 'classes'. In Cornwall, for example, there is no evidence that the county committees made any attempt to put the scheme into practice. In Northumberland in 1645, out of sixty parishes hardly one classis could be made due to the scarcity of godly ministers. The Kent committee had to inform the Speaker of the House of Commons that a committee of twenty gentlemen and an equal number of ministers appointed for this specific purpose had found 'the ministers in generall and the major part of the gentry to be desirous yet a while to wayte the further directions of the Parliament therein . . .', a statement which, *mutatis mutandis*, sums up the attitude of a great many other local authorities outside London.[109]

XII

While county committees might be less responsive to centralist pressures than was desired at Westminster, this did not affect the tendency locally to fix blame on them rather than on the central government and from time to time to appeal to parliament against their oppression. A newsletter of January 1647 mentions a 'great Combustion . . . about an appeale to the Parliament against the iniustice and oppressions of the Kentish Committee', whose members were called up to Westminster about it.[110] On 21 May 1648 a frightened but none the less indignant Mayor of Rochester appealed to Parliament on receipt of news that the Kent committee had dispatched a regiment to that city 'for the stifling of the Petition intended to bee humbly presented to this honorable howse from the Countie of Kent', and that one committeeman had declared that two of the petitioners in every parish ought to be hanged.[111] Not all complaints were stifled before they reached Westminster, however, and even when they were, this naturally fed the belief that it was the local committee rather than Parliament which was the chief offender in matters of fiscal oppression, imprisonment without trial, and, more especially, in notorious cases of cruelty. The charges brought against the Henley committee in February 1646 'of most cruelly using a woman, and forcing out her Tongue, and nailing it to a Sign Post, while Three Companies might march by' made the Commons set a day aside to consider specifically the oppressions of county committees.[112] Even during the war there were probably many MPs who sympathized with the viewpoint expressed in a speech by Sir John Holland asserting that the county committees had outlived their usefulness and ought to be abolished, and 'that the people ... never groaned under soe heavy a burthen ... as these Committees are in most places become through their vsurpations'.[113] Such complaints which become more frequent after the end of the war came mostly from conservative sources, such as the petitions of the lord mayor and aldermen and the apprentices and young men of the City of London in July 1647.[114] But although under fire from the right, the committees, not least in their role of paymasters of troops stationed in their counties, were by no means exempt from attack from more radical quarters, especially in declarations, pamphlets and petitions from and in support of the so-called agitators and other radical elements in the army in 1647-8.[115] The resentment of unpaid and often hungry soldiers often went beyond expression in petitions and declarations and boiled over into acts of violence against those whom they deemed responsible for their condition. During the summer of 1647 the county committeemen of Devon, Dorset, Leicestershire and the deputy lieutenants of Cheshire, who were a county committee in all but name, were all victims of violent attacks from soldiers. In Leicestershire in July the committeemen were marched 'vpp and downe the county in what disgracefull manner they can'. The Cheshire deputy lieutenants were stuffed into Northgate gaol in Chester, 'a Common prison for Rogues & Murtherers', and left without food 'nor any accommodation for nature, but publicly like beasts amongst ourselves'. Small wonder that the committee of the neighbouring county of Lancashire begged Parliament to send on at least £20,000 of the soldiers' arrears of pay lest its members suffer a similar fate.[116] It is significant that, in his proposals of October 1647 pressing on Parliament the need to make adequate provision for the soldiers' arrears and so to prevent them having recourse, *faute de mieux*, to free quarter, Lord General Fairfax urged that any assessment for these purposes ought to be made 'by the way of the High-Sheriffe, etc. as it used to be in the Case of Subsidies, the Names and power of Committees being so unpleasant to the people'.[117] At least in this the army and conservative county gentlemen spoke with the same voice. The committees were the villains of the piece.

Just as the fiscal oppression of Charles i's personal government in the 1630s had produced its martyrs, champions of the freedoms of Englishmen, so did the situation created by the oppression and revolutionary illegality associated with the county committees produce its own champions of conservative constitutionalism and county tradition. At first sight the Lincolnshire gentleman Colonel Edward King is an unlikely candidate for such a role.[118] In 1643, as the supporter of Manchester and the enemy of the Lord Lieutenant of Lincolnshire, Lord Willoughby of Parham, he had stood firmly for the subordination of county to Eastern Association and national interest, on which account he had been *persona grata* with the radical elements both at Westminster and in the county. But his later attack on Independents and sectaries in the army of the Eastern Association had lost him the support of the radicals without reconciling him with his conservative enemies of 1643 whose memories were too long for them to lend wholehearted support to the attacks which he mounted on the county committee in 1644-5. But his renewed attacks in 1646-7 which achieved great publicity through the charge which he delivered to the Grand Juries at the Folkingham sessions in October 1646 and the Sleaford sessions in January 1647 became a rallying cry for the nationwide discontent against the oppressions of the county committees. This discontent found further expression in the petition which the citizens of London delivered to the House of Commons on 19 December 1646, and which the Independents in the House failed to prevent being considered by the substantial margin of 156 votes to 99.[119] The general tone of the petition is conservative, attacking lay preachers and schismatics as well as 'the exorbitant Practices of many Committees' - all the things which King had denounced at the October sessions and was to denounce again at Sleaford the following January. 'But I can say with Daniell, My God hath shutt ye Lyons Mouths that they haue not hurt me : forasmuch as before him Innocencie was found in me.' However, the analogy which suggested itself to most contemporaries was not so much that of Daniel in the lions' den as Hampden in the Court of Exchequer Chamber. For, *mutatis mutandis*, King was protesting against many of the illegalities which had provoked opposition to royal government in the 1620s and 1630s : levying taxes without proper constitutional authority, in excess of what had been voted by Parliament; failure to employ the proceeds for the purposes for which they had been voted; and imprisonment without trial and contrary to due process of law. As is the case with the agitation against the county committees everywhere, King was careful to draw a distinction between the will of Parliament and the oppressions of the committees which, like Egyptian taskmasters - a common simile - 'compell us to make brickes without straw, and beat and imprison us without fault'. Not the least significant of his strictures, calling to mind the Ship Money agitation of the 1630s, was the committee's failure to employ 'the usual proportions and divisions of Rates' whereby financial burdens had customarily been apportioned.

King's denunciation of the Lincolnshire committee and his incitement to a taxpayers' strike seem to have worked only too well, for on 2 April 1647 the hard-pressed county committee complained that this hitherto quiescent county, which had always dutifully paid its taxes, had not only become the scene of widespread refusal to do so but also of demands for repayment of taxes already paid, 'as vniustly imposed on them'. King's attack of 1646–7 took place at a time when his strictures were likely to receive the maximum of attention nationally – during the period of the Presbyterian ascendancy at Westminster. The attack made by William Prynne on the Somerset committee at the beginning of 1648 came at a less favourable time – though Prynne had for a long time been trying to undermine John Pyne's hold on the county. It was less general in the issues which it raised, resting chiefly on the committee's alleged determination to take it out on Prynne's local associates. Nevertheless the political as well as the personal differences between the radical Pyne and the conservative Prynne clearly emerge from the heat of the charges and counter-charges.[120]

Perhaps the most expressive voice of all, echoing the conservative aims of those who had gone to war for local autonomy and against royal centralization, and far from being delivered from Solomon's whips, had been chastised with Rehoboam's scorpions, was that of another Somerset man, Clement Walker. Here surely was the genuine conservative voice of the Country, bitterly opposed to innovation and desiring to bring peace and settlement by restoration and not by revolution:

> If there be any intention to restore our Laws and Liberties and free us from arbitrary Government, it is fit that these Committees and all associations be laid-down . . ., and that the old form of Government by Sheriffs, Justices of the Peace, &c. be reestablished, and the Militia in each County settled, as before, in Lieutenants and deputy Lieutenants, or in Commissioners.

Restoration was the keynote. Just as fiscal oppression would be checked by the restoration of the ancient course of the Exchequer, so would the essentially conservative aims of the Country be realized and the usurped power of the county committees, 'far higher than ever *Strafford* or *Canterbury* durst advise the King to exercise', be ended by the restoration of the traditional forms of county government.[121] The programme of those conservative men who had gallantly gone to war for King and Parliament in 1642 and who formed the backbone of the parliamentarian cause was finally achieved not as a result of the victory of the cause which they had espoused but of the restoration of the king whose father they had fought.

ELEVEN *Between Two Civil Wars 1646–8*

Samuell hewed Agag in peeces before the Lord in Gilgal: your toys of evill Councell and the King can doe no wrong would not serve *Agags* turne, nor *Adonibezeck*, nor the five Kings that Joshua hang up, who all might have pleaded *evil Councell* and the like.

> Henry Marten, *A corrector of the answerer to the speech out of doores* (Edinburgh 1646), p. 6.

With what face can ye endure a smal Councel of war to controul and disobey the great Councel of state? Are ye weary of the Common Law, or rather willing the Marshal Law should rule you? wil ye delight to see Souldiers in Buff, than Nobles in their Parliament Robes? Had ye rather the Land should run down with tears and blood than flow with milk and honey? ... wil ye suffer the Army under pretence of justice to bring you into bondage, and under the name of Saints of light to act the part of the Angels of darkness?

> *Works of darkness brought to light* (1647), p. 7.

If we cannot have Peace but upon these terms, viz. the Will of the King, and the Advantage of the Crown in the Kings esteem; upon these terms we needed not to have had any war. . . .

> *A declaration of the Lords and Commons . . . concerning the paper of the Scots Commissioners*, 13 March 1648, p. 20.

I

AS THE FIRST CIVIL WAR came to an end with the king in Scottish
hands, the Scots appeared to be in a stronger position than any they
had enjoyed since the winter of 1643-4. Nevertheless, the question of
the disposal of the king sparked off a fierce controversy which, as the
Scottish commissioners in England observed as early as August 1646,
threatened to bring about a complete rupture of relations between the
two kingdoms.[1] The English position was put, if in a somewhat extreme form, by the Independent MP Thomas Chaloner, who argued
that, although Charles was king of both countries, there was a fundamental difference between his person *in abstracto* and *in concreto* – shades
of the king's two bodies! – and, as to the latter, 'his Person must be
disposed of by the Supreame power of that Countrey wheresoever he
shall happen to abide'.[2] By contrast, the Scots argued that 'allegeance
hath no limitation of place', in which circumstances Charles 'ought to
be disposed of . . . with the consent of both Kingdomes'. Moreover, the
English claim unilaterally to dispose of the person of the king was a
violation of the Solemn League and Covenant and the Anglo-Scottish
treaty of alliance;[3] to which the English countered by claiming that
it was the Scots who had violated the Covenant and treaty by accepting
the king in their midst in England, which argued for their determination to conclude a separate peace with him.[4]

The fact that the anti-Scottish arguments cited above came from
political Independents reflects the difficult and embarrassing position
of the English Presbyterian associates of the Scots. Given the unpopularity of the Scots in England, the best hope for the Presbyterians was to
get them out of the country with the maximum of expedition and the
minimum of fuss. The Presbyterian ascendancy in the House of Commons, which lasted on and off until Pride's Purge in December 1648,
dates in fact from the removal of the Scottish army from England at the
beginning of 1647. Their success on 1 September 1646, after an initial
rebuff four days earlier, in securing a further £100,000 in addition to the
£300,000 already voted for the Scots in return for their departure, was
at one and the same time an acknowledgement that their interest lay in
getting them out of the country and an earnest of their eagerness to do
all they could for them. The second motive is also apparent in Presbyterian sponsorship of a number of other motions pleasing to the Scots
in the summer and autumn of 1646.[5]

In so far as the Scots were conscious of the fact that their departure would remove the most important obstacle to the achievement of the parliamentary ascendancy which had eluded their English Presbyterian allies for so long, and that the king's person would be safe enough in the hands of a Presbyterian-controlled Parliament, it was only to royalists who shared Charles's forlorn hope that the Scots would reopen hostilities on his behalf that their handing him over to Parliament invited comparison with the treachery of Judas.[6] It is in fact difficult to see what else they could have done, for, as Lord Chancellor Loudoun made clear at a conference with the English parliamentary negotiators on 6 October, it would be highly dangerous to carry the king off to Scotland, where he would serve as a rallying point for the Amalekites. On the other hand, if the Presbyterians controlled Parliament in England, the king's safety was assured, and the doubts expressed not only by Loudoun, but also by the far more radical Argyll, that the English Parliament's claim to dispose of the person of the king, 'may in some sense be to depose or worse', could be disregarded.[7] No doubt anyway they paid too much attention to unrepresentative outbursts such as the demand made by Henry Marten and by the anonymous author of a paper of June 1646 against the return of the militia to royal control, that the king should be brought to trial and punished for his alleged crimes.[8]

One anonymous pamphlet and one outrageous utterance by an MP who delighted to shock his hearers and had long held extreme views about the monarchy do not add up to the general prevalence of anti-monarchical views in Independent circles.[9] But although neither his Crown nor his life was in any real danger at this stage, the defeated Charles had no reason to expect that the peace propositions shortly to be presented to him would make very pleasant reading. At first sight the so-called Newcastle Propositions which were presented to the king on 13 July 1646 do not appear to be notably more severe than those discussed at Uxbridge the previous year.[10] But it must be remembered that it was the stiffness of those terms which had made the failure of the Uxbridge Treaty a virtually foregone conclusion, and, even in defeat, the king was unlikely to consent easily to the abolition of episcopacy, the taking of the Covenant by both king and subjects and the exemption of fifty-seven leading royalists from pardon for capital offences; or, despite Presbyterian attempts to moderate the terms,[11] to the vesting of the militia in parliamentary hands for twenty years without any assurance that it would revert to the Crown thereafter.

One difference between the Uxbridge and the Newcastle Propositions is that the latter were not up for negotiation; rejection of them and resumption of hostilities was no longer an option open to the king. In these circumstances Charles set his hopes on procrastination and intrigue with the object of dividing his opponents, Scotsmen from Englishmen, and Presbyterians from Independents, despite his disavowal in a letter of 10 June of 'any Intention to make a Division'.[12] But his Machiavellian exercises availed him nothing. As the Scottish chancellor forcibly pointed out to him in July, refusal to accept the Newcastle Propositions would have the effect of dismaying his friends and uniting them with his enemies. And so, he went on prophetically, '. . . all England will joyne against you as one man, and . . . it is feared they will . . . depose you, and set up another government; they will charge us to deliver your Majesty to them . . . and . . . will be constrained . . . to . . . settle Religion and Peace without you'.[13]

Loudoun's predictions proved to be astonishingly accurate. Almost all is there: the departure of the Scots, the delivery of the king to Parliament, the Vote of No Addresses, and (perhaps) the ultimately republican solution – at any rate a solution without Charles. Before the end of the second week of February 1647, the Scots had departed and the king was in the hands of the English Parliament.[14] Charles's policies, designed to divide and sow confusion among his enemies had, if anything, had the reverse effect. The Scots had refused to be divorced from their English allies and both Presbyterians and Independents, after some initial hesitation, had stuck out for the terms of the Newcastle Propositions. The second half of 1646, however, was to see a number of divisions in the House of Commons in which Presbyterian motions critical of the armed forces foreshadowed what was to become the central issue of the following year,[15] once the departure of the Scots had left their English allies free to concentrate their attention on what was now the outstanding grievance of many Englishmen – the size and cost of the military establishment.

II

By the time that they had handed the king over to the English Parliament in February 1647, the fine flower of Scottish hopes, which had been so notably raised by the events of the summer of 1646, had withered. The mood of disillusionment is well captured by Chancellor Loudoun's remark that although the Scots were still resolved to 'live and dye with their brethren of England in the prosecution of the ends expressed in the Solemne league and Covenant', they were 'scandalized and greved' by the neglect of the Directory of Worship, the continued use of the Book of Common Prayer and by the proliferation of sectaries in England. All of these things were, needless to say, products of the failure to set up what the Scots regarded as a proper Presbyterian Church in England.[16] But at least they could be thankful for the mercy, however small, that so long as the king remained in the hands of a Parliament in which their 'Presbyterian' allies – however unworthy of the name – were in the ascendancy, and so long as Denzil Holles and his colleagues were resolved to cut the army – that breeding-ground *par excellence* of Independency and sectarian excesses – down to size, the king was in safe hands and the worst dangers of religious heterodoxy and social and political anarchy were likely to be avoided. No doubt the Scots also took heart at the welcome given by the leaders of the Presbyterian party in the House of Commons to petitions from Suffolk and other Eastern Association counties calling for a stricter Presbyterian orthodoxy, an end to religious toleration, and the disbandment of the army.[17]

These safeguards were removed, and the situation transformed at a stroke on 4 June by the abduction of the king from Holdenby House in Northamptonshire by a detachment of soldiers under a junior officer, acting, if not under orders, at least with the connivance, of the principal army commanders, with the possible exception of the Lord General, Fairfax. Whatever the truth about the origins of Cornet Joyce's coup it is straining credulity to argue that the incident was no more than an 'Accident, which had befallen by the Disorder of the Soldiers'. Certainly the army commanders were quick to accept the new situation as conferring a strong advantage on both the army and its Independent allies in parliament.[18] For the Scots and their Presbyterian allies, of course, the reverse was true. It was one thing, as Lauderdale put it forcibly to a meeting of both the English Houses of Parliament on 7 June, for the Scots to have agreed to hand the king over to Parliament, for Parliament was controlled by responsible men, 'of one Religion with us, and engaged in the same Covenant'. It was quite another, and a realization of their worst fears, for Charles to be 'violently torn away from that Place [Holdenby] by some Soldiers of Sir Thomas Fairfax's Army', who were as likely as not Independents, sectaries or even republicans.[19]

Needless to say, the army leaders did their best to pooh-pooh such fears. According to John Rushworth, the Secretary of the army, writing to Lord Fairfax, the Lord General's father, on 9 June, the only people who had anything to fear from the coup of 4 June were the Presbyterian leaders, 'Holles, Stapleton, Clotworthy and such incendiaries', who had plotted to raise a counter-revolutionary force and would not have hesitated to bring in the Scottish army to force the New Model to disband on their terms.[20] The twin spectres of a Scottish invasion coupled with the raising of a counter-revolutionary force in England were to constitute one of the dominant themes of the politics of 1647-8, and, of course, the danger was intensified once the army had pre-empted the situation by taking control of the king's person.[21] For the army coup of 4 June might reasonably be held to provide a justification for calling in the Scots to restore the king to parliamentary custody, as well as to rescue the threatened Presbyterian leaders into the bargain. It is to these considerations, and to the events which precipitated the army coup of 4 June and dominated the political scene in the succeeding months, that we must now turn.

III

It has already been remarked that the departure of the Scots at the beginning of 1647 freed the Presbyterian leaders from the unpopularity which was a product of their close association with a discredited and expensive ally. With the Scots mercifully out of the way, and drawn on by their dislike of the Independent and sectarian New Model Army as well as by their consciousness of the opportunist advantages presented by the increasingly prevalent desire of the political nation to return to normal, the disbandment of the army, or at least of those soldiers not needed at home or in Ireland, was an expedient which had an obvious appeal for Holles and his colleagues. As Dr Morrill has reminded us, the attempted disbandment of the New Model in 1647, which was to have such momentous political consequences, was not the first exercise of this sort undertaken by Parliament, nor was the New Model the only force under arms. Massey's disorderly western army had already been disbanded in October 1646, while Major-General Poynz commanded a force in the north which was in itself about two-thirds the strength of the New Model. Nor were either the grievances of the New Model soldiers about arrears of pay and other matters or their disobedience to Parliament peculiar to them, as the examples of mutinies in provincial armies cited in the last chapter will have already made clear.[22] What was different was the element of political agitation which was, at least at first, peculiar to the New Model, though its members ultimately attempted to extend it to other forces.[23]

But as far as can be ascertained, this feature is something which developed in the course of events rather than being inherent in the soldiers' original demands. While there were doubtless elements within the army who were alarmed at the new-found Presbyterian hegemony in Parliament, and were only too pleased to use the army as a political base for radical ideas, there is scant sign of their influence in the original demands of the soldiers in the spring of 1647, which are completely innocent of any overtly political content and not markedly different from those of their counterparts in provincial armies. There is, in fact, no need to doubt the verdict of the anonymous informant of Colonel Edward Harley in a letter of 27 March, who while stressing the deep discontent existing in Harley's regiment, had no doubt that Parliament would be able to 'doe as they please with the Army', provided that proper account was taken of the soldiers' grievances about arrears of pay and other matters relating to their employment.[24] It is true that this would be a very formidable undertaking, given the fact that these arrears have been estimated as totalling about £2½ million in March 1647.[25] But if only a relatively small part of these huge arrears were to be paid on demobilization, in return for vague promises of full satisfaction when times were better, the problem might prove less intractable. Buoyed up by the general dislike of high expenditure and the high taxation associated with what was widely regarded as an inordinately swollen military establishment in relation to peacetime needs, Holles and his colleagues resolved to try out this approach which had worked well enough with Massey's troops the previous autumn. In doing so, they were no doubt also conscious of the extreme distaste of well-born taxpayers for the army's role as a status-elevator. As one pamphlet published later in 1647 put it, echoing Holles's own dislike of servants riding horses, officers, who 'from being cloathed in raggs are now arrayed in Scarlet', were not unnaturally reluctant to return to mean civilian occupations. Such men being 'used so long to Command . . . have forgotten [how] to obey'.[26] And the price was being paid by the much enduring taxpayer.

The Presbyterian leaders may have correctly estimated the mood of the taxpaying public, but they grossly and fatally misjudged that of the soldiers. Their first shock came in the response of the rank and file to their attempt to suppress the petition which was circulating in the army during the last week in March, asking for payment of the soldiers' arrears and the settlement of other matters, such as provision for the dependants of the fallen, the exemption of volunteers from future impressment, and the indemnification of soldiers for acts done under military discipline which might also be civil offences. The last demand was a constantly recurring feature of the first half of 1647, which saw a number of cases of soldiers being called to answer for such offences in the courts.[27] Although none of the soldiers' demands was in any way outrageous, Parliament was horrified by what it saw as an attempt by the military to dictate the terms on which they would disband. Accordingly on 30 March it issued a stern declaration condemning the soldiers' action. It also commanded the Lord General to suppress all petitioning in the army, even though, as Fairfax gently reminded them, the petition in question was to be directed to him, and he was to be the judge of how much of its contents were matters fit to be transmitted by him to Parliament. Parliament's over-reaction to a petition which was totally devoid of any politically subversive content was to precipitate a chain of events whose chief features were to be the emergence of the army as an autonomous political force, as well as the development within it of extremist movements which were to be a threat to Presbyterians and Independents alike.[28] It was inept, not least because it brought the aggrieved soldiers and their commanders more closely together.

IV

Among the first signs of these developments are a *Vindication of the officers of the Army* presented to Parliament and the letters addressed by the so-called agitators, or elected representatives of the rank and file of eight out of the ten cavalry regiments in the New Model Army,[29] to the three generals, Fairfax, Cromwell and Skippon, at the end of April. While the autonomous professional grievances of the soldiers bulk largest in these letters, prominence is also given to the idea that Parliament's plan to disband the army was part of a counter-revolutionary plot which could be countered effectively only if the army remained under arms. This emphasis is to be found in all the public statements issued by the army in May and June, both before and after it made its allegedly pre-emptive strike on 4 June by seizing the person of the king, and it culminates in the celebrated and momentous 'Solemn Engagement of the Army' which followed a mass rendezvous on Newmarket Heath on the day after the king had been taken.[30] The soldiers avowed that they would not disband until their grievances – which were no longer solely the professional grievances of soldiers *qua* soldiers as in March – had been redressed. The other main achievement of the 'Engagement' was the setting up of the General Council of the army, which was given the task of formulating the army's programme. Given the constitution of this body, which included two elected representatives both of commissioned officers and of other ranks in each of the regiments, it is not difficult to see that the pressures for the army to take a distinctly radical stand would be very considerable, more especially given the tendency of the common soldiers to elect radical representatives.

But for the army to formulate a political programme of any sort, whether influenced by Leveller notions or not, was a matter of the utmost alarm to the Presbyterian leaders at Westminster and in the City. On 10 June following a further army rendezvous on Triploe Heath, twelve senior officers, including the Lord General Fairfax, the Independents Cromwell and Sir Hardress Waller and the more radical colonels Pride and Rainsborough, sent a letter, not to Parliament, but to that other centre of Presbyterian counter-revolutionary activity, the City of London. The letter voiced the army's demand for satisfaction against the guilty men who had tried to disband it and had calumniated the soldiers and misrepresented their demands. But the army's demands now were very different from those of March, and took in 'a settlement of the Peace of the Kingdom and of the Liberties of the Subject ... which ... we ... have as much right to demand ... as we have to our money, or the other common interests of Souldiers'.[31]

Parliament had panicked in March when the soldiers had set about petitioning their commander-in-chief to settle their as yet entirely non-political grievances. That they should within the short space of two months have proceeded from demanding redress of grievances peculiar to soldiers to asserting rights common to all Englishmen was no doubt regarded by those who had over-reacted in March as the consequence of the failure to take a strong enough line then rather than as the avoidable outcome of their mistaken political strategy. The precise nature of the liberties of Englishmen of which the soldiers now claimed to be the champions was to become the subject of fierce debate within the army council in November. But for the moment the army was presenting a united front to its enemies. On 15 June the parliamentary commissioners with the army were presented with a Representation or Declaration of the Army which had been prepared by the newly created army council and which Gardiner has described as 'the first deliberate attempt of the army to set forth a political programme'. In emphasizing that the need to defend their liberties as Englishmen against malignant counter-revolutionary designs was at least as important a motive of the soldiers in resisting disbandment as the obtaining of satisfaction of their grievances as soldiers, the declaration was probably reading the political circumstances and aspirations of June into the events of March. A great deal had indeed happened during the intervening weeks, and notably the politicization of the aspirations of the soldiers. The declaration demanded a purge of disaffected MPs – the heads of charges by the army against eleven leading Presbyterians, including Holles and Stapleton, were appended – and the abrogation of the act that Parliament might not be dissolved except by its own consent, on the grounds that the danger against which the statute was designed no longer existed. Arrangement should be made for the dissolution of Parliament, for new elections and for a limited life for the newly elected Parliament. The declaration steered clear of specific recommendations about the franchise, though it specifically recommended a measure of redistribution of seats at the expense of scandalously rotten boroughs. The powers of both deputy lieutenants and county committees should be severely curtailed. There should be a very generous measure of religious toleration, and it was recommended that 'such who, upon Conscientious Grounds, may differ from the established forms may not be debarred from the common Rights . . . belonging equally to all'. Here was the army's first integrated political programme – a platform worthy of men who 'were not a mere mercenary Army, hired to serve any arbitrary Power of State, but called forth . . . by the several Declarations of Parliaments to the Defence of our own and the Peoples just Rights and Liberties'.[32]

In the process whereby the army had obtained control of the person of the king and had come to assume a positive political stance the role of the so-called 'agitators' is of crucial importance, and it has frequently been too readily assumed that this role was strongly Leveller inspired as distinct from proceeding naturally from Parliament's hostile reaction to autonomously military grievances. The Leveller movement had, of course, achieved some prominence before the appearance of agitators in the army. Leveller influence has already been noted in the petition from radical elements in London on 2 June 1646, and the following month had seen the appearance of Richard Overton's celebrated *Remonstrance of many thousand Citizens*, with its emphatic assertion of royal, as distinct from ministerial, responsibility for the war and the oppression of Englishmen; its assertion of popular, as distinct from parliamentary, sovereignty; and its denunciation of Parliament itself for perpetuating and even increasing the oppression of the subject.[33] During the spring and early summer of 1647, when the army was rapidly moving from voicing its autonomously political grievances to the assumption of a distinctively political role, the House of Commons was bombarded by Leveller petitions, some of which, to judge from the names of the tellers in divisions on such motions as whether these petitions should be considered by the House or burnt by the common hangman, received some support from the Independent parliamentary allies of the army leaders.[34] But there is little to indicate that the agitators were in the Levellers' pocket. In his admirably balanced account of their role Professor Woolrych has emphasized the agitators' supreme concern to maintain the army's unity and to ensure that the army should be disbanded on fair terms. 'The perpetuation of the army', he writes, 'was not the agitators' aim.'[35] It was obviously the concern of the army grandees that their demands would keep within these limits.

V

A classic way of diverting popular attention from radical and revolutionary ends is to direct them against an easily identifiable enemy, opposition to whom can be construed as being the shared concern both of those who were alarmed by, and of those who it was feared might espouse, radical objectives. The dilemma in which the army leaders found themselves in the summer of 1647 was that if they moved too far in a radical direction – which anyway they had no wish to do – they would antagonize the vast mass of the political nation, both in and out of Parliament. On the other hand, if they were content to espouse a policy of moderate reform, as their eleven principal Presbyterian opponents were later to put it, 'outstripping all others in acting for his Maiestie',[36] they would find it difficult to retain control of the agitators and the army, rank and file. To no small extent the army's insistence on retribution on the eleven Presbyterian leaders should be seen as an attempt to divert and canalize militant energies in pursuit of scapegoats whose counter-revolutionary activities had, it was claimed, threatened to plunge England into the horrors of a second civil war.

This is not to represent the dangers of counter-revolution in the early months of 1647 simply as a convenient bogey used by Machiavellian army grandees as a means of preserving the unity of the army. The dangers had, in fact, been – and, as the events of late July were to demonstrate, were again to be – only too real. The creation of a counter-revolutionary force and the disbandment of the New Model were two distinct but complementary parts of the Presbyterian strategy in the spring and early summer of 1647. 'The commanding party in the house', asserted the radical army chaplain Hugh Peter, 'had more force upon them to disband us, than we put upon the house in refusing'.[37] The main source of this force applied to the parliamentary Presbyterians was to be found in the City of London. As Valerie Pearl has demonstrated,[38] a central feature of the counter-revolutionary strategy was the creation of an armed force consisting of divers elements: army units whose commanders – such as Major General Poynz – were trusted by the Presbyterians; the trained bands of London, which necessitated the capture of the City Militia Committee from the control of Independents such as Fowke and Pennington – a process which took place during April and was the subject of a number of divisions between Presbyterians and Independents in the House of Commons during that month;[39] deserters, whose forsaking of the New Model was positively encouraged by the Presbyterian leaders in Parliament; and finally, and perhaps most sinister of all, the recruitment of already disbanded officers and men – some of them ex-royalists – who were popularly known as 'reformadoes', and who were to be the main instruments of counter-revolutionary terror in London during the summer. These counter-revolutionary preparations were stepped up in the early part of June as a result of the transformation of the political situation consequent upon the abduction of the king from Holdenby. Clearly there was something in the notion, stressed in most of the public statements of the army and in Fairfax's letter to the City on 10 June, that the disbandment of the army would open the way to counter-revolution and perhaps to a Scottish invasion.[40] As the army moved on London to quell this counter-revolutionary threat, the City fathers capitulated and ordered the disbandment and dispersal of the reformadoes, disclaiming 'the least Intention to do any Prejudice to that Army whom God had made so eminent an Instrument of our Deliverance and Safety'. This deceived nobody, and what ensued was a lull rather than a permanent detente.[41]

The charges brought by the army against the eleven members included peculation in the case of Sir John Clotworthy, acceptance of bribes by Recorder Glyn and Anthony Nicholls, and political manipulation in Wales, including the favouring of ex-royalists, by Glyn and Sir William Lewis. In addition, there was the rehashing of the charges of complicity with the royalists which Lord Saville had brought against Denzil Holles two years earlier.[42] The group was accused of holding clandestine meetings at Lady Carlisle's house with the aim of bringing about a Scottish invasion, creating a counter-revolutionary force and plunging England into a second civil war to restore the king 'upon their own terms'. This was, of course, the great centrepiece of the indictment, but there can be little doubt that the charges relating to the alleged intimidation of petitioners and the deceiving of the House as to the nature of the soldiers' grievances, together with the role of the eleven members in the plan to disband the army without settlement of full arrears of pay or redress of other grievances, bulked largest in the minds even of the more politically conscious soldiers.[43]

One factor which may have worked in the army's favour by lessening the force of objections to the possibility of a military occupation of London was that the capital had already been subjected to military terror of a quite different sort. Just as the disciplined behaviour of the New Model troops had stood out in strong and favourable contrast to the disorders of Goring's and Grenville's royalist troops in the west country in 1645, so did the prospect of the occupation of the capital by the same New Model seem to many a far less terrible fate than subjection to the excesses of the 'reformadoes' and their like. The fact that the encouragement of such elements was one of the main charges levelled by the army against the eleven members doubtless made their case against the latter the more acceptable in the eyes of many citizens. These in turn would be responsive to the army's repeated complaints that nothing was being done either to disband the 'reformadoes' or to dismiss and bring the eleven members to justice.[44]

In spite of such procrastination, by the third week in July it looked as if a military occupation of London might be avoided. The eleven members withdrew from Parliament with a resultant softening of the Presbyterian backbone, facilitating a series of votes which conceded a great deal of what the army leaders and their Independent allies desired. On 17 July the motion appointing Fairfax as commander-in-chief of all the armed forces in the country was carried by seventy-six votes to thirty-nine. On 21 July a Presbyterian attempt to prevent discussion of the army's propositions in the House of Commons was defeated by the narrower margin of eighty votes to sixty-eight. On 23 July control of the London militia was taken from the hands of the City Presbyterian supporters of Holles and his colleagues, in whose hands it had been since the beginning of May.[45]

Naturally, in the view of the diehard Presbyterian opponents of the army the votes passed in July simply demonstrated in Holles' words, that 'the Parliament was but a Cypher, and only cried Amen to what the Council of War had determined'. In particular, the ordinance relating to the London militia was represented as 'a design of the Army, merely to provoke the City'.[46] If this was so, it spectacularly succeeded. On 21 July, the day after the House of Commons had voted that precautions should be taken to protect its proceedings against 'Multitudes and Tumults',[47] large numbers of Londoners, urged on and doubtless also intimidated by 'reformadoes' and apprentices, signed the so-called Solemn Engagement of the City to bring the king to London to treat with Parliament, to restore him to his rights, and to implement the Covenant, a development which was denounced by Parliament two days later.[48] But Parliament was soon to eat its words. On 26 July the storm broke and both houses were invaded by a counter-revolutionary mob demanding – and obtaining – *inter alia*, the repeal of virtually all the offensive acts of July, the restoration of the eleven members and a parliamentary resolution inviting the king back to London.[49]

The newly established harmony between Parliament and the army which had precipitated the counter-revolutionary storm was now shattered. It could be restored only by the military occupation of London which Cromwell and the grandees had resisted when its necessity had been pressed upon them in late June and early July. But there was a significant difference between what the agitators had then demanded in vain and what was actually done on 6 August when London was occupied by the army. For that occupation could now plausibly be represented as rescuing Londoners from the brutal attentions of the counter-revolutionary mob and Massey's and Poynz's 'reformadoes' who were terrorizing the streets.[50] Secondly, and even more important, the occupation could be represented as designed to restore the integrity of Parliament, through the return to their seats of those Members – not all of whom were Independents and who included the Speakers of both Houses[51] – who had fled to the army following the violence of 26 July.[52] That it also involved the driving away of the eleven Presbyterian leaders, whose restoration had been one of the fruits of the counter-revolutionary coup, was, of course, also true, but the events of those days were held to furnish unmistakable proof – if further proof were indeed needed – of the malignant designs of the eleven.

If a primary aim of the army's occupation of London was to restore Parliament's freedom of action, that body can hardly be said to have distinguished itself by gratitude for being rescued. Although the Lords were compliant enough, the Presbyterians in the Commons appear quickly to have recovered strength, despite the departure of the eleven Members once again. On 9 August the lower House – albeit by the narrow margin of only two votes – refused to pass an ordinance coming down to it from the Lords to the effect that, since Parliament had acted under duress from 26 July onwards, its subsequent measures should be declared null and void. Two days later the House rejected – this time by 34 votes – a draft declaration drawn up in the Lords vindicating the army's action in restoring the integrity of Parliament. Further, on 13 August the Commons rejected by 25 votes an ordinance, again coming to them from the Lords, which condemned the reconstituted London militia committee of 26 July for continuing to act without legitimate authority. While it is true that on the same day the House did pass an amended ordinance whose effect was to repeal all the measures of the July days, the force of the amendment was, by substituting repeal for annulment, to preserve the legitimacy of parliament after the driving away of the Speakers following the tumult of 26 July. This was hardly enough to placate the army, but on 19 August the Commons again refused to pass an ordinance of repeal, this time by only three votes. On the same day the General Council of the army issued a Remonstrance which, as well as resolutely vindicating its march on London to bring order to the capital and restore the Speakers and the fugitive MPs to their places, firmly emphasized the need for Parliament to put its house in order and to right the counter-revolutionary wrongs of late July. This time the Commons at last reacted in the desired manner and consented to the annulment – as distinct from the repeal – of those objectionable measures, with all that this involved in terms of its legal standing during those stormy days. A crucial chapter in the history of the relations between the army, the City and the parliament had ended.[53]

VI

The summer of 1647, culminating in the events of the last weeks of July, had seen the dramatic appearance of a phenomenon which was to play an important, if intermittent, part in the history of England over the next century and a half. Londoners had become accustomed, more especially during the two years before the war, to the spectacle of the mob, used by Pym and his associates as a means of intimidating their opponents. What was new about the London mob of the July days was its counter-revolutionary character, which in a sense made it the direct precursor of the Church and King mobs of the late seventeenth and eighteenth centuries. One royalist sympathizer observed gleefully how 'the same kind of riotous Rascles which rabled [sic] the King out of town, did drive away the Speakers in like manner with many of their Members ... to seek shelter of their Janizaries'.[54] Another derived even greater hope from the phenomenon. Counter-revolutionary tumults were a clear manifestation of the growing popular sympathy for the king 'as the only *Restorer* of Liberty upon whose *Restauration* depends their owne'. Tumults had driven the king from Westminster in 1642; tumults might well bring him back.[55]

Even if some royalist observers were disappointed at the failure of the counter-revolutionary movements of July to bring the king back to power, by no means all of them reacted pessimistically to the army's triumph in August. Some indeed were absurdly optimistic, like the writer who forecast the restoration of the king to his old rights within a matter of days.[56] Nevertheless, it would be a mistake to see the triumph of the army and the Independents in August as necessarily a blow to a peaceful settlement of the kingdom and a victory for extremist solutions. It was partly because of the moderate line taken by the army that the counter-revolutionaries had failed to muster all the support they had hoped for during the period following the abduction of the king from Holdenby. Time and time again the public statements issued on behalf of the army were at pains to emphasize that it was looking for a monarchical settlement with the king exercising his just rights, though the exact nature of these was not specified.[57]

It is now time to turn from the negative side of the army's programme, the attack on the Presbyterian leaders, to its more positive aspect. At first sight the idea of the army leaders and their Independent allies, of whom as one of their Presbyterian opponents put it, ''tis notoriously known how their principles are directly against Monarchy',[58] seeking a settlement with the king seems perhaps more than a trifle odd. But one must beware of reading the attitudes of the end of 1648 back into the middle of the previous year. The army had not taken possession of the king in June 1647, as it was later to do in December

1648, in order to bring him to justice, but to employ him as a powerful weapon in the struggle to save itself from disbandment and the kingdom from counter-revolution.[59] If in some respects the terms of any treaty which the army might make with the king were likely to be more stringent than he might obtain from a Presbyterian-controlled Parliament, in others, and more especially in religious matters, the soldiers might well be able to offer him more. Indeed there were a number of significant ways – not least in his being allowed the ministrations of his own Anglican chaplains – in which the king, on his own admission found the army a more congenial jailer than either the Parliament before June, or the Scots before February 1647.[60] As one perspicacious Scotsman put it, the Independent allies of the army might in theory be 'wors principaled for magistracie then . . . the other partie'. But more important than theoretical considerations was the fact that neither the king nor the Independents had much to hope for from the Presbyterians in matters of religion, in which circumstances they might have more to hope for from one another. For example, the Independents desired nothing more strongly than religious toleration. 'How then . . . can they houp [sic] to injoy this priveleidge more frelie or fullie, then by receiving it from him who hath the sole power . . . to grant it?'[61] It was not for nothing that Sir John Berkeley, the royalist governor of Exeter, had remarked to Cromwell's subordinate officer, Lambert, at the time of the surrender of that city towards the end of the first Civil War, that the king was more likely to obtain a just settlement from the Independents than from the Presbyterians. Significantly it was the same Berkeley who was now dispatched from France by the queen to explore the army's intentions towards their royal captive, and who found Cromwell and the other leaders genuinely disposed towards a settlement with the king.[62] There were other royalists who took a similarly favourable view of the army's intentions, notably the Welsh ex-judge David Jenkins, then under restraint and due to stand trial for his denunciations of various forms of illegality practised by Parliament.[63]

VII

There are three important points to be made about the so-called *Heads of the Proposals*, the peace propositions which were hammered out in the army council in July and presented to the king at the beginning of August.[64] In the first place it was emphatically a monarchical settlement which was envisaged, and on a number of matters, including the retention of the royal veto and the reduction of the period during whichex-Cavaliersweretobedisqualifiedfromofficefromtentofiveyears, significant modifications seem to have been made as a result of Charles's own comments on an early draft. Secondly, although the ecclesiastical provisions were not completely to the king's liking, they were enormously more generous than anything he might expect from the Presbyterians or the Scots, both of whom stuck by the terms of the Newcastle Propositions. Again probably in deference to royal suggestions, the army's proposals did nothing to confirm the sale of episcopal lands, and tacitly assumed the continued existence of bishops, though without any coercive power. In addition the taking of the Covenant was not to be enforced on those who conscientiously objected to it, a provision which would be as welcome to sectaries and radicals in the army as it was to the king. Finally the army's proposals envisaged an end to the present parliament, and the election of a new one based on a wider and uniform franchise and with its duration strictly limited. Some of these last items may, as Professor MacCormack has suggested, reflect the desire to placate the agitators on the army council,[65] though their precise interpretation was soon to become a matter for fierce controversy. But at the time they were produced, the *Heads of the Proposals* must have occasioned deep misgivings among the parliamentary Presbyterians.

The fact that when the *Heads of the Proposals* were presented to the king, the political situation appeared to be promisingly fluid, may well have proved to be his undoing. Despite his specific disavowal, in a letter of 4 August to Fairfax, of any complicity in the counter-revolution of 26 July in London,[66] there can be little doubt that these events, in conjunction with the possibility of a Scottish invasion which his recent interview with Lauderdale had given him reason to see as a distinct possibility, had raised Charles's hopes, and may well have persuaded him to yield to the temptation of playing off his former enemies against one another or, at the very least, to make difficulties about the army's terms. If this is true, he got the worst of every possible world. If he chafed at some of the provisions of the *Heads of the Proposals*, he was also totally unwilling to accept the Covenant and the other religious conditions without which there was no hope of bringing the Scots in on his side. Refusing to make significant concessions on any count, he lost on all. But if the king's stubborn attitude to the *Heads of the Proposals* had no other positive effect, it was undoubtedly an important cause of the temporary break-up of the unity of the army and of the parliamentary Independents, as a result of which the grandees' aims of reaching agreement with the king were made the more difficult to attain.

During the autumn of 1647 one can discern three main sources of opposition to these aims. The first was the parliamentary Presbyterians and the Scots to whom they had, of course, been anathema from the beginning. But the second was to be found in the more radical wing of the parliamentary Independents who originally had not opposed the army's design publicly whatever doubts they may have felt about them in private. Charles's refusal to accept the *Heads of the Proposals* and Cromwell's and Ireton's insistence on continuing to press for accommodation altered that. One observer reports a fierce attack being delivered sometime in October by that *flagellum principum* Henry Marten on Cromwell, whom he described as being 'King-ridden', while references were made to Oliver as a would-be Hotham and worthy of the same fate.[67] A royalist newsletter of the previous month mentions the stormy reception given not simply by the Presbyterians but by the more radical Independents such as Thomas Scot to the suggestion that the House of Commons should give serious consideration to the army's propositions to the king.[68] The split within the ranks of the Independents is also reflected in divisions of the House on these matters, at least if the names of the tellers are anything to go by. On 22 September the two radical and, as they may now be described, anti-Cromwellian, Independents Sir Peter Wentworth and Colonel Thomas Rainsborough acted as tellers against the motion that the House should resolve itself into a Grand Committee to consider 'the whole Matter concerning the King'. The motion passed the house by eighty-four votes to thirty-four with Cromwell and the former middle-grouper Independent Sir John Evelyn of Wiltshire acting as tellers in favour. On the following day Wentworth and Henry Marten were tellers against a similar motion that the House should make application to the king, which was successful by seventy votes to twenty-three. The Independents were clearly split, though the size of the votes and the fact that Sir Arthur Haselrige, whom one usually considers as an MP well on the left of the movement, acted with Evelyn as teller on the other side makes clear the as yet limited strength of the radical dissidents. The association of Cromwell and Henry Marten, an odd and ill-assorted partnership, as tellers in favour of another motion on 16 October that the House should consider the mode of another application to the king does not necessarily contradict this thesis. The motion was lost by sixty-six votes to forty-six, and neither probably expected it to succeed. But it would have suited Marten's book quite well if the House had passed the motion, for it would then have devised peace terms which the king would never accept, which might, in turn, provide the occasion for more radical action. Cromwell, on the other hand, disillusioned by Parliament's obstructive attitude to the army's peace terms, may have welcomed the failure of the motion as justifying the army in going it alone.[69]

VIII

The opposition of Rainsborough to one of the motions mentioned above affords a link between the left wing of the parliamentary Independents and the radical Leveller groups, with whom he was shortly to be associated. Rainsborough had himself been an observer of an incident on 2 August which may well have been a crucial watershed in his own attitude and in that of others. This was the king's ill-advised and petulant rejection of the *Heads of the Proposals* at a conference with representatives of the army. In his invaluable memoirs the royalist Sir John Berkeley tells how Rainsborough departed from the conference in disgust and also of the growing distrust of the agitators on the army council for Cromwell and Ireton which came with the consciousness that they were moving further away from them and closer to the advisers of the king.[70] In a newsletter of 27 September, the royalist William Smith found cause for comfort in this fissure in the army, as a result of which 'the officers of the army will come to an agreement with the King for fear of their own factions and the odium they contract from the kingdom'.[71] At any rate the suspicion of the agitators, and through them, no doubt, of the rank and file, continued to grow and seriously to threaten the army's hard-won unity of June. In September Major Francis White gave eloquent voice to the fears of the agitators about the dangers of coming to an agreement with the king.[72] Far from giving first priority to the provisions of the army's momentous declaration of 14 June, observed the enormously influential radical pamphlet *The Case of the Army Truly Stated*, which appeared in October, the grandees were planning to restore the king first without making any provision that these things would follow.[73] These fears were intensified after the long debates on the franchise and the power of the monarch in the army council at Putney between 28 October and 1 November.[74] As one complainant was to put it on 11 November, if any power whatever were to be restored to Charles, 'he will improve it to the utmost to inslave and ruine you that conquered him'.[75] Who, after all, had won the war?

But despite the importance of the agitators' claims that the army's original aims had been forgotten in the eagerness of its leaders to come to terms with the king, there was more to their disagreement with Cromwell and his colleagues than that. *The Case of the Army* was in fact the product of a radically new situation consequent upon the election by five regiments of new and more radical agitators, this time in close touch with Leveller elements in London. While the precise circumstances of their election have never been adequately explained, the fact and its crucial importance are not in doubt. For in *The Case of the Army* there was developed a programme of constitutional, legal, and – to some extent – social, reform, whose constitutional aspects were to be embodied in the celebrated *Agreement of the People*, which was debated at Putney at the end of October and beginning of November and which presented a radical contrast to the programme embodied in the *Heads of the Proposals*.[76]

Just how radical a contrast it was has been a matter of debate, more especially since the appearance in 1962 of the late Professor Macpherson's study of Possessive Individualism.[77] While not denying that the Levellers' views on the franchise were different from those of the army grandees, Macpherson goes a long way towards minimizing the differences. If, as he argues, the views of one Leveller spokesman at Putney, Maximilian Petty, were typical of them all, they can hardly have been advocates of universal manhood suffrage, as is often claimed, for Petty specifically excludes servants and recipients of alms from the franchise. If this were granted, statements from Rainsborough, Wildman and other Leveller spokesmen to the effect that 'every man that is to live under a government ought first by his own consent to put himself under that government'[78] must be interpreted as meaning a great deal less than the advocacy of universal manhood suffrage. In this view the position of the Levellers is much nearer than is normally assumed to that of the grandees, who would limit the franchise to those who had, in Ireton's phrase, 'a permanent fixed interest in the kingdom',[79] in which category Cromwell at least would have put 'virtual' freeholders such as copyholders of inheritance as well as 'real' freeholders.[80] What was at issue at Putney, in Macpherson's view, was a clash between two restrictive views of the franchise, one of which was simply more restrictive than the other. The typical Leveller view, which is equated with that of Petty, is reckoned, on the basis of some rather dubious backward projections of Gregory King's late seventeenth-century figures, as excluding two-thirds of the adult male population from the franchise.

This interpretation raises a number of questions, the first of which relates to nomenclature. Sir Keith Thomas has sharply questioned Professor Macpherson's inclusion of almsmen under the category of 'beggars', and wage-earners in general under that of 'servants'. In addition he has criticized Macpherson's estimate of the numbers and proportion of wage-earners in England, based, as it is, on some rather shaky extrapolations from Gregory King's already shaky figures.[81] It is, moreover, not unreasonable to add that the very notion of wage-earners as an easily identifiable category raises serious difficulties when applied to early modern England. Day-labourers and labourers taken on by the week are clearly wage-earners in Macpherson's sense, but the contention that they would be included under the category of 'servants' is both unproven and unlikely. The weaver in the west country and other branches of England's most important manufacture, the woollen textile industry, who owned his own loom and worked at home for several capitalist clothiers, was in the modern sense of the term, a wage-earner in so far as while he owned fixed capital, he had no property in the circulating capital of his trade, and therefore in its finished product. The modern economist might classify him as a wage-earner, but, despite the economic realities, he still thought of himself, and was generally thought of, as getting a price for his product, not for his labour. Domestic industry abounded with such people whom nobody even in the wildest flights of fancy would classify as servants. Yet they were the typical and not the exceptional products of contemporary industrial organisation, whose abundant numbers suggest that the proportion of the adult male population constituted by Petty's and Macpherson's 'servants' may well have been a great deal smaller than the latter suggests.

Be this as it may, there remains the question of why it is necessary to equate all other Leveller views on the franchise with those of Petty, or, to put it another way, why should complete consistency as between different Leveller spokesmen be expected?[82] Is there any more reason to expect consistency of political behaviour or aspirations among the Levellers than (say) among the Presbyterians or the Independents? Like the two latter groups, the Levellers were, in the words of one of them, 'an heterogenial body, consisting of parts very diverse from one another, settled upon principles inconsistent one with another'.[83] To those Levellers who held Rainsborough's view of the franchise, the resolutions excluding servants and beggars which were passed by the army council after the conclusion of the debates at Putney fell far short of their desires; while to those who accepted Petty's view, they represented a significant step in the direction of political realism – in fact the first of a number of such steps. Doubtless there were any number of intermediate positions. In the face of the evidence, it is in fact difficult to accept Macpherson's verdict that the resolutions of the army council conceded what *all* the Levellers had been demanding all along, and that in consequence they were the winners not the losers at Putney.

If this in fact was the case, the aftermath of Putney is not easy to explain. That the *Agreement of the People* when presented with an accompanying petition to the House of Commons on 9 November should have been rejected as 'destructive to the Being of Parliament and to the fundamental Government of the Kingdom' is, of course, not very surprising.[84] Parliament had shown no more liking for the far less radical *Heads of the Proposals*. What is more difficult to explain is why, if the resolution of the army council was in fact a victory for the agitators, the public display of the *Agreement* by the soldiers at the famous rendezvous at Corkbush Field near Ware on 14 November should have been accounted such an act of flagrant defiance by Oliver Cromwell.[85]

The traditional view of the confrontation at Corkbush Field, more especially that between Cromwell and the mutinous regiment of Robert Lilburne, has in it all the elements of true tragedy. On the one hand was the fearless and resolute lieutenant-general who had led victorious troops in battle after battle and whose stern unflinching courage was now to reduce a very nasty situation to order. On the other were the mutinous soldiers whose hats, bedecked with copies of *The Agreement of the People*, and the motto 'England's Freedom, Soldiers' Rights' testified eloquently to that naïve and touching faith in the redemptive powers of a new and radical constitution which was also to inspire their Chartist successors two centuries later. Such men, however unsophisticated their political views, had not, as Rainsborough had put it at Putney, gone to war in order to be enslaved.[86] 'Do you [not] think', the agitator Edward Sexby had asked rhetorically in the same debate,

> it were a sad and miserable condition that we have fought all this time for nothing? All here, both great and small, do think that we fought for something. I confess, many of us, fought for those ends

which, we since saw were not those which caused us . . . to venture all in the ship with you. It had been good in you to have advertised us of it, and I believe you would have [had] fewer under your command to have commanded.[87]

That there was again a crisis of confidence between the army grandees and some of the soldiers is hardly in doubt. Fairfax and Cromwell were surely right to see the unbidden appearance of Rainsborough's and Robert Lilburne's regiments at the rendezvous at Corkbush Field as an act of mutiny and defiance, albeit in the case of Lilburne's regiment of a prolonged mutiny which had begun earlier at Dunstable. Rainsborough's regiment had been ordered to another of the three designated rendezvous, but the appearance of Lilburne's regiment at Corkbush Field or any other rendezvous was an act of especial defiance, since the soldiers had been diverted to Ware through the influence of the new agitators, when the regiment had been under orders to march to the north. Kishlansky's argument that the junior officer who had taken command of the mutinous soldiers and led them to Ware had requested and been granted permission from Fairfax to attend the rendezvous is somewhat specious. With the disobedient and mutinous regiment now in the immediate vicinity of the rendezvous, it was the only sensible response to attempt to restore discipline by calling it into the field in the presence of the enormously superior numbers of obedient soldiers, who by now also included Rainsborough's regiment. Paradoxically, both Fairfax and the dissident soldiers were acting with the same aim in view: to restore the unity of the army. But while to Fairfax the prime objective of the three separate rendezvous had been to reassert army discipline and unity in the face of the new danger arising from the king's absconding from Hampton Court on 11 November, to the dissident soldiers the object of the attempt to turn Corkbush Field into a general rendezvous was the reassertion of army unity on a new basis, that of *The Agreement of the People*. Just as the general rendezvous on Newmarket Heath in June had as its end-product *The Solemn Engagement of the Army* and the restoration of unity through the creation of the General Council of the Army, so should another general rendezvous – separate rendezvous called up memories of the efforts of Holles and Stapleton to destroy the army earlier in the year – have as its end-product a new unity cemented by the acceptance of *The Agreement of the People*.

Whatever the reality may have been concerning Cromwell's role at Corkbush Field, order was successfully restored without any concessions with regard to *The Agreement* and at the cost of the life of only one mutineer. Nevertheless, the spectacle of dejected soldiers yielding what Fairfax later described as 'an absolute submission and Conformity to the ancient Discipline of the Army', and casting the symbols of their new-found political aspirations on to the ground before them is among the most poignant and unforgettable scenes in English history. In a few weeks' time a Leveller pamphlet, taking as its title the motto which had been ruefully discarded by the soldiers, *England's Freedome, Souldiers' Rights*, was to appear. The pamphlet roundly condemned the exercise of that martial law under which one of the three ringleaders at Corkbush Field had been shot to death, as contrary to the Petition of Right, the Solemn Engagement of June, and as bad as any of Strafford's and Laud's oppressions. However unrealistic, there is something magnificent about its argument that, following its Solemn Engagement, the army was held together only by the 'mutuall consent' of its members, in which circumstances martial law had no place.[88] But while dissident soldiers might deplore the alleged breach of the Engagement by their commanders, two of the latter, Ireton at Putney on 29 October and Fairfax on 14 November on the eve of the rendezvous, gave expression to a very different view about army disunity. Far from being due to the backsliding of the grandees from the principles of the Solemn Engagement, it was rather the disobedience and indiscipline of some of the soldiers, 'the Dissolution of all that order, Combination and Government which is the Essence of an Army', which constituted the principal threat to the unity of the army and to its engagement not to divide or disband.[89] However tentatively and tardily, the Levellers had threatened to establish an important power base in the army and the incident at Corkbush Field marked an effective end to the Leveller menace there for the time being. When a civilian Leveller petition was presented to the House of Commons, which it described as 'the Supream Authority of *England*' on 23 November, it was suppressed forthwith and the petitioners imprisoned.[90]

IX

In the debate in the army council at Putney on 1 November on the role of the monarchy and the House of Lords in the constitution Cromwell had given no sign of yielding to critics of the army grandees' policies of seeking an accommodation with the king. It had been forcefully argued that the disunity of the army and the 'wilderness conditions' in which it found itself, as compared with the days of unity and victory in the first Civil War, were due, as Captain Bishop put it, to 'a compliance to preserve that man of blood, and those principles of tyranny which God from heaven by his many successes [given to the army] hath manifestly declared against'. In Sexby's words,

> We find in the word of God 'I would heal Babylon, but she would not be healed'. I think that we have gone about to heal Babylon, when she would not. We have gone about to wash a blackamoor, to wash him white, which he will not. We are going about to set up ... the power of kings, some part of it, which God will destroy. . . .

Oliver's reply is a classic of Cromwelliana and offers no hint of regrets for his policies. How could his critics be so positive about God's intentions and in identifying the monarchy with biblical Babylon? He himself had had no indication of the divine will on this matter, and he, after all, was 'one of those whose heart God hath drawn out to wait for some extraordinary dispensations'. In a matter of such fundamental importance, his radical critics must not rush to conclusions. They must 'wait upon God for such a way when the thing may be done without sin and without scandal too. Surely what God would have us do, he does not desire we should step out of the way for it.'[91]

In Cromwell's notion of revolutionary action which ought to be undertaken only without stepping out of the way for it, we catch a genuine glimpse of the elusive character of the conservative revolutionary whose advocacy of accommodation with the king was, however, not to continue much longer. This prompts the question of what was the nature of the divine dispensation vouchsafed to him to impel him to abandon that policy. There are a number of possible candidates for the honour. The first in terms of chronology and perhaps also of likelihood is the abscondence of the king from Hampton Court to the Isle of Wight ten days after Cromwell had defended at Putney the need to come to terms with him. Certainly Charles's attempts to reopen negotiations after his flight to Carisbrook met with a hard and cold response in complete contrast to the attitudes of the period before 11 November.[92]

The king's flight to the Isle of Wight had also raised the possibility of his escape by sea either to the continent or, perhaps worse, to Scotland, which revived the fears of a Scottish invasion which had bulked so large in men's minds during the summer. If the carefully guarded terms of the so-called Engagement which the king concluded with the Scots on 26 December had been generally known, they would have provided ample confirmation of these fears, for a Scottish invasion on the king's behalf was envisaged in the Engagement – and, of course, was actually to take place in the following year – in the event of the king and Parliament failing to reach agreement. Indeed the terms of the Engagement were astonishingly favourable to the king: an interim establishment of Presbyterianism for only three years with the nature of the permanent establishment to be decided thereafter; the taking of the Covenant not to be compulsory for all; the king and his household to be free to worship as they pleased, a concession which made Charles the more indifferent to the undertaking, dear to Scottish Presbyterian hearts, that there should be no toleration for sectaries or, for that matter, Independents.[93] These were better terms than Charles had had either from the Scots or the English Parliament in 1646 or the army in 1647, and, just as the counter-revolutionary coup in London in July had probably been a factor emboldening him to make difficulties over accepting the *Heads of the Proposals* – though he continued to do so after the counter-revolutionaries had been quelled – so did his newly concluded engagement with the Scots help to steel him to reject the parliamentary peace proposals in the form of the four bills which were presented for his assent on Christmas Eve.[94] The king's statement in his reply to the four bills, that they did not meet with the approval of the Scottish commissioners, was particularly infuriating to his English subjects, as was the lengthy and spirited protest from the Scottish commissioners seven days before the bills were presented to the king, not least because they claimed a voice in the settlement of matters which were looked on as of purely English significance.[95]

To many of those who even after the king's flight still required further proof of the futility of trying to heal Babylon, Charles's rejection of the four bills clinched the issue, at least for the time being. Yet the king's action is hardly surprising in view of the fact that the provisions of the bills were far more severe either than the army's terms in the *Heads of the Proposals* or those of the Scots in the Engagement. Parliament was not only to control the militia for twenty years, but there was to be no guarantee that it would be restored to the king or his successors after that time. The abolition of episcopacy and the sale of episcopal and dean-and-chapter lands was probably only to be expected, though this did not make it any the more acceptable to the king, and the provision banning 'the use of the Book of Common Prayer in any place whatsoever', including the royal household, offered a striking contrast to the terms both of the Scots and of the *Heads of the Proposals*, in a matter which was particularly dear to the king's heart. If we add to these things the humiliating provisions of the second and third bills, whereby the king was to eat his words by revoking his wartime declarations against Parliament as well as the titles of honour which he had conferred since 20 May 1642, it becomes easy to see that he had some grounds for complaint that, far from being a valid test of his good intentions, the bills represented a notable stiffening of Parliament's terms, which at the very least called for negotiation rather than the demand for a simple affirmative or negative response. Such an argument might, of course, provoke the reply that the stiffening of terms – at least as compared with the *Heads of the Proposals* though not with the Newcastle Propositions – itself reflected the new situation created by the king's flight and the consequent loss of confidence in the sincerity of his intentions.

In actual fact, the reply that the king's rejection of the four bills did provoke was the passing by the House of Commons on 3 January 1648 of the vote that no further addresses be made to the king, a clear resolution that Parliament should proceed to settle the kingdom without the agreement of the king.[96] The vote and the parliamentary declaration which followed in February marked the final abandonment of the by now rather tattered doctrine that the king can do no wrong. Like the Grand Remonstrance of November 1641, the Declaration contained a synthetic history of the reign, but one in which emphasis is placed on the king's independent behaviour rather than on his being deceived by evil counsellors. No detail is spared, and even the old charges about the poisoning of James I are raked up with more than a hint of complicity between Charles and the Duke of Buckingham in this matter. The recourse to such patent absurdities was likely to be counter-productive, and the declaration provoked dignified replies both from a royalist writer and from the king himself.[97]

In Clarendon's view the Vote of No Addresses was a prelude to regicide and republicanism, employed by the republicans to 'feel the pulse of the people, and discover how they would submit to another form of government'.[98] Some parliamentarians entertained similar doubts about the vote. On 15 January 1648 in the Upper House the Earls of Warwick and Manchester entered protests against the concurrence of the Peers with the Commons in the vote.[99] In the great debate in the Commons on 3 January, the leading Presbyterian Sir John Maynard, among others, opposed it vigorously on the grounds that it set the king aside, an act which had horrifying social implications:

> If the argument ... hold that there was another government,
> before that of Kings etc., so husbandmen was before gentlemen,
> and they before Lords etc. and so we must com to the Levellers
> doctrine.[100]

For many radical Independents probably the central problem was indeed how to set the king aside without coming to the Levellers' doctrine. For this reason alone fears that the Vote of No Addresses inescapably meant a big step in the direction of republicanism may have been exaggerated. It is true that Sir Thomas Wroth, seconding the vote on 3 January, stated roundly that 'our Kings of late had carried themselves as if they were fit for no Place but Bedlam', arguing not only that the kingdom should be settled without the king, but that he ought to be impeached. As to the form of government set up by Parliament, he cared 'not what Form of Government they set up, so it were not by Kings and Devils'. It is true that Ireton and Cromwell, who, a few weeks earlier at Putney, had argued so resolutely for treating with the king, now unhesitatingly supported the Vote of No Addresses. Employing the familiar argument from the fiduciary nature of government but putting it to a radical use, Ireton argued that subjection to the king 'was but in lieu of his Protection to the People; this being denied, they might well deny any more Subjection to him, and settle the Kingdom without him'. For Ireton at least there had clearly been a moment of truth sometime between 1 November and 3 January. Of Cromwell at this time, nothing can be certain. It is true that he observed in the course of the debate that the people ought not 'any longer to expect Safety and Government from an obstinate Man whose Heart God had hardened', and cited Scripture to the effect that 'Thou shalt not suffer an hypocrite to reign'. But he also pronounced himself in favour of a monarchical constitution, 'unless necessity force an alteration'.[101] For Cromwell at least, the Vote of No Addresses was no irreversible step in the direction of a republican constitution. Ludlow tells of a meeting at Cromwell's house in King Street in May 1648 between Cromwell and some of his parliamentary and army allies on the one hand and some of the more radical Independents, of whom Ludlow was one, on the other. On this occasion, which is best known for having ended in horseplay, with Cromwell and Ludlow hurling cushions at one another, Ludlow and the so-called Commonwealth-men took the view that 'monarchy was neither good in itself, nor forus', which, likethecertaintiesoftheagitatorsatPutney, wasboundtoir-ritate Cromwell beyond measure. Oliver and his associates, by contrast, 'kept themselves in the clouds, and would not declare their judgments either for a monarchical, aristocratical or democratical government; maintaining that any of them might be good in themselves, or for us, according as providence should direct us'.[102] For Cromwell, at least, Providence had not yet directed, necessity had not yet forced an alteration. The manner in which it came to do so will be a central theme of the final chapter of this book.

TWELVE *Revolution Contained 1648–9*

So ye shall not pollute the land wherein ye *are*; for blood it defileth the land: and the land cannot be cleansed of the blood that is shed therein, but by the blood of him that shed it.

Numbers, 35:33.

... Our constitution is what the dissensions of our time will permit: not such as were to be desired, but such as the persistent strife of wicked citizens will suffer it to be. But any state soever which in the throes of partisan strife takes up arms for safety, surely does full justice if it maintains relations with its sound and uncontaminated part alone, and expels or removes the rest....

> *John Milton an Englishman His Defence of the People of England against Claudius Anonymous, alias Salmasius his Defence of the King (1651)* in *Works* (New York 1932), p. 29.

> The same arts that did gain
> A power, must it maintain.

> Andrew Marvell, *Horatian Ode Upon Cromwell's Return From Ireland* (1650)

I

IT IS DIFFICULT to turn from 1647 to 1648 without experiencing some sense of *déjà vu*, for in many ways events followed a strikingly similar pattern, though with an even fiercer intensity. The previous twelve months had ended on a distinctly anti-monarchical note with the Vote of No Addresses; the next ended with the execution of the king on 30 January 1649 and the establishment of a republican form of government, a more extreme solution but one reached by what was in some respects a similar road; the foiling of a counter-revolutionary threat which this time eventuated in what everyone had feared but had been avoided in 1647, a Scottish invasion and a second Civil War. Once again the prelude to firm anti-monarchical action was the quelling of counter-revolution, though on a far more serious scale than in 1647. Once again this was succeeded by a round of fruitless negotiations with the king. Once again negotiations produced a split in the Independent party, though this time, on account of the greater intensity of the crisis, the split went deeper and was permanent, and some of those who had been most actively engaged in negotiations with the king in the previous year, and notably Henry Ireton, were now on the other side. And just as the idea of a purge of their opponents had been actively canvassed on both sides in 1647, so was the essential prelude to the last act of the drama, the Purge of Parliament by the army on 6 December 1648. As befits a development in which the tendencies of the previous year were in some measure repeated, but now writ much larger in every respect, the final act is not simply, as at the end of the previous twelve months, a decision to settle the kingdom without reference to the king, but his trial and execution as the revolutionary prelude to such a settlement.

The final chapter falls into three distinct phases. The first is the defeat of militant counter-revolution in the second Civil War; the second the exploitation of the possibility of a peaceful solution of the problems of settlement, which many regarded as an attempt to achieve counter-revolutionary ends by stealth where force had failed; and the third is the forcible breaking off of the treaty and the proceeding to the radical solution demanded by the army and its parliamentary allies.

II

The English Government was indeed fortunate in 1648 in the failure of its external and internal enemies to synchronize their military designs against it. One of the most important features of the situation was the delay of the Scots in mounting their long-awaited invasion, and this in turn reflects the fact that the Scottish nation was deeply divided on this issue. If the so-called Engagers, led by Hamilton, Lauderdale, Lanark and Loudoun – though the last named was soon to defect – commanded a substantial majority in the Scottish Parliament, their opponents, led by Argyll, controlled the General Assembly of the Kirk.[1] It was not that the Presbyterian ministers who constituted the majority of the General Assembly had any objection to the idea of a holy war against the godless sectaries and Independents of the New Model Army. It was rather that any war to achieve the object of the Engagement was, by the standards of the Kirk, a good deal less than holy. Both Argyll and the English were quick to point out that the Engagers 'seem to take the measure of their desires rather from what may please the King than from what may preserve the Kingdomes', and that the Covenant took second place.[2] The Engagers might stress the importance of the ends of the Covenant in their war aims[3] but they invited the inevitable retort that, if this were indeed the case, they had chosen strange allies in the ex-Cavalier, Sir Marmaduke Langdale, who had plotted rebellion in Scotland along with the Engagers, and many of whose associates in the business were 'Papists and grand Delinquents ... and ... notorious Oppozers of the Ends of the Covenant'.[4]

The acute differences within Scotland and the delays consequent upon the desire of the Engagers to convert as many as possible of the waverers greatly disconcerted their potential English allies. Certainly there is abundant evidence that Cavaliers and other English malcontents in England and Holland had very serious doubts about the efficacy of a Scottish war effort which lacked the support of Argyll and the Kirk. Indeed, Argyll did his utmost not only to prevent the invasion, in which he was unsuccessful, but also – and here he may well have had more success – to dissuade English Presbyterians from offering any support for it.[5] In its turn the English Parliament attempted to spike the Scottish guns by inviting the Scots to join them in reopening a peace initiative with the king, notwithstanding the Vote of No Addresses. But this was treated, in the words of the Earl of Lanark's correspondent in England who was desperately anxious that the promised invasion might come about, as a device 'to foment and perpetuat [sic] your [viz. the Scottish] present dissentions',[6] which in part it certainly was. However, if it failed in its primary aim of staving off a Scottish invasion, it may have made a significant contribution to keeping moderate Englishmen from throwing in their lot with the invaders.

The failure to coordinate the Scottish invasion and the risings in various parts of England and Wales was fatal to the hopes of invaders, insurgents and king alike. The Engagers' hopes of risings in many parts of England and Wales, which in the event remained quiescent, were based on wildly optimistic reports from their agents in England.[7] In actual fact the risings were not so extensive as had been feared and the dangers not concurrent, for the Scottish invasion was delayed until the beginning of July, largely due to difficulties at home. Indeed, it may well be that the English insurgents were in two minds about the advantages of associating themselves with the Scots, whose departure from England at the beginning of 1647 had been the occasion of profound and almost universal relief. As Lanark's chief informant warned him on 30 April 'if they can carie on the work without you . . . they will be readyer to exclud [sic] you then to receaue your assistance'.[8]

Whatever the causes, the English Government was able to pick off its enemies piecemeal. Bad timing and endemic localism were the two greatest enemies of the insurgents, and the government's fear of tightly-knit inter-county associations of malcontents, manifesting themselves in such things as coordinated rendezvous at Blackheath (Kent), Putney Heath (Surrey) and Wanstead (Essex) both overstate the degree of coordination between local risings and understate the local antipathy to the outsiders who flooded into the disturbed areas to join the anti-parliamentarian cause.[9] Indeed, when the much feared junction of Kentish and Essex insurgents did finally take place in early July, to culminate in the rebels' occupation of, and Fairfax's successful siege of, Colchester, the Kentish contingent was the pitiful remnant of a county revolt which had already been crushed at Maidstone. The Kentish insurgents had been at their most dangerous when they had stood alone. Their junction with the men of Essex was a product of weakness, not of strength.[10]

III

It must already be clear that the second Civil War was more than simply the revolt of the counties, and, quite apart from obviously non-localist elements in the war, such as the Scottish invasion, the revolt of part of the Fleet and the rising, however contemptible and easily crushed, led by the Earls of Holland and Peterborough and the young Duke of Buckingham, there was an influx of Cavaliers from all over the country to the main localized areas of conflict. Moreover, in so far as it is possible to explore the aims both of the insurgents and of those malcontents who stopped short of actual revolt, such as the men of Dorset whose ardour seems to have expressed itself in fiery sentiments rather than in deeds of arms, a number of common factors emerge.

These include the demands for Parliament to arrange a personal treaty with the king, for the country to be ruled by known and ancient laws, for the army to be disbanded and for the burden of taxation to be reduced.[11]

The strongly royalist sentiments of most of the local insurgents should be seen as complementary to their localist aspirations. Notwithstanding the fact that localist country gentlemen had leaned towards the Country rather than the Court and, indeed, had gone to war for King and Parliament in 1642 on account of their bitter opposition to the royal centralizing pressures of the 1630s, once having sampled chastisement by parliamentary scorpions in place of the royal whips of which they had formerly complained, they were unlikely to find slogans such as 'For God, King Charles and Kent' in any sense incongruous. If their hatred found any particular focus it was on the local county committees, especially where the arbitrary and tyrannical behaviour of men such as Weldon and Livesey in Kent and Pyne in Somerset, had made many enemies, not only among royalists and neutrals but also among people who had not been unsympathetic to the parliamentarian cause. Even the declaration of Holland, Peterborough, Buckingham and their adherents, whose revolt was not notably linked with localist aspirations, was at pains to stress the arbitrariness and illegalities of the county committees as a prime national grievance.[12]

With the exception of northern England and North and South Wales, where one of the worst affected counties, Pembrokeshire, had anyway largely been in Parliament's hands for the latter part of the first Civil War, the government did not experience a great deal of trouble from areas of former royalist strength. In the south-west, where the parliamentary commander Sir Hardress Waller warned Parliament of impending disaster, there were some minor incidents in Devon, unfounded rumours of plans for a rising of eight thousand men under the Marquis of Hertford in Somerset, and an easily quelled revolt in Cornwall. The one solid counter-revolutionary success in this region was the recovery of the Scilly Isles, which were to provide a useful base for royalist privateers until their recapture in May 1651.[13] But trouble was by no means confined to former royalist strongholds, as is clear from the case of East Anglia where there were risings in Essex, and disturbances in Cambridgeshire, Bury St Edmunds, Norwich and Thetford.[14] Above all there was Kent, where Weldon and his committeemen had achieved an unpopularity which was probably exceeded by none of their counterparts anywhere, not even by Pyne's men in

Somerset. Out of the disturbances caused by the committee's officious attempts to suppress Christmas festivities in Canterbury in 1647, the riots following the trial and acquittal of the offenders in the spring, the subsequent petition of the inhabitants of Kent, and the committee's threat of reprisals against the petitioners, there arose the most serious of all the county revolts.[15]

Personal animosities and rivalries were important contributory factors in the revolt in most affected areas, nowhere more strongly than in south-west Wales. Here there occurred the most dramatic turn-around of loyalties, with the former parliamentarian commanders Colonels John Poyer and Rice Powell and Major-General Rowland Laugharne going over to the other side. Laugharne was furious at being superseded in his command, and Poyer apprehensive that he would be forced to disgorge some of his wartime gains. The ranks of the insurgents in South Wales were composed of very diverse elements; ex-Cavaliers, conservative parliamentarians, 'reformadoes' and even former clubmen.[16] Similar, if perhaps not quite so wide-ranging, diversity characterizes the dissidents and insurgents in most other areas of disturbance. In Somerset, where the threatened revolt never materialized, the potential material for Hertford's reported counter-revolutionary undertaking certainly included former parliamentarians as well as royalists.[17] The two elements might join forces, but they were ill-assorted and uneasy partners. It was the presence of Cavaliers, who, like extremist elements in modern demonstrations, had an interest in turning orderly processions into riots, which seems to have been responsible for the disorder and bloodshed accompanying the presentation of the Surrey petition on 16 May. In Kent there was certainly no love lost between the localist gentry, who were outraged by the behaviour of Weldon and his committee, and their royalist allies, some of them wild local men and others equally wild Cavaliers from outside the county.[18] Indeed, at the end of May a government-sponsored attempt by the Earl of Thanet to drive a wedge between the Kentish moderates and the Cavaliers, via the offer of an indemnity and the right of orderly petitioning to those who dispersed, seems to have had some success, and might have had more, had it not been for the not unnatural unwillingness of the Derby House committee to respond to a petition from some Kentish gentlemen accepting most of the government's terms, but asking to be allowed to remain in arms until the county committee, the cause in their view of all the disturbances, was brought to book.[19]

Besides the Cavaliers another violent element which helped to bring discredit on the insurgents was, as in 1647, the 'reformadoes', or disbanded soldiers, jealous of the favours which, in their view, had been heaped upon the men of the New Model Army, more especially in the matter of disbandment and arrears of pay. Among them were some high-ranking officers of considerable military experience, such as the Dutchman Colonel John Dulbier, who had served as Commissary General of the Horse under Lord General Essex and was killed at St Neots on 10 July when assisting the ineffectual rising of the Earls of Holland and Peterborough; and Colonel John Morrice, who had served in both the royalist and the parliamentarian armies in the first Civil War, and was responsible for one of the most daring and well-planned feats of arms in the second, the taking of Pontefract Castle and the killing of Colonel Thomas Rainsborough in an audacious sally from there to Doncaster.[20] According to Sir Hardress Waller, writing on 15 August, a key role in the plan for Hertford's rising in the southwest, which never came to fruition, was to be played by two of Sir William Waller's ex-officers, one of whom had been a major-general.[21]

IV

The case of the 'reformadoes' serves as a reminder that the reaction of soldiers to grievances such as arrears of pay could as easily assume a counter-revolutionary as its more familiar revolutionary form. This applies even more strikingly to one of the most serious threats to the regime in the second Civil War, the revolt of a considerable part of the Fleet.[22] The dangers presented by the defection of ships to the royalists were manifold. The cordial relations of renegade naval commanders, such as ex-Vice-Admiral Batten and Lord Willoughby of Parham, with the Scots highlighted the possibility of intimate cooperation between the revolted ships and the Scottish invaders. Even more urgent were the actual links achieved by the royalist sailors in the Downs with the Kentish insurgents, whose political programme they enthusiastically adopted.[23] It was also feared that the revolt might easily spread from the ships to ports such as Portsmouth, Great Yarmouth and Hull.[24] With the aid of such a fleet the king might conceivably be rescued from the Isle of Wight, foreign troops – and perhaps especially Irish troops – might have safe passage to England to come to the aid of the insurgents, and the trade of the country might be subjected to damaging attacks, a possibility which would certainly not be lost on the

City of London, which might in consequence be impelled to take an active counter-revolutionary part in events.

Compared with the army, the navy – despite the fact that it had followed the Earl of Warwick into the parliamentarian camp in 1642 – was a very conservative force with the strongest suspicion of interference in its affairs by uncomprehending landsmen. In June 1647 the radical agitators in the army had in a publication addressed to 'all the honest seamen of England' tried to interest them in the Leveller programme, as far as can be seen, entirely without success.[25] It was in fact the interference of one who, despite some naval experience, was regarded as a landsman, and a Leveller at that, which was probably the most important single factor in producing the ill will which was to come to fruition in the naval revolt. The crucial event here was the replacement in October 1647 of Vice-Admiral William Batten by, of all people, the notorious radical Colonel Thomas Rainsborough, an event which, as Batten was later to suggest, was all of a piece with the way in which experienced and proved army commanders such as Waller, Laugharne and Poynz had been cast on one side.[26] It is no exaggeration to characterize the profound unease resulting from this appointment as being due to apprehension that it was the prelude to a new modelling of the navy.

Rainsborough's appointment no doubt had a good deal to do with the fears expressed in the Declaration of the revolted ships in July 1648 that 'there was a design of introducing land-soldiers into every ship, to master and overawe the seamen'. To these reasons for his unpopularity must be added his 'insufferable pride, ignorance and insolency', and profound distrust on account of his reputation as a radical. The officers of the ships who refused to serve under him and put him ashore in June claimed to have done so because he was 'a man of destructive principles both in religion and policy'. As to religion, while little is known of Rainsborough's views, they were probably in marked contrast to Batten's strict Presbyterianism, and connected in the popular mind with the disorderly state of affairs described in the revolted ships' declaration in July: 'no settled form of divine worship, no communions, little or no preaching on board, but by illiterate and mechanic preachers'. The analogy with the dreadful goings-on in the New Model Army was only too clear. As to politics, Rainsborough's Leveller activities at Putney and Corkbush Field in 1647 were a matter of common knowledge, and his well-publicized recantation after the latter event did not prevent his predecessor, and doubtless many other naval

men, from characterizing him as unfit to exercise command since he
'openly confessed himself to be a leveller'.[27] No less unfit, however,
was the renegade parliamentarian Lord Willoughby of Parham, whose
appointment by Prince Charles as Vice-Admiral of the revolted ships
was disliked by many royalists both on account of his total lack of
experience in naval matters, and of his past opposition to the king.[28] It
is perhaps ironical that when the fears of the Commonwealth Government on account of the naval revolt were finally put to rest, this was the
result, not of the recall of the old sea-dog Warwick to command the
remainder of the parliamentarian fleet, but of the naval victories of an
ex-soldier, Admiral Robert Blake.

V

In the heady days of July 1647 the City of London had been in the
forefront of counter-revolution, as a result of which the lord mayor, Sir
John Gayre, the former opponent of royal policies in the 1630s and the
moderate of 1642, had been deposed and replaced by a reliable Independent, John Warner, just as the royalist Sir Richard Gurney had
been replaced by Isaac Pennington in 1642. Articles of impeachment
were drawn up against Gayre and his principal aldermanic colleagues
of the July days, who were consigned to prison to await trial.[29] In these
circumstances it is hardly surprising that the mutual hostility between
the City Presbyterians and the army with its Independent allies in
parliament persisted into 1648.[30] The summer of 1647 had seen a counter-revolutionary coup in London, but no Scottish invasion and no
provincial revolts. In 1648 the situation was reversed, when there was
both an invasion and provincial revolts but neither received any help
from the City. But it is easy to be wise after the event, and there were
a number of things which seemed to reinforce the soldiers' suspicions
about collusion between the Scots and the citizens; among them the
Scottish demand for a treaty with the king in London itself, thus
inviting counter-revolutionary tumults on at least the scale of July
1647; their demand on 26 April that 'the City of London may enjoy its
Liberties and Privileges which it had before the later Encroachment of
the Army' – in other words the restoration of the situation which had
prevailed between 26 July and 6 August 1647; and their request for the
liberation of Recorder Glyn and the other aldermen in the Tower.[31]
But in the event the citizens were to gain many of their objectives from
Parliament and without Scottish assistance. These included the long-

desired moving of Barkstead's and Rich's regiments from Whitehall and the Mews; their replacement as the guards for Parliament by the City trained bands; the putting of the Tower under an officer acceptable to the City, and – miraculous transformation – the City militia into the hands of a committee appointed by the City, though subject to parliamentary approval. The process culminated in June with the dropping of the charges against the imprisoned aldermen, including Recorder Glyn, who had, of course, incurred the particular hatred of the army as one of the eleven members. Given these concessions, together with an assurance from Parliament that it had no intention of altering the government of England, by King, Lords and Commons, and that an approach would shortly be made to the king on the basis of the Hampton Court propositions which had formerly been agreed with the Scots, the City had every reason to feel satisfied with its lot.[32]

Another factor which probably predisposed citizens in the same way was their experience of the excesses of the 'reformadoes' and the spectacle of resurgent Cavalierism in the summer of 1647. Consistent moderate support for a policy of concessions to the king was one thing; rampant, resurgent Cavalierism quite another. All this helps to explain why the expectations of the Scots that they would receive help from the City[33] were sadly disappointed; as were those of the Kentish insurgents that they would be allowed passage through the City when they were *en route* for Essex after their defeat at Maidstone. Likewise the appeal directed at the Londoners by the rebel peers Holland, Peterborough and Buckingham fell on very stony ground.[34] On 1 June, the same day as the lord mayor forwarded to Parliament a private petition from some 'well affected citizens' asking for the Kentish rising to be settled, if possible, 'by way of Accommodation and not by any Engagement of Blood', the Common Council made the City's official position unequivocally clear by resolving 'that if any Blood was shed in Kent, they were the Causes of it themselves who refused the Offers made to them by the Parliament and their General'.[35] The City's behaviour thus gave the lie to the radical Independent MP John Weaver, who declared that both the Scottish invasion and the domestic insurgency 'were all begun and carried on in the City of London'.[36] Even the radical Independent Edmund Ludlow had grudgingly to admit, with reference to the City's refusal to grant free passage to the Kentish rebels, that it 'was not willing absolutely to espouse the Cavalier party, especially in a flying posture'.[37] The same is true of its attitude to the naval revolt. Notwithstanding its petition for the reinstatement of the deposed Batten early in June before Batten's defection to the royalists, there proved to be no foundation for counter-revolutionary hopes that 'this Citty must goe with the [rebel] fleet, and neither can nor dare doe other'.[38] The fact that the City had kept its hands clean during the second Civil War added force to its arguments for a treaty with the king, and made it difficult for radical opponents of peace such as Weaver to nail these arguments to the coffin of militant Cavalierism.

What the release of the imprisoned aldermen was to the City, the dropping of the charges against the survivors of the eleven members – Stapleton had died at Calais the previous year – was to the parliamentary Presbyterians. The members were, moreover, allowed to take their seats again, a decision which was bitterly opposed by the radical Independents, Sir Peter Wentworth, John Gurdon, Thomas Scot, John Venn, and the inevitable Weaver.[39] But whatever the designs of the Presbyterian leaders may have been in 1647, they were far more circumspect in 1648, and the charge of their opponent Ludlow that they had encouraged Batten's defection to the royalist fleet,[40] seems to have been groundless. As in the case of the City, the refusal of the parliamentary Presbyterians to succumb to counter-revolutionary temptations added force to their enthusiastic advocacy of a treaty with the king.

VI

It is difficult to over-emphasize the impact of the second Civil War on the political nation. To Cavaliers it had been the great opportunity to undo the work of 1642–8, and, for some, even of 1640–2. The motives of other insurgents were compounded of exasperation at central interference and committee oppression, unprecedentedly high taxation continued after the end of the first war and the negation of the limited localist aims for which they had gone to war in 1642. For them and for many others insurgency was a basic conservative response to the growing radicalism of soldiers, levellers and sectaries. On the other hand to those other conservatives, who, like the parliamentary Presbyterians and the City of London, had sided with the Parliament when they might have been expected to support its opponents, the renewed bloodletting was inexcusable, not least because it jeopardized the settlement of the nation along the only lines in which a limited restorative settlement consonant with the war aims of 1642 could be achieved – that is a monarchical settlement. However, to those high army officers issuing forth

from their prayer meeting at Windsor on that late April day, to depart
on campaigns from which they might never return, the issue was now
crystal clear. While to some, like Ireton, the revelation of what needed
to be done seems to have come somewhat earlier, to others the renewal
of hostilities was – in Cromwellian terms – that divine dispensation
of God's will that they ought not to sheath their swords until Charles
Stuart, that man of blood, had been brought to account.[41]

The difference in the attitude to those who had opposed Parliament
in the first and in the second Civil Wars is clearly reflected in the much
stiffer terms for compounding which were imposed on the latter.[42]
Cromwell remarked in November that even these terms were not stiff
enough, arguing that

> the former quarrel was that Englishmen might rule over one
> another; this to vassalise us to a foreign nation. And their fault
> who have appeared in this summer's business is certainly double
> to theirs who were in the first, because it is the repetition of
> the same offence against all the witnesses God has borne. . . .[43]

That even the austere, non-political, and certainly non-regicide and
non-republican Lord-General Fairfax felt the same relentless fury
against those who had chosen to plunge the country into blood again, is
indicated by his polite but entirely unaccommodating reply to a letter
from the Prince of Wales asking him to use his influence to spare the
lives of the Welsh renegades Poyer, Powell and Laugharne, only the
first of whom was, however, executed in the event; also in his summary
execution of Sir Charles Lucas and Sir George Lisle after the surrender
of Colchester.[44]

Of course, there were Independent politicians, old war party-men,
not to speak of army men, who had not needed the second Civil War to
provide them with proof of the futility of negotiations, even if they saw
in it a golden opportunity to gain converts to their point of view. In a
debate in the House of Commons on 24 May, Thomas Scot argued
vehemently that the king was the cause of all the bloodshed in the three
kingdoms and that rather than treat with him, it was fitter he should
be brought to his trial and hanged, drawn and quartered,[45] a fate which
Scot himself was to suffer in 1660. But even now there were many
Independents – and notably the former middle-group members of the
Independent alliance – who recoiled in horror from such arguments.
Given their support for the Vote of No Addresses, it is likely that this
was not so much due to their enthusiasm for a treaty as their conscious-

ness that, on account of the hardening of radical Independent attitudes as a consequence of the second Civil War, the alternative to a negotiated settlement looked like being republicanism and regicide. It was above all on this issue that there occurred that irreparable split in the Independent alliance for an understanding of which we are indebted to the brilliant work of David Underdown.[46] It was in a sense an archetypal middle-group situation with the radical Independents playing the role of the old war party of 1642–4, the Presbyterians that of the peace party, and the middle-groupers going along with the latters' policy of negotiations, but, in their declared preference for stiffer terms, hoping to retain the support of at least some of the former.

In a sense this can be seen as the reappearance of the Independent split of the autumn of 1647, which had also been over the issue of negotiations with the king, which had alienated not only the Levellers but also the radical Independents against Cromwell and his colleagues, though some of the latter, and notably Ireton, who had then supported negotiations and a monarchical settlement, had now changed sides. On 28 April an Independent amendment to weaken the force of a declaration in favour of the government of England by King, Lords and Commons was defeated. Although both the tellers against the amendment were Presbyterians rather than middle-groupers the unusual size of the majority – the vote was won by 165 votes to 99 – suggests the defection of some of those who normally voted with the Independents; Lanark's English correspondent specifically mentions the middle-grouper Pierrepoint, and Vane, the latter certainly no middle-grouper but at this stage no republican either. Similar considerations may explain the even larger majority on 24 May – 169 votes to 86 – for the motion that the Hampton Court propositions should form the basis for negotiations with the king.[47] For all that, we must beware of burying the Independent alliance too early. For instance, the debates on 17 June on the alleged plot to poison the king and on 3 and 28 July on the terms of a treaty with the king all provide evidence of middle-group Independents such as Sir John Evelyn of Wiltshire, Edmund Harvey and John Swynfen ranged alongside radicals such as Thomas Scot and Herbert Morley.[48]

To proceed to a treaty would involve the abandonment both of the Vote of No Addresses and of the insistence on the king's accepting prior conditions before the treaty could take place.[49] This sort of treaty was, after all, what many of the insurgents in the second Civil War claimed to be fighting for, which put those advocating it in Parliament and the City dangerously near to the position of some of the rebels. This is the significance of the attempts of radical Independents such as Weaver, backed by the Independent London aldermen MPs Pennington and Venn, to bring the cause of peace into disrepute by associating it with the dominant party in the City and *vice versa*. Pennington, attempting to revive the fears of the previous summer, affected great sorrow 'to see his Brethren of the City and the Reformadoes to be all one in Malignancy'.[50] But the radical case would have been stronger if the City had occupied the relatively isolated position of a year earlier. As it was, other petitions for a treaty with the king had been pouring into Parliament from May onwards,[51] outnumbering the radical petitions which, like that from the 'well-affected' inhabitants of London and the suburbs in September deplored Parliament's casting away the advantages of the army's victory by proceeding so soon to a treaty with the grand delinquent.[52] While the latter sort of petition was to become increasingly prominent once the treaty with the king had got under way in September, for the moment it was the more general desire for a peaceful settlement and a return to normal which occupied the forefront of the parliamentary stage.

That the radical Independents did their level best to put every conceivable obstacle in the way of a treaty is hardly surprising. Thomas Scot, for example, spoke eloquently if unsuccessfully against the repeal of the Vote of No Addresses on 17 August, and was soundly put in his place for doing so.[53] That the radicals sometimes continued to carry some middle-groupers along with them, at least in some divisions, is perhaps more surprising.[54] Needless to say, of all political groups in the House of Commons, the voting behaviour of middle-group Independents is the least predictable of all. However, the nature of the issue at stake is by no means always a sure guide to the attitude of parliamentary Presbyterians. In the debate on 17 August on the king's request to be allowed advisers for the Treaty at Newport, without whom, as he put it, 'I can no more treat then a blind man iudg [*sic*] Colours or one run a Race who hath both his feet fast tied', the radical Independents were predictably obstructive towards this entirely reasonable request, as they were again on 11 September to Charles's request for the Scots to be allowed to send representatives to Newport. Conversely, the question propounded in the House that the king be asked to send to parliament the names of those whom he wished to act as his advisers is not the sort of motion one would expect to come from the parliamentary Presbyterians. On the face of it, the successful amendment, excepting persons under restraint and those specifically exempted from pardon by Parliament from acting in this capacity, looks like a characteristic middle-group compromise, stiffening an otherwise unacceptable proposition without relinquishing its essence. Yet two impeccably Presbyterian MPs, Sir Thomas Dacres and Sir Anthony Irby, acted as tellers for the amendment which passed by ninety-five votes to eighty, to be then included in the substantive motion. Whatever its origins, such an amended motion might be expected to win substantial support from middle-group Independents.[55]

While these were still issues on which former middle-group and radical Independents voted alongside one another, if the names of the parliamentary commissioners appointed to treat with the king at Newport reflect anything, it is the growing rapprochement of the very significant section of the middle-group Independents with the Presbyterians. With one exception all were either political Presbyterians or middle-group Independents.[56] The exception is the radical Independent Sir Henry Vane, whose motives are not easy to unravel, and who later, on 2 December, was to deliver a devastating attack on the proposal to continue treating.[57] At this stage, however, he seems to have favoured negotiation, and indeed, as early as 24 May, had been denounced in an anonymous letter to Fairfax for voting 'with the malignant partie against the honest partie' in favour of negotiations with the king.[58] Of the other commissioners, five were middle-group Independents and nine Presbyterians, the latter including two of the former eleven Presbyterian firebrands, Denzil Holles and Recorder Glyn. Glyn himself was an ex-middle-grouper who had moved to the right rather than to the left during the transformation of politics in 1644–5. As a negotiator he now joined forces with five of his former middle-group colleagues who had moved in the other direction, into the Independent camp. These were Lord Saye and Sele, the ex-radical peer who had once been anathema to Charles I; William Pierrepoint, himself the son of an earl; John Crewe, Samuel Browne and John Bulkeley. For all of them – and for other middle-group Independents such as Sir John Evelyn of Wiltshire and Saye and Sele's son, Nathaniel Fiennes, who early in the very same year had been responsible for the radical declaration on the Vote of No Addresses – the threat to stability and the social order, which they deemed to be an inescapable consequence of the radical solutions canvassed in the army and by the more extreme parliamentary Independents, dictated a significant shift to the right, ranging them alongside the Presbyterians.[59] Uneasy partners they might be, but at least they were united in the conviction that the preservation of the monarchy was essential to the social order of which they themselves were prominent pillars. To that extent they were equally desirous that the treaty which opened at Newport on 18 September should be successful.

VII

Given the fact that none of the earlier treaties between Charles I and the Parliament had been successful and our knowledge that the Treaty of Newport had a similar outcome, there is a temptation to regard that treaty simply as the prelude to Pride's Purge, regicide and republicanism.[60] It requires a conscious and very determined exercise of the historical imagination to think away the known outcome and enter the minds of the men who early in September had every hope, as well as of others who had every fear, that the treaty would succeed. As to the latter, the treaty certainly had formidable enemies. The events following the king's flight to Carisbrooke in November 1647, his refusal of the four bills and his Engagement with the Scots had convinced many of the futility of negotiating, and the outbreak of the second Civil War had convinced many more. Most of the waverers in the army had been won over to sterner courses and, of course, they found allies among the more radical Independents in Parliament. But with the Independents split between the radicals who stood by the Vote of No Addresses and those middle-groupers who, faced by the stark alternative of negotiation or revolution, chose the former, the parliamentary situation favoured the search for a settlement with the king. The crucial question was for how long would the parliamentary situation be allowed to remain unaltered.

While to the opponents of the treaty the second Civil War was the final God-given revelation of the iniquity of the king, its supporters hoped that a product of the defeat of the insurgents would be to make Charles more tractable. In a sense they were right, since the king yielded far more at Newport than he had been prepared to do on any previous occasion. In the event, he was not prepared to yield quite enough, but, as the impartial observer must admit, whether he would ultimately have done so was not put to the test, since Pride's Purge brought the proceedings to a brutal end.

It is one of the ironies of history that many of those who most desperately desired a settlement with the king were, next to the avowed enemies of the treaty, those who were most responsible for frustrating it. These were the strict Presbyterians, using the term in the religious rather than the political sense. Presbyterians in this sense were to be found over the whole political spectrum at Westminster from the far right to the far left. For men such as Edmund Prideaux, William Purefoy, Hugh Boscawen, Roger Hill and John Venn, who were strict Presbyterians in the religious, but radical Independents in the political sense, the royal refusal to concede a full Presbyterian settlement of the Church simply had the effect of harmonizing their religious and their political convictions. On the other hand men such as Recorder Glyn, Major-General Richard Browne and William Strode, who were Presbyterians in both senses of the word, must have experienced agonizing ambivalence as a result of the fact that their political and religious inclinations were tugging them in opposite directions. The same is true of such ex-Independent middle-groupers as Robert Goodwin and John Swynfen who had broken away from the radical Independents because of their desire for a settlement and their fear for monarchical institutions, but who were also strict Presbyterians in the religious sense. An illuminating contrast between different middle-group attitudes is provided by the correspondence between Swynfen and John Crewe,[61] one of the Commissioners at Newport, but, unlike his correspondent, no diehard religious Presbyterian. Crewe's Presbyterianism was, at the most, nominal, and in the best of all possible worlds he would, like the political (but not religious) Presbyterians William Jesson and Denzil Holles, have opted for primitive *iure humano* episcopacy.[62] Crewe did his best to impress on Swynfen the dangers of over-rigidity in religious matters which might bring about the very ends desired by their radical Independent opponents, and thus discredit the case for religious Presbyterianism in the eyes of many moderates.

In the dismal, wet autumn of 1648 the drama which was to culminate on the tragic scaffold in Whitehall was played out on three main scenes: the Parliament House in Westminster; the town hall in Newport, Isle of Wight, where the king met the parliamentary commissioners for the treaty; and in the army council in St Albans Abbey, and at Windsor. In the last week of November the three scenes converge on one another, culminating in the army's seizure of the king and Pride's Purge on 1 and 6 December.

There had, of course, been contact all along between the army leaders and the radical Independent politicians at Westminster, who shared their views that, whatever concessions were made by the king, the treaty must not be allowed to succeed. And the MP was not far wrong who asserted in a debate on 24 October that so far it was the king who had made all the concessions.[63] By that time Charles had agreed to rescind all his wartime declarations against the parliament and had yielded to its demands on the militia, Ireland, the public debt, the annulment of titles of honour conferred since May 1642, the disposal of offices by Parliament for twenty years and the abolition of feudal wardship and the Court of Wards in return for £100,000 per annum, though he had argued that it was worth double that sum. Even here the radical Independents raised difficulties, as in Blakiston's objection to paying any compensation for the Court of Wards, that 'very Bane of the Fatherlesse'.[64]

As the king himself put it in a letter of 9 November to the Scottish Lord Chancellor Loudoun, he had made massive concessions, 'reseruing only to ourselfe the Liberty of our Conscience in some few particulars'. If only Parliament would allow him these, he was confident of the success of the treaty.[65] But these were just what Parliament was unwilling to allow him. For it was on precisely these things, and more specifically on religion, that the conscience both of many of the well-wishers to the treaty and of the king himself allowed least leeway. And even though there were some, like John Crewe, who were only too aware of the need to move some way to meet the king, those who opposed treating at all were quick to exploit the potential divergence within the ranks of the peace-seekers. For the concessions which Charles was prepared to make on religious matters, while no doubt representing real sacrifices of principle on his part, were unacceptable to the Parliament.[66] To Parliament's demand for the extirpation of episcopacy and all the other distinctive elements of the Anglican hierarchy, the king ultimately yielded only to the extent of the abolition of archbishops, episcopal chancellors, deans and chapters, archdeacons and prebendaries. His attempt to provide for the possibility of a revival of episcopacy after a trial period of three years of Presbyterian government, by associating bishops and presbyters, the latter chosen by him and the Parliament, in the act of ordination, was not taken up. Indeed for all his unconvincing statements about his belief in primitive, as opposed to *iure divino*, episcopacy Charles held the Laudian view of the apostolic origins of the institution to his dying day, and, indeed, landed himself in some awkward dialectical tangles on account of his failure to distinguish adequately between the two. Not that it made any difference, since Parliament was resolved to get rid of all bishops of whatever variety. Nothing better illustrates Charles's determination not to do anything that would jeopardize the possibility of the ultimate revival of episcopacy than his refusal to consent to the permanent alienation of episcopal lands, which he regarded as a form of sacrilege, and to go any further than to confirm an estate of ninety-nine years in the purchasers.[67]

It must be clear from the above that Charles's answer fell far short of Parliament's demand for a full and permanent Presbyterian ecclesiastical polity. A trial period of three years was the best he could do and even during that time he demanded freedom of conscience and worship for himself and 'any others who cannot in Conscience submit therevnto'. Charles also returned an uncompromising negative to the parliamentary demand that the Covenant be taken by all, including the king, informing the parliamentary commissioner, John Bulkeley, that he could neither take it himself nor force it upon others who conscientiously objected to it.[68]

Charles agreed readily enough to most of the stringent regulations demanded by Parliament against papists, but he indignantly rejected the demand that the queen and her household should not be allowed to worship according to the Catholic rites as a violation of the terms of his marriage treaty. Nor was it only this that worried him, for he knew that to consent to Parliament's demand would amount to 'an entire banishment of the Queene out of England'. Charles felt very deeply the continued separation from his wife, whom he was never to see again, and it accentuated the melancholy induced by his miserable state, even if his condition was exaggerated by the sympathetic observer who reported in a letter of 1 November that he 'was more a Prisoner than ever and ... could not goe to pisse without a guarde nor to Goffe [i.e. golf]'.[69]

It will be recalled that a year earlier the king had been very liberally treated in respect of his private worship by the army, which had allowed him use of his own chaplains and the form of worship he desired in his household. But the Parliament's terms at Newport demanded the use of the Presbyterian Directory of Worship and an end to the use of the Book of Common Prayer even in the royal household. Counselled by his spiritual advisers, Charles's defence of the book, 'compiled by ye blessed martyrs & champions of ye church against ye corruptions of Rome' was couched appropriately in the language of the Foxeian tradition of mainstream Puritan Protestantism, but this cut no ice with Puritans most of whom had passed far beyond Foxeian prescriptions.

Nor did Charles gain anything by the eventual reluctant withdrawal of his insistence on the use of the Prayer Book in the royal chapel, for the value of this concession was neutralized by his declared intention of using some other form of worship than the prescribed Directory. This point, as might be expected, was made much of by Thomas Scot and Vane in the debate on the royal concession on 11 November, Vane suggesting that the preferred form would, as like as not, be 'even more Popish than the Common Prayer itself'.[70]

While there can be no doubt that religion was the main sticking-point, each concession made by Charles from mid-September onwards being rejected by the Parliament,[71] there were also difficulties on other matters, and notably on the parliamentary exemption of thirty-seven of his former followers from pardon for capital offences and the king's refusal to repudiate the Marquis of Ormond, his lieutenant in Ireland. Ormond, 'a man that . . . hazards all for mee', was not to go the way of Strafford, whose never-to-be-forgotten death Charles was soon to expiate by his own.[72]

VIII

The radical Independents had left no stone unturned in their determination to obstruct the treaty. They had opposed the measures facilitating it from the repeal of the Vote of No Addresses onwards. They had used their connections with the local committees to organize radical petitions in the provinces, such as the three blood-thirsty petitions which were presented in the House of Commons on 10 October by Cornelius Holland, Alderman Thomas Hoyle and Sergeant Wylde, from Newcastle upon Tyne, Yorkshire and Somerset respectively, demanding justice on delinquents and an end to treating. In the ensuing debate the middle-group Independent Harvey seems to have gone along with the radicals. However, another middle-grouper, Sir John Evelyn of Wiltshire, proposed and carried a typical compromise between the Presbyterians who wanted the petitions thrown out and the radical Independents who wanted them adopted, arguing that they should be laid aside for the time being and considered only if the treaty proved unsuccessful.[73]

Some of the radical Independents were also giving serious consideration to the idea of aborting the treaty by a purge of its supporters from Parliament. The idea of a purge had been mooted on a number of occasions in 1647 by the radical army officers and their Independent allies,[74] and the fact that Leveller agitators were among the earliest and most consistent proponents of a purge had given a golden opportunity to Presbyterians to treat it as the planned prelude to social revolution.[75] Be this as it may, the basic cast of mind which lies behind the idea is sickeningly familiar to the student of revolutionary action. It is the idea that the virtuous or the godly minority (who, of course, know best) are justified in imposing their will and their solutions on a majority who do not want them. *Mutatis mutandis*, such notions governed the behaviour of the godly people in 1648–9, the virtuous Jacobins in France in 1793, the Bolsheviks in Russia in 1917, and the totalitarians of both left and right who are convinced both of the rightness of their cause and that all who think otherwise must needs be silenced. The army's remonstrance of 14 June 1647 had expressed the wish that the rulers of the state should be 'such Men, and such only . . as are approved at least for Moral Righteousness'. To the radical Independent MP John Lisle, speaking in the debate in the House of Commons on 26 September 1648, the fact that there was a clear and substantial parliamentary majority in favour of negotiating with the king cut no ice. What really mattered was that the treaty was 'contrary to the Wishes and Desires of all the truly Godly and Well-affected in the Kingdom'. Such views find their most eloquent expression in the quotation at the head of this chapter from Milton's *First Defence* of the Commonwealth which had come into existence as a result of their triumph.[76]

It is, however, all too easy to condemn the army and its radical Independent allies for forcing a solution which was contrary to the wishes of the majority in Parliament and almost certainly in the country also. But before doing so, an attempt must be made to penetrate the minds of those favouring such extreme courses. For, as in 1647, the disbandment of the army was seen by the soldiers and their civilian allies as the prelude to counter-revolution. In the context of the autumn of 1648, if the Treaty of Newport were allowed to succeed, there was nothing to stop a restored king from taking advantage of the strong (if mistaken) desire of the overburdened taxpayer to get rid of the army. And to get rid of the army was to remove the only obstacle to counter-revolution. It was along those lines that Edmund Ludlow seems to have argued before both Fairfax and Ireton on his visit to the army before Colchester early in September, and Major-General Harrison made a similar point when trying to convince Lilburne at Windsor in November that the army had to act immediately and that there was no time for constitutional safeguards to be worked out first.

In Harrison's argument, as in the army's Remonstrance of 16 November, the scenario of 1647 was reproduced in 1648, even down to the detail of the planned creation of a counter-revolutionary army under Major-General Browne.[77]

This seems to have been the view of the situation taken both by the radical Independent politicians and by the army leaders, of whom in the continued absence of the still indecisive Cromwell, Ireton seems to have been much the most important figure at this juncture. But agreement on ends did not necessarily denote agreement on the means by which these ends were to be achieved. The radical Independent Edmund Ludlow tells how while he favoured quick and decisive action to abort the treaty, Ireton was originally in favour of giving its supporters enough rope to hang themselves and waiting until the treaty had been concluded and its dangers apparent to all. Even after he had come around to Ludlow's view on this matter, there still remained crucial differences between them. Ireton's plan was for the treaty to be aborted by the withdrawal of the radical Independents from Parliament as a prelude to its dissolution, the creation of a caretaker government and the election of a new Parliament on the basis of a new franchise, no doubt similar to that advocated by the Heads of the Proposals or ultimately adopted in the Instrument of Government of 1653. This did not at all suit the book of the radical Independents, who favoured not a dissolution but a purge of Parliament, partly no doubt because this would leave them ruling the roost at Westminster, whereas no one could be sure that an election to a new Parliament would not – even if conducted on an extended franchise – produce a counter-revolutionary majority at Westminster. Ireton's last-minute reluctant agreement to a purge seems to have been forced by the radical Independents' refusal to go along with his plan that they should withdraw from Parliament.[78]

IX

The above account anticipates in some measure some important political decisions which were made in the army between the beginnings of the treaty in mid-September and Pride's Purge on 6 December. On 20 November the army presented to Parliament a massive Remonstrance which had been approved by the Council of Officers two days earlier.[79] Essentially the work of Ireton, the Remonstrance exudes throughout the spirit of righteousness, certainty and godly determination. It was only when the nation had departed from these certainties and, in

342 THE ENGLISH CIVIL WAR

Sexby's earlier phrase, had tried to heal Babylon, in the regrettable backslidings from the Vote of No Addresses which had produced the treaty in the Isle of Wight, that the favour of Providence had been withdrawn.[80] The way was now clear. Regicide was both the necessary expiation for bloodshed and a supreme exercise in that exemplary punishment which plays such a vital part in contemporary notions of public order. It was absurd 'to punish only Instruments, and let the Head . . . go free'. The army at least had moved from the doctrine of ministerial, to that of regal, responsibility.[81]

If it is a revolutionary expedient to recommend the trial and execution of the king and the setting up of a constitution which would vest all effective power in a Parliament which, in turn, based its authority on the sovereignty of the people, whose safety was the supreme law, then the Remonstrance was emphatically a revolutionary manifesto. And herein lay Ireton's first difficulty in his attempt to get it through the Council of Officers. For while the Remonstrance was in fact far too revolutionary for the more conservatively minded officers, it was not nearly revolutionary enough for the radicals. The story of how Ireton successfully overcame the opposition of both groups has recently been retold by Professor Underdown, whose account significantly modifies Gardiner's verdict that the army council finally accepted the Remonstrance[82] on the rebound from the summary rejection by the king of a peace initiative which had been independently made to him by the army council, an explanation which Underdown demonstrates to be chronologically impossible.[83] The tale of the overcoming of the opposition of those whose revolutionary expectations were disappointed by the Remonstrance has been vividly told by the Leveller leader, John Lilburne, in his treatise *Legall Fundamentall Liberties*.[84] Having been 'couzened in the last year' by the grandees, the Levellers approached with the caution born of bitter experience the proposition put to them that 'the chief things first to be done by the Army was first to cut off the Kings Head . . . and throughly [*sic*] purge if not dissolve the Parliament'. They might take some comfort at the apparent conversion of Ireton and his associates to the views which they had attacked when expounded a year earlier by the agitators at Putney, about the futility of negotiations with the king; and at the provision in the army programme for an end to the present Parliament and a limited life for its successor. But they were correctly suspicious that Ireton was planning only a very limited revolution, 'without . . . some good security to the Nation for the future settlement of their Liberties and Freedoms'. To them this meant acceptance of a new *Agreement of the People*, but the army's timetable did not allow of this, more especially in view of the belief, no doubt assiduously fostered by Ireton, that agreement between the king and the parliamentary commissioners at Newport was imminent. In the circumstances the Levellers had to content themselves with a few hastily tacked-on amendments to the Remonstrance and some vaguely worded promises. Not surprisingly, they were soon to conclude that they had been 'couzened' once again.

X

When the Remonstrance was presented to the Commons on 20 November, it received a predictably enthusiastic welcome from the radical Independents Cornelius Holland, Sir Peter Wentworth and Thomas Scot, all of whom were shortly to become regicides. Equally predictably, it was denounced by the Presbyterians Sir Ralph Assheton and William Prynne, and, much to the chagrin of the officers who had delivered it, it was laid aside for consideration a week later. On 30 November, despite the news that the army was marching on London, a radical Independent motion to consider the Remonstrance was rejected by a large majority, by 125 votes to 58.[85] No doubt many members were reacting indignantly to the pressure which was now all too visibly being applied by the army. On 1 December the House by implication refused to accept the reasons given by Fairfax in a letter of 29 November for the army's advance on London,[86] and a letter was sent to the Lord General asking him to arrest the advance. Indeed it was only by forty-four votes to thirty-three that an intemperate (even if true) amendment to the text of the letter to the effect that the army's advance was 'derogatory to the freedom of Parliament' was defeated. It might in fact just as well have been included, for Fairfax's reply informed the House that the army's arrangements had gone too far for the orders to be countermanded. This was true in more senses than the simple one intended to be conveyed, for what shines out of the letter is the army's indignation at Parliament's neglect of its Remonstrance, which had proceeded not from 'our own wills or judgments, but for the reason and righteousness that is in them'. All the revolutionary determination implicit in these words was soon to be needed.[87]

The situation was beginning to look dangerously like that of July 1647, but the stakes were now higher and the ultimate solution was to be more drastic. On 2 December the radical Independents with Prideaux, Wroth, Wentworth and Vane to the fore, tried to force the issue by moving an immediate debate and vote on the king's last answers from Newport. Prynne's argument against debating such issues in the shadow of 'the Terror now brought on us by the present Approach of the Army' may well have been decisive and it was decided by 133 votes to 102 that the question should not be put. It is interesting to find one middle-group Independent, John Bulkeley, himself a commissioner at Newport, acting along with the Presbyterian Sir Samuel Luke as a teller against the motion, and another, Robert Goodwin, as a teller on the other side. Moreover, if the journalist Mercurius Pragmaticus is to be believed, Richard Norton, another middle-grouper, spoke strongly on the radical side in the debate, reprimanding Prynne for his allegation that this was no free Parliament on account of army pressure, and ominously warning the House that the army was 'resolved to have a free Parliament to debate the King's Answer if we refuse'.[88]

On 4 December, after formally deploring the army's seizure of the king in the Isle of Wight and the bringing of him to the mainland, the House decided against the putting of another radical Independent motion by 144 votes to 93. This was on the face of it a somewhat improbable motion to come from the radicals – that the House should proceed to debate the motion that the king's last answers from Newport were satisfactory. It was, of course, put forward in the certain knowledge that no parliamentary majority could possibly be obtained for it, for the royal answers were plainly inadequate even to the most ardent advocates of a settlement. On the following day the moderates put an alternative motion, that the king's answers were 'a Ground to proceed upon for the Settlement of the Peace of the Kingdom', and, after long debate, this passed by 129 votes to 83. Despite the arguments of the radicals that the House had no alternative but to comply with the army's wishes, it had refused to be intimidated.[89]

From the point of view of the army and their radical Independent allies it would have been bad enough if the king had accepted all of the Parliament's proposals at Newport. That Parliament was now contemplating a prolongation of the treaty despite unsatisfactory royal answers was a resolute slap in the face of the army, which, given the determined and self-righteous mood prevailing among the soldiers, admitted of only one possible answer. This was the event known to history as Pride's Purge, the seclusion on 6 December and the succeeding days of 231 MPs of whom 45 were also imprisoned for varying lengths of times,[90] an action which in the view of some of its victims was 'the highest and most detestable Force and Breach of Privilege and Freedom ever offered to any Parliament of *England*'.[91] For once they did not exaggerate. When set beside these events, the king's attempted arrest of the five members in January 1642 or even the alleged plot of army officers to overawe the Parliament in 1641 were relatively minor incidents. The attempts of the purgers to justify their action rested very shakily on notions such as that the secluded members 'had soe abused the priviledge [of Parliament] by their perpeteutie [*sic*] there', and that most of the legislative achievements of the Long Parliament since 1642 had anyway been made by a patently incomplete Parliament from which malignants – in this case royalists – had been excluded. Such arguments were no doubt meat and drink to the faithful, but can have convinced few others.[92]

While there can be little doubt that Ireton and the army had eventually danced to the tune of Ludlow and the radical parliamentary Independents in purging rather than dissolving Parliament, most observers probably saw things the other way round, seeing the Rump as the willing tool of the army in its design for 'the converting of our well-regulated Monarchy into a military Anarchy, with a popular Parliament, only at the beck of the Army'.[93] Needless to say, one of the loudest, as well as the most prolix, denouncers of the army's coup was one of its most notable victims, William Prynne. Prynne roundly accused Fairfax and his subordinates of treason, but ruined an otherwise impressive treatise against the illegalities of the regime by finding at the heart of the republican conspiracy 'an whole Conclave of Jesuits, *popish Priests* and Jesuited Papists'.[94] In Prynne's view, no doubt, denunciations suitable for the case of Laud were equally applicable to the Rump and the army. But it was hardly necessary to resort to such patent and counter-productive absurdities to make a good case against these bodies.

XI

The traditional view of Pride's Purge as having been directed against the parliamentary Presbyterians by the Independents cannot survive the magnificently thorough analysis of the personnel of the purgers and the purged which has been made by Professor Underdown.[95] While it is true that all the Presbyterian MPs were in fact secluded, and some of them imprisoned as well, not all of the secluded – or even of the imprisoned – MPs were, in fact, Presbyterians. Some of them were middle-group Independents like Nathaniel Fiennes, Sir John Evelyn of Wiltshire, John Crewe and John Bulkeley, who had broken with the more radical Independents over the issue of negotiations with the king, but had not become political Presbyterians in the process. Nor were all those middle-groupers exempt who continued to vote with the radicals, as is demonstrated by the cases of John Boys and the Somerset clothier John Ashe, who acted as teller on the radical side in a crucial motion on 2 December and yet was imprisoned afterwards.[96] In these circumstances it is hardly surprising that more than twice as many former middle-groupers were victims of the purge as supported it, and that as many as one-third neglected to attend Parliament until the spring of 1649. Pride's Purge was directed against many Independents as well as against all Presbyterians.

The second traditional verdict on Pride's Purge is that its basic historic function was to clear the way for revolution, and that after 6 December the rest followed easily and relentlessly; the setting up of the court to try the king; his trial and execution on 30 January; the abolition of the Upper House of Parliament and the establishment of the republic.[97] But the actual course of events is by no means so straightforward. While it is true that these things are unthinkable without Pride's Purge, it should not be assumed that it made them inevitable. During the period immediately before the purge and following what Charles I, in a letter to his son on 29 November, had called 'the thundering declaration [viz., remonstrance] of the army ... against us'[98] the driving force behind the army's revolutionary determination had been Henry Ireton, now completely won over from his conservative monarchism of twelve months earlier, even if still conservative on most other matters. Cromwell was away in the north for most of the time, his mind still apparently not completely made up. Professor Underdown is almost certainly right to see Cromwell's return to London immediately after the purge as the most important factor in the attenuation of the revolutionary certainties expressed in the Remonstrance.[99] Nor was it only in the army that such doubts prevailed. It is fatally easy to regard the parliamentary remnant after the purge as a homogeneous revolutionary minority. But there were in fact soft as well as hardliners at Westminster. While there is no firm evidence that this is in many cases applicable, as in that of Cromwell, to the matter of the fate of the king, there is certainly no reason to believe that if Cromwell had managed, via the mission of the Earl of Denbigh to the king in late December, to reach a settlement with Charles which would have left the latter with life and throne if little else, this would not have attracted some support in Parliament. To say this is not to deny that, in still looking for a last-minute settlement, Oliver was going even more dangerously out on a limb than he had done over the same issue in 1647.

At least these moves gave hope to some royalists that all was not quite lost. In letters written probably to Sir Edward Nicholas in France on Christmas Day and 28 December, the royalist John Lawrans suggests that the significance of Pride's Purge and the army's seizure of the king was not that they cleared away the obstacles to bringing him to trial, but rather, like the seizure of the king at Holdenby in June 1647, that they were an attempt to dish the Presbyterians by acquiring control of the person of the king. Charles was, in fact, too valuable an asset to be eliminated and the Independents were reputed to be planning for him 'to have a share of government in ye same equipage (perhaps) as the Duke of Venice'. There was, Lawrans added, every hope to be drawn from the presence of moderate men on the committee appointed to draw up charges against the king, and, indeed, one of Lawrans's royalist acquaintances had been told by the radical Independent MP Nicholas Love that 'the charge would be nothing but what we knew the King could cleerely acquit himselfe of'. In a later letter of 29 December, however, Lawrans made it clear that his optimism was not shared by many other royalists.[100]

How far the fact that the latter were proved right and Lawrans wrong was due to the ultimate impossibility of persuading the army and the bulk of the radical politicians to swerve from the path laid down in the Remonstrance, and how far it was due to the king's rejection of the terms of Denbigh's mission, is a matter for conjecture. To Cromwell at least the king's final rejection of the terms of Denbigh's mission may well have been the final and unequivocal dispensation from which there could be no turning back. Whatever men's convictions about the king's responsibility for the two Civil Wars, what now had to be done required a strong nerve and complete assurance. In executing the king and establishing a republican form of government, Englishmen were cutting the ship of state free from its moorings; sons were murdering their fathers; the sin of revolt against the Lord's anointed, formerly softened by the now abandoned doctrine of the king's two bodies, was compounded a thousand times over. The implications of the end of royal authority for the problem of authority in general and political authority in particular, though played down by the government, were not lost on some radicals. As early as October 1647, long before regicide could be officially mooted, one Leveller had drawn attention to certain alarming corollaries of the fact of rebellion against the king, arguing that 'There is no forme of government by divine appointment, but the voice of the people is the voice of God . . . For the father hath not power to ingage the sonne but by consent'.[101] It was not for nothing that Oliver Cromwell was to seek incessantly thereafter for a constitution 'with something of the monarchical in it'.

Kings had of course been killed by their subjects before, 'in darkness and in corners basely murdered'. By contrast, 'Parliament held it more agreeable to Honor and Justice, to give the King a fair and open tryal . . . in the most publike place of *Justice*';[102] words which were later to be echoed by Thomas Harrison, the first of the regicides to suffer the horrible penalties of treason in 1660:

> It was not a thing done in a corner. I believe the sound of it hath been in most nations. I believe the hearts of some have felt the terrors of the presence of God that was with his servants in those days.[103]

Thus blood was again to be shed in 1660 in expiation for the royal blood shed in 1649, which in turn was an expiation for the blood guilt of two wars. But there were those for whom the regicide of 30 January invited comparison with another act of expiation, with the supreme atonement. That, whatever his faults, Charles died a martyr for his Church and his religious convictions is beyond dispute. In the words of a future Archbishop of Canterbury who was in his turn not only to stand up for that same Church against Charles's second son, but also to sacrifice his office because of his refusal to acquiesce in the denial of the indefeasible hereditary right of that same king:

> The black act is done, which all the world wonders at, & which an age cannot expiate & the waters of the Ocean we swimme in cannot wash out the spotts of yt blood, than which never any was shedd with greater guilt since the sonn of God powr'd out his.[104]

The image of Charles I as a Christ-figure was soon to become familiar through the illicit circulation of the *Eikon Basilike*. This image, more powerful than all the intellectual arguments of James I in defence of royal absolutism, is among the main reasons why the age of absolute monarchy *par excellence* in England came after 1660 rather than before 1640.

XII

When the parliamentary commissioners had taken their final leave of the king at Newport on 28 November, he had warned them that 'in my Fall and Ruine you see your own'.[105] Was his warning borne out by events? Were the fates of the nobility and the leading gentry of England inextricably bound up with that of their monarch?

In the short run, the king's words might appear to have been all too true. Pride's Purge, the seclusion of the moderate MPs, the dictatorship of the army and the godly party, the rise of new men to power both at Westminster and in the counties, and the abolition of the House of Lords must have seemed like unmistakable pointers in this direction. The execution of the king and the establishment of the republic was a revolutionary act, accomplished by revolutionary means. But it was the end and not the beginning of revolution. Thereafter, with the exception of the brief and disillusioning experience of the rule of the Saints in Barebones so-called Parliament in 1653, and the false dawn of the re-establishment of the Rump after the collapse of Richard Cromwell's Protectorate in 1659, the norm was virtual standstill, or, even – and especially between 1653 and 1658, and again in 1660, a gradual move back in the direction of monarchical institutions. The high point of revolution came on 30 January 1649, the date at which this book closes.

Why was this? Why was it that a House of Commons purged of non-revolutionary elements so rapidly lost its revolutionary momentum?[106] Two alternative, though not necessarily mutually contradictory, explanations have recently been offered, the first in Professor Underdown's magnificent study of Pride's Purge which has been drawn on so heavily in the final chapter of this book. In Underdown's view, the parliamentary remnant following the purge, while reasonable material for carrying out a revolution, was too narrow a base on which to build a stable regime. But stability and revolution stand in inverse relationship to one another, and the broadening of the base of the regime via the gradual readmission of many of the excluded members was, despite the use of a variety of political tests such as the repudiation of the vote of 5 December and the taking of the oath of Engagement to the new regime, a process of dilution whereby its revolutionary edge was blunted. Certainly as more and more secluded members came back, along with those who had voluntarily stayed away, the army's original intention – that the purge would be a temporary expedient to be followed by a dissolution and the election of a new parliament on a new franchise and for a limited term – moved even further from realization and had to wait until Cromwell's illegal dissolution of the Rump in 1653, which even then was followed not by an election but by a nominated assembly.

While Professor Underdown is at pains to emphasize that the aims of some of the Rumpers of December 1648 were decidedly less revolutionary than those of others, his main stress is on the process of subsequent dilution. Dr Blair Worden, while not disputing the importance of this, stresses even more strongly the limited revolutionary inclinations of the original Rumpers, and even of the regicides themselves, the men normally regarded as the cream of the revolutionary cream.[107] There were, of course, regicides like John Carew and Thomas Harrison, to whom the execution of the king heralded the beginning of the millennium, men whose revolutionary expectations were indeed very high, as high as those of the Levellers and the even more radical Diggers, who got very short shrift in the months following the establishment of the Commonwealth. For Harrison and Carew at least the day of the Saints did finally dawn in 1653, and when it did, in Barebones Parliament, it was not at all to the liking of most of their fellow regicides in 1649. To Saints like Carew and Harrison, and to such long-standing republican enthusiasts as Thomas Chaloner, Edmund Ludlow and Henry Marten, regicide was indeed to be the prelude to revolution, though their revolutionary expectations were disappointed in the event. To Henry Ireton, regicide was rightly or wrongly the lesser political revolution undertaken to avoid a greater social revolution, though, ever since his disenchantment with monarchical institutions after Putney, it was a political revolution which he was prepared to accept with enthusiasm. There were others, and Cromwell may have been one of them, who saw regicide as regrettably necessary if peace were to be established – at the very least a peace that would satisfy the soldiers. It may well have been the case that, if the regicide had been compatible with the preservation of the monarchy, most of the regicides would have opted for an institution with something of the monarchical in it. There were probably relatively few out-and-out republicans on principle, such as Ludlow, Marten and Chaloner. For most republicans republicanism was an *ex post facto* belief, born of necessity rather than conviction.

It was only to very few, if any, that the establishment of the Commonwealth marked a new dawn. For far more it was the return to pristine English freedoms which had been usurped by innovating

kings. Just how important it was to use history as a validating charter
for revolutionary programmes in this neo-Cokeian manner is apparent
from the way in which the thinking even of radical figures is permeated
by the notion. It is almost as if the further one appeared to be moving
the greater one's need to seek reassurance from history – not in the
Hegelian sense of acting as its agent, but in the Cokeian sense of re-
creating one's origins. Thus Henry Marten on 27 November 1647
emphasized that the Civil War was not a conquest but the recovery
of ancient liberties.[108] Speaker Lenthall informed the JPs of Yorkshire
on 3 April 1649 that the king had not been executed nor the Commonwealth established in order to facilitate innovation but for 'ye perfect
recoverie of ye Liberties . . . lost in that long succession of Tyrannie'.[109]
In so doing he was echoing the words of the parliamentary declaration
of 16 March where the abolition of the monarchy was described as 'a
most happy way . . . for this Nation . . . to returne to its Just and
Ancient right'.[110] The new great seal of England bore the significant
inscription: 'In the first year of freedom by God's blessing restored,
1648 [viz. 1649]'.[111] 'Restored', be it noted, not begun.

Nor was this basic conservatism confined to the political establishment. The Levellers have justly attracted the interest of political theor-
ists on account of their emphasis on natural rights justified by rational
argument rather than by their historicity. But it is no less important to
emphasize that they too felt the need to describe these rights as having
existed in remote antiquity, in which circumstances they too needed to
be recovered rather than established *ab initio*. Richard Overton's disre-
spectful description of Magna Carta, that hallowed Cokeian repository
of English liberties, as 'but a beggerly thing, containing many markes
of intollerable bondage',[112] does not mean that the Levellers were
indifferent to history, but simply that they regarded Magna Carta as a
product of Norman oppression, and the Norman Conquest not (as
Coke saw it) as the confirmation but as the negation of Anglo-Saxon
liberties which were the essential birthright of Englishmen which it
behoved them to restore.[113] There was apparently nothing, however
novel it might seem, which could not be authenticated by an appeal to
the past, an idea which naturally evoked the scorn of royalist writers.[114]
Even in the case of the farthest out of all radical groups, the so-called
Diggers or true Levellers, there is the same looking back for inspiration, the same reading of current desiderata into past golden ages.
For Winstanley, the Fall and the Norman Conquest seem almost to be
interchangeable. In *The True Levellers' Standard Advanced* (1649) he looks

back to a pre-lapsarian state when the earth was 'a common treasury of relief for all'. Enclosures and private property were the products of the Fall, a view with which Aquinas would not have quarrelled, though he would have rejected the implication that man should strive to re-attain this pre-lapsarian perfection. In *A Declaration from the Poor Oppressed People of England* (1649) it is the Norman Conquest that is the chief villain of the piece, back beyond which the revolutionary must go in his search for a perfect society.[115]

Thus to Levellers and Diggers what governments revered as the ancient constitution was in fact the apparatus of oppression. But it was in not a less but a *more* ancient state of affairs that they found the true freedoms of Englishmen. Revolutionaries in most ages have derived strength from seeing themselves as agents of an historical process. For the revolutionaries of seventeenth-century England, almost without exception, the aim of that process was to return to ancient ways, not to innovate.

XIII

Moderate and conservative men were no less alarmed at the phenomenon of revolution on account of the fact that its proponents looked backwards for inspiration. This book has provided numerous examples of erstwhile radicals moving steadily rightwards, and assuming ever more conservative positions: the great radical parliamentarians of the 1620s, Strangeways, Seymour and Denzil Holles, the first two of whom served with the king at Oxford, while the last became the leading figure of the parliamentarian right wing, one of the five members of 1642 becoming one of the eleven of 1647; Sir William Waller, darling of the war-party radicals in 1643, but apostle of counter-revolution, 'reformado', and one of the eleven in 1647; Saye and Sele and his son Nathaniel Fiennes, Independents *par excellence* in the winter of 1647-8 but desperate defenders of the Newport Treaty before the year was out.

Of course there were some who moved in the other direction. During the great political transformation of 1644-5, while some middle-groupers like Glyn and Clotworthy went into alliance with the Presbyterians, others like Evelyn, St John and Fiennes cooperated with the Independents, though, as the last of those cases has just demonstrated, such moves were often less permanent than the rightward slide of the likes of Glyn and Clotworthy. It is indeed difficult to imagine a more telling illustration of our thesis than the transition from Fiennes's probable authorship and certain support of the militantly radical Declaration on the Vote of No Addresses at the beginning of 1648 to his impassioned defence on 1 December of the king's final answer at Newport as sufficient 'to secure religion, laws and liberties'.[116]

There is, however, another even more spectacular example. Over the period between his blistering attack on episcopacy (but defence of monarchy) in 1641 and his violent attack on monarchy in *The Tenure of Kings and Magistrates, Eikonklastes* and his first and second *Defence*, John Milton moved steadily with - and sometimes ahead of - the radical tide. As the new regime lurched from crisis to crisis it is possible to discern two revolutionary circles completed; the first a smaller circle beginning where this book leaves off in 1649 and completing its revolution ten years later with the restoration of the Rump. But here was no permanent resting-place, and, seen in historical perspective this circle seems rather to be a part of a second and greater revolution; from 1641 to 1660, which sees the restoration not only of the Stuart monarchy but of the ancient form of government both at Westminster and in the counties. And when John Milton, the apostle of regicide and republicanism, and one who was fortunate to keep his head on his shoulders in 1660, made his final appeal for the good old cause on the eve of the Restoration, to whom did he appeal? Freedom and civil rights, he informs us,

> may be best and soonest obtained, if every county in the land were made a kind of subordinate ... commonwealth .... where the nobility and chief gentry ... make their own judicial laws ... and execute them by their own elected judicatures.... So shall they have justice in their own hands, law executed fully ... in their own counties and precincts, long wished and spoken of, but never yet obtained.[117]

When the apostle of revolution appeals to the idea of the community of the county, the wheel has indeed come full circle. If there were few to heed Milton's appeal, this was because the localist millennium - or something not far short of it - which he dangled before them in his desperate attempt to stave off the inevitable was about to be achieved in the context of an ancient constitution which offered a real earnest of its permanence.

Notes

NOTES ON DATING AND ABBREVIATIONS

ALL dates are old style, except for the fact that the year is assumed to begin on 1 January, not 25 March. The following abbreviations and short titles are used in the notes. The place of publication is London unless otherwise stated. Contemporary published materials are normally accompanied by the appropriate reference in D.G.Wing, *Short Title of Books . . . 1641–1700* (New York 1945–51), here denoted as [Wing].

Acts and Ordinances   C.H.Firth and R.S.Rait (eds.), *Acts and Ordinances of the Interregnum 1642–1660* (1911)

Amer. Hist. Rev.   *American Historical Review*

A.P.C.   *Acts of the Privy Council*

Baillie, *Letters and Journals*   D.Laing (ed.), *The Letters and Journals of Robert Baillie . . . 1637–1642* (Edinburgh 1841–2)

Bell, *Memorials*   R.Bell (ed.), *Memorials of the Civil War comprising the Correspondence of the Fairfax Family* (1849)

B.I.H.R.   *Bulletin of the Institute of Historical Research*

B.M.   British Museum (viz. British Library)

Cal. Clarendon S.P.   O.Ogle and W.H.Bliss (eds.), *Calendar of the Clarendon State Papers preserved in the Bodleian Library* (Oxford 1872)

Cal. S.P.D.   *Calendar of State Papers Domestic*

Cal. S.P. East Indies (and Persia)   *Calendar of State Papers East Indies (and Persia)*

Cal. S.P. Ven.   *Calendar of State Papers Venetian*

Carlyle, *Cromwell*   Thomas Carlyle, *Oliver Cromwell's Letters and Speeches* (1857)

Cary, *Memorials*   H.Cary (ed.), *Memorials of the Great Civil War in England from 1646 to 1652* (1842)

C.D. 1621   W.Notestein, F.H.Relf and H.Simpson (eds.), *Commons Debates 1621* (New Haven 1935)

C.D. 1629   W.Notestein and F.Relf (eds.), *The Commons Debates for 1629* (Minneapolis 1921)

Charles I in 1646   J.Bruce (ed.), *Charles I in 1646: Letters of King Charles the First to Queen Henrietta Maria*, Camden Soc. old ser. LXIII (1856)

Clarendon, *Great Rebellion*   W.D.Macray (ed.), *The History of the Rebellion and Civil Wars in England ... by Edward Earl of Clarendon* (Oxford 1958 edn.)

Clarendon State Papers   R.Scrope and T.Monkhouse (eds.), *State Papers collected by Edward, Earl of Clarendon commencing 1621* (Oxford 1767–86)

C.L.R.O.   City of London Record Office

D'Ewes, *Journal* (ed. Coates)   W.H.Coates (ed.), *The Journal of Sir Simonds D'Ewes from the first Recess of the Long Parliament to the Withdrawal of King Charles from London* (New Haven 1942)

D'Ewes, *Journal* (ed. Notestein)   *The Journal of Sir Simonds D'Ewes from the Beginning of the Long Parliament to the Opening of the Trial of the Earl of Strafford* (New Haven 1923)

D.N.B.   *Dictionary of National Biography*

Econ. Hist. Rev.   *Economic History Review*

Eng. Hist. Rev.   *English Historical Review*

Everitt, *Kent*   A.M.Everitt, *The Community of Kent and the Great Rebellion 1640–60* (Leicester 1966)

Everitt, *Suffolk*   A.M.Everitt, *Suffolk and the Great Rebellion 1640–1660*, Suffolk Record Soc. III (1961)

Fast Sermons   R.Jeffs (ed.), *The English Revolution*, I. *Fast Sermons to Parliament* (1970–1)

Fletcher, *Outbreak*   A.Fletcher, *The Outbreak of the English Civil War* (1981)

Fletcher, *Sussex*   A.Fletcher, *A County Community in Peace and War: Sussex 1600–1660* (1975)

Gardiner, *Civil War*   S.R.Gardiner, *History of the Great Civil War 1642–1649* (1893)

Gardiner, *Constitutional Documents*   S.R.Gardiner (ed.), *Constitutional Documents of the Puritan Revolution 1625–1660* (Oxford 1962 edn.)

Gardiner, *History 1603–1642*   S.R.Gardiner, *History of England From the Accession of James I to the Outbreak of the Civil War 1603–1642* (1883–4)

Haller, *Liberty and Reformation*   W. Haller, *Liberty and Reformation in the Puritan Revolution* (1963 edn.)

Haller, *Tracts on Liberty*   W. Haller (ed.), *Tracts on Liberty in the Puritan Revolution 1638-1647* (New York 1933)

Hist. J.   *Historical Journal*

H.M.C.   Historical Manuscripts Commission

H. of Commons J.   *Journal of the House of Commons*

Holmes, *Eastern Association*   C. Holmes, *The Eastern Association in the English Civil War* (Cambridge 1974)

H. of Lords J.   *Journal of the House of Lords*

Hughes, *Warwickshire*   Ann Hughes, *Politics, Society and Civil War in Warwickshire* (Cambridge 1987)

Hutchinson Memoirs   C.H. Firth (ed.), *Memoirs of the Life of Colonel Hutchinson . . . by his Widow, Lucy* (1906)

J. Brit. Stud.   *Journal of British Studies*

J. Mod. Hist.   *Journal of Modern History*

Journal   Journal of the Court of Common Council of the City of London

Knyvett Letters   B. Schofield (ed.), *The Knyvett Letters (1620-1644)* (1949)

Leveller Manifestoes   D.M. Wolfe (ed.), *Leveller Manifestoes of the Puritan Revolution* (1967 edn.)

Ludlow Memoirs   C.H. Firth (ed.), *The Memoirs of Edmund Ludlow* (Oxford 1894)

Luke Letter Books   H.M.C. J.P.4. *The Letter Books 1644-5 of Sir Samuel Luke* (ed. H.G. Tibbutt) (1963)

Maseres, *Select Tracts*   F. Maseres (ed.), *Select Tracts relating to the Civil War in England in the Reign of King Charles the First* (1815)

Morrill, *Provinces*   J.S. Morrill, *The Revolt of the Provinces: Conservatives and Radicals in the English Civil War 1630-1650* (1976)

P. & P.   *Past & Present*

Parliamentary History   *The Parliamentary or Constitutional History of England . . . collected by several hands* (1751-62)

P.C.   Privy Council

P.C.R.   Privy Council Register

Pennington and Roots, *Stafford*   D.H. Pennington and I. Roots (eds.), *The County Committee at Stafford 1643-1645* (Manchester 1957)

Private Journals (1)   W.H. Coates, A.S. Young and V.F. Snow (eds.), *The Private Journals of the Long Parliament 3 January to 5 March 1642* (New Haven 1982)

Private Journals (2)   V.F.Snow and A.S.Young (eds.), *The Private Journals of the Long Parliament 7 March to 1 June 1642* (New Haven 1987)

P.R.O.   Public Record Office

Remembrancia Index   Analytical Index to the Series of Records known as the Remembrancia preserved among the Archives of the City of London (1878)

Ren. and Mod. Stud.   Renaissance and Modern Studies

Repertory   Repertory of the Court of Aldermen of the City of London

Roy. Hist. Soc. Trans.   Transactions of the Royal Historical Society

S.P.   State Papers Domestic

Trans. Amer. Phil. Soc.   Transactions of the American Philosophical Society

Underdown, *Somerset*   D. Underdown, *Somerset in the Civil War and Interregnum* (Newton Abbot 1973)

Walker, *Sufferings*   J.Walker, *An attempt towards recovering an account of the Numbers and Sufferings of the Clergy of the Church of England ... in the late times of the Grand Rebellion* (1714)

Westminster Assembly Minutes   A.F.Mitchell and J.Struthers (eds.), *Minutes of the Sessions of the Westminster Assembly of Divines* (1874)

Whitelock, *Memorials*   Bulstrode Whitelock, *Memorials of the English Affairs* (1682 edn.)

Wood, *Nottinghamshire*   A.C.Wood, *Nottinghamshire in the Civil War* (Oxford 1937)

CHAPTER 1   MONARCHY AND SOCIETY

1. P.Laslett (ed.), *Patriarcha ... and Other Political Works of Sir Robert Filmer* [hereafter Filmer, *Works*] (Oxford 1949), Introduction pp. 1-43. See also G.Schochet, *Patriarchalism in Political Thought* (Oxford 1975), and 'Patriarchalism, Politics and Mass Attitudes in Stuart England', *Hist. J.*, XII (1969), 413-41.
2. See, for example, A.O.Lovejoy, *The Great Chain of Being* (New York 1960 edn.); E.M.W.Tillyard, *The Elizabethan World Picture* (1963 edn.); W.H.Greenleaf, *Order, Empiricism and Politics 1500-1700* (1964). For a 'revisionist' view of James I, see J.Wormald, 'James VI and I. Two Kings or One?', *History*, LXVIII (1983), 187-209.
3. A good contemporary example is E.Forset, *A Comparative Discourse of the Bodies Natural and Politique* (1606).
4. James I, 'The Trew Law of Free Monarchies' (1598) [hereafter

'Trew Law'] in C.H.McIlwaine (ed.), *The Political Works of James I* [hereafter James I, *Works*] (New York 1965 edn.), pp. 64-5.

5. James I, *Works*, p. 307 (speech of 1610).

6. James I, 'Basilikon Doron' (1599) in *Works*, p. 12; cf. 'Trew Law' in *Works*, pp. 54-5.

7. Filmer, 'Patriarcha' in *Works*, pp. 84-5; cf. James I, 'Trew Law' in *Works*, pp. 56-61, and J.W., *Obedience active and passive due to the supream power* (Oxford 1643), p. 22.

8. Sir John Spelman, 'Certain CONSIDERATIONS upon the Duties both of Prince and People', *Lord Somers Tracts*, 2nd coll., II (1750), 69.

9. For an excellent modern treatment of this subject, see K. Thomas, *Religion and the Decline of Magic* (1971), pp. 192-206. On Charles I's restrictions on its exercise, see J.Richards '"His Nowe Majestie" and English Monarchy: The Kingship of Charles I before 1640', *P. & P.* 113 (1986), 86-94.

10. Bodleian, Tanner MSS. 58(a), fo. 74; Gardiner, *Civil War*, III, 241-2. For James I's views, B.M., Add. MSS., 22587, fos. 4-4(b).

11. *Richard II*, iv, i, 201, 203-11.

12. ibid., 255-7.

13. ibid., 145.

14. ibid., 239-41.

15. cf. also the Bishop of Carlisle's prophecy about the fate of England in *Richard II* with that of *Eikon Basilike*, ch. 28.

16. James I, *Works*, p. 310 (speech of 1610).

17. An example is Sir William Morton, 'Ius Monarchiae Anglicanae', Bodleian, Clarendon MSS., 132. fo. 35(b).

18. 'Directions for Obedience in Dangerous or Doubtful Times' (1652) in Filmer, *Works*, p. 233.

19. James I, 'Trew Law', *Works*, pp. 55, 64.

20. On the view of the constitution as immemorial, see J.G.A. Pocock, *The Ancient Constitution and the Feudal Law* (Cambridge 1957), especially pp. 30-55; and see pp. 18-21.

21. Filmer, 'The Anarchy of a Limited or Mixed Monarchy' (1648), *Works*, p. 289. My italics. For a similar argument from family subordination in a state of nature, see Spelman in *Lord Somers' Tracts*, p. 67.

22. Schochet, *Patriarchalism in Political Thought*, p. III.

23. See ibid., pp. 88-9, 136-58; but cf. Greenleaf, *Order*, pp. 86-7, where the similarities between the two theories are emphasized.

24. Introduction to Filmer, *Works*, p. 41.

25. James I, 'Basilikon Doron' in *Works*, p. 12.

26. T. Jordan, *Rules to know a royall king* (1642), p. 1. On Capel, see *State Trials*, IV (1809), 1232. For another late example of the identification, see Oxford. All Souls College, Codrington Library, *Great Britain's Vote* (1648), p. 34.

27. Filmer, 'Patriarcha' in *Works*, p. 57. For similar views in other treatises by Filmer, see *Works*, pp. 231, 284–9. See also James I, 'Trew Law' in *Works*, pp. 55–6, 64–6. For attacks on the idea of paternalistic monarchy, see e.g. *A discourse upon the question in debate* (1642), p. 5; *Maximes unfolded* (1643) pp. 18–22; *Tne subject of supremacie* (1643), pp. 22, 42; John Milton, '[First] Defence of the People of England' in *Works* (New York 1932), pp. 44–7. For an interesting reversal of roles comparing the king with a child and the people with his parents, see [Henry Parker], *The Cordiall of Mr. David Jenkins Answered* (1647), pp. 21–2.

28. Cited by Schochet, *Patriarchalism in Political Thought*, p. 113.

29. On this see P. Laslett, *The World We Have Lost* (2nd edn. 1971), especially ch. 1. For another valuable treatment of these problems, see Schochet, 'Patriarchalism, Politics and Mass Attitudes', art. cit.

30. E. Forset, *A Comparative Discourse of the Bodies Natural and Politique* (1606), p. 46.

31. T. Hobbes, 'Behemoth' in Maseres, *Select Tracts*, I, 360–1.

32. *A collection of severall speeches, messages and answers* (1642), pp. 75–76.

33. B. M. Stowe MSS. 154, fo. 10.

34. 'Memoirs of Sir John Berkley', in Maseres, *Select Tracts*, I, 360–1.

35. James I, 'Basilikon Doron', in *Works*, p. 18.

36. James I, *Works*, pp. 309–10 (speech of 1610).

37. *Richard II*, I, ii, 37–41.

38. The Bye and Main Plots in 1603 and the Gunpowder Plot in 1605.

39. These arguments are in part a summary compiled especially from James I, 'Trew Law' in *Works*, pp. 60–1, 66–7, 70, also p. 309; J. M. Kemble (ed.), *Certaine Considerations upon the government of England by Sir Roger Twysden Kt. and Bart.*, Camden Soc. old ser. XLV (1849), 102; Spelman, 'Certain Considerations', *Lord Somers' Tracts*, 73–79; 'The Rebels' Catechism' (1643), *Harleian Miscellany*, V (1810), 410–3.

40. Bodleian, Tanner MSS., 62, fo. 467.

41. Filmer, 'Patriarcha' in *Works*, p. 62.

42. Baillie, *Letters and Journals*, I, 116–17.

43. T. May, *A Discourse concerning the svccesse of former Parliaments* (1642), especially pp. 2, 4.

44. For example, by the anonymous author of a treatise somewhat incongruously entitled *England's absolute monarchy* (1642), no pagination.

45. L. Alston (ed.), *De Republica Anglorum by Sir Thomas Smith* (Cambridge 1906), p. 17.

46. *His Majesties answer to the XIX propositions* (1642), especially pp. 18 *et seq.* On the royal use of mixed monarchy, see C.C.Weston, 'The Theory of Mixed Monarchy under Charles I and After', *Eng. Hist. Rev.*, LXXV (1960), 426–43.

47. J.R.Tanner (ed.), *Constitutional Documents of the Reign of James I 1603–1625* (Cambridge 1960 edn.), pp. 260–1, 340–1.

48. F.D.Wormuth, *The Royal Prerogative 1603–1649* (Ithaca 1939), pp. 76–7.

49. H.Hulme, *The Life of Sir John Eliot 1592–1632* (1957), p. 375.

50. R.W.K.Hinton, 'English Constitutional Theories from Sir John Fortescue to Sir John Eliot', *Eng. Hist. Rev.*, LXXV (1970), 410–25, especially 421–4.

51. C.Russell, 'Parliamentary History in Perspective, 1604–1629', *History*, LXI (1976), 1–27. See also his *Parliaments and English Politics 1621–1629* (Oxford 1979), passim, and 'The Nature of a Parliament in Early Stuart England', in H.Tomlinson (ed.), *Before the English Civil War* (1983), pp. 123–50; and K.Sharpe (ed.), *Faction and Parliament* (Oxford 1978), pp. 1–42.

CHAPTER 2   TRADITION AND INNOVATION

1. See T.B.Macaulay, *Critical and Historical Essays* (Everyman edn. 1916), I, pp. 292–3 for a good example.

2. H.Butterfield, *The Whig Interpretation of History* (1959 edn.), pp. 45 *et seq.*

3. J.M.Kemble (ed.), 'Certaine Considerations upon the Government of England by Sir Roger Twysden, Kt. and Bart.', Camden Soc., XLV (1849), p. 15.

4. H.Hulme, *The Life of Sir John Eliot 1592 to 1632* (1957), p. 253.

5. Bodleian, Tanner MSS., 321, fo. 4.

6. J.G.A.Pocock, *The Ancient Constitution and the Feudal Law* (Cambridge 1958), pp. 30–55. For another useful account of the connec-

tion between history and politics, see P. Styles, 'Politics and Historical Research in the Early Seventeenth Century' in L. Fox (ed.), *English Historical Scholarship in the Sixteenth and Seventeenth Centuries* (1956), pp. 49–72, especially pp. 53–64.

7. James I informed the Commons in a letter of 11 December 1621 that most of their privileges 'grow from precedents, which shews rather a toleration than inheritance'. See J. R. Tanner (ed.), *Constitutional Documents of the Reign of James I 1603–1625* (Cambridge 1960 edn.), p. 286.

8. On Magna Carta see the works cited in note 6; also F. Thompson, *Magna Carta: Its Role in the Making of the English Constitution 1300–1629* (Minneapolis 1948), especially pp. 233–374; M. P. Ashley, *Magna Carta in the Seventeenth Century* (Charlottesville 1965).

9. Pym even spoke of William I as making a compact with the English nation, included in the provisions of which was parliamentary control of taxation. ['A DECLARATION of the Grievances of the Kingdome, delivered in Parliament by John Pym ESQUIER, 1642' in *Lord Somers' Tracts*, 2nd coll., II (1750), 161.]

10. Cited in Gardiner, *History 1603–1642*, VI, 313–14. For similar views see for example, Kemble (ed.), 'Certaine Considerations', pp. 22–62, 70–6, 82–7; *Questions resolved and propositions tending to accommodation* (1642) [Wing 186], p. 12.

11. *A short discourse tending to the pacification* ... (1642) [Wing 3587], pp. 6–7.

12. Bodleian, Willis MSS., 57, fo. 473; Carte MSS., 119, fos. 27–8.

13. W. Prynne, *An humble remonstrance to his Majesty against the tax of Ship-money* ... (1641), pp. 32–51.

14. W. Hakewill, *The manner of holding parliaments in England* (1641), no pagination.

15. See pp. 124–6, 155, 179–86.

16. On this subject, see P. Zagorin, *The Court and the Country* (1969), pp. 5–18.

17. See, e.g., Charles I's answer to the House of Commons petition of 28 January 1642 [*A Collection of severall speeches, messages and answers* (1642)] [Wing 2159], especially pp. 28–9.

18. *His Majesties answer to a book entituled the declaration or remonstrance* (1642) [Wing 2092], p. 8; *His Majesties answer to the XIX propositions* (1642) [Wing 2122], p. 20.

19. The best treatment is still probably J. N. Figgis, *The Divine Right of Kings* (Cambridge 1934 edn.).

20. James I, *Works*, pp. 309-10.
21. See pp. 124-5.
22. *Troilus and Cressida*, I, iii, 83-136.
23. M.D.Whinney and O.Millar, *English Art 1625-1714* (Oxford 1957), p. I.
24. ibid., p. 6; O.Millar, *The Age of Charles I* (1972), p. 60.
25. Whinney and Millar, *English Art*, p. 4.
26. E.Waterhouse, *Painting in Britain 1530-1790*, 3rd edn. (Harmondsworth 1969), p. 33.
27. See ibid., pp. 31-6.
28. Van Dyck described his picture as a portrait 'a cavallo ad imitatione di Carlo Quinto espresso da Titiano'. [O.Millar (ed.), *The Tudor, Stuart and early Georgian Pictures in the Collection of H.M. the Queen* (1963), p. 18.] On the equestrian portraits, see also R.Strong, *Charles I on Horseback* (1972). For some refreshingly sceptical observations about the limited impact of royal portraits, see J.Richards, *P. & P.* art. cit., 73-5.
29. Waterhouse, *Painting in Britain*, p. 46.
30. J.Summerson, *Architecture in Britain 1530-1830* (Harmondsworth 1970 edn.), p. 112.
31. On Scamozzi and other influences on Jones, see ibid, pp. 117-18, 123, 131; J.Summerson, *Inigo Jones* (Harmondsworth 1966), pp. 36, 43; Whinney and Millar, *English Art*, pp. 21-2, 24-5; J.Harris, S.Orgel and R.Strong (eds.), *The King's Arcadia: Inigo Jones and the Stuart Court* (1973), pp. 56, 146-7; J.Sumner-Smith, 'The Italian Sources of Inigo Jones', *Burlington Magazine*, XLIV (1952).
32. On this see Summerson, *Architecture in Britain*, p. 131; Summerson, *Inigo Jones*, p. 48; Whinney and Millar, op. cit., pp. 22-3, 24-5.
33. City of London R.O., *Remembrancia*, VII, 88, 105, 122; VIII, 85, 122, 125; H.R.Trevor-Roper, *Archbishop Laud 1573-1645*, 2nd edn. (1963), pp. 121-6, 346-7, 350-1, 428-9.
34. For some evidence relating to work attributed to Jones, see Summerson, *Architecture in Britain*, pp. 141-4; Whinney and Millar, op. cit., pp. 43-6.
35. Summerson, *Architecture in Britain*, pp. 142-3; L.Stone, *Family and Fortune* (Oxford 1973), pp. 77-82. Stone's attribution of the Hatfield south front to Jones has not found general acceptance. If true, it would be a very early work.
36. On such influences on design, see Summerson, *Architecture in Britain*, pp. 51-9.

37. See below pp. 34–6, 39–40.
38. See below pp. 100, 102, 111–14, 124–5.
39. W.R.Fryer, 'The "High Churchmen" of the Earlier Seventeenth Century', *Ren. and Mod. Stud.*, v (1961), 128.
40. W.L.Woodfill, *Musicians in English Society from Elizabeth to Charles I* (Princeton 1953), pp. 194–7.
41. M.Lefkowitz, *William Lawes* (1960), p. 150.
42. I owe this information and general guidance about the musical developments of the time to my colleague Professor Peter Aston.
43. Woodfill, *Musicians*, p. 169; Lillian M.Ruff and D.A.Wilson, 'The Madrigal, the Lute Song and Elizabethan Politics', *P. & P.*, 44 (1969), 14–16.
44. *The Correspondence of John Cosin, D.D.* (Surtees Soc. LII, 1869, I, 165, 166, 189). See also pp. 155–6, 183–5 and G.Abraham (ed.), *The New Oxford History of Music*, IV: *The Age of Humanism 1540–1630* (1968), pp. 469–70. For a similar attack on organs and Church music made by Edward Thomas in the House of Commons on 15 June 1641, see J.Rushworth, *Historical Collections* (1691), IV, 287–8.
45. On the connection between Laudianism and the increased interest in organs, see Woodfill, *Musicians*, pp. 154–5.
46. See A.Harbage, *Cavalier Drama* (New York 1964).
47. ibid., p. 71.
48. The Puritans got the best of both worlds, since they also objected to males playing female parts. [E.N.S.Thompson, *The Controversy between the Puritans and the Stage* (New York 1966 edn.), pp. 58–60, 106, 139–40, 165–7, 169–70; G.E.Bentley, *The Jacobean and Caroline Stage* (Oxford 1941), I, pp. 25–6]. For a not very convincing attempt to challenge the traditional view which sees the Puritans as opposed to the theatre, see M.Heinemann, *Puritanism and the Theatre* (Cambridge 1980), passim.
49. Harbage, op. cit., pp. 36–45.
50. ibid., p. 40.
51. On this see L.Stone, *The Crisis of the Aristocracy* (Oxford 1965), pp. 34, 464, 501.
52. Harbage, op. cit., p. 35.
53. Ben Johnson, *Works*, VII, p. 229, cited by P.Palme, *The Triumph of Peace* (1957), p. 140.
54. See Sir John Davis, 'Orchestra, or a Poem on Dancing' (1596).
55. S.Orgel, *The Jonsonian Masque* (Cambridge Mass.), pp. 5–7.

56. *A Book of Masques in Honour of Allardyce Nicoll* (Cambridge 1967), pp. 240-2.

57. I acknowledge my indebtedness to Professor Orgel's brilliant treatment of this masque in *The Jonsonian Masque*, pp. 167-85.

58. *Cal. S.P. Venetian 1617-19*, pp. 110-14.

59. Cited in E. Welsford, *The Court Masque* (New York 1962 edn.), p. 230.

60. *A Book of Masques in Honour of Allardyce Nicoll*, pp. 236-7.

61. ibid., p. 238.

62. P.R.O., S.P. James I, xcv/8.

63. For a contemporary description of the ante-supper by Francis Osborne, see *Secret History of the Court of James the First* (Edinburgh 1811), I, pp. 270-3. For the orgy at Theobalds, T. Park (ed.), *Nugae Antiquae by Sir John Harington, Knight* (1804), I, pp. 348-53. Extracts from both are printed in R. Ashton (ed.), *James I by his Contemporaries* (1969), pp. 232-3, 242-4.

64. *A Book of Masques in Honour of Allardyce Nicoll*, pp. 279, 291-3.

65. See L. C. Knights, *Drama and Society in the Age of Jonson* (1957 edn.), pp. 215-18.

66. *A Book of Masques in Honour of Allardyce Nicoll*, p. 357.

67. Cited by A. Nicoll, *Stuart Masques and the Restoration Stage* (1963 edn.), p. 28.

68. ibid., pp. 29, 170-1, 211.

69. Tanner (ed.), *Constitutional Documents*, p. 359.

70. Cited in C. H. Herford and P. Simpson (eds.), *Ben Jonson* (1925), II, 289.

71. On the genre, see the admirable article by G. R. Hibbard, 'The Country House Poem of the Seventeenth Century', *J. of Warburg and Courtauld Institutes*, XIX (1956), 159-74.

72. Ben Jonson, 'Penshurst', 1-5.

73. ibid., 99-102.

74. ibid., 45-7.

75. Robert Herrick, 'A Panegyricke to Sir Lewis Pemberton', 115-26.

76. ibid., 84-90.

77. Park (ed.), *Nugae Antiquae*, I, 353.

78. Ben Jonson, 'To Sir Robert Wroth', 3-4; 'To Penshurst', 90-2.

79. Ben Jonson, 'To Fine Lady Would-bee'.

80. Thomas Middleton, *A Chaste Maid in Cheapside*, III, iii, 55-7.

81. For a cruder comment on the artificiality and servility of the life of the courtier, see Nicholas Breton, 'The Court and the

Country' (1618), reprinted in W.H.Dunham and S.Pargellis (eds.), *Complaint and Reform in England 1436–1714* (New York 1938), p. 460.

82. Robert Herrick, 'A Country-Life: to His Brother, M.Tho. Herrick', 3–6, 39–42.

83. Millar, *The Age of Charles I*, pp. 66–9, 71–4.

84. Summerson, *Architecture in Britain*, pp. 134–7, *Inigo Jones*, pp. 83–96; Harris, Orgel and Strong, *The King's Arcadia*, pp. 184–6.

85. On this, see P.V.Marinelli, *Patoral* (1971), pp. 57–74.

86. E.StJ.Brooks, *Sir Christopher Hatton* (1947 edn.), p. 159. On the ideal and reality of 'hospitality', see F.Heal, 'The Idea of Hospitality in Early Modern England', *P. & P.*, 102 (1984), 66–93.

87. M.Prestwich, *Cranfield. Politics and Profits under the Early Stuarts* (Oxford, 1966), p. 432.

88. For an illuminating treatment of this cultural dichotomy with a somewhat different emphasis from my own, see P.V.Thomas, '"Two Cultures", Court and Country under Charles I', in C.Russell (ed.), *Origins of the English Civil War* (1980 edn.), pp. 168–93; also G.Parry, *The Golden Age Restor'd: The Culture of the Stuart Court* (Manchester 1981).

CHAPTER 3   CENTRALISM AND LOCALISM

1. E.R.Foster (ed.), *Proceedings in Parliament 1610* (New Haven 1966), II, 279–81.

2. On the idea of the county community and critics of the idea, see especially Everitt, *Kent*, and his *The Local Community and the Great Rebellion* (Historical Association pamphlet 1969); C.Holmes, 'The County Community and Stuart Historiography', *J. Brit. Stud.* XIX (1980), 56–73; A.Fletcher, 'National and Local Awareness in County Communities', in H.Tomlinson (ed.), *Before the English Civil War* (1983), pp. 151–74, and especially pp. 151–2.

3. See A.Fletcher, *Reform in the Provinces* (1986), pp. 354–7; for similar problems in an Elizabethan context, see A.Hassell Smith, *County and Court: Government and Politics in Norfolk, 1558–1603* (Oxford, 1974), passim.

4. ibid, pp. 110, 152.

5. B.M.Stowe MSS. 743, fo. III. For some sceptical observations about the efficiency of such supervision, see Fletcher, *Reform*

in the Provinces, especially pp. 6, 47–58, 92–4, 162–5, 208, 215–16, 355–6.

6. Those arguing for the durability and success of the policies before 1640 include T. G. Barnes, *Somerset 1625–1640* (1961), pp. 172–202; K. Sharpe, 'The Personal Rule of Charles I', in Tomlinson (ed.), *Before the English Civil War*, especially pp. 60–1, 65–8; and L. M. Hill, 'County Government in Caroline England 1625–1640', in C. Russell (ed.), *The Origins of the English Civil War*, especially pp. 77–83. Those taking a more sceptical view include Fletcher, *Sussex*, pp. 150–1, 154–5, 157–8, 224–5 and his *Reform in the Provinces*, especially pp. 56–60, 123–5, 128, 132, 206–7, 215–16, 356; P. Clark, *English Provincial Society from the Reformation to the Revolution* (Hassocks 1977), pp. 350–3; J. S. Morrill, *Cheshire 1630–1660* (1974), pp. 26, 230–1; and especially B. W. Quintrell, 'The Making of Charles I's Book of Orders', *Eng. Hist. Rev.*, xcv (1980), 553–72.

7. W. Rye (ed.), *State Papers relating to Musters, Beacons, Ship Money etc. in Norfolk from 1626* . . . (Norwich 1907), pp. 175–7, 180–7.

8. Hassell Smith, *County and Court*, pp. 120–4, 229–34, 245–76.

9. Foster (ed.), *Proceedings in Parliament 1610*, II, 270–1.

10. M. W. Beresford, 'The Common Informer, the Penal Statutes and Economic Regulation', *Econ. Hist. Rev.*, 2nd. ser., x (1957), 233–4.

11. *ibid*, pp. 234–7.

12. *C.D. 1621*, II, 118.

13. *ibid*, v, 482–3. For a similar comment relating to the patent for inns, see *ibid*, II, 182. Although the latter patent did not directly usurp the functions of JPs, it was no less objectionable to them, since innkeeping licences were sometimes issued to former alehouse keepers who had been refused licences by JPs.

14. *ibid*, II, 109–10; v, 252, 479–80.

15. *ibid*, II, 119, 127–33; v, 485–6; vi, 4–5.

16. *ibid*, II, 123–4, 265–6; 91–92; v, 52–53, 311. On the patent, see M. G. Davies, *The Enforcement of English Apprenticeship . . . 1563–1642* (Cambridge, Mass. 1956), pp. 34 and note, 36–7, 75–6.

17. P.R.O., S.P. James I, LXXXVIII/41, 97.

18. W. B. Willcox, *Gloucestershire: A Study in Local Government, 1590–1640* (New Haven 1940), pp. 165–70. For a similar example of the refusal of Yorkshire JPs in the last years of Elizabeth to enforce the statute of 1597 against tenter-frames, see H. Heaton,

The Yorkshire Woollen and Worsted Industries . . . to the Industrial Revolution, 2nd edn. (Oxford 1965), pp. 140–3.

19. Both patents and commissions normally contained the provision that JPs should aid and assist the patentees and their deputies.

20. 'A Declaration of the Grievances of this Kingdome delivered in Parliament by John Pym, ESQUIER, 1642', *Lord Somers' Tracts*, 2nd coll., II, 169.

21. For Heveningham, Hassell Smith, *County and Court*, pp. 259–64, 268, 301; For Mitchell, *C.D. 1621*, III, 224.

22. See G. Scott Thomson, *Lords Lieutenant in the Sixteenth Century* (1923).

23. J. C. Sainty (ed.), *Lieutenants of Counties 1585–1642* (*B.I.H.R.* Special Supplement no. 8) (1970), pp. 3–4.

24. Scott Thomson, op. cit., p. 79.

25. On Provost Marshals see Lambarde in C. Read (ed.), *William Lambarde and Local Government* (Ithaca 1962), p. 107. And for modern accounts, Hassell Smith, op. cit., pp. 131–3; L. Boynton, 'The Tudor Provost-Marshal', *Eng. Hist. Rev.*, LXXVII (1962), 437–55.

26. For examples of these functions, see Scott Thomson, op. cit., pp. 116–21, 126–37; Hassell Smith, op. cit., pp. 63, 129; W. P. D. Murphy (ed.), *The Earl of Hertford's Lieutenancy Papers 1603–1612* (Wilts. Record Soc., XXIII, Devizes 1969), pp. 179 *et seq.*

27. F. W. Jessup, *Sir Roger Twysden 1597–1622* (1965), p. 148; T. G. Barnes, *Somerset 1625–1640* (1961), p. 293.

28. On the social status of lord lieutenants, see Sainty (ed.), op. cit., pp. 4 *et seq.*

29. Murphy (ed.), op. cit., p. 5.

30. I owe this information to the kindness of Dr Hassell Smith.

31. J. Wake (ed.), *A Copy of papers relating to Musters, Beacons, Subsidies, etc. in the County of Northampton A.D. 1586–1623*, Northamptonshire Record Soc., III (Kettering 1926), p. xxii; J. H. Gleason, *The Justices of the Peace in England 1558–1640* (Oxford 1969), p. 73.

32. For Wiltshire, S. J. Sears, 'Conscription and English Society in the 1620s', *J. Brit. Stud.*, XI (1972), 12. For Norfolk, Rye (ed.), *State Papers relating to Musters . . .*, pp. 102–3; R. W. Ketton-Cremer, *Norfolk in the Civil War* (1969), p. 34.

33. Murphy (ed.), op. cit., pp. 97–8, 99–100, 113, 118–19, 138–9, 151–2.

34. For some examples see Murphy (ed.), op. cit., p. 9; J. Wake (ed.), *The Montague Musters Book 1602–1623*, Northants Record

Soc., VII (1935), p. xx; G. Scott Thomson (ed.), *The Twysden Lieu-tenancy Papers 1583-1668*, Kent Arch. Soc. Records Branch, x (1926), p. 9; Sainty, op. cit., pp. 8-9; A. Clark, 'A Lieutenancy Book for Essex', *Essex Rev.*, XVII (1908), 168-9.

35. Murphy (ed.), *Earl of Hertford's Lieutenancy Papers*, p. 4. On this see also Scott Thomson, *Lords Lieutenant*, p. 48; Hassell Smith, *County and Court*, p. 128. C. Russell, *Parliaments and English Politics 1621-1629*, p. 21.

36. *Cal. S.P.D. 1628-9*, pp. 541-2.

37. Scott Thomson, *Lords Lieutenant*, p. 79; Hassell Smith, op. cit., pp. 127, 242; L. Boynton, *The Elizabethan Militia 1558-1638* (1967), pp. 14-15. On militia training in general, see ibid., passim; and Fletcher, *Reform in the Provinces*, pp. 286-316.

38. 4 & 5 Philip and Mary, cc. 2, 3.

39. 1 Jac I, c. 25.

40. C. L. Hamilton (ed.), The Muster-Master by Gervase Mark-ham', *Camden Miscellany XXVI*. Camden Soc., 4th ser. *XIV* (1975), p. 58.

41. P.R.O., S.P. James I, CVIII/62; *Cal. S.P.D. 1619-23*, p. 117; *Cal. S.P.D. 1629-31*, pp. 200, 490; Murphy (ed.), op. cit., pp. 46-7, 107-8; Boynton, *Elizabethan Militia*, p. 227.

42. B.M. Add. MSS., 26,639, fos. 6(b)-7; Rye (ed.), *State Papers relating to Musters . . .* , p. 141.

43. P.R.O., S.P. James I, CVIII/62; *Cal. S.P.D. 1629-31*, p. 451.

44. Murphy (ed.), op. cit., pp. 50, 53-5; Wake (ed.), *Montague Musters Book*, pp. 78-9.

45. Murphy (ed.), op. cit., p. 63. For similar cases in Northampton-shire and Hertfordshire in 1629, see P.R.O., S.P. Charles I, CXLVII/40, 45; *Cal. S.P.D. 1629-31*, pp. 30-1.

46. P.R.O., S.P. Charles I, CCXCVII/15, 15(1).

47. Murphy (ed), op. cit., pp. 30-1, 32-5, 46-7; Willcox, *Gloucester-shire*, p. 83.

48. For Norfolk, see Boynton, op. cit., p. 225. For Gloucestershire, ibid, and Willcox, op. cit., p. 83. For London, C.L.R.O., Jour-nal XXXVIII, fos. 212, 284; Journal XXXIX, fo. 12; Repertory L, fos. 1(b)-2, 155-7; *Cal. S.P.D. 1635-6*, p. 286; *Analytical Index to the Remembrancia . . .* , pp. 536-9. For Durham, *Cal. S.P.D. 1629-31*, p. 200. For Shropshire, *Cal. S.P.D. 1635*, p. 304.

49. On the 'exact militia', see Boynton, op. cit., pp. 244-97. For

an admirable account of local opposition to the idea, see Barnes, *Somerset*, pp. 244–80.

50. Murphy (ed.), op. cit., pp. 102–4. Italics mine.

51. Rye (ed.), op. cit., p. 74.

52. Murphy (ed.), op. cit., pp. 38–9. See also pp. 62–3.

53. S. R. Gardiner, *History of England, 1603–1642*, VI, 219; Rye (ed.), op. cit., p. 141; Willcox, *Gloucestershire*, pp. 98, 105; E. A. Andriette, *Devon and Exeter in the Civil War* (Newton Abbot 1971), pp. 27–8; L. Boynton, 'Billeting: The example of the Isle of Wight', *Eng. Hist. Rev.*, LXXIV (1959), 23–40; G. E. Aylmer, 'St. Patrick's Day 1628 in Witham Essex', *P. & P.*, 61 (1973), 139–48. A study of billeting and free quarter between 1625 and 1649 is being undertaken by Mrs Anne Williams of the University of East Anglia.

54. Bodleian, Rawlinson MSS., A78, fo. 196; MSS. Eng. Hist. c. 330, fos. 55(b)–56; *A.P.C. 1629–30*, pp. 52–53; Rye (ed.), op. cit., pp. 97–8, 141; Gardiner, *History of England, 1603–1642*, VI, 246–8; Andriette, *Devon and Exeter*, p. 28; Barnes, *Somerset*, pp. 255–8; H. Hulme, *Sir John Eliot 1592–1632*, pp. 198–9; Boynton, 'Billeting: the Example of the Isle of Wight'.

55. Bodleian, MSS. Eng. Hist. c. 330, fos. 2, 166(b)–7(b); Rawlinson MSS. A78, fos. 179–9(b); Barnes, *Somerset*, p. 258.

56. L. G. Schwoerer, *'No Standing Armies', The Anti-army Ideology in Seventeenth-Century England* (Baltimore 1974), pp. 19–32; C. Russell, *Parliaments and English Politics*, pp. 17–18, 324–5, 333, 337, 359.

57. *Cal. S.P.D. 1623–5*, p. 416; Rye (ed.), op. cit., p. 206.

58. On the Council of the North, see especially R. R. Reid, *The King's Council in the North* (1921) and F. W. Brooks, *The Council of the North* (Hist. Assoc. Pamphlet, 1953). On the Council of the Marches, P. Williams, *The Council in the Marches of Wales under Elizabeth I* (Cardiff 1958), and especially 'The Attack on The Council in the Marches, 1603–1642', *Trans. Hon. Soc. Cymmrodorion* (1961), pp. 1–22. For an example of conciliar jurisdiction in the border counties, see Willcox, *Gloucestershire*, pp. 22–8.

59. E. R. Foster (ed.), *Proceedings in Parliament 1610*, II, 261–3, 353–4, 396.

60. Cited in Williams, *The Council in the Marches of Wales under Elizabeth I*, p. 324.

61. Clarendon, *Great Rebellion*, I, 315–18. J. T. Cliffe, *The Yorkshire*

Gentry from the Reformation to the Civil War (1969), pp. 295, 299, 301, 326.

62. On Somerset, Barnes, *Somerset*, p. 204. On London, C.L.R.O. Journal XXXVII, fos. 12-12(b), 19-20; Repertory XLIX, fos. 18, 18(b), 45-6, 46(b), 97(b)-8(b).

63. P.R.O., P.C. 2/XLVIII, fos. 528-9; *Cal S.P.D. 1635*, pp. 446, 560; P. Lake, 'The Collection of Ship Money in Cheshire during the Sixteen-Thirties', *Northern History* XVII (1981), pp. 252-70.

64. For specific charges of inequitable assessments, see W. Prynne, *An Humble Remonstrance to his Maiesty against the Tax of Ship Money* (1641), p. 23; *Cal. S.P.D. 1637*, pp. 52, 208-9 (Huntingdonshire); P.R.O., P.C. 2/L, fos. 396-7 (Oxfordshire); H. Stocks (ed.), *Records of the Borough of Leicester ... 1603-1688* (Cambridge 1923), doc. CCCCII.

65. M. D. Gordon, 'The Collection of Ship Money in the Reign of Charles I', *Roy. Hist. Soc. Trans.*, 3rd ser., IV (1910), 141-62, and especially 145-51.

66. Barnes, *Somerset*, pp. 211-14, 217-18.

67. For examples from Gloucestershire, see Willcox, *Gloucestershire*, p. 128; Somerset, Barnes, op. cit., pp. 204, 209-10, 214-19; Cheshire, J. S. Morrill, *Cheshire 1630-1660* (1974), pp. 29-30. For the cases of Essex and Northamptonshire, A. Clark, *Essex Review*, loc. cit., p. 159: P.R.O. P.C. 2/LI, fos. 313,355-6; *Cal. S.P.D. 1639-40*, p. 527.

68. *Cal. S.P.D. 1636-7*, p. 181.

69. P.R.O., P.C. 2/XLIX, fos. 140-1.

70. Barnes, *Somerset*, pp. 204, 214-16.

71. P.R.O., 2/XLVIII, fos. 28, 484-5.

72. P.R.O., 2/XLIX, fo. 373; P.C. 2/L, fo. 48.

73. V. L. Pearl, *London and the Origins of the Puritan Revolution* (1961), pp. 88-9. For a different view, see R. Ashton, *The City and the Court 1603-1643* (Cambridge, 1979), pp. 185-8.

74. P.R.O., P.C. 2/XLVIII, fos. 517-18; P.C. 2/LII, fos. 559, 620; C.L.R.O. Repertory L, fos. 75-75(b); Repertory LI, fos. 68(b)-9; Repertory LII, fos. 70-70(b); Repertory LIII, fos. 81, 142(b), 232, 317(b); Bodleian, Tanner MSS., 65, fo. 93; Bankes MSS., 5/41; *Cal. S.P.D. 1637-8*, p. 165; *H.M.C. XIIth Rep.*, II, 175; IV, 521.

75. Barnes, *Somerset*, pp. 255, 261, 263-71, 281-98.

76. On Wiltshire, Murphy (ed.), *Earl of Hertford's Lieutenancy Papers*,

pp. 49–50. On Northamptonshire, P.R.O., S.P. Charles I, CXLVII/40, 45; Wake (ed.), *The Montagu Musters Book*, p. 80. On Suffolk and Dorset, P.R.O., S.P. Charles I, VI/16. On Gloucestershire, Willcox, *Gloucestershire*, pp. 82–83. On Norfolk, Rye (ed.), *State Papers relating to Musters* . . . , p. 172. On Herefordshire, P.R.O., S.P. Charles I, CCXXVII/15, 15(i). On Bedfordshire, *Cal. S.P.D. 1635*, pp. 411–12. On Durham, *Cal. S.P.D. 1629–31*, p. 200. On other northern counties, *Cal. S.P.D. 1638–9*, pp. 310, 468–9, 561; Cliffe, *Yorkshire Gentry*, pp. 313–4. For examples in the matters of billeting and coat and conduct money, see Boynton, *Eng. Hist. Rev.*, LXXIV, 29–30; *Cal. S.P.D. 1640*, pp. 154–5.

77. See especially W.K.Jordan, *Philanthropy in England 1480–1660* (1959).

78. W.K.Jordan, *The Charities of London 1480–1660* (1960), pp. 48–9.

79. V.Morgan, 'Cambridge University and "The Country"', in L.Stone (ed.), *The University in Society* (Princeton 1974), I, pp. 183–245.

80. W.R.Prest, *The Inns of Court under Elizabeth I and the Early Stuarts* (1972), pp. 32–40.

81. A.Harding, *A Social History of English Law* (1966), p. 250.

82. *C.D. 1621*, II, 75–8; IV, 49–50.

83. ibid., II, 366–7; III, 255–9; IV, 352–5; V, 121–3, 356; [Edward Nicholas], *Proceedings and Debates* . . . (ed. Tyrwhitt), (1766), I, 360–2.

84. *H. of Commons J.*, I, 635; *C.D. 1621*, III, 287.

85. Foster (ed.), *Proceedings in Parliament, 1610*, II, 261–3.

86. For an interesting contribution to this problem, see D.Brentnall, *Regional Influences in the House of Commons 1604–1660*, University of East Anglia, M.Phil. thesis (1980).

CHAPTER 4   GENTLEMEN AND BOURGEOIS

1. *A moderate and most proper reply to a declaration* (1642) [Wing 2321], no pagination.

2. Bodleian, MSS. Add. C., 132.

3. *Harleian Miscellany* (1809), IV, 352.

4. *Lord Somers' Tracts*, 2nd coll., II (1750), 167. On the threat to private property which would result from a royalist victory, see 'The Vindication of the Parliament and their Proceedings', *Harleian Miscellany*, V (1810), 286, 298.

5. K. Marx and F. Engels, *Manifesto of the Communist Party*, ed. F. Engels, trans. S. Moore (1888), p. 14.

6. On Harrington see James Harrington, *Commonwealth of Oceana*, ed. S. B. Lilijegren (Heidelberg 1924); P. Zagorin, *A History of Political Thought in the English Revolution* (1954), pp. 132–45; R. H. Tawney, 'Harrington's Interpretation of His Age', *Procs. of Brit. Academy*, XXVII (1941), 199–224.

7. H. R. Trevor-Roper, 'The Gentry 1540–1640', *Econ. Hist. Rev. Supplement*, 1 (n.d.), pp. 44–50.

8. C. H. Firth, *Essays Historical and Literary* (Oxford 1938), pp. 103–28, C. Hill, *Puritanism and Revolution* (1958), pp. 199–214.

9. C. V. Wedgwood, *The King's Peace 1637–1641* (1956 edn.); *The King's War 1641–1647* (1966 edn.).

10. Stone's two chief contributions are his massive *The Crisis of the Aristocracy 1556–1641* (Oxford 1965), and his brief but suggestive *The Causes of the English Revolution 1529–1642* [hereafter *English Revolution*] (1972). Trevor-Roper's (Lord Dacre's) views are scattered over many places, but see especially his *The Gentry 1540–1640*, and 'La Révolution Anglaise de Cromwell', *Annales, Economies, Sociétés, Civilisations*, x (1955), 331–40: also his brilliant 'The General Crisis of the Seventeenth Century', *P & P.*, 16 (1959).

11. L. Stone, *English Revolution*, pp. 33–4, 146.

12. R. H. Tawney, 'The Rise of the Gentry 1560–1640', *Econ. Hist. Rev.*, XI (1941), 18. Prof. Tawney was even more emphatic in his Introduction to D. Brunton and D. H. Pennington, *Members of the Long Parliament* (1954), pp. xix–xxi.

13. This is a summary view of the definition given by C. Hill, *The English Revolution 1640* (1955 edn.), p. 4.

14. This passage summarizes the argument developed at greater length in my 'Cavaliers and Capitalists', *Ren. and Mod. Stud.*, v (1961), 158–9; and 'The Civil War and the Class Struggle' in R. H. Parry (ed.), *The Egnlish Civil War and After 1642–1658* (1970), pp. 99–102.

15. For excellent examples, see M. E. Finch, *The Wealth of Five Northamptonshire Families 1540–1640* (Oxford 1956), *passim*; A. Simpson, *The Wealth of the Gentry 1540–1640: East Anglian Studies* (Cambridge 1961), pp. 179–216; J. T. Cliffe, *The Yorkshire Gentry from the Reformation to the Civil War* (1969), pp. 34, 49–57, 95–8.

16. For examples, see G. E. Aylmer, *The King's Servants: The Civil Service of Charles I 1625–1642* (1961), pp. 283–4.

17. For full details and Dr Aylmer's calculations, see ibid., pp. 322-36.

18. Everitt, *Kent, passim*; *Suffolk*, pp. 13-14; C. Holmes, *The Eastern Association in the English Civil War* (Cambridge 1974), pp. 34 *et. seq.* ; Underdown, *Somerset, passim*.

19. D. Brunton and D. H. Pennington, op. cit., pp. 19-20.

20. Pennington and Roots, *Stafford*, pp. xvii-xxii; Clarendon, *Great Rebellion*, II, 449 (bk. VI, para. 240); [J. Corbet?], *An historical relation of the military government of Gloucester* (1645), p. 17; Everitt, *Suffolk*, pp. 17-20; Everitt, *The Local Community and the Great Rebellion* (Hist. Ass. pamphlet, 1969), pp. 14-22; A. C. Wood, *Nottinghamshire in the Civil War* (Oxford 1937), pp. 33-4; Cliffe, op. cit., pp. 351-6; Morrill, *Cheshire 1630-1660* (1974), p. 71; R. N. Dore, *The Civil Wars in Cheshire* (Chester 1966), p. 21.

21. Cliffe, op. cit., pp. 341-2, 352-5; Everitt, *Kent*, pp. 116-24.

22. M. F. Keeler, *The Long Parliament 1640-1641* (Philadelphia 1954), pp. 22, 23.

23. Aylmer, *King's Servants*, pp. 337-421; 'Attempts at Administrative Reform 1625-1640', *Eng. Hist. Rev.*, LXXII (1957), 229-59; 'Charles I's Commission on Fees 1627-40', *B.I.H.R.*, XXXI (1958), 58-67.

24. Misuse of statistical method is no less of a danger. It has been argued that economic mobility was a crucial determinant of the political affiliation and ultimate allegiance of members of the Long Parliament: viz. that 70 per cent of those MPs experiencing upward mobility supported Parliament in the war as against only 27 per cent who supported the king. Conversely, 75 per cent of those experiencing downward mobility supported the king as against only 25 per cent who supported Parliament. But these figures are open to serious question on the grounds both that the evidence on which they are based is a great deal less than conclusive, and that, even if it were, the statistical inferences drawn from it are not unchallengeable, for a statistical correlation is not *per se* proof of a causal relationship. On this see S. D. Antler, 'Quantitative Analysis of the Long Parliament', *P. & P.* 56 (1972), 154-7, and R. S. Schofield in *P. & P.* 68 (1975), 124-9.

25. Clarendon, *Great Rebellion*, II, 296. See also Underdown, *Somerset*, pp. 39-40.

26. Morrill, *Cheshire*, p. 70; Everitt, *Kent*, pp. 117-19; Holmes, *Eastern Association*, p. 14; Cliffe, *Yorkshire Gentry*, pp. 357-8.

27. For the 'industrious sort of people', see C. Hill, *Society and Purita-*

nism in Pre-Revolutionary England (1964), pp. 124–44. For a more detailed version of my argument, see R. Ashton, 'Puritanism and Progress', *Econ. Hist. Rev.*, 2nd ser., XVII (1965), especially 585–6.

28. Clarendon, *Great Rebellion*, II, 464; Cliffe, op. cit., pp. 339–40; Underdown, *Somerset*, pp. 39–40; J. de L. Mann, *The Cloth Industry in the West of England from 1640 to 1880* (Oxford 1971), p. 4; G. D. Ramsay, *The Wiltshire Woollen Industry in the Sixteenth and Seventeenth Centuries*, 2nd edn. (1965), p. 113.

29. For Underdown's views, see D. Underdown, *Revel, Riot and Rebellion. Popular Politics and Culture in England 1603–1660* (Oxford 1985), passim, and 'The Problem of Popular Sovereignty in the English Civil War', *Roy. Hist. Soc. Trans.*, 5th ser. XXXI (1981), 69–94, and 'The Taming of the Scold: the Enforcement of Patriarchal Authority in Early Modern England', in A. Fletcher and J. Stevenson (eds.), *Order and Disorder in Early Modern England* (Cambridge 1985), pp. 116–36. For their applicability to neutralism, see below, pp. 261–2. For the connection between popular culture and religious affiliation, see below, p. 106. For some penetrating criticism of these views, see J. Morrill, 'The Ecology of Allegiance in the English Revolution', *J. Brit. Stud.* XXVI (1987), 451–67, and for Underdown's reply, 'A Reply to John Morrill', ibid., pp. 468–79. Of course, in East Anglia textile production was by no means confined to wood pasture areas, though very prominent there.

30. See eg. K. Wrightson and D. Levine, *Poverty and Piety in an English Village: Terling 1525–1700* (New York 1979). But see also M. Spufford, 'Puritanism and Social Control', in Fletcher and Stevenson (eds.), op. cit., pp. 41–57.

31. J. Corbet, *An historical account of the military government of Gloucester* (1645), pp. 9, 14, 17.

32. The next two sections summarize material and arguments which are developed in greater detail in R. Ashton, *The City and the Court 1603–1643* (Cambridge 1979), passim, and 'Charles I and the City' in F. J. Fisher (ed.), *Essays in the Economic and Social History of Tudor and Stuart England* (Cambridge 1961), pp. 138–63.

33. R. Brenner, 'The Civil War Politics of London's Merchant Community', *P. & P.*, 58 (1973), especially pp. 72–85.

34. For more detailed treatment of this problem, see my 'Conflicts of Concessionary Interest in Early Stuart England' in D. C.

Coleman and A.H.John (eds.), *Trade, Government and Economy in Pre-Industrial England* (1976), pp. 113-31.

35. Ashton, 'Charles I and the City' in Fisher (ed.), *Essays*, p. 156; L.Stone, *The Crisis of the Aristocracy 1558-1641*, p. 432.

36. Evidence in B.M., Lansdowne MSS., 152, fo. 231; Lansdowne MSS., 160, fos. 291-304(b); Harleian MSS., 1878, fos. 79-80; P.R.O., S.P. James I, XIII/70, XVIII/127-8, XXII/23; S.P. Charles I, XCIV/107; P.C. 2/XLII, fos. 87, 294; *Cal. S.P.D. 1611-18*, p. 476; *Cal. S.P.D. 1625-6*, pp. 99, 376, 407; *Cal. S.P.D. 1629-31*, p. 496; *Cal. S.P.D. 1635*, pp. 311-12, 513; *Cal. S.P.D. 1637*, pp. 53-4, 100, 480, 513; *Cal. S.P.D. 1639*, pp. 45, 363-4; *Cal. S.P. East Indies and Persia 1630-4*, pp. 266, 273, 289, 315, 317-19; *A.P.C. 1629-30*, p. 201; W.Foster (ed.), *Court Minutes East India Company 1635-9*, pp. 49-50, 76, 101-2, 131-2; *C.D. 1621*, II, 371-2; III, 50-1, 232-3; VII, 455-7; *H.M.C. Salisbury MSS.*, XVI, 380-1; Ashton, 'Charles I and the City' in Fisher (ed.), *Essays*, pp. 142-5.

37. *H. of Commons J.*, I, 595; *C.D. 1621*, IV, 408.

38. On the companies and the 1624 parliament see *H. of Commons J.*, I, 672, 676, 681, 689, 695, 698-9, 702, 706, 710-12, 717, 754, 758-9, 771, 773-4, 780-1, 783-4, 787, 793-6; A.Friis, *Alderman Cockayne's Project and the Cloth Trade* (1927), pp. 428-31; R.W.K.Hinton, *The Eastland Trade and the Common Weal in the Seventeenth Century* (Cambridge 1959), pp. 64-5; R.Ashton, *The City and the Court*, pp. 112-16, 118-20.

39. 21 and 22 Jac. I. cap 3.

40. *A.P.C. 1625-6*, pp. 122, 125-6; *Cal. S.P. East Indies 1625-9*, pp. 489, 490, 491, 492-3, 496; *H. of Commons J.*, I, 893; London Guildhall, *The Petition and Remonstrance of the Governor and Company ... Trading to the East Indies exhibited to the honorable House of Commons ... Anno 1628*; W.Lefroy (ed.), *Memorials of the Discovery and Early Settlement of the Bermudas or Somers Islands 1615-1685* (1877), I, 439-40, 480; W.R.Scott, *Joint Stock Companies* (Cambridge 1912), II, 291-2.

41. On Ormuz, *Cal. S.P. East Indies 1625-9*, pp. 174-5; Gardiner, *Constitutional Documents*, pp. 12-14. On the French company, see S.R.Gardiner, *History 1603-1642*, VI, 39-48, 65-7, 88-9, 145-8.

42. On these incidents concerning the East India Company, see my 'Charles I and the City' in Fisher (ed.), *Essays*, pp. 154-5, 156-9, and *The City and the Court*, pp. 125-9, 139-41.

43. For this view see Brenner, 'Civil War Politics ...', *passim*. It

is more cautiously advanced by Pearl, *London and the Outbreak of the Puritan Revolution* (1961), p. 92 and note.

44. P.R.O., S.P. Charles I, CXL/24; *Cal. S.P.D. 1628–9*, pp. 507, 524, 550; *A.P.C. 1628–9*, pp. 123, 154–5, 292–3, 295, 356–7; *Cal. S.P. Ven. 1629–32*, pp. 7, 8, 19, 29, 44–5, 56, 75, 178, 290; *H. of Commons J.*, I, 929, 930, 931, 932; *C.D. 1629*, pp. 60–3, 73–4, 93–5, 102–3, 140–4, 155–61, 162–71, 195–201, 217–18, 221–4, 225–38, 241–2, 259–61; Gardiner, *History 1603–1642*, VII, 1–7, 31–7, 57–65, 82–7; Gardiner, *Constitutional Documents*, p. 83.

45. The evidence is reviewed in my article in Fisher (ed.), *Essays*, pp. 138–63, and in *The City and the Court*, pp. 135–41.

46. e.g. the hostility of the Eastland and Greenland Companies to the soapboiling monopolies of the 1630s. See ibid., p. 142, and Scott, *Joint Stock Companies*, II, pp. 71–2; Hinton, *Eastland Trade*, p. 45.

47. The aldermen listed in the first biographical appendix in Pearl, *London . . .* , pp. 285–308.

48. I attempt a much more detailed account of these disputes in Chapters V and VI of *The City and the Court*.

49. C.L.R.O., Journal XXXVII, fos. 345–5(b); Journal XXXVIII, fo. 103(b).

50. For the Londonderry plantation, see T. W. Moody, *The Londonderry Plantation 1609–1641* (Belfast 1939), passim; also *Londonderry and the London Companies 1609–1629, being a Survey and other Documents submitted to King Charles I by Sir Thomas Phillips* (Belfast 1928), passim.

51. R. Ashton, *The Crown and the Money Market 1603–1640* (Oxford 1960), pp. 142–53.

52. P.R.O., S.P. James I, LII/42, LXXVI/10–15; S.P. Charles I, CCCXLVIII/44, CCCLXXVII/107; C.L.R.O., Journal XXXVII, fos. 202–2(b), 345–5(b); Journal XXXVIII, fo. 103(b); Repertory XXIX, fos. 212(b), 219(b)–20, 222(b), 226(b)–7; Repertory XXXI, pt. ii, fos. 290(b)–1, 322(b); Repertory XXXIV, fos. 195(b)–6; Repertory XLII, fos. 3, 10(b), 13–13(b), 58(b), 296(b)–7; Repertory XLIII, fos. 23–23(b), 47(b), 83, 95(b), 107; Repertory XLIV, fos. 89(b)–90, 115–115(b); Repertory XLVI, fo. 220(b); Repertory LIII, fos. 50(b), 130–130(b); Pearl, *London . . .* , pp. 21–2, 84–5.

53. Pearl, op. cit., pp. 81–7.

54. A detailed treatment of these problems and full supporting references are provided in Chapter II of *The City and the Court 1603–*

1643. See also G. Unwin, *Industrial Organization in the Sixteenth and Seventeenth Centuries* (1957 edn.), pp. 126–47, 152–69, and *The Gilds and Companies of London* (1963 edn.), pp. 304–6, 315–16, 319–21.

55. P.R.O., S.P. Charles I, CCXXV/71, CCL/51; P.C. 2/XLVII, fos. 242–3, 254–5; P.C. 2/XLVIII, fo. 356; P.C. 2/XLIX, fos. 137, 211; P.C. 2/L, fo. 173; Bodleian, Bankes MSS., XII/46; C.L.R.O., Repertory XLVI, fos. 330–330(b); Repertory L, fos. 151(b), 191(b), 205(b); Repertory LIII, fos. 28–28(b); Repertory LIV, fos. 322–2(b); *Cal. S.P.D. 1635–6*, pp. 359–60; *Cal. S.P.D. 1636–7*, p. 10; *Cal. S.P.D. 1637–8*, pp. 19, 417; *Cal. S.P.D. 1638–9*, p. 20; *Remembrancia Index*, pp. 227–9; N. G. Brett-James, *The Growth of Stuart London* (1935), pp. 223–47; Pearl, op. cit., pp. 31–7; Ashton, *The City and the Court*, pp. 164–7.

56. C.L.R.O., Repertory XXXIV, fos. 202, 223, 238(b)–9(b); Repertory XXXV, fos. 155–5(b); Repertory XLVII, fo. 9; *C.D. 1621*, VI, 24, 292; Pearl, op. cit., pp. 20–1; Ashton, *The City and the Court*, pp. 167–71.

57. See pp. 62, 64. For the 1626 levy, see M. C. Wren, 'London and the Twenty Ships, 1626–7', *Amer. Hist. Rev.*, LV (1950), 321–35.

58. P.R.O., S.P. Charles I, LXXI/39, 59; LXII/60, 63–5; *Cal. S.P.D. 1627–8*, pp. 253, 262, 275; *Cal. S.P.D. Addenda 1625–49*, p. 178; *A.P.C. 1627*, pp. 208–9; *Remembrancia Index*, p. 195; R. R. Sharpe, *London and the Kingdom* (1894), II, 102–3; Pearl, *London . . .* , pp. 74–5; D. A. Kirby, 'The Radicals of St. Stephen's Coleman Street, London 1624–1642', *Guildhall Miscellany*, III (1970), 105–6.

59. C.L.R.O., Journal XXXVIII, fos. 212, 284; Journal XXXIX, fo. 12(b); Repertory L, fos. 1(b)–2, 155, 157; *Cal. S.P.D. 1635–6*, p. 286; *Remembrancia Index*, pp. 536–9; A. Raikes, *A History of the Honourable Artillery Company* (1878), I, 92–3, 107–9.

60. C.L.R.O., Repertory XLV, fos. 499–500(b), 514; Repertory XLVI, fo. 203; Repertory XLVII, fos. 210–210(b); Repertory XLVIII, fos. 320–1(b); Remembrancia VIII, 85, 122; *Remembrancia Index*, pp. 327–9; W. S. Simpson (ed.), *Documents illustrating the History of St. Paul's Cathedral*, Camden Soc. new ser. XXVI (1880), 134–5; H. R. Trevor-Roper, *Archbishop Laud* (2nd edn., 1963), pp. 121–6, 346–7, 350–1, 428–9; W. K. Jordan, *The Charities of London 1480–1660* (1960), pp. 270, 297, 301, 304–5; Ashton, *The City and the Court*, pp. 196–8; D. A. Williams, 'Puritanism in the City Government 1610–1640', *Guildhall Miscellany*, I (1955), 2–14.

61. Ashton, *The Crown and the Money Market*, pp. 180–4.

62. See below, pp. 133-4, 172-3.
63. R. Howell, *Newcastle upon Tyne and the Puritan Revolution* (Oxford, 1967), especially pp. 35-62; A. M. Johnson, 'Politics in Chester during the Civil Wars and the Interregnum', in P. Clark and P. Slack (eds.), *Crisis and Order in English Towns 1500-1700* (1972), especially pp. 204-10.

CHAPTER 5   RELIGION AND POLITICS

1. Bodleian, Tanner MSS. 65, fo. 179.
2. For Bowles, see [Edward Bowles], *Manifest Truths* (1646), fos. 50-51. For a similar view, see *Harleian Miscellany* v (1810), 34-36. For Cromwell, see W. C. Abbott (ed.), *The Writings and Speeches of Oliver Cromwell* (Cambridge, Mass. 1937-47), III, 586, cited by B. Manning (ed.), *Politics, Religion and the English Civil War* (1973), p. 85.
3. J. Stephens, 'Fundamental errors of the Presbyterians' (1650), Bodleian, Bodley MSS. 307, fo. 38; Sir William Morton, 'Ius Monarchiae Angliae' (c. 1660), Bodleian, Clarendon MSS, 132, fo. 6(b).
4. A. Peel (ed.), *The Notebook of John Penry 1593*, Camden Soc. 3rd. ser. LXVII (1944), 85-93. See C. Hill, *Economic Problems of the Church* (Oxford 1950), pp. 42-45.
5. J. Morrill, 'The Religious Context of the English Civil War', *Roy. Hist. Soc. Trans.*, 5th ser. XXXIV (1984), 155-78.
6. On this tradition, see W. Haller, *Foxe's Book of Martyrs and the Elect Nation* (1967 edn.) and W. M. Lamont, *Godly Rule* (1969), especially pp. 17-73. On the rôle of bishops in general, see P. Collinson, *The Religion of Protestants 1559-1625*, (Oxford 1984 edn.), pp. 1-91.
7. B.M., Stowe MSS., 184, fo. 28(b).
8. See pp. 153-5.
9. On Prynne, see W. M. Lamont, *Marginal Prynne 1600-1669* (1963).
10. S. R. Gardiner (ed.), *Documents relating to the Proceedings against William Prynne in 1634 and 1637*, Camden Soc., new ser., XVIII (1877), 16. For similar views expressed by other councillors, see ibid., pp. 21-2, 23, 24, 26-7.
11. M. Walzer, *The Revolution of the Saints* (1966), p. 2.
12. ibid., pp. 13-14, 32-3, 47-51, 186-9. See above, pp. 4-9.
13. Parker's ideas below are drawn from Henry Parker, *Observations vpon some of his Majesties late answeres* (1642), pp. 18-19; cf. *The Cor-*

diall of Mr. David Jenkins or his reply to H.P. . . . answered (1647), p. 7. The last point is made even more emphatically in *Maximes unfolded* (1643) [Wing 1375], pp. 19–20.

14. *Some speciall arguments for the Scottish subjects* (1642) [Wing 619], no pagination.

15. *The Cordiall of Mr. David Jenkins . . . answered*, p. 22.

16. It must be apparent that I follow the thesis of W. M. Lamont rather than that of M. Walzer in this matter. For a particularly acute criticism of Walzer's arguments along these lines, see W. M. Lamont, 'Puritanism as History and Historiography', *P. & P.*, 44 (1969), 137–9. For a salutary emphasis on the conservative, rather than revolutionary, social implications of Puritanism, see P. Collinson, *The Religion of Protestants*, especially ch. IV.

17. Walzer, *Revolution of the Saints*, p. 14; cf. C. Hill, *Economic Problems of the Church*, pp. 108–9.

18. E. Cardwell (ed.), *Documentary Annals of the Reformed Church of England* (Oxford 1844), II, 201–6. For a similar view by Francis Bacon, see F. Bacon, *Works* (1824 edn.), II, 521: cf. T. Hobbes, 'Behemoth, or an epitome of the civil wars' in Maseres, *Select Tracts*, II, 508, 511–12, 523.

19. *His Majestie's declaration to all his loving subjects of August 12, 1642* [Wing 2241], (Cambridge 1642), p. 21.

20. C. H. George, 'A Social Interpretation of English Puritanism', *J. Mod. Hist.*, XXV (1953), 327–42.

21. C. Hill, *Puritanism and Revolution* (1958), p. 216.

22. ibid., p. 236; italics author's. For a similar view of Perkins' thought and that of other contemporary Puritans, see M. M. Knappen, *Tudor Puritanism* (1965 edn.), pp. 412–4.

23. M. Weber, *The Protestant Ethic and the Spirit of Capitalism* (1968 edn.), passim.

24. Robert Sanderson, *XXXVI Sermons* (1689), p. 215, cit. C. H. and K. George, *The Protestant Mind of the English Reformation 1570–1640* (Princeton 1961), p. 127.

25. W. Perkins, 'A Grain of Mustard Seed', in I. Breward (ed.), *The Work of William Perkins* (Appleford 1970), p. 408.

26. George Herbert, 'The Elixir'. Herbert also stated that '*Idleness is twofold* the one in *having no calling*, the other in *walking carelessly in our calling*'. ('A Priest to the Temple', in *Works* (1859 edn.), I, 239.)

27. W. Perkins, 'A treatise of the Vocations or Callings of Men',

380 NOTES TO PAGES 103-6

in Breward (ed.), op. cit., pp. 455-6. 'An Instruction touching Religious or Divine Worship', in ibid., pp. 318-20. For Hill's arguments about this and similar notions, see C. Hill, *Puritanism and Revolution*, pp. 215-38.

28. W. Perkins, 'A Dialogue out of the State of a Christian Man', in Breward (ed.), op. cit., pp. 383-4.

29. For these views, see R. H. Tawney, *Religion and the Rise of Capitalism* (1944 edn.), pp. 215-18; R. Ashton, 'Usury and High Finance in the Age of Shakespeare and Jonson', *Ren. and Mod. Stud.*, IV (1960), 23-6.

30. Roger Fenton, *A Treatise of Usurie* (1612), p. 61.

31. For a very different view, see P. White, 'The Rise of Arminianism Reconsidered' *P. & P.* 101 (1983), 34-54, *P. & P.* 115. (1987), 217-29. For restatements of the view equating Calvinism with orthodoxy, see P. Collinson *The Religion of Protestants*, especially pp. 81-83, 177-82, 187-8; P. G. Lake 'Calvinism and the English Church, 1570-1635', *P. & P.* 114 (1987), 32-76; N. Tyacke, 'Debate: The Rise of Arminianism Reconsidered'. *P. & P.* 115 (1987), 201-16, and *Anti-Calvinists. The Rise of English Arminianism c. 1590-1640* (Oxford 1987).

32. H. R. Trevor-Roper, 'The Social Origins of the Great Rebellion', *History Today*, V (1955), 379. See also the same author's 'The Gentry 1540-1640', *Econ. Hist. Rev. supplement*, I (n.d.), pp. 30-31, and 'The General Crisis of the Seventeenth Century', *P. & P.*, 16 (1959), 50, 60.

33. D. Brunton and D. H. Pennington, *Members of the Long Parliament* (1954), p. 5; W. Prest, *The Rise of the Barristers. A Social History of the English Bar 1590-1640* (Oxford, 1986), pp. 274-6. On lawyers and politics, see ibid., pp. 256-82; J. D. Eusden, *Puritans, Lawyers and Politics in Early Seventeenth Century England* (1968), especially pp. 86-94; B. P. Levack, *The Civil Lawyers in England 1603-1641* (Oxford, 1973), especially pp. 1, 50, 72-81, 157-60, 167, 172-3, 177-8, 196-8; C. Hill, *Intellectual Origins of the English Revolution* (Oxford, 1965), pp. 247-50.

34. On the south-west, see D. Underdown, *Revel, Riot and Rebellion. Popular Culture and Politics in England 1603-1660* (Oxford 1985), especially pp. 44-105; T. G. Barnes, 'County Politics and a Puritan Cause Célèbre: Somerset Church Ales, 1633', *Roy. Hist. Soc. Trans.* 5th ser. IX (1959), 103-22. For other examples, see C. Hill, *Society and Puritanism in Pre-Revolutionary England*,

especially pp. 166–76, 182–202, 242–9; P. Collinson, *The Religion of Protestants*, pp. 145–9, 170–1, 203–17, 220–41; P. Clark, '"The Ramoth Gilead of the Good": Urban Change and Political Radicalism at Gloucester 1540–1640', in P. Clark, A. G. R. Smith and N. Tyacke (eds.), *The English Commonwealth 1547–1640* (Leicester 1979), pp. 167–87, and especially pp. 181–7: W. Hunt, *The Puritan Moment. The Coming of Revolution in an English County* (1983), especially pp. 130–55. Prof. Hunt's account of Essex Puritanism draws heavily on the conclusions of a seminal Cambridge Ph.D. thesis by K. Wrightson, 'The Puritan Reformation of Manners' (1973). See also K. Wrightson and D. Levine, *Poverty and Piety in an English Village: Terling 1525–1700* (1979). For some refreshing scepticism about the alleged uniqueness of Puritan social control and about the notion that Puritanism was simply a discipline imposed on the lower orders from above, see the admirable essay by M. Spufford, 'Puritanism and Social Control', in A. Fletcher and J. Stevenson (eds.), *Order and Disorder in Early Modern England* (Cambridge 1985), pp. 41–57.

35. Hassell Smith, *County and Court: Government and Politics in Norfolk, 1558–1603* (Oxford 1974), pp. 283–4, 317, 338–40; Walzer, *Revolution of the Saints*, p. 187.

36. Thomas Scot, *The High-Waies of God and the King* (1623), p. 83. I am grateful to Mr V. Morgan for drawing my attention to this sermon.

37. Thomas Scot, *The Proiector* (1623), p. 21; cf. *The High-Waies of God and the King*, pp. 79–80, where Scot denounces 'the Courtly Thief, who begges a Patent'.

38. W. Prynne, *An Humble Remonstrance to his Maiesty against the Tax of Ship Money* (1641).

39. Lamont, *Marginal Prynne*, p. 15.

40. *Cal. S.P.D. 1637*, p. 52.

41. P.R.O., P.C. 2/49, fos. 15–16, 103; *Cal. S.P.D. 1637–8*, p. 285. For Sibthorpe, Puritans and Ship Money, see *Cal. S.P.D. 1639*, p. 23.

42. *Cal. S.P.D. 1639–40*, p. 246.

43. T. G. Barnes, *Somerset 1625–1640* (1961), p. 277; R. W. Ketton-Cremer, *Norfolk in the Civil War* (1969), pp. 100–2; R. Howell, *Newcastle upon Tyne and the Puritan Revolution* (Oxford 1967), pp. 116–17.

44. Scot, *The Proiector*, pp. 6, 19. On godly magistracy, see P. Collin-

son, *The Religion of Protestants*, pp. 141–88. For another example, see R. Cust and P. G. Lake, 'Sir Richard Grosvenor and the Rhetoric of Magistracy', *B.I.H.R.* LIX (1981), 40–53.

45. Levack, op. cit., pp. 186–95.

46. Clarendon, *Great Rebellion*, I, 241.

47. On Preston, see I. Morgan, *Prince Charles's Puritan Chaplain* (1957); C. Hill, *Puritanism and Revolution*, pp. 239–74.

48. Lamont, *Godly Rule*, pp. 68–70.

49. Bodleian, Tanner MSS., 65, fos. 236–6(b); D'Ewes, *Journal* (ed. Notestein), p. 169.

50. William Laud, *A Relation of the Conference between William Laud ... and Mr. Fisher the Jesuit* [hereafter *Relation of the Conference*], ed. C. H. Simpkinson (1901), Epistle dedicatory to the King, p. xxx.

51. George Herbert, 'The British Church'.

52. *The Correspondence of John Cosin, D.D.*, Surtees Soc., LII (1862), pt. i, p. 21.

53. Laud, *Relation of the Conference*, Epistle dedicatory, p. xxvi.

54. J. Ley, *A Discourse Concerning Puritans. A Vindication* ... (1641) [Wing 1875].

55. Gardiner, *Constitutional Documents*, pp. 77–82.

56. B.M., Add. MSS., 29,975, fo. 128(b). For other statements of this view, see e.g. *The humble petition of Nottinghamshire men to the King the 30th of August 1642* [Wing 1413], pp. 2–3; D. Gardiner (ed.), *The Oxinden Letters 1607–1642* (1933), p. 163; Gardiner, *Constitutional Documents*, pp. 203–4; *Harleian Miscellany*, IV (1809), p. 469; *Reasons why the kingdome ought to adhere to the Parliament* (1642) [Wing 592], p. 6; *The second part of Vox Populi* (1642) [Wing 2323], sig. B3; *A declaration and vindication of John Pym* (1643) [Wing 4259], p. 5.

57. Laud, *Relation of the Conference*, p. xxix.

58. ibid., pp. 146–52.

59. R. Montague, *A gag for the new gospel! No! a new gag for an old goose* (1624). On the Montague controversy, see Tyacke, *Anti-Armenianism*, pp. 125–63.

60. On Laud and courtly Catholicism, see H. R. Trevor-Roper, *Archbishop Laud* (1963 edn.), pp. 306–12, 332–4, 370–1; M. Havran, *The Catholics in Caroline England* (1962), pp. 128, 131, 146–9.

61. 'The vindication of the Parliament and their proceedings' (1642) in *Harleian Miscellany*, V (1810), 281.

62. S.R.Gardiner (ed.), *Documents relating to the proceedings against William Prynne in 1634 and 1637*, Camden Soc., new ser., XVIII (1877), 87.

63. *The Correspondence of John Cosin, D.D.*, I, 32.

64. B.M., Stowe MSS., 743, fos. 163-4.

65. Ley, *A discourse* . . . , p. 15; *Prelacie is miserie* (1641) [Wing 3211], p. 8.

66. See Nathaniel Fiennes's speech in the Root and Branch debate on 9 February 1641, J.Rushworth, *Historical Collections* (1692), IV, 179.

67. W.Scott (ed.), *The Works of . . . William Laud D.D.* [hereafter Laud, *Works*] (Oxford 1847), I, 5-6. For another sermon on this theme, see ibid., 64-90.

68. ibid., VI, pt. i, pp. 190-1.

69. Ley, *A Discourse* . . . , p. 37.

70. Laud, *Works*, I, 82.

71. On the jurisdiction of the ecclesiastical courts, see R.A.Marchant, *The Puritans and the Church Courts in the Diocese of York 1560-1642* (1960), and *The Church under the Law* (Cambridge 1969); C.Hill, *Society and Puritanism in Pre-Revolutionary England* (1964), pp. 298-353.

72. See C.Hill, *Society and Puritanism in Pre-Revolutionary England*, pp. 335-7; H.R.Trevor-Roper, *Archbishop Laud 1573-1645* (1963 edn.), p. 359.

73. J.Rushworth, *Historical Collections* (1691), IV, 178. For a similar statement by Falkland, see ibid., p. 185(b).

74. S.R.Gardiner (ed.), *Reports of Cases in the Courts of Star Chamber and High Commission,* Camden Soc., new ser., XXXIX (1886), 275, 280, 298.

75. C.Hill, *Society and Puritanism in Pre-Revolutionary England*, p. 373.

76. R.G.Usher, *The Rise and Fall of the High Commission* (Oxford 1968 edn.), pp. 242-3, 246-55, 330-3.

77. Clarendon, *Great Rebellion*, I, 372.

78. C.Hill, *Economic Problems of the Church* (Oxford 1956), pp. 6-8, 14-18, 35-8, 315-16; P.M.Hembry, *The Bishops of Bath and Wells 1540-1640* (1967), pp. 241-2.

79. Cardwell (ed.), *Documentary Annals of the Reformed Church of England*, II, 231, 246-51; Hill, *Economic Problems of the Church*, pp. 12-13, 310-16. Dr Hill writes that Laud's policy 'brought to a head the antagonism between the new and the old forces in

society' (p. 12). But on this issue at least it was again the Archbishop who was the innovator in the adoption of a rational commercial policy of estate management.

80. Cited in Cardwell (ed.), *Documentary Annals* . . . , 11, 246-7, note.

81. On these policies, see Hill, *Economic Problems of the Church*, pp. 310-31, 336-7.

82. On the Feoffees, see I.M.Calder (ed.), *Activities of the Puritan Faction of the Church of England 1625-1633* (1957), pp. 59, 82-83, and 'A Seventeenth Century Attempt to Purify the Anglican Church', *Amer. Hist. Rev.*, LIII (1948), 760-75; Hill, *Economic Problems of the Church*, pp. 245-74; E.W.Kirby, 'The Lay Feoffees: A Study in Militant Puritanism', *J. Mod. Hist.*, XIV (1942), 1-25.

83. London, Guildhall MSS., 4384/1 [Vestry Minutes, St Bartholomew by the Exchange 1547-1643], fos. 364-5, 391, 406; W.K.Jordan, *The Charities of London 1480-1660* (1960), pp. 115, 287. On lectures see Hill, *Society and Puritanism in Pre-Revolutionary England*, pp. 79-123; and P.Seaver, *The Puritan Lectureships* (Stanford 1970), *passim*.

84. B.M., Stowe MSS., 744, fos. 13-13(b).

85. See, for example, Milton's views in 'Animadversions upon the Remonstrant's Defence against Smectymnuus' (1641), in J.A.St.John (ed.), *The Prose Works of John Milton* (1888), III, 78.

86. On patronage, benefices and advowsons, see Hill, *Economic Problems of the Church*, pp. 53-73.

87. Haller, *Tracts on Liberty*, 1, 47.

88. Hill, *Economic Problems of the Church*, p. 29; Hembry, *Bishops of Bath and Wells*, p. 226.

89. Hutchinson, Memoirs, p. 71. For a similar view, see K.M. Burton (ed.), *Milton's Prose Writings* (1965), p. 18.

90. *Cal. S.P.D. 1644-5*, pp. 280-1.

91. Clarendon, *Great Rebellion*, 1, 125.

92. *Harleian Miscellany*, IV (1809), 463.

93. I owe this point to Professor J.J.Scarisbrick.

94. Clarendon, *Great Rebellion*, 1, 131.

95. In the first edition of this book (pp. 120-3) I took a more extreme view, following the argument of W.Lamont (*Godly Rule*, especially pp. 35-64) in seeing *iure divino* episcopacy as a belief peculiar (among English Protestants) to the Laudians and some of their high church predecessors. I owe the change of emphasis

in this edition especially to the work of P. Collinson, *The Religion of Protestants*, especially pp. 16–21, and J. P. Somerville, 'The Royal Supremacy and Episcopacy "Jure Divino", 1603–1640', *Journal of Ecclesiastical History*, XXXIV (1983), 548–58. I am most grateful to Dr Somerville for drawing my attention to his findings.

96. Cited by Collinson, *The Religion of Protestants*, p. 17. For Knollys's own statements, see C. Cross (ed.), *The Royal Supremacy in the Elizabethan Church* (1969), pp. 176–7. The argument is reiterated in the Root and Branch Petition of December 1640 (see Gardiner, *Constitutional Documents*, pp. 137, 142).

97. For examples, see Rushworth, *Historical Collections*, IV, 186; *Harleian Miscellany*, IV, 469; Ley, *A discourse* ... , pp. 19–20; Haller, *Tracts on Liberty*, I, 61; Lamont, *Marginal Prynne*, pp. 3, 15, 17, 36–37.

98. See, for example, 'The Vindication of the Parliament and their Proceedings' (1642), in *Harleian Miscellany*, V (1810), 282; *Questions resolved and propositions tending to accommodation* (1642) [Wing 186], p. 14: *A declaration and resolution of the Lords and Commons in answer to the Scots declaration* (1642) [Wing 1320], pp. 12–13; Gardiner, *Constitutional Documents*, p. 207 (the Grand Remonstrance of December 1641).

99. Laud, *Works*, I, 83. See also his sermon of 5 July 1626, ibid., pp. 131–2.

100. See above, pp. 7–12.

101. Rushworth, *Historical Collections*, IV, 186.

102. R. Hooker, *Works* (Oxford 1890 edn.), II, 327–8.

103. T. Hobbes, 'Behemoth', in Maseres, *Select Tracts*, II, 540; Clarendon, *Great Rebellion*, I, 406–7.

104. K. M. Burton (ed.), *Milton's Prose Writings*, pp. 41–43, 46–48. Milton writes with guarded approval of primitive episcopacy, but it is clear that he is referring to something very different from what is usually meant by that term (pp. 10–15). For a more detailed treatment of these issues, see below, p. 153–4.

105. For Digby, Rushworth, *Historical Collections*, IV, p. 171. For the Root and Branch Petition, Gardiner, *Constitutional Documents*, pp. 137–44. For the apprentices' petition, B.M., Egerton MSS., 1048, fos. 26(b)–27. For the mariners' petition, *Lord Somers' Tracts*, 2nd coll., II (1750), 38–40.

106. *The case of the King stated* (1647) [Wing 1099], p. 2.

107. See, e.g., Bodleian, Tanner MSS., 64, fo. 150(b); *A declaration of the Lords and Commons* ... *setting forth the grounds, August* ... *1642* [Wing 1450], pp. 13, 15; *A declaration of the Lords and Commons in answer to his Majestie's declaration* (1642) [Wing 1442], pp. 3-6; *A moderate and most proper reply to a declaration* (1642) [Wing 2321], p. 6; *Observations upon his Majesties answer* (1643) [Wing III], pp. 3-5; 'The Vindication of the Parliament and their proceedings' (1642) in *Harleian Miscellany*, v (1810), 283.

108. K. Lindley, 'The Part Played by the Catholics' in B. Manning (ed.), *Politics, Religion and the English Civil War* (1973), pp. 127-76. P. R. Newman, 'Catholic Royalists of Northern England 1642-1645' *Northern History* xv (1979), 88-95. See also his 'Catholic Royalist Activists in the North 1642-6' *Recusant History* xiv (1977), 26-38.

109. *Cal. Clarendon S.P.*, 1, 51.

110. M. J. Havran, *The Catholics in Caroline England* (1962), especially pp. 27-8, 31, 39-60, 91-4, 99, 134-5, 156.

111. See pp. 17-21.

112. *Lord Somers' Tracts*, 2nd coll., 11, 26-8.

113. *A speech in Parliament of William Fiennes, Viscount Saye and Sele* (1643) [Wing 791], pp. 3-4, 7.

114. See p. 10.

115. Hooker, *Works* (Oxford 1890 edn.), 1, 351-4.

116. Bodleian, Rawlinson MSS., AII4, fo. 34. For a similar argument see *Considerations touching the late treaty for a peace* (Oxford 1645), pp. 8-15.

117. See pp. 19-20.

118. Ley, *A discourse* ... , pp. 18-19; cf. the arguments of the Parliamentary Commissioners at Newport in November 1648 against the relevance of the argument from the apostolic origins of episcopacy (Bodleian, Rawlinson MSS., AII4, fos. 58(b)-59).

CHAPTER 6   FROM CONSENSUS TO CONFRONTATION 1640-2

1. M. F. Keeler, *The Long Parliament 1640-1641* (Philadelphia 1954), p. 6. Some of those fifty-nine MPs, the evidence for whose political attitudes in 1640 is insufficiently decisive to justify any positive statement about their political affiliation, may also have belonged to the consensus of 399 MPs, the evidence for whose anti-Court sympathies ranges between the completely certain and the highly probable.

2. G. R. Elton, 'Tudor Government: the Points of Contact. 1: Parliament', *Roy. Hist. Soc. Trans.*, 5th ser., XXIV (1974), 183-200.

3. C. Russell, 'Why did Charles I call the Long Parliament?', *History* LIX (1984), 375-83.

4. Clarendon, *Great Rebellion*, I, p. 183.

5. This account draws on the list provided by D. Brunton and D. H. Pennington in *Members of the Long Parliament* (1954), pp. 225-45, with additional details from M. F. Keeler, and other sources too numerous to be cited in full. In these reckonings both the replacements of original members *and* the original members themselves have been included. However, the eighteen MPs who died between the opening of the Parliament and the outbreak of the war have not been included. In so far as the political affiliations of the latter can be discovered they were as follows: five definitely anti-Court men; six probably anti-Court men; three probably Court supporters; and four about whom no significant facts can be determined.

6. Charles Cavendish (East Retford), Sir Edward Alford (Arundel), Sir Gervase Clifton (East Retford), Francis Gamull (Chester), Francis Godolphin (Helston), Ralph Goodwin (Ludlow), Sir Edward Griffin (Downton), Sir Robert Hatton (Castle Rising), Henry Killigrew (West Looe), Francis Newport (Shrewsbury), Dr George Parry (St Mawes), William Price (Merioneth), and Sir Ralph Sydenham (Bossiney).

7. *D.N.B.*; Brunton and Pennington, op. cit., p. 245; Keeler, op. cit., p. 395. The one disabled MP who is not included, though he fought for the king in the war, is Henry Benson (Knaresborough), expelled for the disreputable, but unpolitical, offence of selling parliamentary protections (Keeler, pp. 107-8).

8. Edward Wyndham (Bridgwater), Sir Nicholas Crispe (Winchelsea), Sir John Jacob (Rye), William Sandys (Evesham), Fitzwilliam Coningsby (Herefordshire), Thomas Webb (New Romney), and the two MPs for Bristol, Richard Longe and Humphrey Hooke, who were expelled in the summer of 1642 for monopolistic activities in Bristol. In addition, William Watkins (Monmouth), who was ejected for election malpractices, was also censured for monopolistic practices. The fact that three of these MPs sat for Cinque Port constituencies, a traditional area of Court patronage, is worth noting (Brunton and Pennington, op. cit., pp. 56-8).

9. D'Ewes, *Journal* (ed. Notestein), pp. 23 note, 36, 224, 267-8, 537; Keeler, op. cit., pp. 139-40, 147, 221-2, 231-2, 333-4, 381, 382-3, 395-6; Brunton and Pennington, op. cit., pp. 54-8, 61; R. Ashton, *The Crown and the Money Market 1603-1640*, pp. 95 note, 101-3, 105; *The City and the Court 1603-1643*, pp. 152-3.

10. Keeler, op. cit., pp. 143, 373-4, 381; Brunton and Pennington, op. cit., pp. 2, 56, 134; D. Hirst, *The Representative of the People?* (Cambridge 1975), pp. 61, 63, 74. The MPs were William Coryton (Launceston), Henry Vernon (Andover) and William Watkins (Monmouth).

11. William Ashburnham (Ludgershall), Henry Percy (Northumberland), Hugh Pollard (Berealston) and Henry Wilmot (Tamworth). [D'Ewes, *Journal* (ed. Coates), pp. 16, 235, 238-9, 258-9; Clarendon, *Great Rebellion*, I, 325-30, 334 note, 351, 352-5; II, 102, 106; Gardiner, *History 1603-1642*, IX, 308-9, 313-18; Keeler, op. cit., pp. 89-90, 303-4, 308, 395].

12. William Taylor (Windsor). [Rushworth, *Historical Collections* (1692), IV, 248; Keeler, op. cit., pp. 357-8.]

13. Clarendon, *Great Rebellion*, I, 576-7; Keeler, op. cit., pp. 89, 192-3, 197-8, 234-6, 311, 380; Brunton and Pennington, op. cit., pp. 57, 67, 86-7; G. Huxley, *Endymion Porter: The Life of a Courtier 1587-1649* (1959), *passim*.

14. Rushworth, *Historical Collections*, IV, 248; Keeler, op. cit., pp. 152-3, 302-3, 383-5; J. T. Cliffe, *The Yorkshire Gentry from the Reformation to the Civil War* (1969), pp. 87, 91, 238, 240, 252-3, 298, 317, 322, 324, 328, 341-3. The Straffordians were the two Sir George Wentworths (brother and cousin, both MPs for Pontefract) and Thomas Danby (cousin) and Sir William Pennyman, both representing Richmond.

15. D'Ewes, *Journal* (ed. Notestein), pp. 83, 128 and note, 175 and note, 464, 465 note, 544-5; Keeler, op. cit., pp. 115-16, 228-9, 395; Hirst, op. cit., pp. 74, 78, 88, 136, 137, 148, 206. Windebank was also a notorious Laudian sympathizer.

16. B.M., Egerton MSS., 2978, fo. 76; Keeler, op. cit., pp. 317, 318-19, 329; Brunton and Pennington, op. cit., p. 131; Aylmer, *The King's Servants: The Civil Service of Charles I 1625-1642* (1961), pp. 338, 352-3, 357, 360-1, 380-1; E. Gore and C. Russell, 'John Pym and the Queen's Receivership', *B.I.H.R.*, XLVI (1973), 106-7.

17. See pp. 85-91.

18. The thesis of Dr Valerie Pearl, *London and the Outbreak of the Puritan*

Revolution (1961), *passim*, especially p. 276. See also R. Brenner, 'The Civil War Politics of London's Merchant Community', *P. & P.*, 58 (1973), 72.

19. ibid., especially 65-72, 76-82. For full details of the City MPs, see Pearl, *London* . . . , pp. 176-93.

20. This thesis is argued at length in R. Ashton, *The City and the Court 1603-1643*, especially pp. 201-21.

21. Clarendon, *Great Rebellion*, I, 250.

22. ibid., I, 207, 217, 225; C. V. Wedgwood, *Thomas Wentworth, First Earl of Stafford* (1964 edn.), pp. 320, 332, 364.

23. cited in ibid., p. 370.

24. Rushworth, *Historical Collections*, IV, 248-9.

25. On Strafford's role in Ireland and the parliamentary attack upon it, see Wedgwood, *Thomas Wentworth, passim*; and H. F. Kearney, *Strafford in Ireland 1633-41* (Manchester 1959), *passim*.

26. For the Long Parliament's attack on the regional councils, see pp. 62-3.

27. See pp. 64-5.

28. *H. of Commons J.*, II, 50, 56, 66; Rushworth, *Historical Collections*, IV, 98-9; D'Ewes, *Journal* (ed. Notestein), pp. 145, 243 and note, 284-5; Clarendon, *Great Rebellion*, I, 229, 236, 239-40; Cliffe, *Yorkshire Gentry*, pp. 313, 316, 327.

29. Rushworth, *Historical Collections*, IV, 146-9; *Harleian Miscellany*, IV (1809), 350-5; D'Ewes, *Journal* (ed. Notestein), pp. 263-4; Clarendon, *Great Rebellion*, I, 371-2; Gardiner, *History 1603-1642*, IX, 359-60.

30. Bodleian, Tanner MSS., 65, fo. 191; Rushworth, *Historical Collections*, IV, 147-8; *Harleian Miscellany*, IV, 352-3; Gardiner, *History 1603-1642*, IX, 353.

31. Gardiner, *Constitutional Documents*, pp. 164, 250; C. Roberts, *The Growth of Responsible Government in Stuart England* (Cambridge 1966), p. 113: A. Fletcher, *The Outbreak of the English Civil War* (1981), pp. 43-4, 48-9, 55-9 offers a more radical interpretation of the Ten Propositions.

32. Clarendon, *Great Rebellion*, I, 280-2, 333-6. Bedford's death is even more crucial to those who, like Professor Paul Christianson, lay particular stress on the role of the peers and of clientage in the reforming consensus of the first session of the Long Parliament. See P. Christianson, 'The Peers, The People and Parlia-

mentary Management in the first six Months of the Long Parliament,' *J. Mod. Hist.* XLIX (1977), 575-99.

33. Clarendon, *Great Rebellion*, I, 431.

34. On the queen's intrigues, see the interesting account by Dr B. Manning, in B. Manning (ed.), *Politics, Religion and the English Civil War* (1973), pp. 47-55. For the army plot, I am most grateful to Lord Russell for making available to me an advance copy of an article to be published in *Roy. Hist. Soc. Trans.*

35. The list here employed is in Rushworth, *Historical Collections*, IV, 248-9. It contains fifty-six names, not all of them members of the House of Commons, and is certainly incomplete.

36. The name of Benjamin Weston (Dover), who was also a parliamentarian in the war, is almost certainly a case of mistaken identity for Nicholas or Richard Weston.

37. Rushworth, *Historical Collections*, IV, 248-9: *D.N.B.*; Keeler, *Long Parliament*, pp. 220, 335, 336-7, 402-3; Brunton and Pennington, *Members of the Long Parliament*, pp. 155, 226-45: Wedgwood, op. cit., pp. 319, 333, 366, 376, 385.

38. Rushworth, *Historical Collections*, IV, 146-9, 170-4, 225-8, 248-9, D'Ewes, Journal (ed. Notestein), pp. 337, 421; D'Ewes, *Journal* (ed. Coates), pp. 199-204; *Harleian Miscellany*, IV, 350-5: Gardiner, *History 1603-1642*, VI, 76-77, 79; VIII, 271; IX, 270, 285; X, 86-87; Keeler, op. cit., pp. 157, 218, 353-4, 367-8; Brunton and Pennington, op. cit., pp. 132, 155-6, 159-60, 167; Wedgwood, op. cit., pp. 358, 366-7, Fletcher. *Outbreak*, pp. 34-35.

39. Sir William Carnaby (Morpeth), Thomas Coke (Leicester), Sir John Strangeways and Gerard Napier (Weymouth), Giles Strangeways (Bridport), George Lord Digby (Dorset), John Digby and Edward Kyrton (Milborne Port), Robert Holborne (Mitchell), Sir Thomas Bowyer (Bramber), Sir John Culpepper (Kent), Joseph Lane (Liskeard), John Mallory (Ripon), Sir William Savile (Old Sarum), and Edmund Waller (St Ives). Waller remained at Westminster after the outbreak of war but his royalist sympathies are not in doubt. Savile was not elected until January 1641. Digby was raised to the peerage and the House of Lords in May 1641.

40. Arthur Capel (Hertfordshire), Sir Richard Cave (Lichfield), Anthony Hungerford (Malmesbury), William Mallory (Ripon), Edward Phillips (Ilchester), Sir John Poulett (Somerset), John Russell (Tavistock), Peter Sainthill (Tiverton), Sir Henry

Slingsby (Knaresborough), Thomas Smith (Bridgwater), John Vaughan (Cardigan). The evidence for Hungerford's anti-Court sympathies in 1640 is rather thin. Slingsby was a 'Straffordian', but otherwise had 'Country' sympathies. Smith and Russell did not take their seats before 1641.

41. B.H.G.Wormald, *Clarendon* (Cambridge 1964), *passim.*

42. D'Ewes, *Journal* (ed. Notestein), pp. 7, 19, 23 note, 98, 149, 162 note; Clarendon, *Great Rebellion*, II, pp. 185-6; Gardiner; *History 1603-1642*, V, pp. 199, 342, 407-8, 425, 425-6 note, 429; VI, pp. 125-6, 233, 269; VII, p. 62; IX, pp. 100, 224; Keeler, op. cit., pp. 337-8; Brunton and Pennington, op. cit., p. 132.

43. The Remonstrance is printed in Gardiner, *Constitutional Documents*, pp. 202-32. For a good modern account see Fletcher, *Outbreak*, pp. 145-51.

44. In 1642 Dering published *A collection of speeches* in justification of his defection. See also Everitt, *Kent*, pp. 84-95; D.Hirst, 'The Defection of Sir Edward Dering 1640-1641', *Hist. J.*, XV (1972), 193-208; Fletcher, *Outbreak*, pp. 255-6.

45. D'Ewes, *Journal* (ed. Notestein), pp. 160, 338, 411 note, 468 note, 470 note, 493-4; D'Ewes, *Journal* (ed. Coates), pp. 196-7, 192-200, 249; *D.N.B.*; Gardiner, *History 1603-1642*, X, pp. 77, 79; Keeler, op. cit., p. 293; Wedgwood, *Thomas Wentworth*, p. 338.

46. *H. of Commons J.*, II, 328; Rushworth, *Historical Collections*, IV, 436; *D.N.B.*; Keeler, op. cit., p. 222; Barnes, *Somerset 1625-1640* (1961), pp. 22, 35-6, 90 note, 117-18, 221 note, 242; Underdown, *Somerset*, pp. 25-8; F.T.R.Edgar, *Sir Ralph Hopton* (Oxford 1968), pp. 11-26; T.G.Barnes, 'County Politics and a Puritan Cause Célèbre: Somerset Church ales, 1633', *Roy. Hist. Soc. Trans.*, 5th ser., IX (1959), 103-22.

47. Clarendon, *Great Rebellion*, I, 493-6; *Parliamentary History*, X, 105-11.

48. On Hyde's authorship of the declaration, see Wormald, *Clarendon*, pp. 34-42.

49. ibid., pp. 32-3; Gardiner, *History 1603-1642*, X, 127. Fletcher (*Outbreak*, p. 180) is properly sceptical about the rumoured offer to Pym.

50. ibid., X, 108, 111-12.

51. *The manner of the impeachment of the XII bishops* (1642) [Wing 472]; Clarendon, *Great Rebellion*, I, 471-7; Gardiner, *History 1603-1642*,

x, 122–6; C.H.Firth, *The House of Lords During the Civil War* (1974 edn.), pp. 105–6; Wormald, *Clarendon*, pp. 42–4.

52. Rushworth, *Historical Collections*, IV, 519; *A collection of severall speeches, messages and answers* (1642) [Wing 2159], p. 14.

53. *The petition of both Houses of Parliament presented . . . March 26th 1642* [Wing 2164], p. 3; Clarendon, *Great Rebellion*, II, 8; cf. 'Vox Populi: or the People's Humble Discovery of their Own Loyalty' in *Harleian Miscellany*, v (1810), 267.

54. *A collection of severall speeches, messages and answers*, p. 45; cf. 'The vindication of the Parliament and their proceedings' (1642) in *Harleian Miscellany*, v, 280. See also *Private Journals*, pp. 9–12.

55. *A collection of severall speeches, messages and answers*, p. 14.

56. Rushworth, *Historical Collections*, IV, 503–11.

57. For examples, see *Two declarations of the Lords and Commons assembled in Parliament* (1642, 18 August), pp. 3,7; *Exceeding joyfull news from the Prince* (1642) [Wing 3706], no pagination; *A declaration of the Lords and Commons . . . in answer to his Majesties declaration* (1642) [Wing 1442], pp. 3–6, 11–12; *A moderate and most proper reply to a declaration* (1642) [Wing 2321], no pagination; *Harleian Miscellany*, v, pp. 265, 282, 283; *Lord Somers' Tracts*, 2nd coll., II (1750), 158–60, 172–3; Clarendon, *Great Rebellion*, II, 92. For royal denials, see e.g., *His Majesties declaration in answer to a declaration* (Cambridge 1642) [Wing 2208], pp. 3–4; *Orders and Institutions of War* (1642) [Wing 2530], p. 3; *His Majesties declaration to all his loving subjects after his late victory* (Oxford 1642) [Wing 2222], pp. 2–4. For Newcastle's own frank observation as reported by his wife, Margaret Duchess of Newcastle, *The Life of the Duke of Newcastle* (1915 edn.), p. 167.

58. Gardiner, *History 1603–1642*, IX, 132–4, 215; Pearl, *London . . .*, pp. 107–8.

59. Clarendon, *Great Rebellion*, I, 271–2. See also Pearl, op. cit., pp. 210–28.

60. Digby's speech in the House of Commons' Root and Branch debate on 9 February 1641 is very eloquent on this [Rushworth, *Historical Collections*, IV, 171–2].

61. B.M., Stowe MSS., 184, fo. 131.

62. Bodleian, Tanner MSS., 66, fos. 83(b)–84.

63. C.L.R.O., Journal XL, fos. 10–10(b); *The Manner of the impeachment of the XII bishops* (1642), no pagination; *Lord Somers' Tracts*, 2nd

coll., II, 18; Clarendon, *Great Rebellion*, I, 548-9; Gardiner, *History 1603-1642*, X, 117-18; Pearl, op. cit., p. 224.

64. *The humble petition of divers baronets, knights, esquires of Lincolne* (1642) [Wing 3452], p. 6.

65. Bodleian, MSS. Add. C132, fo. 35(b).

66. Bodleian, Clarendon MSS., 20, fo. 129.

67. See, e.g., Haselrige's speech of 5 January 1642 (*Lord Somers' Tracts*, 2nd coll., II, 24), and, rather surprisingly, D'Ewes' speech in answer to Waller's allegations on 2 December 1641 [D'Ewes, *Journal* (ed. Coates), pp. 225-6].

68. Rushworth, *Historical Collections*, IV, 506, 509.

69. R.B.Manning, 'The Outbreak of the English Civil War' in R.H.Parry (ed.), *The English Civil War and After, 1642-1658* (1970), especially pp. 8-13.

70. B.M., Add. MSS., 29, 975, fo. 128(b).

71. *Lord Somers' Tracts*, 2nd coll., II, 17.

72. Bodleian, MSS. Add. C132, fo. 92.

73. See p. 121-2.

74. B.M., Egerton MSS., 1048, fos. 26(b)-27; *Lord Somers' Tracts*, 2nd coll., II, 38-40; Clarendon, *Great Rebellion*, I, 549-50.

75. *The humble petition of the clothiers of Leeds* (1642), no pagination.

76. Examples are: Bodleian, Clarendon MSS., 21, fo. 69; *A collection of severall speeches, messages and answers*, pp. 54, 55, 63-5, 80; *His Majesties declaration to all his loving subjects of August 12, 1642* (1642) [Wing 2241], pp. 16-17, 29-32, 70-1; *His Majesties answer to the XIX propositions* (1642) [Wing 2122], p. 11; *His Majesties answer to the petitions of the Lords and Commons* (1642) [Wing 2137B], pp. 8, 11-13; *His Majesties answer by way of declaration to a printed paper* (1642) [Wing 209A], p. 7; *His Majesties answer to a book entituled The declaration or remonstrance* (1642) [Wing 2092], pp. 5-6; Rushworth, *Historical Collections*, IV, 633-4; *Lord Somers' Tracts*, 2nd coll., II, 16.

77. Holmes, *Eastern Association*, pp. 35-6, 43-5, 51-2; see also Manning in Parry (ed.), *The English Civil War and After*, pp. 13-16.

78. K.M.Burton (ed.), *Milton's Prose Writings* (1965), pp. 9-10, 41-3, 46-8; J.A.St John (ed.), *Select Prose Writings of John Milton* (1836), II, 18-19; J.A.St John (ed.), *The Prose Works of John Milton* (1888), III, 53, 92, 137-9.

79. Rushworth, *Historical Collections*, IV, 171; Gardiner, *History 1603-1642*, IX, 285-6 note; D'Ewes, *Journal* (ed. Notestein), pp. 339-40.

80. Rushworth, *Historical Collections*, IV, 293-6; Sir Edward Dering, *A collection of speeches* (1642), pp. 66-78.

81. B.M., Stowe MSS., 184, fos. 27, 43-4.

82. *Lord Somers' Tracts*, 2nd coll., II, 258-9. A similar point is made in the Kentish petition of April 1642 [Bodleian, MSS. Add. C132, fo. 91(b)].

83. Dering, op. cit., pp. 98-101; *Lord Somers' Tracts*, 2nd coll., II, 37. For similar fears expressed by Sir Benjamin Rudyerd, see Bodleian, Tanner MSS., 66, fos. 186-6(b).

84. *The speech of a warden* (1642) [Wing 4862], sig. A2-A3.

85. *Questions resolved and propositions tending to an accommodation* (1642) [Wing 186], p. 12.

86. *Knyvett Letters*, p. 103.

CHAPTER 7   CONFLICT 1642-6

1. J.Rushworth, *Historical Collections* (1691), IV, 637.

2. See Clarendon, *Great Rebellion*, II, 14-15, 193-5; *His Majesties declaration to all his loving subjects of August 12, 1642* (Cambridge 1642) [Wing 2241], pp. 70-1.

3. See p. 152.

4. For these measures, see Gardiner, *History 1603-1642*, x, pp. 153-6, 161-2, 165, 171.

5. An example of Pym's approach is provided in some posthumously disinterred notes in *Harleian Miscellany*, x (1810), 51. Another is the parliamentary declaration of 19 May 1642 [Clarendon, *Great Rebellion*, II, 90, 99-100]. On Hotham and Hull, see *Private Journals* (1), pp. 37, 41, 46-47, 48, 78, 81, 112-3, 114-5; *Private Journals* (2), pp. 213, 216, 223-31, 242-3, 245-7.

6. Clarendon, *Great Rebellion*, I, 487-8, 505-6, 515-16, 524-5. For an excellent modern account of the effect of these events on Hyde, see Wormald, *Clarendon* (Oxford 1964), pp. 48-53.

7. On this see Wormald, *Clarendon*, pp. 104-5.

8. H.M.C. *House of Lords MSS.*, XI, 346.

9. *Clarendon State Papers*, II, 139; cf. *His Majesties answer to a book entituled The declaration or remonstrance* (1642) [Wing 2029], p. 25.

10. *The petition of both houses of Parliament presented . . . March 26th 1642* (1642) [Wing 2164], pp. 3-4; Clarendon, *Great Rebellion*, II, 8-9.

11. *A collection of severall speeches, messages and answers* (1642), pp. 20, 53-4; Rushworth, *Historical Collections*, IV, 522, 536; Clarendon, *Great Rebellion*, II, 3-4.

12. Rushworth, *Historical Collections*, IV, 503-11; *Parliamentary History*, x, 233-51. On the speech, see above, p. 151. For Fletcher's views, see *Outbreak*, pp. 191-227.

13. *An appeale to the world in these times* ... (1642) [Wing 3659], p. 3. Examples of such petitions are those from Sir Francis Wortley and some Yorkshire gentlemen against the removal of the royal magazine from Hull (Gardiner, *History 1603-1642*, x, 191); the Kentish petition of 25 March (Bodleian, MSS. Add. C132, fos. 91-2; *The humble petition of the commons of Kent* (1642) [Wing 3498]; and in the summer of 1642 from inhabitants of Cornwall (Bodleian, Clarendon MSS., 21, fo. 44; Rushworth, *Historical Collections*, IV, 638-9); Flintshire: *A petition of the gentry, ministers and freeholders of the county of Flint* ... *1642 August 12* [Wing 1799]; Lincolnshire: *The humble petition of divers, baronets, knights, esquires* ... *of Lincoln* ... *(1642)* [Wing 3453].

14. For the Herefordshire declaration, Bodleian, MSS. Add. C132, fos. 35-6(b). For the Kentish petitions, ibid., fos. 91-92; *The humble petition of the commons of Kent* (1642); Everitt, *Kent*, pp. 95-105, and T.S.P. Woods, *Prelude to Civil War 1642* (1980); for the London petitions, C.L.R.O., Journal XL, fos. 25-6, 27-8(b); *H. of Commons J.*, II, 489, 499, 501, 502; *H. of Lords J.*, IV, 651-2; *A perfect diurnall of the passages in Parliament* ... number II (1642), pp. 1-2; *Lord Somers' Tracts*, 2nd coll., I, 413-14; V.L.Pearl, *London and the Outbreak of the Puritan Revolution* (1961), pp. 149-50, 228. On 9 August it was reported that money belonging to Benion to the value of £4,000 or £5,000 had been intercepted on the way to the king at York (*Cal. S.P.D. 1641-3*, p. 368).

15. Rushworth, *Historical Collections*, IV, 635-9, 653-4.

16. Bodleian, Tanner MSS., 63, fos. 1-1(b).

17. *H. of Lords J.*, V, 31-32; *Private Journals* (2), pp. 153, 190-2, 206, 254, 257; *A collection of severall speeches, messages and answers*, pp. 15-17, 20; *His Majesties answer by way of declaration to a printed paper* (1642) [Wing 2090A], p. 11; Rushworth, *Historical Collections*, IV, 548. For a detailed treatment of the militia issue, see L.G.Schwoerer, *'No Standing Armies!' The Anti-army Ideology in Seventeenth-Century England* (1974), pp. 33-50, and 'The Fittest Subject for a King's Quarrel', *J. Brit. Stud.*, XI (1971), 45-76.

18. See pp. 53-8.

19. The propositions are printed in Clarendon, *Great Rebellion*, II, 167-70 and Gardiner, *Constitutional Documents*, pp. 249-54; the

text of the king's answer in *His Majesties answer to the XIX Proposi-tions* (1642) [Wing 2122] (hereafter cited as *Answer*).

20. See especially C.C.Weston, 'The Theory of Mixed Monarchy under Charles I and After', *Eng. Hist. Rev.*, LXXV (1966), especially pp. 426-33.

21. *Answer*, p. 25.

22. *Answer*, p. 28.

23. *Answer*, pp. 6-8, 10. On ministerial responsibility, impeachment and the Nineteen Propositions, see the admirable account in C.Roberts, *The Growth of Responsible Government in Stuart England* (Cambridge 1966), pp. 105-7, 112-14, 117, 433, 438.

24. Clarendon, *Great Rebellion*, II, 69.

25. On this concept, see pp. 12-15, 17-18.

26. *Answer*, pp. 10-11, 17-23. For a later royal comment in criticism of the Propositions, see *His Majesties declaration to all his loving subjects of August 12, 1642* (Cambridge 1642), pp. 66-7. For details of their late modification, see Fletcher, *Outbreak*, p. 275.

27. *H. of Commons J.*, II, 496, 497; Rushworth, *Historical Collections*, IV, 534; *A perfect diurnall of the passages in Parliament*, no. II (1642), pp. 6, 7. In addition Lord Strange and the Marquess of Hertford refused to accept parliamentary nominations as Lieutenants of Cheshire and Somerset and were replaced by Lords Saye and Bedford.

28. *H. of Commons J.*, II, 499-500, 502; Rushworth, *Historical Collections*, IV, 532; *H.M.C. 4th Rep.*, p. 307; *A perfect diurnall of the passages in Parliament*, no. II, p. 8; *A joyfull message sent from both houses . . . to Portsmouth . . . August 8* (1642) [Wing 1128], p. 4.

29. *A learned speech made by . . . Sir John Hotham . . . 23 May 1642* [Wing 2905], no pagination; Henry Parker, *Observations upon some of his Majesties late answeres* (1642), pp. 33, 45; Clarendon, *Great Rebellion*, II, 125-33; *Parliamentary History*, XI, 89-115. A similar answer was returned to the king by the parliamentarian defenders of Gloucester on 10 August, 1643 (Clarendon, *Great Rebellion*, III, 133).

30. See p. 53-4.

31. Rushworth, *Historical Collections*, IV, 659-61; *His Majesties answer to the petition of the Lords and Commons* (1642) [Wing 2137B], p. II; *Questions resolved and propositions tending to accommodation* (1642) [Wing 186], pp. 9-10; Clarendon, *Great Rebellion*, II, 196-206 and note.

32. Gardiner, *History 1603-1642*, x, 202. For good modern accounts of the Commission of Array and the Militia Ordinance, see Fletcher, *Outbreak*, pp. 322-3, 347-68; J.L.Malcolm, *Caesar's Due: Loyalty and King Charles 1642-1646* (1983), passim.

33. P.R.O., S.P. Charles I, CCCCXCI 88; *Cal S.P.D. 1641-3*, pp. 368, 369-71, 375-6; *H. of Lords J.*, v, 332; H.M.C. 5th Rep., p. 44; Rushworth, *Historical Collections*, IV, 661-2; Clarendon, *Great Rebellion*, II, 295-6; E.A.Andriette, *Devon and Exeter in the Civil War* (Newton Abbot 1971), pp. 57-9, 64; Underdown, *Somerset*, pp. 31-2, 38-40; F.T.R.Edgar, *Sir Ralph Hopton* (Oxford 1968), p. 31.

34. Bodleian, Tanner MSS., 63, fo. 146; Everitt, *Kent*, pp. 108-10; Holmes, *Eastern Association*, pp. 38, 51-3, 57-8, 61; R.W.Ketton-Cremer, *Norfolk in the Civil War* (1969), pp. 137, 144-8.

35. B.M., Add. MSS., 36,913, fo. 122(b). On the Commission in Cheshire, see Morrill, *Cheshire 1630-1660* (1974), pp. 56, 60-5.

36. Rushworth, *Historical Collections*, IV, 669-70.

37. Washington D.C., Folger Shakespeare Library, Folger MSS., Xd. 483(5); Andriette, *Devon and Exeter in the Civil War*, pp. 55-64.

38. [John Corbet?], *An historical relation of the military government of Gloucester* (1645), pp. 7-8.

39. *Two letters, the one from the Lord Digby . . . Likewise the opposition . . . the Marquesse of Hertford received in executing His Majesties Illegal Commission of Array in Somersetshire* (1642), no pagination; *The Lord Marquesse of Hertford his letter sent to the Queen August 8* (1642) [Wing 4649], pp. 5-6; *A copy of the Commission of Array granted to the Marquesse of Hertford* (1642) [Wing 2168]; *Exceeding joyfull newes from the Earl of Bedford* (1642) [Wing 3757]; Clarendon, *Great Rebellion*, II, 295-9; Underdown, *Somerset*, pp. 31-43; Edgar, op. cit., pp. 31-43.

40. Washington, D.C., Folger MSS., Xd. 483(4); *H.M.C. 4th Rep.*, p. 307; M.Coate, *Cornwall in the Great Civil War and Interregnum 1642-1660* (Truro 1963 edn.), pp. 30-1, 34-7; Edgar, op. cit., pp. 45-8.

41. Everitt, *Kent*, pp. 107-8.

42. *Clarendon State Papers*, II, 144; Clarendon, *Great Rebellion*, II, 181-2.

43. Rushworth, *Historical Collections*, IV, 676-7; *H. of Lords J.*, v, 115, 116, 117; *H.M.C. 5th Rep.*, pp. 27, 28.

44. Gardiner, *History 1603-1642*, x, p. 217. On the eve of Edgehill, a similar proclamation of conditional pardon was to be circulated

to unsettle the parliamentary troops, but it was overlooked in the heat of preparation for the battle (*H. of Lords J.*, v, 423; *H.M.C. 5th Rep.*, p. 55). Waller refused to receive a royal messenger with a similar message before the battle of Cropredy in 1644 (Clarendon, *Great Rebellion*, III, 369-70).

45. B.M., Add. MSS., 36,913, fos. 94-94(b), 96, 98(b)-99. On the behaviour of the Cheshire Commission of Army, see Morrill, *Cheshire*, pp. 60-4. On 17 August 1645 a royal proclamation offered a pardon to all in Yorkshire who returned to allegiance to the king within ten days. (*Cal. S.P.D. 1645-7*, pp. 74-5).

46. *Knyvett Letters*, pp. 102-3.

47. Bodleian, Tanner MSS., 63, fos. 119-19(b), 126. For the neutrality pact, see p. 258.

48. D. Gardiner (ed.), *The Oxinden Letters 1607-1642* (1933), pp. 308-9, 311-13.

49. C.L.R.O., Repertory LV, fo. 456(b); *H. of Lords J.*, v, 72, 192, 280, 284; *H. of Commons J.*, II, 484, 492, 499, 657, 662-3; *H.M.C. H. of Lords MSS.*, XI, 320; *H.M.C. 5th Rep.*, I, 24, 36, 37, 42; *H.M.C. 12th Rep.*, II, 321; *A continuation of the true diurnall of all the passages in Parliament*, no. 10 (1642), p. 67; *A perfect diurnall of the passages in Parliament*, no. 11 (1642), p. 4; *The King's Majesties Resolution concerning the Lord Maior of London* (1642); Clarendon, *Great Rebellion*, II, 246; Pearl, *London . . .*, pp. 228, 250.

50. See p. 133-4.

51. See R. Ashton, *The City and the Court 1603-1643*, pp. 204-21.

52. Gardiner, *Civil War*, I, 4.

53. Bodleian, Clarendon MSS., 21, fos. 120-120(b).

54. Gardiner, *Civil War*, I, 5.

55. Clarendon, *Great Rebellion*, II, 356.

56. *Acts and Ordinances*, I, 37; Clarendon, *Great Rebellion*, II, 380. See above pp. 8-9.

57. B.M., Add. MSS., 36,913, fo. 122(b); Clarendon, *Great Rebellion*, II, 342, 470-1; R. Robinson (ed.), *The Life of Adam Martindale written by Himself*, Chetham Soc., IV (1845), 31-2; E. Broxap, *The Great Civil War in Lancashire 1642-1651* (Manchester 1973 edn.), p. 6; B.G. Blackwood, *The Lancashire Gentry and the Great Rebellion 1640-60* (Manchester 1978), pp. 47-8. G.H. Tupling, 'The Causes of the Civil War in Lancashire', *Trans. Lancs & Cheshire Antiq. Soc.*, LXV (1955), 30-1 and note.

58. *Exceeding joyfull newes from the Earl of Bedford* (1642), no pagination.

59. D.Underdown, *Revel, Riot and Rebellion*, p. 183. For his general observations, see above pp. 83-4. For a stronger emphasis on political commitment in the army, especially towards the end of the war, see A.Woolrych, *Soldiers and Statesmen . . . 1647-1648* (Oxford 1987), pp. 19-23.

60. Bodleian, Tanner MSS., 63, fo. 43; Holmes, *Eastern Association*, pp. 36, 38-41. W.Hunt, *The Puritan Moment. The Coming of Revolution in an English County* (1983), *passim*.

61. B.M., Egerton MSS., 2647, fo. 354.

62. *The requests of the gentlemen of the Grand Jury of the county of Oxford* (1642) [Wing 1121], p. 5.

63. B.M., Egerton MSS., 2647, fo. 201.

64. ibid., fos. 89, 125; *Cal. S.P.D. 1644*, p. 423; Bell, *Memorials*, I, 79.

65. See, for example, *The ordinance and declaration of the Lords and Commons for the assessing* (Oxford 1642) [Wing 1768], pp. 7-8; cf. the documents cited in Clarendon, *Great Rebellion*, II, 232-7, 424.

66. Clarendon, *Great Rebellion*, II, 85-6.

67. Bodleian, Tanner MSS., 58, fos. 54, 62(b), 118; *The ordinance and declaration of the Lords and Commons for the assessing* (Oxford 1642), pp. 12-15; Clarendon, *Great Rebellion*, II, 425, 427; L.Wormock, *Sober Sadness: or historical observations* (Oxford 1643), pp. 39-42; *Three letters: the first from an officer* (Oxford 1643) [Wing 1102], pp. 32-3; D.Jenkins, *Lex Terrae* (1647), *passim*; Gardiner, *Constitutional Documents*, p. 286.

68. Rushworth, *Historical Collections*, V, 183; Clarendon, *Great Rebellion*, II, 85-6.

69. James Howell, *A letter to the Earl of Pembroke* (1647), pp. 10-11. For other statements to this effect, see *The ordinance and declaration of the Lords and Commons for the assessing* (Oxford 1642), pp. 14-15; Clarendon, *Great Rebellion*, II, 407, 427-8; *A letter from a scholler in Oxfordshire to his uncle* (Oxford 1643) [Wing 1436], no pagination; *Three letters: the first from an officer* (Oxford 1643), pp. 4-5, 20-2; 'The rebels' catechism' (1643) in *Harleian Miscellany*, V, 420.

70. Clarendon, *Great Rebellion*, III, 8, 35; *His Majesties declaration to all his loving subjects in answer to a declaration . . . 3 June 1643*, pp. 36-7.

71. On the Oxford Parliament, see pp. 211-15.

72. *A discourse between a resolved and doubtful Englishmen* (1642), cited in J.W.Allen, *English Political Thought 1603-1660: I, 1603-1644*

(1938), p. 470; see also *A discourse upon the questions in debate* (1642) [Wing 1628], p. 13.

73. 'The vindication of the Parliament and their proceedings' (1642) in *Harleian Miscellany*, v (1810), 281; *The subject of supremacie* (1643) [Wing 6104], pp. 26–7.

74. *A remonstrance of the Lords and Commons . . . or the reply* (1642) [Wing 2220], pp. 14–15.

75. *A discourse upon the questions in debate* (1642), pp. 13–14.

76. Clarendon, *Great Rebellion*, II, 125; *Parliamentary History*, XI, 100.

77. Henry Parker, *Observations upon some of his Majesties late answers* (1642) (hereafter *Observations*), especially pp. 1–2, 5, 8–9, 28, 30, 37, 45–6; *Some few Observations upon his Majesties late answer* (1642) (hereafter *Some few observations*), p. 9; and *A political catechism, or certain questions* (1643), pp. 2–3. On Parker and parliamentary sovereignty see Allen, *English Political Thought*, pp. 426–35, and especially M.A.Judson, 'Henry Parker and the Theory of Parliamentary Sovereignty' in *Essays in History and Political Theory in honour of Charles Howard McIlwain* (New York 1967 edn.), pp. 138–67, and especially pp. 146–8, 152–3, 164. For similar views, see *An appeale to the world in these times* (1642), pp. 1–2; *The unlimited prerogative of kings subverted* (1642) [Wing 84], sig. A2–A3; *The subject of supremacie* (1643), pp. 22–4.

78. *Maximes unfolded* (1643) [Wing 1375], p. 5.

79. *His Majesties answer to a book entitled the declaration or remonstrance* (1642), p. 7; Clarendon, *Great Rebellion*, II, 138.

80. *Lord Somers' Tracts*, 2nd coll., II, 257.

81. See J.H.Hexter, *The Reign of King Pym* (Cambridge, Mass. 1941), especially pp. 92–3, 113–14, 133–4, 137–9, 147.

82. See pp. 230–2.

83. For examples of renewed parliamentary allegations of royalist designs to alter the frame of government and religion and denial of any such intentions themselves, see *Two declarations of the Lords and Commons assembled in Parliament* (August 1642), p. 7; *A declaration of the Lords and Commons for the raising of all power, August 9, 1642*, p. 4; *A Declaration of the Lords and Commons . . . in answer to his Majesties declaration* (October 1642) [Wing 1442], pp. 9–10; *A remonstrance of the Lords and Commons or the reply* (3 November 1642), p. 4. See also Henry Parker, *Some few observations*, p. 7.

84. *A remonstrance of the Lords and Commons . . . or the reply* (1642), pp. 25–6, 29–40. Prynne in his treatise on parliamentary sovereignty

argued that this was also clear from the text of Magna Carta. [Allen, *English Political Thought*, pp. 427, 439-49, citing W. Prynne, *The soveraigne power of Parliaments and Kingdoms* (1643).] But see W. M. Lamont, *Marginal Prynne 1600-1669* (1969), pp. 93-8, on Prynne's scepticism about Magna Carta.

85. *Questions resolved and propositions tending to accommodation* (1642), p. 6.

86. B.M., Egerton MSS., 2651, fo. 123; *A remonstrance of the Lords and Commons . . . or the reply . . . November 3, 1642*, pp. 2, 18-23; Henry Parker, *Observations*, pp. 4-5, 35, 36-7, *Some few observations*, pp. 6-8, *A political catechism, or certain questions* (1643), p. 7; Peter Bland, *Resolved upon the question* (1642), pp. 10, 13-14; *Maximes unfolded*, pp. 24-5, 33-7; *The subject of supremacie*, pp. 19, 41-2.

87. *The subject of supremacie*, pp. 41-2.

88. Clarendon, *Great Rebellion*, II, 121; *Parliamentary History*, XI, 92.

89. *A declaration against Prince Rupert* (1643) [Wing 149], p. 6.

90. See *The unlimited prerogative of Kings subverted* (1642) [Wing 84], no pagination; *Maximes unfolded*, pp. 22-3; 'An exhortation for the taking of the Solemne League and Covenant' in *Lord Somers' Tracts*, 2nd coll., II, 269.

91. John Goodwin, 'Anti-Cavalierism' (1642) in Haller, *Tracts on Liberty*, II, 229.

92. *The unlimited prerogative of kings subverted*, no pagination; cf. *Maximes unfolded*, pp. 22, 46-7.

93. *A letter from a scholler in Oxford-shire to his vncle* (Oxford 1643), pp. 14-15.

94. *Some speciall arguments for the Scottish nation* (1642) [Wing 4619], p. 3; 'The vindication of Parliament and their proceedings' (1642), *Harleian Miscellany*, V, 297. On the godly magistrate, see above pp. 106, 107.

95. *The right character of a true subject* (1643) [Wing 1502], no pagination; J.W., *Obedience active and passive due to the supream power* (Oxford 1643), pp. 16-22; 'The rebels' catechism' (1643) in *Harleian Miscellany*, V, 412-13.

96. *A declaration in vindication of John Pym* (1643) [Wing 4259], p. 6.

97. Henry Parker, *Observations*, pp. 33-4.

98. Washington, D.C., Folger Library, Folger MSS., Xd. 483(5).

99. *Powers to be resisted* (1643) [Wing 3111], p. 20; cf. 'The vindication of the Parliament' (1642) in *Harleian Miscellany*, V, 292; Goodwin,

'Anti-Cavalierism' in Haller, *Tracts on Liberty*, pp. 228-9; Parker, *Observations*, p. 45.

100. Gardiner, *Constitutional Documents*, p. 269. One of the disciplinary ordinances of the Scottish expeditionary force made soldiers speaking irreverently of the king liable to be treated as traitors. [*Harleian Miscellany*, v, 423.]

101. See *His Majesties declaration to all his loving subjects of August 12, 1642* (Cambridge 1642), pp. 69-70; *His Majesties declaration in answer to a declaration* (Cambridge 1642) [Wing 2208], pp. 4-5; Clarendon, *Great Rebellion*, 11, 187.

102. *His Majesties declaration to all his loving subjects after his late victory* (Oxford 1642), p. 6.

103. *A declaration of the Lords and Commons ... in answer to his Majesties declaration* (1642) [Wing 1442], p. 10. See also Rushworth, *Historical Collections*, iv, 552; *The second part of Vox Populi* (1642) [Wing 2323], no pagination; *The censure of the Earl of Berkshire* (1642) [Wing 1667], pp. 3, 5. *An appeale to the world in these times* (1642), p. 7; *Harleian Miscellany*, v, 264-5, 292, 294; Gardiner, *Constitutional Documents*, pp. 256-7.

104. Clarendon, *Great Rebellion*, 11, 355-6 note; 111, 25-6.

105. See, for example, *Two declarations of the Lords and Commons assembled in Parliament* (1642), p. 7; *Maximes unfolded*, pp. 17-18; *The Kingdoms case* (1643) [Wing 583], pp. 3-4; *A declaration against Prince Rupert*, pp. 3-5; *The subject of supremacie*, p. 4; *An ordinance of the Lords and Commons to appoint and enable committees ...*, June 1644 [Wing 2090], p. 3. For royalist counter-arguments, see, e.g., J.W. *Obedience active and passive due to the supream power*, p. 15; Francis Quarles, *The loyall convert* (Oxford 1643), p. 6.

106. *A remonstrance of the Lords and Commons ... or the reply* (1642), p. 53. See also Parker, *Observations*, p. 45; *Maximes unfolded*, pp. 42-3, 46-8; *A declaration against Prince Rupert*, pp. 7-8.

107. The distinction of Allen, *English Political Thought*, pp. 393, 467-8.

108. Bodleian, Tanner MSS., 63, fo. 74. See also the declaration made in February 1644 by the so-called 'Parliament' called by the king at Oxford, *Parliamentary History*, xiii, 102, 106. The point was laboured at length by later royalist commentators such as Judge David Jenkins; see D. Jenkins, *A vindication of Judge Jenkins* (1647) [Wing 593], and *Lex Terrae* (1647) [Wing 593]; James Howell, *A letter to the Earle of Pembroke* (1647), p. 11. For a criticism

of Jenkins' views, see *The cordiall of Mr. David Jenkins or his reply to HP . . . answered* (1647), especially pp. 23–4.

109. *Harleian Miscellany*, v, 416–17. See also Wormock, *Sober Sadness*, p. 37.

110. *The King's cabinet opened* (1645) [Wing 591]; *H.M.C. H. of Lords MSS.*, xi, 347.

111. *Clarendon State Papers*, ii, 218–19.

112. For royal denunciations of Marten's and Ludlow's views, see *His Majesties declaration to all his loving subjects of August 12, 1642* (Cambridge 1642), pp. 62, 72. See also *Lord Somers' Tracts*, 1st ser., i (1748), 31.

113. Gardiner, *Civil War*, i, 133, 202–3.

114. Clarendon, *Great Rebellion*, ii, 547.

115. 'Memorial of Denzil Lord Holles' in Maseres, *Select Tracts*, i, pp. 200–1, 210.

116. C.H.Firth, *Cromwell's Army* (1962 edn.), pp. 346–8.

117. See pp. 314–5.

118. Gardiner, *Civil War*, ii, 327–9; Firth, op. cit., pp. 316–18.

CHAPTER 8   THE POLITICAL SPECTRUM AT WESTMINSTER
         AND OXFORD 1642–4

1. See pp. 161 *et seq.*

2. Details are obtained from a very wide variety of sources, and notably M.F.Keeler, *The Long Parliament 1640-1641* (Philadelphia 1954), *passim*, and D.Brunton and D.H.Pennington, *Members of the Long Parliament, passim.*

3. Keeler, op. cit., pp. 137–8, 175–6, 222–3, 294–5, 338; Gardiner, *History 1603-1642*, vi, 33, *Civil War*, i, 41.

4. The half-brother of the later regicide and Fifth Monarchy Man, John Carew, who was executed in 1660.

5. Clarendon, *Great Rebellion*, ii, 56, 259–65, 468; iii, 236, 526–9; Gardiner, *Civil War*, ii, 194; iii, 204, 211; Keeler op. cit., pp. 126–7, 134–5, 222–3, 373; Brunton and Pennington, op. cit., p. 29; M.Coate, *Cornwall in the Great Civil War*, pp. 30, 34, 56 note, 103, 126–7; J.T.Cliffe, *The Yorkshire Gentry from the Reformation to the Civil War* (1969), *passim* (sub Hotham and Cholmeley).

6. *Answer*, pp. 21–2.

7. *A declaration of the Lords and Commons . . . for the appeasing and quieting . . .* (1642) [Wing 1411], no pagination.

8. *A declaration of the Lords and Commons . . . in answer to His Majesties*

declaration (1642) [Wing 1442], pp. 10-11. For a similar charge, see [Thomas Povey], *The moderator expecting svdden peace* (1643), p. 15.

9. B.M., Egerton MSS., 2647, fo. 354.

10. *Questions resolved and propositions tending to an accommodation* (1642), p. 13; see also p. 15.

11. B.M., Harleian MSS., 164, fos. 270(b)-3, and especially fos. 272-2(b).

12. *Lord Somers' Tracts*, 1st ser., 1 (1748), 15 note.

13. Maseres, *Select Tracts*, 1, 214.

14. L. Mulligan, 'Property and Parliament Politics in the English Civil War', *Historical Studies*, xvi (1975), 341-59. On the war, peace and middle groups, see pp. 194-200.

15. B.M., Harleian MSS., 164, fo. 345.

16. On this, see pp. 272-3.

17. *H.M.C. 4th Rep.*, p. 268.

18. *His Majesties declaration to all his loving subjects of August 12, 1642* (Cambridge 1642), p. 48. For other and later examples, see *His Majesties declaration to all his loving subjects after his late victory* (Oxford 1642), pp. 6-7; *The ordinance and declaration of the Lords and Commons for the assessing* (Oxford 1642), pp. 11, 14; *The humble petition of the inhabitants of the county of Hartford* (Oxford 1643) [Wing 3519] (the royal reply), no pagination; *His Maiesties declaration to all his loving subjects in answer to a declaration . . . 3 June 1643* (Oxford 1643) [Wing 2232], p. 9; *Three letters: the first from an officer* (Oxford 1643), p. 34; Francis Quarles, *The loyall convert* (Oxford 1643), pp. 11-12, 17; L. Wormock, *Sober Sadness: or historical observations* (Oxford 1643), pp. 26-8; Clarendon, *Great Rebellion*, 11, 426, 428, 445.

19. *A declaration of the Lords and Commons in answer to his Majesties declaration* (1642) [Wing 1442], p. 10. See also Bodleian, Tanner MSS., 62(a), fo. 118; *A declaration in vindication of John Pym* (1643) [Wing 4259], p. 4; *Observations upon his Majesties answer* [to the City of London petition] (1643) [Wing 111], p. 3.

20. Bodleian, Tanner MSS., 62(b), fos. 345, 346. These are two mutually contradictory petitions from different townsmen.

21. *H. of Lords J.*, v, 346, 360; *H.M.C. 5th Rep.*, pp. 45-6, 46-7, 48-9; R. W. Ketton-Cremer, *Norfolk in the Civil War* (1969), pp. 232-5; Underdown, *Somerset*, p. 44; Gardiner, *Civil War*, 1, 66.

22. Gardiner, *Civil War*, 1, 102.

23. ibid., I, p. 132; *Acts and Ordinances*, I, 265-6; J. Rushworth, *Historical Collections* (1691), V, 358-9; *Harleian Miscellany*, V (1810), 441-3.

24. *Archaeologia*, XXXV (1853), 311-14, 319.

25. e.g. *His Majesties declaration to all his loving subjects in answer to a declaration* (1643) [Wing 2232], p. 45; cf. Wormock, *Sober Sadness*, p. 28.

26. J.H. Hexter, *The Reign of King Pym* (Cambridge, Mass. 1941).

27. See ibid., pp. 51-5 for Professor Hexter's account of what he describes as the phenomenon of 'political foreshortening'. On Holles see P. Crawford, *Denzil Holles 1598-1680* (1979), especially pp. 83-98.

28. *Parliamentary History*, XII, 26-7.

29. See pp. 207-8.

30. *H. of Lords J.*, V, 327; *H.M.C. 5th Rep.*, p. 44; Clarendon, *Great Rebellion*, II, 300-11.

31. *Cal. S.P.D. 1641-3*, pp. 405-7, 410; Rushworth, *Historical Collections*, IV, 58-9, 60-2; *Parliamentary History*, XII, 38-9; Clarendon, *Great Rebellion*, II, 392-5.

32. For the propositions, see Gardiner, *Constitutional Documents*, pp. 262-7.

33. Rushworth, *Historical Collections*, V, 202. For the whole picture of this side of the negotiations, see ibid., pp. 195-261; Clarendon, *Great Rebellion*, III, 1 *et seq.* The best modern account is still Gardiner, *Civil War*, I, ch. V.

34. For an excellent example of such adjustments, see Hexter, *Reign of King Pym*, pp. 67-72.

35. B.M., Harleian MSS., 164, fo. 163.

36. Clarendon, *Great Rebellion*, II, 495.

37. *His Majesties declaration to all his loving subjects in answer to a declaration ... 3 June 1643* (Oxford 1643), especially pp. 10-30.

38. Rushworth, *Historical Collections*, V, 183.

39. Hexter, op. cit., p. 8.

40. B.M., Add. MSS., 31116, fo. 295.

41. On the assessment which passed the House in February 1643 and was renewed in July, see Hexter, op. cit., pp. 21-2, 134. The Excise failed to get through the House in March which suggests that it was opposed by more than the peace party, but succeeded in July, when parliamentarian fortunes were at their lowest point. *An ordinance of the Lords and Commons for the speedy raising and levying of moneyes*, 27 July 1643 [Wing 2032]; *Acts and*

Ordinance, I, 202–14; Clarendon, *Great Rebellion*, III, 34, 307; Gardiner, *Civil War*, I, 101–2, 179; Hexter, op. cit., pp. 25 and note, 134.

42. B.M., Harleian MSS., 164, fo. 243.

43. ibid., fos. 292(b)–3.

44. See Hexter, op. cit., pp. 107–32, 137–47; V.F.Snow, *Essex the Rebel* (Lincoln, Nebraska 1970), pp. 354–8, 375–92.

45. See Snow, op. cit., pp. 383–97; Holmes, *Eastern Association*, pp. 109–11; Crawford, *Denzil Holles*, p. 93.

46. See, for example, the letter of the Scottish Presbyterian Robert Baillie from London on 2 December 1640 (Baillie, *Letters and Journals*, I, 275).

47. e.g. Bodleian, Tanner MSS., 65, fo. 27; *A declaration of the Lords and Commons setting forth the grounds* (1642) [Wing 1450], p. 6; *A declaration and resolution of the Lords and Commons in answer to the Scots declaration* (1642) [Wing 1320]; Rushworth, *Historical Collections*, V, 387–93; Clarendon, *Great Rebellion*, II, 380–1, 387; Gardiner, *History 1603–1642*, IX, 377.

48. My analysis of the origins of the Scottish alliance owes much to D.Stevenson, *The Scottish Revolution 1637–44* (Newton Abbot 1973), pp. 248–98, and H.R.Trevor-Roper, *Religion, the Reformation and Social Change* (1967), pp. 403–10. There is also an admirably clear survey of the course of events leading up to the war by L.Kaplan, 'Steps to War: the Scots and Parliament 1642–3', *J. Brit. Stud.*, IX (1970), 50–70.

49. Rushworth, *Historical Collections*, V, 402–10, 459–66; *H.M.C. 5th Rep.*, p. 67; Clarendon, *Great Rebellion*, II, 510–20.

50. Bodleian, Tanner MSS., 64, fos. 6–7; *H. of Lords J.*, V, 411; *H.M.C. 5th Rep.*, p. 49.

51. Baillie, *Letters and Journal*, II, 45; cf. the statement by the General Assembly of the Scottish Church in September 1643 (Rushworth, *Historical Collections*, V, 470–1).

52. Rushworth, *Historical Collections*, V, 492.

53. B.M., Harleian MSS., 164, fos. 272(b).

54. Maseres, *Select Tracts*, I, 197–8. See Crawford, *Denzil Holles*, pp. 92, 99–102.

55. For a forthright statement of this view, see Hexter, *Reign of King Pym*, p. 195.

56. The Solemn League and Covenant is printed in Gardiner, *Constitutional Documents*, pp. 267–71. I have drawn heavily on the excellent accounts in Gardiner, *Civil War*, I, 228–36; Stevenson, op. cit., pp. 283–93; and Kaplan, 'Steps to War', loc. cit., pp. 61–6.

57. Bodleian, Tanner MSS., 65, fo. 50. Italics mine. The memorandum which is certainly datable from internal evidence at 1643 is wrongly included in the Bodleian catalogue with documents of 1640.

58. ibid., Gardiner, *Civil War*, I, 233; Hexter, op. cit., pp. 195–7.

59. B.M. Harleian MSS., 164, fos. 279–9(b).

60. Hexter, op. cit., pp. 96–99.

61. Baillie, *Letters and Journals*, II, 117–8. See also ibid., pp. 120–2.

62. Rushworth, *Historical Collections*, V, 390. This view was shared by royalists who were also unconvinced by Scottish claims that Presbyterianism and monarchical government were entirely compatible. (ibid., p. 409; Clarendon, *Great Rebellion*, II, 508).

63. Bodleian, Tanner MSS., 62, fo. 332(b).

64. L. Kaplan, 'Presbyterians and Independents in 1643', *Eng. Hist. Rev.*, LXXXIV (1969), 246, 249–50, 253–4. On the 'parties' in the Westminster Assembly, see Haller, *Liberty and Reformation*, pp. 100–28.

65. J. A. St. John (ed.), *The Prose Works of John Milton* (1888), pp. 194–6, 209–10.

66. *H. of Commons J.*, III, 713, 715–6.

67. Clarendon, *Great Rebellion*, II, 536–7, III, 189–90, 223–4, 344–7, 388, 443–4, IV, 117; R. Hutton, *The Royalist War Effort 1642–1646*, (1986 edn.), pp. 133–5, 'The Structure of the Royalist Party 1642–1646', *Hist. J.*, XXIV (1981), especially pp. 556–7, 558–9, 562–3, 565–7; J. Daly, 'The Implications of Royalist Politics 1642–6', *Hist. J.*, XXVII (1984), 749.

68. Henry Parker, *A petition or declaration to be presented to the view of His most excellent Majestie* (1642), pp. 1–2.

69. *An item to His Majestie concerning Prince Rupert* (1642), [Wing 1089], pp. 4–5. See I. Roy, 'England turned Germany? The Aftermath of the Civil War in its European Context', *Roy. Hist. Soc. Trans.*, 5th ser. XXVIII (1978), 127–44.

70. B.M. Harleian MSS., 164, fo. 233.

71. Clarendon, *Great Rebellion*, II, 310; E. Warburton (ed.), *Memoirs of Prince Rupert and the Cavaliers* (1849), III, 26–27. Before the end of 1645 Rupert's attitude to peace negotiations changed radically.

72. Clarendon, *Great Rebellion*, III, 189.

73. See the brilliant case made by Wormald, *Clarendon* (Cambridge 1964), pp. 119-22.

74. For Bristol's and Dorset's arguments, see Rushworth, *Historical Collections*, V, 127-30.

75. Clarendon, *Great Rebellion*, II, 496-7; J.A.R.Marriott, *The Life and Times of Lucius Cary, Viscount Falkland*, 2nd edn., (1908), pp. 294-5.

76. Marriott, *Falkland*, pp. 297-301. Like so many other people, Marriott appears to have been misled by Pym's version of the incident.

77. Clarendon, *Great Rebellion*, III, 42-43. I am entirely convinced by Mr Wormald's judicious analysis of the episode (Wormald, op. cit., pp. 127-8).

78. Rushworth, *Historical Collections*, V, 383; Everitt, *Kent*, pp. 205-8.

79. *Parliamentary History*, XIII, 4-6.

80. Bodleian, Tanner MSS., 62, fos. 117-9.

81. Clarendon, *Great Rebellion*, III, 293 note (from Clarendon's *Life*); Gardiner, *Civil War*, I, 300. This letter is probably the source of information used in a compilation produced in 1656 which gives the same totals. (*A Catalogue of the Names of the Knights, Citizens and Burgesses that have served the last Four Parliaments* (1956), pp. 20-25). I am indebted to Professor J.R.Jones for making his personal copy of this available to me.

82. Keeler, *Long Parliament*, pp. 167, 240-1, 270, 283-4, 297-8, 353-4, 381; Brunton and Pennington, *Members of the Long Parliament*, pp. 2-3, 56, 63.

83. Clarendon, *Great Rebellion*, III, 193-200; Firth, *The House of Lords during the Civil War* (1974 edn.), pp. 135-6.

84. *Parliamentary History*, XIII, 105. See also ibid., pp. 107, 111-2.

85. ibid., pp. 114-20.

86. ibid., pp. 87-116; BM., Add. MSS., 25,277, fos., 60-61; Clarendon, *Great Rebellion*, III, 303-5.

87. Bodleian, Tanner MSS., 62, fo. 548(b).

88. Bodleian, Tanner MSS., 61, fos. 18(b)-19; *Parliamentary History*, XIII, 118-20.

89. See Gardiner, *Civil War*, I, 260, 299-300, 331.

90. Cited in ibid., II, 181.

91. Cited by P.R.Newman, 'The Royalist Party in Arms: the Peerage and Army Command, 1642-1646', in C.Jones, M.Newitt and

S. Roberts (eds.), *Politics and People in Revolutionary England* (Oxford, 1986), p. 82.

92. On Hopton, see F. T. R. Edgar, *Sir Ralph Hopton. The King's Man in the West (1642-1652)*, (Oxford, 1968).

93. R. Hutton, *The Royalist War Effort 1642-6*, passim, 'The Structure of the Royalist Party 1642-1646', *Hist. J.*, xxiv (1981), 553-69; J. L. Malcolm, *Caesar's Due: Loyalty and King Charles 1642-1646* (1983), especially pp. 92-94, where, however, the aristocratic Capel's local popularity is stressed; P. R. Newman, 'The Royalist Party in Arms' in Jones, Newitt, and Roberts (eds.), op. cit., pp. 81-93, and 'The Royalist Officer Corps 1642-1660. Army Command as a Reflexion of Social Structure', *Hist. J.*, xxvi (1983), 948-58. For a sharply critical challenge to Hutton's view, see J. Daly 'The Implications of Royalist Politics, 1642-1646', *Hist. J.*, xxvii (1984), 745-55.

94. See J. R. MacCormack, *Revolutionary Politics in the Long Parliament* (Cambridge Mass. 1973), pp. 1-19; L. Glow (Mrs L. Mulligan). 'Political Affiliations in the House of Commons after Pym's Death', *B.I.H.R.*, xxxviii (1965), 48-70. For a criticism of these views, see R. Ashton, 'Revolutionaries and Rumpers', *Hist. J.*, xviii (1975), 178-80.

95. V. Pearl, 'Oliver St. John and the "middle group" in the Long Parliament. August 1643-May 1644', *Eng. Hist. Rev.*, lxxxi (1966), 490-519, and 'The "Royal Independents" in the English Civil War', *Roy. Hist. Soc. Trans.*, 5th ser., xviii (1968), 69-96. For a different view see W. G. Palmer, 'Oliver St John and the Middle Group in the Long Parliament 1643-1645: A Reappraisal', *Albion*, xiv (1982), 20-26.

96. On the creation of the Committee, see W. Notestein, 'The Establishment of the Committee of Both Kingdoms', *Amer. Hist. Rev.*, xvii (1912), 477-95; Pearl, 'Oliver St. John', loc. cit., 508-15.

97. See MacCormack, op. cit., pp. 21-2; L. Mulligan, 'Peace Negotiations, Politics and the Committee of Both Kingdoms', *Hist. J.*, xii (1969), 4-6, 10 note. Notestein argued that the Committee was dominated by Independents, but, in the light of recent work on political groups, this application of what was at this time an exclusively religious category to politics is an anticipation of later distinctions. (*Amer. Hist. Rev.*, xvii, 483-9.)

98. For a very different view of both Pym's and his successors' attitude to Essex, see MacCormack, op. cit., pp. 6 note, 20-44.

99. B.M., Add. MSS., 33,051, fos. 182(b)-3(b); Gardiner, *Civil War*, I, 356; Snow, *Essex the Rebel*, pp. 435-6. On Essex's relations with the Committee of Both Kingdoms, see ibid., pp. 418-20, 425-6, 429-37, 451.

100. See Pearl, 'Oliver St. John', loc. cit., pp. 507-8; Holmes, *Eastern Association*, p. 112.

101. MacCormack, op. cit., pp. 27-8.

102. Holmes, *Eastern Association*, pp. 112-15.

103. *Fast Sermons*, IX, 147-87; Haller, *Liberty and Reformation*, pp. 121-2; Trevor-Roper, *Religion, the Reformation and Social Change*, pp. 315-16.

104. W.M. Lamont, *Marginal Prynne 1600-1669* (1963), pp. 149-57; *Godly Rule* (1969), pp. 109-18.

105. Haller, *Tracts on Liberty*, II, 321.

106. Baillie, *Letters and Journals*, II, 191-2, 211.

107. For some comments by Baillie on Williams, see ibid., II, p. 212.

108. Haller, *Liberty and Reformation*, pp. 115-17, 'The word of God in the Westminster Assembly', *Church History*, XVIII (1949), 199-219. On the Independents and toleration, see also G. Yule, *The Independents in the English Civil War* (Cambridge 1958), pp. 45-6, 59.

109. Gardiner, *Civil War*, II, 29-31.

CHAPTER 9   THE TRANSFORMATION OF POLITICS 1644-6

1. See, e.g., Pennington and Roots, *Stafford*, p. lxxiv, where he is contrasted with Sir William Brereton, 'who in general favoured the most energetic and uncompromising prosecution of the war'.

2. This paragraph is based on material in Bodleian, Tanner MSS., 62, fos. 402-2(b), 404-4(b), 407-8, 420-1(b), 422-2(b), 428, 453-5(b), 482-3; *H. of Lords J.*, VI, 321, 334; *Cal. S.P.D. 1644*, pp. 120-1; *H.M.C. 4th Rep.*, pp. 263, 271, 272, 275; *H.M.C. 5th Rep.*, p. 115; *H.M.C. H. of Lords MSS.*, XI, 359; *Luke Letter Books*, p. 32; Pennington and Roots, *Stafford*, pp. lxx-lxxi, lxxiv-lxxxiii, 152-3; Morrill, *Provinces*, p. 121. See esp. Hughes, *Warwickshire*, pp. 220-38, and below pp. 271, 275.

3. B.M., Add. MSS., 31,116, fos. 175(b)-6; *Cal. S.P.D. 1644*, pp. 545-6; *Cal. S.P.D. 1644-5*, pp. 138, 139, 143-4, 146-61; *H. of Commons J.*, III, 704; J. Bruce and D. Masson (ed.), *The Quarrel between the Earl of Manchester and Oliver Cromwell, Camden Soc.*, new ser., XII (1875), pp. 32-3, 67-70, 78-94.

4. A.N.B.Cotton, 'Cromwell and the Self-Denying Ordinance', *History*, LXII (1977), pp. 211–31.

5. Holmes, *Eastern Association*, pp. 195–212. I am deeply indebted to Dr Holmes's brilliant and convincing reinterpretation of this episode.

6. Carlyle, *Cromwell*, I, p. 152.

7. L.Kaplan, 'The Plot to depose Charles I in 1644', *B.I.H.R.*, XLIV (1971), 216–23.

8. *Cal. S.P.D. 1644–5*, p. 152, the testimony of Colonel John Pickering.

9. 'Memorial of Denzil Lord Holles', in Maseres, *Select Tracts*, I, p. 191.

10. C.Hill, *God's Englishman* (1970), pp. 65–7.

11. Bruce and Masson (ed.), *Quarrel*, pp. 72–4.

12. ibid., pp. 74–5. cf. B.M. Add. MSS., 31, 116, fos. 177(b)–8; *H. of Commons J.*, III, 713.

13. See pp. 217–18.

14. Holmes, *Eastern Association*, pp. 207–11.

15. V.F.Snow, *Essex the Rebel* (Lincoln, Nebraska 1970), pp. 452–3.

16. *Luke Letter Books*, pp. 69, 79–80.

17. Whitelock, *Memorials*, pp. 111–13; J. Rushworth, *Historical Collections* (1691), VI, 2–3.

18. Cotton, 'Cromwell and the Self-Denying Ordinance', loc. cit.

19. Baillie, *Letters and Journals*, II, p. 247.

20. Whitelock, *Memorials*, pp. 113–14; Rushworth, *Historical Collections*, VI, 4–7; *Ludlow Memoirs*, I, 115; *Parliamentary History*, XIII, 380–6.

21. Maseres, *Select Tracts*, I, 210, 337–8.

22. Gardiner, *Civil War*, II, 188–90; C.H.Firth, *The House of Lords during the Civil War* (1974 edn.), pp. 146–9. The Ordinance is printed in Gardiner, *Constitutional Documents*, pp. 287–8.

23. B.M., Harleian MSS., 166, fos. 173–3(b); *Parliamentary History*, XIII, 386–9.

24. B.M., Harleian MSS., 166, fo. 194; Add. MSS., 31,116, fo. 200(b); *H. of Commons J.*, IV, 88; Whitelock, *Memorials*, p. 113.

25. Snow, *Essex the Rebel*, p. 314; Holmes, *Eastern Association*, pp. 175–7.

26. Clarendon, *Great Rebellion*, III, 437.

27. Maseres, *Select Tracts*, pp. 276–7; *H.M.C. 12th Rep.*, pt. ix, pp. 28–9.

28. C.H.Firth, *Cromwell's Army* (1962 edn.), pp. 46–7; A.H.Wool-rych, *Battles of the English Civil War* (1966 edn.), pp. 103–4; M.Kishlansky, *The Rise of the New Model Army* (Cambridge 1979), pp. 39–46, 50, 62–6, 218–21.

29. B.M., Egerton MSS., 2647, fo. 165.

30. The contrast is, of course, overdone, if only in that most of the soldiers were probably illiterate. On promotion from the ranks see Firth, *Cromwell's Army*, pp. 40–1; L.G.Schwoerer, *'No Standing Armies'* (Baltimore 1974), p. 52.

31. Firth, *Cromwell's Army*, p. 36; M.Kishlansky, *New Model Army*, p. 66.

32. Firth, *Cromwell's Army*, p. 315.

33. On King and Crawford, see Holmes, *Eastern Association*, pp. 199–205, and 'Colonel King and Lincolnshire Politics 1642–6', *Hist. J.*, XVI (1973), 452–7.

34. Firth, *Cromwell's Army*, pp. 317–18.

35. *H.M.C. 4th Rep.*, pt. i, p. 273.

36. J.R.MacCormack, *Revolutionary Politics in the Long Parliament* (Cambridge, Mass. 1973), p. 72. Over 300 Scottish officers were compulsorily retired. (L.Kaplan, *Politics and Religion during the English Revolution* (New York 1976), pp. III–12.)

37. B.M., Add. MSS., 31,116, fos. 188, 191; *H. of Commons J.*, IV, 26, 43.

38. D.Underdown, 'Party Management in the Recruiter Elections 1645–1648', *Eng. Hist. Rev.*, LXXXIII (1968), 238. For an admirable terse and informative summary of the party developments, see the same author's *Pride's Purge* (Oxford 1971), pp. 65–73.

39. V.Pearl, 'The "Royal Independents" in the English Civil War' in *Roy. Hist. Soc. Trans.*, 5th ser., XVIII (1968), pp. 69–96.

40. For an excellent recent account of the circumstances of the Uxbridge Treaty, see Kaplan, *Politics and Religion during the English Revolution*, pp. 97–113.

41. Dr Kaplan, however (ibid., pp. 105–7), lays greater stress than most historians on the Scottish concern about civil matters, notably the militia and Ireland.

42. Bodleian, Tanner MSS., 61, fo. 151; Clarendon, *Great Rebellion*, III, 417; *Parliamentary History*, XIII, 283.

43. *Parliamentary History*, XIII, 336–41.

44. ibid., 348–9; and, for Parliament's reply, 351–2.

45. For the parliamentary and royal propositions, see Gardiner, *Constitutional Documents*, pp. 275-87. For the parliamentary reply to the latter, *Cal. S. P. D. 1644-5*, pp. 276-7.

46. Whitelock, *Memorials*, pp. 107-9; Rushworth, *Historical Collections*, v, 842-3. There is a contradiction between this account and that given by Whitelock to the House of Commons on 4 July 1645 in answer to Saville's charges that Holles and Whitelock were guilty of collusion with the royalists. Here he asserted that 'In all our discourses Mr. Holles and myself did justifie your [viz. Parliament's] Propositions, and vindicate your Proceedings' (Whitelock, *Memorials*, p. 150). See Crawford, *Denzil Holles*, pp. 108-10.

47. Clarendon, *Great Rebellion*, III, 494-5; Whitelock, *Memorials*, p. 125.

48. *Clarendon State Papers*, II, 186-7.

49. *Considerations touching the late treaty for a peace* (Oxford 1645) [Wing 5920], p. 34.

50. *The King's cabinet opened* (1645) [Wing 591], pp. 25-7.

51. *Cal. S. P. D. 1644-5*, p. 373; Rushworth, *Historical Collections*, VI, 132-3; Clarendon, *Great Rebellion*, IV, 74-5; *Parliamentary History*, XIV, 95-7.

52. Bell, *Memorials*, I, 155.

53. There is a full and thorough recent account in MacCormack, *Revolutionary Politics*, pp. 77-91.

54. On the caginess of the parliamentary commissioners at Uxbridge, see Clarendon, *Great Rebellion*, III, 472.

55. Whitelock, *Memorials*, pp. 148-9, 151-2, 153, 155-6; Rushworth, *Historical Collections*, VI, 177, 179.

56. For evidence of charges brought later against peace party men in 1645-6, see B.M., Harleian MSS., 166, fos. 267-7(b); B.M., Add. MSS., 31,116, fo. 268(b); *H. of Commons J.*, IV, 639-40. The process culminates with the impeachment of eleven Presbyterian MPs in 1647 (see pp. 301-3).

57. Whitelock, *Memorials*, p. 154.

58. On these developments, see V. Pearl, 'London Puritans and Scotch Fifth Columnists: a mid-seventeenth century phenomenon' in A. E. J. Hollaender and W. Kellaway (eds.), *Studies in London History presented to Philip Edmond Jones* (1969), pp. 317-31.

59. *Clarendon State Papers*, II, 242-4, 247-8, 254, 313-14; *Charles I in 1646, passim*; Clarendon, *Great Rebellion*, IV, 203-6.

60. Bodleian, Clarendon MSS., 29, fos. 52-52(b).

61. Clarendon, *Great Rebellion*, III, 497.

62. J.H.Hexter, 'The Problem of the Presbyterian Independents', reprinted in his *Reappraisals in History* (1963), pp. 163-84.

63. G.Yule, *The Independents in the English Civil War* (Cambridge 1958), pp. 35-41; 'Independents and Revolutionaries', *J. Brit. Stud.*, VII (1968), 11-32; 'Presbyterians and Independents, Some Comments', *P. &P.*, 47 (1970), 130-3.

64. D.Underdown, 'The Independents Reconsidered', *J. Brit. Stud.*, III (1964), 57-84; 'The Independents Again', ibid., VIII (1968), 83-93, and 'The Presbyterian Independents Exorcized: a Brief Comment', *P. & P.*, 47 (1970), 128-30. This view characterizes Underdown's magnificent study of civil war politics, *Pride's Purge*. It is also held by V.Pearl, 'Oliver St. John and the "middle-group" in the Long Parliament. August 1643-May 1644', *Eng. Hist. Rev.*, LXXXI, especially 490-2, and 'The "Royal Independents" in the English Civil War', art. cit.

65. S.Foster, 'The Presbyterian Independents Exorcized. A Ghost Story for Historians', *P. & P.*, 44 (1969), 52-75. For criticisms of this article by B.Worden, V.Pearl, D.Underdown, G.Yule and J.H.Hexter, and Dr Foster's own rejoinder, see *P. & P.*, 47 (1970), 116-46.

66. For the Accommodation Order, see p. 220.

67. *House of Commons J.*, III, 721, 733; *Westminster Assembly Minutes*, pp. 17, 19.

68. Whitelock, *Memorials*, p. 123.

69. B.M., Add. MSS., 37,978, fos. 9(b), 30(b); W.H.W.Meikle (ed.), *Correspondence of the Scots Commissioners in London 1644-1646* (Edinburgh 1917), pp. 111-12, 130. For the ordinance, see *Acts and Ordinances*, I, 789-93.

70. *Acts and Ordinances*, I, 833-8; *Parliamentary History*, XIV, 280-9. In June a standing committee of Parliament replaced the parliamentary commissioners; (B.M., Add. MSS., 31,116, fos. 270-2; *H. of Commons J.*, IV, 552).

71. *Westminster Assembly Minutes*, p. 121.

72. B.M., Add. MSS., 10,114, fo. 12; Add. MSS., 31,116, fos. 261-1(b); *H. of Commons J.*, IV, 506. See also ibid., pp. 511, 518.

73. *Westminster Assembly Minutes*, pp. 193-5, 196-206, 251-2; Baillie, *Letters and Journal*, II, 360-1.

74. *Parliamentary History*, XIV, 340; Baillie, *Letters and Journals*, II,

360; *Charles I in 1646*, p. 71. The King's statement comes from a letter of 17 October 1646.

75. W.M.Lamont, *Marginal Prynne 1600-1669* (1969), pp. 149-74, *Godly Rule* (1969), pp. 106-31. See also Haller, *Liberty and Reformation*, pp. 229-37.

76. The fullest accounts of the debate are in Whitelock, *Memorials*, pp. 163-4 and Rushworth, *Historical Collections*, VI, 203-5. There are shorter accounts in B.M., Harleian MSS., 166, fo. 260(b); Add. MSS., 18,780, fo. 112(b); Add. MSS., 31,116, fo. 229(b) and *H. of Commons J.*, IV, 262.

77. B.M., Add. MSS., 10,114, fos. 12; Add. MSS., 31,116, fos. 261-1(b); *H. of Commons J.*, IV, 428, 506.

78. Rushworth, *Historical Collections*, VI, 123-4.

79. *Harleian Miscellany*, V, 511-14.

80. B.M., Add. MSS., 37,978, fos. 21(b), 23(b)-25, 26-26(b); Washington, D.C., Folger Library, Folger MSS., Ga. 6, fos. 1-3, 5-7, 28-29; *Cal. S.P.D. 1644-5*; pp. 412, 413-14, 422-3, 531-2, 574-6; *Cal. S.P.D. 1645-7*; pp. 49, 56-7; *Parliamentary History*, XIV, 77-80, 85-9, 103-4.

81. B.M., Add. MSS., 31,116, fo. 472; Bodleian, Tanner MSS., 60, fos. 287-8(b); *Cal. S.P.D. 1645-7*, pp. 215, 255-6; *H. of Commons J.*, IV, 305-6; *H. of Lords J.*, VIII, 34-6; *Parliamentary History*, XIV, 81-4, 144-52.

82. B.M., Add. MSS., 37,978, fo. 34.

83. B.M., Add. MSS., 31,116, fos. 272(b)-3; Bodleian, Tanner MSS., 59, *passim*; Tanner MSS., 60, fos. 361, 368, 391-1(b), 556; Meikle (ed.), *Correspondence...*, pp. 160-1, 183, 189-90, 215-16; *Parliamentary History*, XIV, 199, 205-6, 238-40, 269-72.

84. Bodleian, Tanner MSS., 60, fos. 172-2(b), 207-7(b); *Parliamentary History*, XIV, 36-7, 46-7, 67-70.

85. Bodleian, Tanner MSS., 60, fos. 209-9(b); *Cal. S.P.D. 1645-7*, pp. 114-15; *Parliamentary History*, XIV, 29-30, 145-7.

86. B.M., Add. MSS., 31,116, fo. 270; *H. of Commons J.*, IV, 551.

87. *Parliamentary History*, XIV, 335-42. See also ibid., pp. 344-5, 366-71.

88. B.M., Add. MSS., 31,116, fo. 224(b); Add. MSS., 37,978, fo. 9(b); *Cal. S.P.D. 1645-7*, p. 64; *H. of Commons J.*, IV, 246; *H. of Lords J.*, VII, 539-40; Rushworth, *Historical Collections*, VI, 237; *Parliamentary History*, XIV, 38-41, 136, 154-6, 161-81, 194-5, 342-5.

89. MacCormack, *Revolutionary Politics*, pp. 92-3, 101-2.

90. For examples of party contention, see B.M., Harleian MSS., 166, fos. 267-7(b); Add. MSS., 31,116, fo. 235; *H. of Commons J.*, IV, 296.

91. B.M., Add. MSS., 31,116, fos. 345(b)-6; *H. of Commons J.*, IV, 359-61.

92. *Ludlow Memoirs*, I, p. 132.

93. B.M., Add. MSS., 31,116, fos. 227-7(b); *H. of Commons J.*, IV, 249; Whitelock, *Memorials*, p. 161.

94. Underdown, 'Party Management', loc. cit., pp. 235-64. See also Gardiner, *Civil War*, II, 335-6; III, 77-8; D. Brunton and D. H. Pennington, *Members of the Long Parliament* (1954), pp. 21-37; MacCormack, op. cit., pp. 99-101, Gardiner believed that the elections made little difference to the state of the parties.

95. Whitelock, *Memorials*, pp. 212-13.

96. B.M., Add. MSS., 10,114, fos. 20, 21(b); Add. MSS., 31,116, fos. 284(b), 285, 286(b)-7; *H. of Commons J.*, IV, 659, 680, 687-8, 700; Underdown, 'Party Management', loc. cit., pp. 256-8.

97. *H. of Commons J.*, IV, 662.

98. For more detailed treatment of the role of the City in 1645-6 see V. Pearl, in Hollaender and Kellaway (eds.), *Studies . . .*, pp. 317-31, and 'London's Counter-Revolution' in G. E. Aylmer (ed.), *The Interregnum, The Quest for Settlement 1646-1660* (1972), pp. 29-44.

99. B.M., Add. MSS., 18,780, fos. 167-9; Add. MSS., 31,116, fos. 243(b)-4; *H. of Commons J.*, IV, 348; Whitelock, *Memorials*, p. 187.

100. Hollaender and Kellaway (eds.), *Studies . . .*, p. 329.

101. B.M., Add. MSS., 31,116, fos. 271, 272; *H. of Commons J.*, IV, 555-6, 561; Whitelock, *Memorials*, pp. 212, 213; Pearl in Aylmer (ed.), *The Interregnum*, pp. 35-7.

102. *Parliamentary History*, xiv, 273-7, 318-65.

103. *Charles I in 1646*, pp. 3-4, 16-17.

104. *Clarendon State Papers*, II, 213-16.

105. Clarendon, *Great Rebellion*, IV, p. 164.

106. *Charles I in 1646*, pp. 31-3; *Parliamentary History*, xiv, 442-3.

107. *Charles I in 1646*, pp. 36-8.

108. Bodleian, Tanner MSS., 59, fo. 117; *Cal. S.P.D. 1645-7*, p. 433; for other letters to similar effect see Rushworth, *Historical Collections*, VI, 268-9; *Parliamentary History*, xiv, 381-4, 389-92; xv, 8-12, 17-19.

CHAPTER 10   CENTRALISM AND LOCALISM 1642–8

1. B.M., Stowe MSS., 744, fos. 2–2(b).

2. Gardiner, *Constitutional Documents*, p. 259.

3. B.M., Egerton MSS., 2643, fo. 7.

4. For examples, see *Cal. S.P.D. 1644*, p. 335; Bell, *Memorials*, I, p. 136; Underdown, *Somerset*, p. 74.

5. Bodleian, Tanner MSS., 62, fo. 224.

6. Holmes, *Eastern Association*, pp. 59–60, *The Declaration of the Associated Counties*, 26 August 1648, B.M. E.460 (37), p. 3.

7. B.M., Egerton MSS., 2647, fo. 361. For a similar request from Colchester the following spring, see B.M., Stowe MSS., 189, fo. 19.

8. B.M., Add. MSS., 15,916, fo. 15(b); Clarendon, *Great Rebellion*, II, 451, III, 126–7; Gardiner, *Civil War*, I, 194–5, II, 235, 292; Underdown, *Somerset*, p. 89.

9. E. Warburton (ed.), *Memoirs and Correspondence of Prince Rupert and the Cavaliers* (1849), II, 434–5.

10. B.M. Egerton MSS., 2647, fo. 125.

11. B.M. Stowe MSS., 189, fos. 21, 29, 35; *Cal. S.P.D. 1644–5*, pp. 330–1.

12. Morrill, *Provinces*, pp. 36–7.

13. ibid, pp. 160–1; Clarendon, *Great Rebellion*, II, 469; J.S. Morrill, *Cheshire 1630–1660* (1974), pp. 65–9; Ketton-Cremer, *Norfolk*, pp. 167–9; Holmes, *Eastern Association*, pp. 55–62.

14. *The declaration and vote of the Lords and Commons ... concerning the late treaty* (1642) [Wing 1327]; Clarendon, *Great Rebellion*, II, 460–3.

15. ibid, II, 459–60; *H.M.C. 4th Rep.* Appendix, p. 308; M. Coate, *Cornwall in the Great Civil War and Interregnum 1642–1660* (Truro 1963), pp. 54–7: E.A. Andriette, *Devon and Exeter in the Civil War* (Newton Abbot 1971), pp. 82–4.

16. Morrill, *Cheshire*, pp. 57–9, *Provinces*, pp. 37, 159–60; Pennington and Roots, *Stafford*, p. xx.

17. There is a very good general account of the clubmen in Morrill, *Provinces*, pp. 97–114. For other interpretative accounts see D. Underdown, 'The Chalk and the Cheese: Contrasts among the English Clubmen', *P. & P.* 85 (1979), 25–48, and *Revel, Riot and Rebellion ... 1603–1660* (Oxford 1985), especially pp. 156–9, 167–8, 276–7; R. Hutton, *The Royalist War Effort 1642–1646* (1984 edn.), especially pp. 159–65, 170–2, 180–2, 189–90.

18. Bodleian, Tanner MSS., 60, fos. 163–4; A.R. Bayley, *The Great*

Civil War in Dorset (Taunton 1910), pp. 472–5; Morrill, *Provinces*, pp. 199–200.

19. Hutton, *Royalist War Effort*, p. 156.
20. Underdown, *P. & P.*, art. cit. p. 27.
21. B.M. Add. MSS., 24862, fo. 48: Bodleian, Tanner MSS., 60, fos. 196, 197, 198–8(b); Whitelock, *Memorials*, p. 151; *Parliamentary History*, XIV, 16–19; Bayley, *Great Civil War in Dorset*, pp. 475–6; Morrill, *Provinces*, pp. 196–7.
22. *Cal. S.P.D. 1645–7, passim*, pp. 146–8, 151–3. On the Sussex clubmen see Fletcher, *Sussex*, pp. 272–5.
23. Bodleian, Tanner MSS., 60, fos. 251–5; Washington, Folger Library, Folger MSS., Ga. 6, fos. 31–2.
24. Underdown, *P. & P.*, art. cit. p. 28; Hutton, *Royalist War Effort*, especially pp. 160–5, 170–1, 189–90.
25. On all this, see Morrill, *Provinces*, especially pp. 80–4.
26. *A second remonstrance or declaration of the Lords and Commons . . . concerning the commissions of array* (1643) [Wing 2287], p. 43.
27. *Cal. S.P.D. 1644*, pp. 344–5.
28. Morrill, *Cheshire*, pp. 82–6.
29. B.M., Harleian MSS., 164, fos. 243–3(b).
30. Clarendon, *Great Rebellion*, II, 274; C. Hill, *Puritanism and Revolution* (1958), p. 207.
31. [J. Corbet?] *An historical relation of the military government of Gloucester* (1645), p. 7.
32. B.M., Add. MSS., 15,903, fo. 55; Morrill, *Cheshire*, p. 83 and passim.
33. *Harleian Miscellany*, V, 50; *Cal. S.P.D. 1641–3*, pp. 356–7.
34. On the phenomenon of royalists sitting on the post-war benches in Somerset and Wales, see Underdown, *Somerset*, p. 140; Bell, *Memorials*, II, pp. 378–80.
35. This short passage on the Norfolk JPs is based on very extensive materials kindly put at my disposal by Mr D. Howell James; on Ketton-Cremer, op. cit., passim; and on information from my colleague, Dr V. Morgan.
36. G.C.F. Forster, 'County Government in Yorkshire during the Interregnum', *Northern History*, XII (1976), 100–4, and 'The East Yorkshire Justice of the Peace in the Seventeenth Century', *East Yorkshire Local History*, ser. no. 30 (1973), pp. 20, 25–6.
37. Underdown, *Somerset*, pp. 69–70, 140, 149.
38. Fletcher, *Sussex*, pp. 131–4, 355 (Appendix V).

39. Morrill, *Cheshire*, pp. 184-5, 223-5, 233-4.
40. Everitt, *Suffolk*, pp. 15-16, 25, 26-7; Ketton-Cremer, op. cit., pp. 172, 204-5, supplemented by the materials of Mr D. Howell James and the observations of Dr V. Morgan.
41. Fletcher, *Sussex*, pp. 325-7.
42. Everitt, *Kent*, pp. 143-55.
43. Underdown, *Somerset*, pp. 47, 124-5.
44. On these developments see C. Holmes, 'Colonel King and Lincolnshire Politics 1642-1646', *Hist. J.*, XVI (1973), 451-84.
45. Wood, *Nottinghamshire*, pp. 124-34.
46. Pennington and Roots, *Stafford*, pp. xxii-xxiii; Hughes, *Warwickshire*, especially pp. 169, 174-80.
47. A. H. Dodd, *Studies in Stuart Wales* (Cardiff 1952), pp. 110-76; Everitt, *Suffolk*, especially pp. 15-16; Morrill, *Provinces*, pp. 118-9.
48. Everitt, *Kent*, pp. 144-6; Holmes, 'Colonel King', art. cit., p. 483; Hughes, *Warwickshire*, pp. 220-54.
49. Hughes, *Warwickshire*, pp. 223-4, 228-9, 234-5.
50. On this see D. H. Pennington, 'The Cost of the English Civil War', *History Today*, (Feb. 1958), 126-33. For some useful comparisons, see Morrill, *Provinces*, pp. 84-7.
51. For examples, see Everitt, *Kent*, pp. 157, 170-1; R. Ashton, 'From Cavalier to Roundhead Tyranny 1642-9', in J. Morrill (ed.), *Reactions to the English Civil War 1642-1649* (1982), pp. 185-207.
52. [Edward Bowles], *Manifest Truths* (1646), p. 51. Italics author's.
53. Pennington and Roots, *Stafford*, pp. xvi, lix.
54. Everitt, *Kent*, pp. 133, 139.
55. Underdown, *Somerset*, pp. 125-6.
56. B.M., Egerton MSS., 2646, fos. 273-3(b); *Cal. S.P.D. 1644*, pp. 281-2. On Denbigh and Warwickshire, see above, pp. 223-4.
57. Bodleian, Tanner MSS., 57, fos. 21, 22(b)-23, 352, 378(b); Tanner MSS., 58, fo. 507; Tanner MSS., 59, fos. 230, 232-2(b), 418, 446; Tanner MSS., 62, fo. 514; Everitt, *Kent*, pp. 139-40, 158-60; G. H. Fowler (ed.), 'The Civil War Papers of Sir William Boteler 1642-1655', *Bedfordshire Historical Record Society*, XVIII (1936), 15.
58. Pennington and Roots, *Stafford*, pp. xxvi-xxvii, xxxi-xxxii; Hughes, *Warwickshire*, pp. 184-8, 212, 234. See *Acts and Ordinances*, I, 56-7, for an example of such an ordinance. For another example of fiscal localism see Morrill, *Cheshire*, p. 100.
59. Morrill, *Cheshire*, p. 161. For examples of such requests from

the committees of Yorkshire, Lancashire, Nottinghamshire, Leicestershire and the Northern Association, see Bodleian, Tanner MSS., 57, fos. 74, 171, 265, 352, 454; Tanner MSS., 59, fos. 195, 345, 550; Tanner MSS., 60, fos. 556-6(b). Some requests for decentralization of dues other than for compounding pre-date 1645, e.g. the Ely committee's request for decentralization of the Excise in December 1643 and the Suffolk committee's for decentralization of the fifteenth and twentieth parts in January 1644 (Tanner MSS., 62, fos. 469, 514).

60. Bodleian, Tanner MSS., 60, fos. 119-20, 125, 126.

61. Bodleian, Tanner MSS., 59, fo. 59; Tanner MSS., 60, fo. 569; *Cal. S.P.D. 1645-7*, pp. 381-2, 409-10, 447-9, 454; Rushworth, *Historical Collections*, VI, 264.

62. On Manchester's leniency, Bodleian, Tanner MSS., 61, fo. 14; Tanner MSS., 62, fo. 273; Ketton-Cremer, op. cit., pp. 295-7. For similar cases see Morrill, *Cheshire*, pp. 112-13, 116-17 and *Provinces*, p. 182; Everitt, *Kent*, pp. 227-8.

63. Bodleian, Tanner MSS., 321, fos. 8-8(b).

64. Morrill, *Provinces*, p. 181; Holmes, *Eastern Association*, p. 192; Underdown, *Somerset*, pp. 126-7; Hill, *God's Englishman* (1970), p. 70; R. Howell, *Newcastle upon Tyne and the Puritan Revolution* (Oxford 1967), p. 187.

65. B.M., Egerton MSS., 2646, fos. 197, 247; Egerton MSS., 2647, fo. 162.

66. Everitt, *Kent*, pp. 187-8, 201-4 and *Suffolk*, pp. 16-17.

67. For examples of reminders to the committees of Essex, Norfolk and Hampshire, see B.M., Egerton MSS., 2646, fo. 267; Egerton MSS., 2647, fo. 51; Bodleian, Tanner MSS., 64, fos. 116, 118(b), 129; *Cal. S.P.D. 1644-5*, p. 142.

68. Bodleian, Tanner MSS., 59, fos. 52, 247, 420.

69. B.M., Egerton MSS., 2643, fo. 17; Egerton MSS., 2647, fos. 51, 64, 74, 197, 231.

70. *Cal. S.P.D. 1645-7*, pp. 96-7.

71. Bodleian, Tanner MSS., 62, fos. 561-1(b), 573; *Cal. S.P.D. 1644*, p. 377.

72. Bodleian, Tanner MSS., 62, fos. 402-2(b), 404-5(b), 407-8, 420-1(b), 422-2(b), 428, 453-5(b), 480; *Cal. S.P.D. 1644*, pp. 120-1; *H. of Lords J.*, VI, 321; *H.M.C. 4th Rep.*, pp. 262-3, 269-70, 275; *H.M.C. 5th Rep.*, p. 115; *H.M.C. H. of Lords MSS.*, XI, *Addenda 1514-1714*, 359. And see pp. 223-4.

73. *Luke Letter Books*, pp. 31-2, 337-8 and *passim*.

74. Bodleian, Tanner MSS., 60, fo. 75; *Cal. S.P.D. 1644*, p. 525; *Cal. S.P.D. 1644-5*, pp. 52-4, 112, 186-7, 190-1, 266-9.

75. *Cal. S.P.D. 1644-5*, pp. 12, 55, 111-12, 117; *Hutchinson Memoirs*, *passim*.

76. Holmes, *Eastern Association*, pp. 188-9; 'Colonel King', art. cit.

77. For a detailed and admirable account of these developments, see Holmes, *Eastern Association*, pp. 119-41, 186-94.

78. See B.M., Egerton MSS., 2647, fo. 68; Egerton MSS., 2651, fo. 156; Bodleian, Tanner MSS., 62, fos. 156, 301.

79. B.M., Egerton MSS., 2643, fo. 17.

80. *Cal. S.P.D. 1644*, pp. 545-6; *Cal. S.P.D. 1644-5*, p. 139; J. Bruce and D. Masson (eds.), *The Quarrel between the Earl of Manchester and Oliver Cromwell*, Camden Soc., new ser., XII (1875), pp. 11-12, 32-3.

81. An account of the proceedings at the Bury conference is printed in Everitt, *Suffolk*, pp. 83-9.

82. On the Committee of Safety, see L. Glow, 'The Committee of Safety', *Eng. Hist. Rev.*, LXXX (1965), 289-313; Morrill, *Provinces*, pp. 57-8.

83. *Cal. S.P.D. 1644*, pp. 34, 38-41, 177; *Cal. S.P.D. 1644-5*, pp. 275, 288, 294, 331, 350, 358, 423, 437, 540, 566-7; *Cal. S.P.D. 1645-7*, pp. 56, 358.

84. For a full account of the operations of these bodies, see D. H. Pennington, 'The Accounts of the Kingdom 1642-1649', in F. J. Fisher (ed.), *Essays in the Economic and Social History of Tudor and Stuart England*, pp. 182-203.

85. Bodleian, Tanner MSS., 59, fo. 680. See also Morrill, *Provinces*, pp. 184-5, for a report made to the House of Commons on 10 October 1646. For further complaints in March 1648, see *H. of Commons J.*, V, 492.

86. Everitt, *Suffolk*, p. 23.

87. Morrill, *Provinces*, p. 70.

88. *Cal. S.P.D. 1645-7*, p. 338; Fisher (ed.), *Essays...*, pp. 195-7; Hughes, *Warwickshire*, pp. 192, 215-9, 238-9, 242-7, 249; Morrill, *Cheshire*, pp. 90-1; Holmes, 'Colonel King', loc. cit., 474-5; Underdown, *Somerset*, pp. 141-2.

89. Fletcher, *Sussex*, pp. 333-6.

90. Everitt, *Kent*, pp. 172-84; P.R.O., S.P. 28/234, no piece refer-

ences; for a similar complaint from the Sussex sub-committee, see S.P. 28/245, no piece reference.

91. Pennington and Roots, *Stafford*, p. 343.

92. D.Underdown, *Pride's Purge* (Oxford 1971), p. 74, and 'Party Management in the Recruiter Elections 1645-1648', *Eng. Hist. Rev.*, LXXXIII (1968), 253-4, 256-7.

93. B.M., Add. MSS., 19,399, fo. 45.

94. Underdown, *Somerset*, pp. 140-1, 149.

95. Bodleian, Tanner MSS., 58, fo. 283.

96. See Coate, *Cornwall* . . . , pp. 330-8; Everitt, *Kent*, pp. 225-6. In Kent many committee-men opposed such actions, which were the work of the radical core of the committee dominated by Weldon.

97. Fletcher, *Sussex*, p. 107.

98. Bodleian, Walker MSS., C.4, fos. 218-19, 221-2(b), 224, 226-6(b); Walker, *Sufferings*, p. 24; A.G.Matthews, *Walker Revised* (Oxford 1948), p. 120; Coate, *Cornwall* . . . , pp. 331, 333-5.

99. Fletcher, *Sussex*, p. 108. For similar examples, see Coate, *Cornwall* . . . , p. 338.

100. Bell, *Memorials*, I, 191-3.

101. Bodleian, Walker MSS., C4, especially fos. 176-80(b), 340, 343-9(b), 350, 352, 354-9, 361, 369, 374-6, 378-9(b); Walker, *Sufferings*, pp. 194-7; Matthews, *Walker Revised*, p. 109; J.F.Chanter, *The Life and Times of Martin Blake, B.D.* (1910), especially pp. 96-131.

102. *Luke Letter Books*, pp. 85-6.

103. Everitt, *Kent*, pp. 127, 225-6; J.Webb, *Memorials of the Civil War . . . as it affected Herefordshire and the adjacent counties* (1879), II, 312; Howell, *Newcastle upon Tyne* . . . , pp. 225-6.

104. Ketton-Cremer, *Norfolk in the Civil War*, pp. 250-2.

105. J.W.Packer, *The Transformation of Anglicanism 1643-1660* (Manchester 1969), p. 12. On Anglican resistance, see Dr Morrill's article in J.S.Morrill (ed.), *Reactions to the English Civil War*, pp. 89-114.

106. C.Holmes (ed.), *The Suffolk Committees for Scandalous Ministers 1644-1646*, Suffolk Record Soc., XIII (1970), 31-2.

107. *Harleian Miscellany*, V, 331. On scandalous ministers in general, see I.M.Green, 'The Persecution of "Scandalous" and "Malignant" Ministers During the English Civil War', *Eng. Hist. Rev.*, XCIV (1979), 507-31.

108. B.M., Add. MSS., 15,669, fos. 10, 11; Bodleian, Tanner MSS.,

60, fos. 68-68(b), 69-69(b); *H. of Lords J.*, VII, 309; C. Holmes (ed.), *The Suffolk Committees* . . . , pp. 56-7 and *passim*.

109. Bodleian, Tanner MSS., 60, fo. 77; Coate, *Cornwall* . . . , p. 338; Howell, *Newcastle upon Tyne* . . . , pp. 224, 228-9; Everitt, *Kent*, pp. 127, 225. J. S. Morrill, *Reactions to the English Civil War*, pp. 95-7.

110. Bodleian, Clarendon MSS., 29, fo. 72; Everitt, *Kent*, p. 225.

111. Bodleian, Tanner MSS., 57, fo. 93.

112. *H. of Commons J.*, IV, 435; Whitelock, *Memorials*, p. 197.

113. Bodleian, Tanner MSS., 321, fos. 7-7(b).

114. *H. of Lords J.*, IX, 330, 353-4; *H.M.C. 4th Rep.*, pp. 187, 190; *Parliamentary History*, XVI, 53, 109.

115. Hugh Peter, 'A Word for the Army' in *Harleian Miscellany*, V, 69; *A copy of a letter sent by the agents of severall regiments* . . . November 11, 1647 . . . [Wing 6134], p. 3; *A letter sent from several agitators*, 14 November 1647 [Wing 1604], p. 7; Bell, *Memorials*, II, p. 26.

116. Bodleian, Tanner MSS., 58, fos. 325, 329, 429, 432, 448, 469, 507, 590; Cary, *Memorials*, I, 277-82, 295-7; Morrill, *Cheshire*, pp. 200-3, and 'Mutiny and Discontent in English Provincial Armies 1645-1647', *P. & P.*, 56 (1972), especially 61-71.

117. *Proposals from* . . . *Sir Thomas Fairfax*, 17 October 1647, especially pp. 3-5.

118. This passage on King is based on Bodleian, Tanner MSS., 58, fo. 39; Tanner MSS., 59, fos. 668-9(b); Edward King, *A discovery of the arbitrary, tyrannicall and illegal action* (1647); and the excellent article by C. Holmes, 'Colonel King', loc. cit., pp. 451-84.

119. B.M., Add. MSS., 31,116, fos. 293(b), 294; *H. of Commons J.*, V, 20-1, 24-5; *Parliamentary History*, XV, 221-35 and especially 230.

120. Bodleian, Tanner MSS., 58, fos. 587-7(b); *Cal. S.P.D. 1648-9*, pp. 4, 12-13; Cary, *Memorials*, I, 368-75.

121. Clement Walker, 'The Mystery of the two Juntoes, Presbyterian and Independent' in Maseres, *Select Tracts*, I, especially 338-42.

CHAPTER II   BETWEEN TWO CIVIL WARS 1646-8

1. H. W. Meikle (ed.), *Correspondence of the Scots Commissioners in London 1644-6* (Edinburgh 1917), p. 203.

2. See *The answer of the Commons* . . . *to the Scots Commissioners Papers*, 28 November 1646 [Wing 2520], especially pp. 8, 21-2, 31-2, 43-7, 59-60; Thomas Chaloner, *An answer to the Scotch papers* (1646), pp. 3-5. Chaloner's paper was attacked by the ex-royalist pamph-

leteer Sir John Berkenhead in *An answer to the speech without doores* (1646), who in turn was attacked by C.G., *A reply to a namelesse pamphlet intituled An answer to a speech without doores* (1646) and by Henry Marten, *A corrector of the answerer to a speech without doores* (1646). On Berkenhead's part in the controversy, see P.W.Thomas, *Sir John Berkenhead 1617-1679* (Oxford 1969), pp. 130-3.

3. *Some papers given by the Commissioners of the Parliament* [of Scotland] (Edinburgh 1646) [Wing 1343], pp. 2-6, 8; Loudoun, John Campbell, Earl of, *Several speeches spoken by* (Edinburgh 1646), pp. 21-8; Meikle (ed.), op. cit., pp. 217-18.

4. *The answer of the Commons ... to the Scots Commissioners Papers*, pp. 11-16, 22-5, 27-8, 44-6, 50-3, 54. For similar points made in the pamphlet controversy, see Chaloner, *An answer ...* , p. 2; Marten, *A corrector ...* , p. 4; [John Lilburne] *An vnhappy game at Scotch and English* (Edinburgh 1646), pp. 2-4, 7, 16-23.

5. See, e.g., B.M., Add. MSS., 10,114, fos. 17(b)-18, 22; Add. MSS., 31,116, fos. 282(b), 290, 290(b)-1; *H. of Commons J.*, IV, 593, 644, 655-6.

6. For one such denunciation, see *The Case of the King stated* (1647) [Wing 1099], p. 5. For a later Scottish comment to similar effect see *H.M.C. Mar and Kellie MSS.*, I, 204-5.

7. *Parliamentary History*, XIV, 465; Loudoun, *Several speeches*, pp. 23-6, 28-30; Meikle (ed.), op. cit., pp. 220-1; for similar views, see S.R. Gardiner (ed.), *The Hamilton Papers ... 1638-1650*, Camden Soc., new ser., XXVII (1880), 124-5.

8. Marten, *A corrector ...* , pp. 5-6; *Cal. S.P.D. 1645-7*, pp. 451-2.

9. For a more balanced view, see Bodleian, Clarendon MSS., 29, fos. 42(b), 52-2(b), and above, pp. 185-6, 241.

10. The Newcastle Propositions are printed in Gardiner, *Constitutional Documents*, pp. 290-306. On the Uxbridge negotiations, see above, pp. 234-7.

11. B.M., Add. MSS., 31,116, fos. 274-4(b); *H. of Commons J.*, IV, 575-6.

12. *Parliamentary History*, XIV, 448.

13. Loudoun, op. cit., pp. 28-30; *Parliamentary History*, XV, 83-7.

14. ibid., XV, 279-316; Gardiner, *Civil War*, III, 188-90.

15. B.M., Add. MSS., 10,114, fo. 16(b); Add. MSS., 31,116, fos. 277(b), 279-9(b); *H. of Commons J.*, IV, 617, 631-2; Whitelock, *Memorials*, p. 222.

16. Bodleian, Tanner MSS., 59, fos. 736-7.

17. Gardiner, *Civil War*, III, 216.

18. *Parliamentary History*, xv, 414-16. Holles, of course, argues that Joyce was acting under Cromwell's orders. (Maseres, *Select Tracts*, I, 246.)

19. *Parliamentary History*, xv, 401-6.

20. Bell, Memorials, I, 353, 354. See also Sirrahnino [John Harris?] *The Grande Designe* (1647) cited in W.C.Abbott (ed.), *The Writings and Speeches of Oliver Cromwell* (Cambridge, Mass. 1937), I, 452.

21. See e.g. the Army Council's resolution of 16 July about the danger of invasion (Bell, *Memorials*, I, 369).

22. J.S.Morrill, 'Mutiny and Discontent in English Provincial Armies, 1645-1647', *P. & P.*, 56 (1972), 49-74. And see above, p. 286.

23. For Poynz's complaints to this effect, see Bell, *Memorials*, I, 360-4. On the development and character of this agitation and, in particular, its separateness from Leveller agitation, see M.A. Kishlansky, *The Rise of the New Model Army* (Cambridge 1979), pp. 179-222, and 'The Army and the Levellers: The Roads to Putney', *Hist. J.*, xxII (1979), 795-824.

24. Bodleian, Tanner MSS., 58, fo. 16; Cary, *Memorials*, I, 183. Sir Keith Thomas notes that in 1649 the radical demands of most of the soldiers seem to have evaporated once their grievances as to pay had been redressed. (G.E.Aylmer (ed.), *The Interregnum. The Quest for Settlement 1646-1660* (1972), p. 58.)

25. I.J.Gentles, 'The Debentures Market and Military Purchases of Crown Land 1649-60' (London Univ. PhD thesis 1969), cited by Morrill, 'Mutiny...' loc. cit., p. 49. Prof. Gentles estimates that arrears were to reach almost £3 million by the following January. (I.Gentles, 'The Sales of Crown Lands during the English Revolution', *Econ. Hist. Rev.*, 2nd ser., xxvI (1973), 615. See also his 'The Arrears of Pay of the Parliamentary Army at the End of the First Civil War', *B.I.H.R.*, xLvIII (1975), 52-63, and 'Arrears of Pay and Ideology in the Army Revolt of 1647', in B.Bond and I.Roy (eds.), *War and Society* (1970), pp. 44-66. For scepticism about Gentles' figures, see M.A.Kishlansky, 'The Army and the Levellers...' *Hist. J.*, xxII (1979), 5 and note.)

26. *Works of darkness brought to light* (1647) [Wing 3585], p. 5. For Holles, see Maseres, *Select Tracts*, I, 191. For other examples, see

Some Queries propounded to the Common Councell and Citizens of London (30 July 1647) [B.M. E400(26)], pp. 11-12: *Vox Civitatis or the cry of the City of London* (28 September 1647), [B.M. E409(10)], p. 4; *A Paire of Spectacles for the Citie* (4 December 1647), [B.L. E419(9)], pp. 4-5.

27. *Parliamentary History*, xv, 339, 355-6, 486-7; Cary, *Memorials*, I, 233-4. On the legislation relating to indemnity, see ibid. pp. 374, 406, 430; Bodleian, Clarendon MSS., 29, fo. 236; *H. of Commons J.*, v, 181, 199; *Acts and Ordinances*, I, 936-7, 953-4. On the issue of indemnity in general, see R. Ashton, 'The Problem of Indemnity 1647-1648', in C. Jones, M. Newitt and S. Roberts (eds.), *Politics and People in Revolutionary England* (Oxford 1986), pp. 117-40.

28. For these events, see B.M., Add. MSS., 31,116, fos. 306-6(b); Add. MSS., 46,374, fo. 52; *H. of Commons J.*, v, 127, 129, 132; *H. of Lords J.*, ix, 115; J. Rushworth, *Historical Collections* (1691), vi, 446-8; *Cal. S.P.D. 1645-7*, pp. 543-4; Whitelock, *Memorials*, 183-8. There are good accounts in Gardiner, *Civil War*, iii, 223-30, Kishlansky, *Rise of the New Model Army*, pp. 179 et seq., and A. Woolrych, *Soldiers and Statesmen . . . 1647-1648* (Oxford 1987), pp. 24 et seq.

29. *Parliamentary History*, xv, 358-60; Cary *Memorials*, I, 201-6, 238. There is a lively popular account of the election of agitators and the preceding and subsequent events in the 'Solemn Engagement of the Army' of 5 June 1647, printed in *Leveller Manifestoes*, pp. 146-53. For the Vindication, see B.M. E385(19); A. Woolrych, *Soldiers and Statesmen . . . 1647-1648* (Oxford 1987), pp. 55-56.

30. Rushworth, *Historical Collections*, vi, 510-12; *Parliamentary History*, xv, 424-30; *Leveller Manifestoes*, pp. 146-53. See also Gardiner, *Civil War*, iii, 279-82: M. Kishlansky, *New Model Army*, pp. 231-2; A. Woolrych, *Soldiers and Statesmen*, pp. 116-20.

31. *A letter sent to the right honourable the lord mayor* (10 June 1647) [Wing 1622], especially pp. 4-5; *Parliamentary History*, xv, 431-4. This concern for political as well as religious considerations had already been expressed as early as April 1647 in *The Vindication of the Officers* (B.M. E385(19), p. 2).

32. Rushworth, *Historical Collections*, vi, 564-70; *Parliamentary History*, xv, 455-75; W. Haller and G. Davies (eds) *The Leveller Tracts 1647-1653* (Gloucester, Mass. 1964), pp. 51-63. See Gardiner, *Civil War*, iii, 293-5; Kishlansky, *New Model Army*, pp. 242-3; Woolrych, *Soldiers and Statesmen*, pp. 126-8.

33. *Leveller Manifestoes*, pp. 109-30. For the petition of 2 June 1646, see above p. 252.

34. ibid., pp. 131-43; B.M., Add. MSS, 31,116, fo. 304(b); *H. of Commons J.*, v, 179-80: *Parliamentary History*, xv, 374.

35. Woolrych, *Soldiers and Statesmen*, pp. 55-136, especially pp. 66-67. See also Kishlansky, *New Model Army*, pp. 205-14.

36. *Parliamentary History*, xvi, 122.

37. 'A Word for the Army' (1647) in *Harleian Miscellany*, vi (1810), 67. For the Presbyterian reply, see *A Word to Mr. Peters and two Words for the Parliament and Kingdom* (1647), [B.M. E413(7)], especially pp. 19-23.

38. Aylmer (ed.), *Interregnum*, pp. 44-48.

39. C.L.R.O., Journal 40, fos. 215, 215(b); B.M., Add. MSS., 31,116, fo. 307; Add. MSS., 46, 374, fo. 52; *H. of Commons J.*, v, 132, 143.

40. For a sceptical view about the dangers of a Scottish invasion, see J.R. MacCormack, *Revolutionary Politics in the Long Parliament* (Cambridge, Mass. 1973), pp. 197-9.

41. C.L.R.O., Journal 40, fos. 227, 228(b), 229(b); Bodleian, Tanner MSS., 58, fo. 234; *Cal. S.P.D. 1645-7*, pp. 590-2; *A letter sent to the right honourable the lord mayor* (1647), pp. 3-5; *Parliamentary History*, xv, 38-40, 472, 476-9, 489-91; xvi, 14-19, 24-27.

42. See above, pp. 237-40.

43. For the charges, see *Parliamentary History*, xv, 470-3; xvi, 69-93; Bell, *Memorials*, I, 367-83; *Leveller Manifestoes*, pp. 167-73. For the eleven members' answer see *Parliamentary History*, xvi, 116-59.

44. On counter-revolutionary excesses in London and the army's complaints, *Cal. S.P.D. 1645-7*, pp. 565, 590-1; *H. of Lords J.*, IX, 322-3; *Parliamentary History*, xv, 472, 476-7, 479; xvi, 14-19, 26-27, 37, 99; Aylmer (ed.), op. cit., pp. 48-49.

45. *H. of Commons J.*, v, 248, 251-2, 253, 254, 255, 256-7; Rushworth, *Historical Collections*, vi, 634-5, 640-2; *Parliamentary History*, xvi, 162; Gardiner, *Civil War*, III, 327-8.

46. Maseres, *Select Tracts*, I, 272-3. See also *Vox Civitatis, or the cry of the city of London* (1647) [Wing 713], pp. 5-6. For a similar comment from a royalist standpoint, see Clarendon, *Great Rebellion*, IV, 241-2.

47. *H. of Commons J.*, v, 252.

48. *To the Lord Mayor ... the Aldermen and Commons ... The humble*

Petition of the Citizens (1647) (B.M. 669, f. II(47)); Rushworth, *Historical Collections*, VI, 636-9.

49. C.L.R.O., Journal 40, fo. 240(b); Rushworth, *Historical Collections*, VI, 642-3, 648-51; *Parliamentary History*, XVI, 173-84.

50. For example, their treatment of petitioners at Guildhall on 2 August (*H. of Lords J.*, IX, 401-2; *H.M.C. 6th Report*, p. 193).

51. See Speaker Lenthall's criticism that Parliament was acting under *force majeure* (*Parliamentary History*, XVI, 196-9). The flight of the more conservative Manchester, the Speaker of the Upper House, is even more significant.

52. *Cal. S.P.D. 1645-7*, pp. 567-8; *H. of Lords J.*, IX, 375-8; *Parliamentary History*, XVI, 210-12, 223-37. For contemporary comment on this from two radically different points of view, see Clarendon, *History*, IV, 244-5; Bell, *Memorials*, I, 379-84.

53. On the votes, B.M., Add. MSS., 46,374, fo. 68; *H. of Commons J.*, V, 270, 271, 273, 275, 277-8, 279, 280; *H. of Lords J.*, IX, 379, 384, 397-8; *H.M.C. 6th Rep.*, p. 191; *Cal. S.P.D. 1645-7*, p. 569. The army's Remonstrance is printed in *H. of Lords J.*, IX, 391-7; B.M. E402(30); *Parliamentary History*, XVI, 251-73.

54. James Howell, *A letter to the Earle of Pembroke* (1647), pp. 6-7.

55. *The case of the King stated* (1647), p. 8.

56. Bodleian, Clarendon MSS., 30, fo. 30. For similarly optimistic views, see ibid., fos. 24, 35.

57. See e.g. Bodleian, Clarendon MSS., 29, fo. 236; Bell, *Memorials*, I, 356: *Cal. S.P.D. 1645-7*, p. 591; *Parliamentary History*, XVI, 15, 262-3. For an admirable account of the army's negotiations with the king, see Woolrych, *Soldiers and Statesmen*, pp. 174-81, 183-4.

58. *Works of darkness brought to light* (1647), p. 10.

59. See e.g. the letter of 22 June 1647 from John Rushworth, Secretary to the Army Council, to Lord Fairfax (Bell, *Memorials*, I, 357-8).

60. *Clarendon State Papers*, II, 373-4, 381-2; Clarendon, *Great Rebellion*, IV, 228-32, though Clarendon emphasizes that the king received less consideration later (ibid., IV, 256-7). For a Presbyterian disapproval of the army's concessions, see *Works of darkness brought to light*, pp. 5-6.

61. *H.M.C. Mar and Kellie MSS.*, I, 204-5.

62. See Berkeley's Memoirs printed in Maseres, *Select Tracts*, I, especially pp. 356-66, for a very sagacious account by no means uncritical of the king.

63. D.Jenkins, *An apology for the army touching* (1647), especially pp. 2, 8. For a more hostile royalist view of the intentions of the army leaders, see *The Case of the King stated* (1647), especially pp. 6–8, 11–16.

64. The Heads of the Proposals are printed in Gardiner, *Constitutional Documents*, pp. 316–26.

65. MacCormack, *Revolutionary Politics*, pp. 208–9.

66. *Parliamentary History*, xvi, 205–6.

67. Cary, *Memorials*, i, 354–5 (N.Hobart to J.Hobart). For Hotham, see above, p. 189.

68. *H.M.C. 5th Rep.*, pt. i, p. 173.

69. *H. of Commons J.*, v, 312, 316, 335–6.

70. Maseres, *Select Tracts*, i, 368–73.

71. *H.M.C. 5th Rep.*, pt. i, p. 173.

72. Francis White, *The Copy of a letter sent*, 3 September 1647, especially pp. 5–6.

73. *Leveller Manifestoes*, pp. 203–4.

74. The version used here is that of A.S.P.Woodhouse (ed.), *Puritanism and Liberty* (1966 edn.), pp. 1–124. See M.A.Kishlansky, 'Consensus Politics and the Structure of Debate at Putney', *J. Brit. Stud.*, xx (1981), 50–69: A.Woolrych, *Soldiers and Statesmen. The General Council of the Army and Its Debates 1647–8* (Oxford 1987), pp. 214–63.

75. *A copy of a letter sent by the agents of severall regiments*, 11 November 1647 [Wing 6134], p. 2; cf. *A letter sent from several agitators*, 14 November 1647 [Wing 1604], pp. 4–5.

76. For good accounts of these events see Kishlansky, 'The Army and the Levellers...', *Hist. J.*, xxii (1979), 822–3: Woolrych, *Soldiers and Statesmen*, pp. 202–17, and 'Political Debate in the New Model Army' in C.Jones, M.Newitt and S.Roberts (eds.), *Politics and People in Revolutionary England*, pp. 106–9. The Agreement of the People is printed in Gardiner, *Constitutional Documents*, pp. 333–5.

77. C.B.Macpherson, *The Political Theory of Possessive Individualism* (1964 edn.), pp. 107–59.

78. Woodhouse (ed.), *Puritanism and Liberty*, p. 53. See also ibid., especially pp. 55–6, 66. For Petty's statements about the franchise, see ibid., especially pp. 53, 61–2, 83. For an ingenious and plausible argument that Petty moved to his more restrictive view of the franchise in the course of debate as a compromise

solution in search of a consensus position, see C. Thompson, 'Maximilian Petty and the Putney Debate on the Franchise', *P. & P.*, 88 (1980), 63–69.

79. Woodhouse (ed.), *Puritanism and Liberty*, pp. 54–5, 57–8, 62–3, 70–3, 77–8.

80. ibid., p. 73.

81. K. Thomas, 'The Levellers and the Franchise', in Aylmer (ed.), *Interregnum*, pp. 59, 69–78.

82. See ibid., pp. 57–78; J. C. Davis, 'The Levellers and Democracy', *P. & P.*, 40 (1968), 174–80. Further evidence of the heterogeneity of Leveller views is provided by Roger Howell Jr. and D. E. Brewster, 'Reconsidering the Levellers: the Evidence of *The Moderate*', *P. & P.* 46 (1970), 68–86.

83. Henry Denne, *The Levellers Designe Discovered* (1649), p. 8, cited by Davis, 'The Levellers and Democracy', *P. & P.* loc. cit., p. 176.

84. *H. of Commons J.*, v, 354.

85. For an account of the rendezvous, see William Clarke, *A full description of the proceedings at the rendezvous of that regiment*, 16 November 1647; *Ludlow Memoirs*, I, 172–3. For Fairfax's account, see *Parliamentary History*, xvi, 333–6. For Cromwell's report of the matter to the House of Commons on 19 November see D. E. Underdown (ed.), 'The Parliamentary Diary of John Boys, 1647–8', *B.I.H.R.*, xxxix (1966), 151–2. For critical use of this and other evidence and a sceptical view of Cromwell's role at Corkbush Heath, see M. Kishlansky, 'What happened at Ware?', *Hist. J.*, xxv (1982), 827–39. For an examination of the same evidence and a measured reassertion of the traditional view of the significance of the rendezvous and Cromwell's role, see A. Woolrych, *Soldiers and Statesmen*, pp. 277–99.

86. Woodhouse (ed.), op. cit., p. 71.

87. ibid., p. 74.

88. *Leveller Manifestoes*, pp. 242–58.

89. *Parliamentary History*, xvi, 341–2; Woodhouse (ed.), op. cit., pp. 86–87.

90. *Leveller Manifestoes*, pp. 235–41; Underdown (ed.), 'Parliamentary Diary of John Boys', *B.I.H.R.*, loc. cit., pp. 152–3.

91. Woodhouse (ed.), op. cit., pp. 103–7.

92. B.M., Egerton MSS., 2618, fo. 21; [H. Tracey], *His Majesties most gracious message to the Speaker of the House of Peers*, 17 November

1647; *Parliamentary History*, XVI, 397-8; Maseres, *Select Tracts*, I, 383-4. The view that the king's flight inevitably resulted in a worsening of relations with parliament and a stiffening of parliament's peace terms is challenged by John Ashburnham, the king's confidant [Oxford, All Souls College, Codrington Library; *The Copy of a Letter from Mr. Ashburnham to a Friend*, (1648), especially p. 5]. However, not only is Ashburnham's judgment unreliable, but his own reputation was involved on account of his personal role in the king's flight from Hampton Court.

93. The Engagement is printed in Gardiner, *Constitutional Documents*, pp. 347-53.

94. For the four bills and accompanying propositions and the king's reply, see ibid., pp. 335-47, 353-6.

95. *Parliamentary History*, XVI, 430-73, 480; *An answer to the chief or materiall heads of passages in the late declaration*, 4 January 1648, *passim*.

96. The Vote is printed in Gardiner, *Constitutional Documents*, p. 356.

97. *Parliamentary History*, XVII, 2-24, 27-42.

98. Clarendon, *Great Rebellion*, IV, 283.

99. *Parliamentary History*, XVI, 490.

100. Underdown (ed.), 'Parliamentary Diary of John Boys', *B.I.H.R.* loc. cit., pp. 155-6.

101. ibid., p. 156; *Parliamentary History*, XVI, 491-3; Abbott (ed.), *Writings and Speeches of Oliver Cromwell*, I, 576.

102. *Ludlow Memoirs*, I, 184-6.

CHAPTER 12   REVOLUTION CONTAINED 1648-9

1. G. Donaldson, *Scotland: James V to James VII* (1965), p. 337.

2. See *A declaration of the Lords and Commons concerning the papers of the Scots Commissioners*, 13 March 1648 [Wing 1392], p. 36.

3. See, e.g., B.M., Add. MSS., 15,750, fo. 34; *Parliamentary History*, XVII, 124-6, 311-12, 314-32.

4. ibid., pp. 300-3.

5. Gardiner (ed.), *Hamilton Papers*, Camden Soc., new ser., XXVII (1880), pp. 172-3, 196, 202-3, 205, 222.

6. ibid., pp. 198, 202-3; *Cal. S.P.D. 1648-9*, pp. 56, 117; *Parliamentary History*, XVII, 231-3, 261-4, 286-7.

7. Gardiner (ed.), *Hamilton Papers*, pp. 165-7, 170-2, 181-2, 200.

8. ibid., pp. 194; see also pp. 228-9.

9. *Cal. S.P.D. 1648-9*, pp. 79-80, 82; *Parliamentary History*, XVII, 174-5. See also Everitt, *Kent*, pp. 252-3.

10. *Cal. S.P.D. 1648-9*, pp. 94-5, 105, 118-19.

11. ibid., pp. 63-4; *H. of Lords J.*, x, 260; *H.M.C. 7th Rep.*, p. 30; A.R.Bayley, *The Great Civil War in Dorset 1642-1660* (1910), pp. 351-3; A.L.Leach, *The History of the Civil War (1642-1649) in Pembrokeshire and on its Borders* (1937), p. 161; Everitt, *Kent*, pp. 238-9; Fletcher, *Sussex*, pp. 291-2.

12. *Parliamentary History*, XVII, 289.

13. ibid., pp. 159-61, 163-7; Bodleian, Tanner MSS., 57, fos. 124, 127-9; Washington, Folger Library, Folger MSS., Xd. 483, (23-5); *Cal. S.P.D. 1648-9*, pp. 276-7, 279, 297; Gardiner, *Civil War*, IV, 145; M.Coate, *Cromwell in the Great Civil War and Interregnum 1642-1660* (Truro 1963), pp. 239, 241-2; Underdown, *Somerset*, pp. 147-8.

14. See Everitt, *Suffolk*, pp. 14, 15, 94-108; R.W.Ketton-Cremer, *Norfolk in the Civil War* (1969), pp. 331-54; J.T.Evans, *Seventeenth Century Norwich* (Oxford 1979), pp. 172-82; B.Lyndon, 'Essex and the King's Cause in 1648', *Hist. J.*, XXIX (1986), 17-39.

15. *Cal. S.P.D. 1648-9*, pp. 88-9, 95-8; Underdown (ed.), 'The Parliamentary Diary of John Boys', *B.I.H.R.*, XXXIX (1966), 159-60. On the Kentish revolt, see Everitt, *Kent*, pp. 231-70.

16. H.A.Lloyd, *The Gentry of South-West Wales 1540-1640*, pp. 126-7; A.H.Dodd, *Studies in Stuart Wales* (Cardiff 1952), pp. 118, 137-8; Leach, *History of the Civil War in Pembrokeshire*, pp. 125-7.

17. Underdown, *Somerset*, pp. 147-8.

18. Bodleian, Clarendon MSS., 31, fos. 83(b)-84, 86; *Cal. S.P.D. 1648-9*, p. 63; C.H.Firth (ed.), *Clarke Papers*, Camden Soc. new ser., LIV. (1894), II, 11-13; *Parliamentary History*, XVII, 169-70; Underdown (ed.), *B.I.H.R.*, loc. cit., p. 164; Gardiner, *Civil War*, IV, 127-8.

19. B.M., Add. MSS., 44, 846, fo. 44(b); *Cal. S.P.D. 1648-9*, pp. 76, 95-8, 194; *H. of Lords J.*, x, 279; Firth (ed.), *Clarke Papers*, II, 17-18; Everitt, *Kent*, pp. 254-7.

20. Clarendon, *Great Rebellion*, IV, 385-6, 396-407; *Ludlow Memoirs*, I, 198; Gardiner, *Civil War*, 159-61.

21. Washington, Folger Library, Folger MSS., Xd., 483(23).

22. For good narrative accounts of the naval revolt, see J.R.Powell, *The Navy in the English Civil War* (1962), especially pp. 138-91; J.R.Powell and E.K.Timings (eds.), *Documents relating to the Civil*

War 1642-1648, Navy Records Soc. cv (1963), especially pp. 300-11. For documents, ibid., pp. 311-406.

23. ibid., pp. 333, 335-6, 337-9; *Parliamentary History*, xvii, 199-204.

24. *Cal. S.P.D. 1648-9*, pp. 200-1, 216-17, 223; Powell and Timings (eds.), *Documents* . . . , pp. 356-9.

25. *Leveller Manifestoes*, pp. 142-53.

26. Powell and Timings (eds.), *Documents* . . . , pp. 291, 365.

27. ibid., pp. 332-4, 354-5, 365.

28. ibid., p. 353; Gardiner (ed.), *Hamilton Papers*, pp. 221, 222-3, 229.

29. *Cal. S.P.D. 1645-7*, p. 600; *H. of Commons J.*, v, 315-16, 317, 318, 493-5, 507; *H.M.C. 5th Rep.*, p. 179; *Parliamentary History*, xvi, 308-9; xvii, 85, 96-103; Underdown (ed.), 'Parliamentary Diary of John Boys', loc. cit., 146-7, 149.

30. For examples, B.M., Stowe MSS., 189, fo. 39 (Wm. Clarke to Lieut.-Col. Rede); *H. of Lords J.*, x, 234-5; *H. of Commons J.*, v, 246; *H.M.C. 7th Rep.*, p. 23; *H.M.C., Ancaster MSS.*, p. 414; Gardiner (ed.), *Hamilton Papers*, pp. 181, 190-1; *The true answer of the Parliament to the petition of the Lord Major*, 25 April 1648 [Wing 2378]; *Parliamentary History*, xvii, 92-6, 120-1. On the city's position in 1648, see I. Gentles, 'The Struggle for London in the Second Civil War', *Hist. J.*, xxvi (1983), 277-305.

31. *An answer to the chief or materiall heads and passages in the late declaration* (1648), pp. 1-3; *A declaration of the Lords and Commons . . . concerning the papers of the Scots Commissioners*, 13 March 1648 [Wing 1392], especially pp. 21-2, 25-6, 61-2, 73-4; Henry Marten, *The Parliament's proceedings justified* (1648), pp. 5-6; *Parliamentary History*, xvii, 126, 320-1, 325.

32. *H. of Lords J.*, x, 249; *H. of Commons J.*, v, 555, 562, 583-4, 586; *H.M.C. 7th Rep.*, p. 24; Underdown (ed.), 'Parliamentary Diary of John Boys', loc. cit., 164; *Parliamentary History*, xvi, 367; xvii, 132, 147-8, 171-3, 197, 212, 220.

33. Gardiner (ed.), *Hamilton Papers*, p. 247.

34. C.L.R.O., Journal 40, fo. 285(b); *H. of Lords J.*, x, 367-8; B.M., E451/33, E451/36 (declarations of the insurgent peers); *Parliamentary History*, xvii, 291.

35. *H. of Lords J.*, x, 295-6; *H.M.C. 7th Rep.*, p. 28; *Parliamentary History*, xvii, 194-8.

36. ibid., p. 306, citing Walker, *History of Independency*, p. 121.

37. *Ludlow Memoirs*, i, 194.

38. Gardiner (ed.), *Hamilton Papers*, p. 221; Powell and Timings (eds.), *Documents* . . . , pp. 336, 353.

39. *H. of Commons J.*, v, 583-4, 586, 589-90; *Parliamentary History*, XVII, 212, 226-8.

40. *Ludlow Memoirs*, I, 183.

41. *Lord Somers' Tracts*, VI, 500-1.

42. *H. of Commons J.*, VI, 73.

43. W.C.Abbot (ed.), *The Writings and Speeches of Oliver Cromwell* (Cambridge, Mass. 1937), I, 691-2.

44. B.M., Add. MSS., 19,399, fos. 58, 60. For a letter of 19 June from Lucas to Fairfax attempting to justify his part in the rebellion, see Add. MSS., 15,858, fo. 66; Bell, *Memorials*, II, 56-7.

45. Cited in Gardiner, *Civil War*, IV, 130.

46. D.Underdown, *Pride's Purge* (Oxford 1971), especially pp. 96-7, 100-5.

47. *H. of Commons J.*, v, 547, 572; Gardiner (ed.), *Hamilton Papers*, p. 191.

48. *H. of Commons J.*, v, 622, 650; *Parliamentary History*, XVII, 241, 276-9.

49. *H. of Commons J.*, v, 617, 673-4; *Parliamentary History*, XVII, 273-4, 292-4, 333-6, 348, 405-6, 412-17.

50. *H. of Lords J.*, x, 295-6, 349-50; *H. of Commons J.*, v, 613-14; *H.M.C. 7th Rep.*, pp. 28, 33; *Parliamentary History*, XVII, 264-6, 387-95.

51. e.g. *H. of Lords J.*, x, 30; *H.M.C. 7th Rep.*, p. 30; *Parliamentary History*, XVII, 139-41, 228-9, 255, 269-72, 280-1, 307-8.

52. ibid., pp. 451-60.

53. ibid., pp. 406-7.

54. e.g. ibid., pp. 383-4, 434-6.

55. Bodleian, Tanner MSS., 57, fos. 179, 180, 204, 213; *H. of Commons J.*, v, 674; VI, 18.

56. Bodleian, Rawlinson MSS., A114, fo. 4; *Cal. S.P.D. 1648-9*, p. 277; *Parliamentary History*, XVII, 436-7. See Underdown, *Pride's Purge*, pp. 104-5.

57. On Vane's attitude to the Newport negotiations, see V.A.Rowe, *Sir Henry Vane the Younger* (1970), pp. 109-14.

58. Firth (ed.), *Clarke Papers*, II, 17.

59. For sketches of the careers of these middle-groupers, see V.Pearl, 'The "Royal Independents" in the English Civil War', *Roy. Hist. Soc. Trans.*, 5th ser., XVIII (1968), 69-96.

60. This seems to be the view of Professor MacCormack, *Revolutionary Politics in the Long Parliament* (Cambridge, Mass. 1973), p. 286.

61. *Cal. S.P.D. 1648–9*, pp. 296–7, 300, 302–3, 306–7, 319.

62. See Jesson's intervention in the debate on 26 October (*Parliamentary History*, XVIII, 102–3). For Crewe's religious views, see Underdown, *Pride's Purge*, pp. 15–16, 63, 64–5, 114; Pearl, *Roy. Hist. Soc. Trans.*, art. cit., pp. 83–4.

63. *Parliamentary History*, XVIII, 100–1.

64. B.M., Add. MSS., 32,093, fos. 259–62; Bodleian, Ballard MSS., 45, fos. 3, 7a; *Cal. S.P.D. 1648–9*, p. 304; *H. of Commons J.*, VI, 67; *Parliamentary History*, XVIII, 46–51, 53–4, 56–9, 96–8, 124–5.

65. B.M., Add. MSS., 15,750, fo. 37.

66. For the parliamentary demands on religion, *Parliamentary History*, XVIII, 2–5.

67. B.M., Add. MSS., 32,093, fos. 249, 250–3, 254–8, 263–3(b); Bodleian, Rawlinson MSS., A114, fos. 25(b)–6(b), 27(b)–31, 32–4(b), 35(b)–6, 45–6, 49(b), 53, 58(b)–60(b); Bodleian, Ballard MSS., 45, fo. 10(b); *H.M.C., Ancaster MSS.*, p. 416; *Parliamentary History*, XVIII, 7, 42–4, 142, 243, 245–51, 278–9.

68. B.M., Add. MSS., 32,093, fo. 264(b); Bodleian, Ballard MSS., 45, fo. 12.

69. Bodleian, Ballard MSS., 45, fos. 2a–2aᵛ, 5; Rawlinson MSS., A114, fos. 36(b), 45(b), 50.

70. Bodleian, Rawlinson MSS., A114, fos. 50, 53(b); Tanner MSS., 57, fo. 400; Ballard MSS., 45, fo. 15; *Parliamentary History*, XVIII, 109, 143, 146.

71. Bodleian, Rawlinson MSS., A114, fos. 26(b)–7, 44(b)–5(b), 49–50, 58(b)–60; *H. of Commons J.*, VI, 74, 86; *Parliamentary History*, XVIII, 38–41, 79–82, 107–13.

72. Bodleian, Ballard MSS., 45, fo. 8aᵛ; *Parliamentary History*, XVIII, 126–8, 156–8; Gardiner, *Civil War*, IV, 225–6.

73. *Parliamentary History*, XVIII, 30–5.

74. *Parliamentary History*, XV, 461; XVI, 99–100; Bell, *Memorials*, I, p. 365; Underdown (ed.), 'Parliamentary Diary of John Boys', loc. cit., pp. 148–9. See also Underdown, *Pride's Purge*, p. 80.

75. *Works of darkness brought to light* (1647) [Wing 3585], p. 5. For examples of Leveller arguments for a purge, see Francis White,

The copy of a letter sent, 16 October 1647, p. 13; *Leveller Manifestoes*, pp. 167, 176-9, 200, 203, 204-5, 211.

76. *Parliamentary History*, xv, 462; xvii, 478-9; John Milton, *Works* (New York 1932), p. 29; see above, p. 321.

77. *Ludlow Memoirs*, i, 203-5; *Parliamentary History*, xviii, 168, 170, 200-6; Haller and Davies (eds.), *The Leveller Tracts 1647-1653* (New York 1944), pp. 418-19.

78. *Ludlow Memoirs*, i, 206-7. For Lilburne's clear account of these matters in his 'Legall Fundamentall Liberties', see Haller and Davies (eds.), *Leveller Tracts*, pp. 418-22. For an admirable modern account, see Underdown, *Pride's Purge*, pp. 132-3, 140-2.

79. The Remonstrance printed in *Parliamentary History*, xviii, 161-238.

80. ibid., pp. 165-7, 171-2, 211, 226.

81. ibid., especially pp. 214-15, 230.

82. Firth (ed.), *Clarke Papers*, ii, 54.

83. Gardiner, *Civil War*, iv, 241-5; Underdown, *Pride's Purge*, pp. 119-22.

84. Haller and Davies (eds.) *Leveller Tracts*, pp. 415-24. For detailed modern accounts see Gardiner, *Civil War*, iv, 238-41, and Underdown, *Pride's Purge*, pp. 125-6, 128-31.

85. *H. of Commons J.*, vi, 81, 91; *Parliamentary History*, xviii, 238-9.

86. ibid., pp. 266-72.

87. Bodleian, Tanner MSS., 57, fos. 448, 452; Cary, *Memorials*, ii, 73-4; *H. of Commons J.*, vi, 92.

88. ibid., p. 92; *Parliamentary History*, xviii, 290-3; Underdown, *Pride's Purge*, p. 137 and note.

89. *H. of Commons J.*, vi, 93; *Parliamentary History*, xviii, 301-447, most of it Prynne's enormous speech.

90. I owe these figures to the detailed researches of Professor Underdown. See his *Pride's Purge*, especially pp. 210-13.

91. *Parliamentary History*, xviii, 473-4.

92. Firth (ed.), *Clarke Papers*, ii, 67-9; *A declaration of the Parliament of England expressing the grounds*, 22 March 1649 [Wing 1499], pp. 22-3.

93. *The Parliament under the power of the sword* (1648) [Wing 508], pp. 3-4.

94. B.M., Egerton MSS., 2618, fo. 31; William Prynne, *A briefe memento to the present vnparliamentary ivnto*, 16 January 1649, especially p. 16.

95. Underdown, *Pride's Purge*, pp. 208-56, especially pp. 230-6.
96. ibid., pp. 159-60; *H. of Commons J.*, VI, 92.
97. For good surveys of these developments see Gardiner, *Civil War*, IV, 272-330; C.V.Wedgwood, *The Trial of Charles I* (1964); Underdown, *Pride's Purge*, pp. 163-207.
98. *Clarendon S.P.*, II, 452.
99. Underdown, *Pride's Purge*, pp. 143, 148-50, 158, 166-72.
100. Bodleian, Clarendon MSS., 34, fos. 17-18(b).
101. White, *The copy of a letter sent*, p. 7.
102. Bodleian, Tanner MSS., 57, fo. 497.
103. Cited in Wedgwood, *Trial of Charles I*, p. 222.
104. Bodleian, Tanner MSS., 57, fo. 525; Cary, *Memorials*, II, p. 117 (William to Francis Sancroft, 12 February 1649).
105. Bodleian, Tanner MSS., 57, fo. 427(b).
106. The passage which follows is an only slightly amended version of my arguments in 'Revolutionaries and Rumpers', *Hist. J.*, XVIII, (1975), especially pp. 183-5.
107. B.Worden, *The Rump Parliament* (Cambridge 1974), especially pp. 33-60.
108. Underdown (ed.), 'Parliamentary Diary of John Boys', loc. cit., p. 153.
109. Bodleian, Tanner MSS., 56, fo. 3.
110. Whitelock, *Memorials*, p. 380.
111. Gardiner, *Civil War*, IV, 294.
112. *Leveller Manifestoes*, p. 124.
113. For an interesting variation on this theme in the Leveller 'earnest petition' of January 1648, see ibid., p. 269.
114. An example is Sir William Morton, 'Ius Monarchiae Anglicanae' (Bodleian, Clarendon MSS., 132, especially fos. 75-85).
115. G.Winstanley, *The Law of Freedom and other Writings*, ed. C.Hill (1973), pp. 77-8, 84-6, 107.
116. Gardiner, *Civil War*, IV, 60-1, 265.
117. 'The Ready and Easy Way to Establish a free Commonwealth' (1660) in Milton, *Prose Writings*, ed. K.M.Burton (1965), pp. 240-1.

Bibliographical Note

The number of books and articles, particularly those published in the twentieth century, is so enormous as to have inspired whole bibliographical guides, one of the most useful of which is the recent study by R.C.Richardson, *The Debate on the English Revolution* (1977). For full bibliographical guidance readers should refer to this and to G. Davies and M.F.Keeler, *Bibliography of British History: Stuart Period 1603–1714* (Oxford 1970). What follows can necessarily be only the briefest selection.

Of the general histories the best is the account by a contemporary who played a notable part in the events which he described, Edward Hyde, Earl of Clarendon, *The History of the Rebellion and Civil Wars in England*, ed. W.D.Macray (Oxford 1888, repr. 1958, 6 vols). Vital to an understanding of this essential work is the essay in C.H.Firth's *Essays Historical and Literary* (Oxford 1938) and B.Wormald's masterly *Clarendon. Politics, History and Religion 1640–1660* (Cambridge 1951, repr. 1965). The only modern works to bear serious comparison with Clarendon are the nineteenth-century masterpieces by S.R.Gardiner, *History of England . . . 1603–1642* (1883–4, 10 vols) and *History of the Great Civil War* (revised edn. 1893, 4 vols). The best modern narrative accounts are in C.V.Wedgwood, *The Great Rebellion: i. The King's Peace* (1955) and *ii. The King's War* (1958). See also the same author's excellent *The Trial of Charles I* (1964).

Useful modern volumes of collected essays by various authors are C.Russell (ed.), *The Origins of the English Civil War* (1973). In the same series are J.Morrill (ed.), *Reactions to the English Civil War 1642–1649* (1982) and G.E.Aylmer (ed.), *The Interregnum: The Quest for Settlement 1646–60* (1972), in which the essays by V.Pearl and K.Thomas especially fall within the period covered by this book. Other collections are R.H.Parry (ed.), *The English Civil War and After, 1642–1658* (1970), B.Manning (ed.), *Politics, Religion and the English Civil War* (1973) and the *festschriften* for Christopher Hill and Ivan Roots: D.Pennington and K.Thomas (eds.), *Puritans and Revolutionaries* (Oxford 1978), and C.Jones, M.Newitt and S.Roberts (eds.), *Politics and People in Revolutionary England* (Oxford 1986).

The doyen of Marxist historians of the Civil War is C.Hill, whose collected essays *Puritanism and Revolution* (1958) contain pieces on a variety of topics relating from general interpretative essays to socio-literary history. Among Hill's other important general contributions are *Economic Problems of the Church* (Oxford 1955), *Intellectual Origins of the English Revolution* (Oxford 1965) and *Society and Puritanism in Pre-Revolutionary England* (1964). Another Marxist interpretation is B. Manning, *The English People and the English Revolution 1640–1649* (1976). Among the most individual and original of modern non-Marxist and post-Whig accounts are H.R.Trevor-Roper, *The Gentry 1540–1640 (Econ. Hist. Rev. Supplnt.* no. 1, Cambridge 1953), 'The General Crisis of the Seventeenth Century' in *P. & P.*, no. 16 (1959), and L.Stone, *The Causes of the English Revolution 1529–1642* (1972), which makes use of some of the techniques of modern social science.

Other than Gardiner's work, there is no good general history of early seventeenth-century England. On the politics of the pre-war years the most important modern revisions are to be found in M. Prestwich, *Cranfield, Politics and Profits under the Early Stuarts* (1966) and Conrad Russell's article in *History* LXI (1966). For studies of the personnel of Parliament in the 1640s, see D.Brunton and D.H.Pennington, *Members of the Long Parliament* (1954) and the more detailed and exceptionally valuable study by M.F.Keeler, *The Long Parliament 1640–41* (Philadelphia 1954). Two modern works on the politics of the 1640s are outstanding. They are J.H.Hexter, *The Reign of King Pym* (1941) and D.Underdown, *Pride's Purge* (1971). J.R. MacCormack, *Revolutionary Politics in the Long Parliament* (1973) covers similar ground to Underdown, but less satisfactorily. Underdown's, *Revel, Riot and Rebellion. Popular Politics and Culture in England 1603–1660* (Oxford 1985) has, as its subtitle suggests, a radically different and refreshingly unorthodox thesis.

The literature on the Levellers and ultra-radical politics is voluminous, but there have been two modern reinterpretations, both of which have the effect of playing down Leveller radicalism. The first is

C.B.Macpherson, *The Political Theory of Possessive Individualism* (Oxford 1962), ch. 3, a brilliant study but one which bears the stamp of mind of the political theorist rather than the historian and makes insufficient allowance for variation in Leveller views, and has excited some criticism (see above pp. 309-12). The second, D.Hirst, *The Representative of the People?* (1975) is not about the Levellers at all, but its study of the franchise before 1642 has had the startling effect of rendering Leveller notions on the subject a great deal less novel than they previously appeared. Christopher Hill's *The World Turned Upside Down* (1972) is a novel and important study of radical ideas which hitherto have received far less attention than those of the Levellers. On the army and politics see C.H.Firth, *Cromwell's Army* (3rd edn. 1921, pb. 1962), and more recent and in some respects, conflicting accounts in M.Kishlansky, *The Rise of the New Model Army* (Cambridge 1979) and A.Woolrych *Soldiers and Statesmen, The General Council of the Army and its Debates* (Oxford 1987).

The most important single development in the historiography of the Civil War since the last war has been the emphasis on local and regional studies. While the tendency was in some measure anticipated in the 1930s by M.Coate, *Cornwall in the Great Civil War and Interregnum 1642-1660* (Oxford 1933) and A.C.Wood, *Nottinghamshire in the Civil War* (Oxford 1937), in terms of distinctive emphasis and methodology the process begins with A.Everitt's truly seminal *The Community of Kent and the Great Rebellion* (Leicester 1966), which has been followed by a number of similar county studies (see Richardson, Debate . . . , ch. 7). To these should be added Ann Hughes, *Politics, Society and Civil War in Warwickshire* (Cambridge 1987). The appearance of a volume of printed sources with a long and excellent historical introduction by J.S.Morrill, *The Revolt of the Provinces* (1976), is a sure indication of the coming-of-age of this approach. A regional as distinct from a county study with a sharply different emphasis from that of Everitt is C.Holmes, *The Eastern Association in the English Civil War* (1974). See also Holmes's article 'The County Community and Stuart Historiography', *J. Brit. Stud.* XIX (1980), 56-73. Urban history has been less well served than county history. Valerie Pearl's *London and the Outbreak of the Puritan Revolution 1625-1642* (1961), though indispensable, makes insufficient allowance for changes of aldermanic attitudes over the period and is too apt to assume that the attitude of the municipal governors in 1642 was that which prevailed over the whole reign before the war. For a different view see R.Ashton, *The City and the Court*

1603–1643 (Cambridge 1979). One of the all too few good studies of a provincial town is Roger Howell Jr., *Newcastle upon Tyne and the Puritan Revolution* (Oxford 1967). There is an interesting essay on Chester during the war by A.M.Johnson, in P.Clark and P.Slack (ed.), *Crisis and Order in English Towns 1500–1700* (1972). Three valuable recent studies relating to Civil War in Scotland are David Stevenson, *The Scottish Revolution 1637–44* (Newton Abbot 1973) and his *Revolution and Counter-Revolution in Scotland 1644–1651* (1977), and Lawrence Kaplan, *Politics and Religion during the English Revolution. The Scots and the Long Parliament 1643–1645* (New York 1976).

Among the many works on the religious history of the period valuable recent studies include W.Lamont, *Godly Rule* (1969), an outstandingly original study. Michael Walzer's *The Revolution of the Saints* (1965), however, while stimulating, is an exercise in political theory rather than history. William Haller's *The Rise of Puritanism* (New York 1938) and *Liberty and Reformation in the Puritan Revolution* (2nd ed. 1955) are valuable. H.R.Trevor-Roper's illuminating, valuable and entertaining *Archbishop Laud* (1940) was likened, not altogether unjustly, by the late Professor R.H. Tawney to a study of Wordsworth by an author who didn't like poetry. For an account of the movement connected with Laud, see N.Tyacke, *Anti-Calvinists. The Rise of English Arminianism c. 1590–1640* (Oxford 1987). See notes on text, p. 380 for articles challenging Tyacke's views. The whole literature of Puritanism and Church history is voluminous and the reader is referred to the aforementioned Oxford bibliographical volume of Davies and Keeler.

It is again emphasized that a bibliographical note of this length can do no more than scratch the surface of a subject which continues to attract a flood of monographs and not least of articles in journals where much of the most fundamental work has been done. The footnotes to this book give some idea of the volume and variety of the work and the reader is reminded again of the need to refer to the large-scale bibliographical guides mentioned at the beginning of this note.

Index

War party, *cont.*

military commanders, 199–200,
217–18, 223–8, 233, 352; Committee
of Both Kingdoms and, 217;
Eastern Association army loses
favour with, 276–7; issues on
which allied to middle group, 203;
issues on which middle group
opposed to, 199–200; merges with
Independents, 222–3, 240; New
Model Ordinance and, 233; royal
declaration denounces, 197–8;
Scots and, 203, 222–3, 233, 234–5;
Self Denying Ordinance and, 228–
30; social status of adherents of,
190–2; some middle groupers
move towards, 234, 237, 238;
taxation and, 199
Warwick, Earl of, *see* Rich, Robert
Warwick, Sir Philip, 132
Warwickshire, 223, 271; committee
of, 223, 268, 269, 271, 275, 279
Watkins, William, 212, 388
Weaver, John, 329, 330, 333
Weldon, Sir Anthony, 266–7, 270,
279, 324, 324–5, 422
Wells Cathedral, 193
Wentworth, Peter, 244
Wentworth, Sir Peter, 238, 308, 330,
344
Wentworth, Sir Thomas, Viscount
Wentworth, Earl of Strafford, 41,
61, 67, 95, 131, 132, 135, 136, 138, 139–
40, 141–3, 144, 147, 149–50, 179, 288,
314, 339
Wentworth, Thomas, 33
West Midlands Association, 274–5
Westminster Assembly of Divines,
205–6, 219–21, 244–6
Westmorland, 65, 123
Weston, Sir Richard, first Earl of
Portland, 39
Wharton, Philip, Lord, 249
Whig interpretation, 16–17, 20, 72–3,
101

Whitacre, Lawrence, 252
White, Major Francis, 309
Whitelock, Bulstrode, 227, 229–30,
236, 238–9, 241, 245, 250, 413
Whitelock, James, 13
Whitgift, John, Archbishop of
Canterbury, 100, 110, 113, 118
Wight, Isle of, 58, 59, 315, 326, 335,
344; *see also* Treaty of Newport
Wildman, John, 310
Williams, John, Bishop of Lincoln,
118, 122
Williams, Roger, 220, 410
Willoughby of Parham, Lord, 170–1,
192, 249, 267, 326, 328
Wiltshire, 50, 51, 54, 55, 56, 57, 58,
65, 83–4, 106, 260, 261, 262, 270;
committee of, 281
Windebank, Sir Francis, Secretary
of State, 131, 132, 135, 139, 388
Windham, Thomas, 108
Wogan, Charles, 55
Wood, Mr, 193
Worcester cathedral, 193
Worcester, Earl of, *see* Somerset,
Henry
Worcestershire, 60, 261
Wren, Matthew, Bishop of Norwich
and Ely, 97, 118
Wriothesley, Thomas, fourth Earl of
Southampton, 207, 208
Wroth, Sir Robert, 34, 35–6, 37
Wroth, Sir Thomas, 318, 344
Wrothe, Thomas, 108
Wylde, John, 339
Wynn, Sir Richard, 141–2

York, 61, 158, 162, 173, 174
Yorkshire, 52, 61, 65, 67, 79, 80, 82,
83, 122, 132, 136, 137, 152, 167, 177,
247–9, 257, 258, 265, 271, 283, 339,
351, 395